19.25

SOCIAL DEVELOPMENT

A Series of Books in Psychology

Editors: Jonathan Freedman
Gardner Lindzey
Richard F. Thompson

SOCIAL DEVELOPMENT

THE ORIGINS AND PLASTICITY OF INTERCHANGES

Robert B. Cairns

The University of North Carolina
Chapel Hill

W. H. Freeman and Company
San Francisco

To Beverly

Library of Congress Cataloging in Publication Data

Cairns, Robert B   1933–
  Social development.

  Bibliography: p.
  Includes index.
  1. Socialization.   2. Social interaction.
  3. Developmental psychology.   4. Sociobiology.
  5. Social behavior in animals.   I. Title.
  HQ783.C336   301.15'7   78-12199
  ISBN 0-7167-0195-2

Printed in the United States of America

9 8 7 6 5 4 3 2 1

CONTENTS

PREFACE

I decided to write this textbook during a year that I spent on Mt. Desert Island, working on research at the Jackson Laboratory and exploring the Maine coast with my young family. I finished the book in another splendid setting with my family, now much older, while I participated in an advanced studies group on ethology and psychology at the Zentrum für interdisziplinäre Forschung in northern Germany. This was a civilized way to begin and end a book whose aim is to synthesize current streams of thought in social behavior. My goal was—and is—to bring together in a readable and coherent fashion the ideas and evidence central to a contemporary perspective on social behavior and personality.

Simple enough, but what are the essential elements of this perspective, and how does it differ from earlier views? Since much of the book is concerned with answering these questions, I'll mention only that it examines social behavior within a developmental framework and deals explicitly with the network of interchanges in which social patterns occur. Neither approach is novel; J. M. Baldwin discussed interactions in children in 1897, and C. R. Darwin explored ontogenetic-phyletic concerns in 1872. Nonetheless, the incorporation of these approaches into contemporary views has had an explosive impact on the field, its method, and its concepts. Although several biology texts discussing social behavior from an evolutionary perspective have recently appeared—and have led to the formation of the new subdisciplines of human ethology and sociobiology—there have been few attempts to deal with the issues within a developmental framework, and none with principal focus on child social behavior.

The basic outline of this volume has remained remarkably constant. Initially, because of the dearth of relevant literature on children, I thought that the book would be short. However, as the literature grew, so did the book. Since I felt it important to present an up-to-date picture, virtually all of the volume has been rewritten within the past year. The new literature has been mostly in the area of interactional analysis and has added greatly to our understanding of reciprocity and the ontogeny of social patterns. In any case, the scope of the field has been expanded, and happily so.

The material in this book has been used at Chapel Hill for the past three years in a course entitled Social Development and Personality. My hope is to promote the teaching of the subject matter on a broader basis than in the past and to help establish social development as an interdisciplinary course of study. In keeping with that aim, and to cover the major concepts and findings in the area, I have interlaced discussions of child behavior with those of the biological and comparative aspects of social behavior. If one wishes to divide the text—as some instructors probably will—fifteen of the chapters are concerned mostly or exclusively with child social patterns (Chapters 1, 2, 6, 7, 8, 11, 12, and 15-22). As a whole, these chapters constitute a comprehensive introduction to the main issues, problems, and accomplishments of studies of the social development of children. The remaining seven chapters provide an introduction to parallel issues in the social development of nonhumans.

Several years ago I was lucky enough to be a graduate student at Stanford University when social learning theory was undergoing a major transformation at the hands of Albert Bandura and Richard H. Walters. Al was my major supervisor during all of those years, and Dick was an older graduate student with whom I worked closely and argued a lot. In addition, there was Robert R. Sears, a teacher and guiding force. I suspect that much of what is in this volume reflects those influences, directly and indirectly.

In more recent years I have been blessed with a succession of stimulating colleagues and graduate students who have left their imprint on my thinking and work. Gilbert Gottlieb, in particular, has reminded me of the unfinished business of this book and has contributed in multiple ways to bringing this volume to completion. My colleagues at the University of North Carolina, Indiana University, and elsewhere have kindly read earlier chapters of the manuscript, and I thank Harriet Rheingold, Robert T. Brown, Meredith West, Scott Paris, and Ross Parke for criticizing sections of the book. I am also grateful to Eleanor Willemsen and Sandra Scarr-Salapatek for their reading of an earlier draft in its entirety. As graduate students, my research collaborators in this enterprise helped to provide empirical information on issues where it was meager or missing altogether. For their contributions, I wish to thank Don E. Fleener, Susan D. Scholz, Scott Paris, Linda C. Monahan, Albert Einsiedel, Jr., Michael Hall, Robert Quilty, Judith Milakovich, Samuel Sherman, Margaret Holmberg, Dennis

MacCombie, James Green, Gwen Gustafson, Jane Perrin, and Diane Scott. Much of the unpublished research that I cite from my laboratory was supported by the National Institute of Child Health and Human Development. Elaine Morrow typed several versions of the manuscript, and her good nature and efficiency have been many times appreciated.

My greatest debt remains to my main collaborator, Beverley D. Cairns, to whom this volume is dedicated.

Robert B. Cairns
October 1978

SOCIAL DEVELOPMENT

I

INTRODUCTION AND CONTEMPORARY THEMES

Discoveries over the past two decades have brought about a fresh developmental view on the nature of social patterns and personality. This new perspective was much needed, since the traditional ideas that have grown up with separate disciplines (psychology, sociology, psychiatry, and biology) have long been recognized to be partly or wholly inadequate. Even so, the scientific advances that paved the way for the new perspective cannot be assigned to a single research "breakthrough" or to a single discipline. The credit must be shared, because there have been several productive lines of research that managed to leap across traditional boundaries. The key findings—on the origins of social synchrony, on continuity and change in personality and social patterns, on social organization and social cognition—have prompted a common focus on developmental processes. These findings have also required a realignment among disciplines concerned with social development and have thereby helped to create a new major area of scientific study.

This volume provides an introduction to the main concepts and accomplishments of the area. Special attention will be given to its implications for understanding human social patterns and personality. The first two chapters present some ideas and themes that distinguish the developmental perspective from earlier ones.

1

THE DEVELOPMENTAL SYNTHESIS

This book is concerned with the development of social interchanges: how they originate and how they are maintained and changed over an individual's lifetime. By social interchange, we mean a special kind of behavior organization in which the acts of one individual contribute to the direction and control of the acts of another individual (or individuals). The interchanges that we will examine include those that are recognized as "attachment" and "aggression," "altruism" and "anger," "gender role" and "sexual development." Hence the issues that we shall deal with concern living, and all of us have had a good deal of living experience of one type or another. Any fresh data or novel claims may produce uncommon resistance, or else may be modified so that they fit what we already know, or *think we know.* Personal preconceptions are more deeply rooted than scientific ones. In teaching undergraduate and graduate courses, I have explored a number of different ways to avoid some of the more obvious pitfalls. The method that students like best and the one that I will adopt here is slightly unconventional, so I shall explain it.

Traditional expositions about development and personality have usually begun with earlier theories,

and have then covered the data. However, I will reverse this procedure and cover first the impressive body of information and ideas on specific problems of social development. Most of the concepts that have evolved in the course of these investigations cut across disciplines, and therein lies their power. For example, the concept of *social reciprocity*[1] brings together the psychoanalytic-ethological explanation of mother-infant attachment (Bowlby, 1969) and the neobehavioristic explanations of that attachment (Gewirtz, 1972; Sears, 1972). Reciprocity is not solely the property of either the psychoanalytic or the behavioristic child psychologist, however. The idea and term appeared earlier in zoologist N. Collias' (1956) masterful description of the maternal bond in sheep and goats, and in the classic description by T. C. Schneirla and J. S. Rosenblatt (1961) of the maternal behavior of cats.

Rather than attempt to make the new findings and concepts fit the molds of earlier theories of development, then, it has seemed more direct to de-

[1] *Social reciprocity* is a property of certain interchanges in which the acts of two organisms influence each other, and similar though not necessarily identical acts can be observed (see Chapter 17).

scribe, in their own terms, the key ideas and discoveries that gave rise to them. I have therefore relegated the major comparisons and the extended discussion of general theories to the last section of the book. The decision was made not because I considered the general theories unimportant, but because I thought that a definition of the concepts of the synthesis would permit us to view old issues and controversies in a new light. Theories, like organisms, develop and adapt to changing times and discoveries.

An introduction is in order to help us establish where we are and where we are going—to orient us as to the areas to be covered and the major issues to be solved. So I will begin by presenting a few key definitions, a short history, and a brief overview of what the developmental synthesis is all about. If the coverage seems too brief—if it only stirs up questions without answering them—then I will have succeeded in my aim.

The Meaning of Social Development

Compared with other terms used in psychology and in everyday life, "development" seems to be a rather straightforward word, one that hardly ranks with the jargon that most of us have become accustomed to in psychology. We might even wonder why a definition is called for. That in itself is a reason to be wary because there are a good many terms that are entirely satisfactory for use in everyday discussions but that are too vague for technical purposes. In this regard, one of my colleagues at the University of Pennsylvania questioned whether the research that I was doing at the time had much of anything to do with developmental psychology. Since he was a good-hearted, earnest fellow who knew that I was studying the family constellations of 7-year-old children, I was at first puzzled by his question, but subsequently found that it was simply his way of opening a discussion of the question of what is real developmental research. According to

his view, merely working with children, no matter how young or old they may be, is not sufficient to qualify as developmental research. Instead, the work should focus on age-related changes in behavior and potential, or should be directed at the elucidation of those processes that might be associated with those changes. William Kessen (1960) has brilliantly expanded that argument, and his article is well worth consulting.

Nonetheless, research in the field of developmental psychology in general and social development in particular has proceeded on the assumption that just about anything that concerns the behavior of children and adolescents, and more recently, the elderly, qualifies as being developmental. If the work is not done with humans, it is more than slightly suspect in terms of applicability or relevance. Probably the most astute definition of the traditional developmental boundaries is the one-genus hypothesis of Harry Stack Sullivan (1953) that "everyone is much more human than otherwise." Historically, such sentiments have led many to think of social interchange as a unique and singular creation of human beings. This definition of the field of developmental psychology faithfully reflected the way it has been perceived by most psychologists; however, to consider biological and comparative research as irrelevant or tangential is merely to insulate that area from the very ideas and results that are required to solve its most compelling problems.

It does seem important, then, that we clarify what is meant by "development." Some writers have simply stopped trying to define the term and have used others, such as "ontogeny" or "epigenesis," in its stead. This was Zing-Yang Kuo's solution, and his definition of behavioral epigenesis is worth quoting:

> The epigenesis of behavior is a continuum of the dynamic process of interlocking reactions between the organism and the environment, resulting in the reorganization or modification of the existing patterns of both the behavioral gradients and the environmental context. . . . We shall define behavioral epigenesis as a continuous developmental process from fertilization through birth

to death, involving proliferation, diversification, and modification of behavior patterns both in space and in time, as a result of the continuous dynamic exchange of energy between the developing organism and its environment, endogenous and exogenous (Kuo, 1967, pp. 11–12).

The breadth of this definition reflects Kuo's protest against the narrow constraints placed on the concept and underscores his view that the study of behavior is a synthetic science. Because he broadened the concept, he was criticized for making it too vague and too inscrutable to be useful.

Happily, Kuo's definition can be shortened and simplified without sacrificing his essential ideas. Accordingly, our working definition of behavioral development will be *the dynamic organization of behavior over time, from fertilization to death.* "Dynamic organization" means that there is an ongoing fusion throughout life between the effects of functional stimulation ("experience") and the processes of maturation and growth. Even seemingly stable conditions of the organism, such as behaviors that continue from one time to another and from one setting to another, reflect a continuing adaptation to internal and external change. Though such an abstract definition of development is necessary, it can be mind-boggling at this stage of the discussion, and I shall not dwell on it any longer at this point.[2]

The second term that requires definition is "social." What kinds of phenomena are social? For instance, is the sexual transformation of human female embryos into males or hermaphrodites by means of hormonal injections a matter of embryology or a matter of social development? In our view, it depends on one's focus. If the concern is only with the hormonal mechanisms that permit the transformation to occur in ontogeny, the research task and outcomes fall primarily in the domain of embryo-

logical science. But if the concern is with how these changes influence the developing infant's and child's interactions with other persons, and contribute to his or her self-concept, expectations, and eventual sexual practices, then the phenomena surely fall in the domain of social development. More generally, the word "social" refers to *all the effects that organisms produce on one another.* These effects may be behavioral or biological, direct or indirect, intended or unintended, benign or destructive, normal or neurotic.

These definitions will guide what will be covered in this volume. Accordingly, the information and research described here will not be restricted to children, although they will indeed be a special focus. Further, some issues will be discussed that have rarely been seen to be relevant to social development, such as biosocial influences and socio-sexual behavior, and other issues that have usually been considered matters of individual motivation and personality, such as altruism and aggression.

Three Fundamental Questions

One other matter that should be clarified is the issues with which the field of social development has been concerned. In analyzing the quintessential concerns—the origin, continuity, and change in social interaction patterns—it will be helpful to ask three questions:

1. How are social interchanges and relationships initially established?
2. How are social interchanges and relationships maintained over time and across settings?
3. How are interchanges and relationships modified and transformed?

Some would restrict the analysis to what might be called normal, "species-typical" social behaviors; others would concentrate only on abnormal or deviant behaviors. I have not made such a distinction,

---

[2] I should add that the concepts of behavioral epigenesis, behavioral ontogeny, and behavioral development are used interchangeably in this volume. Some nuances of difference in meaning can be identified, but such clarification would not add materially to an understanding of the main issues of social development.

primarily because there is no conclusive evidence that the processes that control "normal" social development are necessarily different from those that control "neophenotypic" development, whether supernormal or abnormal.

Nor does listing the questions separately imply that their answers will also be distinct. As a matter of fact, there is good reason to expect that the events that control the origin of the behavior exhibited in certain social interchanges are related to those that contribute to its maintenance and modification. Nonetheless, there is some advantage to be gained by differentiating these three concerns because it is rare that a single investigator or group of investigators has focused simultaneously on all of them. Hence it should not be too surprising to find that orientations that offer the clearest solution to the problem of determining origin tend to be ineffective in helping us to determine events that contribute to maintenance and change, and orientations that explain maintenance and change are not very helpful in explaining establishment.

Perhaps an illustration may be useful. In the summer of 1974, a research team at the University of North Carolina observed a young boy, Peter, who was 5 years old when he was placed in school. Along with 25 other children of the same age, Peter had been enrolled in a special summer preschool program before entering kindergarten in the fall. The only thing that made this session unique was that the preschool does not ordinarily meet during the summer months, but in this particular year the research budget permitted an extra 8 weeks of participation. The class consisted of a typical mixture of children that one finds in a university community in the summertime. A team of researchers observed Peter and several of his classmates throughout the summer to obtain an overview of how they got along with the other children and with adults. The "target" children, of whom Peter was one, were observed daily for one hour by one person, for one-half hour by another, and at irregular intervals by two additional observers, for a total of slightly more than 300 hours over the course of the summer. Following is an account of some of their observations.

Figure 1-1. Peter.

Peter had originally been selected because he had been one of the most passive, withdrawn children on the first day of the program when he was brought to class by his mother. By the third week of school, his behavior had changed dramatically. He was no longer withdrawn, as he had been during the first week; rather he had become one of the leaders of one of the most influential groups of boys, and was the most popular boy in class.

When Peter was observed in small-group activities, such as listening to the teacher read stories and then discussing them, Peter participated in some of the discussions, making small jokes but rarely getting into trouble. Outside the classroom, however, Peter was often found in the company of 2 or 3 boys who constituted the most physically active and rambunctious group.

Friendship patterns were in flux during much of the summer. Although the friendships that Peter established were generally stable, specific associations would last only 2–3 days—that is, Peter typically selected his friends from a group of 4 boys, but at any given time in the summer he would have one friend with whom he spent more time than the others. Why were there cyclic shifts in friendship patterns and why were the cycles of such short duration? The research team found no single answer to these questions, because there appeared to be multiple reasons for the shifts, including changes in Peter's activities and in those of his playmates, as well as modifications in the structure of the school program. Activity preferences seemed to play a significant role. Peter liked to ride his bike, play ball, and splash in the water tank, but these activities were enjoyed to different extents by others. Hence the context and Peter's choice of activity helped to determine whether he was to be found with a given peer on a particular day. The researchers were sometimes able to identify a specific incident that precipitated the beginning or ending of a cycle. For example, a friend was overheard yelling a racial slur at Peter. This particular association was terminated for a few days, and then was resumed.

Some aspects of Peter's behavior were most stable. For instance, Peter infrequently sought other children's company, but they sought his. During the entire observation period, he was sometimes provoked by other boys, but he rarely fought back. Instead, he merely terminated the relationship and went on to some other activity. On some occasions, other boys were observed to take up his cause, and as he walked away, they would become involved in scuffles in his defense. Moreover, Peter showed the same good-natured tolerance in his relationships with girls as with boys. The teasing in which he became involved rarely escalated to more hostile forms of behavior, as did teasing among other children.

Some of Peter's other relationships were also quite stable. In his interchanges with one teacher,

he was noticeably unrestrained, and there was a great deal of mutual bantering and joking. Similar interchanges were rarely observed with the rest of the teachers; even though they would initiate conversations with Peter, he rarely reciprocated.

At this point, we might wonder about the origin of Peter's interactions. To what extent were the interaction patterns controlled by events that occurred within the school, and to what extent had they been established in infancy or later in the familial interactions and then generalized to the school? To what extent did the degree of Peter's physical coordination determine the initial nature of the interchanges—whether with boys or with girls, whether active or passive, whether aggressive or good-natured? Peter's actions and attitudes changed strikingly during the course of the summer. Similarly, Peter's behaviors and attitudes changed in the course of a single day, depending on whom he was with and the setting in which the interchanges occurred. Who was the "real" Peter, or was he merely showing the different ways in which he adapted to various situations? What accounted for the dyadic and contextual relativity of interactions, so that seemingly incompatible activities were elicited, depending on the time and place? More generally, we might ask whether Peter's unique social adjustment to the preschool can be considered predictive of his behavior later on. For instance, will Peter be assertive or passive as a young man, and what might account for the persistence of these characteristics, or their failure to persist? We might also compare his actions with those of another 5-year-old, Frederick, who was brought to a clinic at the University of California at Los Angeles for the treatment of extreme effeminacy (Chapter 16). Finally, what aspects of Peter's behavior were a result of the broader cultural context of which he, a bright 5-year-old living in a progressive Southern community in the mid-1970's, was a part?

A major finding that is a byproduct of the developmental synthesis is that the answer to these complex problems of living cannot be obtained by relying on traditional concepts of heredity, learning, and cognition, and their interactions, no matter how ex-

pertly they are formulated. The contributors to social development lose their separate identities as
they become uniquely fused in the course of the
ontogeny of an individual, and the product itself is
subject to continual elaboration and modification.
This view of social development as being one part
of biological-social system is not a traditional one in
psychological theory, and we will at this point examine its antecedents and alternatives.

The Developmental Synthesis: A Brief History

Over the years, social development has intrigued
investigators in several scientific disciplines from anthropology and zoology to psychiatry and psychology. Charles Darwin and Sigmund Freud were vitally concerned with the matter, as were John B.
Watson, J. Mark Baldwin, William James, Arnold
Gessell, and a great many others both before and
since. Because our aim here is to put into perspective the present-day issues and ideas, we have a li-
cense to be selective. The basis of selection will be
the extent to which an approach or discipline has
contributed to the contemporary synthesis, the details of which will be described more fully later in
this book.

Developmental Psychobiology

The first major stream of thought is the developmental psychobiology of T. C. Schneirla and Zing-
Yang Kuo, the two scientists who are credited with
having independently enunciated the principles of
the modern approach to behavioral development.
These principles have since been extended and refined by D. S. Lehrman, G. Gottlieb, J. S. Rosenblatt, and others and have become the dominant
theme in American comparative psychology; but to
Kuo and Schneirla belongs the credit for having pioneered in the early 1930's an idea before its time.

Despite the fact that both men established distinguished scientific reputations over a period of 40
years of active and creative research, each worked
in relative obscurity during much of his lifetime.
They died at a time when their ideas were at the
threshold of gaining general acceptance—Schneirla
in New York in 1968, Kuo in Hong Kong in 1970.

A casual reading of Kuo's only book published in
English, a brilliant and controversial work entitled
The Dynamics of Behavior Development (1967),
leaves one with the immediate impression that Kuo
was a scientific revolutionary, a scientific agnostic,
or both. He saw clearly that the study of behavior
must be grounded in biology and must repudiate
both mechanistic and teleogical concepts. But the
fact that he managed, successively, to reject most of
the essential ideas of Darwin, Pavlov, Lorenz, and
virtually all American learning theorists since Watson did not endear him to the scientific establishment, and explains why the book went out of print
shortly after it was published, as he predicted it
would. But his ideas did not go out of circulation.
An exceedingly important message survived the po-
lemics—namely, that the

> behavioral process is not just a stimulus-response
> relationship, a conditioning process, nor just a
> revelation of innate actions in the form of "court-
> ship," "threat," food-begging, egg-rolling in the
> nest, and the like. In other words, *the study of
> behavior is a synthetic science.* It includes com-
> parative anatomy, comparative embryology, com-
> parative physiology (in the biophysical and bio-
> chemical sense), experimental morphology, and
> qualitative and quantitative analysis of the dy-
> namic relationship between the organism and the
> external physical and social environment (p. 25;
> emphasis by Kuo).

The integration of scientific areas is necessary to
deliver up the secrets of behavioral development,
which is necessarily fused with biological development. A static state is anathema to an adapting biological organism: it is death. Mechanistic stimulus-
response concepts of learning are "extreme over-
simplifications" of complex organizational processes. The goal Kuo set for himself was to redefine

the essential problems of behavior according to the potential of the organism for organization over the course of development.

The goal of the holistic developmental theory of T. C. Schneirla is similar, and although it is stated in less controversial terms, it is just as radical. Schneirla claimed, as did Kuo, that the study of development is the study of living, and that it requires an emphasis on the "whole organism" and its integrated processes. Although he was a founder of modern comparative psychology, Schneirla was wary of the dangers of haphazardly generalizing across species, and was aware of the pitfalls in leapfrogging from studies of primates and rodents to the solution of human problems. He stressed the differences as well as the similarities in the behavioral organization of various species, and pointed out the fallacies of both anthropomorphism and zoomorphism.[3] He argued that the proper study of any given behavioral pattern, such as an aggressive act, must begin with an analysis of the activity in the light of the biosocial organization of the individual, the structure of the group of which it is a part, and the nature of the interchanges in which the acts occur. Holistic theory thus parts company with the theories of a good many contemporary animal behaviorists, which may account for its rather slow acceptance. Since Schneirla, Kuo, and their students have rarely addressed themselves to the study of children, and have eschewed making superficial generalizations from nonhuman organisms to humans, the infiltration of these ideas into the mainstream of developmental psychology has been minimal.

Social Learning and Social Development

A second major stream of thought is the social learning approach to social development—the still-dominant view in child psychology. At the time the de-

velopmental orientation was evolving, rather important events were taking place in learning theory that permitted its extension to the problems of social development. Between 1935 and 1940, R. R. Sears, N. Miller, J. Dollard, and J. Whiting, working together at Yale University, explored the possibility of reinterpreting psychoanalytic principles using the terms and concepts of learning theory. This seminal work, along with the contributions of B. F. Skinner, J. B. Rotter, and their colleagues that began in the late 1940's and have continued to the present, provided the basis for the social learning approach that has been exceedingly influential in guiding socialization research and thinking in the fields of psychology, anthropology, and sociology.

There is no single "social learning theory"; the label refers to a family of theories that span three generations and 40 years of development (see Chapter 19). Despite differences in emphasis, all social learning theories accept the proposition that social behaviors are acquired, maintained, and changed primarily through learning processes. The differences arise because (1) there is disagreement about how animals and children learn and whether the same principles can be applied across species; and (2) learning principles can be used in different ways to explain social phenomena.

It will be useful to identify some of the general concepts of the social learning approaches. The original social learning theories emphasized internal controls of social behavior and how new motives, such as dependency, achievement, and aggression, are learned. The next generation of social learning theories underscored the importance of external, environmental controls. Hence behavior modification emphasized the importance of reinforcement, and the environmental consequences of an action, in determining whether social behavior will be repeated and maintained. What are the reinforcers? The social behaviors of other persons presumably gain reinforcement potential, in that *social reinforcers* such as approval and attention can be expected to maintain social patterns. Another influential social learning view focuses not on the consequences, but on the environmental events that

---

[3] "Zoomorphism" refers to the assignment of animal-like qualities to human beings; anthropomorphism refers to the assignment of human-like qualities to animals.

elicit (stimulate) the behavior. Accordingly, persons whom the child has available to imitate, and the structure of the social network in which the child is observed, are seen as basic to the prediction and control of the child's social patterns. Finally, having come almost a full circle during the past 40 years, the social learning-cognitive approaches of the mid-1970's refer again to the internal controls of social action, including the child's cognitive constructions and the biological constraints on what may be learned.

Social learning ideas were extended and invigorated by the pivotal contributions of Albert Bandura and Richard Walters, who together were responsible in 1963 for bringing social learning formulations closer in line with the phenomena of childhood. Like any scientific theory, social learning views have been responsive to new data and have been undergoing continual reformulation since their introduction. The story of these changes is partly the story of this volume. The point to be made here is that social learning ideas have proved to be a necessary complement to the developmental approach, particularly when it has been applied to problems of the social interactions of children.

Cognitive Development and Social Behavior

A third major stream of thought concerning social development reflects the pivotal contributions of Jean Piaget and Heinz Werner, whose views have been ably expanded by a cadre of contemporary theorists (including J. Flavell, B. Inhelder, L. Kohlberg, and J. Langer). Originally a zoologist, Piaget viewed changes in cognitive capabilities as analogous to the metabolic exchanges that occur in the course of physical development. In discussing the relationship between the two, Piaget (1952) wrote:

> Life is a continuous creation of increasingly complex forms and a progressive balancing of these forms with environment. To say that intelligence is a particular instance of biological adaptation is thus to suppose that it is essentially an organiza-

tion and that its function is to structure the universe just as the organism structures its immediate environment (pp. 3–4).

Hence the core Piagetian ideas of "assimilation" and "accommodation" refer to processes by which an organism maintains a mental equilibrium between itself and the stimulating environment. These ideas follow from the assumption that a continuous reciprocating relation exists between mental structure and mental function. If this view of mental development seems to fit with the earlier statements of Kuo and Schneirla regarding behavioral development, the similarity should be hardly surprising. Both general theories are built on biological-organizational foundations; Piaget applied the ideas to the epigenesis of information-processing in children, and the developmental psychobiologists applied them to the comparative study of behavior. But if the similarities are striking, so are the differences, because the respective research areas have evolved with reference to different problems, different methodologies, and different organisms.

One of the major contributions to recent studies of child development has been the attempt to reorganize social learning concepts so that they take into account the information-processing capabilities of children. The result has been that some of the key concepts of social learning, including imitation, have recently been redefined in terms of their informational properties (Aronfreed, 1968; Bandura, 1971; Mischel, 1973). The acceptance of the view that the child is a thinking, adaptive, and active organism has paved the way for a rapprochement with the cognitive orientation.

Ethology and Evolution

The final major stream of thought, ethology, also had its roots in zoology. Konrad Lorenz and Niko Tinbergen are credited for having systematized ethology and for having brought it to the scientific forefront. Lorenz's classic paper on the development of species identification in precocial birds appeared in German in 1935, but the full impact of his ideas was not felt by the American scientific audience until 1951, when Tinbergen's short book, *The Study of Instinct,* was published. Modern statements of ethology began as a protest against the narrow constraints of the then-dominant learning statements of C. Hull, E. R. Guthrie, and E. C. Tolman. Some 35 years were required to achieve recognition, but the protest has undoubtedly been successful. The ethological view, that there is a relationship between the biological constraints on the organism and what it may learn, has had a massive effect on contemporary learning formulations (Hinde and Stevenson-Hinde, 1973). The shift in perspective has stimulated, among other things, the discovery of the ways that organisms are "prepared" biologically to learn certain relationships more easily than others (Bolles, 1972; Seligman and Hager, 1972).

But ethology is much more than a protest. The main emphasis of ethology, "the biology of behavior," has been that behavioral adaptations must be viewed from an evolutionary perspective. The ramifications of this focus have been multiple: the study of diverse species, the use of naturalistic observation, and the identification of instinctual controls of behavior.

Especially relevant to recent discoveries concerning social development have been the attempts of British psychoanalyst John Bowlby, beginning in the late 1950's, to integrate the psychoanalytic view of the child with the evolutionary emphasis of ethology. The fit is surprisingly harmonious, and Bowlby has written a most influential analysis of the relation between the biological foundations of social behavior and the social attachment between the human mother and her infant. Bowlby's integration renewed interest in the infant in the mid-1960's and thus reopened a field that had been virtually dormant for a period of 30 years, except for the notable work of Myrtle McGraw, Harriet Rheingold, Mary Ainsworth, H. R. Schaffer, and others.

Sociobiology is closely related to ethology in terms of its emphasis on the evolutionary controls of social behavior. E. O. Wilson's volume, *Sociobiology: The New Synthesis* (1975), was the birth announcement for the "new science," which is defined as "the study of the biological bases for all social behavior" (Wilson, 1975, p. 4). This definition would seem to indicate that there is an overlap with the concerns and content of ethology. And there is. But the aim of sociobiology is unique in that it attempts to integrate the principles of modern population biology and ecology with those of sociology. Another major goal is to identify the quantitative genetic mechanisms that underlie the evolution of societies and, thereby, to account for the evolution of social behaviors. A distinctive feature of Wilson's proposal is his belief that the study of social behavior best proceeds by "decoupling" (divorcing) the issues bearing on individual social development from those concerned with the evolution of societies. Hence the label "sociobiology" (sociology-biology) rather than "psychobiology" (psychology-biology). The question of whether decoupling is necessary or useful will come up repeatedly in this volume.

So brief an outline of the history of social development is barely a skeleton. As I suggested in the first paragraph of this chapter, the major credit for the contemporary synthesis is due the researchers whose work has pinpointed the shortcomings of narrow approaches to the problem. Even a mini-history is to be faulted if it fails to mention the catalytic contributions made by Harry F. Harlow's study of primate social ontogeny, John Paul Scott's analyses of genetics and social behavior, Robert R. Sears' pioneering studies of the effects of different child-rearing methods, and Roger Barker's efforts to establish the usefulness of ecological methods in child research (that is, the study of individual children in a natural setting). But to go further, I am afraid, would only delay the explanation of how the conflicts between theories and data have begun to be resolved.

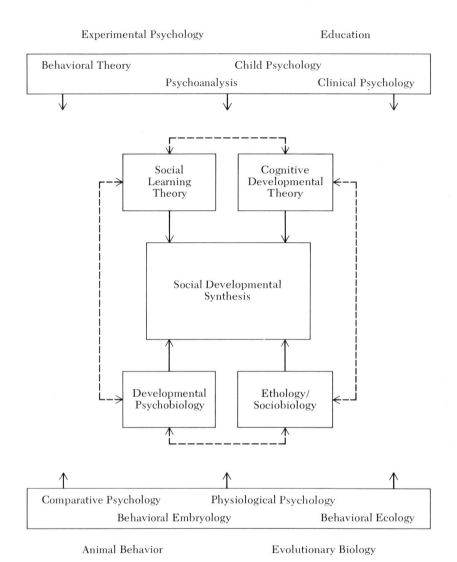

Figure 1-2. The relationships among the major contributors to the developmental synthesis. A division has historically been made between developmental orientations concerned with children (*top*) and those concerned with animals (*bottom*). Further subdivisions have been made between cognitive approaches to child development and behavioral ones, and between functional analyses of animal development and phyletic-evolutionary ones. Linkages between approaches are indicated by dotted lines.

Pathways to the Developmental Synthesis

As shown in Figure 1-2, the streams of thought that contribute to the developmental synthesis emerge from two different traditions: one concerned with child development and education, and the other concerned with animal behavior and evolution. The academic disciplines (education, child and clinical psychology, philosophy *versus* zoology, behavioral ecology, comparative psychology) associated with the streams of thought differ in orientation, problems, and solutions. Transcending the differences is a common concern for the essential issue of development: how social actions are established, maintained, and changed in ontogeny and phylogeny. Linkages of these disparate approaches to development, indicated by the dashed lines in Figure 1-2, have paved the way for the present synthesis.

What Is to Follow

This book is organized into four parts. Part I consists of this introductory chapter on the scope of the field of social development and Chapter 2 on contemporary themes. Part II deals mainly with the foundations of social development as they have been studied in very young organisms. Our concern will be not only with the processes of establishment, but also with the processes of maintenance, adaptation, and change. The first three chapters of Part II focus on animal research from a comparative perspective; the last three deal with the special concerns of the early social development of humans. The last chapter in Part II (Chapter 8) deals with the social interchange strategies of older children and how they relate to dependency behavior.

Part III, the longest part, deals with different important aspects of social development: aggression, sex-typing, reproduction, altruism, play, and related topics. I have included a separate set of chapters on each to show how these problems of social adaptation have been solved by nonhuman species. There follows a more detailed discussion of the available information on these aspects of the development of children. I have chosen to not mix studies of children and studies of animals, because I have found, in teaching, that the literature on neither is understood very adequately if animals are used to illustrate human problems, or vice versa. Rather, the similarities and the differences can be grasped more readily when the principles resulting from the study of each are stated separately. After analyzing this information, we will be in position to see areas of agreement, disagreement, and, ultimately, synthesis.

In the final section of the book, the issues that were touched on lightly in Chapters 1 and 2 are reexamined. I present an overview, a comparison, and an evaluation of general theories and processes. This is not so formidable a task as it appears to be. These last chapters are intended not merely to summarize, but to clarify which of the early principles are consistent with the findings that have emerged as a result of the developmental synthesis, and which are not. A synthesis is not eclecticism; it demands a rejection of ideas that do not logically fit each other or the data, and a fusion of the ideas that do.

My task, then, is to describe the work and ideas on social development that have come out of the quiet revolution in child psychology and psychobiology of the last 20 years. Almost unrecognized, even by many who are near to them, the advances in the developmental sciences have brought us closer than ever to a scientific explanation of the nature of social behavior and personality. Now it is time to provide support for this claim. The next chapter presents an overview of the main themes of the new perspective.

2

CONTEMPORARY THEMES

In this chapter I will introduce and discuss some empirical themes and concepts that have emerged recently in the study of social development. For the most part, the concepts cannot be confined to any one discipline or orientation; they have been independently developed by investigators of social development from many different backgrounds. The study of socialization is no longer the exclusive province of child psychologists, as it was once thought to be.

The aim here is to get acquainted with some of the key ideas that will be returned to when we consider particular problems of social development.

Interchanges in Social Development

Social actions require the participation of two or more persons; their analysis requires *interactional* or *dyadic* research methods. How do dyadic procedures differ from *monadic* ones? Robert R. Sears (1951) answered that question for us more than 25 years ago in his pioneering analysis of social inter-

change phenomena.[1] He pointed out that many of the immediate controls over the actions of one member in a relationship are provided by the other individual in the interchange. Research procedures then, should be concerned with the mutual controls that are operative. At the least, research designs should preserve the essential nature of the relationship by observing the two (or more) individuals simultaneously and noting their influence on each other. Sears objected in particular to the practice of restricting experimental procedures to the observation of single individuals alone in relatively barren, asocial settings in order to achieve experimental "control," because the experimenter thus "controlled" or eliminated those sources of influences that most directly affected social development. So-

[1] The fundamental concepts of interchange analysis have a long and distinguished history in the fields of sociology and social psychology. Sears himself drew on the contributions of Leonard Cottrell (1942), who in turn had been stimulated by the interchange concepts of George H. Mead (1934) and H. S. Sullivan (1940). Earlier, James Mark Baldwin (1897) provided a brilliant statement on the relations between cognitive development and social interactions. The ideas have been "discovered" anew on several occasions in the past 80 years (Cairns and Ornstein, 1979).

cial actions should be studied in the interactional contexts in which they occur. This eminently reasonable idea was a corrective to the then-prevalent position that social patterns are too complex to be studied directly (Hull, 1951). Figure 2-1 includes a simplified representation of a dyadic interchange.

Interactional methodologies have now had a significant effect on research designs for the study of social development. They influence both the kinds of questions that are asked and the way that the results are analyzed and interpreted. A major stimulus in the field of child psychology, in addition to the work of Sears, has been a series of provocative papers by R. Q. Bell (1968, 1971), asserting that children can influence their parents as much as their parents influence them. But the *pedogenic* view (that the child controls the parent) has encountered as many pitfalls as did the earlier *adultogenic* one (that the parent controls the child). To the extent

that the essential reciprocity of influence is ignored, either interpretation can be faulted.

Obviously the interactional approach is not devoid of conceptual implications. However, it is less a theory of social development than a methodological proposal about how social phenomena should be analyzed. As Sears originally outlined the methodology, it must focus upon the sequential nature of interchanges. The object is to preserve information about how the responses of one individual provide stimuli for the subsequent behavior of the other. Attention should first be given to the actual behaviors of each individual, and to the events that immediately precede and follow these behaviors. The investigator thus attempts to learn what are the immediate determinants of the behavior to be explained, and how the activities of the "other" individual synchronize, facilitate, inhibit, or redirect the course of the interchange.

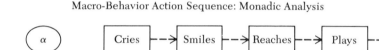

Macro-Behavior Action Sequence: Monadic Analysis

α (6-month-old infant)   Cries --→ Smiles --→ Reaches --→ Plays --→

Macro-Interactional Sequence: Dyadic Analysis

α (6-month-old infant)   Cries --→ Smiles --→ Reaches --→ Plays --→

β (Father)   Picks up --→ Laughs --→ Tickles

Figure 2-1. Two ways to view social behavior patterns. The monadic analysis focuses on just one individual; the dyadic analysis requires simultaneous attention to both members of the interchange. This simplified dyadic schema does not consider the influence of social and physical contexts, the internal states of the two or more persons involved, and the expectations that they may or may not have about the course of the interchange.

An essential feature of the interactional method is that it requires the investigator to view a given social act in the social system in which it occurs.[2] It is necessary to zoom in on the process and to examine the content and the minutiae of the interchange itself. Consider aggressive behavior. In instances of fighting, the events that *precede* the conflicts are of nuclear importance. The interactional procedure, by focusing upon the actions of both participants, can yield information about the provocations of the victim and about the role that he plays in the process. Studies of the injury-producing acts of children (Patterson and Cobb, 1971) and adults (Toch, 1969) indicate that the responses of the "victims" are significant determinants of the seriousness of the encounter. Essentially the same methodology can be used to analyze other social phenomena, such as mating, maternal care, and peer relationships.

Two additional points should be made concerning the nature of interactional research. First, the method is not limited to field observation work. Because the methodology has been typically employed in the context of field work, the assumption is sometimes made that it is limited to and has its primary value there. In point of fact, it has been successfully used in the laboratory analysis of sexual, affiliative, competitive, and fighting interchanges. Indeed, the procedure is suitable for use in any setting where the relationship itself may be the determining factor of the behavior of the individual or individuals. This includes virtually all interchanges, from psychotherapy and behavioral modification to traditional laboratory analyses of social reinforcement and modeling.

Second, interactional procedures do not solve the problems created by basically inadequate and ill-conceived experiments or theoretical analyses. There is no substitute for asking thoughtful and precise questions before the research, whether dyadic or monadic procedures are employed. Useful field

experiments and valuable interactional analyses begin with clearly defined problems and questions. In the case of social development, the problem is one of determining how specific interchanges early in life are translated over time and space to influence later interactions.

Social Organization and Social Systems

The child, from birth, develops particular styles of social interchange. The interpersonal styles may change from situation to situation, and over time, but they are the stuff of which personality is made. The fact that certain behavior patterns become increasingly predictable and characteristic of the individual is one of the more basic phenomena of social development. The social patterns of the child or even of the infant are more than a patchwork of unrelated sequences that have somehow been drawn together; they ordinarily form distinctive and easily recognizable patterns and networks. And it is these patterns that make for individuality—for likes and dislikes, for trust and suspicion, for love and hate.

The interchanges in which organisms become involved contribute to the integration of behavior patterns, as we just observed. But the interchanges themselves are constrained by (1) the broader social network in which the interchanges occur, and (2) the inherent properties of the individuals, including their action capabilities, developmental status, and prior experiences. In other words, interchanges are embedded in a social system and are controlled by the capabilities of each participant.

The social system "beyond the dyad" has been conceptualized in various ways. The essential point to be made is that the understanding of social development

> demands going beyond the direct observation of behavior on the part of one or two persons in the same place; it requires examination of multiper-

---

[2] The term "social system" refers to the recurrent network of interchanges that is characteristic of a group of individuals. The "group" can be as small as 2 persons, a family, or a colony, or as large as a clan, a community, a society, a culture, or a species.

son systems of interaction not limited to a single setting and must take into account aspects of the environment beyond the immediate situation containing the subject (Bronfenbrenner, 1977, p. 514).

What kinds of "multiperson" systems must be considered? A primary candidate for developmental analysis has been the family system, consisting of the members of the primary family (father, mother, siblings, aunts, depending on the social organization of the species). Among children, other systems would include those in which the child is involved in school or preschool, peer groups, as well as other, loosely structured groups. On still a broader scale, Bronfenbrenner identifies a "macrosystem" as "the overarching institutional patterns of the culture or subculture . . ." (p. 515). Such macrosystems provide the "blueprints" or the norms for the individuals and subgroups within the culture.

Infants are introduced at birth to pre-existing social systems that help to support and organize social behaviors. The properties of social systems and their requirements for the infant differ markedly. The pigtail monkey has but one caretaker, but the bonnet monkey has several; the Chinese infant is assigned to community care, but most American children remain home until the second year; the chaffinch female raises her own young, but the cowbird female fosters her offspring to other birds. Moreover, variations within subgroups are themselves significant. It would be as gratuitous to believe that all Chinese mothers behave alike as it would be to believe that the family living in the next-door apartment treats its child the way we do. Such societal influences do not operate only on mothers and infants; they continue to operate on persons from birth to maturity, and into old age.

Other "support" for the organization of behavior is basically structural-biological, and some patterns of response come about with little or virtually no specific prior experience. "Swimming" in many neonatal mammals, including newborn babies, is one example (see Figure 2-2). Even 10-day-old infants can perform coordinated and effective swimming actions. The socially relevant actions having to do with fighting (Chapter 9) and sexual reproduction (Chapter 13) are two other instances where behavioral coordination seems less dependent on specific experience than on the development of the reflexive and physiological substrate for the behavior. Even though the initial organization of these behavior patterns does not reflect the social training conditions, such patterns are highly vulnerable to experiential modification and reorganization. Swimming, again, illustrates the point. Although it is true that this behavior is innately organized, the activity becomes patterned by the subsequent experiences of the young. A smooth freestyle or a breaststroke is the product of spending several hundred hours in the water, practicing and correcting minute components of coordination. Swimming only looks "natural" after arduous practice. Other action patterns, including those of a social nature, such as fighting and sex, are drastically modified and/or perfected following their initial occurrence.

Much of this volume will be devoted to exactly how social patterns are organized, changed, and reorganized. This brings us to another general theme: individual adaptation in social development.

Plasticity in Social Development: Malleability and Reversibility

Most developmentalists would agree that the early experiences of the child—those occurring during the first 3 years of life—are critical for his social development. The consensus on this matter has not changed greatly over the past 30 years. The general assumption has changed in one way, however, and this change has had a monumental impact on developmental theory and research. It is simply that nowadays the *subsequent* experiences of the child—those occurring after the age of 3—are being seen as potentially having as much impact as earlier ones on the organization of social patterns at maturity. In

18

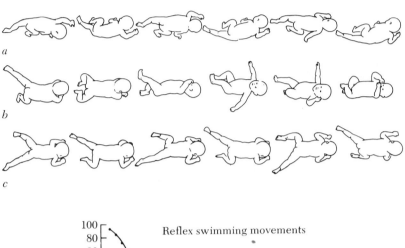

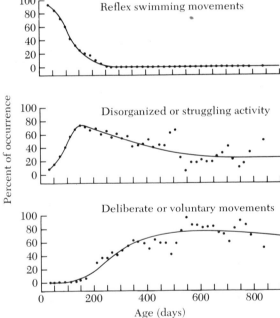

Figure 2-2. Relation between coordinated swimming movements and stage of development. M. McGraw found that human infants (from birth to approximately 3 months) made coordinated reflexive swimming movements when placed in water (stage *a*). From 3 months to about one year, the infants struggled in the water and their movements were disorganized (stage *b*). From about the end of the first year, the infants were capable of making voluntary or deliberate movements (stage *c*). The outlines of the infants were made by tracing successive frames of movie film; the graph shows the frequency with which the different kinds of movement were observed (adapted from M. B. McGraw, 1939, with permission).

other words, not only are the first 3 years "critical," but so are the next 3, and the following 6, 9, and 12 years, up through adolescence and early maturity. A major concern of contemporary developmental research—and of this volume—will be to determine precisely how the developing organism continues to adapt throughout ontogeny and into maturity.

The concern with adaptation and change throughout development has not been limited to studies of children. Indeed, a major impetus for the re-evaluation of the continuity and early experiences has come from studies of nonhuman young that had been raised under various conditions of privation or enrichment. Attempts to "rehabilitate" or reverse the effects of the early isolation can be remarkably successful, if the experiences at maturity are appropriately arranged.

At quite a different level, we find that young men and women in later adolescence and early adulthood show considerable potential for change. The shifts can be toward either greater or lesser conformity with the standards of society. The "lesser conformity" instances sometimes turn out to be the more newsworthy ones. Two examples are the events at My Lai IV in South Vietnam, when young soldiers indiscriminately killed infants and aged, defenseless women; and the activities of the members of the Manson family that culminated in a series of brutal murders in Southern California. It would be easier to dismiss the horror stories of My Lai and "Helter Skelter" if we could assume that *all* of the participants were unbalanced psychologically. But much of the evidence that has been gathered in recent years about these events, and others like them, suggests that that explanation is too simple. Rather, there is a strong possibility that these incidents reflect the behavior of otherwise normal persons who have adapted to demands that are alien to "accepted" societal values. In the course of normal development, each social system has particular requirements that shape, maintain, and direct behaviors and values.

Although it may seem reasonable to view the young as being capable of adapting, we must antici-

pate two of the problems generated by this view. First, the notion of individual adaptiveness, which seems eminently reasonable when considered alone, conflicts with another primitive idea that is equally compelling. Each of us has a sense of identity, about our own life and the lives of those around us. Events and circumstances and times may change, but each of us endures. But acceptance of the idea of adaptation implies that we change as well. The conflict between continuity and change has generated difficult empirical and conceptual problems that are basic to the developmental synthesis and to this volume.

The second problem is to determine the importance of early experiences and how they influence later behaviors. As a result of the adoption of a developmental perspective, either-or questions of development, such as "Can the sexual orientation of homosexuals be reversed?", can be restated so that the concern is not *whether* changes can be produced, but *how*. The relationships of infancy are modified by the experiences of preschool, of later childhood, and of adolescence. At each stage, there is the possibility for modification, exaggeration, or elimination, either by the young or by the social system in which they develop.

In the discussion of social adaptation, I will make frequent use of the terms "plasticity," "malleability," and "reversibility." Since there is some danger of their being misunderstood (or worse, of having meaning projected into them, that is, to each his own), some definitions are called for. My definition of *social plasticity* will be faithful to the dictionary definition: "capable of being molded, receiving shape, or being made to assume a desired form" (see Figure 2-3). A corollary concept, *malleability*, refers to the extent to which a given characteristic of the individual can be modified from the norms for his age, sex, and species *during the period of initial establishment*. The agents of malleability can be hormonal, surgical, contextual, experiential, or social. All that is required is that the behavior or structure be shown to be outside the range normally found in the group of which the individual is a part. If the

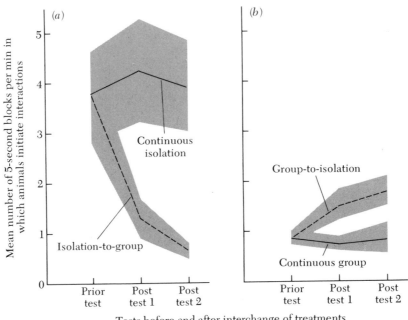

Figure 2-3. The plasticity of effects produced by long-term isolation. One of the effects of long-term rearing of male mice in isolation is to produce animals that are highly likely to initiate interactions that often result in aggressive bouts. Animals raised in small groups are less likely to initiate aggressive interactions. These effects may be modified drastically at maturity by shifting the experimental conditions in which the animals are maintained. Animals moved from the isolation treatment to the group-rearing treatment at maturity behave in a manner that is virtually identical to that of animals raised in small groups from birth. However, animals moved from small groups to isolation at maturity are less likely to behave as if they had been continuously isolated. (Adapted from Cairns and Nakelski. Copyright © 1971 by the American Psychological Association. Reprinted with permission.)

behavior rarely occurs, it can be called a *neophenotype*. *Reversibility* refers to the extent to which the characteristic can be reorganized, *once it has been established*. In circumstances where the aim is to institute normal or "species-typical" forms of interchange, reversibility is synonymous with therapy. More generally, the concept has been employed in determining whether some prior state of organization can be modified by experiences or internal readjustments later in life.

Behavior, Biology, and Bidirectionality

When originally offered, the proposal that maturational events can be disregarded in systematic accounts of the social development of children (Bandura and Walters, 1963; Sears et al., 1957) was in part a backlash against the view that social changes were caused by growth and maturation. Learning theorists argued, and rightly so, that such terms gave the illusion of having *explained* development when they only *described* age-related changes. What was needed, it was further argued, were accounts of why and how distinctive social patterns are learned in development.

In retrospect, it seems clear that the movement for reform was too successful. Not only were maturational-growth processes taken out of the spotlight, they were not included in the social learning program. To achieve precise experimental control, social learning investigators in the 1950's and 1960's typically studied children only at a single age (usually early childhood). Such procedures inevitably highlighted the effects of the experimental manipulation while showing (not surprisingly) that modest effects could be due to age-maturational factors. Problems arose when the "general" principles derived from such observations turned out to be less "general" than they had been supposed to be. Concepts that adequately described short-term effects produced in 4-to-6-year-old children, such as imitation and social reinforcement, had to be extensively revised in order to be applied to the social behaviors of 6-month-old infants. The concepts were even less adequate when used to explain social development from an evolutionary perspective, a point emphasized by John Bowlby (1969). Maturation and species-typical processes clearly place a constraint on what may be learned, and when.

But the major advances in understanding maturational influences have been more general. The contemporary turnaround in the appreciation of the role of biological factors in social development came when it was discovered that they were necessarily interrelated at each stage of the explanatory process. Psychobiological events have now been shown to play a definite, constructive role in the establishment and organization of social behaviors, including the most basic ones. The recent findings on the determination of sexual characteristics and behavior patterns illustrate what I mean. One of the more dramatic recent discoveries has been that the sex of the mammalian embryo is not wholly determined at conception (Young, 1961). The male fetus—across the class Mammalia—produces hormones that help to direct its own sexual development, including the formation of male internal and external structures and the inhibition of the formation of female ones. Without this suppression of the feminine and accentuation of the masculine, the infant at birth would have some of the physical features of both male and female.

This phenomenon of the fetus helping to shape its own development illustrates what Gottlieb (1970, 1976b) has called the *probabilistic conception of prenatal development*. According to this interpretation, prenatal behavior is not determined merely by the biological structures of the young. Rather, the relation is a *bidirectional* one between structure and function. Stated more simply, the experiences of the individual—even self-produced ones—can change its biological properties. These changes, in turn, help to control and direct social behavior. Development is a two-way street; it is not just the unfolding of potentials, nor the shaping by experience. The course of development is not fixed either by internal events or by environmental events; instead it is bidirectional and, therefore, probabilistic (see Figure 2-4).

Let us consider another example, one that is closer to the usual concerns of students of child development. The bidirectionality between structure and function can extend to cultural attitudes and sex-role typing. Paradoxically, there are negligible differences in the actual capabilities of boys and girls at the very ages (3–10 years) when extreme differences first appear in play preferences and other sex-role behaviors. In other words, stereotyped sex-typing differences in play are present in the fourth year of life, even though *sexual dimorphism* (that is, differences in physical structure related to sex, such as size and strength) is not pronounced until 7–10 years later, in adolescence. When they are given equal opportunities, 8-year-old boys and girls show minor differences in the time they require to swim 50 meters or run 100 yards. The ubiquitous

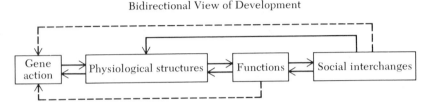

Unidirectional View of Development

Bidirectional View of Development

Figure 2-4. A revision in the conceptions of development. The older view of development considered only the unidirectional relationship between genetic and biological controls and social interchanges; the former was seen as contributing to the control of the latter. The bidirectional view of development indicates that there are a host of feedback effects, some of which concern the social control of physiological states and their development (adapted from Gottlieb, 1976b, with permission).

differences in play preferences between young boys and girls thus are predictive of later sexual dimorphism; they do not merely reflect the children's contemporaneous status. Because cultural expectations, opportunities, and the development of actual skills are interrelated, it would be inaccurate to conclude that play patterns are either "biologically" or "culturally" determined. The biological differences are anticipated, and augmented, by the culture.

Given the spectacular advances that have been made in other areas of biological science in recent years, these comments on the use of developmental information in predicting subsequent behavior may seem elementary. In one sense, they are. Extensions of the ideas of control systems to biology were necessary to pave the way for the acceptance of behavior as one element in the biological process. The classic work of Schneirla (1971) on the synchronous relations between brood maturation and the migration in army ant colonies, of Parkes and Bruce (1961) on the prevention of pregnancy in mice by exposing newly mated females to the odors of unfa-

miliar males, and of Lehrman (1961) on the external controls on patterns of reproduction and maternal care in birds, teach a significant lesson about development. These phenomena underscore the necessity of viewing basic social interchanges as being both an *outcome* and a *determinant* of physiological conditions of an individual and the others with whom he interacts at each stage of social development.

Social-Cognitive Development: The New Behaviorists

A developmental synthesis requires the introduction of new concepts and the revision of old ones. I have already mentioned a good many of the "new" concepts, such as the bidirectionality of influence in structure and function and the dyadic conception of social interchanges. Now a few comments are called for on the revisions that have been made, particularly in behavior theory.

Discovery of the *constraints on learning* is a case in point. Some relations are more rapidly learned than others; such "prepared" (more easily learned) associations often are closely related to the survival requirements of the species. For example, rats rapidly associate the taste of poisoned foods with nausea, even though they do not get sick until several hours after eating such foods. Taste, as it turns out, is a better indicator of which foods are adulterated than are, say, appearance and odor. Hence the association is "prepared" in two ways: the rodent is prepared to learn about things that can poison him; and the stimulus (taste) is more readily associated with poisoned foods than is sight or smell.

Essentially the same "preparedness" can be observed in the learning experiences of the neonate. Activities related to the survival of the infant, including the conservation of heat and energy, are most readily organized around appropriate environmental events. For instance, rhesus monkey infants spend 50 percent or more of their time sleeping or resting. When awake, they have a high probability of sucking. At this stage of development, the environmental events that are most likely to support these responses are "preferred" and become capable of supporting ongoing responses. As the animals grow older and become capable of performing more complex and different acts, the preferences for certain environmental events also change. Similarly, when the individual's responses change in the course of development, he becomes "attached" to different environmental events. More generally, there is a *developmental synchrony of learning*. This concept means that the young respond selectively to particular environmental events and that this selectivity is paced by the individual's developmental status. At each stage of development, response patterns are more readily organized around some environmental events than others.

A related extension and equally important advance in social learning theory is the integration of this theory with cognitive principles. It is noteworthy that the way has been led by two of the theory's more prominent spokesmen. Albert Bandura, a major architect of modern social learning theory, has offered a revision of ideas concerning imitation that relies heavily on the cognitive and information-processing capabilities of the child. Bandura writes that

. . . modeling influences operate principally through their *informative* function, and that observers acquire mainly symbolic representations of modeled events rather than specific stimulus-response associations (Bandura, 1971, p. 16; my italics).

The emphasis on informational functions represents a sharp departure from the earlier, noncognitive view of Bandura and Walters (1963). Walter Mischel (1973) has recently offered an even more sweeping reconceptualization of the social learning position, which has moved it closer to cognitive principles. Mischel argues that persons differ in their cognitive competence (intelligence), encoding strategies (how they categorize the environment), expectations, motives, and self-guided rules. These individual variables, in turn, operate differentially in specific settings and interactions.

The picture, then, is not one of learning principles merely interacting with cognitive and maturational ones. In an interaction, the contributing events can maintain their separate identities. The requirement for a synthesis, by contrast, is a fusion of the fundamental ideas and principles. The concept of a developmental synchrony in learning involves such a synthesis. And, as we shall see later, so do the revised views of social reinforcement and modeling.

Of Mice and Men

The problem of comparative generalization is not a new one. From the publication of Charles Darwin's *The Expression of the Emotions in Man and Animals* more than one century ago (1873) to the publication of Lorenz's *On Aggression* (1966) and Wilson's *Sociobiology: The New Synthesis* (1975), there has been a continuing controversy concerning the relevance of nonhuman behavior to human behavior. As documented by Darwin, close similarities in at least some basic emotional and social response systems exist across species. Extending the Darwinian proposal, G. J. Romanes argued that nonhuman animals can make "intelligent" adaptations to the idiosyncratic demands of the settings in which they are maintained. These adaptations were presumed to reflect the operation of conscious and intelligent processes, not unlike those observed in humans; hence there was a direct linkage between man and animals. Further, once the adaptation had occurred, the behaviors were thought to be directly transmitted to the offspring.

When the "intelligent adaptation" assumption is carried to its extreme, as Romanes did in *Mental Evolution in Animals* (1884), it fades rapidly into anthropomorphism, according to which animals are seen as humanlike in the basic ways in which they respond and adapt. [3] This position found considerable support in the beliefs of the day, popular as well as scientific. An influential counter-proposal was offered by Lloyd Morgan (1896), who marshaled evidence against both (1) Lamarckian genetics and (2) the view that consciousness and intelligence accounts for both behavioral plasticity and adaptation. In a statement admirable for its clarity and forceful logic, Morgan (1896) concluded that it was superfluous to attribute consciousness and intelligence to animals if the behavior could be explained by physiological and habitual mechanisms, without reference to mental events.

---

[3] It would be most unfair to Romanes and to his contributions to fail to add a comment on his pivotal role in the establishment of a scientific framework for comparative analysis. He is sometimes referred to as the "father of comparative psychology" because of his vigorous and influential efforts to identify the relatedness of behavior among species. He laid the groundwork for the subsequent contributions of Whitman and Jennings in the United States and of Heinroth and Lorenz in Europe (see Klopfer and Hailman, 1967).

Instead of interpreting the behavior of animals in terms of human experience, some influential writers early in this century interpreted human experience in terms of animal behavior. This perspective on evolution paved the way for J. B. Watson's rejection of cognitive phenomena in humans, and for the direct application to man of terms and concepts established in studies of invertebrate and vertebrate organisms. The more easily recognized errors of generalization have been labeled "zoomorphism." As Barnett (1973) observed, the use of animal stories to make points about human behavior was a favorite pastime of medieval moralists. He also observed that modern writers are still capitalizing on the propensity of humans to see something of themselves in animals, and vice versa. The errors that have been made in drawing parallels have sometimes been overlooked. The same term—aggression, altruism, or attachment—has been used to refer to particular classes of social interactions from ants to fish to man. Although a term—say, aggression—may be defined so that it refers to a given feature of animal behavior, there is no assurance that the same definition will fit the several properties of human interchanges that have been given that label.

The shortcomings of zoomorphism are not merely semantic. Analogues fail to come to grips with the ways in which the behaviors are established in the first place, and are controlled and maintained, once established. To explain the occurrence or absence of a specific interaction pattern (fighting, mating), it is useful to know what is the function of the behavior in the social organization of the individual's species or subgroup. What roles do physiological events, including hormonal development, play in the instigation or inhibition of the activity? What is the history of the behavior in the repertory of the individual? How do events in the immediate relationship control the occurrence or inhibition of the behavior? What mechanisms account for the very first occurrence of the behavior and how do the responses of others control the recurrence of the activity? The answers to such questions are necessary in order to evaluate whether the behavior can be traced to a common ancestry.

There is a fundamental difference in the aims of investigators who approach social behavior from a developmental perspective and those who approach it from a phyletic perspective. The former are concerned with the identification of *proximal* controls of social behavior—that is, those hormonal, morphological, neural, cognitive, or social events that limit and direct a person's interchanges. Their aim is to identify the functions, the antecedents, and the consequences of social actions. Evolutionary determinants are to be found on quite a different level of analysis. These are the factors that operate in phylogeny, or the history of the species rather than the history of the individual, to increase reproductive fitness. E. O. Wilson has labeled these phyletic mechanisms the *ultimate* determinants. He also observes that the difference between the functional and evolutionary approaches to behavior parallels the difference between functional and population biologists (Wilson, 1975).

One insightful proposal on how these two lines of analysis can be drawn closer together deserves our attention. Following a recent trend in zoological classification, D. D. Jensen (1967) has proposed that evolutionary/developmental approaches should adopt *polythetic criteria* in determining the generality of behavioral concepts. (Polythetic criteria demand that we have detailed information about the interchanges in both species before we can judge their relatedness with regard to a particular characteristic.) According to Jensen, polythetic generalizations require that a matrix of similarities and differences be built when an attempt is made to apply the same concept to two different species or to two different stages of the same species. In other words, consideration must be given to the multiple features of the concept and the behaviors that it subsumes—their functions, controls, development, and roles in social organization. It is not sufficient to focus on a

single "key" feature to justify commonality (*monothetic* generalization) (see Figure 2-5).

What are the implications of polythetic analysis for the study of social development? One is that we must attend to the multiple properties of the characteristic, whether it is sex-typing, aggression, or affiliation, in each of the species that are initially presumed to be similar to each other. For instance, we cannot automatically assume that an intensive study of aggression in, say, free-ranging chimpanzees, will necessarily tell us much of value about fighting in preschool children. Similarly, we cannot assume that the "thrashing" of the infant is linked to the antisocial aggression of the juvenile simply because of their similarity on a single dimension (being hurtful). The points that Jensen makes about generalizing across species apply with equal force to generalizing across developmental stages in children.

Premature extrapolation, whether about species or over ages, makes for poor science because it results in (1) an incomplete analysis of the phenomenon, and (2) a failure to examine directly the mechanisms that control the behavior in the individuals about which the generalization is made. The polythetic method does not prohibit the induction of common principles; it simply requires that they be based upon a full and accurate description of the behavior in the first place.

It has sometimes been suggested that child psychologists should simply make a quick overview of the animal literature, paying particular attention to monkeys, and then get on with the job of studying children directly. The position is a curious one for developmental scientists to take. Moreover, in practice, studies of animal social behavior are not simply ignored. Often they are cited selectively when they appear to provide especially cogent support for a basic proposition, such as the harmful effects of maternal separation or the innateness of aggression. Such a pick-and-choose process is virtually guaranteed to result in a biased view of the events that control social behavior both in the species cited and in children. A basic implication of polythetic analy-

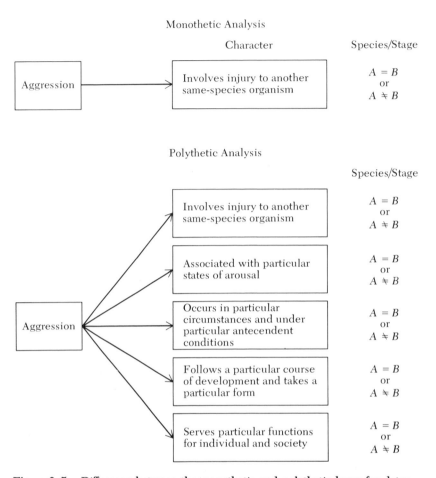

Figure 2-5. Difference between the monothetic and polythetic bases for determining whether particular acts that occur at two different age or phyletic levels may be classified as instances of "aggression." The monothetic approach focuses upon a single key characteristic. The polythetic analysis requires that the act be viewed from multiple perspectives, including antecedent conditions, circumstances, associated internal conditions, developmental sequences, and functions for self and society.

sis is that studies of the development of nonhumans and humans should proceed along parallel lines, in order to permit the corroboration and revision of our primary ideas about development. To be unaware of comparative contributions can hardly be justified by modern science or by common sense.

Whence It Came: Theoretical Precursors of the Synthesis

The heart of any scientific explanation of social development is the processes—the behavioral, evolutionary, and biological mechanisms—that it considers critical for establishment and change. Psychology in general and social development in particular have been blessed with a variety of theories.

The assignment of sorting out the claims of the precursors to the developmental synthesis is not as formidable as it may appear at first blush. The disputes among orientations have been general rather than specific; that is, they have been concerned with general conceptual issues rather than ways of interpreting a given set of observations. Why the diversity? One reason is that different methods have been adopted, different research strategies have

been employed, and different subject populations have been studied by the various orientations. In theory building, there is a self-fulfilling relationship between aims, methods, and processes. The processes that are discovered at the least reflect, and at the most are predestined by, the particular procedures and methods of the orientation. Accordingly, as Alfred Baldwin (1967) cogently observed, developmental theories are prone to "talk past each other rather than at each other."

Figure 2-6 is a simplified outline of the differences among the five major orientations to social development with regard to aims, methods, populations, and concepts (of establishment and maintenance).

	Social Learning	Cognitive Development	Ethology and Sociobiology	Developmental Psychoanalysis	Developmental Psychobiology
Major Concerns	Learning of social behaviors	Cognitive controls of social behaviors	Evolution of social behavior	Development of behavior disorders	Behavior-biological interactions
Primary Populations	Normal pre-school-age and school-age children	Infants to adolescents; humans	Invertebrate and vertebrate behavior	Human infant Clinic patients	Nonhuman mammals and birds
Representative Methods Employed	Short-term behavioral experiments	Interviews; verbal assessments	Naturalistic observations, controlled observations	Observation Clinical study	Physiological and behavioral manipulation, observations
Representative Concepts of Establishment and Maintenance	Imitation, social reinforcement	Stage concepts Autogenesis	Innate controls, species-typical patterns	Preprogrammed attachment: separation, anxiety	Bidirectional organization, reciprocal controls

Figure 2-6. Simplified view of relation between the aims, methods, subjects, and representative concepts of five approaches to social development. The concepts and aims help to determine, and are determined by, the methods employed and the populations studied.

Although each orientation may be entirely consistent and coherent within itself, it may be quite irrelevant to the aims and phenomena of other developmental theories.

If each orientation were as independent as implied in the outline, there would be no cause for concern, no overlap, and no conflict between competing ideas. Nor would there be any pressure to move toward a common approach to the problems of development. But a considerable amount of conflict has been generated by attempts to trace the logical implications of the concepts that appear on the bottom line of the figure. Because of these differences, significant steps have been taken toward a synthesis of comparative psychology and ethology, on the one hand, and of social learning and cognitive development, on the other. The outcome of these integrations is one of the main topics of this volume.

An apparent bias in the outline requires comment. Psychoanalysis, the grandfather of personality theories, seems only modestly represented. The slight is only apparent, however, since the pivotal contributions of Sigmund Freud and his successors are an integral part of the entire outline. In some instances the debt is explicit—for example, the ethological-psychoanalytic integration of John Bowlby and Mary D. Ainsworth and the social learning formulations of R. R. Sears, Neal Miller, and John Dollard. However, in a broader sense, there has been common though not universal acceptance of certain fundamental psychoanalytic concepts. These would include the assumptions of the early determination of social behavior, the homeostatic distribution of energy, and the critical role of interpersonal influence. Beyond Freud stand the fundamental insights of Charles Darwin and George Romanes on the functions and evolution of social behaviors.

But to go further at this point would defeat the purpose of presenting just enough of a theoretical framework to permit us to proceed. After we become acquainted with the primary phenomena and how they are controlled, we shall explore the concepts in greater depth. The facts of social development can both guide and amend the speculations.

Concluding Comments

During the past 80 years, interest in social development appears to have taken roughly the form of a sine curve. Research in the area has waxed and waned. Socialization was the principal concern of behaviorally oriented child psychologists from the end of World War II through the 1950's. But it became obvious by 1960 that learning theories could not explain all of the complex phenomena of human social development. Attention then shifted back to the mental development of the child, according to the cognitive model of development outlined by Jean Piaget. Significant advances were made in our understanding of early perceptual learning, language development, memory organization, and ethical development. By the mid-1970's the pendulum of interest and research had swung back to the issues of social adaptation and development. New data and new ideas have been contributed by the fields of biology, education, and comparative psychology.

Four key themes have emerged in the course of this revival. The *bidirectionality of structure and function* theme emphasizes that social behavior is not just a consequence or end product of maturation. Social acts also direct developmental processes, in both the young and those with whom they interact. Once the biophysical structures of the organism develop, they direct and organize social patterns. Social behaviors themselves are an integral part of biological life processes. A second major theme emphasizes the *interactive nature of the behaviors to be explained*. Beyond the truisms and the potential circularity of interactional approaches, there is a significant and revolutionary idea. It is that social actions cannot be considered apart from the context and the social interactions in which they occur. Children shape their parents, just as parents shape their children. Both the methods and the concepts of social development must reflect the fact that the reference behaviors interact. The third theme is an extension of the second. *Social activities are organized;* they occur in patterns and clumps, as functions of social systems and the synchronized acts of individuals. Recognition of the coherent and integrated nature of social relationships is a necessary corollary of interactional emphases; such recognition ensures that they are not dismissed as trivial or buried by the minutiae of behavior. The fourth theme is that *social relationships are malleable and reversible to varying degrees.* As we will see, the range of plasticity depends on the nature of the responses, the type and timing of the manipulation, and the social organization of the society and the species. Much of this volume will be concerned with identifying the conditions necessary for malleability and change.

These themes have helped contemporary scientists to transcend the traditional metaphors of social development. "New wine" will burst old bottles, and new data and emphases have required basic revisions in social learning concepts. Perhaps the major change has been the accommodation of social learning principles to the biological and cognitive conditions of the organism. Some interchange patterns are more likely to occur at one age than at another. The individual's learning capabilities change markedly with age, as do his cognitive capabilities. There is a *developmental synchrony in learning.* The individual is not only "prepared" to learn particular relationships more easily at one stage of development than at another, he is also predisposed to perform particular classes of social responses at different ages. What is learned is jointly controlled by the behavioral dispositions and the social systems into which the individual is integrated. The maturation-linked dispositions themselves are paced by the age and the phyletic and cognitive status of the individual.

New facts continue to support and augment the changes in perspective. One decade ago, research on infancy had produced only a handful of studies; today the study of infancy is a dominant area of developmental psychology. Studies of animal behavior and ethological studies of social development have enjoyed not only scientific but popular support. The development of powerful and relatively inexpensive technologies (including closed-circuit television and computer analysis) has made practical the implementation of new methods of studying social interaction.

What goals, then, might we aim for in the study of social development? Despite the diversity of interests, species, and problems, serious developmental researchers have had a common objective: to determine what events in ontogeny promote the establishment, maintenance, and plasticity of social interchanges. Although the goals are bold ones, they are not necessarily unobtainable. Indeed, recent advances indicate that they are within reach. Let us now turn to an examination of those advances and their implications.

THE FOUNDATIONS OF
SOCIAL INTERACTION

The chapters in Part II focus on the development of basic social patterns in man and animals. In keeping with the emphasis of the rest of the book, these issues are examined according to a life-span developmental approach. This means that the phenomena that occur *following* infancy are considered to be potentially as important for social adaptation as those that occur *during* infancy.

One of the problems that appears in the study of certain early social relations is that newborn infants can hardly "learn to be social." They don't have the time. Mammalian infants must be able to perform some basic interchanges immediately after birth, including those involved in the synchrony of their feeding activities and the control of their bodily temperatures, in order to survive. Hence Chapter 3 is concerned with the question of how mammalian young and their mothers solve these problems and thereby establish "foundational" relationships.[1] Chapter 4 focuses on the malleability of early social interactions in mammals, including the question of how susceptible they are to changes from "normal" conditions and what consequences are produced by these changes. Chapter 5 deals with devel-

---

[1] You will soon discover that it was necessary to extend the coverage of social foundations to nonmammals in two instances. In one instance—prenatal determinants of social behavior—the extension was required because of the meager amount of information available concerning mammals in this critical area. In the other instance—imprinting reversibility—the literatures on birds and mammals have overlapped, and the reader would have been given a biased view of the problem if one were presented without the other.

opmental transformations in the social actions of mammals over time and space. It addresses the question of how social behaviors can be reorganized in early maturity and beyond.

Early human social development is the subject of Chapters 6 through 8. So that similarities and differences may be noted, the chapters on human and animal development parallel each other. Accordingly, Chapter 6 deals with the establishment of social relationships between infants and other persons, and Chapter 7 is concerned with the continuity of social relationships and the effects of abrupt changes in maternal care on child behavior. Chapter 8, the last chapter in this section, is an introduction to the distinctively human interaction patterns that have been called interpersonal competency, dependency, and affiliation. These relationships rely on the child's unique capabilities to anticipate, diagnose, and otherwise think about social interchanges.

3

THE ORIGIN OF SOCIAL RESPONSIVITY AND SOCIAL ATTACHMENT

What is the origin of the infant's first social relationship? How does the behavior of the neonate become synchronized with the actions of other individuals? In attempting to answer these questions, we will immediately become aware of the relation between biology and behavior, and the relation between the organic states and acts of the infant and those of the parents and siblings.

Life Before Birth: Prenatal Determinants

No single event did more to encourage behavioral scientists to take a fresh look at socialization than Konrad Lorenz's rediscovery of the curious way that young birds seem to form social bonds. Lorenz (1937) focused attention on the fact that newly hatched chicks and ducklings approach and subsequently (within hours after hatching) prefer the first salient object to which they are exposed. Usually the object is the maternal hen or duck, but it could be an affectionate human caretaker or a flashing light. It is a credit to the genius of Lorenz that he saw in this simple observation an explanation of why young animals become identified with and prefer to remain with, mate, and care for members of their own kind rather than other species. According to Lorenz's classic statement, infant birds of many species are genetically programmed to respond positively after hatching to objects that have some of the properties of their own species. Once the response has been made, the young animal becomes "imprinted" to the characteristics of the object and, presumably, to those of its own species. [1]

Is imprinting necessary for species identification? Overlooked in the classical statement was the possibility that some basic events that determine initial social preferences may have already taken place before birth. The social preferences of the newborn are not neutral. In an important study, newly hatched ducklings were found to demonstrate a strong preference for the maternal call of their species when it was heard at the same time as the calls of other species—even though the ducklings had been hatched and incubated in isolation and the

[1] Imprinting is the process whereby newly hatched precocial birds become socially attached to and identify with their species or species surrogate (see Chapter 5).

calls were nearly identical (Gottlieb, 1966). After having watched one of these demonstrations in Dr. Gottlieb's laboratory, I became convinced that the ducklings were hearing something that I was not, since the difference between calls is almost impossible for the average human ear to detect. Indeed, the selective response of the young birds fits the criteria that are usually employed to categorize a behavior as innate: it appears shortly after birth, it is universal for the species, and it occurs without prior training or experience.

But categorizing a behavior as innate does not explain how it develops. It has been known for some time that the embryonic duckling is active and responsive—that it influences others and is influenced by its own experiences. For example, ducklings and other precocial birds vocalize several days before hatching.[2] The onset of vocalization occurs soon after the bill penetrates the interior membrane at the large end of the egg, and before it cracks the shell. Hence the embryonic duckling can "talk to itself." Also, in the natural setting, the maternal duck emits calls during the incubation period. Ei-

ther source of stimulation, self-produced or mother-produced, could operate to sensitize the young to the distinctive calls of its species or to speed up a naturally occurring process.

These possibilities were explored in a series of experiments recently conducted by Gottlieb (1975a, b, c). To control for the effects of self-stimulation, he devised a surgical procedure for devocalizing the embryo before hatching. These muted ducklings (which hatch normally and later regain their voices) can then be incubated in auditory isolation or exposed to any range of experimentally selected sounds. The combined evidence, summarized in Figure 3-1, leaves no doubt that the experiences of the embryo, including those that it produces for itself, influence post-hatching preferences.

These experiments make clear that social behavior is continuous through ontogeny; birth or hatching is just one stage in the life cycle that has been ongoing. The work also emphasizes the hazards of drawing premature conclusions as to the importance or lack of importance of experience in controlling the "normal" maturation process. Just as the original observations of imprinting permitted a basic revision of the then-current ideas about socialization, contemporary studies of the bidirectionality of social influence in birds have made possible a reassessment of what mammals learn in the course of development. But the prenatal activities of the

---

[2] The word "precocial" is derived from a Latin root that means "early ripening"; hence it refers to species whose young are active and able to move about freely at hatching. The word "altricial" refers to species whose young are relatively helpless at hatching and require parental care for an extended period. These terms may also be used to refer to mammalian infants.

Figure 3-1. Peking ducklings prefer the maternal calls of their own species even when they have been incubated in isolation, without having been exposed to the maternal calls.

Top: Given the choice between approaching the maternal call of a Peking duck and a chicken, Peking ducklings prefer the maternal call of their own species to that of other species. Developmental studies of the prehatching activities of the embryo indicate that the duckling vocalizes to itself before hatching (during penetration of air space). Surgical procedures have been devised to "devocalize" the embryo before it hatches and before it can vocalize to itself.

Middle: Late embryonic and early postnatal stages of

Peking duckling. The embryo vocalizes before hatching, after penetration of the air space at the large end of the egg. The devocalization operation can be performed early (during the tenting stage and before penetration) or late (after penetration of the air space and after some prehatching vocalization has occurred).

Further studies have shown that this "self-vocalization" is a key factor in the young duckling's preference for maternal calls.

Bottom: If the devocalization occurs early (before the duckling has heard itself), the maternal preference is disrupted. If the devocalization occurs later, but before hatching, the maternal preference is stronger (adapted from Gottlieb, 1976b, with permission).

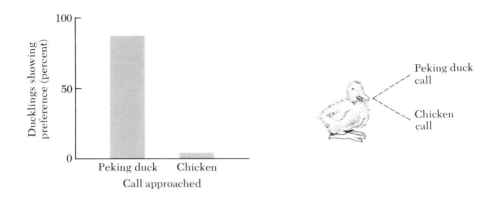

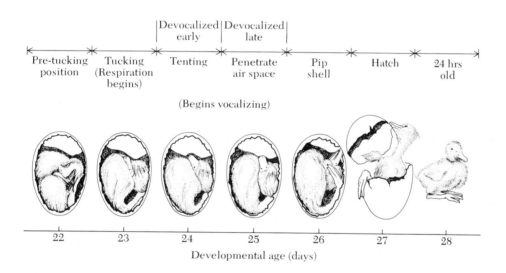

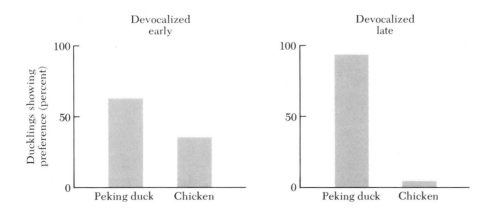

infant constitute only half the story (or less). The mother herself is active during this period, and her activities have an impact on the developing young, on societal organization, and on herself.

Dyadic Interactions at Birth

Activities of the Mother

Detailed observations of mammalian mothers before birth indicate that pre-partum [3] self-stimulation contributes significantly to subsequent maternal-infant adaptation. One of the more interesting changes is the way in which the mother effectively prepares herself for giving birth and taking care of her infant. Some of the most accurate observations have been made of the activities of female rats just before they give birth (Roth and Rosenblatt, 1967). The toilet behavior of female rats that are not pregnant follows a predictable pattern. The animals start from the front of their bodies and work backward (forepaws, neck, back, sides, and rear). Just before giving birth, pregnant females reverse the order: they begin at the anogenital region and nipple lines. This activity seems, at parturition, to contribute significantly to the birth process, during which the maternal animal persists in bursts of licking at the vaginal opening. Upon appearance of the fetus, she draws it to her mouth, while licking and rotating it. Turning then to the placenta, she engorges it while holding the pup with her forepaws. The birth fluids and membranes are licked from the fetus. This ingestion of the afterbirth is called *placentophagia*. In the process of licking the pup, the maternal animal

[3] Some technical terms are used in this discussion of the birth process that the reader should become familiar with. *Pre-partum* refers to the period just before birth; *parturition* refers to the birth process; and *post-partum* refers to the period following birth. *Perinatal* refers to the events occurring immediately before, during, and immediately after birth. *Primiparous* refers to females who have borne one child and no more or who are parturient for the first time; *multiparous* refers to females who have given birth at least once before.

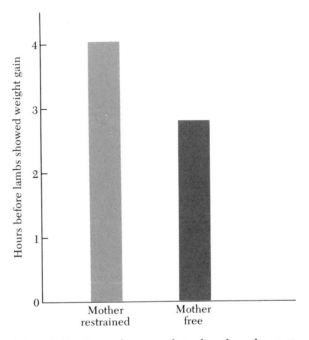

Figure 3-2. Do mothers contribute directly to the onset of suckling in their offspring? The lambs whose mothers had been restrained took longer to show weight gain than did lambs whose mothers were free to stimulate and direct them (data from Alexander and Williams, 1964).

gradually begins to concentrate upon the neonate's anogenital region. This stimulation evokes urination and defecation. The products of elimination are consumed by the mother, and the area thereafter becomes one of "special attractiveness" (Rosenblatt and Lehrman, 1963).

Maternal stimulation thus arouses and maintains activity in the young. Evidence obtained from studies of other mammalian species suggests that the adult animal's stimulation during grooming has a directive function as well, in that the offspring are brought into close proximity with the mammary areas (Alexander and Williams, 1964; Blauvelt, 1955). Infant lambs, like most other mammalian young, tend to suck indiscriminately at any objects around which their mouths fit, including their own paws, the clothing of the experimenter, or maternal wool. During the first 12 hours following birth, the experimental lambs (whose mothers' heads had been yoked and restrained) gained significantly less weight and showed less "teat-seeking activity" than did offspring of ewes that had not been restricted (Alexander and Williams, 1964) (see Figure 3-2).

For the purposes of interaction analysis, it should be observed that the suckling behavior of the young serves a dual function. Suckling reduces hydraulic pressure in the mammary glands of the mother and simultaneously provides nourishment for the offspring. It also seems likely that anogenital stimulation of the young by the mother has dual significance. In the neonate, stimulation is required for anal elimination. The neonatal young of some mammalian species will die if such stimulation is not provided (Lehrman, 1961). Hence the same act that promotes infant survival also produces a most attractive substance for the mother. In both instances of interaction, essential biological functions are served for both members of the pair.

The behavior of maternal mammals toward their offspring at birth varies markedly between individuals and between births. First-born are treated less adequately than later born; in some species, it appears that initial birth is for practice. Inexperienced chimpanzee mothers in captivity seem to be afraid of their first-born. They refuse to touch them and do not permit them to cling. Maternal mutilation of the neonate sometimes occurs. Van den Berghe (1959) reported the abnormal behavior of a gorilla mother who first bit off a hand of her neonate, then a foot, and finally crushed its skull.

Not all first-born nonhuman primates are treated so badly. Nearly all the captive-reared mother chimpanzees who were observed to experience successful births ate the afterbirth (Tinklepaugh and Hartman, 1930; Yerkes, 1943). Van Lawick-Goodall (1968) has speculated that, in the wild, primate mothers have considerable interactive experience that may prepare them for parturition and for caring for their young. They should be less fearful of the neonate and better prepared to meet its demands. This idea is certainly plausible and is supported by at least some anecdotal information, such as the observation by Jane van Lawick-Goodall. She reports:

> In 1960 I observed the behaviour of a very young (almost certainly primiparous) velvet monkey with a newborn infant (still wet when I first saw it). The mother, who was some 100 yd. from the rest of the troop, sat on one branch for nearly 4 hr., occasionally touching her genital area and then licking her fingers. During this time she occasionally appeared to relax her cradling position so that the infant slipped very low in her lap. Each time, after it had struggled violently for several seconds, the mother adjusted its position and cradled it again. When she finally got up prior to joining the other monkeys she kept one hand under the infant for several seconds before moving off after which the infant seemed to have no difficulty in maintaining its ventral position. The mother appeared to have difficulty in keeping her balance as she walked along branches. She was only observed to eat six small berries between 10 a.m. and 5:30 p.m. (p. 224).

Overall, the picture that emerges is that during the *post-partum* period a behavioral interdependency rapidly develops between the mother and her offspring. The interactions are not immediately smooth or predictable. Rather, the behaviors of the offspring elicit a synchronous response in the mother, and vice versa (see Figure 3-3). As the interactions recur, the sequences themselves become more predictable and the behavior episodes become more regular. The interactions ensure that in the critical hours shortly after birth, the mother will attend to her young and they will survive. Figure 3-4 is a summary of the contributions of the mother and her offspring to the basic interchange that occurs following birth.

Although most of these observations are the result of studies of rodents and ungulates, similar observations have been reported for other domestic species, including dogs (Rheingold, 1963), cats (Schneirla,

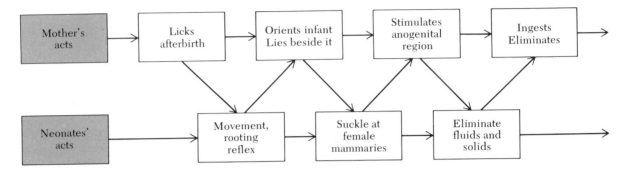

Figure 3–3. Some of the bases for the synchrony of the acts of the mother and of the infant. The *rooting reflex* is observed in mammalian infants. Touching the infant's head elicits (1) orientation toward the source of stimulation and (2) sucking movements.

Rosenblatt, and Tobach, 1963), and goats (Collias, 1956). Obviously, it is difficult to obtain comparable information by observing nondomesticated species. The reports obtained from field observations (for example, Altmann, 1963; Rheingold, 1963) suggest that the basic aspects of early *post-partum* interactions are the same in both domesticated and nondomesticated species. However, it should be observed that not *all* mammals exhibit all aspects of the behaviors described. The camel, for instance, is not a placentophage. Furthermore, not all animals within the same litter are treated alike. The last arrival in a litter of kittens is typically given considerably less maternal attention than is the first-born animal. Finally, drastic modifications in the biophysical status of the mother do not necessarily inhibit or change maternal behavior. Even rodent females whose mammary tissues have been surgically removed exhibit normal maternal behavior (Moltz, 1970; Moltz et al., 1967).

Clearly there is considerable diversity in the physiological and behavioral mechanisms that shape and consolidate maternal-infant interaction sequences. The events that evoke and maintain mutual responses must be sufficiently redundant so that one process can fail without producing disastrous consequences. It is not uncommon, of course, for biological systems to have "fail-safe" features, particularly those systems that are essential for survival.

Activities of the Infants

Young animals, even at birth, are not passive agents in the interaction-establishment process (see Figures 3-3 and 3-4). Infant mice and rats, for example, will group together even when not placed together (retrieved) by the mother. This phenomenon can be simply demonstrated by removing 24-*hour*-old mice from the mother and scattering them randomly in a new compartment. Even though they cannot see and their hearing and olfaction capabilities are seemingly primitive, each of them rolls and swims about in the wood shavings until contact with another infant is established. As this activity continues, the original "clump" of 6–8 animals rapidly becomes organized. Experimental analyses indicate that such behavior is at least partly controlled by the need to regulate bodily warmth (see Figure 3-5). Homeothermia (the capability to maintain a constant internal blood temperature) is not observed in rodents until approximately 2–3 weeks after birth.

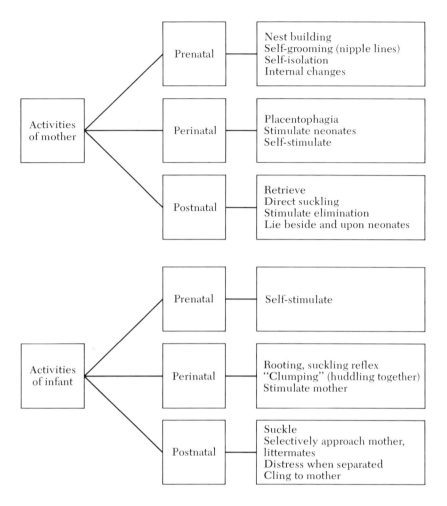

Figure 3-4. The acts of the mother and of the infant, observed in many but not all nonhuman mammals, that have been presumed to facilitate the establishment of the mother-infant relationship.

Alberts (1978) has recently shown that neonatal mice also rely on the sense of smell to direct their movements toward each other.

Whatever may be the later significance of the early interactive behaviors, there can be no doubt that they are essential for the infant's immediate sur-vival. The conditions also seem to encourage the rapid development of an inter-response dependence between the mother and her offspring, as well as between the offspring and each other. The mother-infant pair or mother-litter combination is typically removed from the other animals. Among animals

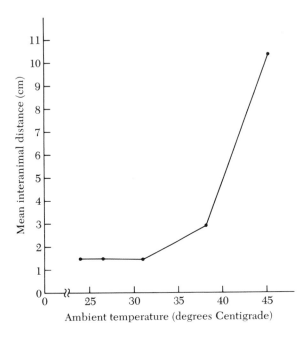

Figure 3-5. The distance between 8 neonatal mice (less than 24 hours of age) and littermates is a direct function of the ambient temperature. Mean interanimal distance is the average distance that each infant maintains between itself and other infants. Locomotion is independent, achieved primarily by "swimming" through the litter material (from Cairns, 1973, with permission).

that bear precocial young, a type of functional isolation is frequently produced by the mother. The maternal elk or deer, for instance, separates herself from other members of the herd before parturition. The mother keeps her infant away from the conspecific group for periods as long as several days or weeks before rejoining (Altmann, 1963). Such maternal-infant isolation has also been observed in free-ranging chimpanzees (van Lawick-Goodall, 1968). Among animals that bear altricial young, mother-infant interactions are assured by the incapability of the neonates. They either remain in the nest, as do rodents and canines, or they cling to the

mother, as do the young of various subhuman primate species. The mother-as-an-interactor is a ubiquitous event.

Consolidation of the Early Social Interchanges

Maternal-infant interaction patterns are established in the first hours after birth; they become consolidated and organized in the days and weeks that follow. Nursing, for instance, becomes more efficient as each participant—the mother and the infant—becomes more skilled in its role and in "reading" the subtle cues of the other (see Figure 3-6). Since there are multiple opportunities for feeding each day, there is considerable opportunity for each participant to discriminate and to learn the social responses of the other. With each feeding, both the form of the mother's response and her lactational state are influenced. Simultaneously, mutual anticipations evolve.

Other dyadic skills are involved in transportation. It is essential that patterns of support (such as holding by the mother and clinging by the infant) are established early by primates that necessarily move with the troop or subgroup. R. A. Hinde and his collaborators at the Sub-Department of Animal Behaviour at Cambridge University have completed a thorough study of the mutual clinging activity of the rhesus monkey mother and her offspring during the first 7 months of life (Hinde and White, 1974). In the rhesus, the normal form of clinging is the "ventro-ventral" position, in which the infant is pressed against the abdomen and breast of the mother. During the first week of life, the infant clings ventrally almost continuously. But by the twenty-fifth week of life, it is on the mother less than 50 percent of the time during the morning hours. The ventro-ventral position facilitates sleeping, feeding, and digestion as well as transportation. The closeness also encourages the development of mutual dependencies. For example, changes in the balance and position of one

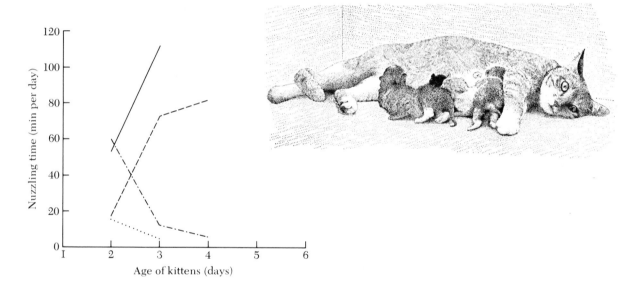

Figure 3-6. The establishment of feeding patterns and the learning of nipple preferences in kittens.

Top: Nursing is initiated by the mother cat shortly after the kittens are born. She lies on her side to expose her nipples and licks the blind kittens, thus orienting them to her body. They crawl to her, nuzzle in her fur, and, while maintaining constant contact with her fur, move along her body to the nipple region. There nuzzling changes into gentle nose-tapping until a nipple is touched. The touch of the nipple stimulates the kitten to make mouthing movements that change into sucking when the nipple is grasped.

Middle: Nipple preference is developed by the kittens within a few days. They show rapid improvement in the speed with which they find the preferred nipple. If a kitten accidentally takes another kitten's nipple, it readily abandons that nipple when the rightful owner nuzzles it. When a kitten is sucking from its preferred nipple, it will hold on tenaciously if another kitten tries to take it.

Bottom: Identification of a milk-filled nipple by the texture or odor of the surrounding flange is rapidly learned by newborn kittens. The kitten nuzzles the textured flange around the milk-filled nipple (*solid line*) much more than textured flange around a sealed nipple (*dotted line*) and learns to feed itself independently at the age of 3 days. It needs more time to learn to discriminate the odor of the milk-filled nipple (*dashed line*) from the odor of the sealed nipple (*dashed/dotted line*). (Adapted from J. S. Rosenblatt, Learning in Newborn Kittens. Copyright © 1972 by Scientific American, Inc. All rights reserved.)

elicit complementing changes in the activity of the other.

Mutually dependent interchanges also occur during grooming and play. A considerable part of the waking hours of young monkeys and baboons and their mothers is devoted to reciprocal grooming. This activity serves both communicative and hygenic functions. Marler (1965) has observed that grooming may control behavior through redirection. The action appears to promote relaxation in both the recipient and the grooming agent. Grooming also helps to curb infection by mites and other micro-organisms; the fur is often a rich source of small edible beasts for the individual during the grooming.

The preceding discussion has focused on the consolidation of interaction patterns in maternal-offspring pairs. Similar interactions can be observed between infants and nonmaternal members of a species. The range of alternative partners is dependent on the species and on the opportunities that are available. In some species, such as sheep and elk, the infant is insulated from alternative interactions. When ready to give birth, the mother separates herself from the group of which she is a part and does not return until the infant has learned to be responsive to her. However, the young of other species, such as mice and dogs, are maintained in a communal setting and learn to respond early to the parental animal, to littermates, and to nonmaternal females.

Psychobiological events not only establish interactions, they help to maintain them. Changes in morphological/physiological status can be either a *determinant* or an *outcome* of changes in dyadic interaction patterns. The type of social-physiological feedback pattern that sometimes occur is illustrated by the reaction of rat mothers that are separated from their young (see Figure 3-7). Compared with a group of control mothers (who kept their litters), the mothers whose young had been "kidnapped" showed a sharp decrement in their readiness to nurse, to retrieve the infants, and to build nests. Correlated changes occurred in their physiological condition. Normally, the estrous cycles of maternal rats are inhibited until about the fourth week after they have given birth, so they cannot immediately give birth to a new litter. However, the estrous cycles of females whose litters have been removed begin shortly after parturition (Rothchild, 1960). Even more remarkable, the physiological state of the mother at parturition—in terms of lactation, retrieval, and nest-building—can be prolonged indefinitely by constantly replacing her growing litter with pups that are less than 10 days of age (Wiesner and Sheard, 1933). Maintaining the filial interaction provides for the continuation of the maternal condition, which in turn leads to the persistence of filial interactions, and so on (see Figure 3-8).

Although synchronization in lactation and estrous cycling has been most clearly demonstrated in rodents, it is not just a rat or hamster phenomenon. The physiology of maternal hormonal systems is similar in all mammals in that the feedback that occurs in stimulation is required to keep the mother in a maternal state (Gorbman and Bern, 1962). The infant helps to "design" its own mother, and to keep her in synchrony with its own needs (Figure 3-9).

Changes in the Relationship Between Parents and Their Young

A normal social relationship is dynamic and flexible. In most species, the movement of the infant away from the mother, litter, and nest is as inevitable and crucial for survival as is its early social dependence. *Separation* is generally viewed as inevitably traumatic, both for the young and for the parental animal. However, most offspring can and must eventually fare on their own. The achievement of an independent existence ordinarily requires repeated separation.

The typical patterns and timing of "detachment" from the mother are almost as diverse as the species that have been studied. Social organization patterns differ as a function of ecological demands and of the sex and species of the individual. Nevertheless,

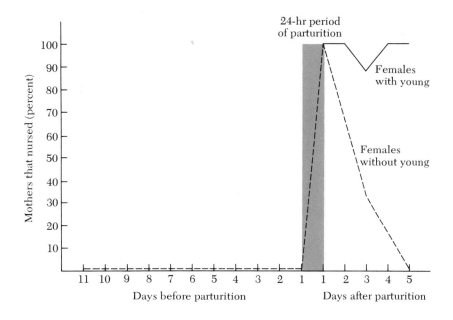

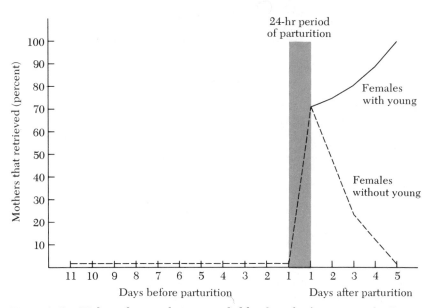

Figure 3-7. Without the stimulation provided by the infant's activities, the "maternal condition" in rats rapidly disappears. In this figure, mothers whose infants were removed at birth are compared with mothers whose litters were not removed. Note that there is a precipitous drop in the percentage of females that are willing to nurse (*top*) and to retrieve (*bottom*) unfamiliar infants (adapted from Rosenblatt and Lehrman, 1963, with permission).

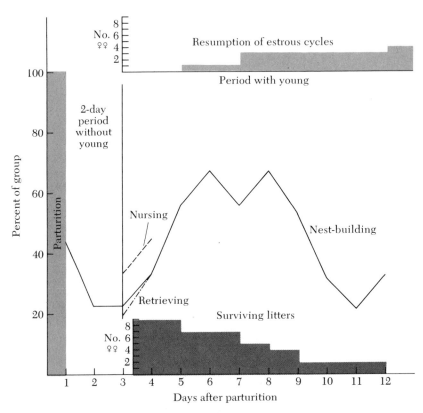

Figure 3-8. Removal of infant rat pups for only 60 hours after birth can drastically decrease the likelihood that they will survive if returned to their mother. When infants are returned, the mothers resume nest-building, but they have difficulty nursing and show little interest in retrieval. Hence most of the infants die within the next 2-7 days, and the mothers become physiologically ready to have another litter (adapted from Rosenblatt and Lehrman, 1963, with permission).

some consistencies emerge across species and circumstances. For example, the males of some matriarchal species (such as sheep) tend to show a more drastic change in the relationship with their mother than do the females. The females tend to remain with the mother, but the males tend to form bachelor bands or to travel alone at about the end of the first year (Grubb and Jewell, 1966).

Other species form family units. How these units develop in ontogeny depends in part on the nature of the unit and the nature of the maternal-infant relationship. One of the more interesting patterns occurs in the Hamadryas baboon and has been observed by Kummer (1968). He finds that the adolescent male tends to spend progressively more time away from the family unit, beginning at about the

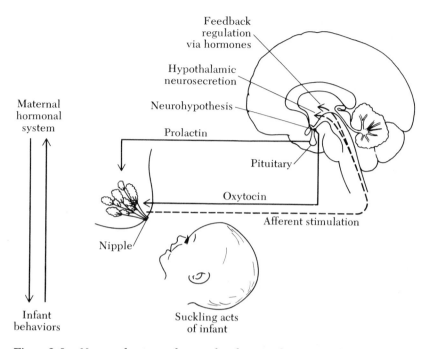

Figure 3-9. Neuroendocrine pathways of prolactin and oxytocin release. Prolactin is a primary hormone that, in cooperation with other hormones, promotes the manufacture and secretion of milk. Prolactin is released as a result of the afferent stimulation provided by the suckling actions of the infant. Oxytocin helps to trigger the ejection of milk from the mammary glands.

end of the first year. The male's social activities center around the other males. At about age 4 or 5, young adult males are observed playing with, and caring for, young females. Not infrequently, the male takes over the maternal role in transporting and protecting the young female. Kummer speculates that the male's attentiveness to the young female marks the beginning of a new single-family unit, with the young male as its leader.

A controversy has recently arisen among researchers as to why there is a change in the mother-infant relationship and who is responsible for the separation of mother and infant. One position that has been vigorously defended is that the mother herself initiates separation by forcing the young away—either by punishing them or by not meeting

their needs. The alternative position, just as strongly held, is that the separation reflects the normal independence and curiosity of the young and is a natural consequence of increasing maturity. The reader may wonder whether it makes any difference which view is correct or why both positions are not tenable, so some background information is in order.

At least part of the problem is that the two views tap more fundamental differences about the nature of the young and about who is directing whom in the maternal-infant relationship. On the one hand, the social behavior of the young animal is often viewed as being controlled by a fundamental attachment to the mother. This bond is seen as being not only basic to all other social relations but also enduring and of singular importance. From the perspective of attachment theory, it seems puzzling that the young should be the ones to *initiate* changes in the fundamental relationship. Nonetheless, separations reliably occur across mammals. Why?

Of the two possibilities, the one that is more consistent with attachment models is that the mother herself brings about the separation. Indeed, direct observations of young mammals indicate that the mother does actively discourage approaches from her young. Schneirla and Rosenblatt (1961) made detailed observations of the maternal cat-kitten relationship to determine how the weaning comes about.

In stage 3, which generally begins shortly after the 30th day, the initiation of suckling depends more and more and finally almost altogether upon the kittens. They now follow the female about the cage with greater frequency and increasing persistence, remaining at the place of her disappearance when she leaps to the wall shelf. When she happens to be accessible to them, they persist with vigor in attempts to nuzzle which at times result in attachment and suckling, but with increasing frequency, as through prompt counteraction by the female, may end in little more than a brief social exchange. In various ways, consequently, the kittens forcibly influence the female's behavior more and more. Her changing attitude toward the kittens is indicated clearly by the increasing frequency and duration of her stays on the shelf, at least until the kittens themselves can reach the shelf. From the time the kittens can get to the shelf, at about the 45th day, the female avoids it increasingly. In the third stage, therefore, the intimacy of the social bond between female and young has decreased with their changing behavioral relationships—i.e., as their social distance has increased (pp. 236–237).

Schneirla and Rosenblatt concluded that the mother contributes to weaning and to the development of response independence in her offspring in two ways: by leading them to sources of solid food

and by making sucking more and more difficult, thus forcing the kittens to obtain their food independently (see Figure 3-10).

Not all mammalian mothers are so benign in simply denying food to their offspring. Some species take more direct measures. From her observations of maternal behavior in dogs, Rheingold (1963) reports that in the later stages of weaning, "mothers punished pups when they suckled or tried to suckle." There was no doubt that these acts were intended as punishment, in that the mother was "growling or barking at a pup, snapping or baring her teeth to it, catching its head in her mouth and

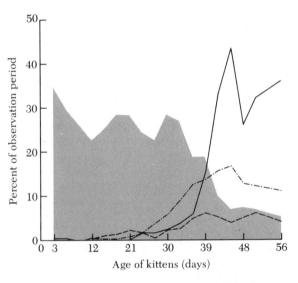

Figure 3-10. How actions of mother cat affect changes in the feeding and play patterns of her kittens. The amount of nursing that occurred during the daily observation period is indicated by the shaded area. Play activities of kittens directed toward the mother (*dashed line*) and toward each other (*dashed/dotted line*) began to increase about 30 days after birth, and at the same time the mother began to spend time on a shelf, out of reach of the kittens (*solid line*). (From J. S. Rosenblatt, Learning in Newborn Kittens. Copyright © 1972 by Scientific American, Inc. All rights reserved.)

shaking it, holding it down with a paw, or pouncing on it, but [such behavior was] in distinction to the same acts in apparent play." When these maternal acts occurred, nursing and contact between the mother and her offspring decreased. The mothers in fact cleared a space around themselves free of pups. Unmistakable maternal discouragement of approach activities has been observed also in various primates. For instance, a monkey mother will slap, bite, and sit on her offspring when their approaches to her become too vigorous or bothersome (Rosenblum and Kaufman, 1968).

The other possibility is that the young animal is the effective agent in changing the relationship. There is indeed ample evidence that young animals become increasingly curious and adventurous as a function of age. Their basic biological systems—ingestion, elimination, temperature control, locomotion—become more efficient and physiologically independent. Furthermore, the animals become more capable of pestering and otherwise provoking their mother, as well as others in their immediate environment. Some adult animals respond to impertinences by retreating; others respond with rebuff and punishment.

Debates about the "nature" of the young (whether they are attached, dependent infants or active, independent organisms) tend to oversimplify the actual dynamics of the infant-parental relationship. Hinde and Spencer-Booth (1967) stated the problem clearly when they wrote, "we feel that it cannot be too strongly emphasized that the relationship between mother and infant is a developing, interacting pattern" (p. 195). Clearly the actions of both contribute to the detachment. The mother punishes, but the young provoke. As the behavior of the one changes in response to maturational and environmental events, reciprocal adjustments occur in the behavior and physiology of the other. The behavioral and biological feedback then augments and stabilizes the change. The young animal helps to shape its own future, but the continuing contribu-

tions of those with whom it interacts are of equal or greater importance.

Attachment Behaviors in Mammals

According to modern usage, "attachment" refers to an exclusive, relatively enduring, affective bond "that one individual (person or animal) forms between himself and another specific individual" (Ainsworth, 1972). The prototypic attachment is that which develops between mother and child. That a strong tie develops early in life is certainly no new revelation. However, the systematic study of attachment behavior in animals and man began only recently. Scott (1962) and Harlow (1958) opened the door for the systematic study of this early affectional relationship with their now classic studies of the young puppy and infant rhesus monkey. At about the same time, Bowlby (1958) and Gewirtz (1961) made theoretical statements about human infants that have been most influential.

Direct observations of the behaviors of very young mammals toward their mothers leave no doubt about the intensity of this early relationship. Three phenomena of the mother-infant relationship have been taken as evidence of the strong, specific bond: separation-disruption, approach and preference, and fear of strangers.

Separation-Disruption

Possibly the most dramatic phenomenon that occurs in a filial relationship is the behavior disorganization that is produced when there is a forced separation of mother and infant. When a one-month-old monkey is separated from its mother, a relaxed, contented infant can be abruptly transformed into a restless, crying, and sometimes extremely agitated organism—even in the absence of physical irritation or injury. Jensen and Tolman (1962) have written a graphic description of the immediate effects of separating two pigtail macaque infants (5 and 7 months of age) from their mother:

> Separation of mother and infant monkeys is an extremely stressful event for both mother and infant as well as for the attendants and for all other monkeys within sight or earshot of the experience. The mother becomes ferocious toward attendants and extremely protective of her infant. The infant's screams can be heard almost over the entire building. The mother struggles and attacks the separators. The baby clings tightly to the mother and to any object to which it can grasp to avoid being held or removed by the attendant. With the baby gone, the mother paces the cage almost constantly, charges the cage occasionally, bites at it, and makes continual attempts to escape. She also lets out occasional mooing-like sounds. The infant emits high-pitched, shrill screams intermittently and almost continuously for the period of separation (pp. 132–133).

The phenomenon is as dramatic in herd animals as in primates. The separation of young sheep from their mother is particularly striking. The extreme agitation and disorganization that result might lead one to believe that the young animals were enduring great pain or physical duress. These 20- to 30-pound animals run full speed around the isolation chamber. On occasion, the circling pattern gives way to a line drive directed at the door or the wall. Finally, some lambs leap vertically upward. Others run head first into the ceramic tile wall. After recovering, the animals repeat the running and head-banging with groggy redundancy. Throughout, their activity is punctuated by distressful, plaintive, high-pitched "baa's" (see Figure 3-11).

Not all mammals display such extreme separation-disruption behavior (see Figure 3-12). Maternal rats, for instance, show intense disorganization only if the separation-reunion occurs under particular conditions, such as removal of half of the pups rather than the entire litter (Scholz, 1974). And

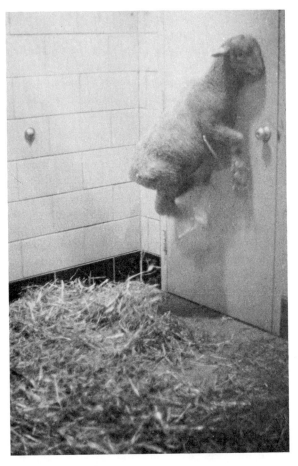

Figure 3-11. Photograph showing behavioral disorganization in young lamb separated from other members of the flock.

there are significant differences—both within individuals and between individuals—in the degree of reaction. Not all instances of separation produce spasms of distress and vocalization. As will be discussed in Chapter 7, that a human infant will be separated from his mother is usually taken as a matter of course. Otherwise, it would be virtually impossible for the mother to perform the necessary

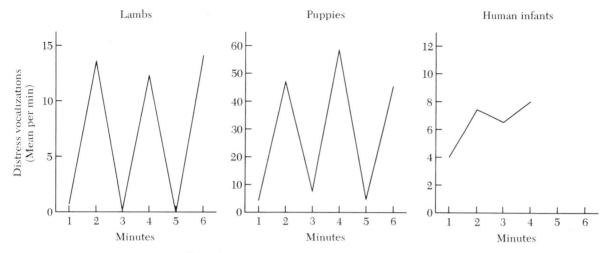

Figure 3–12. Effect of removal and replacement of the mother or littermates on the emotional arousal and physical activity of the infant. Note that replacement is highly effective in decreasing arousal in lambs, somewhat less effective in puppies, and even less effective in human infants. (Removal occurred during the *even* minutes, and replacement during the *odd* minutes. The infants were observed with the mother in the first minute.)

day-to-day activities. Knowledge of the reasons for these variations and how they arise can provide a key to understanding why the behavior occurs when it does.

Approach and Preference

A second general phenomenon is the physical closeness that the infant seeks to maintain with the principal "other" in its world. The metaphor of a psychological umbilical cord between the mother and her offspring probably led to the use of the descriptive term "attachment" in the first place. Systematic studies have confirmed that the activities of both the young and the mother help to maintain this proximity. The young of most orders of placental mammals, including nonhuman primates, rats, carnivores (dogs, cats), and various types of ungulates (horses, sheep, deer) have been observed to approach their mother. That the very young like to be with their

mother is hardly news, no matter how sophisticated the apparatus or how ingenious the test. Their very survival depends on her.

But young mammals, including children, are not continuously "attached" to their mother. They sometimes prefer to be with other individuals. Although proximity-seeking behavior is common and occurs in general across species, it is not constant. Young lambs, for instance, "wander." Only after rebuffs by other members of the flock will they return to the mother. Similarly, children are active, curious, and exploratory (Corter, Rheingold, and Eckerman, 1972). In these instances, it is the activity of the mother or of other adults, and ecological circumstances that help to maintain maternal-infant closeness. These differences occur both within the individual (sometimes closeness is preferred by the offspring and sometimes it is not) and between individuals. The tie that binds the infant and its mother is rather elastic. It may change from one situation to another; in some settings it is not present at all. In all mammals, the tendency to remain with the mother changes over time; "independence" increases with age.

Fear of Strangers

A third phenomenon that has been associated with attachment propensities is the distress that is sometimes observed in infants when they meet unfamiliar individuals. In human infants, this phenomenon has been called *fear of strangers*. The phenomenon of stranger-fear in young nonhuman mammals has received less attention. When it is observed, it is ascribed to the infant's *neophobia*, or fear of the new, a characteristic that is not limited to the young. (One example is their avoidance of strange and possibly poisoned foods.)

In overview, those who have attempted to identify the origin of social interchanges have used two different methods. One has been to analyze the ways in which the infant begins to respond to all social stimuli, including those provided by the mother. The other method has focused upon the social bond that typically forms between the mother and her young. Although attachment behaviors have been singled out for special attention, it is well to remember that they are merely piecemeal events abstracted from the organized and complex interactions that evolve between the immature organism and its caretakers.

Social Controls of Attachment Behavior

One aim of investigators of attachment behavior has been to identify the processes that cause variations in the intensity of the bond. What is it that other individuals around the infant do, or fail to do, that increases the infant's specific dependence upon them?

Is Feeding Necessary?

By definition, all mammals have one property in common: their young must suckle to survive. Since the initial relationships that develop inevitably involve the mother, it has seemed entirely reasonable to assume that the bond arose because of suckling.

The proposition that the feeding interaction is a necessary and essential step in the development of social cue properties was later incorporated into general behavior theory (Dollard and Miller, 1950; Sears, Whiting, Nowlis, and Sears, 1953). The nursing mother, in that she is necessarily associated with reduction of the infant's biological drive, was assumed to acquire motivational properties (that is, it was assumed that the infant would attempt to be with her and remain in her presence even when it was not hungry or in pain). These properties were subsequently generalized to other persons. The feeding interaction thus was considered to be a primary determinant of the course and nature of the young animal's (and child's) social behavior development. In view of the plausibility of this line of reasoning, and the obvious biological facts upon which it was based, it is small wonder that the assumption was not seriously challenged until the recent past.

The challenge, when it came, produced startling results. In their now classic studies, Harlow and his colleagues at the University of Wisconsin demonstrated that the delivery of milk is not a necessary condition for the establishment of enduring social cues and preferences. In a representative study (Harlow and Zimmerman, 1959), infant monkeys were isolated at birth and were maintained with two different objects that had some of the stimulus properties of a real mother. One object was a wood cylinder covered with a sheath of terry cloth, and the other was simply a wire cylinder. The wire model was so made that a bottle containing milk could be installed in the upper part in order to permit suckling. The terry cloth "mother" did not deliver milk. Both cylinders were inclined at an angle so that they could easily be climbed upon and clasped.

After the infants had been maintained in these conditions for 25 days, their preference for one or the other cylinder "mother" (surrogate) was assessed in different circumstances. The primary measure used throughout the experimental series was the amount of time that the infants spent on one or the other cylinder. The results were clear and impressive: the infants tended to spend more time in contact with the terry cloth-covered object than the wire one. Whether or not the model had "lactated"—that is, had delivered milk to the infant during rearing—made surprisingly little difference in terms of the preferences demonstrated in the test setting. Harlow and Zimmerman (1959) thus conclude that "feeding, in contrast to contact comfort, is neither a necessary nor a sufficient condition for affectional development."

We might reasonably ask how the two objects differed in terms of their respective response-support properties—that is, their capabilities to support the behaviors of the infants. According to the results of these initial studies, the cloth-draped object tended to support such activities as lying down, clinging, and sleeping. It is unclear whether the infants performed any behaviors with respect to the wire "mother" that they did not perform with respect to the wire cage in which they were enclosed—possibly little else except suckle. Most of the nonfeeding activities of the monkeys during rearing seemed to be centered around the cloth-covered object, whereas few of their behaviors (except feeding) were organized around the wire object. Thus one object had the capacity to elicit and support a variety of behaviors, including clinging and sucking; the other could support only feeding and climbing.

Is Contact-Comfort Necessary? The Impact of Sight and Other Senses

The results of these initial studies of the infant rhesus monkey suggest that feeding may not be necessary for social attachment development but that contact comfort is.

However, there is ample evidence that some young animals form strong bonds even in the total absence of direct interchange, or physical contact. Even from a distance, some stimuli—including those seen, smelled, and heard—can provide the basis for the development of strong preferences in some species (see Walters and Parke, 1965, for a review of the evidence). The role of sight and sound in imprinting in birds has long been recognized (Bateson, 1964; Gottlieb, 1971). Sight can play a major role for mammals as well (Walters and Parke, 1965). For instance, Cairns and Johnson (1965) accidentally discovered some years ago that lambs do not require interactions or physical contact. The problem that led to this discovery was an entirely practical one of devising a way that young lambs and an adult ewe could be raised together in reasonable harmony without allowing the ewe to reject and batter the lamb. One solution was simple: the ewe was separated from the young lambs by a wire fence. The animals could see, smell, and hear, but not touch each other. Later the investigators were surprised to find that the effects of "separated" rearing—that is, the young lamb's preference for the ewe across the fence—were no different from the effects produced when unlimited physical contact was permitted. In both instances, the lambs developed an exceedingly strong preference to approach and follow their adult partners, and became disrupted when separated from them. Subsequent studies of the role of distance receptors showed that the development of preferences is not limited to animate partners. For instance, isolated lambs develop a strong preference for visual patterns produced by operating television sets that they are reared with (Cairns, 1966b).

Studies of other young mammals (guinea pigs, dogs) indicate that they too can develop a selective responsiveness to events with which they have had no physical interaction. The role of distance receptors in the development of social preferences, and nonsocial ones, cannot be minimized. The extent to which young mammals are dominated by particular sensory systems differs with age and species. Lambs rely largely upon visual stimuli to orient themselves to their environment. It seems not entirely unreasonable, then, to assume that they will be highly responsive to visual stimuli in the course of social preference formation. The behavior of young puppies seems to be controlled less by visual stimuli than by tactile, olfactory, and auditory cues. Rodents, on the other hand, rely primarily on odor for species identification (Alberts and Galef, 1973). Given the diversity in sensory and response systems across species, a single stimulus modality would not be expected to be of universal effectiveness for all mammalian young—not even tactile stimulation.

The Curious Effects of Punishment on Social Preferences

Surprisingly enough, several studies of mammalian social development have indicated that social attachment behaviors are not necessarily inhibited or extinguished by punishment. This was effectively shown by Harlow and his co-workers (Arling and Harlow, 1967; Seay, Alexander, and Harlow, 1964). Rhesus monkeys that are reared in isolation, even in the constant company of a cloth surrogate, exhibit "strange" social behavior at early maturity—they are socially and sexually inept. Even in those cases where previously isolated females have been impregnated by a male and bear offspring, they typically behave in an entirely unmotherly manner toward their young. According to work done at the Wisconsin Primate Laboratory, motherless mothers are most inadequate mothers. Those studied either abused their offspring or were indifferent to and

ignored them (see Figure 3-13). The investigators felt that few of the infants would have survived if intervention measures had not been taken by the laboratory staff. In one instance "the mother passively accepted the baby to the breast by Day 3 [after birth], and attempts to remove and hand feed the baby were abandoned on Day 4 since such efforts provoked violent attacks directed against her infant. These attacks included crushing the infant's head and body against the floor . . . and jumping up and down with her full weight on the infant" (Seay, Alexander, and Harlow, 1964, p. 347).

To determine what effect such rearing experiences had upon the social preferences of surviving infants, Sackett (1967) permitted them to approach and remain with one of three different individuals, one of whom was the infant's punitive mother.

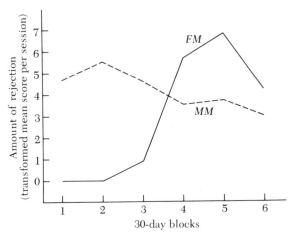

Figure 3-13. Punitiveness of "motherless monkey" during the first 3 months of life, indicated by the rejection of offspring by the motherless monkey females. (*MM* = motherless monkey mothers; *FM* = feral-reared or normal mothers.) Note that in the succeeding 3 months, the *FM* mothers began to reject their offspring, while the *MM* mothers became more accepting of them. (Adapted from Seay et al. Copyright © 1964 by the American Psychological Association. Reprinted with permission.)

Comparisons were made between infants that were normally reared, those reared on a cloth surrogate, and those reared by a punitive "motherless monkey" mother. Surprisingly, of the various groups tested, the punitively reared animals showed the *strongest* preferences for spending time in the area of the mother.

In a preliminary experimental study of this phenomenon Rosenblum and Harlow (1963) devised a cloth cylinder that would irrationally punish its infant. During the first 5½ months of life, the baby rhesus monkeys were blasted with compressed air approximately every 30 minutes if they were clinging to the surrogate. The animals reared with the punitive model spent more time on their surrogate than same-age animals spent on a standard, nonpunitive surrogate (see Figure 3-14).

How might we account for such infantile masochism? One possible interpretation is suggested by the detailed observations that Seay et al. made of one of the more punitive mothers. As the preceding description indicates, some of the more violent attacks occurred when attempts were made to remove the infant or when the infant attempted to separate itself from the mother. The infant found that an effective way to minimize such treatment was to cling to the central or dorsal surface of the mother's body. The "punitive" behavior thus might simply constitute a particular reaction by the adult to which the infant's own responses must become adapted. Sackett (1967) reports that the offspring of motherless monkeys were subjected to extreme aggression only during the first 2–3 months of life. "After this time overt hostility by the mothers rarely occurred *because the infants learned to avoid attacks by the mothers*" (p. 365, my italics).

Cairns and Johnson (1965) found that when the young of other species are placed with a punitive adult, they too adopt behavior patterns that seem to make the most of a very bad situation. For instance, if a young lamb is placed in a small compartment with an adult ewe, she will vigorously and violently rebuff the young lamb's approaches by battering the

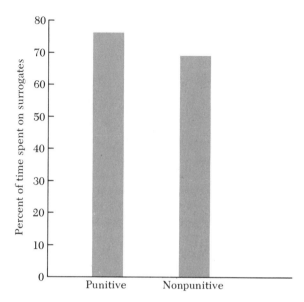

Figure 3-14. An infant monkey is more likely to approach and remain with an experimental "rejecting" mother than with a comparable "accepting" mother. The "rejecting" mother was a standard Wisconsin surrogate model that was programmed to blast the infant with compressed air at various intervals. The control model did not punish, but was otherwise identical to the rejecting model. From days 21–160, the infant monkeys that had approached the rejecting model spent more time in contact with it than did the infants that had approached the control model (data from Rosenblum and Harlow, 1963).

animal against the walls. Since the ewe uses her head to butt, the lamb can avoid these onslaughts by remaining behind her. Indeed, the abused lamb rapidly learns to follow, rather than remain in front of, the rejecting female. In both cases—monkeys raised by a motherless mother and lambs raised by a rejecting ewe—the behavior of the adult provides the occasion for the development of adaptive responses in the young. Once these interaction sequences are acquired, they are—like other avoidance responses—highly resistant to change.

These studies were conducted, it should be noted, under special conditions of environmental restriction. Neither the young nor the "mothers" were permitted to escape, and alternative objects were not available that would support the performance of the young animals' response patterns. Quite a different outcome is obtained when experiments are conducted under less restrictive conditions. In the natural or seminatural setting, continued punishment is typically associated with physical separation and diminution of the filial bond (Altmann, 1960). Unfortunately, no attempts have been made to rear a single infant simultaneously with a "good" and a "bad" mother—that is, one that accepts and another that rebuffs the approaches of the young. It would be remarkable indeed if the more tolerant one failed to become the event around which the infant's behavior was organized. Observations of herd animals suggest that rebuffs by other potential mothers maintain the coherence of the relationship between an infant and its *real* mother. The young animal does not become "attached" to the punishing female.

In summary, punitive events can organize the young animal's behavior. Far from being ineffective, punishment can be most influential in development. In some rearing situations, punishment has the paradoxical effect of increasing the preference of the young animal for the punisher. When the punishment organizes the young animal's activity toward the "other," rather than away from it, then punishment is not reciprocated "tit-for-tat"; rather, it helps to consolidate the relationship. This appears to be a special case of the general phenomenon that was mentioned earlier. The degree of preference that an infant shows for a person or object reflects the extent to which that infant's behavior is organized around it, whether such behavior is brought about by coercion or by kindness.

Behavioral Dependencies and Relationship Organization

The foregoing discussion has indicated that properties and behaviors of other animals are significant in the development of social preferences in young ani-

mals to the extent that they support and maintain the young animals' responses. For instance, grooming has been recognized by several investigators in the field (Goodall, 1965; Kummer, 1968, 1971) and in the laboratory (Mason, 1967) as being important in maintaining patterns of mutual response. Similarly, mild reactivity by the other animal (or object) to the actions of the infant elicits play in most young mammals. When these play patterns have been consistently elicited, the stimuli with which they have been associated acquire significant cue or signal properties. Further, as William Mason has shown, whether a young chimpanzee will approach a person associated with playing or a person associated with clinging depends on the young animal's current state. If the animal has just been given a heavy dose of an amphetamine, it is more likely to approach the person who permits clinging and less likely to approach the person who has previously handled it roughly (Mason, 1967).

Attempts to mimic the "reactive" properties of organisms by making inanimate objects capable of counter-responsiveness have been most successful, both in producing a tendency to interact with the object and in establishing a new social preference. S. D. Scholz and I devised a "reactive" companion for lambs by merely suspending a common wastebasket from the ceiling of the compartment in which the lamb was isolated. The object was wired so that any slight movement would close an electric circuit, making the basket "beep" softly. When the basket was initially introduced to the compartment, the 8 individually tested 10-week-old lambs became distressed, and, on occasion, attacked and butted it. Within 24 hours, however, the animals tended to remain near the basket and to press against it. Removal of the basket for brief intervals then produced distress and the species-typical separation-disruption (R. B. Cairns and S. D. Scholz, unpublished study) (see Figure 3-15).

What can be said then about the properties of environmental events that facilitate the development of social preferences by the young animal? No single activity—such as suckling or physical contact—seems to be required if the young organism's behavior is organized around the distinctive features of the other. To the extent that environmental events become synchronized with and supportive of the ongoing activities of the young, a "bond" or preference tends to evolve. However, both species-typical biases for specific stimulation and prior adaptation experiences of the young animal are important. One of the lessons of recent work is that the psychobiological controls have a continuing impact on the nature of the preferences that are formed. The organismic status of the young, and of those with which the young interact, help to determine what are the "dominant" ongoing activities and how or whether they can be supported. This brings us to a discussion of the several organismic controls of social preferences.

Organismic Controls of Social Attachment

Certain characteristics of the young individual have been associated with its readiness to form specific social relationships and bonds. Two such "organismic" features deserve special attention here: the age of the young, and its species.

Contributions of Developmental Status

Developmental status, as it is correlated with age, is considered to be of importance for two related but separate reasons. First, the assumption is often made that there is a particular time in the life of the young animal when it is most likely to form a "primary" social bond. This notion that there is a *critical period*

Figure 3-15. Photograph of approach of a young lamb to a salient inanimate object. Removal of the object is sufficient to trigger severe separation-disruption, including vocalization, activity, and hyperventilation.

for the development of social relationships has been stated in a number of ways and has inspired considerable debate and some research. Since the concept and its implications seem best discussed in terms of the more general issue of social behavior plasticity, discussion of the matter will be deferred until the next two chapters.

The second reason, which seems more relevant here, is that age-correlated changes influence the sensory and response processes that underlie preferences. Conditioning processes change as a function of age. Acquisition of conditioned responses is typically slower in the younger members of the species (Pavlik, 1958), and their retention is typically poorer (Campbell, 1967). How much slower and how much poorer depends on the nature of the response and species being studied. Similarly, the ability to make visual and auditory discriminations increases with the age-developmental status of the infant (Carmichael, 1954; Gibson, 1969). To the extent that the learning and retention of the stimulus properties by which the other animal is recognized depend upon these processes of conditioning and perceptual discrimination, they also reflect the age-maturational status of the young animal.

The response apparatus also changes as a function of age. In the early stages of life, primate infants spend a great deal of time sleeping or suckling. (During the first week of life, the primate infant sleeps approximately 85 percent of the time.) Events or individuals that support these behaviors, invariably the mother or her substitute in the natural state, will be the ones toward which the early "attachment" is directed. But as the response capabilities of the organism change, and as locomotive and food-getting skills develop, the kinds of environmental events that support the animal's responses also change. To the extent that these "new" behaviors become linked to alternative stimuli in the environment, either because the performance of the response requires such an association or because of contextual conditioning, new preferences and interaction sequences will evolve. Response systems, not organisms, become "attached" to stimuli, and as

response patterns change, so must the events that support them.

As we have already seen, biophysical changes in the mother reflect, support, and are synchronized with thermal, eliminative, and feeding changes in her offspring. This synthesis occurs not only with respect to the mother but with respect to others as well, including littermates and adult members of the group.

The mechanisms that are responsible for the development of social responsiveness in the young do not disappear as the animal matures. Mothers form "new" social bonds, if only with their own young. Young animals demonstrate a capacity for the rapid development of new preferences in adulthood. Likewise, subadult and adult primates form alliances that are as enduring as were those developed between the infant and its mother. DeVore (1965) has observed that the study of such alliances is exceedingly important to understanding the social structure and organization of baboon troops. For instance, two males who themselves are not dominant alone may, in coalition, dominate the other male members of the troops.

Diversity and Distinctiveness

In view of the differences among mammalian species in terms of morphology and breeding and rearing patterns, we should not be too surprised to find that there are extreme differences among species in the development of social interchange patterns. Some phyletic differences have already been commented upon. These include species-characteristic differences in response to separation from the mother, speed with which the young achieve recognition by the mother, and the kinds of stimuli by which the young animal recognizes others. More generally, the degree to which animals form specific dyadic relationships with particular "others" differs markedly across species. Rats, for instance, do not show strong preferences for specific individuals. Cat and mouse mothers are typically willing to adopt offspring other than their own, and their infants readily "adopt" new mothers, if they fit some general species-typical specifications. On the other hand, ewes are highly discriminative about which offspring they permit to approach them, as are some species of monkeys.

The task of determining the mechanisms that account for species differences in social behavior is not unlike the task of identifying ontogenetic mechanisms. Just as the response propensities of the individual differ in the various stages of his life, so do the response capabilities of species differ as a function of evolutionary adaptation. The environmental events that support the behaviors of young monkeys are not likely to be the same as those that support the behavior of young lambs or rodents. For species that have finely differentiated structures for grasping, environmental events (either individuals or objects) that permit clinging and grooming should have particular behavior-support properties. For species that do not have these behavior capabilities, because of differences in peripheral structure or central neural organization, such attributes of objects would be less relevant for behavior control. One outcome is that "contact comfort" is less important for the development of social interchanges in certain species (such as sheep and birds) than in others (such as monkeys and dogs). And among some species of ducks, the calls of the members of the species are of greater significance than the sight of them, at least in the initial establishment process.

In addition, the social organizations of the species have themselves evolved. For instance, the ecological requirements for some species demand exceedingly rapid and intense social preference formation in infants, while other environments promote slower, less exclusive relationship formation (Crook, 1970; see also Chapter 21). As the work of Rosenblum and Kaufman (1968) shows, the distinctions between genetic and ontogenetic contributions tend to blur when a detailed analysis is made of the social interactions. And it is just that type of detailed analysis that is required to clarify the developmental processes.

Summary

At the end of this overview of early social responsiveness as it occurs in nature, some generalizations about the nature and course of the process are in order. The literature itself keeps us from being too expansive—only a few mammalian species have been studied, and even fewer have been intensively analyzed. Nonetheless, much of the work that has been completed gives us a coherent if incomplete picture of the process.

■ Attempts to discover *the* age of the "onset" of social responsiveness are futile. Questions that imply that there is an abrupt beginning of reactivity to others are based upon too simplistic a view of the developmental process. Social development is a continuous phenomenon, a stream of events that occur from conception to maturity and death. Even the principal reference point that was selected in this chapter—birth—is arbitrary. During the fetal period of development, the animal undergoes a series of behavioral transformations that pave the way for, and become incorporated into, the "social" responses that are observed following birth. The analyses of Gottlieb (1976b) and others (Kuo, 1967; Prechtl, 1965) have helped to explicate the relationship between such *prenatal* experiences and *postnatal* behavioral development.

■ At birth, a complex set of internal events controls the maternal reactions to the young and their reactions to the mother. The specific ways in which the initial interaction is facilitated, and the particular biological processes that are operative, differ among species. Nonetheless, some of the mechanisms appear to be rather general. These include maternal cleaning of the young and the stimulation of their basic digestive processes (sucking, defecation), and the maintenance of body temperature by huddling together (Alberts, 1978; Barnett, 1963; Welker, 1959).

■ The offspring are not passive recipients of maternal care. In most species, the young act to shape and direct maternal responses. The exogenous stimulation that they provide the mother is ordinarily necessary to keep her in a "maternal condition." An understanding of this interplay between the endocrinological states of the mother and the behavioral development of the offspring is of basic importance to any systematic analysis of social development.

■ Maturation-paced events contribute directly to the initiation and control of social interaction patterns throughout infancy and childhood. The effects of biochemistry and biological structure are not limited to a brief period during infancy. Evidence to support this assertion is found in detailed accounts of the processes involved in initial social response, weaning, detachment, and separation-reunion. Endogenous factors are pacemakers in an active sense in that they provide the stimulus for particular behaviors. Structural changes also have an indirect influence upon behavior, in that changes in sensory encoding and learning capabilities are linked to an individual's age-maturational status. Such variables determine in part what an animal can learn, and when.

■ The early social development of most mammals is marked by the development of a strong emotional bond between the infant and its mother, and sometimes others (father, siblings, mother substitutes). The tendency to approach a specific "other" is, for altricial mammals, necessary for survival. The "attachment" arises out of a specific mutual dependence of behaviors, particularly those that are dominant in the response repertoire of the infant (clinging, sucking, grooming, playing, defecating) and the mother. No single activity—such as feeding or giving tactile comfort—is necessary for the attachment to develop, even though these activities facilitate the development of specific preferences. The extent to which a particular stimulus or activity is effective depends on the sensory and response capabilities of the pair involved, and these in turn vary systematically with age and species.

■ The individual continuously adapts to its social environment and nonsocial environments. To a greater or lesser degree, the young of all species "detach" themselves from the mother and littermates. The timing of the process and its extent are determined partly by maturational changes that occur in both the young and the mother and partly by ecological and survival demands. Social relations are themselves dynamic and are responsive to internal as well as external shifts. Adaptation is not the exclusive property of the very young; younglings, juveniles, and adults also change and are changed by the actions of others.

4

PLASTICITY IN SOCIAL DEVELOPMENT: MALLEABILITY, SEPARATION, AND NEOPHENOTYPES

What happens to the development of the infant when its normal relationships are disrupted, either by nature or by design? How adaptable is the infant to marked variations from the pattern of social interchanges for which it has been "prepared" by biological and social conditions? A good deal has been written about the negative implications of the disruption of the "preadapted" relationships of the infant. However, except for making some comments about "fail-safe" mechanisms and the robustness of normal development, I skirted these questions about the flexibility and resiliency of the young in Chapter 3. It is now time to deal with them, for they relate to two of the principal goals that draw investigators to the study of social development.

One of the goals is psychiatric. Studies of disruptions of early relationships promise, on the surface, to reveal something about the bases of later emotional distress. What that "something" is has been a matter of considerable concern. A principal aim of at least some leading investigators of social development has been to evaluate, using animals, the assumption that early separation or bad mothering accounts for the infant's vulnerability to psychopathological disorders (Bowlby, 1973; Har-

low, 1958). Others have focused on the etiology of early autistic disorders (Tinbergen, 1974).

The other goal is related to W. F. Dearborn's dictum, "If you want to understand something, try to change it" (Bronfenbrenner, 1977). Following the lead of Z. Y. Kuo, investigators have recently been concerned with the ways in which new or unusual interchanges can be established. Such neophenotypic studies have concentrated on how the young organism adapts to and is modified by extremes in rearing conditions.

The first orientation has thus been concerned with the development of psychopathology; the second, with the development of new levels of social competence and adaptation. The distinction should be kept in mind because it has made a big difference in the kinds of observations that investigators have made, and in the kinds of conclusions that have been drawn. Both orientations are worthy of scientific recognition. Both help us to understand how social adaptation is achieved. Taken together, they help to explain malleability and change in social relationships. In this chapter we will first examine the outcomes of brief separation and longer-term privation on the course of social development and then look at attempts to create social neophenotypes and new social competencies.

Brief Mother-Infant Separations

The Immediate Effects

For most young mammals, forced separation from the mother is a traumatic and disorganizing experience. The following passage describes what happens when an 8-week-old female lamb is isolated in a 15 × 15 foot sound-insulated room.

> Upon placement in the isolation-observation room, the animal immediately freezes for a brief interval. Then she begins to circle the room, head erect, breathing rapidly and nostrils flaring. No vocalizations are heard in the first 15–30 seconds, but as she moves she also emits an audible "baa." The initial vocalization is rather weak, but the second and succeeding ones re-echo through the observation room. The vocalizations are short in duration at first (.5–.7 seconds) but they become more prolonged (1.5–2.0 seconds) as they recur at the rate of about 9 per minute. The animal becomes increasingly more agitated, and the pace is quickened. She defecates as she moves. On one of the circular trips, she breaks into a full run. At the moment before crashing headlong into the wall, she leaps, propelling herself upward, with her forelegs reaching 6–7 feet above the floor. On landing, she resumes circling and baaing. Approximately 30 seconds later, the animal makes another leap against the wall, rising slightly higher and landing with greater force. Grain, hay, and water are available in one corner of the observation room. During one of the excursions, she pauses to sniff and nose the food, but does not eat or drink anything. After about 10–15 seconds, she resumes the pattern of moving about the room. From time to time, she stops suddenly, head erect and immobile. Movement of the head is jerky. When the air-conditioning clicks on, she looks fixedly at the duct in the upper corner of the room.

Movement through the room is resumed. It is interrupted by pauses to orient with head erect, or to browse through hay-straw floor cover. Initially the floor-grazing activities last for about 15–30 seconds, followed by more locomotion-vocalization. Subsequent grazing bouts become increasingly longer, although they are occasionally punctuated by lifting the head and baaing, then a resumption of grazing (R. B. Cairns, unpublished observations).

Although there are significant individual differences in the intensity of the agitation, the basic pattern of hyperactivity and response disruption is found in almost all young, isolated sheep. The survival features of this behavior, for the individual, have not escaped attention. Individual sheep can be recognized by the distinctive properties of their vocalizations. It is entirely likely that this stimulus serves as a signal for the mother. The heightened activity of the young may also increase the likelihood that the isolated animal will be brought into contact with an adult member of its species.

Studies of the short-term isolation of other mammals confirm that the separation-disruption response is a general one. Descriptions of the behavior of young puppies when they are first removed from their mothers parallel the account of lamb behavior. There are, of course, species-typical patterns of reaction. The most obvious response of the young dog is vocalization. Rates of yelping in some breeds are astounding, ranging up to 200 instances per minute. Pups 3–4 weeks of age are unable to move about and jump as readily as young lambs of the same age. But as the pups mature, a strikingly similar pattern of reactivity is observed. The immediate response of the subhuman primates to separation is also one of heightened agitation, vocalization, and general behavioral disruption (Jensen and Tolman, 1962; Mason, 1965).

Although most research has concentrated on the young, observations of the mother during the separation interval indicate that she too undergoes considerable disruption. Jensen and Tolman (1962) report that the rhesus monkey mother grimaces, screams, and in general seems to be in a state of emotional duress. Kittens cry when separated from their mothers, and the mothers are stimulated to retrieve their offspring (Haskins, 1977). The general conclusion seems to be that both the infants and their mothers are affected by the separation. Even though the manner of expression may differ, states of emotional distress are observed in both.

Adaptation

When the young animal is kept away from its mother for an extended period, the effects are less dramatic but equally important. The bouts of vocalization and heightened activity of the 8-week-old lamb become shorter and less frequent, and the grazing and ruminating become more prominent. After 24 hours, the following observation was made:

> The animal is lying in the corner beside the food and water receptacles, chewing in a fashion characteristic of ruminants. She maintains this activity for the first five minutes of the observation. External disturbances, such as the noise of the activities in adjacent experimental rooms, are sufficient to elicit an orienting response (i.e., head erect, cessation of rumination). In response to one disruption, the animal arises, circles the room, and baas. The movement itself is markedly slower than observed on first being separated. It resembles the characteristic walking gait normally observed in the home compartment. After circling the room twice, she returns to the food area, grazes for another two minutes, and lies down and ruminates. Rumination continues for the remainder of the observation period (R. B. Cairns, unpublished observations).

Subsequent observations during the next days and weeks indicated that the animal became quite used to, and apparently comfortable in, its new motherless and companionless surroundings. In terms of weight, appearance, and resistance to disease, the isolated lambs were not different from animals that had been left with conspecific partners. Similar adaptations have been observed in puppies (Figure 4-1).

Available information on other species indicates that the pattern of agitation, followed by recovery to preseparation levels of activity, is a rather general one (see Cairns, 1972, 1977, for a review of the evidence). As might be expected, the pattern of adaptation to separation differs significantly both across species and among individuals within a given species. Analyses of the recovery process of nonhuman primates indicate, however, that some experimentally orphaned infants sometimes go into a state of prolonged "mourning" after the agitation and before recovery (Hinde, 1969; Hinde and Spencer-Booth, 1971).

This variability points up the need to specify the precise conditions under which the individual is maintained during the time that it is separated from the mother—especially if the infant is left with other animals. The interaction patterns and social organization of the group that the individual is left with influence the course of the adaptation. The time required for the process and the extent to which the young animal shows aberrant responses, such as withdrawal or motor depression, are affected by the activities of others with respect to it.

The results of studies of the differential response by two species of macaque monkeys to short-term maternal separation underscore the importance of the maintenance conditions (Rosenblum and Kaufman, 1968). The usual response of the pigtail macaque infant to maternal separation is first extreme agitation, then marked depression, followed by gradual recovery of preseparation levels of activity. The depression stage is marked by virtual cessation of activity, withdrawal, and nonresponsiveness to stimulation. Bonnet monkeys, on the other hand, typically fail to show any behavior that is even remotely like the depression of the pigtails. Following a period of agitation, the bonnet infants settle down to an activity level that is similar to that observed in the preseparation periods. Rosenblum and Kaufman (1968) observed that these separation-induced behavioral differences between the two species were directly correlated with differences in the way that the nonmaternal animals responded to the infants in the motherless context. The adult pigtail macaques tended to ignore the orphaned infants, whereas the adult bonnet macaques freely interacted with the

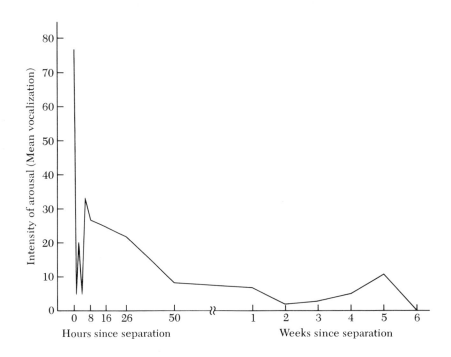

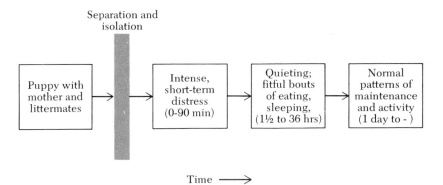

Figure 4-1. *Top:* Course of adaptation to isolation by 28-day-old puppies that have been removed from their mothers and littermates. Yelping (vocalization) is a convenient and useful index of arousal and excitement. *Bottom:* The effects typically observed in young puppies following separation from the mother.

young (see Figure 4-2). The joint effect of differences in prior maternal care and postseparation nonmaternal care produced dramatic differences in the offspring, including differences in their response to maternal separation. The lesson that the investigators learned from their work was that

the line between phylogenetic and ontogenetic

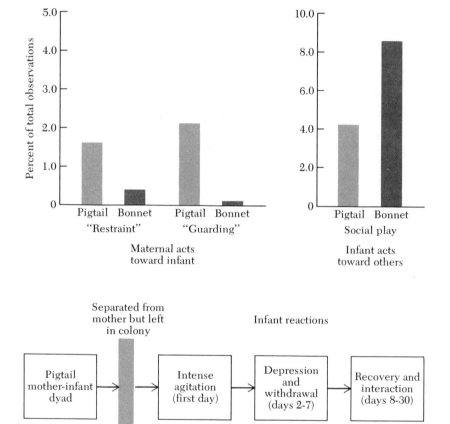

Figure 4-2. *Top:* Differences in maternal-infant interchange between pigtail and bonnet monkeys before separation. *Bottom:* Different reactions to separation by pigtail and bonnet infants (from Rosenblum and Kaufman, 1968).

forces, as is so often the case, becomes at least increasingly blurred with intensive study. It seems evident here that behaviors which, because of their species specificity . . . might appear to have a specific genetic base, may well be highly influenced by ontogenetic factors, in ways that might be overlooked without detailed comparative studies (Rosenblum and Kaufman, 1968, p. 426).

Similar conclusions were reached by investigators at the Louisiana State primate laboratory (Preston, Baker, and Seay, 1970; Seay, Schlottmann, and Gandolfo, 1972). In their studies of maternal separation in the patas monkey (also called the African red monkey), these investigators found that immediately on separation, the typical infant showed the now-familiar pattern of "intense cooing, frantic searching about in all three sections of the apparatus, and wide-eyed scanning of the room" (Preston et al., 1970, p. 302). An important discovery was that the "intense," "frantic" activity lasted less than half an hour (although the extent of some visual exploration apparently remained above normal "for several days"). Preston et al. (1970) analyzed the total pattern of the typical infant's response to separation and concluded that the separation experience facilitated development, or at least made the animals appear more mature. During the separation period, the

> . . . patas infants remained alert. They attended to each other and the daily laboratory activities going on around them. Their motor activity was not severely depressed, as the high-home- and other-home-cage-location scores indicated. *In general, the infants seemed to have suddenly grown much older.* This impression is supported by the appearance during separation of adult behaviors of aggression, thrusting, grooming, and just sitting watching the activities of the people and animals around them. Almost all of a mother patas's time is spent in the latter two activities (Preston et al., 1970, p. 304—my italics).

Why the difference between this apparent adjustment pattern and the pattern of depression and

withdrawal that has sometimes been observed in the rhesus monkey? The investigators speculate that one essential reason for the difference may be the role of the typical patas mother in controlling her offspring. The typical patas mother inhibits rough-and-tumble play among infants. In contrast, certain other macaques, such as the rhesus and java monkey, hold freer reins with respect to play-fighting and physical contact among infants. Hence when the patas mother is away, the baby monkeys play. When she returns, the rough-and-tumble activities are inhibited—that is, return to "normal."

Two main points are illustrated by these cross-species comparisons of monkeys. The first is that the differences among species appear to be closely linked to the interactional network that is present *before* separation and the nature of the new opportunities for interaction that are present *during* separation. The second is that we had best be cautious when labeling the changes that are provoked by change as being either good or bad, normal or abnormal. What appears to be a "deviant" response to separation may simply indicate that the young animal's "normal" development has been facilitated by the experience.

Reunion: Does Absence Make the Heart Grow Fonder?

Brief separation also provides an opportunity for evaluating the effects of varying periods of maternal absence. When mother and infant are reunited, their interchanges can be observed and then compared with those of pairs that were not separated—or their own preseparation relationship can serve as the reference point.

Reunion, like separation, can be an exciting and potentially traumatic experience. Young primates typically become hyper-responsive at the time of reunion, and so do their mothers. For instance, after a separation period of 3 hours, there is more mutual clinging among chimpanzees than if the temporary separation had lasted only 1 hour (Mason, 1967).

Brief separations also have a direct, temporary effect on the quality of the mother-infant interchanges in monkeys, a fact that has been repeatedly documented (Hinde and Spencer-Booth, 1967, 1971; Schlottmann and Seay, 1972). However, direct effects on the relationship become increasingly difficult to detect in follow-up observations (Hinde and Spencer-Booth, 1971).

If the effects of brief separations on maternal-infant interactions are not enduring, are there any long-term consequences whatever? This important question remains controversial, possibly because the data that may fuel the controversy are themselves meager and only suggestive. Hinde and Spencer-Booth (1971) made one of the more careful attempts to identify the long-term effects of the brief separation of rhesus monkeys. They found some evidence of what appeared to be increased fearfulness on the part of the separated monkey infants when they were tested 5 months later. However, these differences "washed out" in a subsequent test conducted when the infants were 2½ years old. The modest differences in the activity of experimental and control animals that were observed at 30 months were not readily interpretable. These findings must be contrasted with the results of studies of other animals, both primates and nonprimates, which indicate that there are no long-term effects of brief separations (see Cairns, 1977, for a review of the evidence).

Less-than-brief separations, lasting weeks rather than hours or days, may lead to less happy reunions. Indeed, evidence obtained from the studies of extended periods of separation described in the next section indicates that there is a diminution in the tendency of the offspring to approach and remain with the mother following the separation. Although this outcome might be interpreted as being simply what would have happened anyway (after all, the young do undergo weaning), the effects are accelerated and pronounced relative to normal (nonseparation) rearing conditions.

One reason for this result became clear to us when we conducted a maternal-offspring separation experiment with dogs at the Jackson Laboratory in Bar Harbor, Maine (unpublished study). The pups were removed from their mothers at 4 weeks of age and returned to them at 9 weeks of age. They thus had ample opportunity to interact with their mothers and to develop a preference for them before separation. The reunion took place in a maze. The pups were given the choice of approaching their mothers or approaching an empty goal area. We were not surprised to find that the pups showed a strong tendency to select their mothers. However, the maternal dogs attempted to avoid their offspring, and if their attempts failed, they nipped at the pups, pushed them away, or otherwise punished their advances. The treatment worked, and the pups ceased to approach their mothers. Why the rejection? Observation of the pups' reactions to their mothers suggests an answer. When the pups encountered their mothers, their response was one that had been dominant in their prior interactions with them: they attempted to suckle. The mothers, however, had stopped lactating, and the feeding interaction sequence was, for them, impossible to maintain. Furthermore, significant changes had occurred in the offspring's physical appearance and form of response during the period of separation. Although most of the stimulus-response associations may have remained relatively invariant during separation, the suckling response could not be reinstituted because the structures supporting it had changed. Prior learning had been canceled out by development.

The results of these studies of short-term isolation leave no doubt but that the subsequent maternal-infant interaction is influenced by involuntary separation. The effects cannot be attributed solely to changes in the responses of either the infant or the mother—rather, the behavior of both animals seems to have been altered by the separation. The interactions between the mother and her infant are not static; there is a continuous realignment of the behavior of each as a result of changes in the patterns of stimulation provided by the other (see Figure 4-3).

Changes in Mother	Changes in Offspring
Psychobiological Changes in Hormonal Condition (Effects Not Due to Learning)	Psychobiological Changes in Maturational Level (Effects Not Due to Learning)
1. Changes in physiological maternal condition, with consequent changes in cues of mother for infant. 2. Onset of nonmaternal behavior propensities, including sexual activity.	1. Endogenous changes in sensory and motor abilities and emotional sensitivity. 2. Changes in motor coordination and ingestive capabilities. 3. Increase in social competence of infant for establishing and maintaining nonmaternal relationships. 4. Changes in social elicitation properties of the offspring as it passes from the infancy stage (due to appearance, morphology, and physical ability).

Response and Stimulus Changes that Can Be Attributed to Learning/Extinction Processes	Response and Stimulus Changes that Can Be Attributed to Learning/Extinction Processes
1. Extinction of specific stimulus properties of the infant due to competing responses, decay, or counterconditioning. 2. Generalization of "new" stimulus properties that may have been established during the period of separation. 3. Changes in the social setting that provided the background for the mother's earlier responses.	1. Extinction of specific stimulus properties of the mother due to competing responses, decay, or counterconditioning. 2. Generalization of "new" stimulus properties that have been established with respect to other adults (including peers) during separation. 3. Changes in the social setting that provided the background for the infant's earlier responses.

Changes in the Role of Mother in Society	Changes in the Role of the Offspring in Society
1. Changes in the role of the mother due to resumption of estrus and nonmaternal activities. 2. Changes in the actions of the other members of the society/colony toward the mother.	1. Changes in the role of the offspring due to changes in appearance/activity that are a normal consequence of the maturational process. 2. Changes in the actions of other members of the society/colony toward the infant.

Figure 4-3. Summary of events that contribute to changes in the response of the infants to their mothers following separation and vice versa.

Although memory traces of the relationship may be retained, the physical capabilities of the animals change. The younger the infants are when first separated from their mothers, and the longer the period of separation, the greater is the likelihood that these endogenous changes will alter the "reunion" activities. Just because the isolated animals initially perform at reunion the same behaviors toward the mother as they did before separation does not mean that the reunion will be a happy one. The previous activities may now be inappropriate.

Let us return now to the question raised by the heading of this section. Does absence make the heart grow fonder? Or is separation merely the occasion for being "out of sight and out of mind"? Each of these maxims has some truth, depending on the length of separation. However, it is not merely the heart or the mind that undergoes change; it is the entire biological system of both mother and infant. The young animal's adaptation to the new setting begins immediately upon separation. The hyperactivity and disruption are only the first phase of a behavioral reorganization in the separation circumstances. To trace the course of this behavioral reorganization, it is necessary to analyze the young animal's adaptation to the "motherless" context.

Long-term Isolation and Separation

If young animals that have been separated from their mothers for long periods have some difficulty re-establishing a relationship with their mothers, what will be the social reactivity of a youngling that has been removed from its mother before the establishment of a species-typical preference and raised entirely alone? Total disaster? The problem is a difficult one to study experimentally with mammals because of the inability of most mammalian young to survive alone. Not only is the mammalian infant dependent upon the mother for food, but most mammalian young require stimulation to perform

such essential functions as elimination and thermal regulation. The sheer necessity of keeping the animal alive has led to compromises with the "total isolation" ideal.

How then have experimenters solved the problem of rearing the infant without its mother (or another female quite like her)? A widely used and simple technique has been to "hand rear" the infant until it is able to care for itself. Hand rearing is typically done by human caretakers who feed, stimulate, and, depending on the species, diaper the infant. Other procedures do away with, to varying degrees, the physical contact between caretaker and infant. Thoman and Arnold (1968) thus developed a procedure for rearing rat pups that involves intubation (sliding a tiny tube through the infant's mouth into its stomach). Small quantities of a milk substitute are then pumped 4–6 times daily directly into the stomach of the animal (which is virtually transparent in the days immediately after birth). The procedure has recently been improved upon by Hall (1975), who chronically implants a feeding tube and thereby does away with the need to handle the pup when it is fed. Other mechanical procedures permit infant monkeys, kittens, and puppies to suckle virtually without physical contact, so that the young animals do not have social encounters of any sort (Harlow and Zimmerman, 1959; Schneirla et al., 1963; Bacon and Stanley, 1970). Let us now turn to what these procedures reveal about the ways in which such extreme social privation influence (1) the infants' physical health and well-being, and (2) the infants' capabilities for social adaptation to others of their kind.

Physical Consequences of Social Privation: Are Mortality and Growth Affected?

In a report on the physical aftereffects of brief maternal separation in sheep, Liddell (1959) commented that a young lamb that is given a short-term conditioning test ". . . in the absence of its mother (although it rejoins her immediately after the test) invariably dies within the year. Usually death occurs before six months of age" (p. 215). The bulk of the evidence, however, does not support the conclusion that maternal separation by itself leads to illness (see Hafez, Cairns, Hulet, and Scott, 1969). Isolated lambs can thrive, if their basic physical needs are met. Whether the illness observed by Liddell was due to some property of the shock conditioning procedures or to some other, as yet unidentified, variable remains to be determined. Nonetheless, the belief that maternal separation per se produces higher rates of mortality and illness in deprived mammalian babies has persisted (in part, no doubt, because of its presumed relevance to human psychopathology). The matter is as controversial as it is important. However, after 20 years of research on this issue, the results seem to be falling into a reasonably coherent pattern.

One definitive investigation deserves attention. A study by Davenport, Menzel, and Rogers (1961) was one of the first to yield compelling evidence on this matter. Some 79 chimpanzee infants were reared in one of three conditions: "normal" rearing in the presence of the mother, hand rearing by human caretakers, and restricted rearing in an isolation "bubble." Chimpanzee mothers are attentive to their offspring and highly protective of them. Hence the infants in the normal rearing condition could not routinely be removed for weighing at weekly intervals. They were kept with the mothers for periods ranging from 1 to 22 months after birth. When they were finally separated, the infants, if quite young, were hand fed; if older, they were placed with other chimpanzees and treated in much the same fashion as adults.

In the hand-fed or partial privation condition, the infant chimpanzees were taken from their mothers at 2 days of age and reared by human caretakers in a laboratory nursery. They were diapered, fed by bottle and cup, and occasionally allowed to be visited by other infant chimps until they were 2 years of age.

The third condition approximated total privation. The infants were separated from their mothers within 12 hours after birth and placed individually into an isolation bubble. The cubicles, which were about the size of compartments in which premature human infants are placed, were located individually in a darkened, sound-deadened room. A small lamp inside each cubicle permitted the experimenter to see the infant by looking through a nonreflecting screen that did not permit the infant to see out. Feeding was accomplished by inserting a bottle through a removable wall (from birth to 8 months) or by inserting a tube through the wall (from 8 months to 2 years). The infants were placed in an opaque bag once each week and weighed. At no time during feeding, weighing, or cleaning did they see outside their cribs. They were fed a diet that contained approximately 30 percent fewer calories than that given the nursery group, "because of the decreased possibility of energy expenditure imposed by the rearing environment" (Davenport et al., p. 805).

When compared with infants reared under normal conditions by their own mothers, the young chimpanzees maintained in partial or virtually total isolation did not "waste away." On the contrary, mortality rates were in general low, and they did not differ among animals in the three conditions (normal, 12 percent; partial privation, 13 percent; "total" privation, 6 percent). The deaths that did occur in the 2 years following birth were due primarily to pneumonia or congenital disorders; none were traceable to events surrounding separation from the mother.

The growth of the infants in the two "mother-separated" groups was also excellent. They actually showed significantly greater weight gains than did those kept with the mother (Figure 4-4). At 5-7 months (depending on the laboratory condition), the nursery-reared and cubicle-reared infants weighed as much as did the mother-reared infants at 12 months of age. Why the difference in weights? The investigators believe that it directly reflects the differences in diet available to the infants and the differences in caloric intake. They add that "it was impossible, of course, to determine caloric intake of

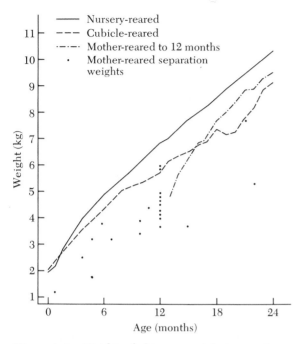

Figure 4-4. Weights of chimpanzee infants reared under three conditions of privation. Note that infants in two mother-separated conditions weighed, on the average, significantly more than infants in the mother-reared condition at virtually every age. After separation, mother-reared infants showed a rapid gain in weight. (From Davenport et al. Copyright © 1961 the American Orthopsychiatric Association, Inc. Reproduced by permission.)

mother-reared infants; however, it is believed to be considerably less than that provided by the nursery feeding regimen" (Davenport et al., p. 808). This conclusion is supported by the fact that separation from the mother at 12 months of age was associated with sharp increases in the weights of the infants. These findings have since been confirmed in studies of various other mammalian species, including lambs, puppies, and rodents. (Cairns, 1977, reviews some of this evidence.)

It must be added that studies of separation have indicated that some growth modification is triggered by separation. In the period immediately following separation at weaning, there is often a short-term decrease in weight gain because of (1) the necessity to shift from one diet and/or form of eating to another, and (2) the overall behavioral disruption occasioned by the separation. There are nonobvious physical needs that the mother, or littermates can meet (such as stimulation of elimination and temperature regulation). "Clumping" does confer some advantages because it minimizes energy expenditure (Alberts, 1978), and, perhaps as a consequence, group-maintained mice are frequently found to weigh more than isolation-maintained ones, and weaning leads to fewer deaths if the mice are placed in a group than if they are isolated (my unpublished observations). To sum up, the available data permit us to dismiss the belief that maternal separation, in itself, has inevitable and irreversible adverse consequences for the physical growth and health of the nonhuman infant.

Behavioral Consequences of Social Privation: Alienation and Withdrawal

Recent research also permits a definitive answer to the question of whether extreme social privation affects an infant's subsequent interactions with members of its own species. In all mammalian young that have been studied, some effects have been identified. The magnitude of the outcome depends on such variables as the action pattern characteristic of the species studied, the testing context, and the features of the privation (such as length in isolation and age at which it was begun).

A representative study should help to illustrate the kinds of outcomes that have been observed. Schneirla and his colleagues reared kittens in isolation for periods of 7–42 days but returned them to the litter to be tested at various intervals (Schneirla and Rosenblatt, 1961; Schneirla et al., 1963). While in isolation, the kittens were fed automatically in a special brooder. The other members of the litter were not removed from the mother and served a dual purpose: they were control subjects, and they maintained the mother in a maternal condition. Even a brief interruption of the maternal-kitten interaction in its early stages tended to disrupt the feeding behavior of the isolated offspring upon reunion with the mother. By the time the control or normally reared kittens were 7 days old, they were highly efficient in the art of suckling. In effect, they were assigned their own nipple. In contrast, 7-day-old kittens that had been isolated and then reunited with the mother were generally inept. The nonisolated animals nuzzled the maternal animal in the mammary region, but the isolated animals indiscriminately nuzzled her back, paws, neck, and genital area. From their observations, Schneirla and his colleagues concluded that the isolated kittens' attempts to nurse were not significantly more efficient than those of neonates.

Reunion effects were sharply intensified when separation was for longer intervals (Table 4-1). None of the kittens maintained in isolation for the longest interval (42 days) demonstrated any species-appropriate suckling upon being reintroduced to the litter and mother. Such a deficiency cannot be attributed to a natural "waning" of the suckling behavior, since kittens that had not been isolated continued to be nursed by the mother. Nor could the effect be attributed to a lack of hunger on the part of the young subjects. Even after 48 hours with the mother, during which time they had no other source of food, the kittens still failed to suckle. At least part of the problem was that they did not try. They failed even to approach the mother, and she did not attempt to retrieve them.

In another significant investigation, Fuller and Clark (1966) isolated puppies from the third week of life until the sixteenth week. During isolation, the dogs were kept in small (2 ft by 2½ ft) compartments. Upon first being removed from the compartment, the 4-month-old dogs behaved in an aberrant manner (Figure 4-5). They failed even to leave the isolation compartment to approach and interact with nonisolated puppies of the same age. The same test was given repeatedly from 16 to 20 weeks of age. The pups' abnormal behavior was reduced merely by gently handling them following each test and by administering a tranquilizer to them immediately after each test. The isolated puppies that were both handled and drugged were more likely to emerge from the compartment and to interact with other animals. From these observations, Fuller and Clark concluded that the release from isolation was a traumatic experience that caused the animals to cower and remain in the corner. When the effects of the emergence experience were so modified, the

Table 4-1. Suckling responses of isolated kittens on test returns to female and litter from the incubator.

Age and duration of isolation (days)	n	Average number of days isolated	Percent suckling on return to female
Kittens that suckled from brooder during isolation			
0, 7	3	7	100
6, 23	5	18	100
18, 33	2	16	100
23, 44	4	22	25
2, 44	4	43	00
Kittens that did not suckle from the brooder during isolation			
34, 49	4	16	100
47, 54	3	7	100

SOURCE: Adapted from Schneirla and Rosenblatt, copyright © 1961. The American Orthopsychiatric Association, Inc. Reproduced by permission.

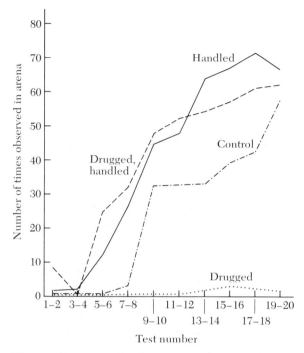

Figure 4-5. How isolated puppies are treated immediately after each test is a significant determinant of the apparent severity of the effects of isolation. If pups that have been isolated are gently petted immediately following each test, they are likely to emerge into an unfamiliar area on subsequent tests. Drugging the animals with a tranquilizer after the test facilitates emergence if the animals have been petted (handled) and retards it if they have not. (From Fuller. Copyright © 1967 by the American Association for the Advancement of Science. With permission.)

isolated subjects behaved in a manner not unlike that of nonisolated dogs.

Studies of puppies and kittens maintained in isolation from birth (or isolated shortly afterward) commonly find that (1) the young tend to fail to approach other members of their kind; (2) if and when they do approach, their actions are initially inept; and (3) previously isolated animals are highly excitable and reactive to stimulation, both elicited and unelicited. Essentially the same outcomes have been observed in studies of rhesus monkeys that have been maintained in isolation over long intervals (1–2 years). The results of experiments conducted at the Wisconsin laboratory (Mason, 1960; Harlow and Harlow, 1965), as well as elsewhere, indicate that the magnitude of the effects is roughly proportional to the length of isolation. Animals isolated early in life and kept in that condition for 1–2 years are hyper-reactive to stimulation and, not infrequently, attack and fight on being introduced to conspecific partners. Infants isolated for a shorter term or later in life tend to be less jumpy, less inept, and less alienated.

Amelioration of Privation Effects

Can the consequences of isolation be made less severe? Yes. The work of Fuller and Clark (1966) indicated that one way to reduce the severity of isolation is to ease the *transition* from isolation to exposure to conspecific partners. Another effective procedure explored by the same investigators was to provide some ameliorative experiences *during* the period of isolation. Even very modest changes in the nature of the isolation experience had remarkable effects on the severity of interpersonal alienation. In one set of experiments, a small window was placed in the wall of the isolation compartment so the puppies (who were isolated at 3 weeks) could see the laboratory room outside. Since relatively little activity was occurring in the lab (merely the caretaking procedures), this modification would appear to be trivial. Nonetheless, the effects were found to be marked when the pups were tested at 4 months. Their behavior was similar to that of dogs of the same age that had been physically removed from the mother, handled, and placed with other dogs.

Working with isolated rhesus monkeys, Mason (1967) found that placing a simple swing in the compartment was sufficient to reduce the undesirable effects of total separation. If the isolated infants were permitted to play on the swing, they responded more positively to human handlers, and were more likely to adapt socially to other monkeys.

The fact that such minor modifications in living circumstances are so effective in ameliorating the effects of isolation underscores why isolation is so effective in the first place. When isolated, animals are not only removed from the specific characteristics of others of their kind, they are simultaneously removed from significant variations in other basic stimulus modalities. The isolated animals view a relatively static and stable environment; they are not touched except by themselves, and they can move around only in a very small area, typically in a circle. The alienation observed in these animals immediately upon removal from isolation could reflect in part the impact of being placed in a changing, less predictable, novel environment. And it could be due in part to the unanticipated movement and touch of other members of their kind. To the extent that the young continue to perform behaviors that were adaptive to isolation, they will appear to be asocial and abnormal. For example, in the tightly confined isolation compartment, dogs run in circles or twirl for exercise. The persistence of this activity following isolation has been labeled the "twirling syndrome" and is taken as evidence of their abnormality.

Explanation by "Absence" or "Presence"

Such findings point up a primary methodological limitation of the isolation or species-separation experiment. Usually the procedure tells us only that certain classes of stimuli, namely those produced during interaction of the animal with other members of the same species, have been withheld from the young animal. Typically, it does not tell much about what events the animal has been *exposed to* during the isolation period. After the young are removed from their mothers, their behavior development is not terminated. They continue to develop distinctive patterns of responding, but in an environment that is different from the one to which the species is typically exposed. The young animal is by no means encapsulated in a contextual vacuum just because it has been removed from the "normal" environment: the animal cannot be deprived of all of the stimuli that are characteristic of its kind. It carries a significant proportion of these cues within itself. Even dogs maintained in complete isolation can hear themselves bark, smell their excretia, bite their tails, and lick their fur. These species-typical cues cannot be eliminated without also eliminating the subject. This methodological restriction can be offset by making the focus of analysis not what the organism is "deprived of," but what it has been "exposed to."

If the experimenter is prepared to cope with the more compelling biological needs of these orphans, their rate of physical growth will be normal. Just as the infant normally adapts its responses to the mother, in experimentally produced motherless environments it must fit its responses to the isolation setting. Such adaptation may preclude, at least temporarily, alternative forms of social organization.

Social Neophenotypes: Cross-Specific Rearing and Adaptation

Given the tendency of the young to adapt to their rearing conditions, some investigators have attempted to produce organisms that are behaviorally quite unlike their own kind by systematically controlling these conditions. The aim of this research on *neophenotypes* differs from that of privation studies. Privation studies were originally proposed to investigate how "abnormal" or neurotic behavior comes about, or to demonstrate which elements of behavior are learned and which are innate. Studies of neophenotypes are concerned not so much with abnormality as with ways that "new" or adaptive interchanges develop.

In view of the reliance of the young upon others for survival, it would be adaptive for them to not be overly selective very early in life. Given their biological needs, too narrow a range of "acceptable" mothers could prove disastrous. Nor, on the other hand, would evolution be best served if the young were entirely without biases. The balance between indiscriminancy and exclusivity must be struck in such a way that survival is optimized for the young, and for the species. What is surprising is the full range of "others" that the young will accept. Interspecific pairings have been created, resulting in such odd couples as kittens with rats, monkeys with dogs, lions with humans, dogs with rabbits, horses with sheep, and rat pups with cats. Proper alignment of the interaction can bring about joint attraction even in some of the oddest couples. We will now analyze how the alignment can be brought about in interspecific adoptions.

Preconditions for Establishment of Cross-Specific Social Preferences

Studies of successful cross-specific pairings tell us as much about what is not required as what is. Suckling, for example, is not a necessary element in adoption. The young develop strong preferences for other animals, pieces of cloth, and even television sets, although none of these has lactational capabilities. Nor is direct physical interaction necessary. Although the evidence on physical interaction is less complete than the evidence on lactation, its meaning is nonetheless clear. Further, punitive "others" do not inhibit a preference. Even young animals that have been mutilated will frequently develop a strong preference for the punisher.

What, then, are the necessary and sufficient conditions for the development of cross-specific attachment behaviors? According to the generalization stated in Chapter 3, preferences evolve when the infant's activities become organized around or dependent on some property or properties of the other animal. Such dependency is fostered by direct inter-

actions that are mutually supportive. However, studies in which only distance receptor information is permitted indicate that interactions facilitate but are not necessary for preference establishment.

Course of Cross-Specific Adaptation

In Chapter 3 we saw that maternal-infant adaptations proceed rapidly under normal rearing conditions. But anecdotes about cross-specific pairings suggest that the relationships can be formed virtually as rapidly with nonmaternal and with non-conspecific partners. From an evolutionary perspective, the rapidity makes sense. If adaptation did not proceed rapidly, then it might not succeed at all. The young would perish.

The results of the few experimental attempts to plot the course of the infant's adoption of a new host have been consistent with the generalization about rapidity. In a representative study (Cairns and Werboff, 1967), 4-week-old puppies were placed individually with an adult rabbit. Checks were made of the course of the establishment of a relationship at close intervals during the first 24 hours of pairing, and at staggered intervals thereafter. A primary test simply involved brief removal, then replacement, of the rabbit. If, during removal, the pup showed signs of disruption and agitation (for example, repeated frantic yelping and increased movement around the compartment), it was assumed that the rabbit had acquired significant social control properties—that is, that the pup had developed an "attachment" for its partner. Within only 2–4 hours of cohabitation with the rabbit, the pups became frantic on being separated from the new companion. As shown in Figure 4-6, the effect was strongest when free physical interaction between the animals was permitted. Subsequent tests of social preference (not shown) indicated that the experimental pups preferred a rabbit over another puppy, whereas animals that had had "normal" social experiences preferred other pups.

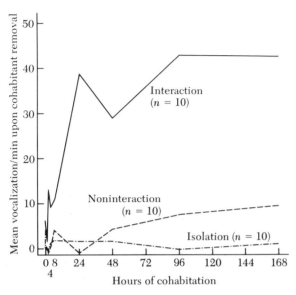

Figure 4-6. Four-week-old puppies that had been separated from their mothers and placed with an adult rabbit showed, within 2 hours, some distress when briefly separated from the rabbit. Peak levels of distress were obtained after only 24 hours of co-rearing. The yelping (vocalization) and agitation began when the rabbit was removed from the rearing compartment; they ceased when the rabbit was returned. If the puppies were not permitted to interact physically with the rabbit during co-rearing, the preference formation took longer and the preferences were less strong. Puppies that were merely removed from the mother showed no inherent preference for the presence or absence of the unfamiliar rabbit. Figure shows mean vocalization difference scores, that is, vocalization when the rabbit was removed for one minute minus vocalization when rabbit was returned (from Cairns and Werboff, 1967).

Equally rapid development of cross-specific acceptance and preference formation has been observed in other pairings. Mason and Kenney (1974) cross-fostered 10-month-old monkeys with adult dogs (see Figure 4-7). The description of their observation of the early adaptation process is informative:

Initially, most monkeys reacted to the dogs with fear, expressed in grimaces, distress vocalization, crouching, and withdrawal. These behaviors usu-

ally disappeared quickly, however. All but one of the eight subjects approached within 2 hours (5 within 30 minutes), and all approached within 7 hours. Clinging to the dog occurred within the first 4 hours of exposure in seven monkeys; one monkey did not cling until after 13 hours of exposure (p. 1212).

Following the initial approach, the animals behaved toward each other in a benign manner. As in the case of puppies, the young monkeys reared with adult dogs preferred the alien species over other monkeys when given a choice. Mason and Kenney (1974) confirmed the earlier reports of Kuo (1967) and Cairns (1966b) in finding that "natural" (species-typical) preferences can be rapidly canceled out by developmental experiences.

Habitats and Preference Formation

Given the range of animals among which attachment behavior has been observed, it should not be surprising to find that such behavior occurs with respect to various nonanimate stimuli as well. In a well-known and classic demonstration, Harlow and Zimmerman (1959) followed the development of young monkeys' preference for cloth-covered objects. The phenomenon is not limited to primates or to cloth-covered objects. Studies of infant puppies and kittens have yielded parallel results. In general, it appears that *any* salient feature of the animal's living conditions, particularly those features that are relevant to its dominant activities, can acquire preferential properties. The preference may be for sleeping areas, for specific lighting conditions, for surfaces to rest upon, and so on. Rosenblatt (1972) has shown that kittens have formed strong location preferences within their home area by the end of the first week of life (see Figure 4-8). It seems reasonable to believe that the basic processes involved in the establishment of preferences for other animals were the same as those involved in the establishment of preferences for particular things, for particular habitats, and for particular activities (see Immelmann, 1975, for a review of the data on habitat and on food imprinting in birds).

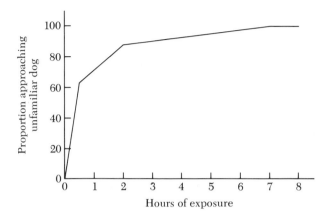

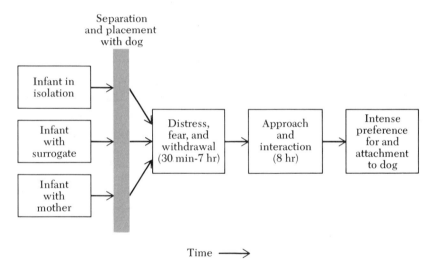

Figure 4-7. *Top:* The tendency for infant monkeys to approach and remain with their adult canine partner was observed soon after the monkeys were separated from their mothers and cross-fostered to an unfamiliar dog. *Bottom:* The course of adaptation to the adult dog appeared to be the same, regardless of the prior rearing condition (adapted from Mason and Kenney, 1974).

The Role of the "Other"

By focusing on the offspring, we learn at best only part of the story of the determinants of early social plasticity. The young must not only accept others; they must be accepted by them. And in light of the delicate balance between survival and death that exists early in life, maternal adoption should proceed rapidly if at all. In at least some species, the process is exceedingly rapid. Studies of adoption by maternal does and ewes indicate that they show recognition and preference as soon as 5 minutes follow-

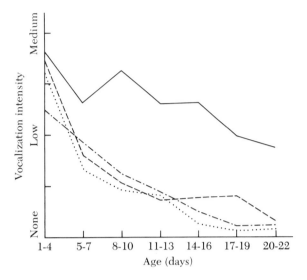

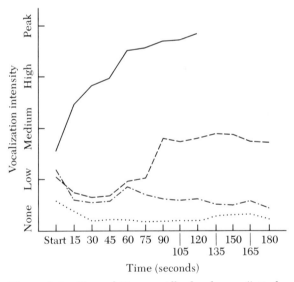

ing birth (Klopfer and Klopfer, 1968; but see also Smith, Van-Toller, and Boyes, 1966).

Further study of the factors that control maternal adoption in mammals is sorely needed. The wide range of pairings that have been casually reported testifies to the plasticity of maternal preferences. Certain species, including those which normally bear litters rather than single or twin offspring, are typically nondiscriminative in their acceptance of unfamiliar young of the same species. Entire litters of mice can be exchanged between their natural mothers without the mothers seeming to care or even notice. When unfamiliar young are introduced into most cat or dog litters shortly after birth, acceptance is routine. Although the time required for maternal acceptance in these pairings has rarely been studied, it appears to proceed rapidly within hours after introduction. If it did not, the survival of the young would be so seriously prejudiced that they would not live. The tolerance of such mothers can extend to the infants of alien species as well.

Among animals whose young are relatively inept at birth, such as primates, it is not so urgent for survival that specific identification be made at parturition. The infants are sufficiently dependent that they either maintain constant contact with the mother or they stay where she deposited them (in the nest, burrow, or crib). It is not surprising, then,

Figure 4-8. Young kittens rapidly develop an "attachment" to particular places in their environment. Graphs show relation between the age of the animal and the intensity of its response to being placed in an unfamiliar area.

Top: Intensity of vocalization in kittens was rated at the start of the tests as a measure of their distress. Within a week the kittens cried much less when they were put anywhere in the home cage (*dashed and dotted lines*) than when they were placed in a strange cage (*solid line*). Cry-

ing decreased equally in the home (*dotted line*) and in adjacent (*dashed/dotted line*) and diagonal (*dashed line*) corners, indicating that the kittens recognized the home cage.

Bottom: Ability to distinguish regions of the home cage is evident in kittens that were tested at 5-7 days of age. Intensity of crying is lowest when kittens are placed in the home corner (*dotted line*). It takes the kittens about a minute to distinguish between the adjacent corner (*dashed/dotted line*) and the diagonal corner (*dashed line*). When the kittens are placed in a strange cage, the intensity of their crying steadily increases (*solid line*). (From J. S. Rosenblatt, Learning in Newborn Kittens. Copyright © 1972 by Scientific American. All rights reserved.)

that primate mothers are not noted for extremely rapid learning of the distinctive features of their young. For instance, rhesus monkey mothers do not distinguish visually between their own young and peers of the same age until about the sixth day postpartum (Jensen and Tolman, 1962). But by the seventeenth day after birth, the monkey mothers make a clear distinction between their own young and others. These findings suggest that the mother monkey's ability to recognize her own infant visually develops during the first days of experience with it, not instantaneously.

Some Cross-Specific Failures: The Dynamics of Interchange

To emphasize only the successes of cross-specific adoptions can be misleading. There have also been failures. One of the primary reasons for an unsuccessful pairing was just discussed: rejection by the mother. Just as natural mothers sometimes reject their own young, and the young reject their mothers, so it is in some instances of cross-specific adoptions. More generally, cohabitation may prove to be unsuccessful because the characteristics of the partner prejudice the survival of the young. Playing too roughly, or mouthing or gnawing, when performed by the partner toward an infant, can have disastrous consequences. Obviously not all female dogs are good cross-specific partners, just as not all are good mothers to their own litters.

Apart from the hazards that occur during the establishment of the relationship, equally important problems may arise during the course of the interchanges. Simply because an early affectional relationship is established is no guarantee that it will persist. Changes in the physical conditions of the individuals involved can trigger significant changes in the nature of the relationship. Skeletal and physical maturation changes are correlated with changes in the nursing-feeding patterns of the young, and thus affect the closeness of the maternal-infant relationship. Maturation-paced changes in the behavior

of young puppies—from sucking on the fur of their cohabitants at 4 weeks of age to gnawing on their heads at 10 weeks—can trigger concomitant changes in the reactions of their partners.

When such "natural" behaviors are permitted to proceed unchecked, the relationship can be adversely affected. What began as playful behavior, in the absence of controlling feedback can become more vigorous and more damaging. The development of early attachment behavior does not necessarily preclude subsequent injury and relational changes.

Can the course of the relationship be shifted by external controls? Kuo (1967) reports that it can. While conducting observations of cross-species rearing, his assistant acted as an equalizer when the interchange became unbalanced. For instance, when a dog began to gnaw or otherwise injure its cohabitant, the assistant immediately punished the activity. Either a command to stop or direct physical punishment proved to be effective. Once the noxious activities were eliminated from the relationship, the animals behaved toward one another in a benign and mutually supportive manner. But it must be emphasized that mere long-term exposure to a partner of another species does not ensure adaptation. Social interchanges are dynamic; they are paced by events that occur during the interaction as well as by the biophysical status of each member of the pair.

Malleability, Species-Preparedness, and Adaptation: A Concluding Comment

Although young mammals show great malleability in their social preferences, the infant is not without species-typical tendencies or propensities. And the fact that these early biases can be modified does not diminish their importance. The adaptation process requires a trade-off between the demands for survival that the species is ordinarily confronted with and the specific challenges that the individual must overcome. Species-typical propensities are clearly present in both birds and mammals. Studies of malleability—when appropriate comparisons are made—usually demonstrate that the infant mammal is more easily fostered to its own kind than to other species. Such behavioral data are consistent with the results of recent studies of the sensory encoding capabilities and preferences of the young (Gottlieb, 1971). For instance, mallard ducklings respond preferentially to the maternal calls of their species.

These biases support the view that the young are "prepared" to acquire species-typical social preferences. Indeed, it would be puzzling, considering the adaptive properties of the biological apparatus, if such species-general propensities did *not* exist. The fact that such biases can sometimes be rapidly and effectively overcome testifies to the existence of processes that make individual adaptation possible. The learning and conditioning capabilities that are necessary for social development allow young mammals to accommodate to the demands of a changing world and to continually modified survival needs. Malleability does not diminish the significance of biological preparedness of the organism. Rather, it underscores how truly efficient is the system that has evolved.

Summary

The material covered in this chapter permits the following summary statements:

■ For many, but not all, young mammals, involuntary separation from the mother triggers behavior disruption and emotional distress. The agitation diminishes rapidly as the young animal becomes reoriented to the isolation setting. The extent and duration of the disruption are dependent upon the circumstances of isolation as well as the species of the animal and the nature of its prior relationships. Most younglings calm within hours, and their behaviors become organized around the events occurring in the new surroundings. The infant's mother reacts similarly. When the two animals are reunited, they again experience a heightened arousal, which may persist.

■ An infant reared in privation is placed in isolation shortly after birth. Animals so reared become adapted to the isolation circumstances. Removal and introduction to a "normal" environment results in behavioral arousal and disorganization. Immediately following the change from isolation to nonisolation, social alienation and a functional re-isolation are frequently observed. These effects of privation can be eased either by slightly reducing the original degree of privation, or by reducing the impact of returning to a "normal" social setting.

■ Just as the young adapt to the conditions of isolation, they also "fit" their responses to members of other species. The adaptation is typically accompanied by the rapid development of a strong dependency and social attachment behaviors. A wide range of cross-specific adoptions has been demonstrated experimentally; such pairings have also occurred fortuitously. Both the preferences and the activities of the fostered young are clearly different from those of other members of their species.

■ Young mammals also develop strong preferences for, and organize their behaviors around, inanimate objects in their environment. Although the data are incomplete, they seem to indicate that the time required for the development of these preferences is similar to that required for the development of social preferences. Moreover, the same principles that account for the development of social preferences are thought to apply to the development of nonsocial ones, such as choice of habitat.

■ The characteristics that are required for adaptation to a "new" animal are possessed by both adult and young animals. Under appropriate circumstances, females readily adopt the young of a different species. Even if there is an initial rejection by the potential "mother," acceptance can sometimes be brought about by extended cohabitation and mutual exposure. Neonatal young rarely reject a potential mother, no matter how different she may be from their real mother.

■ The development of early attachment behavior is no guarantee that the relationship will be a happy one. It is subject to change at each stage of the individual's development. As the young animal matures, it may engage in "playful" activities that prove injurious to the other cohabitant. In the absence of controlling feedback, the behavior of both animals can become increasingly negative. The outcome can be disastrous, despite the initial compatibility. Interchanges are thus dynamic—they are controlled by interactional events as well as by the physical-maturational status of each participant in the relationship.

Social attachment behaviors are directly linked to the support of basic life processes in infants. For young mammals, the actions of others are essential for survival (except in highly contrived environments). As the physical capabilities and social circumstances of infants change, their preferences and social patterns change as well. Studies of malleability indicate that psychobiological events contribute to the establishment and modification of social preferences *at each stage of development*—not merely at birth. Further, they show that learning processes are continually interrelated with psychobiological events, enabling the individual to be uniquely responsive to changing environments and internal states. In short, ontogenetic and phyletic controls are complementary and are fused at each phase of development. In the next chapter we will examine how early social preferences endure, or are reversed.

5

PLASTICITY IN SOCIAL DEVELOPMENT: REVERSIBILITY AND CONTINUITY

A conflict has arisen between two basic areas of developmental research: that concerned with the effects of early experience and that concerned with behavior modification. Findings from early experience research emphasize the malleability of social behavior in early life and its stability later on. A major theme of this work is that once an early pattern has been established, the outlines of the individual's social interchanges are relatively fixed. The results of behavior modification research, on the other hand, point up the malleability of social behavior *throughout* the lifespan. The essential message of behavior modification research is that social behaviors are not fixed: they are continuously vulnerable to changes in circumstances and in reinforcement contingencies (see Chapter 19). It is addressed to teachers, therapists, and others who must deal with children or adults whose "early experiences" are past history. The paradox is this: how can social interchanges appear to be both fixed and plastic at the same time?

Fundamental conflicts of this sort are a source of confusion to the student and an embarrassment to the teacher. But to the developmental scientist, they provide the clues necessary to answer the fundamental questions of the synthesis. The continuity/reversibility question becomes an empirical problem to be analyzed and solved rather than debated. The issue cannot be settled by making a box score comparing studies that show adaptability with those that show reversibility. Both effects have been demonstrated. The problem is to establish what conditions facilitate either type of ontogenetic adaptation.

Up to 10 years ago, longitudinal developmental studies of the aftereffects of early experience were principally concerned with finding out whether there were any. Hence the major research design that was employed (Figure 5-1, top) was concerned with determining whether early experiences had an effect at maturity. The procedures were not designed to clarify how the effects were achieved (translated over time) or whether the consequences were produced only by early experiences (could later ones work as well?). A major advance was the introduction of interchange research designs (Figure 5-1, center). In order to determine whether the social pattern is vulnerable to change in adulthood, the conditions to which the young are exposed in early life are changed at maturity. In addition, the interchange design permits a split-half contrast, in which half of each group is maintained in its original condition. Analysis of noninterchange (original) con-

Early Experience Design

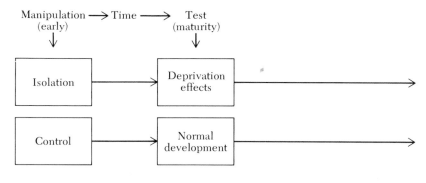

Interchange Design

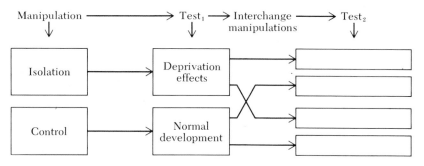

Developmental Interchange Design

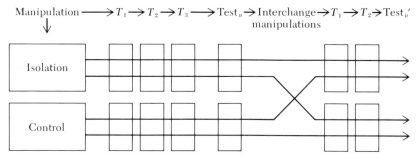

Figure 5-1. Three major developmental research designs. There procedures are designed to yield information about the effects of differential rearing conditions. (Isolation is used in this example, but other conditions, such as enrichment or punishment, could be substituted.) T_1, T_2, ... refer to the repeated tests employed to plot the course of developmental changes. The early experience design (*top*) permits the researcher to determine whether early experiences have enduring effects. The interchange design (*middle*) describes the procedure for shifting half of the subjects in each condition to the alternative condition (for example, from isolation to group living, or vice versa). The developmental interchange design (*bottom*) permits the researcher to plot the processes of development and change. Essentially an extension of the interchange design, this procedure requires repeated observations and tests during the course of development.

ditions at maturity allows an evaluation of changes in behavior that occur simply as a function of maturation.

Finally, developmental interchange designs (Figure 5-1, bottom) were introduced to identify *why* changes occur (or do not occur) in development. Repeated assessments are made using long-term manipulations across the span of development, rather than only at the beginning and at the end of the process. Developmental data from repeated tests permit the investigator to identify the mediators (the proximal causes) of change, *at the time that the changes occur.* As we will see in this chapter, this procedure has become the design of choice for the study of multiple developmental issues, from, say, the processes by which early traumas and social privation affect later social adjustment, to the effects of Head Start on later scholastic performance. More generally, the design has the potential to resolve the apparent paradox between adaptation and continuity in social development.

In view of the practical and theoretical importance of the issues of social reversibility, it seems appropriate that we examine these issues in detail. Accordingly, in this chapter we will be concerned with the persistence and reversal of early social attachment behaviors. In this chapter, we will find that if interactions remain too rigid in a variable environment, then survival is jeopardized. As social conditions change, old patterns of behavior tend to give way to new ones. But all social patterns are not equally adaptable; nor do all "new" conditions support adaptation. Such a mixed bag of results might be expected if the behaviors served different functions and the processes of change were multiple. As we will find, they do, and they are.

Privation and Rehabilitation

In Chapter 4 it was observed that separation from the mother ordinarily has three outcomes. First,

there is initial stress and disruption in both animals. Second, the young animal tends to adapt, rapidly, to the conditions that prevail following separation, adopting activities that "fit" the requirements of the new situation. Third, an extended separation sometimes leads to a progressive alienation of the young animal from members of the original society, including its own mother. She changes, and so do her offspring. In Chapter 4, we did not deal with the extent to which the alienation was permanent. Can animals that have adapted to isolation, or that have never formed a relationship in the first place, ever be successfully brought back to their "normal" living circumstances?

In brief, the answer is yes. Social adaptation is not restricted to very young animals; readaptation or "therapy" [1] can be most successful under some conditions. Since this result seems to conflict with earlier proposals that have enjoyed wide acceptance, some explanation is called for. One of the first clues that rehabilitation is possible was obtained from studies of the first and second offspring of motherless monkeys (Seay et al., 1964)—that is, the babies of monkeys that has been raised in social isolation. The first offspring did well to survive. The motherless mothers treated their first-born infants in a punitive and rejecting manner, but these same mothers treated their second offspring in an entirely normal way. The second time around, the motherless moth-

---

[1] A comment on terminology is in order. *Therapy, rehabilitation,* and *adaptation* have been used loosely in recent experimental reports to refer to seemingly benign changes induced by postisolation experience. Borrowed from a "medical model" of behavior pathology, the first two terms imply a recovery from illness or disability. The "sick" behavior is supposed to be produced by isolation, and the "well" behavior is brought about by the postisolation experience. The main hazard in using these terms in the context of isolation is that the above assumptions may be quite wrong. It is not evident that the isolated animal is "abnormal," or that the postisolation outcomes are "normal." By way of example, the aggressive, reactive male mice produced by isolation rearing may be more like wild-reared *Mus musculus* than are the peaceful, nonaggressive mice produced by laboratory rearing conditions.

The term "adaptation" presents special problems because it has often been used as a synonym for health, normality, and happiness. That is not its usage in this book (see Chapter 21 for further discussion of this issue).

ers apparently could not be distinguished from "normal" (nonisolated) mothers. Whatever might have been the effects of isolation rearing on maternal care, they were not permanent. Why the difference between the treatment of first-born and second-born infants? One possibility is the age of the mother at giving birth to the second offspring: older animals are typically less excitable than younger ones and would therefore show a different response to the birth process and to the unfamiliar infant.

There is another possibility: the mothers may have been socialized by their offspring. The females had experienced several months of interaction with their first-born, and during the course of these interchanges, the isolated females could have become habituated to the activities of other animals in general and to the interchanges of infants in particular.

Follow-up studies have indicated that neither motherhood nor old age is necessary for the reversal of social alienation and are thus consistent with the notion that the young socialize their mothers. Recent work at the Wisconsin Primate Laboratory shows that young male monkeys can also be rehabilitated (Novak and Harlow, 1975; Suomi and Harlow, 1972). In the Novak and Harlow (1975) investigation, males that had been isolated for 6–12 months were permitted to interact with monkeys much younger than themselves. In discussing the results of this investigation, Novak and Harlow (1975) conclude that "monkeys raised without any social experience during the first year of life can learn to be social under appropriate conditions" (p. 461). Here the key seems to have been the age and the response characteristics of the individuals with whom the interaction was permitted. If a previously isolated male is placed with same-age peers, fighting, alienation, and withdrawal result. But if the other monkey is young enough to be nonthreatening yet old enough to play and socially interact, the relationship is typically a benign one. Over time, they developed mutually facilitative patterns of interaction (see Figure 5-2).

The dyadic nature of the therapy process is evi-

dent in the following quote from Suomi and Harlow (1972):

> The isolate subjects did not exhibit spontaneous recovery during initial exposures to the younger, socially normal monkeys, a fact that is not surprising since no isolate monkey had shown spontaneous recovery in previous experimental situations. Rather, the therapist monkeys actively initiated the first social interactions, and only then did the isolates gradually exhibit improvement. Specifically, the therapist monkeys' initial responses to the isolates were to approach and cling, while the isolates were typically immobile and withdrawn. Only after clinging had been initiated did the isolates reciprocate, and only when the therapists had directed play responses toward the isolates did isolate play behavior emerge. Once these interaction patterns were established, the isolates themselves initiated play bouts with progressively increasing frequency (p. 493).

Suomi and Harlow indicate that although the process of rehabilitation was continuous, two overlapping stages of interchange could be identified. The first stage involved breaking down the abnormal self-directed behaviors of self-huddling and stereotyped rocking. As we suggested in Chapter 4, these activities may have been adaptive to the isolation circumstance but were bizarre when they occurred as part of the interaction. Because the infant was crawling over and clinging to the isolate, it became difficult for him to rock and self-huddle, and this behavior diminished. The second stage involved the development of more complex social responses, including grooming and interactive play. The investigators comment that the "therapists apparently provided the crucial stimulation as they themselves developed a complex social repertoire in the course of normal maturation." The situation is one in which withdrawn, timid animals, content to self-stimulate, were effectively drawn into an interchange by active, clinging infants.

In the study just described, 6-month-old animals were given "therapy" by younger ones. However, younger animals are not the only ones that make

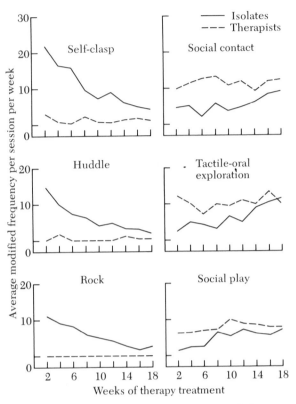

Figure 5-2. Time course of the changes in behaviors produced when isolated monkeys are placed with younger "therapist" monkeys. Note the convergence of actions and the emerging similarities or behavior. (From Novak and Harlow. Copyright © 1975 by the American Psychological Association. Reprinted by permission.)

The male infant-female preadolescent pairs showed much affection and a small amount of hostility which waned with time. During the first control male infant pairing, the observers were surprised and rather amused to see the tiny infant male threatening and aggressing the much larger female preadolescent while she fear grimaced and cowered in a corner. By the second week, this aggression had ceased and much ventral contact, grooming, and play was initiated by the juvenile. The isolate infant pair showed less contact and play than did the control pair. During the second and third weeks, the isolate manually and orally manipulated the female, including her nipples, and in addition, he groomed her. These behaviors were certainly unexpected in an isolate infant animal. The female generally did not respond when he manipulated her and was always calm and gentle with him (Brandt and Mitchell, 1973, p. 226).

In light of the "macho" acts of the male infant monkey, you may have wondered how well the male preadolescents performed as "therapists." In a word, poorly. When the preadolescent males were placed with infant males, the infants seemed adept at bringing out the worst in the older animals. In this relationship, the preadolescent "therapists" behaved like capricious tyrants, and peaceful ventral grooming and contact "quite suddenly turned into aggression" (Brandt and Mitchell, 1973). In the days that followed, relations improved, and "by the third week, both isolate and control infants were attempting to temper aggression and had become adept at avoiding the preadolescent to avoid being aggressed" (p. 226). A similar sequence of events was observed in a companion study in which infants were placed with an adult male rhesus monkey (Redican and Mitchell, 1973). Over a period of 7 months, there was a gradual increase in contact (including grooming) between the infant and the adult, which evolved into an intense mutual dependency and attachment. Though there was some initial ambivalence and fear, the relationship developed into benign behavior and mutual bonding.

good "therapists." Older females (preadolescents, 30 months old) can also reverse the effects of isolation rearing. Young rhesus monkeys (both male and female) that had been isolated for 6 months were paired with either a male or female preadolescent partner (Brandt and Mitchell, 1973). A second group of control infants (nonisolated, reared with their mothers) was also used for comparison purposes. The female preadolescents proved to be highly effective in the rehabilitation process:

This pattern of initial arousal, rejection, and even attacking is not an unusual one, a matter that will be considered in greater detail in Chapter 10. The point to be emphasized here is that the "alienation" of the isolated animal, regardless of its species, is not necessarily self-imposed; it may reflect as well the nature of the reception that the isolate is given by the animal or group with which it is placed. Without the protection of the experimenter, the isolate may not adapt simply because it does not live long enough to enjoy happier days. The "initiation" can run an unhappy course in seemingly docile groups, including domestic female lambs. Death and maiming have been observed in the initial stages of adaptation when weanling and juvenile mice are placed with unfamiliar adult animals (MacCombie and Cairns, 1975). Infant monkeys have been observed to barely survive the first day, if they were totally unfamiliar to members of the colony (Rosenblum and Kaufmann, 1968). These brutal initiation stages do not necessarily preclude the eventual development of positive interchanges.

In primates, the social structure of the species and the circumstances in which the introduction is made, along with such characteristics as age, sex, and species of the isolate and the group, are associated with differences in the intensity of the initial reception (Schlottmann and Seay, 1972). Nonetheless, if the young survive the initiation, mutual accommodation is the rule rather than the exception.[2]

One further comment on the long-term consequences is in order. The isolation experience, or the attempts to revise the effects of isolation, may sensitize the individual to subsequent problems. What is a minor difficulty for a nonisolated animal may be catastrophic for a previously isolated one. For example, the isolation experience (or the subsequent bru-

tal "therapy") may produce a timid, easily aroused animal. In nonstressful circumstances, the behavior of the isolation-reared animal may appear to be identical to that of the group-reared one. But under stress, the adaptation may collapse (see Rogers and Davenport, 1969). Further, as will be examined in some detail in Chapter 14, later privation can lead to changes in the biophysical status of the individual. To the extent that the physiological characteristics of the animal are affected by social influences, the behaviors that are correlated with these characteristics will also be modified. The major lesson to be learned from studies of the reversibility and persistence of isolation-rearing effects is that the alienation consequences are not *necessarily* enduring. They can be modified, although not always completely or in such a way that the individual appears to be indistinguishable from others of its kind.

The Extension and Reversal of Social Preferences

A matter that is closely related to the modification of isolation-rearing effects is the establishment of a new "attachment" subsequent to an initial one. Until the recent past, it was commonly accepted that the first social bond was fundamental for all relationships that followed later in life. This hypothesis can be traced to its psychoanalytic origins (Freud, 1933) and extends to contemporary ethological-psychoanalytic views of human social development (Ainsworth, 1973; Bowlby, 1973) and proposals that there are "critical periods" in animal behavior (Lorenz, 1937; Scott, 1962).

Partly as a result of the evidence concerning the reversibility of isolation-rearing effects, a more relaxed view of the importance of the first relationship has come to the forefront. According to the revised perspective, the young animal is believed to have the capacity for continuing adaptation beyond the

---

[2] The "rehabilitation" of isolated monkeys was not the first or even the most persuasive evidence on the matter. Follow-up manipulations of animals reared in isolation, including dogs, rats, mice, sheep, and precocial and altricial birds, had already shown that the effects of isolation could be significantly modified or altogether reversed (see Table 5–3).

initial attachment. As the conditions for maintenance and interaction change, the preferences and activities of the young can also be expected to change. Accordingly, the early preferences are seen as serving their primary function at that time of the individual's life (infancy). They are instrumental in keeping the infant alive and healthy, and prepared for dealing with events that might arise in later stages. Subsequent preferences reflect, in part, the individual's current interchange and survival requirements. According to this view, continuity in preferences is not determined entirely by early experiences or by species membership; rather, it is a developmental phenomenon that reflects the fusion of these factors with the prevailing psychobiological states of the individuals.

Evidence with regard to the possibility of establishing new relationships is now clear. The stimulus properties of new animals or even a new species can undergo dramatic and rapid changes. The changes may occur if the animal has been previously isolated, or if it was originally raised with, and socially attached to, members of its own kind. The previously described work of Mason and Kenney (1974) makes this point. Not all of the young monkeys used in this study had been previously isolated; some had been reared with their mothers and same-age peers. For them, cohabitation with a mongrel dog was the occasion for the establishment of an additional relationship, beyond the primary attachment. Nonetheless, the course of adaptation for the socially reared monkeys apparently was parallel to that of the previously isolated ones. In each case, the transplanted infants first experienced extreme distress, but this gave way within hours to approach and mutual admiration. The nature of the interchange and the resulting preference are described in the following passage:

> During the continuous cohabitation phase of the experiment, the monkeys and dogs were in frequent contact. They rested together, played together, and groomed each other—the monkeys, with their hands; the dogs, by licking the mon-

keys' fur and anogenital area. The monkeys presented[3] to the dogs for grooming and exhibited social facilitation of feeding, drinking, and investigatory behaviors initiated by the dogs. They often accompanied the dogs when they were taken from the kennels for an exercise period. Most monkeys would cling to the dog, although some of the older ones walked or ran with it, usually keeping within a few feet. If they were prevented from going along, they characteristically vocalized, paced, attempted to escape from the cage, and showed other signs of agitation (p. 1210).

The observations were supported by a series of tests showing that the relationship was strong and specific to the therapy partner and that it overrode choices *for other monkeys.*

The phenomenon is not limited to primates, nor to instances where the "primary" attachment was to members of the infant's own species. Lambs were permitted to form an attachment bond with respect to docile dogs and then reintroduced at early maturity (6 months of age) to the farm where they were born and permitted to flock and to graze with other sheep (Cairns and Johnson, 1965). After spending 3 months in the pastoral setting, the young sheep were returned to the laboratory and retested with their original partners. In every case, the preference was reversed: the subjects preferred other sheep to the dogs, for whom they originally showed an intense preference. The traces of the earlier experience had not been entirely erased, however. Although the experimental sheep did not select their earlier attachment partner, they were less distressed by the presence of dogs than were sheep reared from birth with other sheep.

Whatever are the properties of the relationship that are required for adapting to an alien species, they are not lost by the time the animals reach maturity. The anecdotal reports of Romanes (1884)

---

[3] "Presenting" in primates is an act of submission, in which the submissive animal bows "bottom up," that is, presents to another animal, remaining motionless to permit mounting, grooming, or inspection.

provide early illustrations, such as Dudgeon's (1879) observation of a maternal cat who adopted a litter of weanling rats when her own offspring were removed.[4] More recent and systematic information on cross-specific adoptions is found in Hersher, Richmond, and Moore (1963): maternal sheep and goats treated "foreign" offspring as if they were their own. Rats will also readily adopt and rear alien young (Dennenberg, 1971). In each case, there is a necessary readjustment of behaviors on the part of both the mother and the adopted offspring. Once these adaptations have been made, the relationship appears to have the basic characteristics of the species-typical filial pattern.

So it seems clear that the young and adults of various species can establish new and strong bonds in addition to those originally established. Further, the evidence indicates that the original relationships were not so much displaced by the later ones as they were "extended." That is, nonhuman mammals in a variety of species seem capable of developing, simultaneously, multiple relationships. This should not be wholly surprising. A family dog can get along with, and become attached to, the several members of the household (human and nonhuman), while retaining peculiar and strong sexual and affiliative preferences for other canines. Such capabilities for multiple social discriminations and preferences may be the rule, not the exception.

Is the primacy effect dominant? On this matter,

---

[4] Here is Dudgeon's article in its entirety:

Some years ago the late Hon. Marmaduke Maxwell of Terreglas took me to his stable to show me a cat which was at the time bringing up a family of young rats. The cat some weeks previously had had a litter of five kittens; three were taken away and destroyed shortly after birth; next day it was found that the cat had replaced her lost kittens by three young rats, which she nursed with the two remaining kittens. A few days afterwards, the two kittens were taken away, and the cat very shortly replaced them by two more young rats, and at the time I saw them the young rats—which were confined in an empty stall—were running about quite briskly, and about one-third grown. The cat happened to be out when we went into the stable, but came in before we left; she immediately jumped over the board into the stall and lay down; her strange foster-family at once ran under her, and commenced suckling. What renders the circumstances more extraordinary is that the cat was kept in the stable as a particularly good ratter.

sufficient data are not available to permit a conclusive statement. Certain findings (Mason and Kenney, 1974) suggest that the initial attachment, although not forgotten, does not remain dominant. Moreover, maturation-paced species-typical biases interact with the animal's individual experiences at each stage of development to affect preferences (Immelmann, 1975; Kuo, 1967). What seems important is that even these biases can be greatly extended and modified at maturity if the period of cohabitation is over a sufficiently long interval, or if the interchanges are sufficiently intense.

Imprinting: A Special Case of Plasticity in Birds

In light of the importance of the imprinting phenomenon in precocial birds, I will digress to comment on the extent to which the first-established filial relationships are irreversible. As documented by the excellent recent review by Klaus Immelmann (1975), the concept of imprinting has been applied to a wide range of phenomena, from the establishment of food and habitat preferences to mate selection and the establishment of mother-infant relationships. As originally used by Konrad Lorenz (1937), the term "imprinting" applied only to the establishment of species identity in precocial birds. Imprinting was differentiated from conditioning or learning on the basis of four criteria:

1. The process can take place only during a restricted critical period early in the individual's life.

2. The process, once accomplished, is totally irreversible.

3. The process involves the learning of species-general characteristics (that is, the establishment of a preference for the entire species).

4. The process can be completed before the emergence of the appropriate response. (Hence sexual behaviors can be imprinted even though they

have not yet appeared in the infant's response repertoire.)

The key issue for the present discussion and for discussion of the concept of imprinting is irreversibility. Some of the most thorough analyses of the reversibility-irreversibility assumption have been conducted with birds, following the "interchange" designs shown in Figure 5-1. When birds are removed from their original imprinting conditions following different periods of exposure and placed with a new imprinting object, the preferences themselves undergo rapid change (Einsiedel, 1973; Salzen and Meyer, 1967) (see Figure 5-3).

In Einsiedel's experiment, newly hatched chickens were placed alone with an "imprinting object." The object used in this experiment was a small circular pillow made of blue or green cloth, approximately 2 inches in diameter, which was suspended from the ceiling of the compartment. All chicks were left with the object until they were 72 hours old (post-hatch). At that time, after the birds had become "imprinted" to the object and formed a strong preference for it, half of them were placed with a new object (*interchange* condition). As a control, the rest of the chicks were kept with the original imprinting object (*noninterchange* condition). The new objects differed from the original ones only in color: if the original pillow had been green, the new one was blue, and vice-versa. At regular intervals after being placed in one of these two conditions, the birds were given a choice between the two kinds of objects in a neutral compartment to determine which one they preferred to approach and remain with.

Among animals in the control conditions, the original preferences remained strong and intact: there was virtually no "novelty" effect or preference for the unfamiliar. But in the experimental interchange conditions, new preferences were established in an exceedingly short interval, despite the fact that the second object was exposed at 72 hours, considerably beyond the end of the "critical period" (12–30 hours for this species). Virtually all birds showed some new preference for the new ob-

ject within 5 hours, and often within 5 minutes. They became disrupted and vocalized when it was removed but were contented when it was replaced.

Recall that the question of the primacy of attachment concerned the strength of the new preference relative to the strength of the preference for the primary imprinted object. In situations where a *simultaneous* choice was permitted—that is, the birds could approach either the primary (first-exposed) object or the secondary (second-exposed) one—they showed a progressive tendency to prefer the new object over the old. The preference for the new was a direct function of the number of hours that the birds had been exposed to the new object (and kept from the old one). But it must be added that the primary object was not forgotten. To the contrary, if the birds were permitted to choose the original object or none at all, there was a clear recognition of and preference for the primary object. Albert Einsiedel (1975) makes the important point that the bird can become, simultaneously, attached to two different objects. The second experience did not cancel out the first; rather it extended the number of objects that the bird preferred. Einsiedel points out that objects do not necessarily compete with each other; the bird may have several preferences simultaneously if his prior experiences are appropriately arranged. Hence the preferences were not *reversible* so much as they were *extendible*.

The reversal and extension of imprinting are not limited to laboratory manipulations of precocial birds. Observing the choice of mates in altricial birds, Eric Klinghammer (1967) found few instances of strong "irreversibility" in mate selection. He concluded that choice of a sexual partner can be influenced long after the young have become independent of their parents. In fact, in several species, the final choice of sexual partner occurs close to or at sexual maturity. Most important, he concluded that "there is no *one* way in which the final choice of a mate is achieved." Further, "concern with irreversibility and reversibility diverts attention from the real problems, namely from an analysis of all the factors that affect the choice of mate at sexual maturity." Such factors include the length of exposure

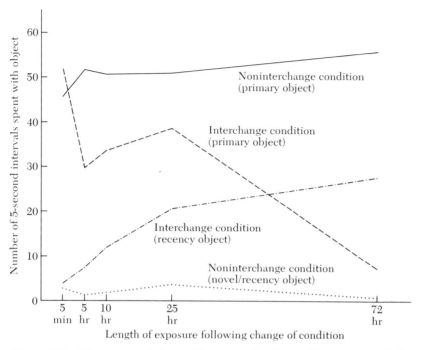

Figure 5-3. Time course of the modification of the effects of imprinting in chickens by subsequent experiences. Virtually no change was obtained among chicks exposed to a single object (noninterchange condition). These chicks continued to avoid the "recency" object (to which they had not been previously exposed) when it was presented in the experiment. Quite the opposite result was obtained among chicks that had been exposed to a second object (interchange condition). By the seventy-second hour, they showed a definite tendency to prefer it (adapted from Einsiedel, 1975, with permission).

to the individual's own species rather than to an alien species, including human beings, and the reactions of members of the other species to the individual's sexual advances.

It is now generally accepted that imprinting is not irreversible; that is, the presence of one preference does not preclude the development of alternative ones (Bateson, 1966, 1978; Zajonc, Reiner, and Hausser, 1973). Nonetheless, the original exposures do indeed have carry-over effects. Although the chicks no longer avoid the new stimulus, they do not necessarily entirely "forget" their earlier preferences. The range of objects with which they will interact has been extended as their experiences have increased. The presence of one preference does not preclude the development of alternative ones. (See Chapter 21 for further comments on the possible species-relativity of these effects.)

When Adaptations Fail

Social adaptation is not inevitable. There are instances where the young utterly fail to adapt to contemporary social requirements. Earlier I commented that a box score of the findings on whether young animals are stable in their initial preferences ("primacy") or showed later adaptability ("recency") would not, in itself, solve the problem. Table 5-1 demonstrates this point; the apparent conflicts in the third and fourth columns suggest why the problem has remained open to controversy. (Table 5-1 summarizes the outcomes of representative studies; it is not intended to be exhaustive.) Despite its apparent disorder, the table is informative in pointing out that:

1. Earlier reports emphasized the *lack* of plasticity (primacy, nonreversal), but in the past 10 years investigators have found that a wide range of outcomes can be obtained in later development; and

2. Evidence for adaptation in later life is not limited to "higher" mammals (primates), but is found as well in birds and nonprimate mammals.

Table 5-1. Early social preferences versus later social preferences.

Investigator	Species	Preference for		Reversal, nonreversal, or extension of preferences	Comments
		Primacy	Recency		
Birds					
Romanes, 1884	Various	Yes	No	Nonreversal	Remained with "alien" species
Lorenz, 1937	Gosling	Yes	No	Nonreversal	Preferred first caretaker
Salzen and Meyer, 1967, 1968	Chicks	No	Yes	Reversal	Reversal of original preferences in 2-choice test
Klinghammer, 1967	Various altricial	Yes/No	Yes/No	Varied	Mating depended on species
Einsiedel, 1975	Chicks	No	Yes	Partial reversal	Reversal of original preferences in 2-choice test
Einsiedel, 1973	Chicks	Yes	Yes	Extension	Extension—chose either in 1-choice test
Zajonc et al., 1973	Chicks	Yes	Yes	Extension	Multiple preferences expressed
Immelmann, 1972	Zebra finch	Yes	No	Nonreversal	Foster species preferred
Mammals					
Scott, 1945	Sheep	Yes/No	Yes/No	Reversal/nonreversal	Two lambs: one hand reared, other socialized
Freedman, King, and Elliot, 1961	Dogs	Yes	No	Nonreversal	Single pup could not be socialized after critical period

As discussed earlier, the problem is to determine the conditions that are responsible for adaptation and plasticity on the one hand and persistence and stability on the other. At the risk of oversimplification (by leaving out consideration of species, test circumstances, and age and sex of the animal, which also have been shown to significantly affect the adaptation process), I have singled out for special comment three major proximal determinants of whether or not there is a "reversal" or "extension" of social preference: (1) the functional isolation produced by the young animal; (2) severe rejection by the group to which the individual is introduced; and (3) dissynchronous (socially inept) behaviors of the young animal that intensify rejection (see Figure 5-4).

Table 5-1. Early social preferences versus later social preferences. *(Continued)*

Investigator	Species	Preference for		Reversal, nonreversal, or extension of preferences	Comments
		Primacy	Recency		
Mammals					
Cairns and Johnson, 1965	Sheep	No/Partial	Yes	Reversal/ extension	Reversal to species-typical but tolerate original partners
Harlow and Harlow, 1965	Rhesus monkeys	None (isolated)	No	Nonreversal	Alienated and possibly rejected by group
Meier, 1965	Rhesus monkeys	None (isolated)	Yes	Reversal	Accepted by "experienced" partner
Cairns and Werboff, 1967	Dogs	Yes/No	Yes	Extension or reversal	Extension to species-typical
Fuller, 1967	Dogs	None (isolated)	Yes	Reversal	"Emergence training"
Kummer, 1968	Hamadryas baboon, female	Not determined	Yes	Extension or reversal	Females and infants accepted by new troop
Kummer, 1968	Hamadryas baboons, male	Not determined	No	Nonreversal	Males rejected by new troop
Missakian, 1969	Rhesus monkeys	None (isolated)	No	Nonreversal	Unsuccessful sexual pairings
Cairns and Nakelski, 1971	Mice, male	None (isolated)	Yes	Reversal	Acceptance following disruption
Suomi and Harlow, 1972	Rhesus monkeys	None (isolated)	Yes	Reversal	Acceptance by infant "therapist"
Brandt and Mitchell, 1973	Rhesus monkeys	None (isolated)	Yes	Reversal	Acceptance by adolescent partner
Mason and Kenney, 1974	Rhesus monkeys	No	Yes	Reversal	Reversal from species-typical to canine
Novak and Harlow, 1975	Rhesus monkeys	None (isolated)	Yes	Reversal	Acceptance by younger partner

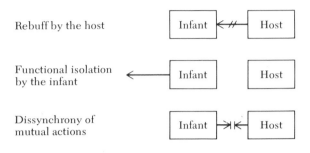

Functional Isolation

In the initial stages of a new relationship, young animals ordinarily persist in whatever activities they have previously learned, and/or show signs of distress and disruption. For isolated animals, the immediately observed withdrawal-alienation is, in effect, a continuation of the isolation experience even though other animals may be available to interact with. Isolation-reared kittens, for instance, fail to approach the mother immediately upon emergence from isolation (Schneirla et al., 1963). Likewise, young dogs that have been reared in isolation fail to leave the holding compartment when another puppy is awaiting them outside (Fuller, 1967). For these animals, the situation produced by withdrawal appears to be a reinstatement of the rearing conditions, in that the animals have produced for themselves a state of functional isolation. If left in the new circumstances, however, the young dogs will eventually become habituated to their new surroundings.

Rejection by the Host

But the "new surroundings" may not permit the young to adapt, for the integrity of the group is maintained by the systematic rejection of nonmembers. The response to the newcomer is a function of the species of the group and its cohesion, as well as the relative ineptness of the intruder. Typically it is characterized by some form of investigation and rejection. The rejection by some species, such as prairie dogs, is highly ritualized, and few physical attacks occur (King, 1955). In other species, including rats (Alberts and Galef, 1973; Barnett, 1963; Eibl-Eibesfeldt, 1961) and dogs (King, 1954), the rejection involves physical attack. Still other species invoke less severe but unambiguous physical signals. For instance, if a young female lamb is introduced to an intact female group, it is intensively examined or butted away (Cairns and Scholz, 1970; Grubb and Jewell, 1966; and Hersher, Moore, and Richmond, 1958).

Kummer (1968) describes a remarkable example of the complex controls that operate to maintain group integrity. In one phase of his field studies of the social organization of the hamadryas baboon in Northern Africa, Kummer captured baboons in one area and transported them approximately 23 miles to an unfamiliar baboon troop. The reception accorded the transplants depended on whether they were young or old, male or female. The adoption of transplanted adult females and infants (whether male or female) was smooth and almost immediate. Infants were adopted by adolescent males, and females were incorporated into a one-male unit of the new troop. Transplanted adult males, however, were not so warmly received. In one instance, Kummer released an intact one-male unit—one male, two adult females, and one infant—into a foreign troop. But the members of this troop threatened and attacked the male and wrested one female and the infant away from him within the first few minutes. Kummer (1968) describes what then happened:

> The other female stayed in close body contact with the beseiged leader. In the fight that followed with another of the troop's males, he barely ever let go of her and in this way was able to maintain her for more than 10 minutes. After leading her through the troop, he sat down on the

plateau above the cliff. As he sat there, continuously holding onto his female, at least 100 of the troop's baboons began to gather about him. While they sat and watched the two, for a few minutes they neither threatened nor attacked them, and limited themselves to watching the pair who sat in the midst of an empty circle about 15 meters in diameter. Later threatening and attacking were again resumed, whereupon the couple withdrew into a field of opuntias. From the noise, it appeared as though the battle continued there. Ten minutes later the released leader appeared on the edge of the cliff, accompanied, strangely enough, by the entire troop of 350 animals going along with him on all sides. The striking thing about this was that none of the troop threatened him nor in any way made contact with him, but rather would merely follow his gradual shifts very carefully. When he sat, they would also sit and watch him, all the while leaving a very marked area around him open. No other behavior could have so clearly illustrated the foreignness of the stranger (pp. 113–114).

Although the variables that diminish the likelihood of rejection have yet to be systematically explored, some transplants are clearly less likely to be rejected than others. The critical factors must surely include age (younger animals are usually more acceptable than older ones), sex (females are more acceptable), and species of the transplant as well as of the host. But the safeguards are not guaranteed by gender or maturity. Both infants and females may be viciously attacked, depending on the circumstances of testing and the species.

Dissynchronous Acts Eliciting Rejection

As was already mentioned, the inept behaviors of the transplanted animal may increase the likelihood of rejection. For example, ambivalence in the approach of a transplanted young lamb can elicit rejection by the potential mother. On the next occasion that the lamb and its mother are brought together, the experience of the prior rebuff can magnify the ineptness of the lamb's approach, and thus may elicit even more punitive acts (Klopfer, Adams, and Klopfer, 1964).

Similarly, previously isolated adult monkeys may be socially and sexually inept. Ineptness elicits noncooperation by potential mates, and the relationship can deteriorate to the point where there is little interest in sexual activity. (This topic is discussed in greater detail in Chapter 14.) The dynamics of such interchanges are, of course, not limited to the mother-infant or male-female relationship. Nor are the outcomes of adaptation guaranteed to be happy; the mutual dependencies that evolve can be destructive for one or both individuals.

In general, an adaptation process is initiated as soon as the animal—adult or infant—is transplanted to a new location. To the extent that the match between prior responses and current requirements is a poor one, and the young animal is permitted to escape, no enduring mutual accommodation will occur. If, however, both individuals are required to remain together and interact, significant modifications can occur for both the young and the host (Hersher, Richmond, and Moore, 1963).

Developmental Continuity and Change

The "paradox" about continuity and change described at the beginning of this chapter becomes less paradoxical when attention is given to the conditions required for either outcome. The processes of development are variable enough so that some systems are structured and fixed by early events and others are relatively uninfluenced. The experimenter's problem is to determine which systems are fixed and which are variable, and how either outcome is achieved. At this point we will consider some theoretical undercurrents that have brought this issue to the surface.

Embryological Analogue and Critical Periods

Early research on the issue of social development fixedness was guided by the assumption that physical growth and development were analogous. A significant breakthrough in embryological research occurred in the 1920's when a Nobel laureate, Hans Spemann, found that living tissue, early in its development, is highly susceptible to the influence of the context in which it is placed. In an elegant series of experiments, Spemann found that presumptive skin tissue of the embryonic newt could be excised and transplanted to areas where the nervous system was to develop. The transplanted cells developed as nerve tissues, not skin. For the induction to be successful, the transplantation must be performed within a narrow span of time, early in the organization of the structure and the tissue. There is a "critical period" of high plasticity, and once this period has ended, the character of the structure and tissue becomes fixed. Attempts to produce plasticity thereafter are rejected. On the basis of these results, Spemann proposed that the surroundings organize the character and functions of the tissues in early development.

The proposal that there are critical periods in development has proved to be of value in the analysis of other embryological events, from the formation of sensory structures to the development of basic organ systems. In each case, there is a limited period of high vulnerability to both endogenous and exogenous events during the formative stages of the system; once established, the systems are relatively irreversible.

Instances of Relative Nonreversibility in Sensorimotor Development

That early visual stimulation is critical in organizing the development of the sensory system is now recognized as one of the more important discoveries in the neurobiology of behavior (Daniels and Pettigrew, 1976; Grobstein and Chow, 1976). If a young kitten is deprived of patterned visual stimulation for the first 12 weeks of its life, it is deficient in form perception, depth perception, and sensorimotor coordination. There are changes in the neural organization of the visual system as well. Studies of the cells in the lateral geniculate (a way station in the neural transmission from the eye to the visual cortex) indicate that the size of the cellular mass itself is decreased by the deprivation. Other analyses show that positive effects are obtained from exposure to only one type or form of visual stimulation. Kittens that have been reared in darkness except for only a few hours of exposure to vertical lines respond selectively to vertical dimensions at maturity. Conversely, kittens exposed only to horizontal lines after being reared in darkness show a selective attention to these stimuli at maturity. Single-unit recordings (obtained by implanting micro-electrodes in the visual cortex) indicate that individual cortical cells are "set" to respond to the exposed stimulus dimension (Blakemore, 1973).

The question of the extent to which the neurological effects are reversible has no simple answer. It depends on the nature of the function analyzed (whether behavioral or neurological), the type of deprivation and "rehabilitation" procedures, the species studied, and the kinds of tests that are used (Tees, 1976). Some efforts to reverse the effects produced by the deprivation of patterned visual stimulation have been quite successful (Grobstein and Chow, 1976). Not only are the behavioral functions recovered (the cats see normally) after the cats are removed from visual privation, but the cell mass in the lateral geniculate returns to normal size. Hence the present evidence on visual privation suggests that some of the neurological consequences (and most behavioral ones) are modifiable by early *and later* experience.

But can these visual effects be induced at adulthood? In particular, can orientational preferences be influenced by special exposure conditions at adulthood as they are in early life? Apparently they can. The recent work of Creutzfeldt and Heggelund (1975) has demonstrated that maintaining adult cats in a visually restricted environment produces neural consequences that are seemingly as profound as those achieved by special rearing in infancy. Their results, shown in Figure 5-5, are problematic. In adulthood, cortical cells show a *decreased* responsiveness (rather than the increased responsiveness produced by early stimulation) to the line orientations to which the animals were exposed. The reason for this reversal of effects has yet to be explained.

There is a more general issue that requires com-

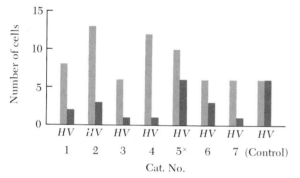

Figure 5-5. Results of testing cells in visual cortex of 7 experimental adult cats and one control cat to determine neural plasticity after cats were kept in darkness for 2 weeks except for exposure twice a day to a visual environment consiting only of vertical stripes. There was a decrease in the number of neurons sensitive to vertical orientations relative to those sensitive to horizontal orientations. *H* refers to the number of cells in the horizontal orientation; *V* refers to the number of cells in the vertical orientation. Figures across the top are: the total number of cells recorded in each animal, the number that could be driven by visual stimuli, and the number that could not be classified according to visual stimulation. (Adapted from Creutzfeldt and Heggelund. Copyright © 1975 by American Association for the Advancement of Science. Used with permission.)

ment. Why should there be experience-produced plasticity in so basic a function as vision (or hearing, taste, or olfaction, for that matter)? It would seemingly be more adaptive for the species *not* to have to rely on the experiences of individual organisms for such basic functions to develop. Possibly the most plausible answer to this question is that experience is necessary to organize components of the system in order to permit it to operate at maximum efficiency. Consider, for instance, the integration by the brain of the information derived from two eyes in order to perceive depth and perspective (stereopsis). This cross-correlative process is performed with staggering accuracy, enabling humans to make judgments that are six times more accurate than can be predicted by the grain of the retinal receptors of the eye. As Daniels and Pettigrew (1976) point out, the fine details of this organization would be hard to predict in advance, given the slight differences in the placement and optical properties of the eyes and the continuous shifting of the relative location of the eyes during the course of development. It is thus reasonable to expect that the organization of binocular signals would reflect individual experience, and that this organization would be susceptible to change as a function of the growth and developmental status of the organism. This proposal is deserving of further exploration.

The findings obtained from the studies of motor development and coordination appear to be consistent with the idea that experience affects the organization of the components, rather than the shaping of the components themselves. The important work of Held, Hein, and their colleagues demonstrates that sensorimotor coordination in the kitten is dependent on the developmental integration of visual and movement experiences. Movement alone, or visual stimulation alone, will not suffice to achieve "normal" sensorimotor coordination. For instance, kittens that are visually exposed to complex stimuli but otherwise reared in the dark are deficient in normal depth perception and placement movements (Held and Hein, 1963; Hein and Diamond, 1972). Hence it is the correlative organization of the two experiences, not either one alone, that is required for normal sensorimotor coordination. With regard to the problem of reversibility, it should be mentioned that these "deficiencies" in coordination are rapidly eradicated. After a few hours in a lighted room, the kittens move normally and efficiently.

Before concluding this section on the role of experience in the development of sensory and motor patterns, Gottlieb's (1976b) distinctions between *maintenance, facilitation,* and *induction* require comment. Gottlieb has emphasized that experience can

> play at least three roles in the development of behavior and the nervous system; it can *maintain* (sustain, preserve) ongoing developmental states or particular end points, it can *facilitate* development, and it can *induce* (channel, determine) development (p. 28—author's emphases).

Although it is too early to draw a firm conclusion, the data available from anatomical/physiological studies suggest that the primary functions of experience in neural development are of the maintaining and facilitating sort—that is, experience serves to keep the nervous system operating effectively and helps to bring about optimal levels of operation. But what about sensory and motor behavior? Here there is also abundant evidence that experience both maintains and facilitates the development of these systems. In addition, there is also evidence that experience plays an "inductive" role in the organization of these systems. Experiences appear to finely tune binocular vision (and possibly biaural hearing) and to provide the basis for organizing birdsong into species-typical or neophenotypic patterns. Once the system has become rigidly stabilized ("crystallized" for Marler and Mundinger, 1971), it appears to become increasingly resistant to change as a result of experience.

Critical Periods in Social Development

Now we can return to the problem of social behavior reversibility. Influential as the "critical period"

embryological analogy has been, there are good reasons to believe that its unquestioned application to *social* development is inappropriate and misleading. A basic problem is that the empirical data show that adaptation, rather than "irreversibility," seems to be the predominant outcome in mammalian social behavior. In addition, criticisms have been raised at the theoretical level, two of which deserve mention here.

First, social acts are, by definition, embedded in interactional relationships. The social actions that an individual performs typically occur within a social organization; as such, they are under the control of the acts of other individuals within that organization. Social acts are often inappropriately viewed as structures of the individual rather than as part of an interaction organization. In this regard, Atz (1970) has observed that the history of the study of animal behavior shows that to think of behavior as structure has led to the most pernicious kind of oversimplification. An interactive view of social development requires that equal attention be given to the activities of the other individuals. The "normality" or "non-normality" may be attributed to the nature of their actions as much as to the initial acts of the young organism. The behaviors of others, in turn, direct or redirect the behaviors of the young.

The other major criticism is that many of the "critical events" responsible for the establishment of social relationships recur (unlike those responsible for the establishment of sensory and motor systems). New relationships can be formed, and old ones changed, throughout the lifetime of the individual.

Studies of social behavior over the life span indicate that it would be incorrect to conclude that a developmental magic moment occurs when social behaviors are set forever. Although there may be critical and dramatic events—as Kummer found when observing integration in baboon troops—they do not necessarily occur early in the life of the individual. The major task for future research will be to determine the mechanisms that govern the organization.[5]

The basis on which sensorimotor and social systems can be differentiated requires comment. Z. Y. Kuo (1967) has proposed a similar distinction, between structural-functional patterns and social behaviors. The former include "dexterity, skilled activities, such as swimming, dancing, athletics, etc., sensory capabilities, vocal expression in songs and speech." Structural-functional patterns, because of their internal dependency and structural supports, are less vulnerable to change once they have been organized. The muscular and anatomical features of an organism help to establish and maintain its distinctive mode of responding.

Social behaviors, on the other hand, can be reordered in sequence and consequence and may or may not result in structural changes. Even though interchange systems do become consolidated and relatively stable over time, they rarely become as rigidly "crystallized" as sensorimotor systems. Social preferences and roles, in particular, remain vulnerable to reorganization when changes occur within the individual (such as growth and maturation) and when social circumstances change. There is no con-

flict, then, between the results of research on social continuity and the results of research on change. Both outcomes are possible—indeed, expected—when it is recognized that social action patterns are subject to organization and reorganization throughout development.

Summary

Questions about whether social attachment is fixed or reversible cannot be answered by tabular summary of positive and negative studies; either result can be obtained. The outcome is multiply determined by the nature of the original experience and the context in which the individual is placed after that experience, the reactions of the others to the young, and the organismic status of the individual (sex, age, species) relative to the "other."

This overview of social attachment reversibility and extendability in nonhuman vertebrates has suggested the following generalizations:

■ Social preferences and attachment behaviors are functional for both the individual and the species. The underlying social processes are sensitive to the adaptational requirements of the organism. As these needs change, either because of changed environmental circumstances or maturation, the individual's social interaction patterns and preferences become realigned. Social adaptation and its byproduct, attachment behavior, reflect processes that continue throughout life. Simply because a social preference is established early in life does not ensure that it will remain functional or primary.

■ Accordingly, isolation-produced effects on social behavior (for example, alienation, withdrawal) are not necessarily permanent. Studies of mammalian young reared in isolation indicate that the more prominent consequences can be significantly if not

---

[5] It is a pity that developmental theorists have borrowed Spemann's concept of critical period and ignored his more fundamental concept of organizers. The organizational process by which the social responses of the young are synchronized into the interactional system remains a key issue for developmental theories of social behavior. This concept would appear to constitute a closer analogue to Spemann's essential contributions than the notion that there is a "magic moment" at which basic socialization occurs.

In embryology, the "critical period" refers secondarily to the stage of development, and only indirectly to the "age" of the individual following conception. At particular stages in the developmental sequence, structures are more easily influenced and tissues are more plastic than at others. It is usually not misleading to equate age with stage of morphological development. However, the distinction between age and developmental stage becomes quite important when social behavior is considered. Social behavior patterns are less rigidly linked to maturational stage than are basic organ systems and tissue development. Interaction patterns may be more vulnerable to modification in their formative stages than later on, but these formative stages do not necessarily occur early in life.

totally ameliorated. Several conditions, including benign interactions with others, tend to facilitate "rehabilitation." Although nonpunitive interactions facilitate the process, they apparently are not necessary. Even punitive interchanges bring about shifts in the isolated animal's social orientation, and in its preferences.

■ Just as privation effects can sometimes be diminished or totally reversed at maturity, "primary" or first-established social preferences can also undergo significant modification. As its circumstances and biological needs change, so do its patterns of interchange and, possibly, preference. Experimental analyses of the process of social adaptation indicate that the "transplanted" individual first goes through a period of behavioral disruption and withdrawal, then adapts its behaviors to the responses of the other individual. The longer the young animal remains in the new situation, the more likely it is that mutual adaptation and preferences will develop. The formation of new relationships does not require, however, that the old ones be displaced or eliminated.

■ Although the social preferences and responses of young mammals are typically adaptive to their current circumstances, several conditions can produce the apparent persistence of early experiences. These include the similarities across time of the social network and nonsocial adaptation requirements, as well as similarities in the individual's biophysical and cognitive capabilities. In natural (nonexperimental) circumstances, there is considerable stability in the individual's environment from infancy to adulthood. Further, "others" with whom the young must deal and the circumstances in which the young must live are often unchanged throughout development.

■ When there is no environmental continuity, previously established social behaviors can persist, even though they are seemingly inappropriate and maladaptive. When first placed in a new setting, the transplanted individual may choose to re-create its prior circumstances. The result is self-produced isolation (withdrawal). Further, the individual's reactions to the new setting may be self-perpetuating: they can elicit rejection and a continuation of alienation.

■ Not all failures to accommodate are due to the social deficiencies of the young animal. They are commonly caused by the responses that others make to the animal and by the constraints that are operative in the new setting. Intruders, including transplanted animals, are often rejected. The severity of this rejection depends in part on the sex, age, and species of the transplant and in part on the social organization of the "adopting" group. What appears to be withdrawal and alienation may be a reaction to the behavior of the new group.

■ Both experimental and nonexperimental studies of the persistence of imprinting experiences in birds indicate that the "total irreversibility" assumption is misleading.

■ Theoretical models of early influence have been re-evaluated in light of the results of recent studies of social interchange. Although the embryological concept of "critical period" seems appropriate for some aspects of nonsocial behavioral development, its application to social development is less certain. Some sensory (visual, auditory) systems are relatively permanently organized early in development, but even these systems may be susceptible to modification at maturity under extreme environmental condition.

Finally, a word of caution about the varied mechanisms of social adaptation is in order. We have found that certain mechanisms apply to the social development of several mammalian species. Perhaps this should not be too surprising, in light of common phylogeny, common physiology and morphology, common environments, and common social organizations. But superimposed on these general processes are species-typical and species-distinctive requirements. Even closely related subspecies of monkeys or sublines of mice can differ markedly among themselves because of "trivial" differences in rearing and social organization. All this points to the importance of analyzing, for each species, the social circumstances and experiences to which the young are normally exposed. It also points to the hazards of generalizing on the basis of the apparent similarity of social outcomes (such as *the* effects of isolation, and primacy) rather than on the basis of the similarity of social processes, which can yield multiple outcomes. Consideration of this problem is especially important when attempting to understand human social development, the topic to which we now turn.

6

ON HUMAN SOCIAL BONDS: THE FIRST RELATIONSHIPS

Taken as a whole, the results of investigations indicate that even the vague and elusive properties of social interchanges of nonhuman mammals can be explained within a behavioral-biological framework. Now we will attempt to ascertain whether a similar analysis will reveal the secrets of early social relationships in children.

The temptation is great to assume that we need merely demonstrate the parallels that exist between monkeys and man because, after all, have not the same basic social processes evolved in humans as in nonhuman primates? Perhaps. Or it may be that novel human capabilities and qualities—such as language, symbolization, memory, and a "higher" sense of ethics—have permitted distinctively human patterns of social development to evolve. In any case, to generalize too readily from animals to humans is a risky business; parallels that are drawn across species remain only semiscientific if we confine our attention to the observations that fit our expectations and ignore those which do not. Polythetic generalizations in sociobiology or psychology require that developmentalists have as detailed a view of children as they have of animals. Happily, since 1960 a

substantial amount of research has focused on human infancy and childhood.

Chapters 6–8 are intended to be an introduction to the early social development of children. The present chapter focuses on relationship establishment in infancy and the events that influence it. Chapter 7 deals with relationship plasticity in children—the development of new relationships and the transformation of old ones. Chapter 8 is concerned with the development of patterns of interchange and the ways that interpersonal games are acquired and perfected in childhood.

The Natural Course of Social Development

Let us begin by analyzing the "natural" course of the relationships that children form with other persons. Despite the obvious differences that exist among children, as evidenced by their behavior toward other persons, children are more alike than different early in their development, regardless of their background and culture (whether reared, say, by an Indian family in Guatemala, by the Bushmen of the Kalahari Desert, or by caretakers in an Israeli kibbutz). Following is a general outline of the normal course of early social development.

1. In the days and weeks following birth, the infant inevitably develops actions that can elicit, maintain, and control interchanges, such as smiling, crying, laughing, and clinging to other persons.

2. The infant shows an increasing capability to discriminate among persons and settings. Gross distinctions are made by the fourth month, and more sophisticated discriminations are made over the next twelve months.

3. By the end of the first year, the infant forms strong and obvious preferences for particular persons and things. He selectively approaches and follows, and becomes disrupted and upset when particular things or persons are removed from him, or he from them. One relationship that has received particular attention is the infant's bond with his mother, though recent investigations have demonstrated that relationships can develop simultaneously with the father, siblings, and other persons.

4. Just as he distinguishes "preferred" persons and things, the infant is wary of and sometimes avoids strange events, persons, and actions.

5. Infants early participate in the exchange of actions and things, including toys. Primitive exchanges of actions may be observed in the first days following birth, and exchanges of objects occur between 12 and 18 months of age. More complex patterns of response are observed from 18 months onward.

6. The infant typically establishes and maintains multiple relationships. Distinctive actions are directed toward several different persons from 6 months of age onward.

7. Significant changes in the child's ability to adapt and to manipulate social interchanges are correlated with changes in cognitive and linguistic abilities.

The infant's social behavior should not be analyzed separately from his cognitive, motor, and physical development (see Table 6-1). The ranges in age must be interpreted loosely; there is much individual variation. Note also that the outcomes of studies of simple perceptual acts show greater agreement than the outcomes of studies of complex social discriminations associated with distress.

Now we will analyze the processes that govern the development of these similarities, and attempt to determine how variations may arise.

Onset

There is some benefit to be gained from identifying the point at which a social pattern or sensory capability is first observed in babies. This information can then serve as a kind of behavioral bench mark that is useful for both practical and scientific purposes. For instance, if there is little evidence that infants possess any social sensitivity at, say, x days of age, adoptions might be less disruptive if they took place before rather than after x.

What, then, is x? What is the date of onset of social responsiveness and social attachment behaviors? Surprisingly, until recently, only meager systematic empirical information was available on this subject. Apparently, the time was ripe in the mid-1960's for the development of techniques for studying early social development. Three different groups of researchers in different parts of the world—East Africa, Europe, and North America—working in virtually independently, developed reasonably comparable measures of the strength of the mother-infant relationship. One measure common to these initial studies was the infant's crying upon being separated from its mother. The activity is highly discernible and dramatic. When separation occurs, the child begins to cry, his cries ranging from a whimper to a violent outburst. This phenomenon has been

Table 6-1. Indexes of social development in infants (mean age in weeks).

Investigator	Sustained visual regard of person	Social smile	Differential response to mother and stranger	Stanger disruption (marked distress)	Separation disruption (marked distress)
Ainsworth, 1963	—	—	—	—	22+
Bayley, 1969	4	6	21	—	—
Bridges, 1933	—	17	21	28	—
Bronson, 1973	—	—	—	28	—
Fleener and Cairns, 1970	—	—	—	—	48–56
Gesell and Amatruda, 1947	4	8	24	28	—
Griffiths, 1954	4	8	14	34	—
Kagan, 1976	—	—	—	—	36–58
Schaffer and Emerson, 1964	—	—	—	—	22–78
Shirley, 1933	—	8	—	—	—
Spitz, 1965	4	8	26	32	34
Tennes and Lampl, 1964	—	—	21	39	17–60
Yarrow, 1967	—	—	—	—	21+

SOURCE: Selected normative data from L. J. Yarrow, 1972, with permission.

called separation protest and behavioral disruption, terms that appear to be virtually identical but imply different things about the determinants of the behavior. The former presupposes that the infant is capable of recognizing the reason for his discomfort and intentionally registering protest to that state of affairs. Since both assumptions are open to question (because they attribute adult-level cognitions and motivations to human and nonhuman infants), the latter term is preferred.

In the first study, Mary Ainsworth of the University of Virginia deserves credit for having conducted an ingenious clinical study of maternal-infant relationships in Uganda, East Africa. Ainsworth (1963, 1967) interviewed the same group of mothers every 2 weeks, for approximately 7 months, and then made a longitudinal plot of the age of onset of the separation-induced disruption. The judgment of disruption was made on two bases: what the mothers said and what the experimeter observed. Since the interviews were conducted in small, one or two-room cottages, the experimenter could sometimes see whether the child cried upon being separated

from its mother. Two results of the African study are particularly noteworthy. First, there was considerable variation in the age at which the infants first began to cry on maternal departure. Some infants cried at 3 months of age; others cried at about 6 months; and two failed to cry at all. Second, the median age of the onset of protest crying was approximately the fifth month.

The second study was conducted in Glasgow, Scotland, by H. R. Schaffer and P. Emerson (1964). The basic procedure was similar to that employed by Ainsworth, possibly because both Ainsworth and Schaffer had worked with psychoanalyst John Bowlby at London's Tavistock Clinic. Compared with the Ainsworth study, the Schaffer/Emerson study was more extensive in scope, and its criteria for determining the age of onset of attachment behavior were somewhat more clearly defined. Sixty-four lower-middle-class mothers were interviewed every month, from the time their infants were 3 months of age until they were 18 months. The mothers were asked whether their infant cried on being left by her, if he cried in his crib at home or in his pram outside the market when left by her, if he cried when left with another caretaker, and whether he cried only when separated from the mother, or also when separated from others (siblings, father, grandparents). On the basis of this inventory, a summary score was derived that reflected the overall propensity of the child to cry on being separated. The results of this longitudinal analysis are shown in the right-hand column of Table 6-1. Although the two studies utilized similar procedures, the "separation protest" began somewhat later in the Schaffer/Emerson study than in the Ainsworth study. (The median onset of crying in the former was 8-9 months following birth.)

The third study was complete at about the same time in Bloomington, Indiana (reported in Fleener and Cairns, 1970). Although the work was undertaken independently of the Ainsworth and Schaffer/Emerson, studies, the same dependent measure (separation-disruption) was used. However, infants were observed in the laboratory, not at home, and their reactions were filmed and recorded on tape. Their mothers left the room (saying "bye-bye, baby") and, after a minute away, returned. For control purposes, an unfamiliar woman also left and returned. In contrast to the researchers in the Uganda and Scottish studies, the Indiana researchers observed the children directly rather than relying on the mother's perceptions and memory. They also required that the crying be discriminative (in response only to maternal departure, not simply to the departure of anyone). Most infants did indeed become upset upon being separated from their mothers. Discriminative crying, however, was only observed in the older infants (11-12 months of age or older). And, as in the studies of the infants in Scotland and Uganda, not all of the infants cried on separation. Some infants in all age groups failed to show signs of great disruption on being separated, even in the unfamiliar surroundings of the laboratory.

The most striking difference among the three studies was the range of the median age of onset—

from 5 months in Uganda to 8-9 months in Scotland to 12 months in Indiana. One possible reason for the difference is that it reflects basic cross-cultural variations that could be due to differences in rearing practices, or to more basic genetic differences in the rates of physical/cognitive maturation. Genetic factors might account for the discrepancy between the Scottish and Uganda samples, but they hardly explain the difference between the Scottish and American results. This raises the possibility that these differences are due to variations in rearing practices; that is, whatever it is that the Ganda mothers did differently, they were presumably more effective in eliciting attachment behaviors than were the Scottish mothers, who in turn were more effective than the American mothers.

There is a third possibility. The differences may reflect variations in the procedures followed by the different investigators, including the frequency with which the behaviors were observed and where they occurred. Separating an infant from his mother is a complex manipulation. *Where* the separation occurs (at home or away) may make a difference (see Parry, 1972). *What* the child is left with (nothing, a pacifier, a toy) may also affect his reaction (Rheingold and Eckerman, 1970). *Whom* the infant is left with (no one, father, stranger) when the mother is away might contribute to the effect (Schaffer and Emerson, 1964). *Duration* of the separation (hours, days, weeks) and *frequency of observations* could determine whether crying occurred and was observed (Littenberg, Tulkin, and Kagan, 1971; Spelke, Zelazo, Kagan and Kotelchuck, 1973).

The most recent evidence on the onset of crying supports this last possibility (that experimental procedures differed). Jerome Kagan (1976) and his collaborators at Harvard University studied infants in four different groups: the aforementioned African Bushmen, Guatemalan Indians, an Israeli kibbutz, and lower-class families living in the city of Antigua, Guatemala. Roughly the same procedures were used throughout the study. Plotted in Figure 6-1 are the percentages of infants in each age group who cried when their mothers left them alone with an

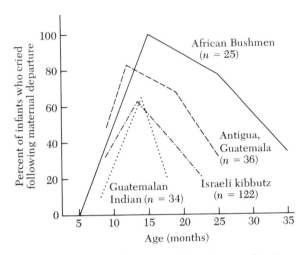

Figure 6-1. Onset of separation disruption as a function of age is remarkably similar across cultures when the same methods are used. Note that there was a sharp rise in reactivity at about the end of the first year, and a marked decline over the next 2 years. These percentages do not, however, tell whether the infant's crying was in response to the mother's departure, or to the departure of the unfamiliar woman (adapted from Kagan, 1976, with permission).

unfamiliar woman. Although the proportion of children who cry differs across cultures, the age of onset, and form of the curves appear to be reasonably similar across cultures. It should also be noted that crying decreased as the infants (again, in all cultures) grew older.

Why Cry?

The fact that procedural variations can yield large differences in infant responsiveness raises a question about what causes separation vocalization. Infants obviously cry in circumstances other than separation: when they are hungry, in pain, or sleepy, and when they are interrupted. Why does an infant cry when mother (or other persons) leaves? Three an-

swers have been offered. One is that crying is a survival mechanism. It signals to the mother that the infant is in distress and tells her where he is located. Bowlby (1958) has concluded that since the noise is unpleasant to the mother, she will probably be motivated to renew contact with her offspring. Bowlby (1958) has proposed that vocalization serves as an innate releaser of maternal retrieval behaviors. Such an explanation seems well taken; it is entirely plausible that the young primate's vocalizations serve to enhance its survival in nature.

A second, related explanation that has been offered is that crying is a manifestation of an "attachment structure" or motive. Crying that is contingent upon maternal absence is seen as an index of the strength of the child's attachment to the mother. The presumption is that the contingency between crying and attachment is inherent. This proposal assigns to separation-induced crying a special motivational status relative to other instances of infant distress.

A third explanation is that crying is a manifestation of a perceptual and behavioral reorganization that occurs as a result of a radical change in the infant's environment (such as maternal departure or being left in an unfamiliar setting). According to this proposal, human behavior around stable features of the environment. The greater the change in the environment, the greater is the disorganization of behavior and perception and the higher the level of arousal. As the infant's behavior and perception stablize in the new setting, there is a concomitant decrease in arousal levels. According to this view, separated-induced crying is one aspect of a more general process; hence one does not need to propose a special mother-infant motivational system to explain the effect.

The experimental evidence that is available seems to support this view, but surely, does not exclude the possible evolutionary functions of the action. Infants can become adapted to being separated. Mothers who work and who leave their offspring at day care centers find that the infants are

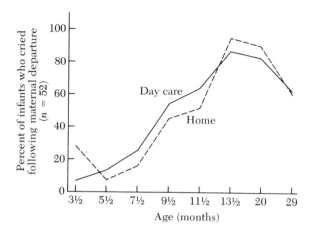

Figure 6-2. This comparison of home-reared and day care-reared children suggests that day care rearing does not make a difference in the onset of social disruption. The procedures and results were similar to those of the separation-disruption experiment (Figure 6-1), except that these data are based on groups of American children who had differential rearing histories (adapted from Kagan, 1976, with permission).

not traumatized daily by the separation. There are no reliable differences in their responses to experimental separation (Figure 6-2). Indeed, many infants are disrupted if the mother appears in a setting where she is not expected. Similarly, infants' behavior may not become disrupted if the mother leaves from an exit to which they are accustomed, but they will cry if she uses an unfamiliar door (Spelke et al., 1973).

Further examination of separation vocalization suggests that the activity requires the development of several basic capabilities of the infant, including the capability to discriminate visually between familiar adult females and nonfamiliar ones. The discrimination must be sufficiently precise to allow the infant to identify her presence or absence in a variety of locations in the setting. This requirement presupposes that the infant can visually "search" (including a scan of areas around him), adjust to

changing background conditions, and identify the mother by subtle cues. Given the prerequisites for the phenomenon, it is remarkable that reliable and sharp discriminations can occur as early as the end of the first year of life.

Social Responsiveness: How Early?

Other criteria for measuring social responsiveness demand less advanced sensory capabilities. Visual orientation, for instance, requires only that the infant distinguish between 2 adult females who stand side by side. The easier the perceptual task, the earlier should be the child's differential responsiveness. In a pairwise visual comparison, even very young infants (3 months old) orient differentially toward their mothers. Similarly, approach tests lessen the importance of the child's ability to discriminate. Paired comparisons between the mother and unfamiliar women indicate that infants will crawl toward the mother, reliably, as soon as they are able (sometimes as early as 6 months). It is likely that infants can distinguish among persons on the basis of vestibular and proprioceptive (nursing, burping, rocking) stimulation even earlier.

In light of these differential sensitivities, when can we say that the onset of social responsiveness occurs? As in the case of nonhuman young (see Chapter 3), the onset is relative to the response measure that is used. If the response is discriminative separation vocalization, the onset is late in the second half of the first year. If the response is approach and orientation, the onset is at age 5-6 months. If the response is visual discrimination and recognition, the onset is about the third month. If the response is distinguishing among caretakers who hold and feed, the onset may be within the first days or weeks after birth. In Chapter 3, it was observed that attempts to determine the age at which onset of social responsiveness occurs in nonhuman young are futile. The social development of human infants is also a continuous phenomenon, beginning at birth and possibly before. We will now examine some of the earliest mother-child interchanges.

Initial Dyadic Interactions

Activity of the Mother. In nonhuman mammals, the actions of the mother immediately following birth are essential for the infant's survival. However, responsibility for the survival of the newborn human infant is assigned to professionals, such as the midwife, obstetrician, and pediatrician, who are institutionalized mother substitutes. For humans, "natural childbirth" means only that the mother is not given analgesic or anesthetic drugs—not that birth is unassisted, as it is in other primates.

Accordingly, the initial interactions between the mother and her infant rarely occur at the time of parturition. In many hospitals, she does not interact with the infant until the first or second feeding, some 12–16 hours after birth. These initial interchanges are of particular interest. The aim of a research team at Stanford University Hospital (Thoman, Turner, Leiderman, and Barnett, 1970; Thoman, Barnett, and Leiderman, 1971; Thoman, Leiderman, and Olson, 1972) was to identify the kinds of neonate-maternal interactions that occurred during the first feeding periods, whether breast-feeding or bottle-feeding procedures were adopted. Different infant-caretaker pairs were observed to determine how the mother contributed to interchange differences. For example, mothers who had borne other children *(multiparous)* were compared with mothers who had not *(primiparous)*. Experienced professional nurses were also compared with the infant's mother, regardless of parity.

Striking and consistent differences were found among the caretakers. Primiparous mothers were enthusiastic but lacked adeptness and coordination in feeding. Compared with multiparous mothers, they took longer to feed their infants. They also spent more time in such nonfeeding activities as talking to and playing with them. Although the nurses (who had worked in the Stanford nursery for more than 10 years) spent less time than mothers in feeding and nonfeeding activities, the infants ingested more milk[1] and more rapidly when fed by caretakers.

The caretakers also differed in number of feedings offered. In general, the more experienced the caretaker, the less frequent the feedings (primiparous mothers were most frequent; nurses were least frequent). Interestingly, these differences sharply decreased when the novices gained a little experience. Within 60 hours, the number of times that primiparous mothers fed their infants was virtually equal to the frequency of feeding by more experienced mothers. Apparently, primiparous mothers learn rapidly. As in other mammals, the responses of the mother become synchronized with the particular needs of the infant.

Activity of the Infant. To what extent does the infant contribute to the observed differences in maternal feeding patterns? We have already seen that the differences between primiparous and multiparous mothers may in fact reflect differences between the behavior of first and later infants. Perhaps it is not so much a matter of the mother's "learning" as it is that the first-born infants become more similar to later-born ones in the days after birth.

First births are typically different from subsequent ones. In first deliveries, more problems are created for both the infants and the mothers. First deliveries are of longer duration (roughly twice as long), first labors are more stressful, and more drugs are given to mothers during their first labor. Such anesthetics or analgesic medications affect not only the mother but her unborn infant as well. The action can be direct; that is, the drug can be transmitted from the mother's blood to the infant's.

---

[1] One parallel between human and nonhuman mothers is noteworthy. Scholz (1974) reports that primiparous rodent females spend more time feeding than multiparous ones but have smaller offspring. It should also be noted that Thoman et al. (1971) found the differences between primiparous and multiparous mothers to be less robust than did Thoman et al. (1970).

These factors—stressful labor, prolonged delivery, and anesthetics administered to the mother—can have a powerful impact on the infant's activity and reactivity in the hours and possibly even days immediately following birth (Conway and Brackbill, 1970; Kraemer, Korner, and Thoman, 1972). [2] Combined with constitutional and genetic differences and differences in maternal care, these factors yield differences among infants in fretfulness, activity, and responsiveness (Brown, Bakeman, Snyder, Fredrickson, Morgan, and Hepler, 1975).

Maternal-Infant Synchrony. How does the maternal-infant synchronization begin and progress? There is now ample evidence that the infant is biologically "prepared" for the synchrony of particular actions, such as feeding. The sucking activities are so organized that they fall within the optimal range to allow the breast to deliver milk. Moreover, according to Osofsky and Danzger (1974), attentive, sensitive mothers have more responsive babies, and vice versa. Since in the latter study the infants were selected from an average hospital population, the effects of parity and of drugs used during and after labor contributed to the outcomes in unknown ways.

In another recent attempt to assess the several factors contributing to the synchronization of newborn baby-mother interactions, a group of investigators at Georgia State University assessed the effects of maternal medication and of the infants' birth weights, birth order, and sex on the patterns of interchange (Brown, et al., 1975). Direct observations were made of the interchanges that occurred be-

tween 45 black inner-city mothers and their healthy newborn babies. In general, the results agreed with those of other studies. The first-born babies were relatively inactive compared with later-born infants, possibly because the mothers of first-born infants had been given more medication while in labor (Figure 6-3). Also, mothers of first-born infants took longer to feed their babies than mothers of later-born infants. The latter difference could have been due to the inexperience of the mothers of the first-born, or to the after effects of the medications that were used in labor, which could affect both mother and infant. The Georgia State research group also found that the sex and size of the child do influence the nature of the interchanges, in that boys and larger infants receive more nonfeeding stimulation than do girls and smaller babies. Why? There is no definitive answer, but since the stimulation was given after all feeding and caretaking activities were taken care of, and since larger infants eat more efficiently and remain alert longer, there may have been more opportunity for "surplus" attention.

One comment should be made about the relation between the nature of the interactive pattern and the development of maternal-infant synchrony. Some action patterns are more readily intergrated with behaviors of the other person than other patterns. That our best examples of synchrony are to be found in the interchanges surrounding nursing-suckling seems not fortuitous: in the feeding interchange, the infant is as likely to be an expert as the mother. The suckling patterns of human infants—as well as nonhuman mammalian infants—are already organized, as they must be, for survival.

Problems arise, however, when this model of organization (feeding) is applied directly to other forms of synchrony for which the infant may be less prepared, or even inept. Condon and Sander (1974) have proposed the intriguing hypothesis that the neonate synchronizes its activities with the speech patterns of its mother, and that the infant's behaviors have a "dancelike" quality because they are coordinated with the rhythms of speech. Tronick, Als, and Brazelton (1977) suggest that the infant not

---

[2] The question of how long the effects of drugs last is still controversial. One problem is that the effects of parity (birth order) are sometimes confounded with the effects of drugs. It is unclear whether enduring differences reflect the difference in maternal handling (of first *vs.* later children) or the direct impact of the drug on the child (see Aleksandrowicz and Aleksandrowicz, 1976; and Federman and Yang, 1976). In addition, fearful and depressed mothers are more likely to be given drugs (Yang, Zweig, Douthitt, and Federman, 1976). The differences in infant behavior, regardless of parity, may thus reflect differences maternal attitudes, which in turn influence the mother's response to the infant's actions toward her.

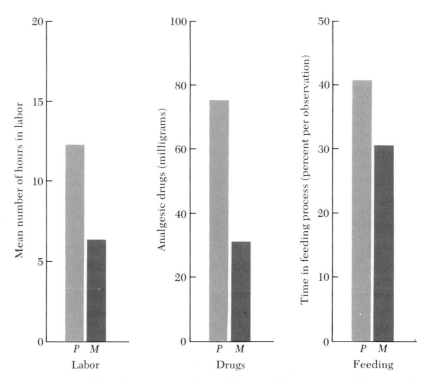

Figure 6–3. Effect of parity on number of hours in labor, amount of drugs used during delivery, and amount of time spent in feeding the infant. Primiparous mothers (*P*), typically experience longer labor, are given more drugs, and take longer to feed their babies than multiparous mothers (*M*) (data from Brown et al., 1975).

only able is to communicate with the mother but also can respond to the expressed intent of the mother: "Thus, long before language, the infant is a skillful communicator" (p. 79). Although the hypothesis is an attractive one and deserves vigorous exploration, the evidence in support of this proposal has not been compelling. One problem with the findings is that they fail to refute simpler explanations, such as the possibility that the mother coordinates her speech with the infant's states and activities, not vice versa.

More generally, interpersonal synchrony does not require equal participation by the two persons (in-

fant and "other") in responding and initiating. It can come about because of:

1. *higher-order events* that affect both persons equally (such as a drug that slows down the behavior of both the mother and infant or changes their affective/expressive states);

2. *response limitations*—the synchrony merely reflects the restricted response range of the infant (for example, to suck when nipples or nipplelike manipulanda are placed in his mouth);

3. *skillful "matching"* of the acts of the partner so that the major burden for synchrony is carried by one member of the pair (for example, the adult can fit his acts to those of the infant, as in pat-a-cake, or peek-a-boo);

4. *mutual contributions* to synchrony—each individual perceives and adapts to the actions of the other.

Instances of social synchrony have typically been assumed to be of the fourth type, when in fact there is good reason to expect that in early development this type of synchrony is quite limited (more on this matter in Chapters 8 and 17).

To summarize, the individual characteristics of the infant and, to a lesser extent, the mother, produce certain variations in the interactions that are observed among mother-child pairs shortly after birth. But transcending these variations are the similarities arising from the biological needs and capabilities of all newborns. The psychobiological processes associated with elementary caretaking functions contribute to a primary synchrony between the infant and the caretaker. Although the elements of the synchrony do not have to be learned (by the infants), the organization is learnable in that infants and their mothers (or other caretakers) become more efficient and fitted to each other over time.

Consolidation of Early Social Interchanges

The mother-infant relationship rapidly becomes a distinctive and predictable set of interchanges. Observations of maternal-infant interchanges in the home have been helpful in pinpointing some of the consistencies. Linda Monahan's (1975) research at Indiana University illustrates one procedure. The observer visited each home on 3 different occasions, 3 days apart. The mother was asked to go about her daily activities as usual, and the observer, who was a young woman about the same age as the mother, merely remained in the background. The behaviors of the mother and her infant were recorded at 5-second intervals, and particular note was made of any activity that occurred between the two. The

behavior-coding scheme permitted the investigator to trace which activity occurred first and the responses of the other (either the infant or its mother) to it, and thus provided a detailed and precise record of the course of the interchanges. Half of the 24 infants in the study were 7 months old, and half were 14 months old. All infants were first-born.

The Monahan study revealed that the infant controls much of the mother's behavior. The younger infants commanded the attention of the mothers by fussing and crying. This action had strong signal properties for all of the mothers. Surprisingly, maternal vocalization failed to produce any significant vocalization in the infant, although it did increase the infant's attention to the mother (see also Beckwith, 1972).

In the Monahan study, neither the behaviors of the mothers nor the activities of the infants could be viewed in isolation from each other without possible distortion of the functions of the actions. An earlier interactional study by Howard Moss indicated that the least active 3-month-old infants had mothers who talked to them the most (Jones and Moss, 1971; Moss, 1967). Moss proposed that the mothers selected the intensity of stimulation that seemed to them most appropriate for their infants' state. Similarly, Monahan discovered that the most active mothers (in terms of talking to their infants and stimulating them) were more likely to be ignored by their offspring. This result is open to two interpretations. Perhaps there is a limit to how often the infant can or will respond, and as this limit is approached, he begins to ignore the mother. Or perhaps the babies' *inattention* stimulates further contact from the mother. In any case, these studies indicate that there is an early dependency of each person on the overt acts of the other, with the mother taking the active role in maintaining the interaction and "reading" the state and cues of the infant.

Recent studies have sought to determine whether the nature of the interchanges that evolve is influenced by such factors as personality characteristics of the mother, presence or absence of other children, the social class of the family, and organismic properties of the child (sex, size). Finally some attention has been given to the other parent in the home—the father.

Maternal Personality. It has been suprisingly difficult to find strong or consistent relationships between maternal personality characteristics and maternal-infant interchanges (Table 6-2; Monahan, 1975). Why should such an intuitively appealing idea fail to be supported? One possible reason is that the fault lies in the personality tests themselves, in that the global dispositions they describe simply are not those relevant to observations made in the home (Mischel, 1969). A second possible reason is that the infants "normalize" both their mothers and the interchange, because their common needs, de-

mands, and activities cancel out personality differences. This normalization was observed, it may be recalled, in the "therapy" of motherless-monkey mothers by their first-born infants.

Birth-Order Effects. As previously mentioned, birth order affects the mother's actions toward her newborn. Follow-up studies indicated differences in maternal actions toward first-and second-born babies at 3 months. In a well controlled study of birth-order effects, Jacobs and Moss (1976), of the National Institute of Mental Health, initially observed a sample of first-born 3-month-old infants and their mothers in their homes. Then, 2 years later, they observed the same mothers in their homes when their second baby was 3 months old. A direct comparison of the two sets of observations indicates that

Table 6-2. Rank correlations between maternal scores on Interpersonal Checklist* and maternal behavior with infant (7 and 14 months old).

Maternal Personality Variable	Maternal Interaction	r†
warmth	Orienting to infant	−.07
	Smiling at infant	.07
	Talking	.08
	Contacting infant	−.06
	Audiovisual stimulation	−.20
	Mutual visual regard	.21
	Noninteraction time	−.01
control	Orienting to infant	.15
	Talking	.07
	Contacting infant	.08
	Audiovisual stimulation	.23
	Mutual visual regard	.12
	Noninteraction time	−.22
dependency	Orienting to infant	.09
	Talking	.00
	Contacting infant	.06
	Audiovisual stimulation	−.21
	Mutual visual regard	.14
	Noninteraction time	−.07

*The "Interpersonal Checklist" is a standard personality questionnaire that was given to the mothers.
†If the correlation equals +1.00 or −1.00, the relation is perfect. None of the correlations in this table are statistically reliable.
SOURCE: Monahan, 1975, with permission.

the first baby received more maternal affection (measured by kissing, smiling, and vocalization). Why the difference? Possibly, because the mother was younger and less experienced, or because the first-born baby was a novelty, or because the second child must compete for both time and affection when there is a child already in the home. The social system that the second child is brought into is clearly different from that which the first child enters. Whether any (or all) of these possibilities is responsible for the differences cannot be determined from available data.

We should be careful to not overemphasize the importance of birth-order effects. There is considerable overlap in the ways in which first- and second-born children are treated, and birth-order effects can be cancelled out by the sex of the second child. Further, mothers tend to maintain their "style" in interacting with the baby from the first to the second (and probably beyond). There was continuity in maternal treatment not only of the infants but of the observers; women who were friendly with the Jacobs-Moss investigators the first time around were also friendly 2 years later.

Social Class. The aim of some recent studies has been to investigate the possibility that maternal-infant interchanges may vary with the socioeconomic class, race, and intellectual level of the parents. Much of this work has been based on the premise that the early experiences of the infant determine his or her intellectual and social destiny.

An overview of these studies shows that lower-class mothers differ from middle-class mothers in communication styles (Baldwin and Baldwin, 1973; Feshbach, 1973; Tulkin and Kagan, 1972). In the study conducted by Tulkin and Kagan, physical contact and other nonverbal interactions did not vary with social class; but virtually every type of verbal behavior assessed did. (The lower-class mothers talked much less to their infants.) Does the type of stimulation affect the infant's response to the mother? At least one follow-up study of the same

infants suggests that it does. Tulkin (1972) has reported that middle-class infants distinguish between their mothers' voices and those of strangers; lower-class infants do not. When tape recordings were played, the middle-class infants quieted more, and vocalized more, upon hearing the mother's voice than they did upon hearing the voice of the stranger. The lower-class infants responded similarly to both. Tulkin speculates that the reason for the difference is that the middle-class infants experienced more verbal stimulation (see also Falender and Heber, 1975).

Father-Infant Interchanges. The preceding studies concerned only maternal-infant relationships. Other recent studies indicate that the father may have more influence over the infant's social development than has been generally assumed. The question is whether this influence is exerted directly, or whether it is mediated via the mother, or whether both parents exert their influence jointly. Rebelsky and Hanks (1971) have devised an ingenious procedure for determining the extent of the fathers' interaction with their very young offspring. Beginning in the second week of the infants' life, 24-hour audiotape recordings were made every 2 weeks. The infants were "bugged" with tiny microphones. Whenever anyone talked to them, or they vocalized, a voice key was activated.

Analysis of the tapes indicated that on the average, fathers interacted with their offspring 2–3 times a day. The mean time spent in interaction was only 37.7 seconds during the entire 24 hours—an average of 0.03 percent of the day. The most active fathers spent an average of 10 minutes, 26 seconds in interaction; the least-active fathers spent no time whatever in talking to their offspring. Surprisingly, the amount of interaction did not dramatically increase as the children grew older. At the end of the 3-month observation period, the fathers spent even less time with their female offspring, but spent about the same amount of time with the males.

Nonetheless, infants demonstrate virtually as

strong an attachment to their father as to their mother (Cohen and Campos, 1974; Kagan, 1976; Lamb, 1977; Ross, Kagan, Zelazo, and Kotelchuck, 1975). Despite the miniscule amount of time spent in interchanges with the father, the children show a strong tendency to approach him and cry when separated from him (see Figure 6-4 and Chapter 7).

Naturalistic analyses of maternal interaction provide data that are obtainable through no other procedure. They represent one of the most important recent advances in the study of human socialization. Nonetheless, the interpretation of interactions observed in natural (nonexperimental) circumstances requires caution. Interactional analyses preserve the sequential flow of the interchange and are helpful in determining who influenced whom. However, changes in the patterns of interchange are also correlated with developmental changes in the capabilities of the infant and in the attitudes, interpretations, and behaviors of the mother. There is a confounding of these potential influences on the relationship, and there are also carry-over effects from prior interactions. To obtain more precise information about the determinants of the relationship, it is necessary to examine the interactions of the infant and the mother under more controlled (that is, laboratory) conditions at each stage. Taken in conjunction with the results of naturalistic observations, such information can help us to specify the essential determinants of social patterns in infancy.

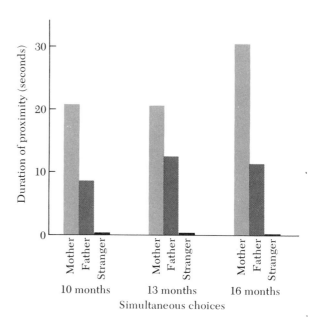

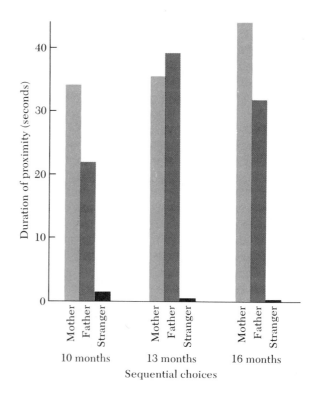

Figure 6-4. How do infants respond to their fathers? When they had to choose between mother, father, and an unfamiliar person (male or female), babies of several ages selected the mother more often than the father, and the father more often than the stranger (*top*). But when the three persons were not simultaneously pitted against one another, and the child could choose to approach (or not approach) one person in sequential tests, the difference between mothers and fathers was slight. However, children still avoided approaching unfamiliar persons (*bottom*) (data from Cohen and Campos, 1974).

The Infant as a Pacemaker: Developmental Changes in the Interchange

Visual Attention and Responsiveness

Early in life infants begin to participate in shaping the course of their own development. Through selective attention to environmental events, they help to determine the nature of the social experiences to which they will be exposed.

To infants, faces—whether smiling or unexpressive, familiar or strange—are very interesting and attractive stimuli. Newborns prefer to look at a face rather than at a variety of alternative objects, including a lighted orange globe, newsprint, or a square (see Fantz, 1963, 1967). By the second month, they also choose to smile at a facelike object (Spitz and Wolf, 1946a). But it has recently been pointed out that there is good reason to believe that the face is interesting to infants less than 2½ months old not because it is a face "but because it is a complex object" (Maurer and Salapatek, 1976). The very young infant seems less attracted by realism than by such basic features of the stimulus as movement, contours, and complexity (Carpenter, 1974). Since faces are "complex" stimuli in several dimensions, there is ample reason to suspect that infants' discriminations and preferences are based on these basic properties of stimuli.

The child's capacity to process the information that he sees in a face is clearly dependent on his age-developmental status. Two-month-old babies are more attentive to faces than are 4-week-old babies and do a more systematic job of inspecting the internal features (eyes, mouth); they do not simply focus on the contour (chin and hairline). From the second month to the fourth month, the infant prefers increasingly more complex patterns (Greenberg and O'Donnell, 1972) and learns to distinguish between familar and unfamiliar faces (Fagan, 1976).

Why does the infant become more responsive to persons than to inanimate objects? Rheingold (1966) has pointed out that persons are, first of all, interest-

ing (complex and mobile) and responsive stimuli. For the infant, facial features are highly salient. Eyes are the first facial features to be discriminated (in the second month, according to Caron et al., 1973). As Piaget (1932) observed, the very conspicuousness of other persons draws the infant's visual attention. It follows that other persons, because of their salience, reactivity, and mobility, rapidly acquire signal (discriminative) properties for the infant—that is, they become capable of eliciting different responses. And the probability that other persons will respond to the infant is enhanced if the child's attention is accompanied by distinguishable changes in his facial expressions and posture.

Smiling and Laughing: Development and Social Functions

Smiling is one of the more effective ways that the child has of registering interest and attention. What is the course of its development? Recent analyses indicate that the earliest smiles of the newborn are under endogenous control; they are correlated with the spontaneous activity of the central nervous system (for a review of the evidence, see Emde and Koenig, 1969; and Sroufe and Waters, 1976). Smiles can be elicited by external events during the first week of life, particularly when the child is asleep (Wolff, 1963). Light touches or blowing on the skin can elicit smiles in the 1- to 2-week old child. In the weeks following, smiles can be elicited by a variety of events, including voices and (in the fourth week) simple tactile stimulation. The ability to see is not necessary for the development of smiling, since it emerges at about the same time in both normal and congenitally blind children (Freedman, 1965). Table 6-3 summarizes the evidence on the development of smiling and laughter and the events that control them.

Once the response is established in the child's repertoire, smiling, like most other primitive response systems (sucking, elimination, crying), can be conditioned and used to condition other persons. By the fourth month, children can learn to smile or cry, coo or struggle, in the presence of particular others. Yvonne Brackbill, in a Stanford University study published in 1958, was the first investigator to demonstrate systematically how infants can be trained to smile.

Investigations during the past 10 years have replicated and extended Brackbill's primary findings. Many of them have been concerned with the point at which the child begins to make differential responses to others as persons. In a variation of Brackbill's experiment, Robert Wahler (1967) of the University of Tennessee used both the infants' mothers and some female experimental assistants to condition smiling behavior. He found that the mothers were effective in training the infants to smile. Curiously, the non-mothers were entirely ineffective. Their tickle-smile-greeting behavior simply did not work as a reinforcer. This result seems strange be-

Table 6-3. The development of smiling and laughter.

Age	Response	Stimulation	Latency	Remarks
		Smiling		
Neonate	Corners of the mouth	No external stimulation		Due to central nervous system fluctuations
Week 1	Corners of the mouth	Low level, modulated	6–8 sec	During sleep, boosting of tension
Week 2	Mouth pulled back	Low level, modulated; voices		When drowsy, satiated
Week 3	Grin, including eyes	Moderate level, voices	4–5 sec	When alert, attentive (nodding head with voice)
Week 4	Grin, active smile	Moderate, or moderately intense	Reduced	Vigorous tactile stimulation effective
Weeks 5–8	Grin, active smile, cooing	Dynamic stimulation, first visual stimulations	3 sec or less	Nodding head, flicking lights, stimulation that must be followed
Weeks 8–12	Grin, active smile, cooing	Static, visual stimulation, moderately intense	Short	Trial by trial effects, effortful assimilation, recognition; static at times more effective than dynamic
		Laughter		
Month 4	Laughter	Multimodal, vigorous stimulation	1–2 sec	Tactile, auditory
Months 5–6	Laughter	Intense auditory stimulation, as well as tactile	Immediate	Items that may have previously caused crying
Months 7–9	Laughter	Social, visual stimulation, primarily dynamic	Immediate	Tactile, auditory decline
Months 10–12	Laughter	Visual, social	Immediate or in anticipation	Visual incongruities, active participation

SOURCE: From Sroufe and Waters, copyright © 1976, by the American Psychological Association. Reprinted by permission.

cause, as Wahler points out, previous studies (including Brackbill's) of the phenomenon did not use the infant's mother to reinforce smiling. Possibly the explanation is not that one woman was the child's mother and the other woman was not, but that one woman had considerably more experience in responding to and handling infants than the other. Recall that Thoman et al. (1971) compared experienced nurses and primiparous mothers and found that the ability to make subtle discriminations directly affects the infant's feeding activities. It may also be that a woman's experience in responding to, and interacting with, infants also significantly influences her ability to elicit or reinforce social smiling.

Mysterious Mona Lisa motivations are not required to explain of why the infant smiles and why smiling is effective. The response appears to be a species-typical behavior pattern that occurs 1–2 months after birth. Initially it simply registers changes in the tonus of the skeletal musculature of the baby, including a mild tensing of the facial muscles. A rather wide range of events seems to be capable of eliciting the required change in arousal level. The reasons why burping or tickling the child elicits general musculature change—including smiling—seem clear: the child is actively responding to direct physical stimulation.

But why, as Piaget and others have observed, do children respond by smiling to familiar or "recognizable" visual or auditory events? Perhaps the psychological impact of recognition is sufficient to produce changes in arousal level, without prior conditioning. Further, in the training-to-smile experiments, the social stimulus (the experimenter) became a reliable signal for physical stimulation capable of evoking mild arousal and musculature involvement. The experimenter thereafter became an effective cue for the elicitation of anticipatory responses and general activity, including smiling. It does not seem unreasonable to suppose that a similar pattern of learning to respond is repeated every day in the life of most children. Such conditioned orienting and responding serve to recruit further dyadic sequences. The games played with infants

help to establish the basic capability for social interchange. Happily, they are also fun—for both the parent and the infant. Smiles early become social detectors that can be used in increasingly complex ways in interpersonal communication and control, by both infants and adults.

Sroufe and Waters (1976) recently offered a similar analysis for the development of laughter (see Table 6-4). The essential proposal is that laughter reflects the operation of a tension-release mechanism that is triggered initially by physical stimulation and later by visual and social events (such as talking to or smiling at the child). Once established, the expressive activity can then serve multiple social and communicative functions for the child. Sroufe and Waters conclude, rightly, that "cognitive and social-emotional aspects of development are inseparable" (p. 187).

Vocalizations and Their Early Development

The infant can produce a wide range of noises, many of them orally. Vocal behaviors could be roughly classified as aversive (crying, fussing) or positive (cooing, gurgling, laughing). Vocalizations can serve a survival function that other responses cannot. They can be heard in the dark as well as in the light, or when the infant is hidden, in distress, or lost. Modulation of the auditory signal (its volume, pitch, rhythm) can communicate considerable information about the state of the infant with only modest energy expenditure. Vocalizations provide a near optimal combination of detectability and versatility for the infant, particularly when he is in danger. (See Marler, 1965, for an excellent discussion of signal properties.)

Several years ago Leonard Carmichael (1954) offered a thoughtful proposal about fetal and neonatal crying. He suggested that neonatal crying is a reflexive response—"the result of appropriately activated muscles, which bring about the expulsion of air in such a way as to cause it to vibrate" (p. 125). Crying is thus simply one component of a response pattern evoked by intense stimulation. In the postnatal period, heightened stress, produced by such events as pain or abrupt changes in the ambient temperature, evokes hyperventilation and crying. All events capable of eliciting this pattern do so by activating the central nervous system, probably by rapidly increasing the metabolites in the bloodstream (Carmichael, 1954). The correlation between stress and crying has been observed in unborn and surgically removed fetuses, as well as in infants at birth.

Empirical analysis of crying in newborns supports Carmichael's view that crying is initially for the infant a reflexive response to intense, painful stimuli, whether chronic or abrupt. Crying is also a positive feedback system: crying begets more crying. How can it be reduced, when the removal of obvious stressors has no effect? One effective experimental technique that has been explored is continuous or monotonous stimulation. The monotony can be produced by swaddling, continuous sound ("white" noise), bright lights, or permitting the infant to suck something (such as a pacifier). The pacification effects of stimulation appear to be cumulative; thus stimulation in several modalities is more effective than stimulation in a single one (Brackbill, 1971, 1975). A loud noise (80 db), sounded for 30 minutes, induces quiet sleep in babies 44 hours old and is considerably more effective than a softer noise or silence. Why does it work? No conclusive answer can be offered at this time, though one explanation is that the intense, monotonous stimulation acts directly on sites in the reticular activating system and lowers arousal (Brackbill, 1975). Another possibility is that the noise is in fact a stressful experience for the neonate and that his adaptive response is withdrawal and sleep (Sostek and Anders, 1975).

Another general way to produce quieting is to use briefer forms of stimulation. To halt crying, the mother often picks up and rocks the infant. Or she may simply hold the baby and sing or talk to him. That quieting result has been taken as support for the general assumption that the infant craves physical contact comfort of the sort that only a mother can provide. However, recent work suggests a less romantic explanation of the phenomenon. Korner and Thoman (1972) point out that maternal "soothing" has several components, only one of which is physical contact. For example, the rocking motion and temperature change may be the effective "quieters." To separate the effects of contact from those of vestibular proprioceptive stimulation, Korner and Thoman evaluated the contribution of each to the reduction of crying. To obtain a rocking effect in the absence of personal contact, an infant was rocked in an infant seat 14 times during a brief (30-second) period. For purposes of comparison, another infant was picked up and put to the shoulder or was simply held close without being lifted. Vestibular proprioceptive stimulation was clearly shown to be more quieting than mere physical contact. It was equally effective whether produced by physical contact (holding) or by an impersonal means. This finding was corroborated by Pederson and Ter Vrugt (1973), who found that the more rapidly the infant is rocked, the quieter he becomes. The point to be made is that crying, like smiling, laughing, and looking, reflects the physiological state of neonates and young infants.

How to Eliminate the Negative. One question that has persistently attracted attention is the altogether practical one of how to handle a crying baby so that the crying will be eliminated, or at least minimized, in the future. Most parents do not wait to check out the most recent theory on the matter; they proceed to find out what, if anything, is causing the baby to cry. But what if there is no identifiable cause—the infant has been fed and is dry and warm—what then should be done? According to one school of thought, parental responsiveness only reinforces crying; therefore, the child will become more and more adept at crying to control the parent. There is evidence to indicate that older children do indeed use crying tantrums as a control technique, and that these displays can be strengthened through reinforcement or eliminated through extinction (Gewirtz and Gewirtz, 1965; Williams, 1959).

An opposing view is that crying is an adaptive

activity of the young infant, the purpose of which is to communicate a message that should be heeded immediately. Hence, by responding, parents will not reinforce crying so much as they will produce contented and nonfrustrated babies. Bell and Ainsworth (1972) report that in a longitudinal study of babies that covered the first year of life, mothers who were more responsive to crying during the first 3 months had infants who were less likely to fuss and cry later in the year. Hence ignoring the babies did not extinguish crying; rather, it seemed to encourage crying.

Which of these views is correct? What started as a showdown between the two basic orientations has revealed the essential shortcomings of both. Although each position has some merit, both seem to overlook the developmental and stimulus changes that were responsible for provoking and inhibiting crying in the first place. The focus of both was on the consequences (responsiveness), not on the determinants. The omission is a nontrivial one because it suggests that both views interpreted the problem too narrowly. Consider, for instance, the correlation between maternal responsivenss and decreased crying during the first year. Women who truly do not like to hear their infant cry are likely to arrange the infant's feeding and bathing schedule, crib materials, and stimulation in order to diminish crying. What the correlations may reflect then, is how successful the responsive mothers are in creating such conditions and in learning the basic lessons of how to interact with their offspring. [3]

It should also be remembered that not only does the likelihood of crying diminish as a function of age-related physiological changes but the environmental events that control its occurrence also change over time. The mother changes as well, in that her perception and interpretation of cries are modified as a function of her experience and the child's age (Fleener and Cairns, 1970). Although the newborn's cry has signal properties for the mother from birth, the nature of its communication function is clarified as the mother gains experience in identifying different kinds of vocalizations. Cries differ in intensity and tone, and occur in different contexts. Different vocalizations may be interpreted as merely fussing or as something to be checked on, or as an emergency. To treat cries merely as acts to be "extinguished" or "reinforced" indicates failure to appreciate the variety of signals and the communication network of which they are a part.

How to Accentuate the Positive. Up to this point we have concentrated on less-than-pleasing vocalizations: cries, fussing, and tantrums. What about more positive ones? How are they controlled and how are they used to exert control? As with negative vocalizations, a variety of conditions can cause or inhibit positive sounds. It was pointed out earlier that laughter begins in about the fourth month of life. In these younger infants, it is elicited primarily by tactile and auditory stimuli. In the second half of the first year of life, visual and social events become increasingly effective (Sroufe and Wunsch, 1972). Studies of the conditioning of positive vocalizations have also been successful, using infants as young as 3 months. [4] The finding of Jones and Moss (1971), that the least active infants had mothers who talked to them the most, is evidence of the mutual control properties of vocalization. Moss (1965, 1967) argues that mothers select the intensity of stimulation that is appropriate for their infants' state.

From the very beginning, infant vocalizations are effective in directing the activities of the mother and others. Nonetheless, there is much for the infant, and the parents, to learn. The infant must learn that a contingency exists between his vocalizations—both positive and negative—and parental acts. The parents must learn to discriminate among the subtle variations in the infant's signals. The evi-

---

[3] And the dispute goes on; see the recent exchange between Gewirtz and Boyd (1977) and Ainsworth and Bell (1977) regarding the nature of the evidence and the problems associated with its analysis.

---

[4] There is some disagreement as to whether the infants are conditioned or whether the vocalizations are elicited. See Bloom and Esposito (1975) for a discussion of the elicitation properties of the stimuli.

dence suggests that this mutual control normally proceeds rapidly and efficiently, providing the basis for further parent-child behavioral synchronization.

Locomotion and Following

Development of the child's ability to move about freely and independently of caretakers has manifold implications for social interchange. It seems reasonable to expect that children who can crawl or walk or run require different patterns of interchange than those who cannot. Moreover, it is not mere coincidence that the tendency of the child to become upset when separated from familiar events and people occurs roughly at the same time that he develops the capacity to get around on his own.

The changes in the infant's social relationships that are directly linked to locomotion development have been given scant attention in studies of children. One exception is a recent doctoral dissertation by Dale Hay (1975). Hay selected 16 infants 9-12 months of age who had just developed the ability to move about on their own. One rather surprising result of her study was that toddlers this age, supposedly at the threshold of strong maternal attachment, were as likely to follow an unfamiliar adult woman (or man) as they were to follow their own mothers (Figure 6-5). Moreover, Hay found that toddlers preferred to follow toys rather than people, including the mother. The toy in this study was pulled by a string across the laboratory floor into a distant room. At the same time, the mothers walked in the opposite direction into still another room. Fourteen children followed the toy; 2 followed the mother.

Hay also attempted to ascertain what the child gains from the experience of following other people or things. Hay explored the reasonable possibility, suggested by Bindra (1974), that the experience would acquaint the child with his environment and would provide information that might facilitate subsequent independent investigation. Hay's results indicate that following, as well as being carried, does indeed have an impact on the child's subsequent learning and exploration. Hay's findings point to one

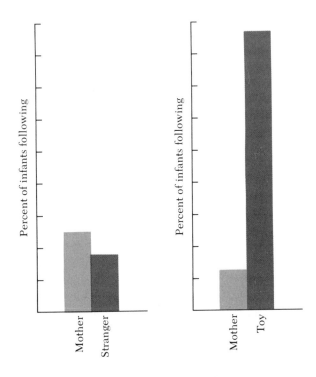

Figure 6-5. In a laboratory analysis of following, 9- to 12-month-old children were found to be about as likely to follow an unfamiliar woman as they were to follow their own mother, and were considerably more likely to follow a moving toy than to follow their mother (data from Hay, 1975).

of several ways in which changes in morphology affect the structure of the child's social interchanges and, possibly, his or her cognitive development.

Exploration and Sharing

Physical exploration begins almost immediately after birth and plays an essential role in the development and organization of basic response systems, including grasping, reaching (White and Held, 1966), and suckling (Thoman et al., 1971). Visual orientation and exploration begin soon after the visual system is functional, in the first 2 months after birth (see Table 6-1).

Environmental Attractions and Exploration. Excursions away from the mother become increasingly frequent in primate young, including human infants, as the infant's locomotive skills develop (Harlow and Harlow, 1965; Jensen, Bobbitt, and Gordon, 1967; Rheingold and Eckerman, 1970). The characteristics of the objects around him—their relative novelty, their reactive properties, their interest value—tempt the infant to explore. Recent studies by Harriet Rheingold and her co-workers (Corter, Rheingold, and Eckerman, 1972; Rheingold and Eckerman, 1970) are of particular interest. In one of these investigations, 24 human infants 10 months of age were placed with their mothers in one of two adjoining rooms. Each infant was permitted free access to both areas: they could either remain with the mother or explore the adjacent room. Although most of the infants were far from agile, all were able to locomote by one means or another. About 2/3 of the group could creep on their hands and knees; 1/6 could only "swim" across the floor on their bellies, and the remainder could toddle on their feet. All infants left their mothers to explore the adjacent room. This result was surprising because most accounts of maternal-infant interactions emphasize infants' dependency and attachment.

In this study, if a toy were placed in the other room, the infant left the mother sooner than if the room were empty. In general, the more toys that were placed in that room, the more time the infants spent away from their mothers. One child made the excursion in and out of the adjacent room 13 times in a 10-minute period.

Rheingold and Eckerman (1970) have assessed the significance of such independent, exploratory behavior as follows:

The infant's separating himself from his mother is of biological importance. It is of consequence for the preservation of both the individual and the species—of the individual since it confers the advantage of greater familiarity with the environment and thus increases the likelihood of adaptation to the environment; of the species, since it

allows the mother to care for the next offspring and leads eventually to the formation of breeding pairs. The infant's separating himself from his mother is also of psychological importance for it enormously increases his opportunities to interact with the environment and thus to learn its nature. For, while he is in contact with his mother, his universe is confined to her person and the environment near her. There are limits to what the most attentive mother can bring to him. Even when he is carried about, his contacts with the universe are necessarily circumscribed. When, however, he leaves her side by himself, many new kinds of learning can occur (p. 78).

In addition to whatever new physical experiences detachment and exploration may provide, they also provide the infant an opportunity for the establishment of new interactions and the modification of old ones. Analysis of how the child interacts in the course of his explorations will help us to understand the processes of interchange establishment and consolidation.

Sharing: Instances of Infant-Initiated Interchanges. In the course of this work, Rheingold made the interesting discovery that even the youngest children "shared" what they found with their mothers. Each infant brought the toy back to the mother, gave it to her, and returned to the other room for another. The infants also laughed and pointed out "new" things in the room, including the wastebasket and the ceiling. Do young children share exclusively with their mothers? Apparently not (Table 6-4). Fathers reliably elicit such behavior, and, to an almost equal extent, so do unfamiliar adults (Rheingold, Hay, and West, 1976). This last finding is of particular interest in the light of the presumed fear that children have of strangers (Chapter 7).

At what point in life do infants begin to share? Although the evidence on this matter is still fragmentary, it is known that the onset of sensorimotor coordination necessary for pointing, possibly one aspect of sharing, reliably occurs at about 9–10 months. Precisely what prompts the infant to point

Table 6–4. The high probability that 2-year-old children will share.

	Mean age of children (months)	Number of children	Person with whom shared	Percent of children showing toy	Percent of children sharing toy
Study 1	18.5	24	Mother	96	83
Study 3a	19.0	12	Father	100	67
Study 3b	19.0	9	Unfamiliar Person	67	67
Study 4	17.9	20	Mother	90	55
Study 5	18.4	10	Father	70	70
Study 6a	15.1	12	Mother	75	42
Study 6b	17.9	12	Mother	92	75
Study 7	18.0	24	Mother	100	88
Overall				92	72

SOURCE: From Rheingold, Hay, and West. Copyright © 1976 by the Society for Research in Child Development, Inc. Reprinted with permission.

remains to be ascertained. Pointing may initially be an abortive grasping for a too-distant object, or it may be an integral part of visual-motor orientation. Once in the infant's repertoire, pointing is easily elicited. In summarizing her field observations, Rheingold has commented that "you can scarcely observe an 18-month-old child out of doors for more than 10 seconds without seeing him point at something."

The interchanges involved in sharing thus appear to be an outgrowth of the explorative and investigatory behaviors of the infants. As they orient toward new and unusual features of their environment, they explicitly direct other individuals to those features as well. Their responsiveness, in turn, elicits further talking, giving, and pointing. And this may be the stuff of which early social relationships are made.

Now we can return to the question of how these interchanges become organized in patterns, and how relationships are established.

Social Attachment Behavior in Humans

The recent surge of professional interest in mother-infant attachment behaviors has been spurred by two major influences. One influence is the commitment of comparative and developmental psychologists to trace the ontogeny of the infant's basic social patterns. The other influence is the attempt made by clinical psychologists and psychiatrists to identify how initial relationships become the basis for pathological emotional and social maladjustment at maturity. The two views held by comparative/developmental and clinical orientations are not necessarily contradictory; nor are they necessarily harmonious. The latter orientation has an implicit concern with the special issues of psychopathology, and it considers the mother-infant relationship to be lasting and stable, the foundation for a healthy personality. In contrast, the developmental orientation is uncommitted with regard to assumptions about the enduring significance of the first interchanges. This orientation even permits the alternative proposal that the initial interchanges of the infant are less stable and less enduring than comparable ones later in life. Accordingly, the first relations may constitute pre-primer lessons in learning how to interact; it could be seen as the beginnings of social adaptation, not a prototype of its end product.

A question that is critical for both the descriptive and the theoretical views of "attachment" is whether individual differences are continuous from one time to another; that is, whether early attachment behaviors are predictive of later ones.

Individual Differences in Attachment Behaviors: Stability and Change

Reliable information on the stability of behaviors taken as indexes of social attachment has been hard to come by. A significant improvement in our knowledge about the social attachment behavior of human infants occurred in 1971 when three closely related but independent laboratory studies of stability were reported (Coates, Anderson, and Hartup, 1971; Lewis and Ban, 1971; Maccoby, 1971).[5]

Taken in conjunction with the earlier work of Fleener (1967) and the later work of Ainsworth and her co-workers (Ainsworth, 1972; Stayton and Ainsworth, 1973), the reports yield a clear and surprising picture of the extent to which individual differences in maternal-child interactions and attachment behaviors are variable during the first 3 years.

Although the relevant investigations were carried out in different laboratories, the procedures followed and the measures used were quite similar. Each of the studies involved direct observation of mother-child interactions under seminatural conditions in a short-term longitudinal design. In two of the studies (Coates, Anderson, and Hartup, 1972; Maccoby and Feldman, 1972), the maternal-infant interaction was manipulated by having the mother absent herself from the room. The observation periods were rather brief, lasting 10–20 minutes. The intervals between observations ranged from 1 day to 1 year.

Because the studies were not precise replications of each other, the consistency of their results is all the more impressive. The findings can be summarized as follows.

1. There is only modest stability of differences among individual children in the measures of mater-

nal-offspring interactions during a 3- to 6-month period. Moreover, the degree to which individual differences are predictable diminishes to nonsignificance as the time between observations is extended to 1 year (see Table 6-5). Nonetheless, there was some suggestion in the data of Maccoby and Feldman that the experimental manipulation of introducing a stranger is, in Maccoby's terms, "a catalyst that produces consistency." For example, even though "remaining close to mother" is not a very stable characteristic over time, that the child will remain close to mother when a stranger is present is moderately predictable from 2 years of age to 2½ or 3 years of age.

2. Individual differences in attachment behavior at one stage are not translatable into differences in more mature behaviors at a later stage. It has been proposed (Ainsworth, 1969; Bowlby, 1969) that even though the overt behavior might change over time, the underlying "attachment structure" will remain relatively stable. The specific hypothesis evaluated by two of the investigators (Lewis and Ban, 1971; Maccoby, 1971) was that the basic motivational difference would remain relatively stable, but that over time, proximal expressions of attachment (touching, proximity-seeking) would be replaced by distal forms (looking, smiling). Virtually no support for this proposal was found in either study. The relevant correlations typically did not differ from zero.

3. Overall, the behaviors of the children with respect to their mothers, and vice-versa, show consistent change during the first two years of life. However, the differences among infant-mother pairs at one stage are not very predictive of differences at a later stage. As several investigators have documented, the onset of discriminative crying by infants upon maternal departure typically occurs at the end of the first year (see Table 6-1). Similarly, infants look at the mother in a normal interchange more frequently at 25 months than at 13 months (Lewis and Ban, 1971). Over the shorter term (3-6

---

[5] Two of these papers later appeared in published form: Coates et al., 1972a, 1972b; Maccoby and Feldman, 1972.

Table 6-5. Individual differences in infant-maternal attachment: temporal stability correlation coefficients.*

Investigator	Age			
	1 week	3-4 months	6 months	12 months
Distress vocalization when separated from mother or surrogate				
Fleener, 1967	.68			
Maccoby and Feldman, 1972			.29 to .35	.37 to .49
Stayton and Ainsworth, 1973		.23		
Stayton and Ainsworth, 1973		.41		
Stayton and Ainsworth, 1973			−.15	
Coates, Anderson, and Hartup, 1972		.08		
		.34		
Proximity seeking with respect to mother or surrogate				
Fleener, 1967	.75			
Maccoby and Feldman, 1972			−.14 to .53	
Maccoby and Feldman, 1972				.10 to .20
Coates, Anderson, and Hartup, 1972		.43		
		.67		

*Correlation coefficients (product-moment or rank-order) shown in body of table.

months), changes in expression are more difficult to discern (Coates, Anderson, and Hartup, 1971).

Three comments seem in order concerning stability-change findings. First, the measures were typically only of the children's behavior. Few attempts were made, in any of the studies, to identify changes in maternal behavior that might be responsible for alterations in the behavior of the children, or to measure the stability of the material-infant relationship. In view of the fact that the responses were dyadic, the nature of the interchange in which they occurred is a significant determinant of their recurrence or disappearance. In brief, the dynamic matrix in which the behaviors of both the child and the mother are embedded is the key to the problem of stability and change in attachment behavior. Such findings emphasize that attachment is a relational concept, involving the contributions of two individuals, simultaneously, not just those of the child.

Second, the measures that are employed in studies of continuity can have a marked influence on the kinds of results that are obtained. Attachment measures are no exception. Subjective, judgmental measures that are designed to capture individual differences in relationships tend to provide better long-term predictions than do objective measures that reflect the actual social behaviors of persons (Cairns and Green, 1979; Waters, 1978). Hence a rating-based typology, such as that employed by Ainsworth (1973) in distinguishing between the responses of "attached" and "anxious-attached" infants to reunion with the mother following a brief separation, appears to yield higher levels of individual difference predictions than do behavior observations (such as were used in the above studies). Why do ratings "work"? Among other things, ratings and typologies permit the judge to eliminate much of what actually occurs in order to focus upon features of actions and emotions in the mother and child that are relevant to the dimension to be rated. This methodological matter and its implications are important, and they will be taken up again (in Chapters 17 and 22).

Finally, one critical finding that is frequently overlooked is that the interactional behaviors of mothers, not their children, are reasonably predictable from one time to another (Bell and Ainsworth, 1972). Recall that Jacobs and Moss (1976) found that mothers tended to treat their second child as they treated their first one and treated the observer similarly during both visits. The focus of attachment studies has been on the child; perhaps more attention should be given to the parents and how their affection for their child grows, develops, and is changed over time.

Attachment or Interaction?

These difficulties in studying "attachment" as an enduring entity have led to revised views concerning how to study parent-infant relationships. Rosenthal (1973a, b) and others have observed that if a researcher is interested in the mother-infant or father-infant relationship, then the dyadic interchanges should be the focus of analysis. Rosenthal feels that researchers have instead spent too much time and effort in the study of attachment indexes. Her proposal has considerable merit. "Preference" is but one feature of interchanges; other properties such as elicitation and reciprocal control are most powerful contributors to social development and change. A related matter concerns the carry-over effects from early interactions to subsequent ones. The relation between maternal-infant and father-infant or peer-infant interactions will be explored more fully in subsequent chapters.

Summary

This overview of the establishment of social responsiveness in human infants is remarkably parallel to the overview of the establishment of social responsiveness in nonhuman young presented at the end of Chapter 3. Consider the following summary points made there:

- Attempts to discover *the* age of the "onset" of social responsiveness are futile.
- At birth, a complex set of internal events controls the maternal reactions to the young, and their reactions to the mother.
- The offspring are not passive recipients of maternal care.
- Maturation-paced events contribute directly to the initiation and control of social interaction patterns throughout infancy and childhood.
- The early social development of most mammals is marked by the development of a strong emotional bond between the infant and its mother, and sometimes others (father, siblings, mother substitutes).
- The individual continuously adapts to its social environment and nonsocial environments.

That most of these statements apply equally well to human infants and their early social interchanges should not be too surprising, because the biological needs and capabilities of the immature human are in many basic respects quite like those of other immature mammals.

However, there are some differences. For example, the first generalization, concerning the role of biological changes at parturition, has no parallel in infant development. Placentophagia and associated maternal activities are notable by their absence. So are opportunities for the infant to synchronize his "preadapted" actions, such as clinging and "clumping," with those of the mother. Nonetheless, children establish adequate relationships in the absence of these biologically determined actions, just as nonhuman mammals do. Specific instigation by the mother (and others) plays a minimal role in the initial occurrence of smiling, crying, positive vocalizations, and exploration. Although the role of other persons in the establishment of sharing has yet to be studied, pointing, an elementary form of sharing, seems to be basically controlled by maturation. These acts do not have to be initially learned; they become woven into the communication network that the child establishes with the parents and other persons.

Although distinctive patterns of maternal-infant interchange can be identified, differences among infants prove to be stable only if the interval between testing is rather short (1 day to 1 week) or if the mother-infant dyad is taken as the unit of analysis. Short-term factors, such as delivery aftereffects, context and time of day of observation, and bodily states, permit more adequate predictions of the immediate relationship than do enduring properties of maternal personality.

These findings are consistent with the proposal that the *interactions that occur at birth and during the first year are vital for survival and for the infant's current well-being, but may be of less importance for later social development. If the infant is kept alive, well, and responsive, a wide range of early rearing conditions qualify him or her for normal social development.*

Although this summary statement is consistent with the available data, two additional comments should be added. First, it would be curious for a developmental analysis to deny that early social interchanges influence subsequent development, for doubtless they do. The foundations for parental affection are laid, and parents learn from their children. Parental behaviors are shaped, expectations are formed, and attitudes are modified by the early responsiveness of the child, but regrettably little information is available on the continuity of these complex parental attitudes over time.

Second, the question must be raised, If not in early infancy, then when? At what point in time does the quality of parental responsiveness begin to make a difference in the kinds of interchange that occur and the types of relationships that are formed? In Chapters 3–5 we reviewed evidence indicating that if an animal is maintained in a new, deprived, or atypical circumstance long enough, carry-over effects from pre-adult rearing conditions do become apparent. To obtain comparable information on children, it is necessary to use a different type of analysis. The effects of "natural disruptions" (such as divorce) or maltreatment or desertion that occur in early childhood are particularly relevant; so are laboratory studies of ways to create new social bonds or to extinguish old fears. It is to these studies that we now turn.

7

SOCIAL ADAPTATION
AND SOCIAL DEPRIVATION

The original mother-infant bond is the wellspring for all the infant's subsequent attachments and is the formative relationship in the course of which the child develops a sense of himself. Throughout his lifetime the strength and character of this attachment will influence the quality of all future bonds to other individuals.

—*Klaus and Kennell (1976), pp. 1-2*

The view that the first few years of life necessarily have crucial effects on later development and adult characteristics . . . must be challenged in the light of growing evidence. . . .

—*Clarke and Clarke (1976), p. 4*

The matters that are covered in this chapter on social adaptation and maternal deprivation are as controversial as they are important. The controversy can be traced to the clash between two ancient speculations on the nature of early experience and its aftermaths. According to the *developmental arrest* view, social development will be retarded or arrested, and children will become vulnerable to later disorders, if they are deprived of normal social stimulation in infancy. Hence Klaus and Kennell propose that "there is a sensitive period in the first minutes and hours of life during which it is necessary that the mother and father have close contact with their neonate for later development to be optimal" (p. 4). The other speculation is that of *develop-*

mental adaptation. Among other things, this proposal holds that both early and later experiences are highly significant in determining the nature of the child's social patterns. According to Clarke and Clarke (1976), "a child's future is far from wholly shaped in the 'formative years' of early childhood," and "early learning . . . serves as no more than a link in the developmental chain, shaping proximate behavior less and less powerfully as age increases" (pp. 18 and 24).

Differences in interpretation on a matter so critical are perhaps inevitable. Nonetheless, developmental studies of the past decade have begun to provide a resolution to this very old problem. Two areas of research have particular relevance to this special issue of social plasticity. One area is concerned with the question of how adaptable very young children and their parents are to conditions that are different from the normal "monotropic" (single-infant, single-mother) relationship. The second area concerns studies that have traced the later effects of maternal "deprivation" or long-term separation of infants from their actual mothers. In this chapter, we will evaluate the results of recent work in these two areas.

Plasticity of Human Infants' Social Bonds

The Extendibility of Social Preferences in Infancy

Recall that the previously described studies of nonhuman infants indicated that their preferences can be rapidly extended to include new animals and new places. Even species-appropriate preferences can be modified, in that young animals can develop simultaneous preferences for various objects and individuals. In these experiments, extension of the young animal's preferences per se did not prejudice its future development or health. The permanence of the changes depended upon the nature of the social network into which the young animal was placed and whether that network was hostile to or accepting of the animal. These results seem to be in disagreement with the view that the immediate success and long-term effects of social adaptation depend primarily on the infant itself and whether it has established a strong social bond with a single mother or mother figure.

The questions of whether human infants have a similar flexibility in their early social preferences and whether the establishment of a single strong bond precludes the establishment of new ones are best answered by analyzing the processes that govern the establishment of social preferences in infants. In a significant investigation of these processes, D. E. Fleener (1967, 1973) attempted to produce, experimentally, a new set of social prefer-

ences in babies. Fleener reasoned, on the basis of the results of comparative studies and an analysis of the learning contingencies involved, that even a brief period of interchange should be sufficient to modify the child's social orientation and preferences. This hypothesis was based on the belief that the child would rapidly accommodate his responses to those of the caretaker, and vice versa. Mutual dependence and recognition should evolve following the accommodation. One byproduct of the mutual dependence should be a change in the nature of the relationship—the infant would develop a preference for the person with whom he interacted.

To test this hypothesis, Fleener arranged to have a mother bring her child to the Indiana University Medical Center 3 hours a day for 3 consecutive days. After a brief period (1–4 minutes), during which Fleener and the infant got acquainted, the mother handed the infant to Fleener, who carried it into a large laboratory room and left it with a woman who had several children of her own. She served exclusively as the child's caretaker for the remainder of the day, and for the next 2 days. She did everything that a mother or a babysitter ordinarily would do for the infant—she played with the child, fed it, changed its diapers, and let it sleep when it got tired. Since there were no telephones or other distractions in the laboratory, she was free to devote her complete attention to the infant. Possibly because of her experience with children, the caretaker was sensitive to and could "read" the infant's needs. The women who served in the role of caretaker knew how to play with and respond to children. Each of 2 women cared for 10 different infants, aged 10–14 months. The babies were cared for one at a time.

To evaluate the effects of this manipulation, preference tests were administered before the first day's interaction and after the third day's interaction. One test measured the effects of abrupt separation-departure. The infant was left in the room, and each of the women, in turn, left the laboratory for a 1-minute interval, then returned. Each experimenter made 2 such departures. The child's response to the

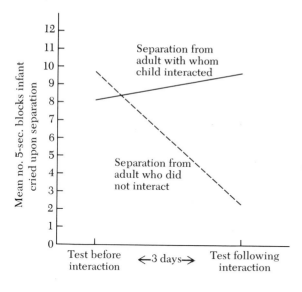

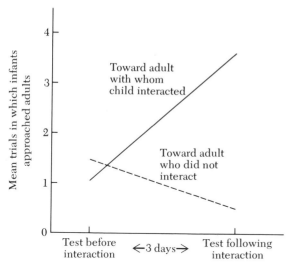

separation was observed and his vocalizations were recorded on tape. The second test measured the child's preference for each of the two women. Again, before any interaction, the child was placed in a two-choice apparatus, which was an oversized T maze runway. One of the women positioned herself at the end of each parallel alley. The child could choose to crawl, swim, or toddle to one of the two women; or he could choose to remain where he was (and perhaps cry). To ensure that the child was not just showing a position preference (going to the right or to the left), the women switched positions in the middle of the trials. The same two tests were repeated after 3 days of interaction.

The experimentally induced relationships were apparently very strong. In terms of the measures used to assess the outcome, the manipulations were singularly successful. Although almost no preferences or differential crying were observed in the pretest series, the infants had developed a strong preference for their caretaker by the end of the third day. They virtually ran to their own caretaker and they cried when she left. They responded to her as if she were their own mother (see Figure 7-1).

What is striking about this research is that the effects were produced in such a short period. The interchanges were restricted to a total of 6½ to 7½ hours, over a period of 3 days. The rapid establishment of "new" preferences in human infants is surprising, but not without precedent. It is precisely what would be expected on the basis of a substantial number of similar experiments conducted with animals (see also Shelton and Slaby, 1975).

Figure 7-1. Infants who are allowed to have brief but intensive interaction with an unfamiliar "motherly" person tend to display "attachment" behaviors towards her that are not unlike those typically observed between infants and their mothers. *Top:* Separation tests given before and after the experimental interaction indicate that before the manipulation, the responses of 10- to 14-month-old infants to the woman who was to be the caretaker did not differ from their responses to another woman. Following the experience, the infants became disrupted when the caretaker left the room (as measured by the number of 5-second blocks that the infants cried during a one-minute separation).

Bottom: The same infants were tested before and after the manipulation to determine their tendency to approach either of the two women. Again, a strong preference was demonstrated after the intensive interaction. Four choice trials were given each day (data from Fleener, 1967).

Although the newly established preferences were impressive, they did not overpower the preference for the infant's actual mother. In Fleener's (1967) pilot investigation of this possibility with 6 of the mother-infant pairs, the real mother and the child's caretaker were pitted against each other at the end of the preference maze following the final test on the third day. In every instance, the infants approached the mother rather than the caretaker. Would parity with the basic mother preference be achieved over time? There are several indications that it would.

First, there is ample evidence that the infant and young child form multiple preferences or bonds, and these include caretakers and acquaintances as well as members of the family (father, siblings, grandparents). Despite the niggardly amounts of time that the average father apparently spends with his infant, he typically elicits strong "attachment" responses from the baby. (The infant approaches him, smiles, and cries when he leaves.) According to recent reports, the father is almost as likely to elicit attachment behaviors as the mother in most situations (Cohen and Campos, 1974; Ross et al., 1975), although when the child must make a choice, it is usually the mother who wins. Such overlap in the child's response to the two parents is striking, in light of the great differences in the amount of time that each one spends taking care of and interacting with the infant.

Second, the child can become attached to inanimate objects and places (such as blankets, toys, clothes, teddy bears, cribs, and homes) to the extent that they can often be substituted effectively for the mother. It seems reasonable to expect that there is in children some relationship between the processes that govern nonanimate attachment and those that govern animate ones, as there appears to be in animals (Chapter 4). In this regard, Passman and Weisberg (1975) found that "blanket-attached" children were quite as content when left in a strange laboratory with their blankets as when left with their mothers. Other studies confirm that the child forms strong preferences for places, such as his crib, favor-

ite room, or nursery school (see Brookhart and Hock, 1976; Fein, 1975; and Ross et al., 1975).[1]

Finally, what has been viewed as a pathological response to separation could be the progress of the child's adaptation to a new set of relationships and evidence of his resilience and robustness. For instance, Heinicke and Westheimer (1966) found that young children left in a hospital for 2 weeks or more do not immediately and joyously respond to their parents on reunion. This withdrawal has been interpreted as evidence of the child's anger at having been deserted (Bowlby, 1973), but it may also be viewed as reflecting the child's initial disorientation and wariness with regard to persons whom he has not seen recently. Heinicke and Westheimer also indicate that several of the children formed new relationships with the nurses who were responsible for them.

Establishment of a Relationship by Orphaned Infants

One of the major concerns that has been voiced with regard to institutional rearing is that the absence of a single "mother" figure can have potentially deleterious effects. The failure to establish a firm and rewarding relationship with a single individual, the principal caretaker, has generally been assumed to prejudice the child's ability to form satisfying relationships with others. Harriet Rheingold's (1956) research was designed to compare the effects of being cared for by one "mother" with the effects of being cared for by many "mothers." The research attempted to answer the question "What effect will an increase in the child's social responsiveness to one person, the 'mother,' have upon his responsiveness to other persons?"

A woman experimenter cared for and mothered 4 orphaned 6-month-old infants exclusively and intensively for 8 weeks. The experimenter:

---

[1] When a child of my acquaintance was 4 years old, one of her dominant attachments was to a 1968 white Pontiac sedan. Her family traveled a lot.

fed, bathed, diapered, soothed, held, talked to, and played with these four babies for seven and one-half hours a day, from 7:30 A.M. to 3:00 P.M., five days a week, for eight weeks, a total of 300 hours. During these hours no one else cared for these babies . . . . The goal was to give the children maximal gratification.

For comparison purposes, an equal number of 6-month-old infants were cared for as part of normal hospital routine. This control group of infants had *several* affectionate caretakers, while the experimental group had a *single* affectionate caretaker.

Changes in the infants' social responsiveness were measured by a series of tests. The investigator was interested not only in changes with respect to herself, but in changes with respect to other persons. Accordingly, two different persons administered the "infant responsivity" tests: the caretaker and an unfamiliar woman. The infants' responsivity to the person was measured by changes in orientation, facial expression, and emotion (laughter or crying).

As in the Fleener (1973) study, the strongest responses were obtained with respect to the caretaker. The "mothered" infants were more responsive to her than were the control infants.

Additionally, they responded more to the caretaker when she tested them than they did to the unfamiliar examiner. An increased responsivity to one person did not necessarily lead to a rejection of unfamiliar ones—rather, establishment of new relationships was facilitated. According to Rheingold, "not only did the experimental babies not show signs of discomfort when approached by strange persons but instead they became more friendly, according to some of the evidence."

Approximately one year later, an attempt was made to trace every child in both the experimental and control groups (Rheingold and Bayley, 1959). All but 2 of the original 16 infants were located and retested in the Chicago area. By this time, the children were 1½-2 years old, and, except for one child, all had been placed in homes. The original experimenter (the surrogate mother) and an unfamiliar examiner administered tests of social responsiveness similar to those that had been used in the original study.

Did the infants remember the person who had provided "maximal gratification" for them? Apparently not (Table 7-1). The differences in the responses of the experimental and control groups to

Table 7-1. Means and ranges of the "social test" used in follow-up study one year after special caretaking.

Subjects	Experimenter		Examiner		Combined score
	Mean	Range	Mean	Range	Mean
Experimental group*					
Total social responsiveness	32.1	27–39	30.9	27–38	31.6
Positive	17.4	2–30	16.0	2–37	16.7
Negative	14.7	1–37	14.7	3–29	14.7
Response to mother	2.3	0–16	5.7	0–19	4.0
Control group†					
Total social responsiveness	28.0	14–39	28.3	22–44	28.4
Positive	19.8	5–32	20.2	4–37	20.1
Negative	8.2	3–12	8.2	2–18	8.0
Response to mother	4.5	0–11	4.8	0–10	5.4

*N is 7.
†N is 6 for responses to experimenter and to examiner, but 7 for combined score.
SOURCE: Rheingold and Bayley. Copyright © 1959 by the Society for Research in Child Development, Inc. Reprinted with permission.

the experimental "mother" were slight and unreliable. The unfamiliar examiner, whom the children had never seen, evoked as strong a response as did the former "mother." Both groups scored in the normal range on the Cattell infant intelligence test, and both responded to the "new" adults in an altogether friendly manner. In summary, there was no basis on which to argue that the experimental and control subjects differed from each other in any significant way after just one year.

These findings are significant because both experimental and control groups spent approximately the first 9 months of life in an institution, then experienced a major change in their life situation and interpersonal relationships. Despite such inauspicious beginnings, they appeared to be adapting well. The following description is from Rheingold and Bayley (1959):

> In general, the group (of experimental and control infants) was marked by a friendliness which seemed warm and genuine. Eleven of the fourteen subjects not only approached the stimulus persons but also allowed themselves to be picked up and held. Only two subjects, both boys, presented a different social response: they clung to their mothers and cried when the stimulus persons approached them. No comparable data are available for children who have lived all their lives in their own homes, but in preliminary testing of the social test on three children not one approached the examiners. Instead, they looked at the examiners from behind their mothers' skirts and retreated whenever the examiners moved in their direction.
>
> No child, furthermore, showed the marked apathy or attention-seeking behavior believed by some to characterize the behavior of children reared in institutions. Differences there were, to be sure, between the children, but none seemed to depart markedly from the normal in temperament or personality. In fact, several of the mothers spontaneously commented upon how easy these children were to handle in comparison with their other children. They mentioned, specifically, their good eating and sleeping habits and their ability to amuse themselves (p. 369).

These results are consistent with a larger body of information on the transient nature of the child's early social responsiveness and his resilience. The rapid adaptation of the infant to new interpersonal circumstances does not mean, however, that his reaction is one of immediate acceptance. To the contrary, studies of children adopted in the first or second year indicate that the *initial* change can be stormy (Yarrow and Goodwin, 1973). The extent of initial disruption is hardly indicative of later adaptation, however. Variations in the intensity of the child's disturbance immediately upon adoption are not correlated with his social adjustment 10 years later (Yarrow, Goodwin, Manheimer, and Milowe, 1973).

Fear of Strangers Reconsidered: Adaptation to Social Change

Such experimental studies of the social adaptation of infants raise a question about the fear-of-strangers phenomenon. After all, the mother surrogates in each study were first of all strangers. Why were not the children fearful? And if they were, why did they become less frightened over time?

As in other instances of apparent conflicts in results, a careful examination of the procedures used suggests an answer to these questions. First, not all children are fearful of unfamiliar persons. According to the norms of Gesell and Thompson (1934), the response "withdrawing from stranger" does not reach 50 percent at any age level. Likewise, fear is not an automatic reaction to all persons. Kindly, sensitive adults can elicit approach and exploration, not avoidance (Maccoby and Feldman, 1972; Rheingold and Eckerman, 1973).

Second, tests of fear of strangers are typically restricted in terms of time. As in the case of separation-disruption, whether distress or adaptation is observed seems dependent upon the length of time the interaction is permitted to endure. The likelihood of wariness and short-term distress is greatest early in the interchanges. The likelihood of adaptation pro-

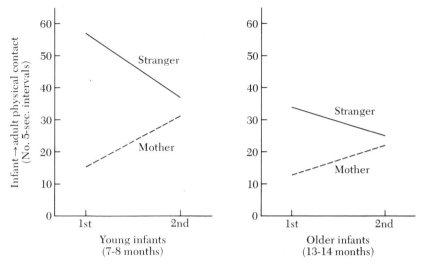

Figure 7-2. In the Monahan (1975) study of interchanges between the child's mother and an unfamiliar woman in the home ("stranger"), it was found that infants moved toward and played with the "stranger" more than they did with their own mother during a comparable interval. The differences were greater in the first 20-minute session than in the second one. *Left:* results for 12 young (7- to 8-month-old) infants. *Right:* results for 12 older (13- to 14-month-old) infants (data from Monahan, 1975).

gressively increases over time. If the test ends with the introduction (and the evocation of disruption), then the adaptation phase obviously cannot be identified.

Third, there are a variety of ways that an experimenter can elicit approach or withdrawal, fear or delight, depending on how he responds to the infant (either intentionally or unintentionally) and/or how long the interaction is observed. For instance, even though the experimenters in the Fleener (1973) and Rheingold (1956) studies were unfamiliar, they were not "strangers" in the foreboding and frightening sense. The infants responded accordingly—in a friendly, accepting fashion. Monahan (1975) found, in fact, that a responsive stranger could be as effective as the child's mother in eliciting all basic measures of conditional reactivity (Figure 7-2). The babies not only contacted and played with the

unfamiliar woman, they cried when she left. This was an instance of "stranger separation" (Figure 7-3). The most recent and perhaps most compelling evidence on the matter was reported by Ross and Goldman (1977b) in their study of 60 one-year-old infants who were exposed briefly (4 minutes) to a friendly unfamiliar woman or to an unresponsive woman who smiled occasionally. The same women (4 in all) played different roles with different children. The infants were sensitive to the difference in adult behavior: they approached and played with the "outgoing" ones and avoided, fussed, and cried with the "passive" ones.

There should be no question that unfamiliar persons can produce wariness and heart-rate changes in some infants some of the time. The intensity of the response is dependent on the age of the child. Children 5 months old and younger rarely become wary

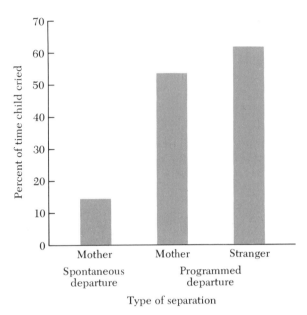

Figure 7–3. In the home setting, infants rapidly become adapted to unfamiliar persons. At the end of two 20-minute interaction sessions, the mother and the stranger left the room (and the infant) in counter-balanced orders and returned 60 seconds later. Children were as likely to cry following such pre-planned separations from the stranger as from the mother, if the stranger had interacted with the child (*middle and right columns*). Note that few children became disrupted if the mother left the room spontaneously (*left column*) in the course of the stranger-infant observations. "Programmed" means that the experimenter told the adults when to leave the room (data from Monahan, 1975).

if the stimulus is visual (Campos, Emde, Gaensbauer, and Henderson, 1975). It is also dependent on the novelty of the stranger (Brooks and Lewis, 1976; Kagan, 1976) and the context of testing (Brookhart and Hock, 1976). But there is a serious question about how these changes in behavior should be interpreted. Infants also smile at strangers (Eckerman and Whatley, 1975). Brookhart and Hock (1976) propose that infants approach the stranger in an unfamiliar laboratory setting because

they "perceive the stranger as a source of comfort" in an alien environment (p. 338).

These outcomes suggest that fear of strangers can be transmuted into new social relationships. If the activity of the unfamiliar person permits it, the arousal reflected in initial wariness can activate a vigorous positive interaction. The process of social adaptation can be facilitated if the behaviors of the "new" individual fit (or support) previously established interchange sequences for the infant. Or the process can be retarded if the behavior of the other person requires the development of totally new dyadic sequences. What has been viewed as a special category of responding—"fear of strangers"—may be more appropriately considered the initial phase of interpersonal adaptation, to be found in virtually all social relationships.

Day Care and the Effects of Having Multiple Mothers

The number of working mothers has increased steadily during the past two decades. There has been a concomitant increase in the number of children placed in day care centers and enrolled in other preprimary programs (Figure 7-4). Is the daily separation from the mother harmful to young children? Lois Hoffman (1974) concludes that it is not. She points out that the problem is not the separation, but the maternal attitudes and the real-life events that made child care a preferred or necessary alternative in the first place. The relationship to the mother—or anyone else—is determined by what occurs when they are together, not when they are apart.

What concerns us here is the extent to which the day care experience hinders or prevents the child's establishment of an adequate pattern of interchange with his mother and other persons. The bulk of the recent evidence—which typically compares the maternal attachment of "home-reared" children with that of children placed in day care centers for varying lengths of time—provides scant basis for distin-

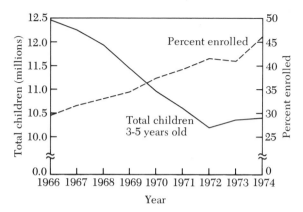

Figure 7-4. Total number of children 3–5 years old and percent enrolled in preprimary programs in the United States, 1966–1974. Although the number of preschool children diminished in the period, the proportion enrolled in day care and preschool increased dramatically (data from *Preprimary Enrollment,* A Report of the National Center for Education Statistics, Government Printing Office, 1975).

guishing between the two kinds of care.[2] This is not to say that the day care experience does not have any effects whatsoever; rather the effects do not appear to be very striking and are not easily traced to any aspect of the mother-child relationship. Those modest differences that have been identified have typically been differences in the child's relationship to other adults and other children (see Schwarz, Strickland, and Krolick, 1974). This finding makes sense because the children have in common a relationship to their mothers, but they differ in the amount and kind of exposure that they have had to other children and adults. Long-term day care rearing appears to lead to children's play that is more spontaneous, free-wheeling, and assertive (Schwarz et al., 1974). In some schools, the children are also more likely to catch the flu (Doyle, 1975). Both results could reflect the policies and actions of

[2] The recent studies include the work of Brookhart and Hock, 1976; Cornelius and Denney, 1975; Doyle, 1975; and Kagan, 1976. The investigations provide impressive confirmation for each other, and for Hoffman (1974)—see Figure 6-2.

the teachers, or the attitudes of parents who keep their children in the center for long periods.

In summary, studies of human infants indicate that there is considerable plasticity in their early relationships. These results are consistent with the results of studies showing the ephemeral nature of individual differences in mother-child and father-child relationships (Chapter 6). They are also consistent with the information on the reversibility of social relationships induced in animals by experimental procedures (Chapter 5). With these findings in mind, we now turn to one of the most hotly debated issues in social development: the effects of extended maternal deprivation on infants' social and emotional development.

Maternal Deprivation and Its Consequences

According to classical psychoanalytic theory, disturbances in very early social relationships are the basis of the more severe forms of behavioral pathology (Freud, 1933). Severely regressive forms of behavioral pathology (such as schizophrenia) thus reflect the inappropriate investment of libidinal energy during the early periods of object relationship formation. In particular, it is assumed that the infant's fear of loss of love (separation anxiety) is directly related to the more severe psychoses and autism. Modern psychoanalytic theories have tended to revise significant portions of Freud's theory of infantile sexuality. But his emphasis on the importance of the maternal-infant relationship remains, although the reasons offered for that importance have changed. With regard to the significance of the oral stage, Munroe (1955) observed that "all Freudians consider that essential modes of relationships to objects and persons stem from this period, and that the infant's expectations of the outer world are profoundly influenced by this initially oral contact" (p. 225). Since the mother is *the* individual with whom the infant is presumed to have the basic "oral contact," her relationship to the child remains fundamental. Separation and long-term absences are thought to engender a fear of loss of the "attachment figure," which renders the child highly vulnerable to chronic anxiety, anger, and emotional disturbance (Bowlby, 1973).

During and immediately following World War II, reports from diverse sources described a maternal deprivation syndrome among children who had been given good physical care. Much of the relevant information was summarized by the distinguished British psychoanalyst J. Bowlby (1952) in an influential review published by the World Health Organization. The primary data for Bowlby's review came from studies of children who had been maintained in institutions for varying periods. The behavioral deficits associated with orphanage rearing included developmental arrest, depression, withdrawal in infants, and a limited capacity for social relationships in older children. Foreboding terms—such as *marasmus* (literally, "wasting away") and *anaclitic depression*—were introduced to describe the extent and depth of the disturbance triggered by "maternal *deprivation*." Other terms, including "affect *hunger*" (Levy, 1937) and "emotionally *starved*" (Spitz, 1945) carried the theoretical message. Presumably an inadequate supply of attention and love could be as devastating to the infant's emotional and social development as starvation could be to his physical well-being.[3]

These assumptions, and the data offered in support of them, rekindled the controversy that had been ignited by an earlier, contradictory proposal of John B. Watson (1928) that social development in children is stifled and retarded by *too much* mater-

nal affection and attention. Love, Watson argued, becomes conditioned when neutral events are associated with or occur simultaneously with pleasurable stimulation. And if the mother coddles the child, "all too soon the child gets honeycombed with love responses for the nurse, for the father and for any other constant attendant who fondles it." Accordingly, a "honeycombed" child is a candidate for social "invalidism," or constant dependency upon the caretaking, support, and good will of others. In Watson's world, presumably the most adaptable infants would be produced by kindly but objective caretaking, without kissing, and other "mawkish" reactions. Watson believed that these displays were intended to satisfy the sexual-affectional cravings of the parents rather than those of the child.[4]

During the past 18 years a sober evaluation has been made of the claims and counterclaims concerning the effects of maternal separation and deprivation (Casler, 1961; Bowlby, 1969, 1973; Rutter, 1972; Wolins, 1970; World Health Organization, 1962; Yarrow, 1961, 1964). On a theoretical level, serious questions were raised about the appropriateness of a homeostatic biological drive analogy in the discussion of social interactions—that is, that hunger drive is equivalent to social drive (Gewirtz, 1961). Then there is the question of what is the critical ingredient in "mothering"—precisely what is the infant being "deprived of" in instances of maternal deprivation? And how little (or how much) interaction is considered "inadequate"? Furthermore, there is the problem of the specificity of the effects—which types of maternal deprivation lead to which behavioral disorders, and why? Finally, as Bowlby (1973) indicated, "some of the workers who first drew attention to the dangers of maternal deprivation resulting from separation have tended on occasion to overstate their case." Specifically, selec-

---

[3] Spitz's article in the first volume of *The Psychoanalytic Study of the Child* was one of the first attempts to produce empirical evidence relevant to the developmental arrest assumption. Unfortunately, Spitz's conclusions and the data base on which they were based are open to devastating criticism on statistical and methodological grounds (Pinneau, 1955). Other early studies, including that of Ribble (1943), are equally vulnerable on scientific grounds, a point that was recognized in reviews that appeared at the time in *The Psychoanalytic Study of the Child*.

---

[4] Watson offered no data in support of his claims. But the lack of evidence did not keep Watson's views from becoming highly influential. Unfortunately, these "scientific" proposals exercised a great effect on child-rearing patterns in the United States during the second quarter of the present century.

tive attention was given to pathological outcomes, and instances of normal or nonaberrant behavior were given scant notice. The investigators viewed the effects through smoke-colored glasses.

Controversies of this sort thrive in the absence of data. The less adequate the empirical information, the greater latitude there is for polemical statements about the awesome effects of one treatment or the other. The issues become less controversial when a precise analysis is made of the relevant concepts and data.

Context in Which the Child Is Placed. The term "maternal separation" tells us only what and who the child has been removed from; it does not yield any information about the setting in which he is placed. Studies of nonhuman primates indicate that the socio-ecological structure of the group is exceedingly important in determining the extent and pervasiveness of the animal's behavioral disturbance. For instance, Rosenblum and Kaufman (1968) found that when members of the group with which the infant was left were responsive to it, the infant's adaptation to the motherless setting progressed rather smoothly. For the same reason, we should not be too surprised to find that the immediate effects of maternal separation in human infants are variable, depending on the type of treatment they receive during separation.

These studies of contextual factors indicate that separation qua separation does not necessarily prejudice the immediate or long-term social adaptation of the child (Yarrow, 1964, p. 109). For example, short-term laboratory separations produce minimal effects if the infant is left with an experienced and able caretaker. Even being left in a hospital for short-term treatment does not necessarily lead to behavioral disruption in the 2-year-old child (Heinicke and Westheimer, 1966). Long-term separation, as when the child is transferred to a foster home for rearing, may or may not be disruptive, depending on the interactions to which the child is exposed in the new setting (Rheingold and Bayley, 1959; Yarrow and Goodwin, 1963). Disruption in

infancy does not necessarily affect the child's social responsiveness 10 years later (L. J. Yarrow et al., 1973).

Few attempts have been made to analyze the processes by which behaviors are transferred across relationships and settings. On the basis of information obtained from studies of nonhumans, it seems reasonable to expect that the degree of similarity between the adaptation requirements of the setting in which the child is reared and those of the setting in which he is later placed will determine whether his behavior is "appropriate" or "normal" when he is removed from one to the other. What might be considered effective and appropriate behavior in the institution could be considered ineffective and "pathological" elsewhere. It is thus conceivable that children reared in institutions may experience a kind of "institutional" deprivation.

Nature of the Relationship with Mother. There has been considerable speculation about whether previously established relationships "insulate" the infant and child from the deleterious effects of stress. Thus a child who has developed a strong attachment to his mother might be expected to be better able to withstand the trauma of stress and maternal separation. There is scant support for this hypothesis. In fact, the opposite result is obtained when the child's adjustment to a motherless environment is traced over a short period. One of the first systematic studies of brief separation was conducted by Spitz and Wolf (1946b) who reported that the children who showed the most disruption after separation were those who were judged to have the closest relationship with their mothers. A more recent longitudinal analysis of maternal separation resulting from adoption showed that "a change in mothers is not likely to be severely traumatic if there is little emotional involvement with the mother figure prior to change" (Yarrow and Goodwin, 1973, p. 1040).

These results should not be too surprising. Those children whose responses are dependent upon the unique cues provided by their mothers should be the ones who would be most seriously disrupted by her absence, because they have the most to lose. Rather than protecting the child from the traumatic effects of separation, the focalized relationship could make subsequent social adaptations even more difficult for the child. Margaret Mead (1962) has observed that children who grow up in cultures where several adults share in the caretaking are better able to tolerate separation. Moreover, analyses of the effects of maternal employment indicate that maternal employment, which requires that others take care of the children, does not necessarily affect their social behavior (Hoffman, 1974; Siegel and Haas, 1963). The nature of the social relationships that children form is determined more by what a mother does with her children when they are together than by the fact that she must be periodically separated from them. Similar nonsignificant findings with respect to the deleterious effects of mother separation have been obtained in studies of children reared in a communal setting, such as the Israeli kibbutzim (Beit-Hallahmi and Rabin, 1977).

Age at Separation.   Though there has been much speculation about the importance of age of separation, reliable information on the differential effects of separation as a function of the child's developmental-maturational status is meager. From the work on short-term separation, we know that older infants tend to become more readily upset upon being separated visually from their mothers than do younger infants. There is marked variability in this relationship, however. Furthermore, two reports suggest that the severity of the initial disruption upon separation is unrelated to the nature of the social adaptation subsequently made by the individual (Hellman, 1962; L. J. Yarrow et al., 1973).

Behavior upon Reunion with Parents.   Studies of children who have been separated from one or both parents for significant periods (2 weeks or more) have shown that problems frequently occur in mutual adaptation. In particular, a 2-year-old child who has returned from the hospital has been ob-

served to actively avoid his parents (Heinicke and Westheimer, 1966). The child may not permit his mother to help him at meals, or he may withdraw from her expressions of affection. After the extended absence of the child, it is not infrequent that the parents demonstrate some ambivalence about how to respond to the child, or are ambivalent about whether to respond to him at all. In one of the families studied by Heinicke and Westheimer at London's Tavistock Clinic, the mother became less involved with (visited less often, showed less interest in) the child as the period of separation was extended (to 23 weeks). When the child finally was permitted to come home, the mother delayed the reunion. A similar difficulty in mutual adaptation has been observed when father-offspring pairs have been separated because of the father's military service (Stolz et al., 1954). Uneasiness in one produces uneasiness in the other, resulting in a temporarily strained reunion.

As in the studies of reunion in nonhuman species (Chapter 4), changes in the behavior of one member of a pair require the adoption of new interaction patterns or the drastic revision of old ones. The period of readjustment that follows an extended separation requires a necessary realignment of the interactions of both individuals. Although the child is likely to be the one who has changed more, new adaptations are required by both participants. Realignments of the behavior of persons who have remained with the child have been continuously occurring.

Long-Term Effects of Maternal Deprivation

The best information available on the persistent effects of a disruption of early mother-child relationships has been obtained from follow-up studies of adults who as children were separated from their mothers. World War II tragically provided the occasion for a great many such separations. At the height of the London blitz, many children were separated from their families and raised in residential nurseries in the relatively safe countryside. According to Anna Freud and Dann (1951), the immediate effect of dislocation was disruption of the children. Twenty years after this experience, a group of these children (now adults) were examined by Maas (1963). He found no instances of severe psychopathology, and the behavior of the individuals appeared to fall within the normal limits. Unfortunately, data from a comparable set of control subjects (children who had remained with their parents) were not presented. Hellman (1962) found that even persons who experienced extremely traumatic separations in childhood appear to function quite adequately in adulthood. However, other reports indicate some persistence of the disruptive effects of early separation and maintenance in an institution (Goldfarb, 1945). Although the latter report and those of Ribble (1943) and Spitz (1945) may "overstate their cases" (Bowlby, 1973), it would be hazardous to ignore them.

But it would be equally misleading to fail to question the view that institutional rearing and disruption of the monotropic (single-child, single-mother) bond will inevitably lead to anxiety, protest, and psychopathological detachment. This is the implication of the statements that "separation is dangerous and whenever possible should be avoided" (Robertson and Robertson, 1971) and that

> the effects of separation from mother can be likened to the effects of smoking or of radiation. Although the effects of small doses appear negligible, they are cumulative. The safest dose is a zero dose (Bowlby, 1973, pp. 72–73).

Such a view of the inherent inviolability of the mother-child relationship does not resonate with the facts. Studies of the social adjustment of children reared in institutions indicate that early separation and/or long-term institutionalization does not necessarily result in social or emotional impairment (Gardner, Hawkes, and Burchinal, 1961; Gavrin and Sacks, 1963; Pringle and Bossio, 1958; Rheingold and Bayley, 1959; Saltz, 1973; Skeels, 1966; Wolins, 1970).

Wolins and his colleagues (Wolins, 1970; Moyles and Wolins, 1971) made cross-cultural comparisons of children reared in European institutions ranging from good to borderline in terms of quality of care. One of the former, the Children's Home, was essentially a large apartment house located in Belgrade, Yugoslavia. The institution was described by Wolins (1970) as follows:

> "Families" consist of some 16–18 children and an "aunt" or "uncle" who often is older sister/brother in age. Contact with natural families is maintained, although considerable misgivings are expressed about their negative genetic legacy. ("What can you expect from children of mental patients, prostitutes, and alcoholics?" is heard more often than one would anticipate.) The objective is to undo early damage to the child to enhance development, and to instill a local version of socialist values which is by no means internally consistent and clear (p. 100).

In general, the intelligence test scores and ratings of social adjustment of children reared in this institution did not differ from those of children reared in homes in Belgrade (Moyles and Wolins, 1971; see Table 7-2). Further, the children who had been admitted to the institution early in their lives (presumably the most deprived) did just as well and frequently better on these tests than children who were admitted later. Personality and social adjustment are more difficult to assess, but in terms of standard inventory and projective test assessments (Table 7-3), these children did not differ from the normal control sample.

Summarizing the results, Wolins (1970) states that the study

> gave little evidence to support the familiar assumptions of deficiencies in intelligence, personality and value development, even though the children were subject to 'early and prolonged deprivation' including separation from the natural mother and many years of institutional care. While these children had seriously deprived backgrounds, and expressed ambivalence about

Table 7-2. Comparison of scores on the cognitive measures achieved by children who were assigned to institutions in early childhood and in late childhood, and children who were reared at home.

Item	Austria: Kinderdorf			Yugoslavia: Children's home		
	Early ($n = 12$)	Later ($n = 54$)	Home ($n = 67$)	Early ($n = 13$)	Later ($n = 23$)	Home ($n = 72$)
Mean age at entry (yr.)	4.4	9.6	—	4.8	11.8	—
Mean age when tested (yr.)	15.6	15.8	13.9	15.2	15.9	15.3
Mean length of stay (yr.)	11.2	6.2	—	10.4	4.2	—
Mean RPM percentile score	52.3	44.2	54.1	20.9	29.3	37.3
IQ				104.0	104.8	105.3

Note—Because of the generally low scores on the Raven Progressive Matrices (RPM) test, most children were retested on a Yugoslav version of the Wechsler Intelligence Scale for Children (WISC) specially constructed for group administration. Belgrade norms were based on a sample of 3,768 children distributed over an age range of 14–18. The WISC has a mean of 100, $SD = 15$. The n was somewhat reduced ($n = 8$ for early entrants, $n = 14$ for later, $n = 26$ for home) because not all children in the original sample were available for retesting.
SOURCE: From Wolins, copyright © 1970, by the American Psychological Association. Reprinted with permission.

institutional living and about their present and future status, they were not markedly different in intelligence and personality variables from those who were separated from their families at a considerably more advanced age or not at all. Also, length of institutional residence (in this case, all in excess of several years) was related to the present status of the child (p. 105).

What can be said, then, about the long-term effects of maternal deprivation? Despite the apparent conflicting interpretations and discrepant findings, certain conclusions are permitted. First, we can be confident that social behavior disruption is not an *inevitable* consequence of early maternal deprivation or separation. The recent literature overwhelmingly supports the conclusion that some children reared in institutional settings can get along exceedingly well in society in adulthood. Apparently the child is affected not by the institutional rearing per se but by the nature of the interaction patterns and responses that it supports and its relation to what the child will be exposed at maturity.

Second, the experiences that intervene between infancy and adulthood have a significant impact upon the kinds of social adaptations that are observed at maturity. Not surprisingly, when the results of maternal deprivation studies are viewed from a developmental perspective, the findings are not uniform. In virtually all studies, the experiences that intervened between the early deprivation and the adult assessment were overlooked. The effects of the "deprived" child's earlier treatment could have been reinstated, supported, or canceled out by these later experiences. The methodological lesson implicit in such findings is that the significant issues of developmental psychology are not likely to be settled by two-shot observations, in which individuals are assessed in infancy and then again in adulthood. In social behavior, the outcome is the cumulative product of preceding interaction patterns, whether early, intermediate, or contemporaneous.

Summary

Recent laboratory studies have shed new light on the nature of early social development in infants. Taken *in toto*, they make necessary a revision of the

Table 7-3. Comparison of measures of security and affiliate responses of children admitted early and later to group programs and of children living at home (percent).

Sentence Completions	Austria: Kinderdorf			Yugoslavia: Children's home		
	Early (n = 12)	Later (n = 54)	Home (n = 67)	Early (n = 13)	Later (n = 23)	Home (n =72)
Personal security						
I am often full of . . . [negative feeling].	33.3	38.9	53.7	53.9	48.0	40.3
I often have the feeling that . . . [negative].	66.5	48.1	62.7	61.6	72.0	45.8
When I am alone I . . . [negative].	8.3	7.4	11.9	7.6	12.0	15.3
Social affiliation						
Working closely with others can be . . . [negative].	0.0	5.6	13.4	23.1	16.0	23.6
Working in groups can be . . . [negative].	0.0	1.9	11.9	0.0	0.0	0.0
I am most happy when . . . [social affiliation].	8.3	5.6	10.5	15.4	16.0	7.0
I am most happy when . . . [family].	41.7	25.9	28.4	0.0	4.0	2.8

SOURCE: From Wolins, copyright © 1970, by the American Psychological Association. Reprinted with permission.

widely held assumption that the "essential modes of relationships to objects and persons stem from this period" of early infancy. When relieved of this burden of presumed implications for adult personality or psychopathology, the social behaviors of the child become interesting in their own right. They can be studied in terms of the functions that they serve for the infant and for those with whom he interacts. The major findings can be summarized as follows.

■ Attempts to manipulate the preferences of 6- to 14-month-old infants experimentally have proved to be successful. Experimental studies (and naturalistic observations) suggest that the expansion of the child's social world does not require the extinction of earlier preferences. New preferences (and social attachments) can be established and cultivated while old ones are maintained. Hence, *extendibility* is considered to be a more appropriate term than

reversibility or extinction to describe the processes of normal social development.

■ Flexibility in the formation of new relationships and their retention and extinction has obvious physical survival properties for the infant. Such malleability promotes adaptation in the event that separation from the mother or caretaker occurs, whether by death, poverty, choice, or divorce.

■ Early social interchanges are tentative rather than rigid or "foundational." Relationships are necessarily interwoven with and determined by the infant's motor learning, and perceptual capabilities. The result of these findings has been a re-evaluation of phenomena that have conventionally been categorized as maladaptive, such as fear of strangers and separation anxiety. Such labels have had the unfortunate effect of diverting attention away from the socially adaptive features of the behaviors they represent. Viewed from the perspective of social development, these reactions constitute the first stage of interchange reorganization and social adaptation.

We may conclude that infants and young children are considerably more robust than they have been credited for being. It is true that some studies have shown that brief maternal separation can be highly disruptive. But the degree of disruption is modulated by the circumstances of separation and the nature of the setting in which the child is left. Furthermore, the disruptive effects do not necessarily, or even typically, persist.

But there is a gap in the evidence. If every child were adaptable and resilient to change, there would be little enduring unhappiness or distress. Stress and anxiety would perhaps exist only in the early stages of a new relationship; separation and loss would be only temporary problems. Although this depiction is generally accurate, it is surely not the whole story. At least it does not agree with many of our own experiences. At some point in development, human relationships do become firmly established and recovery and redirection do become more difficult; patterns of human social interchange and the emotions associated with them become stable and intense. So a question must be raised as to how and when affiliation patterns become stabilized.

The answer to this question requires a different kind of research orientation than one that focuses on the mother or her substitute. In the normal course of events, a child must meet and deal with other children and adults, both at school and at play. We now turn to the outcomes of some attempts to analyze the development of these interpersonal relationships beyond maternal attachment.

8

BEYOND SOCIAL ATTACHMENT: SOME DYNAMICS OF INTERACTIONAL DEVELOPMENT

"Beyond social attachment" has two meanings for us in this chapter. First, the phrase refers to the multiple interchanges in which the child participates outside the family network—in school, at play, and elsewhere. These relationships are "beyond" attachment in both chronological and spatial dimensions of the child's life: they occur after infancy and they occur away from the family. Second, and perhaps more important, we will move "beyond" attachment in a conceptual or theoretical sense. The multiple relationships of early childhood require broader perspectives on the interactions in development than attachment theory provides, and in this chapter we will examine those perspectives.

First, we will examine how parents influence the post-infancy socialization of the child, particularly the child's dependent behaviors. Then we will turn to the major task of this chapter: an overview of how extrafamilial interchanges and social preferences develop and how cognitive processes are involved in their development.

What Do Parents Contribute?
Child-Rearing Antecedents of Dependency

Most psychological theories (and virtually all common-sense ones) assume that the events that occur in the family—especially between parent and child—play a formative role in the basic social orientation of the child. This view has been stated concisely in the social learning concept of *dependency* and how it develops. Dependency behaviors are those acts that maintain positive interchanges between the child and others. More specifically, Sears, Rau, and Alpert (1965) define dependency as the "action system in which another person's nurturant, helping, and caretaking activities are the rewarding environmental events. Dependency actions are actions that elicit such events" (p. 27). Clearly the technical concept of "dependency" is not the same as the everyday notion, which brings to mind a clinging child or "one who relies on another for support or favor." On the contrary, the technical usage of the term is closer to what may be called affiliative or gregarious behavior—in general, the opposite of acts labeled aggressive or antisocial.

A major aim of social learning models has been to determine the relationship that exists between child-rearing practices and the two social orientations of the child—aggression and dependency. The work that has been conducted on this issue is voluminous, constituting the major thrust of developmental research from 1950 through the mid-1960's. Since excellent and comprehensive sources are available, it will not be necessary to discuss the theoretical, methodological, and empirical issues at length here.[1] The salient findings of the research are as follows.

1.   There is no clear evidence that a relationship exists between the child's dependency and parental warmth and love. According to Yarrow, Campbell, and Burton (1968), "the safe conclusion at present is that no strong support for the view that child dependency simply and directly relates to the affectional bond between parents and child has been mustered" (p. 40).

2.   The concept of dependency is multidimensional (Sears, 1963); that is, the behaviors that are usually measured (seeking help, staying near the mother) are not highly intercorrelated. Such multidimensionality makes it difficult, if not impossible, to find direct correlates with antecedent parental behaviors. The child who clings is not necessarily the same one who seeks attention or who is responsive to praise (Ascione, 1975). Composite measures of dependency combine these disparate characteristics, which, on logical and empirical grounds, should be kept separate.

3.   Somewhat more reliable predictions from home to preschool relationships can be made when discrete behaviors (such as "clinging to adults") are assessed; but even these associations are disappointingly small. One cannot predict, say, that the child who constantly clings to his mother will also cling to his teacher.

At first glance, the verdict would seem to be negative for the social learning account of dependency. But such a conclusion would be erroneous because it fails to give consideration to what was learned about social interchanges as a direct outcome of this work. Indeed, the concepts of interchange analysis were introduced into developmental research by R. R. Sears in his pioneering efforts to reformulate the dependency concept (Sears, 1951).

Equally important, the data point to the conclusion that parental rearing practices do affect children's social behaviors. They support the proposition that familial relationships directly influence the way that the child interacts with the family, but the impact of these relationships on the child's other social relations is indirect and, in many instances, marginal. For instance, to the extent that the mother fosters specific dependent behavior patterns, the child can be expected to reciprocate (in that relationship). When and how this behavior pattern becomes generalized to other relationships, including those in the preschool, is a separate matter—that is, the child's experiences in these new relationships determine whether the youngster will continue to behave in a dependent fashion with respect to other children and teachers. *The same interactional learning processes that were operative in the establishment of interactions with the parents continue to be operative in the child's establishment of interactions in the preschool and school.*

Accordingly, the various "dependency" behaviors must be viewed in terms of the interactions in which they take place. When the behavior occurs in a new relationship or setting—(the school or the playground), the counter-responses that it evokes from

---

[1] Of the several books and articles that have been published on the subject, six can be especially recommended: two original reports of R. R. Sears and his collaborators (Sears, Maccoby, and Levin, 1957; Sears, Rau, and Alpert, 1965); a comprehensive review by Eleanor Maccoby and John Masters (1970); an incisive critique of research methods by Yarrow, Campbell, and Burton (1968); and two recent theoretical reassessments by researchers who were active in the field (Alloway, Pliner, and Krames, 1977; Gewirtz, 1972).

others will be significant determinants of its persistence or change. If this elaboration of the original social learning hypothesis is correct, one should not automatically expect to find a close relationship between early child-rearing practices and specific features of the child's social orientation in the preschool. The interaction patterns of the child must be examined in the context of the school itself, and this is an issue to which we now turn.

Peer Interchanges Beyond Attachment

That children become more competent participants in interchanges as they grow older can hardly rank as a major discovery. It has come as a mild surprise, however, to find that children become interpersonally adept as young as they do. By the eighteenth month, children play various games with each other and with adults (Ross and Goldman, 1977a). In their second year, children can be observed to play "run and chase," "king of the mountain" (where the nursery school teacher is the mountain), "roll the ball," and a variety of other games that require interindividual attention and coordination (Eckerman, Whatley, and Kutz, 1975; Mueller and Lucas, 1975). In the third and fourth years, the interchanges escalate markedly in complexity, as verbal skills and motor patterns develop (Garvey and Hogan, 1973; Mueller, 1972). By age 5 or 6, children have graduated to new levels of interpersonal "gamesmanship." They have become adept at manipulating and controlling each other, their teachers, and their parents. Comprehensive studies (described in Chapter 17) confirm that social interchanges occur, in some form, at each developmental stage from birth onward.

Mutual controls are built into the fabric of social interchanges, and it is perhaps for this reason that such controls have proved so difficult to analyze. Certain basic phenomena can be readily identified in the interactions of young children, and they have been rediscovered by various investigators over the past half century. In this regard, Helen McI. Bott deserves credit for being one of the first to observe systematically the phenomenon of social reciprocity among 3- to 4-year-old children. (Her studies were conducted at the University of Toronto in the late 1920's.) Bott was surprised to find a high correlation between the actions that a child initiates toward other children and the actions that they initiate toward him. Bott called the phenomenon a "balance in contacts." This finding agreed with two sets of data later collected by Bott in 1929 and 1930. Bott (1934) wrote that

> these correlations indicate that the give and take of social intercourse is nicely balanced; that the child who is active towards others in the one who received most from them. The shy, retiring child, on the other hand, is little noticed by the group (p. 75).

The child, in effect, gets what he gives; he helps to create his own environment. Although this idea later became a cornerstone of interpersonal theories of personality (Horney, 1937; Sullivan, 1953), scant attention was paid to how the process actually occurs in the course of development. Nonetheless, the phenomenon kept recurring in developmental studies whenever the actions of the child and those with whom he interacted were simultaneously recorded. H. H. Anderson (1939) found, in a preschool-kindergarten sample, that dominative behavior invited domination in return, and that "integrative" (cooperative) acts invited integrative responses. Later, Raush (1965), Kohn (1966), and Hall (1973) confirmed these findings when studying older children and diverse encounters.

Egocentricism Revisited

The recent direct analyses of the process of peer interchange have shed light on some old issues. Egocentricism is a case in point. Following Piaget's lead (1936), observers of the social behavior and speech of young children have traditionally emphasized its "private" or egocentric nature (Flavell, Botkin, Fry, Wright, and Jarvis, 1968). This emphasis seemed entirely consistent with the Piagetian assumption that the young child is incapable of interpersonal communication because he lacks the ability to take the role of the other child. However, the "egocentric child" concept has been effectively challenged recently (Garvey and Hogan, 1973; S. Sherman, 1975; Mueller, 1972). In his studies of previously unacquainted preschool-age children (3½ to 5½ years), Mueller found that the overwhelming majority of verbal utterances of one child elicited some form of response from another. On only 15 percent of the occasions that one child said something to another child did the other child fail to respond.

This work was extended by Catherine Garvey and Robert Hogan (1973) at Johns Hopkins University. To obtain precise information about the child's utterances and the responses that they elicit, these investigators left children 3½–5 years old together to play freely in a playroom with a variety of toys and posters and a large one-way mirror. They were observed in 18 pairs via closed-circuit television; their interactions were recorded on videotape, and recordings of their conversations were subsequently typed in transcript form. The sessions lasted no longer than 15 minutes. From the transcripts and the videotapes, judgments were made of the number and type of "utterance units," which were stretches of one child's speech separated by pauses greater than 1 second or by another child's speech. The other child's response to the utterance were then coded to indicate whether he ignored the utterance, paid attention to it, or performed some appropriate verbal or nonverbal act.

Not only do children in this age range spend considerable time in social interaction, but much of the interaction involves talking. And the children do not simply talk to themselves or engage in socially meaningless babbling. On the contrary, the speech "gambits" (control strategies) employed are basically similar to certain of those observed in adult conversations. For example, one gambit used by

adults to open conversations is the "summon-answer" routine. In the opener, the first speaker elicits attention from the second. In move 2, the second speaker indicates a willingness to respond. Move 3 is up to the first speaker: he must somehow justify getting the second speaker's attention. Both persons are committed at this point. Use of this pattern, Garvey and Hogan (1973) argued, would be "substantial evidence of communicative intent and ability to use a conversational gambit to secure the involvement of the partner" (p. 566).

Children do indeed employ this 3-move pattern, and the result is sometimes much longer interchanges. Typically these 3½- to 5-year-olds used "Do you know what?" or "Guess what?" as the opener. Move 2 was almost invariably "What?" Move 3 could vary from an invitation, to a statement of fact, to an insult, as in the following playful interchange quoted by Garvey and Hogan (1973):

Boy A: "Do you know what?"
Girl B: "What?" (pause, Betty turns to Sammy and moves toward him) "What?" (repetition is louder, with broader rising-falling intonation)
Boy A: (Sammy grins, then laughs before speaking) "You're a nut."
Girl B: "What? What? What's a nut? What?" (both children laugh simultaneously; Betty dashes threateningly at Sammy, shrieking the final, "What?")

It looks as if Sammy got himself into some difficulty by creating a state of involvement from which he was unable to extricate himself. His response was sufficiently inappropriate to be a joke. The playful manipulation of the gambit suggests that the children were experimenting with the uses and consequences of this way of controlling others. From their observations, Garvey and Hogan (1973) concluded that

. . . early language serves, not only to coordinate the children's actions, but also to facilitate mutual engagement which has those actions as its focus.

As children become able to sustain an interaction per se, play activity becomes less important as a vehicle for promoting these relations; this development continues until children can interact solely by verbal means. We propose, then, that early activities which promote the acquisition and use of verbal forms of interpersonal contact are biologically useful, for they must precede those later derivations from basic dialogue, which become monologue, inner speech or thought, writing, and finally, adult dialogue (p. 568).

Since preschool-age children are capable of using these complex forms of mutual control, it should not be entirely surprising to find that they are adept in a wide range of social situations.

Similarity and Reciprocity

In interchanges, there is typically a high level of similarity between how a child behaves toward others and how others behave toward him. We have already noted Bott's (1934) observations on this apparent reciprocity in preschool children. Her work involved observations in "unrestrained" or naturalistic conditions of an ordinary preschool. Other observations of the phenomenon of the balance in contacts (Anderson, 1939, Kohn, 1966) were also made in unrestrained preschool settings. One problem in interpreting such observational studies is that factors other than the child's interactional behavior may have accounted for the similarity. For instance, the apparent reciprocity may reflect factors that draw similar children together (such as similar children being placed together by the teacher or commonality in their play preferences). Such factors yield similarities that would, on the surface, appear to be determined by reciprocities in interchanges. Do children tend to behave in a similar fashion even when these external factors are controlled? One way to answer this question is to conduct laboratory studies of pairs and triads of children who did not choose their playmates. If the behavior of children who have been assigned at random to play together is similar to that of their playmates, we will have

more confidence that the reciprocity phenomenon reflects interpersonal processes (rather than second-order factors that operate on children separately). In such a laboratory study, S. Sherman (1975) repeatedly observed a large number of randomly formed groups made up of 3 children of the same sex. The activities of the children, who were 4-5 years old, were recorded on videotape so that the investigator could later code the activities of each child separately. It was thus possible to follow precisely the actions of each child in the triads as well as the immediate actions/reactions of other children that that child's activities provoked.

Sherman's work confirmed the existence of the reciprocity phenomenon. In virtually all triads, whether made up of boys or of girls, a synchrony rapidly evolved in pairs of children such that performance of an act was followed by the performance of a similar but not identical act by a second child. For example, a typical interchange between 5-year-old girls would involve dolls that had been placed among other toys placed in the playroom. One girl's picking up and dressing the doll was highly likely to elicit a similar act by another girl, and statements such as "My doll has a blue dress" were likely to elicit counterstatements about dolls ("My doll's name is Heather"). Both the acts and the utterances were functionally matched and were similar though not identical in content. The behaviors within the pair of children were synchronized in the sense that each child elaborated on some item mentioned in the ongoing or proceding utterance or act of the other child. At a more general level, when a child initiated an interchange with another child in the triad, there was likely to be counterinitiation by that other child directed toward the first child (see Figure 8-1).

A second finding of S. Sherman (1975) concerned the way that all three children interacted together. Rarely (only 7 percent of the time) did the three children interact simultaneously as a group of three; rather, the triad formed a two-plus-one pattern— that is, three children were indeed "a crowd," in that at any one time in the observation series two of

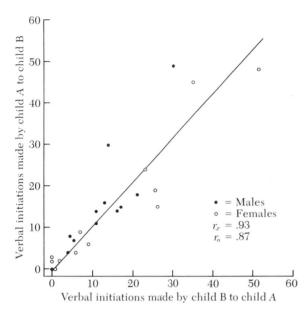

Figure 8-1. Children who initiate a social action receive a counterinitiation. Graph compares the number of occasions that one child in the laboratory directed a remark to another child with the number of times a remark was directed to him by the other child (over 10-minute intervals). The children were 4 ½–5 ½ years old. The correlation was high and positive for both boys and girls (adapted from S. Sherman, 1975).

them tended to be involved together and one child was left out. Rarely did the children act totally independently of each other (replicating the "egocentricism" disconformation), and rarely did they spontaneously interact as a unit of three persons. The pairs that formed were unstable, at least in the initial session, so that different children rotated into (and out of) the two-person interchange.

Further laboratory studies of interaction patterns of groups have indicated that the reciprocity phenomenon is not limited to children in the 4- to 5-year age range; it is found in older children as well. One investigator (Eckerman, 1979) found that even 2-year-old children show a very high level of reciprocity in their activities when paired together at

random. Other researchers (Rabinowitz, Moely, Finkel, and McClinton, 1975) report that the exploration of objects by a 3-year-old stimulates exploration by the child's partner. (The development of reciprocity will be discussed further in Chapter 17.)

One finding of laboratory studies of small groups is that children exercise considerable control over the content, style, and termination of each other's actions. This interactional organization permits us to make highly reliable predictions about the behaviors of one child *even if we do not observe him directly.* The predictions are made merely on the basis of our observations of the person with whom he interacts. Using this procedure, S. Sherman (1975) has been able to predict, with a high level of accuracy, whether 4-year-old children were going to play with dolls, trucks, or blocks; whether they were going to be quiet or rowdy; and whether they were going to be effeminate or masculine. Similarly, W. M. Hall (1973) demonstrated that the number of times a 7-year-old boy would bang a doll around the room could be precisely predicted by watching the other child in the room with him. The unobserved child's behavior and language were not mirror images of those of the partner, but they filled in the missing elements of the observed child's behavior pattern. In a type of feedback operation, each child's pattern of activities was both a determinant and an outcome of the activity pattern of the other child.

Recognition of the pervasiveness of mutual control processes permits a reassessment of why the social behaviors of an individual child are so poorly predicted by focusing exclusively on that child. Children's behaviors depend simultaneously on their own unique characteristics and temperament and on those of the person with whom they interact at a given point in time. As we will see in Chapter 22, reciprocity also helps us to understand the problem of continuity and change (for example, why some social actions of the child appear to be so unstable from one setting to another, and from one day or week to another). Reciprocity is found in both qualitative and quantitative aspects of interchanges, and in both pleasant and unpleasant acts. The finding that reciprocity occurs in both experimental and nonexperimental settings is not an unimportant one. In the classroom, the child can choose his partner and, to some extent, create his own environment; but in the experimental setting, both partner and environment are selected for him. The child's selection of companions in everyday life is described by Kohn (1966) as follows:

> The variety of children available probably offers the individual child sufficient choice to enable him to construct the kind of environment which will keep constant his prevailing mode of adaptation. The mild-mannered, low-initiative child will, in all likelihood, select the nice children who will collaborate with him to maintain his preferred equilibrium between himself and the environment (p. 99).

Some Features of Interactional Control in Young Children

Recent investigations of interchanges have emphasized the control properties (including instructions) of the context in which they occur, the inductive properties of children themselves, and the role of preferences as both determinants and consequences of interchanges.

Contextual Constraints

The nature of the setting in which the interactions occur may limit the range of behaviors possible and hence serve to "level" the differences among children and the differences between children and the persons with whom they interact. Settings may also support differentiation of a child's actions and roles, leading a greater variety of patterns and less similarity from one place to another. The extent to which interactional patterns and the stimulus properties of

other persons are context-relative has been demonstrated repeatedly. A person's role (and anticipated support properties) may be quite different in one setting than in another, and even young children are aware of the differentiation. Bott (1934) observed a striking difference between the child's response to the mother in her role as a nursery school observer and his response to the mother in her role at home. The mother was selectively ignored when in the school. Bott comments:

> Conceivably the reaction to mother-as-observer is quite different to what one would find to mother-as-teacher, or to the mother at home. As far as we were able to judge, children tend to react differently to different situations, e.g., routine or free play, rather than to different individuals. The same person in a different role seems to distract them more than different personalities exerting the same kind of authority or performing the same offices (p. 91).

Rather the same conclusions were reached more recently by Rose, Blank, and Spalter (1975), who found considerable variability in the behavior of preschool-age children in different settings. As the children's activities changed as a function of context, so did their patterns of interchange and social preferences. [2]

Instruction and Interchanges. Although the instructions given in the course of experiments may not be viewed as "changes in context," they appear to operate according to the same principles. Further, "experimental demands" or instructions embedded in the procedure of the experiment itself

---

[2] Children respond differently to their mothers, depending on the context in which the interaction occurs. When mothers appear unexpectedly at a nursery school, a wide range of responses can be provoked in their children. The child may show off, ignore his mother, tell her to leave, cling to her, ask to be held, or demand that she stay. As Schwarz and Wynn (1971) have shown, the mother's presence does not necessarily facilitate preschool adaptation; for some children, her presence retards the process. Out-of-context appearances, even by the mother, can be disruptive after the child's behavior has become organized in the school.

can have a potent influence. For example, indirect instructions can be communicated via films and by interchanges between experimenter and child. Films showing how children relate to each other can elicit social activity from children who are usually shy and socially inactive (Keller and Carlson, 1974). Although these "modeling" effects are transient (they were obtained only in observations immediately following the experimental session but not in later observations), they nonetheless suggest ways in which passive children can be made less so.

Other contextual changes in interactional patterns can be produced by the way in which the experimental task is organized and presented to children. Hartup and his co-workers (French, Brownell, Graziano, and Hartup, 1977) have recently explored the effects of constructing a situation that promotes cooperation (as opposed to competition and independence). Triads of first-grade and third-grade children were confronted with a task (building a tower out of 7.6 cm^3 wooden blocks) that required some degree of coordinated action among children for successful completion. The better (taller, more stable) the tower, the more chips earned (which the children could exchange for an inexpensive toy). Three conditions were established. In the *cooperative* triads, all children in the triad were winners to the extent that the group as a unit scored well, and the booty was shared equally. In the *independent* triads, each child won chips according to his own performance but all could win. (Each child's outcome was independent of the rest of the group.) In the *competitive* triads (called contrient by French et al.), the single triad member who had individually contributed the greatest number of blocks to the tower was awarded chips, but the other triad members received nothing ("winner take all").

Which type of triad produced the best (tallest, most stable) towers? Triads in the cooperative condition inevitably outperformed triads in the competitive conditions, achieving almost twice as many points on the average. The triads assigned to the independent condition scored somewhere between

the cooperative and contrient conditions. (There were, incidentally, no reliable sex or age differences in the triad performances.) Further, the children in the cooperative triads showed a greater differentiation of roles than did children in the independent or competitive ones, a finding that on the surface seems to run counter to intuition. The cooperative groups efficiently subdivided activity and job specialization. For instance, French et al. report that it was not "unusual to observe two children quickly placing several blocks on the tower while the third straightened the tower and warned the builders when it became too high or unstable."

The actions and directions of one's interactive partner also can determine which interactional strategy the child will adopt, and maintain. Robert Quilty (1975) recently devised a novel experimental method of studying how distinctive interpersonal strategies can be elicited and carried over to the next encounter. In Quilty's experiments the interactions between 6-year-old children and an adult were recorded on closed-circuit television. The instructions given to the children were that "we have some new games and we want to see how children like them." The children were first given wooden building materials with which they could construct a variety of objects, such as cars, ships, and houses.

One aim of the experiment was to determine whether the children's interactions with the experimenter could be biased by their preceding interactions with him. Therefore, in the first phase of the study the experimenter tried to direct the children's interchange strategies by dropping not-so-subtle hints as to which kind of activity was expected. The hints ranged from explicit instructions ("Build what I build") to setting an example (by adding onto the children's models) to ignoring the children completely. Not surprisingly, the children got the message. Those children who were expected to build together with the experimenter worked on a joint model; those who were told to imitate made exact duplicates of the experimenter's model; and those who were expected to work independently built their own creations.

Table 8-1. The recurrence of interchange strategies.

Child's acts in test phase (session 2)	Child's condition during interaction phase (session 1)			
	Imitation ("Do as I do")	Imitation (implicit)	Independent ("Do what you like")	Working together ("I'll work with you")
Copying experimenter	9.6	3.4	1.9	2.0
Watching experimenter	21.6	17.3	6.5	7.3
Working independently	0.2	6.5	10.6	1.9
Working together	0	0	0	8.0

NOTE: Table shows the mean number of responses that children in each of the four conditions produced in the second (test) session.
SOURCE: Data from Quilty, 1975.

To determine whether the child would subsequently re-create the interchange strategy that had been induced, Quilty (1975) then set up another "game." It also consisted of materials that the child could build with, but the materials themselves were quite different from those used in the first encounter. Also, in the second session, the experimenter did not give any instructions (to imitate, to work independently, or to work together). Rather, the child was free to select whatever interchange strategy he wished to adopt. In this experimental arrangement, the children showed a strong tendency to reinstitute whatever was the original relationship (Table 8-1). Children who had previously imitated continued to imitate; children who had earlier worked independently continued typically to work independently; and children who had worked together with the experimenter continued to try to build together on the new task. Indeed, the *only* children who worked cooperatively with the experimenter were those who had done so earlier. Overall, the dominant interactional strategy adopted by children in the second session was usually the one that had been induced in the first session.

In general, experimental research as well as studies of preschool and school classroom organization support Roger Barker's emphasis on the significance of the setting and the child's expectations concerning the regulation of social interchanges (Barker, 1963, 1965; Schoggen, 1963; Willems, 1965; Willems and Raush, 1969; Wright, 1967). The more recent work goes a step further to indicate that particular relationships can gain unique control properties of their own. Once the structure in which the interchanges are to take place is established, it has an overriding effect on the nature of the patterns selected and maintained.

The Inductive Properties of Children's Behavior

There has been a good deal of speculation that children "re-create" relationships and thus design their own social environment by inducing particular acts toward themselves. This speculation is doubtless well founded, but there may also be limits to how efficient and effective young children are in this endeavor.

In a relevant study conducted at the National Child Research Center (Yarrow, Waxler, and Scott, 1971), female caretakers of small groups of children were trained to play either a high-nurturant or low-nurturant role. Some children thus were given constant kindness and love; other children were ignored and given little attention or affection. The

Table 8-2. Variations in frequency of adult's contacts with different children: Percent of children receiving designated number of contacts from adult.

No contacts from adult	Positive contacts from high-nurturant adult				Negative contacts from low-nurturant adult			
	Initiated by adult		In response to bids		Initiated by adult		In response to bids	
	Adult 1	Adult 2	Adult 1	Adult 2	Adult 1	Adult 2	Adult 1	Adult 2
0–10	3	0	22	17	20	5	41	29
11–20	12	6	17	22	23	19	33	14
21–30	3	11	20	22	28	43	10	24
31–40	15	17	17	11	23	19	3	14
41–50	30	22	8	11	3	0	5	5
51–60	15	22	8	11	3	5	5	0
61–70	7	17	5	0	0	9	3	9
Over 70	15	5	3	6	0	0	0	5
Mean number of contacts	47.4	49.2	28.4	29.7	22.1	31.0	16.3	27.0
SD	22.8	19.0	20.0	18.1	12.2	14.8	16.1	22.0
n	40	18	40	18	39	21	39	21

SOURCE: From Yarrow, Waxler, and Scott, copyright © 1971 by the American Psychological Association. Reprinted with permission.

caretakers were highly trained and experienced, and, as it turns out, so were the children.

Did all children receive their assigned quota of love or inattention? As shown in Table 8-2, some children appeared to be unlovable no matter whom they were assigned to. Conversely, other children were rarely ignored by the caretakers, even if they were supposed to be. Some 10 percent of the children assigned to the high-nurturant caretakers were involved in more than 70 positive contacts with her, whereas another 10 percent of those assigned to the same caretaker were involved in less than 20 such contacts. An equally wide range was found among the children assigned to the low-nurturant caretakers. At least part of the variation in the caretakers' roles can be attributed to the activity of the children. Those children who made the greatest number of attention-seeking bids were also the ones who received the most nurturance from the caretaker, regardless of her assigned role. Other causes of variation from the assigned role include the sex of the child (boys had more negative contacts with the adults), the number of aggressive contacts with other children (those involved in such contacts had more negative contacts with adults), and kindliness

to the caretakers (the "nicer" children were treated more warmly by the adult).

Experimental reports have recently confirmed that variations in the child's actions do indeed directly influence the adult's response to them. The usual procedure has been to train children to be confederates of the experimenter (that is, to play different roles with respect to college student "subjects"). Typically the children are old enough (9–11 years) to serve as reliable confederates and young enough to be employed cheaply (50 cents a session in one study). Cantor and Gelfand (1977) varied the children's responsiveness to the adult's attempts to help them (the children) finish various art projects (such as copy designs on an Etch-A-Sketch screen or build a model with Tinker Toys). The six-boy and six-girl confederate groups (averaging about 9 years of age) were instructed to be either responsive (smile, initiate conversations, seek evaluations) or to be unresponsive to the adults' overtures (avoid looking at the adult or initiating conversations with them). The manipulation yielded reliable differences in how the adults behaved toward the children (they paid more attention to the responsive children, and they rated them as more likable, more attractive, and more intelligent).

Cantor and Gelfand (1977) conclude:

The present results portray the child as one who helps to create his social world. A child who fails to attend to and converse with adults is seen by the adults as less socially attractive and even as less intelligent than the pleasant, sociable child. This is so even though in the responsive condition the children asked for considerably more guidance in performing the art tasks (thus indicating less skill and less independence) than they did in the unresponsive condition. Apparently, the pleasant child tends to be overrated and the socially withdrawn child to be underrated on a variety of characteristics (p. 237).

Similar findings have been reported by Bates (1976). But a word of caution is in order. Although extremes in the children's behaviors can produce similar extremes in adult behaviors and evaluations, it should be observed that the behavior induction effects in the college student subjects were relatively modest ones. There was in fact considerable overlap between subjects' reactions, despite vast differences in the behavior of the children.

Why do the actions and reactions of children influence the behavior of adults toward them, and vice versa? The evidence suggests that each person's attitude and range of action are, in a cumulative sense, constrained by the preceding events in the interchange and in prior interchanges. Social feedback controls the interchanges of adults as well as of children. The reactions of the partner determine, in part, whether the child imitates or responds reciprocally or plays alone and whether the adult is attentive, smiles, and forms a positive opinion of the child. These effects can be produced in the short term with modest success and are seen as well in the long-term, day-to-day interactions of the school.

Interchanges and Preferences

A point about the relationship between interchanges and preferences should be remembered.

The mere existence of a relationship does not require that the individuals necessarily like or are attracted to each other. Indeed, many (or most) of the interchanges in which children are involved from infancy through the school years are ones in which they have little choice. They are assigned to a school, to a teacher, to a classmate, and so on. Each of these assignments influences the opportunities for interaction and the nature of the actions that will be tolerated and supported. At this point we might inquire as to the relationship between preferences and interchanges: does one lead to the other?

Does "Like Beget Like"?   Intuitively one might expect that children tend to seek out others whose behaviors and attitudes are likely to match their own. There is indeed empirical evidence to support this notion. Specifically:

1. A child who behaves like another child tends to elicit imitation (a special instance of reciprocity), and a child who behaves differently from another child tends to elicit counterimitation (Fouts, Waldner, and Watson, 1976; Fouts, 1975; Miller and Morris, 1974).

2. Same-sex interchanges occur more frequently than heterosexual ones, and the interchanges differ in quality: girls are more verbal than boys (Berk, 1971; McGrew, 1972; Reuter and Yunik, 1973).

3. Children having similar backgrounds find it more easy to cooperate with each other than do those from different backgrounds (Feitelson, Weintraub, and Michaeli, 1972).

But perceived similarity is not the whole basis for initiating interchanges. There is equally compelling evidence that interchange preferences are determined by the apparent competence, attractiveness, and skills of the other person. By the time children are in preschool, they form stereotypes about attractiveness in other children based on their physical appearance (Cavior and Lombardi, 1973; Lerner, 1972; Lerner and Korn, 1972, Lerner and Schroeder, 1971). The stereotypes of physical attractiveness become more stable in middle childhood (8–12 years) and are correlated with whether or not other children are seen as potential friends or partners (Cavior and Dekecki, 1973; Kleck, Richardson, and Ronald, 1974; Staffieri, 1972).

The basis for children's friendship expectations appears to change as a function of the child's developmental/cognitive status. Bigelow (1977) recently compared some 480 children aged 6-14 in terms of what they expected in their best friends that was different from their other acquaintances. Bigelow defined three stages in friendship expectations. Younger children (6-9 years) valued a friend who liked common activities and stayed nearby (Stage I). Older children (13-14 years) valued such characteristics as "genuineness" and "intimacy potential" (Stage III). The intermediate-level children (Stage II) valued "admiration"—presumably a friend who held them in high regard. Bigelow (1977) also found that not all bases for friendship change with age. In particular, two of the characteristics—reciprocal liking and perceived similarity—were relevant for all age groups tested.

Interaction Leads to Liking—Sometimes. If one chooses to interact with persons whom one likes, is the opposite also true? Will the occurrence of interactions lead to the development of mutual preferences and liking? In the case of infants and mothers, or infants and experimenters, the answer seems to be yes (Chapter 7). However, beyond infancy, the story is more complicated.

In one of the few attempts to assess experimentally the effects of classroom interchanges on social preferences, Haskett (1971) arranged a first-grade classroom in pairs of children who would be highly likely to cooperate with each other. The members of each pair had to work side by side for 45 minutes a day for 3 consecutive school days. The *cooperation* pairs were instructed to build models out of Popsicle sticks and tape. The *contiguous* pairs were told to work on their projects individually. The *control* pairs were not seated next to each other but were told to work on their models in their regular seats in the classroom. Tests of social preference were made both before and after the experiment. Even this

very brief experiment showed a change in each child's stated preferences for his partner. The "cooperative" partner was preferred more following the interaction than before. Although this outcome was statistically reliable only when the partner was of the opposite sex, the other findings of the study are consistent with the conclusion that interaction increases liking.

Similar outcomes have been reported in studies of the social behavior of adults (see Byrne, 1971; Homans, 1950). Such findings led Homans to propose the interaction-attraction hypothesis: "If the frequency of interaction between two or more persons increases, the degree of their liking for one another will increase, and vice-versa" (p. 112). Why should interaction make a difference? One possibility is that the behavior of the other person becomes more predictive and supportive of the interchanges of the first person. As has been shown in studies of infants and nonhuman young, the interchange itself is the basis for the mutual synchronization of behavior. The activities of each participant become mutually supportive, and as the individuals become acquainted, there is a concomitant mutual dependency.

But there remains the disturbing fact that in reality close friendships frequently turn sour, children may leave home, and sometimes the better we get to know a person, the more we despise him. Such realities may prevent human life, in the words of Roger Brown (1965), from "melting down into a perfectly uniform sugar syrup." Why might interaction not always engender positive feelings? There are probably several things that can end the happiness cycle: failure to fulfill one's expectations, restriction of one's activity, thoughtless insults without apology. As in the analysis of nonhumans (Chapter 6), simply because an interaction occurs does not mean that it will remain sychronous. Children who have developed some skill in adapting to new relationships are usually less likely to tolerate an unhappy relationship if a more pleasant one is available.

Despite its general accuracy, the hypothesis that interaction leads to liking fails to acknowledge that many preferences are specific to certain situations and activities. Simply because a child is a preferred partner with whom to build a model out of Popsicle sticks does not mean that he will be the preferred partner for a game of catch. Just as nonhuman primates have preferred partners for different activities (grooming, playing, sex), so do children have different playmates according to the activity and circumstance (whether in the playground, in art class, or in small group discussions).

The Recurrence, Consolidation, and Differentiation/Generalization of Interchanges

In the preceding section, we were reminded that social interaction patterns are not only established, they can be changed or transferred to new situations and relationships. These observations bring us to the interesting and provocative question of how interchanges are learned and unlearned, generalized and differentiated. The rest of this chapter is devoted to some thoughts on these questions. First, we will discuss the concepts of interchange recurrence, consolidation, generalization, and differentiation; then we will examine the mechanisms by which they operate.

Recurrence

The available evidence indicates that *once an interchange has occurred between two individuals, the probability of its recurrence in that setting is increased.* The "recurrence principle" is an empirical generalization based on observations of a broad range of relationships, species, and circumstances. Both positive and negative interchanges recur, and negative (abusive and fighting) patterns are as predictable as positive ones (see Chapters 10 and 12).

Indirect support for the recurrence principle in children is found in accounts of the situational speci-

ficity of preschool interactional behavior. Continuity of interactions among preschool-age children has typically been found "only when the situation remained constant" (Rose et al., 1975). Even from day to day, there was considerable variability in the child's associations and actions across settings, as was found with Peter (Chapter 1). But when the setting is held constant, enduring interchange patterns emerge (S. Sherman, 1975). Such interpersonal stability would be expected if there were indeed carryover effects of particular interchanges in particular settings. Typically there are.

Consolidation

With each recurrence, social interchanges become more readily performed and organized. Variations in the acts of others can be tolerated without disruption of the "theme" of the interchange. After the new father has changed his infant's diapers a number of times, both participants become more skilled in their roles. Once our actions with regard to another person are well established, they become increasingly resistant to change. *Consolidation* refers to the process whereby interchanges become more organized with each recurrence. Once an interchange pattern has become consolidated, it can be elicited even in the absence of some of the conditions that were originally required for its establishment, and it becomes increasingly resistant to change.[3]

The clearest evidence of the consolidation of interchanges in various nonhuman mammals can be found in studies of the persistence of aggressive behaviors and sexual behaviors even in the absence of the conditions that were necessary for their original establishment (see Chapters 10 and 14). In our analysis of the establishment of social "attachment" behaviors in children, we have seen how the child's

---

[3] The idea that behavior patterns are consolidated in "themes" is a key one for contemporary views on interchanges (see Chapter 17).

activities become organized around particular things (dolls and pillows), places, and people.

In children, social acts and nonsocial acts persist even when they are no longer appropriate, or are embarrassing, or are inconvenient. The acts, interpersonal and nonpersonal, can seemingly become ingrained and gain an inertia of their own. At a more general level, interpersonal "styles" seemingly become consolidated in particular relationships so that they persist even when the conditions supporting the style have changed. Such persistence provides a basis for predictability, identity, and idiosyncracy.

Generalization and Differentiation

Two concepts, interchange generalization and interchange differentiation, are related to each other and to consolidation. Generalization refers to the phenomenon in which interchanges that have been established and consolidated in one setting or relationship are elicited in novel ones. For example, an interchange pattern becomes generalized if a boy who terrorizes his younger brother at home and calls him a crybaby displays similar acts and attitudes toward his peers at school.

Interchange differentiation, on the other hand, refers to the phenomenon in which the child distinguishes the difference between the two settings or persons and alters his behavior accordingly. Hence, the child might continue to be a terror at home but may be respectful of younger children at school, or vice versa.

Interchange differentiation is linked to a phenomenon—the situational specificity of social behaviors—that has been a source of puzzlement to personality and developmental researchers since it was first emphasized by Hartshorne and May (1928). These investigators found that there is only modest predictability from one setting or relationship to another of those admirable characteristics, "altruism" and "honesty." The attempts to determine why such specificity occurs are still continuing (Chapter 17).

Intuitively most of us expect that there will be stability and generality in interchanges. Despite this overriding faith in the uniqueness and stability of individual behavior, there is surprisingly little evidence from studies of young children to support it. Even in a single day, there is scant generality in a child's social actions from the outdoor playground to the classroom, from the experimental observation cubicle to the playground or classroom (Rose et al., 1975; S. Sherman, 1975).

Nonetheless, it would be premature to conclude that generalization is merely in the mind of the beholder. Experimental studies of attempts to produce interchange generalization, in particular, have yielded provocative results. One such attempt by Donna Gelfand and her colleagues at the University of Utah dealt with the "generational" transfer of techniques of reward and punishment (Gelfand, Hartmann, Lamb, Smith, Mahan, and Paul, 1974). These investigators asked whether children who had been either punished or rewarded in learning a simple task, when they later (as adults) played the role of the experimenter, would adopt the procedures to which they had been exposed. They did. Whatever interactional pattern the child had been exposed to, he tended to repeat, even though his role had been switched from the recipient to the giver. Within the context of interactional analysis, it appears that the child effectively fit the other child into the role that he himself had formerly played, thus permitting a "replay" of the original interchange. In this regard, Cottrell (1969) speculates that parents tend to adopt patterns of rearing that are similar to the ones they experienced.

What about interactional generalization when the child's role remains the same but the persons with whom he deals differ from the persons in the original relationship? This question lies at the heart of some problems of therapy, teaching, and child rearing. Their goal is often to generalize to other persons effects that are produced in the original relationship.

Recent evidence on the matter comes in part from attempts to teach "social skills" by means of various coaching and modeling techniques (Gottman, Gonso, and Rasmussen, 1975; Keller and Carlson, 1974). When television viewing is combined with direct coaching and training in interactional patterns, the likelihood of generalization to new relationships is increased (Friedrich and Stein, 1975). The use of films to promote social interchanges in the classroom usually achieves the desired effect, but it is often short-lived. Related efforts to assess the immediate and enduring effects of television programs have yielded mixed results, a matter that will be discussed in greater detail later (Chapters 12 and 19). On the other hand, extended "coaching" and training withdrawn children to play with other children has had promising, and seemingly lasting, effects (Oden and Asher, 1977). Active participation of children in ameliorative interchanges—with direct instructions and guidelines on how to generalize them to peer interchanges—seems capable of producing success. These results are consistent with the experimental study of Quilty (1975) that showed how children select and generalize interchange strategies.

The Nature of Interchange Learning

We can infer from the research now available that learning processes occur at several stages of interchange establishment. The precise nature of the learning processes involved has been elusive, however. One of the reasons for the elusiveness has been that the basic concept of learning employed for the task of explaining interchange establishment and maintenance—reinforcement—was not derived from the study of interchange phenomena but has been applied to them. The extrapolation has met with mixed success. We will first examine the issues involved and then offer some general comments on the nature of interchange learning.

Varieties of Reinforcement

Positive Reinforcement as an Interchange Concept. In interchanges, persons may behave in a way that is mutually reinforcing—that is, each person provides the positive consequences for the behavior of the other (Skinner, 1953). Gewirtz and Boyd (1977b) have recently demonstrated that mothers' behaviors are indeed reinforced by acts that they perceive to be produced by their infants.[4] Variations in positive reinforcement contingencies have been employed as well in the treatment of withdrawn and isolated children, in the reduction of aggressive behavior (by nonreinforcement of assertive acts), and in an attempt to solve a variety of other problems of behavioral control in prisons and institutions for the retarded.

Because of singular importance of the reinforcement proposal, it is necessary to undertake a careful examination of its application to social interchanges. Certain investigators, such as G. Patterson (1979), who originally adopted a positive reinforcement explanation of interchanges, have modified their stance because of the problems encountered in the application of the idea in specific areas. An outline of some of the disputed issues follows.

1.   Interchanges recur and are generalized in the apparent absence of positive reinforcement.

2.   The incidence of certain social acts (such as assertiveness) tends to increase rather than decrease in the absence of positive reinforcement.

3.   Contexts and instructions often appear to exert a more powerful control over the nature of the interchanges that occur, and their recurrence, than do specific "reinforcement" events, whatever the type.

---

[4] In this experiment, each infant was placed in a laboratory room. The infant's mother remained in another room. The mothers were told that their infants' behaviors (head turning) would be symbolically coded on a matrix of lights. However, the lights were actually totally controlled by the experimenter and were unrelated to the child's behavior. This study was one of the few to control experimentally the acts of one member of the mother-infant dyad in order to determine the effects produced on the other member.

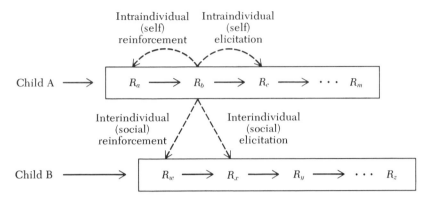

Figure 8-2. Diagram of the theoretical relationships between the social reinforcement and social elicitation functions of interpersonal acts. Terms R_a, R_b, ... R_m refer to the acts of child A; R_w, R_x, ... R_z refer to the acts of child B. The arrows indicate the sequence of events, from left to right, and imply the joint dependency of acts upon intraindividual and interindividual sources. Conceptual problems arise because any act in the sequence can potentially serve as an antecedent (elicitor) and or as a consequent (reinforcer). Intraindividual reinforcement is usually called self-reinforcement (or self-punishment); interindividual reinforcement is called social reinforcement (or punishment). The boxes imply that most activities are organized in patterns, or "themes."

4. It is difficult, and often impossible, to distinguish between the eliciting (stimulus) effects of an interpersonal act and the reinforcing effects (Figure 8-2). A corollary of this statement is that the immediate outcomes of positive reinforcement in interchanges are often different from long-term outcomes.

5. The various concepts that have been labeled "reinforcement" (social reinforcement, vicarious reinforcement, primary reinforcement, secondary reinforcement) appear to subsume different functional relationships and, possibly, different processes.

Each of these issues requires thoughtful consideration; taken together, they suggest than an account of interchanges solely in terms of the positive reinforcement may be incomplete (see Chapter 19).

Negative Reinforcement as an Alternative. Patterson (1979) has recently proposed that interchanges

are controlled by negative reinforcement.[5] Although positive reinforcement is still proposed to be necessary to establish coercive behavior in young children (2–4 years old), negative reinforcement (the reduction of pain or discomfort through cessation of punishment, teasing, and various noxious acts of others) serves to reinforce coercion in later childhood. Patterson's analysis points out that reinforcement processes (whether positive, negative, or social) are not necessarily mutually exclusive. One form of reinforcement may be dominant and then become less important at different levels of the interchange or at different stages of life.

Such a pluralistic view seems to be closer to the facts than is a single-process view of reinforcement.

[5] Note that negative reinforcement has been used in two different ways: (1) to refer to the consequences produced by punishment; and (2) to refer to the consequences produced by the *reduction* of punishment (and of other painful, uncomfortable states). Patterson has employed the concept in the second, or the reduction of discomfort, sense.

Most of the issues just outlined, however, still present a problem for the application of the concepts of positive or negative reinforcement.

Vicarious, Internal, and Social Reinforcement. The reinforcement concept, when applied to normal children and adults, required some modification to take into account the fact that much reinforcement is internal or symbolic. The concepts of vicarious reinforcement, social reinforcement, and internal reinforcement were thus introduced. A discussion of the strengths and weaknesses of these "human" concepts of reinforcement is reserved for Chapter 19.

The Role of Cognitive and Conditioning Processes

Some of the stubborn problems associated with understanding the relationship between learning processes and interchanges can be solved if certain features of interchanges in children are made explicit. Three of the more important ones are that (1) interchanges occur sequentially, and therefore we should pay attention to the forward-acting properties of events (elicitors) as well as possible backward-acting ones (reinforcers); (2) contexts and relationships profoundly influence the nature of the interchanges that are observed; and (3) the child's expectations, attributions, and interpretations—and those of other persons—take on increased significance across development in determining the nature and course of interchanges. These features require concepts of learning that permit us to take into account the eliciting properties of the acts of others, the supportive and directive properties of situations (or stimulus configurations), and the information-processing capabilities of children in anticipating and interpreting interpersonal acts.

No comprehensive theory of interchange learning has yet been formulated, although significant steps have been taken (see, for example, Bandura, 1977; Gewirtz, 1972; Patterson, 1979). It now seems clear that both cognitive and conditioning mechanisms

play prominent roles in interchange consolidation and modification. These roles, however, are not invariant. They depend on such factors as the cognitive capabilities of the organisms (as determined by their species and developmental status), the nature of the interchange (whether, say, species-typical or idiosyncratic), and the stage (initial or later) of interchange consolidation.

Three additional comments on the nature of interchange learning are in order.

1. Children undergo rapid changes in their ability to learn the consequences of interpersonal actions, anticipate and formulate the rules of interchanges, and interpret the expectations of others. Further, this information is stored and recalled seemingly in the same way that information about nonsocial events is processed (through tuition, observation, repetition, association). Hence information processing, memory organization, and concept identification are as relevant to the study of social behavior as they are for the traditionally "cognitive" issues of intelligence and academic performance. Furthermore, the same concepts used in the study of information processing seem directly applicable to the analysis of social interchanges.

2. Various noncognitive learning processes seem to be involved in social behavior, from the coordination of motor actions in interchanges and the consolidation of particular styles of behaving to the association of given contexts with the elicitation of action patterns. The nature of the conditioning that occurs (both within contexts and within interchanges) strongly implies that associative conditioning processes are at work (Atkinson and Estes, 1963; Cairns, 1966a; Estes, 1958). Within this conditioning framework, the occurrence of an interaction in a setting is sufficient to enhance the probability of its repetition when the setting is reinstituted.

3. In analyzing the events that occur within interchanges, we can distinguish between eliciting (activational, short-term) effects and learning effects (carryover to future encounters). This distinction between activation and learning has repeatedly been suggested by theorists concerned with interactional phenomena (see Sears, 1951; Patterson and Cobb, 1971). Patterson and Cobb (1971) refer to events in terms of whether they "facilitate" an ongoing interaction or "inhibit" it. These terms do not necessarily require learning (that is, modification of the probability of future action). The two functions of interpersonal stimuli appear to be intimately linked. The elicitation (or inhibition) of an act is assumed to increase the likelihood of the future occurrence (or nonoccurrence) of the action in that setting.

To summarize, interpersonal expectations and correlated psychobiological states can be influenced not only by direct experiences but by the information embedded in the context, instructions, and what is observed. It seems likely that the most reliable confirmation and disconfirmation of children's social expectations and actions are not vicarious, however. They occur in the give and take of the child's social experiences. Participation in interchanges cumulatively establishes for the child stable ways of acting in interpersonal settings. The child learns what to expect, from whom, and when to expect it. These expectations in turn are integrated with the child's actions and with the actions and attitudes that they provoke from other persons. If the setting and organisms remain reasonably constant, so will the interchanges.

The preceding comment implies that no single learning concept, including reinforcement, is sufficient to explain the recurrence, consolidation, generalization, and differentiation of interchanges.[6] What seems required is the application of learning concepts that are appropriate to the age-develop-

mental status of the organisms under investigation. In the case of children, this requires that explicit attention be given to cognitive processing and memory organization.

When Learning Is Not Required

Just as it is important to recognize the appropriateness of learning mechanisms and to determine their relationship with each other, it is important to specify when they are not required. The ontogenetic study of interchanges indicates that it is unnecessary to invoke learning concepts to explain the "acquisition" of some social patterns (for example, suckling, aggressive, and sexual behavior). Certain basic interchanges appear to become established in the absence of specific learning experiences, although each of the patterns seems "learnable" with respect to determining with whom, when and where the interchange occurs. Nor is prior learning always required for the recurrence and consolidation of interchanges. Psychobiological changes in the child (unlearned) accompany the recurrent performance of certain behaviors and may promote their occurrence in the future. The recognition that unlearned changes contribute to interchange establishment and persistence does not detract from the importance of learning mechanisms. It does remind us that the entire organism is involved in the establishment of social action patterns and that social learning must be viewed in the context of the developmental and psychobiological status of the children involved.

Some Applications

Although the issues of learning and organization are relevant to any theory of interchange development, we might reasonably ask how they relate to our understanding of everyday problems. Perhaps that question can be addressed with a modest example. Suppose that we wish to decrease the likelihood that our friend Peter (Chapter 1) will misbehave

[6] I will not extend this discussion of whether reinforcement is required for interactional learning to occur. Suffice it to say that nothing in this analysis contradicts the empirical law of effect (Postman, 1947). The essential problem is that advanced analyses of reinforcement (Bolles, 1972; Glickman and Schiff, 1967; Premack, 1959; Timberlake and Allison, 1974) have attempted to determine how the empirical "law" can be explained in more basic biological and conditioning terms. Further discussion of these matters can be found in these sources and in Rachlin (1976).

with one of his buddies, Mark. According to the present analysis, several different steps could be taken, each of which should decrease the probability that such an interchange would recur. We could physically separate Peter and Mark by reassigning one of them (say, Mark) to another play group in the school. But this obvious solution may simply transplant the problem to other groups, and generate new problems by virtue of Mark's unacceptablity to the new groups. Or we could concentrate on one (or both) member(s) of the pair and, by suggestion, direction, or coaching, involve him (them) in nondisruptive activities. Teacher involvement in the interchange may be required at first, but as the patterns became consolidated, the teacher could be gradually "phased out" of active participation. Since there is likely to be a reciprocity of behavior, Peter's behavior should also shift in a less disruptive direction. As a third alternative, the supporting context could be changed. The actions and reactions of other members of the group could be modified, or the nature of the group's activities, time of meeting (before outdoor play instead of just after it), or group structure (more rigid or less rigid) could be changed. These alternatives are not mutually exclusive and the choice would depend, in part, on the events that elicited and maintained the behavior.

An interchange analysis also suggests why certain strategies are not likely to be effective. For instance, if the recurrence principle is valid, simply ignoring the boys (nonreinforcement) could be tantamount to asking for more of the same behavior. Not only would the disruptive interchanges be expected to continue, they might escalate and get worse, influencing other children and other groups. If this result were obtained, it would contradict the widely accepted proposal that nonreinforcement of disruptive activities extinguishes them. Ignoring Peter and Mark could be interpreted by them as permission for the behavior and hence promote more disruption. The "gleeful" behavior of preschool children reflects the operation of a mutual facilitation process that has escalated in intensity (L. Sherman, 1975; S. Sherman, 1975).

Other examples that the reader may wish to consider include the effective handling of crying in infants (Chapter 6), the rehabilitation of a child designated as a social isolate in the classroom, or the redirection of peer-directed aggression in a 9-year-old boy. At a more general level, it is useful to consider the implications of the modification of an entire classroom (or school) of disruptive children.

The foregoing analysis forces attention to what supports and maintains the child's social patterns, whether the supports are interactional, contextual, or psychobiological. We have just touched on the issues that underlie the problems of continuity and change. These matters will be returned to in subsequent chapters.

Summary

Empirical studies of the interchanges of children "beyond attachment" have indicated the following.

■ Children's interchange patterns are not "one-dimensional." Even 1-year-old infants discriminate among the persons with whom they interact; and they selectively tease, beg, grab, hug, play, and aggravate. This capacity for interpersonal discrimination develops rapidly, and by the fourth year children have developed multiple and complex interaction strategies that they draw upon, depending on their expectations, the setting, and the actions of other persons.

■ The interaction patterns of children vary with context and relationship. Failure to take into account the conditions and context of the interaction severely limits one's ability to predict social behaviors.

■ Reciprocity in interchanges (where one child's acts are similar to, though not necessarily identical with, the acts of another) continues to be of basic importance beyond infancy. Information about the behavior of one child in an interchange provides a highly reliable index of the behavior of the other child, from 18 months onward. Reciprocity is one outcome of the constraints imposed by the behavior of one child on the behavior of another child.

■ Once an interchange has taken place, the probability of its recurrence is increased, especially if the circumstances are similar or unchanged. Repeated occurrences of an interchange pattern lead to its consolidation and integration. The generalization of interchanges across settings and relations is not automatic; it depends in part on the child's expectations and the nature of the interchange.

■ An examination of the learning mechanisms that are involved in interchanges requires that we consider information-processing concepts, associative conditioning, and the elicitation properties of interpersonal acts and settings. In particular, attention must be given to the special problems presented by the sequential nature of interchanges, and to the changes in cognitive processing and memory organization that occur in the course of development.

■ The same interactional learning processes that operate in parental-child relationships appear to operate in the child's interactions in the preschool and school. In effect, the child continues to adapt his social behaviors to new settings and relationships. We thus find a differentiation of the child's social patterns and a situational and relational specificity in many of his social actions.

In this chapter, I touched only lightly on the ways that changes in the developmental status of children are related to changes in children's interchange patterns, the interpretations they can make, and the reactions they elicit from other persons. This matter, which is basic to the establishment and modification of interchanges, will be returned to in later chapters.

III

SOCIAL INTERCHANGE
DEVELOPMENT

The aim of this part is to extend the developmental synthesis to the social and personality development that occurs after infancy. Accordingly, we will be concerned with the development of interpersonal control processes and the ontogeny of sexual identification, play, reciprocity, and altruism.

Ever since the seminal contributions of Darwin and Freud on the evolutionary and psychiatric significance of aggressive and sexual behaviors, they have been of nuclear concern to investigations of social and personality development. Freud recognized that these interpersonal functions are basic to all individuals and species. How sexual development proceeds—the selection of partners, the ontogeny of heterosexual or homosexual acts, the relation of arousal states to behavior, the dyadic synchronization of mating preferences—is still of central importance. Two key issues that will be covered in this section are the development of gender role in children and the relation of gender identification to sexual activities and attitudes.

Although there are problems in using a single term "aggression" to refer to all unpleasant acts that occur in relationships, the related developmental issues cannot be ignored or denied. "Aggression" covers the full range of interpersonal controls, from injury and punishment to symbolic gestures and threats. As the early major theorists—from Darwin to James to Freud—emphasized, aggression is intimately linked to interpersonal and societal control.

A final comment concerns the content of the next nine chapters. To analyze the essential problems of interchange ontogeny, information from the sister sciences concerned with development—zoology, genetics, sociology, linguistics, and psychology—must be synthesized. In photography, to gain perspective and to focus on detail, it is necessary to "zoom out" as well as to "zoom in." Some of the following nine chapters zoom out on related issues and fields in order to identify the main contributors to the synthesis; other chapters zoom in to show how these contributors complement each other in order to explain origin and change in interactions. As in the preceding part, we will first analyze the different ways that the synthesis occurs in nonhuman animals and then focus on the social systems of childhood.

9

THE DEVELOPMENT
OF AGGRESSIVE BEHAVIOR:
PSYCHOBIOLOGICAL FOUNDATIONS

In 1923 the League of Nations established a committee whose purpose was to define "aggression." In 1974, the group submitted its 350-word report to the United Nations. According to its working definition, aggression is the use of armed force by one state against another state in violation of its sovereignty. However, a key provision of the report was that the ultimate decision about whether or not an act is "aggression" was to be left to the judgment of the United Nations Security Council.

Why did it take more than half a century to arrive at a definition? Obviously the problems were less semantic than they were political and judgmental. The judgments had to do with whether the force had been provoked, what constitutes armed force, and whose independence was being threatened. For instance, was the American blockade of Cuba during the missle crisis of 1962 an act of aggression or an act of defense? Doubtless the answer would differ depending on whether the Kennedy administration or the Castro government was asked to judge.

Although there clearly are differences between the political and the behaviorial definitions of aggression, both definitions are similar in one basic respect. Between individuals, as well as between nations, judgments must be made to determine whether a given hurtful action was provoked or unprovoked, intended or accidental, hostile or benignant. Further, the judgment rendered usually depends on whose perspective is taken: the one injured or the one inflicting the injury.

Formulating a satisfactory definition of the behavioral concept of aggression is so difficult that one theorist gave up (R. Johnson, 1972) and another likened the task to "taking a stroll through a semantic jungle" (Bandura, 1973a, p. 2). Because of the multiplicity of actions that might be classified as aggressive, depending on their interpretation, their severity, and the context and relationships in which they might occur, Johnson reasoned that no single definition would suffice, so he offered none. However, Albert Bandura (1973a) defined aggression as "behavior that results in personal injury and the destruction of property" (p. 5). But he added that not all injuries are caused by aggression, and most aggressive acts involve not actual injury so much as intent to injure. Both agreed that aggression is not a "thing" or entity; rather, it is a social judgment about interchanges.

Happily, a developmental analysis does not require a definitional consensus. The problem of tracing the ontogeny of hurtful interchanges is empirical rather than semantic. Our task here will be to ascertain how physically painful interchanges occur in the course of development and what their consequences are for the relationships concerned. Hurtful interchanges might be called play, or punishment, or fighting. Which seems intuitively to fit will depend on such factors as age of the interactors, their relationships to each other, and the sheer intensity of their behavior. Before one organism can hurt another, it must have developed the capacity to do so. The development of this capacity in nonhuman animals and its elaboration in interactional relationships will be the focus of this chapter and the next.

First we will consider the multiple functions of aggressive acts; then we will trace the ontogeny of aggressive behavior in three different nonhuman species. In the last part of this chapter, we will analyze the biological and genetic factors that have been linked to the development of this behavior. In Chapter 10 we will learn how social learning processes, combined with physiological processes, account for the maintenance and change of aggressive interchanges.

Why Aggression?
An Evolutionary Perspective

Why do hurtful acts occur in the first place? Implicit in many accounts of such behavior has been the assumption that such responses are basically nonfunctional—that they reflect the "dark side" of human nature and are something to be inhibited or redirected. This ancient idea was given endorsement in the psychonanalytic theory of violent and sadomasochistic behavior (Bibring, 1969; Freud, 1959). In one version of the psychoanalytic theory of motivation, Freud viewed aggression as an inevitable behavioral consequent of the Thanatos (death) instinct. The ultimate goal of the Thanatos energy was a "return to the quiescence of the inorganic world," achieved by the destruction of the self and others. According to this view, aggressive behavior was socially nonfunctional and without redeeming features—it was the very antithesis of survival. The individual and the species persisted *despite* the operation of this inborn propensity.

Other psychologists in Freud's time concurred that there was an inborn disposition to behave in a violent and aggressive manner, but, unlike Freud, they acknowledged that there were some useful features of the behavior. William James (1890) felt that the human instinct of pugnacity contributed to fitness, to the betterment of the species, and to population control. He wrote:

> In many respects man is the most ruthelessly ferocious of beasts. As with all gregarious animals, "two souls," as Faust says, "dwell within his breast," the one of sociability and helpfulness, the other of jealousy and antagonism to his mates. Though in a general way he cannot live without them, yet, as regards certain individuals, it often falls out that he cannot live with them either. Constrained to be a member of a tribe, he still has a right to decide, as far as in him lies, of which other members the tribe shall consist. Killing off a few obnoxious ones may often better the chances of those that remain (pp. 409–410).

Partly because of the excesses of early purposive explanations of aggressive behavior, psychologists have been wary of the concepts of "adaptation" and "survival properties." As a result, they have usually ignored these concepts, the problems they represent, and any clarification they may offer. But fortunately, these issues have reappeared, partly because they have been a central concern of behavioral biologists from Darwin's time to the present. For Darwin, agonistic behavior and conflict were essential to perpetuation of the species. The individual's ability to compete with others of his kind for food, shelter, and sexual partners determined who should survive.

Biological theory has extended the Darwinian model to explain particular aspects of social organization and population distribution (see Etkin, 1964; Wilson, 1975). In particular, ecologist V. C. Wynne-Edwards (1962) has argued that aggressive interactions serve a critical function in the control of population density. He proposes that animal populations are regulated by homeostatic mechanisms that strike a balance between the density of the population and the critical resources that are available. Competition and aggressive behavior ensure that there will be an optimal allocation within each group.

But there is a paradox in the Wynne-Edwards proposal. If natural selection results in increasingly more competitive animals, then why are most higher mammals so gregarious? In a reversal of the notion that competition and aggression are disruptive to society, Wynne-Edwards (1962) argues that these activities are necessary for the survival of a cohesive population. Society is thus defined as "an organization capable of providing conventional competition" (p. 14). The key concept here is "conventional competition," which is presumed to be essential for the maintenance of population homeostasis. "Conventional" competition differs from the unrestrained type in that it involves only ritualized visual displays and threats, which ensure the integrity of social hierarchies and territories. If the efficacy of such signals diminishes, then the very integrity of the society is threatened. Unrestrained attack would be disruptive and ultimately devastating for social organization.

Similarly, Konrad Lorenz (1966) proposed that the aggressive drive is fundamental to interindividual attraction and group cohesion. Aggressive acts elicit acts of ritualized appeasement, and these, in turn, permit the behaviors of two or more individuals to become intertwined and mutually dependent. Lorenz has proposed that in addition to providing the basis for social organization, aggression serves three basic species-survival functions:

1. Maintenance of optimal population distribution within a society and between societies.

2. Mate selection and the maintenance of an optimal gene pool.

3. Brood defense and the protection of the young of the species.

Intriguing as the "group selection" evolutionary interpretations offered by Wynne-Edwards may be, they have been for the most part rejected by contemporary population biologists in favor of "individual selection" or "gene selection" explanations. A key difference among the theories is the unit that is presumed to be selected for in evolution—whether it is the group (society or species), the individual organism, or the genes themselves. Hence the recent focus has shifted from what aggressive acts can do for the society to what they can do for individuals in fulfilling their "ultimate" assignment of conveying their genes to later generations. One insight in current formulations is that individuals can perpetuate their genes by enhancing the survival of their own offspring *or* by enhancing the survival of the offspring of their close relatives (many of whose genes are the same as the individual's own). The latter alternative, or "kin selection," underlies the genetic theory of altruism that has been brilliantly formulated by W. D. Hamilton (1964). By helping one's close relatives (such as full siblings or cousins), one can literally help oneself in enhancing one's "inclusive genetic fitness" (conveying one's genes directly plus conveying them via relatives).

Another way of putting the matter is to say that individuals are essentially "gene machines." Richard Dawkins (1976) has thus proposed that organisms are basically huge apparatuses that have been designed by genes to perpetuate themselves. Whatever behavior patterns do the job most effectively—whether aggression or passivity, altruism or selfishness—should be favored in the course of evolution.

But the specific problem remains: Why do most individuals stop short of killing competitors who are not closely related to them (or doing away with obnoxious second cousins)? One individual selection answer to this question has been offered by the game theory analysis of geneticist John Maynard

Smith (1974). To determine the genetic consequences of a behavior pattern that is almost universal in a population, Maynard Smith argues, it is necessary to take into account the nature of the counter-responses that will be provided and initiated by other indivduals. For instance, a "hawk strategy" (fighting to the death) has been calculated by Maynard Smith to be a low-payoff interpersonal strategy if all of one's opponents are likely to reciprocate with the same strategy. Alternative patterns, such as "conventional competition" or a "dove strategy" (running away and making love, not war), would usually yield higher genetic payoffs. If such an "optimal" strategy persists across generations, it is called an "evolutionarily stable strategy" (ESS).

Before we leave this brief (and incomplete) overview of evolution and aggression, mention should be made of recent attempts to reassess the relationship between the two in terms of the dynamics of the social system in which agressive acts occur. Even contemporary selection explanations have tended to view aggression as if it were a unitary characteristic or "strategy" that can be conveyed from generation to generation, much like the color of one's eyes. The alternative would be to view social patterns as growing out of the demands of the socio-ecological system in which they occur (Crook, Ellis, and Goss-Custard, 1976). According to this view, whether fights are destructive, restrained, or inhibited would depend on the total configuration of societal organization. Modest shifts in the energy resources available, predation pressures, or changes in the genetic timing of individual development would produce compensatory changes in the level and intensity of aggressive acts that are favored by the system. The problem, of course, is to specify precisely which changes are most important, and why.

Although these *ultimate* or evolutionary considerations may seem remote from *proximal* or immediate determinants of aggressive behaviors, they cannot be overlooked in a developmental framework. If Crook et al. (1976) are correct, the two levels of analysis are interdependent (see also Hinde, 1970; Kuo, 1967; and Tinbergen, 1972).

Territories and Hierarchies

To maintain itself, a society must somehow achieve an equilibrium between energy supply and energy demand. One way to achieve such a balance in animal societies is to establish "territories." A presumed function of such territories is to distribute the society relative to resources.

Territoriality. The concepts of territory and conventional competition require further elaboration. Consider, for example, the social organization of the prairie dog. These small animals, about 14–17 inches in length at maturity, are members of the squirrel family. Approximately 1,000 of them live together in towns. In the 75-acre prairie-dog town in the Black Hills of South Dakota, studied by King (1955), the property was subdivided by the animals into small units. The members of the subgroups, called clans or coteries, share the burrows and resources of a small area. The area defended by the coterie covers about 7/10 of an acre and accommodates groups, on the average, of 4 adult animals and 6 young animals of both sexes (see Figure 9-1).

The relations between members of a coterie are congenial: the animals frequently groom and play with each other. Interactions with animals from other coteries, however, are characterized by hostility and bluffing.

King (1959) has provided us with an excellent description of the role of "conventional competition" in territorial disputes (see Figure 9-2):

> When a coterie member, foraging at the limits of its own territory, passes into an adjoining territory, a resident of the area rushes up to drive it away. The invader may be only a few feet outside its own territory and, failing to recognize that it is trespassing, may refuse to yield. The ensuing struggle is a stereotyped ritual that consists more of threat than fight. The animals rush toward each other, stop short and freeze face to face. Then, in a kind of reverse kissing encounter, one of the disputants turns, raises and spreads its tail, exposing its anal glands, and waits for the other to approach. The latter cautiously draws near and

Figure 9-1. Prairie dog families divide their "towns" into territories (*a, b, c,* and *d*), the borders of which they zealously guard. Numbered areas at upper left are new territories established by emigrating adults. Territory *c* is in the process of being split. Solid circles indicate large, active burrows; open circles indicate smaller burrows; dots are holes without craters. Each square is 50 feet wide. (From J. A. King, The Social Behavior of Prairie Dogs. Copyright © 1959 by Scientific American, Inc. All rights reserved.)

sniffs. Then they exchange roles; they alternate in this way until the stalemate is broken by an attempt of one to bite the rump of the other. The bitten contestant (prairie dogs are rarely scarred) backs away a few feet and then returns to the fray. The dispute is often accompanied by much rushing back and forth and repetition of the smelling encounters. Finally some arbitrary boundary is established and the antagonists return to their foraging (p. 133).

Boundary disputes in other territorial mammals are similar in many respects to that just described. A salient feature of the encounters is that the "compe-

Figure 9-2. Prairie dog territorial boundaries are maintained by specific interchanges. For example, an identification kiss is exchanged whenever the animals meet (*upper right*). Nonrecognition is followed by a tail-raising ritual in which the animals alternately sniff each other's anal glands (*lower left*), attempt to bite each other's rump, stalk off (*lower right*), and then repeat the ritual until one animal retreats a few feet. Rarely does either suffer more than a nip. (From J. A. King, The Social Behavior of Prairie Dogs. Copyright © 1959 by Scientific American, Inc. All rights reserved.)

tition" is typically settled without lethal or even serious injury. Same-species fighting, as it occurs in the natural setting, is rarely destructive. Even the spectacular bouts that are observed in wild mountain sheep and moose during the mating season rarely terminate in serious injury.

Patterns of territoriality vary with the species and its habitat. Mice and rats defend the areas in which they live only under certain conditions. As the amount of space expands, the number of males that defend territories also increases. Crowcroft (1966) has published a witty and informative account of how this expansion-contraction process operates in a community of mice living in a silo. In sheep, the arrangements are more complicated. Subgroups of female sheep tend to band together and graze in selected areas, or "home ranges." Different subgroups may occupy the same section of the home range, but at different times of the day (Grubb and Jewell, 1966). Thus one subgroup may occupy the hillside in the very early hours of the day but move to shore areas at midday. When the first parcel of land is vacated, another group may move in, without conflict. "Territory" thus can be relative to the temporal as well as to the spatial dimension.

Although it is generally agreed that territories serve, among other things, to distribute the members of a society relative to its resources, it should be pointed out that there are also psychobiological controls of population density. These include the role of social stimuli in controlling estrous cycles (Whitten, 1956), blocking pregnancy (Adler and Zoloth, 1970; Parkes and Bruce, 1961), and preventing infant mortality (Calhoun, 1973). To assign the entire burden for population control to aggression is too restrictive an interpretation; multiple biological and ecological factors interact to achieve optimal levels.

Social Hierarchies. Within an intact group, the rigidity and explicitness of social rank orders differ with the size and species of the group. In some species, such as the common barnyard chicken, "dominance orders" are strict and linear. One hen dominates the other chickens in the living enclosure; she assumes control of their food, water, and roosting places. If and when perogatives are challenged, the subordinate receives a severe peck. In a falling-domino process, the injured party will then often peck any subordinate animal that it encounters, and so on down the line. Hence the term "pecking order." Once established, pecking orders become resistant to change—a type of "social inerita" develops (Guhl, 1968; Guhl and Fischer, 1969). Dyadic interactions are formed such that subordinates tend to maintain their relative rank even when given injections with androgen hormones (known to increase fighting ability). Furthermore, instances of blatant attack diminish as the length of time that the animals are together increases. After the relationships within the society have become consolidated, subtle shifts in posture are sufficient to signify social rank.

Stable social hierarchies have been observed in primate groups, but the social systems of primates are varied and complex, and the hierarchies are not necessarily generalized from one context to another (Strayer, Bovenkerk, and Koopman, 1975). Alliances can form between the mother and her young, between male and female consorts, between entire families, between male-male pairs, and between male triads. In the case of the Japanese macaque, status is a shared or "social class" characteristic (Stephenson, 1975). When threatened, the offspring of higher-class females can recruit help and thus maintain their privileged rank. But most often aggressive acts are unnecessary. In primate groups, as in other stable societies, there is ordinarily little need for attacks and fighting. Dyadic and group relations stablize and become self-maintaining. A consolidated social system can be a powerful catalyst for the continuity of interchanges.

Mate Selection

There is not always a correlation between aggressive capabilities and aggression and sexual potency. The more aggressive male is not always the more successful one in reproduction. For instance, extremely aggressive male mice are sometimes more preoccupied with fighting than with copulating (Crowcroft, 1966; Levine et al., 1965). Similarly, there is not always a correlation between the aggressiveness of male dogs and their attractiveness to female dogs (Beach, 1969).

Nonetheless, that aggression is associated with reproduction cannot be denied. In free-ranging herd animals, such as deer, moose, and wild sheep, bouts of fighting are most likely to occur during the mating season (Altmann, 1963; Darling, 1937; Geist, 1971). Further, the dominant male typically has a reproductive advantage. Field studies indicate that dominant elephant seals, which constitute only 4 percent of the male population, mate with approximately 85 percent of the females (Le Boeuf and Peterson, 1969). The dominant sage grouse accounts for 75 percent of the mating (Wiley, 1973). Similarly, DeFries and McClearn (1970) report that the "autocrat" in a colony of mice sires more than 90 percent of the progeny produced by the colony. After a social hierarchy has been established, the higher-ranking animals have more access to food, water, and mates.

Brood Defense

Do mothers fight to protect their infants? To date, the clearest evidence is provided by laboratory studies of rodent mothers, who viciously attack certain intruders. These studies indicate that maternal females are more likely than nonmaternal females to attack male or female rodent intruders—particularly 3–12 days after birth (Green and Cairns, 1976; Svare and Gandelman, 1973). These females are selective in attacking members of their own kind (Figure 9-3). They typically permit human "intruders" to replace and remove their infants without challenging or attempting to bite them. One exception to this generalization is the finding by Susan Scholz (1974) that maternal rats will attack (or try to attack) the experimenter if only half of their litter is taken from the rearing compartment but show little or no disruption if the entire litter is removed. The reason for this difference is unknown; possibly the disruption results from having to sort through half of the offspring. It seems reasonable to believe that the post-partum aggressive effect is not limited to maternal rats, but information about other species is meager. Similarly, the precise determinants of post-partum attacks have yet to be identified, although changes in hormonal states in the post-partum period have been clearly implicated (Svare and Gandelman, 1973).

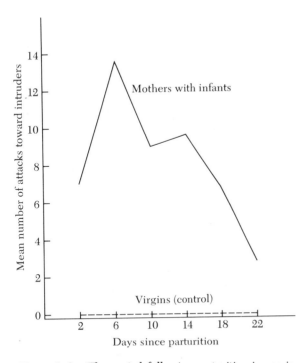

Figure 9-3. The period following parturition is one in which female mice are most likely to attack intruders, whether male, female, or juvenile. The probability diminishes sharply as the young reach weaning age (day 21). Introduction of an intruder into compartments of nonmaternal females rarely elicits attacks (control). (Data from Green and Cairns, 1976.)

Why Not Aggression?
Interactional Functions in Development

Up to this point, the discussion has been restricted to the presumed survival functions of aggressive behavior for the species. These functions have often been sufficient to "explain" why such behavior occurs. But as D. O. Hebb (1953) and D. S. Lehrman (1970) have pointed out, assumptions of evolutionary function, although useful, tend to provide answers when more questions are called for. Speculations about the survival functions of aggressive behavior do not consider the processes that are responsible for the development and instigation of fighting throughout the life of the individual. Why do members of the same species differ in their propensity to attack? The likelihood that an individual will attack varies with his psychobiological status at that moment and the setting in which he is maintained. Why do such day-to-day or place-to-place fluctuations occur? It is known that genetic, biochemical, and neurological manipulations can increase or decrease the probability that particular individuals will fight in particular settings. To obtain a satisfactory answer to the question "why aggression?" we must analyze the development of aggressive behavior.

Notwithstanding psychological legends to the contrary, punishment is a most effective method of inhibiting or redirecting behavior (Church, 1963; Solomon, 1964). When punishment occurs in a dyadic relationship, one of the immediate results is an abrupt change in the ongoing behavior of the other individual. It seems entirely reasonable to expect that in the normal process of growing up, there will be multiple occasions in which hurtful acts will occur in relationships and that the young animal will be both victim and offender. By way of example, in some species the mothers effectively use punishment to disrupt the feeding patterns of their offspring when it comes time for weaning. And puppies that are hurt or too vigorously tossed about by their littermates often curb this behavior by nipping or growling. Pain—or events that signal it—serves to inhibit and redirect activities.

In light of the multiple control properties of aggression throughout development, perhaps we should ask "why *not* aggression?" rather than "why aggression?" The wonder may be that aggressive acts are so rare.

Aggressive Interchanges in Normal Development

The aim of this section is to profile how the development of aggressive behaviors proceeds in three mammalian species: dogs, hamadryas baboons, and mice. The goal is to illustrate, not to catalogue or survey, the range and diversity of the patterns of aggressive development in mammals. There are great differences between, as well as within, mammalian orders in most social behaviors, and aggression is no exception (Crook et al., 1976; Eisenberg, 1977). Nonetheless, there are some advantages to be gained from describing how these differences—and similarities—come about in the course of ontogeny.

Development of Aggressive Behaviors in Dogs

Immediately following birth, the young dog is scarcely able to satisfy independently even his most primitive needs. Thermoregulation is achieved in part by huddling with others of the litter in a heap, and defecation and urination are dependent upon stimulation by the mother. Puppies' eyes do not open until approximately 13 days after birth, and standing is not observed until about 21 days (Fuller and Fox, 1969; Scott and Fuller, 1965). It is all the more noteworthy, therefore, that playful fighting among the puppies begins at about day 15—virtually as soon as the young animal can move around in a reasonably coordinated fashion. At first the pups chew each other's fur or lick each other's faces. Such activity frequently elicits reciprocal licking and chewing. At about the third week, the mouthing and biting increases rapidly. The targets are their own and each other's bodies, and various parts of the mother's anatomy (her ears, tail, leg "feathers," back fur). Nor is the experimenter exempt. The occupational hazards of direct observation include mutilated shoes and gnawed ankles.

Rheingold (1963) observed five purebred litters and described her observations:

On day 27, tossing the head while holding in the mouth some part of another pup's body, head, neck or back, was observed. On the same day, too, crouching of the forepart of the body appeared as a prelude to play. Pouncing on and lunging into each other followed within a few days. These activities were freely combined, often accompanied by mouthing and biting, and they increased in frequency and vigor. During the second month, rough and tumble play with much biting, running, and chasing was observed whenever the pups were not eating or sleeping. Often the play involved the whole litter, at times only a part of it, and occasionally a pup would play by himself, prancing, charging, twirling, and shadow boxing (pp. 196–197).

Soon the activities become less like play and more like fighting. In the second month, the tussling is sometimes accompanied by growling, snarling, biting, and painful yelps. The fights become increasingly severe with the eruption of teeth and the development of the large muscle systems. By the seventh week after birth, puppies that are left together in litters begin to attack each other. The target animal is usually, but not always, the smallest of the litter. In most breeds, the "gang-ups" are episodic and ephermeral. But pups of certain breeds, such as the fox terrier, can be permanently maimed or killed. Scott and Fuller (1965) cite a case in which the three smallest members of a litter of 6 terrier pups were females. When 5 of the pups began to terrorize one of the females, she was removed. Then the others began to attack the next smallest female, until she was removed. At that point, the 3 males directed their attacks at the sole remaining female. The attacks certainly were not of the playful variety. In these groups, "one puppy would get hold of the ears and another the tail, stretching their victim between them, while the third animal attacked in the middle" (Scott and Fuller, 1965, p. 106). For the animal suspended in the center, the behavior hardly seemed like a playful tussle.

In the third and fourth months, dominance relationships clearly emerge in some breeds. Dominance among dogs has been measured in various ways. One of the most popular techniques is to observe the competition between two hungry dogs for possession of food or a bone (James, 1951; Pawlowski and Scott, 1956). Among basenjis and fox terri-

ers, two breeds that are relatively aggressive at maturity (in terms of intragroup fighting), dominance relationships are obvious by the fifteenth week. The dominance patterns of less aggressive breeds, such as cocker spaniels and beagles, are less stable or clearly defined at that age, or even later.

The development of aggressive behavior in the dog is fairly continuous. Biting and gnawing increase as a function of age from the second week on. By the time the dog reaches maturity and begins to fight in earnest, it has a considerable backlog of playful fighting experience to draw upon.

Do early playful fighting experiences affect the development of attack and fighting behaviors? For instance, will a dog that has not had these experiences be handicapped relative to one that has had intralitter training? We have already observed that the mother frequently responds to the playful advances of the pups by engaging in counterplay. But at about the seventh week post-partum, her tolerance decreases. During the weaning process, she becomes increasingly wary of the pups' approaches. She avoids the pups and on occasion nips them when they compete with her for food (Fuller and Fox, 1969; Scott and Fuller, 1965). It seems reasonable to expect that these maternal activities facilitate weaning, but the necessary controlled experiments have not been conducted. The question remains whether her attacks somehow facilitate the development of fighting behavior in her offspring. We will return to these issues after analyzing aggressive development in two other species.

Development of Aggressive Behaviors in Hamadryas Baboons

In an early review of primate behavior, Elliot (1913) wrote that hamadryas baboons are "dangerous animals when adult, possessing savage and ugly dispositions" (p. 116). The classic observations of Sir Solly Zuckerman (1932) in the zoos of London confirmed the reputation of these animals for aggression. Recent field work suggests they are "savage and ugly," but only on occasion and sometimes for good reason (Kummer and Kurt, 1963; Kummer, 1968, 1971). Attacks and punishment play a primary role in the integration and organization of interanimal relationships at virtually every level of the hamadryas society. [1]

The following accounts of baboon behavior (Kummer, 1968) illustrate how aggressive acts can help to consolidate and preserve relationships in the one-male unit, the elementary harem group in the hamadryas social organization.

A male, having just arrived at the sleeping rock, turns suddenly and rushes 30 meters back along the on-coming column. An adult female from the farthest party runs toward him and receives a bite on the back of the neck. Squealing, she follows the male up to the sleeping rock where his other females are waiting (p. 36).

An adult male is leaving the sleeping rock followed by his females. On the way, one of these presents her swelling to a subadult male who then mounts her. As they are copulating, the unit leader looks back, causing the two to separate and the young male to flee. The leader attacks his female and after biting her on the back, mounts her himself p. 41).

A fight breaks out on the sleeping rock. As soon as it begins, Smoke looks up, advances quickly to the farthest of his females and hits her gently on the head with his hand (p. 36).

These observations suggest that punishment for straying has the paradoxical effect of bringing the members of the unit closer together. Apparently the contingency of the punishment largely determines which behavior will be inhibited. In these instances, the females were punished for straying, or for seducing.

---

[1] A note on the organization of hamadryas societies is in order. The social structure is arranged in the following hieraracy: *troop*, the largest social group consists of as many as 750 animals that travel together and sleep in the same area; under certain conditions the group may split up into several *bands*, consisting of 30 to 90 animals; each band is composed of several *one-male units*, comprised of one adult male and 1 to 9 females with their young. Frequently two males cooperate in leading their units; such pairs of unit leaders are called two-male teams (Kummer, 1968).

What is the course of development of these behaviorial propensities, particularly in the male of the species?

1. *Behavior in early infancy (birth to 6 months).* For the first 10 days, the infant receives the mother's constant and solicitous attention. Grooming, the dominant and most time-consuming interaction among baboons, is especially intensive in this period. The infant is kept on the mother's stomach or in her arms virtually all the time. During travel, he clings to her undersides or back.

From birth to 4–6 months of age, baboon infants are distinguished by hair that is completely or partially black, but that changes to brown hair at about 6 months. Infants whose coats are black can crawl over or onto other baboons, including adult males, without reprimand. Sometimes the older black infants form play groups with other black infants. Even at this point in life, young hamadryas baboon males are more likely than young females to become involved in play activities with peers.

Similarly, at the age of 2 months, rhesus monkey male infants become involved in rough-and-tumble play with each other more frequently than do female infants (Harlow, 1965). Rough-and-tumble play appears to be for some primates what playful fighting is for the puppy: noninjurious wrestling, rolling, and sham biting. The basic threat response appears prominently in the rhesus male's behavior in about the second month. It has been described as "stiffening of the posture, staring at the other monkey, flattening the hair on the top of the head, retracting the lips, baring the teeth" (Harlow, 1965, p. 239). Sex differentiation in activity occurs at about the sixtieth day after birth in the rhesus monkey.

2. *Behavior in later infancy (6–12 months).* During this period the male hamadryas infant spends increasingly more time away from the mother and in the company of the peer group. Their interactions include running, chasing, tumbling, nipping, and tail-pulling, each activity lasting up to 10 minutes. Infants that have lost their black coats appear also to have lost whatever special status they had with respect to adults. When the infants exceed the limit in their interactions with adults, they are frequently punished or rebuffed by a mild attack.

3. *Behavior of juveniles (1–3 years).* Play activities with peers occupy an increasing proportion of the time of juvenile males, and these activities become more and more boisterous and energetic. If females are initially involved, they tend to drop out as the "play" becomes more vigorous. Mutual assaults sometimes escalate to attacks; at that point adult baboons intervene, and further "play" is temporarily inhibited. At about 2 years of age, males develop a strong affinity for each other. Male hamadryas baboons may still maintain some ties with the maternal unit during periods of travel, but during rest periods they assemble at the troops' periphery and play with each other.

At 3 years of age, playful fighting among males is much less frequent, although it still occurs. Rather than engage in playful fighting, 3-year-old males tend to groom each other. They continue to remain away from the group, at the periphery of the troop.

Female hamadryas juveniles, from the ages of 1 to 1½ years, are often kidnapped from the home unit by young, low-ranking adult males. Kummer offers the intriguing hypothesis that such "child brides" are the nucleus of new one-male units. Kummer's analysis suggests that the juvenile females form strong social bonds with their captors. At sexual maturity, the females then become the primary members of the single-unit harem.

In summary, the precursors of adult aggressive patterns are found in the interactions of one-year-old, and younger, baboon infants. The playful fighting of juvenile males is gradually replaced by grooming behavior in subadulthood. What fighting later occurs is less playful, particularly when it is between two males. Milder forms of aggressive behaviors—neck bites, threats, slaps—become contingent upon specific transgressions of females and young members of the family unit. The conditions that elicit aggressive behavior change drastically, as do the form and intensity of the responses.

Development of Aggressive Behaviors in Mice

In most basic respects, the ontogeny of the behavior of the mouse in the first 2 weeks following birth is similar to that of the species already discussed. The newborn mouse is, if anything, less physically mature and more dependent than the puppy or primate infant. Mice mature faster, however. By the fourteenth or fifteenth day, their eyes have opened, they are covered with hair, and they can stand and move about independently.

Attempts to trace the onset of aggressive behavior in this species have yielded consistent results (Cairns and Scholz, 1973; Uhrich, 1938). Before day 15, there are few interchanges between members of the group. However, young mice (like most other young mammals) tend to "clump" together or heap themselves on one another. There is little rough-and-tumble play or mutual grooming at this stage of development. Physical interaction usually occurs only as a byproduct of some other activity (such as burrowing into the clump for thermoregulation, suckling from the mother, or digging in the bedding). When such contact is made, the other individual rarely takes notice of it (that is, the ongoing activity is rarely disrupted).

In the third week (days 14–21), the physical and locomotive capabilities of mice undergo dramatic changes, but "intentional" interchanges are still infrequent. From time to time, a young mouse will dart across the compartment, and this darting on occasion creates a Ping-Pong ball effect because the stimulation causes other young mice to dash across the compartment. Attacks (biting at each other's fur or wrestling) do not occur before approximately the twenty-first day if the animals are permitted a normal diet. The onset of such behavior is a function of age, but since the animal's size, stage of sexual maturity, and social actions are highly dependent on maturation status, which in turn depends on the adequacy of post-partum diet, chronological age is relative. As shown in Figure 9-4, attacks occur in the fourth week (days 21–30) in both male and female groups.

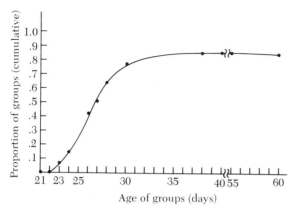

Figure 9-4. Onset of attack behavior in mice reared in small groups occurs typically between weaning and puberty. (Sexual maturity in mice occurs between day 32 and day 40.) Graph shows the cumulative proportion of 14 groups of ICR mice in which fighting attacks were first observed as a function of the age of group members ($n=5$ per group; 7 male groups, 7 female groups). (From Cairns and Scholz. Copyright © 1973 by the American Psychological Association. Reprinted by permission.)

A significant difference between the development of attacking in mice and the development of such behavior in the other species that we surveyed (baboons, dogs) is that adult forms of the behavior are not seen in the interchanges of infantile or juvenile mice. Indeed, there are few extended interchanges of any sort (grooming, playful fighting, or chasing) among young mice. The attacks that occur seem to emerge in the absence of any specific social precursors such as playful fighting or trussling. The playful fighting and shadowboxing of puppies and primates are never observed in mice; rather, aggressive acts in mice emerge in a near adult form.

Are adult mice then relatively docile? No, despite their Disneyland image. Under certain conditions *Mus musculus* (house mice) are brutally vicious toward members of their own kind—sometimes violent enough to kill their victims. The adult male mouse will indeed attack both females and infants. When adult males that have been isolated since

weaning are placed together in groups, they typically become involved in an orgy of violence that often terminates only when the weakest members of the group are literally torn apart. Even though they have had no "practice," these male rodents are exceedingly adept at performing the essential acts of aggression. Adult females, however, are less likely to attack, submit more readily, and rarely "fight."

These descriptions illustrate the events in development that precede the occurrence of hurtful behaviors in the young of 3 different species. The differences among them are perhaps more striking than the similarities, and the three merely illustrate the diversity that exists among mammalian species. Nonetheless, there appear to be some common features despite the diversity. The following list is necessarily both tentative and speculative:

1. Aggressive activities occur early, frequently, and, seemingly, inevitably. Throughout their development, the young are both perpetrators and victims.

2. Despite differences in the precursors of attack onset across species, certain age-related trends are general. In particular, with increasing age there is a diminution in the frequency of attacks and an increase in their intensity and damage-producing potential.

3. Aggressive behaviors occur in a variety of relationships (mother-infant and father-juvenile, as well as among peers of varying ages) and in a wide range of situations.

4. Sex differences in aggressive behaviors emerge early in most but not all species; males are typically more likely than females to become involved in assertive-aggressive actions (but see discussion later in this chapter).

5. Some hurtful acts performed by the young have definite functions in that they disrupt or change the behavior of others. Not all of them can be so interpreted, however. A good many instances of playful fighting appear to be just that—attempts to engage other individuals in vigorous interchanges.

6. Accounts of normal development leave open the question of whether the preadult forms of aggressive behavior are necessary precursors of adult fighting. The fact that mice, an unusually violent species, fail to engage in playful fighting as juveniles suggests that such "training" may not be necessary—in this species, at least.

Descriptions of the normal development of hurtful activities do not explain discrepancies between species. To obtain more precise answers concerning the necessary and sufficient conditions for the establishment of aggressive behavior, we must analyze the results of attempts to isolate the contributions of particular psychobiological factors.

Psychobiological Considerations in the Development of Aggressive Interchanges

In this section we will consider the ways in which the development of aggressive behavior is paced by morphological, neurological, and hormonal factors and will attempt to answer the question of whether differences in aggressive patterns are heritable within species.

Morphological Development

The more violent forms of fighting are obviously paced by the ontogeny of necessary structural and muscular systems. The young dog must develop the bodily strength and canine teeth necessary for waging effective attacks; the hamadryas baboon must develop enormous strength in the forelimbs to compete successfully; and various herd animals cannot effectively fight until specialized antlers and horns have developed. However, it seems misleading to assign only a preparatory role to morphological development. The changes in structure also have consequences that have not usually been viewed as aid-ing aggression but that nonetheless produce pain or injury in the partner. They are associated with a termination of weaning, detachment, and formation of new relationships. Morphological changes can modify the nature of the dyadic relationship.

Doubtless the changes in the morphology of the young that make suckling painful for the mother and other food-getting behavior possible for the juvenile are most important, because they are linked to the onset of weaning, the resumption of estrous cycling in the mother, and the formation of new social patterns by the offspring independently of the mother. Different mammalian groups have evolved unique solutions to problems posed by the inevitable morphological changes in their young. Adult prairie dogs, for instance, escape from the young by migrating from the home territory to the outskirts of the "town." Adult hamadryas baboons achieve the same result but more aggressively. The unit leaders punish the male juveniles, thereby forcing them to form groups at the perimeter of the troop. In both instances, there is a definite change in interactions that occur between the young, their peers, and adults.

What happens if species-typical morphological changes occur in development and such immature behaviors as chewing, gnawing, and chasing others persist? As we have seen, playful fighting in young terriers can persist until the victim is terrorized and/or killed, if there is no inhibitive feedback. "Unintended" homicide can also occur when a puppy is permitted to grow up in the company of a smaller, more vulnerable species, such as a rabbit (Cairns and Werboff, 1967).

Injuries to young animals are obviously not limited to cross-specific pairings. They reflect the more general consequences of a relationship between two animals of grossly unequal physical structure in which the superior one fails to inhibit the more vigorous responses of the other. The mother-young relationship is a case in point. Infant abuse is not limited to human mothers. If the female fails to control her vigorous responses toward her young (recall the motherless rhesus monkeys), then the survival of the

Table 9-1. How hormonal changes affect fighting behavior of quails.

Experimental treatment	Males			Females		
	Number	"Good" fighters		Number	"Good" fighters	
		Percent	n		Percent	n
Normal birds	50	56	28	50	12	6
Gonadectomized birds	40	25	10	40	10	4
"Restored" birds (gonadectomy, implantation)	40	50	20	40	30	12
Testosterone injections (normal before injection)	50	84	42	50	34	17
Testosterone injections (poor fighters before injection)	30	63	19	30	40	12
Gonadectomized birds (good fighters before operation)	30	17	5	20	80	16
Sham operation (good fighters before operation)	20	90	18	20	95	19

SOURCE: Adapted from Kuo, 1960, with permission.

young animal is jeopardized. As a result of growth-determined changes, the relations between the mother and her offspring, and among offspring, undergo continuous realignment. Moreover, the reactions provoked during the interchange not only promote realignment, they require it.

Hormonal Action and the Development of Aggressive Behaviors

Along with changes in morphology, significant modifications occur in the hormonal organization of mammalian young and those with whom they interact. At least some of the changes have been directly related to variations in the occurrence of fighting.

Gonadal Development. At sexual maturity, the fighting of the males of most species begins to differ sharply from that of females. Kuo (1960) attempted to analyze the contribution of hormonal changes to, and the sex differences in, this aggressive behavior. Using Japanese quails, Kuo established that approximately 50 percent of the males could be trained to be "good" fighters. His system for discriminating between a "good" and a "poor" fighter was a complex

one, the details of which need not concern us here. Kuo found that if the birds were castrated by removal of testicular tissue at 8 weeks of age, the proportion of good fighters produced at maturity was only 25 percent of the total (Table 9-1). Compared with a normal (noncastrated) population, sham operations[2] did not yield significant difference. In a conclusive demonstration that the gonadectomy was the effective manipulation, Kuo showed, using two different methods, that it could be reversed. One method used was replacement therapy, in which the animals were given a series of testosterone injections. The other method was reimplantation of testicular tissue in the gonadectomized animals. Both procedures increased the number of successful fighters to approximately 50 percent. Even more interesting was Kuo's demonstration that normal fighters can be transformed into "super" males by hormone treatment. By giving injections of testosterone to animals that had not been

[2] A sham operation is a procedure used in physiological experiments to determine the effects of being-operated-on. In this case, the procedures were the same as castration operation (e.g., the animals were anesthetized, surgical cuts were made), except no testicular tissue was removed.

gonadectomized, the proportion of successful fighters was raised to 85 percent. Parallel treatments with female quail had only modest effects on their fighting behavior (see Selinger and Bermant, 1967). Modification of dominance patterns in chickens has been accomplished through castration, on the one hand, and hormonal injections, on the other (Guhl and Fischer, 1969).

Sex hormones affect the development and expression of aggression in certain mammalian species as well. Castration of male mice has the general effect of reducing their tendency to attack. But the results of such experiments depend not merely on whether gonadal hormones are present or absent. The effects also depend on the stage of development at which the gonadectomy is performed and whether the animal had fighting experiences before the operation. Specifically, mice that are castrated while immature are poor fighters (Bevan, Daves, and Levy, 1960). But if the animals have not had fighting experience before castration, they tend to not attack their partners. On the other hand, castration performed *after* fighting experience has a less strong effect (Bevan, Daves, and Levy, 1960). These investigators found that castrates given replacement therapy were only slightly more aggressive than those not injected with testosterone.

Lee and Naranjo (1974) attempted to determine whether androgen affects ability of "despot" mice to maintain their position in a social hierarchy. These investigators castrated the despot mice in several groups. Almost immediately following postoperative recovery, these mice were displaced in the hierarchy by their competitors. Replacement therapy (modest to massive dosages of testosterone) was at best only temporarily effective. The castrated animals would fight for short periods, but were unable to sustain such behavior even when given exogenous hormones. This experiment showed that the effects of prior experience can be eliminated—if continued challenges are permitted. This point will turn out to be a most important one when we consider the cumulative or consolidation effects of prior experience in Chapter 10.

Some years ago, Scott (1958) concluded, on the basis of the then available evidence, that "the male hormone must be present in order to get the animal to start fighting, but it is not necessary once a strong habit has been established." That generalization remains generally accurate, if certain revisions are made. Male hormones are not necessary for the establishment of fighting in females or in prepubertal mice. Female mice are highly likely to attack in the first few days after giving birth (Green and Cairns, 1976; Svare and Gandelman, 1973). Moreover, virgin female mice will attack animals that are younger and smaller than themselves (Edwards, 1968) or highly reactive animals (Green and Cairns, 1976). Nonetheless, male hormones do contribute to the establishment of fighting, because castration or the absence of androgens greatly diminishes the incidence of attack establishment in most species.[3]

Thus far our discussion of hormonal action has been confined to birds and mice. How do hormones affect the behavior of other mammals? The evidence from studies of primates and humans is consistent with the view that dominant behavior at maturity is not solely dependent on hormonal control. In particular, variations in the levels of testosterone in the blood of the males in a colony of macaque monkeys did not significantly predict social rank or mating frequency (Eaton, 1976),[4] as shown in Figure 9-5.

Further, implantation of gonadal hormones in castrated macaque monkeys fails to change the so-

---

[3] But not all. Nonestrous female hampsters are intensely aggressive toward other hampsters of either sex. Extrous hampster females however, are not aggressive and lordosis (sexual posturing) is easily elicited (Floody and Pfaff, 1977).

[4] There appears, however, to be considerable day-to-day fluctuations in the level of testosterone in the blood, suggesting that this measure is sensitive to such factors as diurnal rhythm, nutrition, momentary states of arousal, as well as to chronic and stable individual differences in testosterone secretion. Cumulative indices of male hormone activity, such as the secondary characteristcs of sex dimorphism (size, coat fullness and color) do appear to be correlated with dominance in primate societies. Ironically the *less* precise measures of testosterone activity (gross secondary sex characteristics as opposed to levels of testosterone in the blood) may prove to be the best predicators of social interchanges.

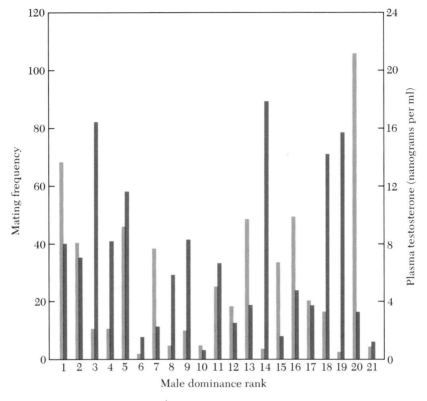

Figure 9–5. Do aggressive monkeys have higher levels of testosterone? A recent analysis of the Japanese macaque indicates that level of testosterone (*light gray bars*) is not correlated with either dominance rank or mating frequency (*dark gray bars*). (From G. G. Eaton, The Social Order of Japanese Macaques. Copyright © 1976 by Scientific American, Inc. All rights reserved.)

cial status of low-ranking macaque monkeys (either male or female) in a stable group (Mirsky, 1955). Clearly no 1-to-1 relationship holds between sex hormones and aggression in primates. Social structure and social experiences can augment, or cancel out, hormonal effects (more on this matter in Chapters 13 and 14).

Workers at the Oregon Regional Primate Laboratory conducted an extraordinary series of studies (to be discussed in greater detail in Chapter 13) and found that the developmental stage at which hormonal manipulations are performed is critical in de-

termining their effects. Hormonal changes that are initiated when the major organ systems are developing in the fetus can have widespread effects. In one experiment, pregnant rhesus monkeys were given a series of testosterone injections in the second quarter of gestation. The treatment produced masculinized females—individuals whose chromosomal analysis indicates that they are female but who have some of the anatomical features (partial internal and external genitalia) of males. The experimentally masculinized females behaved more like males than did control females. The effects of the prenatal treatment were persistent. Even in the third year of life, the masculinized females were more likely to threaten and initiate attacks and to engage in rough-and-tumble play than were the control females. Since testosterone may play an important role in influencing the structure of the brain, as well as the formation of the reproductive apparatus, early injection can have far-reaching effects.

What, then, are the mechanisms by which gonadal operations and testosterone injections exert their effects? The relationship is not a simple one; nor is it the same across species. Hormones have multiple effects on the central nervous system, morphology, and sensorimotor organization, as manifested by sexual dimorphism, activity differences, and variations in reactivity-sensitivity (Chapter 13). Given these behaviorial differences, "masculinized" females tend to be relatively dominant in interactions, and "demasculinized" males tend to be relatively subordinate. Once these interaction patterns become consolidated, they are resistant to extinction and change.

Neurological Organization and Aggressive Responses

It has been known for some time that the destruction or electrical stimulation of particular agreas of the brain can elicit heightened aggression or docility. Surgical destruction or removal of the septal area, for instance, produces rats that are savage and dangerous to handle. They resist capture and attack any object thrust in their direction, including other rats. These effects are typically transitory. They are most pronounced immediately after the operation and decline in the following days and weeks (Miczek and Grossman, 1972). The heightened tendency to fight can be elimiated within 16 days by handling the animals, or by pairing them with other rats. Rats that are housed singly show an increased tendency to attack for up to 45 days after the operation (Ahmad and Harvey, 1968).

The septum can hardly be considered a brain "attack center" for the executive control of aggression. The effects are more general. Ablations in this area produce heightened reactivity to a variety of stimuli, including light, shock, and handling (Schwartzbaum, Green, Beatty, and Thompson, 1967), as well as the curious effect of facilitating the learning of avoidance responses. Apparently the reason is simply that septal-lesioned animals are less likely to freeze and hence more likely to perform responses that permit them to avoid shock (Hamilton, 1972). On this score it has been proposed that the positive relationship between damage to the hippocampus and aggression is a byproduct of a more general failure of the animal's capacity to inhibit responses. Animals with hippocampus damage are also less likely to freeze (Blanchard, Blanchard, and Fial, 1970; Blanchard and Blanchard, 1972). The point to be made is that whether aggressive behavior is exhibited by animals with brain lesions is dependent upon the general behavoral changes produced by the operation. These changes, such as "freezing" or hyper-reactivity, can increase or decrease the likelihood that attacks will occur in an interchange.

Extensive work on brain stimulation and aggression, using cats as subjects, supports this conclusion. Neurological studies have centered primarily on the hypothalamus as a determinant of aggression-related activities. Electrical stimulation of particular loci in the hypothalamus by implanted electrodes yields patterns of attack, defense, or flight (Kaada, 1967). John Flynn and his co-workers at Yale University (Flynn, 1973; MacDonnell and Flynn, 1966) have found that the region surrounding the mouth of the cat becomes highly sensitized during periods of hypothalamic stimulation. Flynn's careful tracing of the neurological pathways by which hypothalamic stimulation is translated into attacks suggests that a key link between brain stimulation and the social act called aggression is a heightened sensitivity of sensory systems.

Moreover, the effects of brain stimulation are not necessarily automatic. Stimulation of a particular area of the hypothalamus can lead to fight or defense, depending on the situation (Gloor, 1967; Grossman, 1972; Valenstein, Cox, and Kakolewski, 1970). Rosvold and his colleagues (1954) found that monkeys who were dominant in their social hierarchy before brain surgery (removal of the amygdala) dropped to the bottom following the operation. But when the same animals were placed in individual cages, they appeared to be more aggressive than they had been before the operation. The social system can augment, or cancel out, major physiological manipulations.

The effects of brain manipulation also depend on the individual's social experiences in ontogeny. Roberts and Bergquist (1968) compared the attack behavior elicited by hypothalamic stimulation of normal cats with that of cats raised in social isolation. Their results indicated that the attacks elicited in isolated animals were similar in form to those elicited in the nonisolated animals. This result is consistent with the general assumption that the aggressive response patterns are species-typical, regardless of individual experiences. But the cats directed their attacks toward different objects. Previously isolated animals did not discriminate between targets as different as a sponge and a rat. Their nonisolated counterparts, however, clearly distinguished between the two targets—the rat was attacked more rapidly and more persistently. Experience made a difference in where the attack was directed, not in how it was performed.

In summary, research on the brain mechanisms associated with aggressive behavior has become increasingly sophisticated in recent years. Such work has tended to go beyond the mere demonstration that a relation exists between aggression and the destruction or stimulation of one area of the brain. Attempts are now being made to determine precisely what aspects of behavior are influenced, and why and how brain manipulations are translated into attack or nonattack tendencies. This trend is nicely illustrated by the elegant work of Flynn and his colleagues in tracing the pathways from hypothalamic stimulation to super-sensitivity of peripheral areas to facilitation of reflexive biting to triggering attacks toward social and nonsocial stimuli.

The main lesson to be learned from the preceding discussion is that the relation between brain manipulation and social behavior is rarely simple and direct. Aggressive acts occur during social interchanges, and these interchanges reflect the internal states and prior experiences of both members of the relationship as well as the social system and context in which the relationship occurs.

Are Differences in Aggressive Behavior Inherited?

In light of these social-biological considerations, it is of interest to note that extreme differences in fighting can be produced by genetic selection. The result has repeatedly been demonstrated—most convincingly in experiments conducted with purebred dogs and genetically controlled strains of mice.

The studies of dogs were part of a 20-year research project conducted at the Jackson Laboratory in Bar Harbor, Maine (Scott and Fuller, 1965). The breeds studied (basenji, beagle, cocker spaniel, and wire-haired fox terrier) were hunting dogs. However, they have been bred to perform quite different tasks in the hunt. For instance, the fox terrier is prized for its tenacity in combat and the vigor of its attacks upon the hunted animal; the cocker has been taught to flush game and then wait.

Not surprisingly, the breeds also differ in aggressive tendencies. In dominance tests, wire-haired terriers become increasingly assertive with their littermates from the fifth week on. Cocker spaniels invariably show less aggressive activity in the test situation than do wire-haired terriers, regardless of age at comparison. To determine whether these effects are related to the biophysical structure of the animals or are due to differential social experiences, James (1951) cross-fostered beagles and fox terrier pups. Some terriers were transferred to the beagle mothers, and beagles were introduced into the terrier litters. The terriers were superior to the same-age beagles by whatever measure of dominance taken and regardless of rearing circumstances. They won in all competitive food contests (2 dogs competing for one bone) and sired all puppies born during the course of the study. Corroborative findings on breed differences in aggressive behavior have been reported in other comparative investigations (King, 1954).

The sharp differences in aggressive behaviors are obviously not limited to breeds of dogs. Few direct comparisons have been made between species, possibly because the differences are so obvious. Nonetheless, it is instructive to find that some species that would be expected to be reasonably similar in terms of aggressive capabilities are not. For example, a series of round-robin bouts arranged between inbred strains of laboratory mice of one species and American field mice (King, 1957) indicated that this was an unfair match-up. The laboratory mice attacked the field mice an average of 20 times per bout and were virtually never attacked in return. To determine whether societies behave differently from individuals, the entire sample of animals of both species was placed in a large observation arena. The events of the next 4 days illustrated why a "hawk" strategy is not always superior to a "dove" strategy. The laboratory mice viciously attacked each other, vying for position, territory, and dominance. The field mice retreated to a single corner of the enclosure and watched the mayhem. At the end of 4 days, most of the laboratory mice were dead or dying. The field mice were virtually unscathed (King, 1957).

Since there are clear differences among species and among inbred strains in terms of the likelihood of fighting, we might ask whether it is possible to produce these genetic differences experimentally. It is. Attempts to breed selectively for aggressive behavior in rodents have been most successful. In Turku, Finland, K. M. and K. Lagerspetz (1971) found a significant difference in the aggressive behavior of the strains in three generations (Figure 9-6). The aggressive strains were also more active (they ran more in a running wheel and were more ambulatory in an open-field test) and defecated less

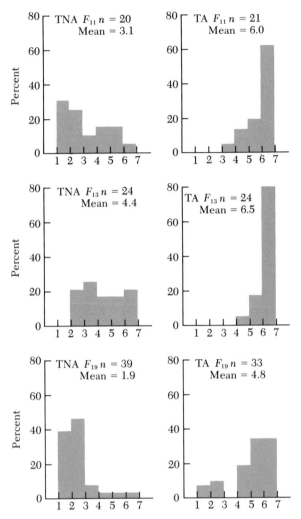

Figure 9-6. Aggressiveness score distributions for male mice of the eleventh (F_{11}), thirteenth (F_{13}), and nineteenth (F_{19}) generations of selective breeding for nonaggressiveness (TNA) and aggressiveness (TA). Aggressiveness was measured with a rating scale of 1–7, with 7 meaning vicious (adapted from Lagerspetz and Lagerspetz, 1971).

when under mild stress (presumed to be related to "emotionality"). These results constitute an interesting parallel to the classic studies on emotionality in rats (Hall, 1951). In the earlier study, it was found that the "low emotional" animals also had lower defecation scores and higher activity or mobility levels. Significantly, the "low emotional" strain was more aggressive than the "high emotional" strain, even though this charactieristic (aggression) was not the characteristic being selected for.

These results, I have found, can be readily replicated (Cairns, 1976). From a foundation stock of standard laboratory mice, the 2 most aggressive males were bred to the most aggressive females, and nonaggressive males were bred to nonaggressive females. The effects were parallel to those of Lagerspetz and Lagerspetz (1971). To rule out the possibility that these effects were due to rearing differences, the day-old infants were fostered to control mothers. The results confirmed that the effects were not due to such influences. Nor was weight the deciding factor. Why, then, did the animals differ in aggressive behavior? Videotape analyses of the two strains indicated a primary difference in the interactional activity of the aggressive and nonaggressive sublines before attacks. The nonaggressive strain tended to "freeze" and reflexively to kick backward or be startled when stimulated by their test partners. Such freezing, combined with heightened reactivity, elicited attacks. Not only did the nonaggressive strain not attack but their behavior typically provoked fights. Quite the opposite effects were observed among the males that had been selectively bred for aggression. Although these males were also highly sensitive to stimulation, they were not immoblized and did not freeze; rather they approached, stimulated, and eventually attacked their partners. Detailed analysis of the videotapes indicates that the typical outcome in relationships involving one animal of the aggressive strain was mutual escalation—increasingly more intense levels of stimulation eventually resulted in attacks by the subject. In summary, the nonaggressive strain elicited attacks from their test partners, whereas the aggressive strain directed attacks toward their test partners.

Does this mean that it is possible to produce strains whose aggressive behavior differs in only 2 or 3 generations? Yes, *if* one is willing to restrict the tests to young male adults. Surprisingly, when the test for aggression was delayed until the nonaggressive males no longer froze and hence no longer elicited attacks, the males behaved like the aggressive strains; that is, they initiated attacks rather than provoked them. The data suggest that the reason is that the primary characteristic that distinguishes aggressive from nonaggressive strains is the rapid of maturation of the systems underlying reactivity, mobility, and freezing. [5] When the nonaggressive strains were tested at a later age, the differences between strains was greatly diminished but did not disappear entirely (Figure 9-7).

A comment on the range of species that have been discussed is in order. Most studies of aggression have used rodents, dogs, and monkeys. Why not rabbits, cows, and pigs? Apart from the obvious size limitations, it might appear that these species were not selected because they simply are not very aggressive. Plausible as this assumption may be, it is not correct. Detailed analyses of rabbits (Mykytowycz, 1965), pigs (Ewbank, Meese, and Cox, 1974), and cows (Syme, Syme, Waite, and Pearson, 1975) indicate that in these species, aggressive interchanges play a significant role in the establishment and maintenance of social patterns. Although the behavior may not seem savage nor lead to the death of the other animal, as it frequently does with rodents (Kinsey, 1976; Poole and Morgan, 1975), it nonetheless can be entirely functional for the individual, in that it inhibits and controls the behavior of other animals.

Let us return to the question posed at the beginning of this section: "Are differences in aggressive behavior inherited?" This question, although it is provocative, is misleading and probably should be

---

[5] It should be noted that the selective breeding procedures that are effective for producing differences among males do not produce differences in females (Cairns, 1976), and effective procedures for producing "aggressive" females do not yield parallel differences in males (Hyde and Ebert, 1976). Similarly, the rearing experiences that lead to heightened fighting in males are necessarily not the same as lead to attacks in females (Chapter 10).

184

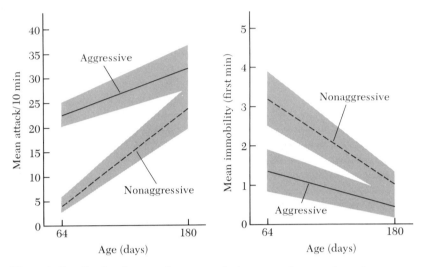

Figure 9-7. The developmental stage at which an animal is tested can determine whether the animal is shown to be aggressive or nonaggressive. *Left*: the difference between selectively bred aggressive and nonaggressive male mice at 64 and 180 days of age. The effect is highly reliable when the animals are about 2 months old, but not statistically significant when the animals are 180 days old. (Shaded area shows the standard error of the mean.) *Right*: similarly, the "freezing" behavior of the two groups of mice differs greatly at day 64, but very little at day 180. Experiment used both a longitudinal and a cross-sectional design (adapted from Cairns, 1976).

dismissed, or at least restated. To the extent that aggressive behavior reflects the operation of a social process, it cannot be "inherited." On the other hand, the psychobiological characteristics that affect the processes by which two organisms become involved in hurtful interchanges are clearly influenced by the genetic background of both individuals. These include such obvious features as size, musculature, and vigor, as well as such nonobvious features as maturation rate and reactivity to stimulation. But even these characteristics do not have automatic or inevitable effects on the interchange processes that lead to hurtful behaviors. A simple "yes" or "no" answer to the question regarding the inheritance of aggression would necessarily be misleading. The roles that genetic factors play in any given aggressive interchange depend on the nature of the social setting, on the particular action/reaction patterns of both organisms, on their momentary psychobiolocal states, and on their prior interactional experience. In short, the fusion is a unique one for each organism, but the processes by which the fusion occurs are general.

Summary

The information in this chapter is closely connected to that of the next (Chapter 10). By way of transition to that chapter, the following points should be remembered:

■ Aggressive acts—whether perceived as attacks, punishment, or coercion—are inextricably woven into the patterns of normal interchanges. They constitute a principal means by which organisms control and direct interactions. Perhaps the question should not be "Why aggression?" but "Why is there not more aggression?".

■ Attempts to identify how aggressive behaviors contribute to the individual's Darwinian (genetic) fitness have led to the investigation of several phenomena, including territoriality, dominance, and brood defense. Although these phenomena have been shown to correlate with reproductive success, their occurrence—and their relationship to aggressive acts of the individual—varies across species and ecological circumstances. Hence the study of ultimate (evolutionary) functions of aggressive strategies requires attention to the socio-ecological systems in which the behaviors occur and to the genetic "pay-off" of aggressive strategies relative to nonaggressive ones.

■ Analyses of the development of the capacity for assertive actions indicate that there is a broad range of internal controls; the developmental status of the individual is important throughout. The morphology, hormone levels, sexual dimorphism, neurological stimulation, and genetic background of the individual all contribute to the likelihood that an animal may become involved in an aggressive interchange.

■ An adequate explanation of the immediate determinants of aggressive acts must consider both the events in the interchange and the structure of the social group.

"Developmental" answers to questions of aggressive control have genetic, biochemical, neurological, and pharmacological aspects. But the precise ways in which biological-genetic-experiential events are fused in ontogeny and influence aggressive behavior must be explained. It is to that issue—synthesis in experience—that we now turn.

10

SOCIAL EXPERIENCE
AND THE DEVELOPMENT
OF AGGRESSIVE BEHAVIOR:
COMPARATIVE PERSPECTIVES

This chapter is concerned with the ways in which developmental experiences contribute to the promotion or prevention of aggressive interchanges in animals. A special problem will be to identify how individual differences arise in ontogeny and how they can be modified or canceled out.

How to Produce Aggressive Juveniles

To determine which environmental conditions are sufficient and necessary for the establishment of aggressive behavior, we might reverse the questions that are usually asked about violence. Rather than asking how to prevent or control hurtful acts, we can ask how to promote them. What can be done to produce a violent juvenile animal? How might its development be manipulated in order to maximize the amount and intensity of aggressive expression?

The answer to this question is interesting because it is concerned more with what is not required than with what is. Contrary to widely held beliefs, the establishment of aggressive behavior does *not* require reinforcement or imitation; nor does it require that the subject animal experience frustration or pain. On the contrary, it has repeatedly been shown that the *absence* of social experiences (including those related to fighting) is associated with intense fighting on the part of the "naive" animal. Paradoxically, the lack of exposure to fighting seems to facilitate the establishment of aggressive behavior.

Ethologists have long emphasized the isolation-aggression phenomenon (Eibl-Eibesfeldt, 1967; Lorenz, 1966). But it has not received much attention from psychologists. Perhaps the problem has been that the phenomenon appears at first to demand an explanation in terms of an innate drive and to be incomprehensible in terms of systematic principles of learning or development. Indeed, it has been offered by Eibl-Eibesfeldt (1967) as compelling proof that aggressive behavior is instinctive and that developmental experiences are not necessary to explain its ontogeny. A careful analysis of the results of studies of the isolation-aggression phenomenon indicates that this conclusion is only partly correct.

Before considering the developmental controls of the phenomenon, we should first identify its main properties. The best demonstrations of the effect are obtained with mice. Mere isolation of male mice from 21 days until maturity is sufficient to produce animals that will rapidly and viciously attack other animals. The result is remarkably consistent across strains; typically only those strains that have been selectively bred for nonaggression fail to attack. Furthermore, additional training experience does not greatly enhance the effect. Attempts to identify an "optimal" period of isolation have shown that similar results are obtained at maturity, following a period of approximately 2 weeks' separation from members of their own kind (Cairns, 1973).

Perhaps even more striking are the results of attempts to evaluate the relative importance of isolation versus training. A representative study is the one conducted by J. L. Milakovich (1970) in the Indiana Animal Behavior Laboratory. Milakovich worked with 3 groups, each consisting of 20 male mice. The first group was trained according to standard procedures.[1] Its training was allotted 10 days and was to involve a progression from mild sparring with a docile partner to vicious attack against a defenseless victim. Another group of 20 animals was given no specific training but was merely exposed to and permitted to interact with another male mouse once each day (equated in exposure time, handling, etc., to first group). Still a third group of 20 animals was not permitted to interact; these animals were placed alone in the test compartment for the

amount of time required for training. Half of the mice in each condition (that is, 10) were raised in 2 groups of 5 each. The other 10 mice of each condition were isolated after weaning (21 days of age). The design of the experiment thus permits a comparison between the effects of training and the effects of rearing.

Which is more important—the experience of having been taught to fight or the experience of having been reared alone? In a test where they were exposed to another male of the same strain, virtually all animals that had been isolated attacked the other animal (see Figure 10-1). There were no differences between the trained and untrained groups, if they had been isolated. Indeed, animals that were given no training whatsoever tended to be *more* vicious. On the other hand, the group-reared animals rarely attacked, whether they had been trained or not. The rearing conditions were clearly more effective than the elaborate training and reinforcement procedures in bringing about attacks.

To what extent is the isolation effect limited to mice? Despite the wide range of isolation procedures used, the effect holds up across several mammalian species. Monkeys are more likely to bite others after isolation rearing than after normal rearing (Mason, 1960; Sackett, 1967). Similar outcomes have been observed in such diverse types as chow dogs (Kuo, 1967), gerbils (Rieder and Reynierse, 1971), wild rats (Galef, 1970), grey quail (Kuo, 1960), and sheep (Cairns and Scholz, 1970). Isolated animals may even attack members of another species (see Figure 10-2). The results are not entirely consistent, however. Not all breeds of dogs that have been isolated have shown a strong tendency to attack. Isolated cocker spaniels and beagles tend to cower after being removed from isolation (Scott and Fuller, 1965). And as was indicated in Chapter 9, not all strains of mice attack after isolation (Cairns, 1976). Such inconsistencies require that we ask why isolation promotes the establishment of fighting and/or why group rearing inhibits it.

---

[1] The procedures described by Scott (1958) involve dangling a docile "target" mouse in front of the recruit and, through successive approximations, eliciting the recruit's approach, investigation, and eventual attack. Each trial requires 3 minutes, with one trial per day over a 10-day period.

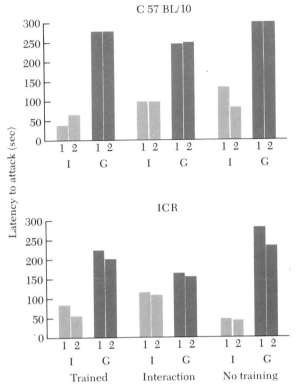

Figure 10-1. The effects of training, mere exposure, and no training on an animal's latency to attack another animal were compared in two different strains of mice— C 57 BL/10 (*top*) and ICR (*bottom*). The major effect was not due to the training conditioning but to the condition in which the animal had been reared. Isolated animals (*light gray bars*), regardless of the training regime to which they had been exposed, were more likely to attack during both of the daily 5-minute tests than were animals that had been maintained in groups (*dark gray bars*). I = isolated, G = grouped; 1 = first test, 2 = second test (Cairns and Milakovich, 1971).

Why Is Isolation Effective?

The form of the question "Why is isolation effective?" carries a hint about its answer. It implies that isolation should be viewed in terms of its positive properties rather than merely as a control for what will develop in the absence of social stimulation.

Two main behavioral consequences of isolation have been identified, along with a host of physiological effects. First, isolates are likely to move toward and investigate other conspecific animals when freed from isolation. This result has been established in a variety of test circumstances and across various species, but most frequently with rodents (Latané, Cappell, and Joy, 1970). Isolated animals treat other nonisolated animals as if they were novel stimuli; they crawl over, under, and around them. But genetic diversity is ever present; not all breeds or strains show a heightened tendency to approach "novel" animals. Isolated beagles, for instance, tend to freeze, as do some strains of mice.

Second, previously isolated animals are highly reactive to stimuli emitted from others of their kind (Ader, 1968; Cairns, 1973). The reactivity is shown in a number of ways. Isolates are jumpy; they are harder to catch; and, when placed with others of their kind, they are sensitive to being touched by them. Precise measurements of reactivity made with finely calibrated stablimeters confirm that there are great differences in the tactile sensitivity of isolated and group-reared animals (see Figure 10-3).

The neurochemical and physiological effects of isolation are numerous, compelling, and, to some extent, conflicting. The physiological effects that have been identified (such as differences in adrenal secretion and relative size of the adrenal glands) have usually been linked to stress responsiveness. The careful studies by Vale, Vale, and Harley (1971) have shown that different strains interact with each other in markedly different ways (in terms of fighting and dominance patterns) when they are reared together. These social differences give rise to differences in endocrine activity, including adrenal secretion. Isolation, then, may either increase or decrease hormonal activity, relative to nonisolated control social groups.

Reactivity and Escalation

We have seen that experience does indeed affect aggressive behavior, in that the gross manipulation

Figure 10-2. Isolated animals will attack not only members of their own species but members of other species as well. This photograph shows an isolated ICR male mouse (weighing approximately 33 g) attacking a young adult albino rat (weighing approximately 300 g). The attacks occurred without provocation shortly after both animals were placed in a neutral compartment and continued until the test was terminated. Typically the larger animal was wounded and bleeding at the end of the observation.

of isolation is clearly associated with fighting at maturity and has other organismic, behavioral, and societal effects (see Figure 10-4). But the way in which these basic response dispositions are translated into aggression has yet to be clarified. How do and why should heightened curiosity and stress responsivity lead to a readiness to attack? Two basically different explanations of the isolation-aggression phenomenon have been offered. One suggests that aggressive acts are innate, and one focuses on the effects induced by the isolation experience.

Innate Propensities. The hypothesis that aggression is linked to isolation appears to be consistent with the hypothesis that the innate propensity for aggressive acts is diminished by the response inhibition and/or response competition that occur in the course of social rearing. According to this hypothesis, aggressive patterns may typically be inhibited by other conspecific animals in the course of normal development. Hence the young animal is socialized by selective punishment in the form of attacks by

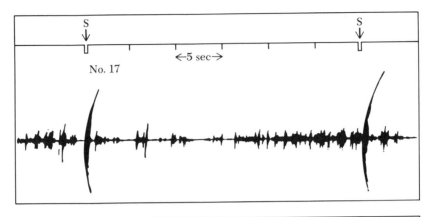

No. 17

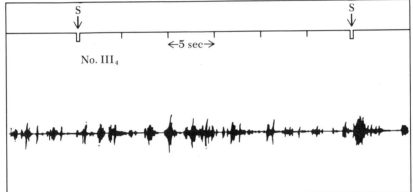

No. III₄

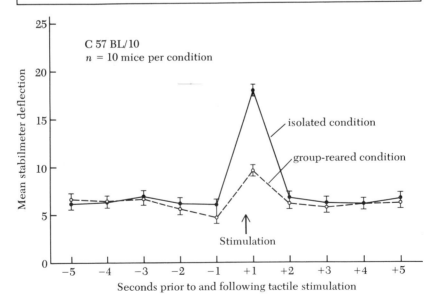

C 57 BL/10
n = 10 mice per condition

isolated condition

group-reared condition

Stimulation

Mean stabilmeter deflection

Seconds prior to and following tactile stimulation

peers, parents, and other adults. Because isolated animals do not "benefit" from such inhibition, they continue to be aggressive into adulthood.

Aggressive patterns may also be displaced (or given strong competition) during prosocial, nonaggressive interchanges. The occurrence and consolidation of such species-typical acts as grooming, playing, and helping may diminish the occurrence of aggressive ones. Animals maintained in isolation presumably are less likely to acquire such competing action patterns.

Induction by Isolation. Although the "innate" hypothesis seems intuitively sound, it does not take into account the possibility that young animals may be predisposed by the isolation experience to initiate interchanges that are mutually painful and hurtful. How might isolation induce a tendency toward aggressive behavior and thus increase the probability and intensity of aggressive interchanges? In a bidirectional process, the psychobiological characteristics induced by isolation may alter an interchange so that (1) the isolate and those with whom it interacts will become increasingly aroused and (2) the behaviors of those participating in the interchange will rapidly escalate in intensity and will have hurtful consequences (Cairns, 1973). Evidence in support of this idea can be obtained from direct observations and from experimental manipulations of interchanges.

Observations of interchanges between naive isolated animals indicate that they tend to increase in intensity and vigor until attacks and counterattacks occur and a full-scale fight erupts. High-speed film and videotape analyses demonstrate that when other animals merely touch or groom an isolated animal, it becomes startled, jumps away, and immediately stops whatever it was doing. Moreover, the isolated animal's fur becomes fluffed (piloerection, a sign of heightened arousal), its eyes may squint, and it may lunge or claw at the other creatures. If these acts occur, they often stimulate similar counterresponses. This feedback elicits further, increasingly intense reactions by the isolate, and so on. In a word, the interchange escalates.

One way to manipulate the interchanges experimentally is to administer drugs to the other animal(s) that diminish their reactivity to the isolated animal. In at least one species, this type of "milieu" therapy has proved quite successful (Cairns and Scholz, 1973). Isolated male mice that might otherwise be expected to be vicious did not attack when they were exposed to a quiet (thoroughly tranquilized) mouse. The effect is a direct function of the drug dosage given to the other animal.

In summary, the puzzle of why isolated animals rapidly attack other members of their kind in a variety of circumstances may be solved by determining how rearing experiences bias interchanges. Isolation-aggression research conclusively shows that specific training is not required for the establishment of aggressive behavior. But it would be inaccurate to conclude that isolation rearing merely

Figure 10-3. Animals reared in isolation are typically highly reactive to the stimuli from which they have been isolated, particularly somatosensory stimuli (being touched lightly), whereas nonisolated animals tend to ignore or to not respond to such stimulation. This figure (*upper*) shows sample records from two mice (No. 17, which had been isolated, and No. III$_4$, which had been reared with other mice). "S" indicates the delivery of the tactile stimulus (a slight touch with a cotton swab). The greater the deflection on the oscillograph, the greater was the reactivity of the animal to stimulation. *Lower*: Second-by-second summary of activity of groups of animals placed in the two rearing conditions before and after the tactile stimulation. Note that the only reliable differences between conditions occurred in the interval immediately following stimulation (from Cairns, 1973, with permission).

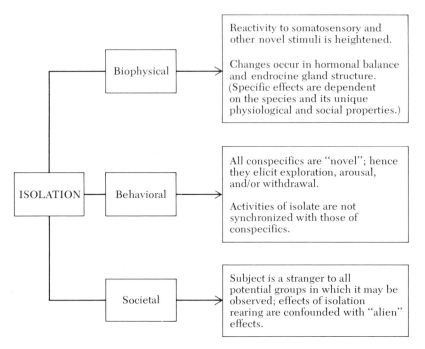

Figure 10-4. The multiple effects of isolation rearing on the young animal's biophysical, behavioral, and societal status.

brings out the innate behavior tendencies of the young animal. On the contrary, isolation rearing may induce new propensities that facilitate the occurrence of attacks when the animal participates in interchanges.

Aggression in Social Animals

Lest it be concluded that isolation is necessary for the development of aggressive behaviors, it should be emphasized that aggression is a problem for social groups, not for solitary individuals. Even in groups composed of animals that have never been segregated from others of their kind, vicious and deadly attacks occur. The following list gives some

idea of the range of events that can elicit fighting among nonisolated animals (see also Marler, 1976).

1. *Disruption of the group.* Events that disrupt the group also increase the probability of fighting. This can be demonstrated in mice merely by changing the bedding material and in monkeys by transferring the animals to a new area. Feeding rhesus monkeys in a new area or feeding them when they are unaccustomed to it produces aggressive interchanges (Southwick, Siddiqi, Farooqui, and Pal, 1976).

2. *Introduction of a new member.* A special way to disrupt the group is to bring in an unfamiliar animal. In most species, this triggers investigation and, subsequently, attack (recall the instance of baboon "transplantation" cited in Chapter 5). Investigators have obtained this result using groups of dogs (King, 1954), rats (Blanchard et al., 1974; Alberts and Galef, 1973), sheep (Hersher, Moore, and Richmond, 1958), and mice (Cairns and Nakelski, 1971).

What is the distinctive characteristic of the outsider that elicits attacks? In rodents, odor, especially of males, is a key stimulus. Dabbing the urine of a strange male mouse on the flank of a group-maintained mouse reliably increases the probability that the strange mouse will be attacked (Mackintosh and Grant, 1966). In general, virtually any stimulus property that communicates unfamiliarity elicits heightened states of arousal.[2] Whether that arousal will be translated into vigorous investigation, sexual activity, or aggressive behavior depends on the responses and characteristics of the stranger.

3. *Transgressions against others (their territory, status, or ongoing behaviors).* Naturalistic studies of fighting indicate that transgression into the domain of another animal and disruption of its ongoing activity can reliably elicit attacks in many species. But the details of territoriality and dominance structure differ markedly across species; extreme differences appear among even closely related breeds of macaque monkeys and baboons (Kummer, 1968).

4. *Administering shock.* For some time it has been known that painful electrical shock elicits attack and/or defense (O'Kelly and Steckle, 1939). A series of studies by Ulrich, Hutchinson, and Azrin (1965) has shown that two animals of the same species maintained in a small compartment and given a simultaneous shock tend to "attack" each other while the shock stimulus is present. The conditions that are basic to shock-elicited aggression have been considered by many to be a prototype of the basic conditions responsible for fighting. But in light of

the attention given to the phenomenon, it is important to note the ways in which it is atypical:

a. In the intershock interval, rats are neither active nor reactive; they remain in almost exactly the same posture they were in at the termination of the shock.

b. The probability that shock-elicited "attacks" will occur between two animals is inversely related to the size of the compartment; the larger the compartment, the less likelihood of fighting or attacks (Powell and Creer, 1969; Ulrich and Azrin, 1962).

c. If the animals were previously exposed to shock when alone, they will be less likely to attack when shocked when another animal is present (Payne, Anderson, and Murcurio, 1970).

d. Either aggressive or sexual responses can be elicited by shocking the tail of one rat when it is in the company of another. Which response occurs depends on the sexual receptiveness of the partner (Caggiula, 1972).

e. Under some conditions, shock inhibits aggression (see discussion later in this chapter).

For these reasons many investigators now question whether shock-elicited aggression reveals anything about the determinants and functions of fighting as it occurs outside the laboratory. Blanchard and Blanchard (1977) conclude that shock elicits defense, not aggression.

5. *Reciprocal aggression.* Another way to trigger fighting is to place an animal in a situation where it is likely to be attacked. Under many circumstances, attacks elicit counterattacks. Even nominally passive male animals will counterattack females that bite them or other males that provoke or injure them. The reciprocation rule is one of the most ubiquitous that has been identified in studies of aggression, but there are exceptions to it. The intensity of the initial attack may be so severe that counterattacks are precluded. Further, at some juncture in each combat, aggression must beget submission,

---

[2] Not just any urine elicits attacks. Applying the urine of female mice diminishes the likelihood of attack (Mugford and Nowell, 1970). In an attempt to identify the effective feature in the urine odor, C. T. Lee and W. Griffo (1974) castrated males and then injected them with the female hormone progesterone. Animals dabbed with urine from the castrated and feminized males were not attacked, while those dabbed with urine from castrated males were attacked.

withdrawal, or escape; otherwise every fight would be continued to the point of exhaustion or death. Aggression begets aggression most predictably when the combatants are relatively evenly matched in hurt-producing capabilities, their actions are painful but not paralyzing, and their prior encounters have not been decisive.

The interactions that precede attacks among socially reared animals are similar in many ways to those that precede attacks among isolated animals.[3] It is relevant at this point to recall the distinction between interaction establishment and interaction maintenance that was made earlier. The isolation-aggression phenomenon seems especially relevant to establishment. It demonstrates that attack sequences do not have to be learned; they appear to be performed adequately on their first occurrence, without specific training. They enter the repertoire through the operation of more fundamental developmental mechanisms.

Although specific learning experiences may not be necessary for the establishment of aggressive behavior, they can be decisive for maintenance or change. Studies of animals in "normal" social settings necessarily confound the carryover effects of prior interchanges with the immediate determinants of the behavior. It seems appropriate now to take a closer look at what some of these carry-over effects are, and how they may affect later social patterns.

What Is Learned?

Recurrence and Consolidation of Aggression

Aggressive interchanges, like nonaggressive ones, tend to recur if the conditions under which they previously occurred are repeated. The recurrence

principle that applies to the affiliative, prosocial interchanges of children (Chapter 8) applies as well to the assertive-aggressive interchanges of nonhumans. In interchanges that follow fighting among animals that are normally separated, less vigorous acts tend to be eliminated and to be replaced by aggressive, defensive behaviors. There is a sharp decline in the latency to attack, a primary index of aggression.

In addition, aggressive interchanges become consolidated, in that the behaviors become efficiently organized and fewer of the original stimuli are required to elicit the behaviors in subsequent interchanges. In an interesting demonstration of consolidation, Lagerspetz and Hautojärvi (1967) briefly exposed previously isolated male mice to other male mice, grouping them in pairs. As might be expected, attacks occurred and were typically initiated by the isolates. A second group of isolated male mice was exposed to a receptive female. Rather than fighting, these males attempted to copulate with her. Then the experimenters made a devious switch. In a second test, the males that had first been tested with a male mouse were exposed to a receptive female, and, conversely, those that had first been tested with a female were tested with another male. In this test, the original patterns persisted; the female partners were bitten, and the male partners were mounted.

Such consolidation effects are not limited to cross-sex testing. Indeed, consolidation is the rule, not the exception. The behavior organization survives the absence of the social feedback that was initially required for its establishment. In the previously cited study of drugged and nondrugged partners (Cairns and Scholz, 1973), it was found that subsequent tests directly mirrored the effects produced in the initial encounter. When all subjects, regardless of their first encounter, were placed with an inactive (drugged) partner, the effects of the first experience carried over. Those animals that had initially been induced to attack, attacked; and those that had not initially been induced to attack remained nonaggressive.

---

[3] Except for the phenomenon of shock-elicited aggression, which has distinctive properties that may disqualify it for inclusion with other attack sequences observed in socially reared animals.

The concept of consolidation helps to explain some otherwise puzzling outcomes that have been obtained in studies of the psychobiological determinants of aggressive interchanges. The problems arise when investigators who use seemingly identical neurological and hormonal procedures obtain opposite results. Castration, for instance, has different effects on aggressive behavior, depending on the prior experiences of the animal. Male mice that were tested for aggressive behavior and then castrated tended to persist in fighting. However, males that were castrated before the test typically did not attack other males. The behavior persisted despite the absence of stimuli that might have been necessary for its initial establishment (Bevan, Daves, and Levy, 1960). (Note the similarity to the persistence of canine and feline sexual behaviors described in Chapter 13.)

A parallel outcome has been observed in septal lesion studies. (Recall from the preceding chapter that knife cuts in the septum lead to temporary hyperreactivity and aggressive behaviors.) If the tests are conducted within 5 days after the operation, heightened aggressive activity is observed; if the tests are conducted 15 days after the test, there is little or no aggressive activity. But repeated testing halts the decay of aggressive behavior. If the animals are tested 5, 10, and 15 days after the operation, attacks occur during all three tests. Miczek and Grossman (1972), conclude that learning processes maintain aggressive behavior in the *absence of the neurological conditions that were initially required for its establishment.*

Attack sequences can be organized (and supported by) settings and circumstances as well as by the individual acts and cues of other animals.[4] Territoriality is a case in point. Prairie dogs will attack within the "boundaries" of their coterie but not out-

side them. Similarly, male hamadryas baboons will attack in their own resting areas but not elsewhere. The dog that is a terror in its own yard becomes a docile visitor in another area. Kuo (1967) is one of the few researchers who has demonstrated experimentally the situational supports and relativity of fighting. He found that chows could be trained to attack cats outside the laboratory, and to treat them entirely civilly inside the laboratory. The reverse effect was also demonstrated: the same dogs that would eat and sleep with a feline companion inside the laboratory viciously attacked cats outside the laboratory. Kuo (1967) called the phenomenon the Dr. Jekyl-Mr. Hyde effect.

As might be concluded from the results of this experiment, "prey" aggression (attacks against other species) can also be consolidated as a result of earlier experience. For instance, once a rat becomes a mouse killer, it remains one. It will kill mice under conditions that do not elicit such behavior from other rats because it has had prior experience in killing (Paul, Miley, and Mazzagatti, 1973). The behavior may under some conditions become generalized to the individual's own species; rats that kill mice are also likely to kill rat pups.

In natural social settings, the supports for consolidation extend beyond the learning experiences of the animals involved. They are woven into the structure of the social network—hence the formation of "roles" and "ranks." The relations within the social group serve as a catalyst for consistency in interchanges, both aggressive and nonaggressive.

Inhibition of Aggressive Acts

How is aggressive behavior inhibited? Perhaps more important, can the inhibition of aggressive behavior be learned? In answer to the first question, a variety of stimulus properties of the individual (such as female odors) can diminish the probability of attack. Immobility, or nonreactivity, also diminishes the likelihood of attack. Ritualized actions, such as "presenting" oneself for grooming or investigation,

---

[4] The training of "war dogs" during World War II and the training of dogs for protection and security today take advantage of the rapid consolidation of aggressive/attack tendencies (Behan, 1946). The eliciting stimulus may be the verbal commands of the handler or the particular characteristics of the individual to be attacked.

also decrease the incidence of aggressive behaviors in prairie dogs, primates, and kangaroos (Kaufmann, 1975). These are instances in which a passive or nonaggressive response tends to be effective. But in at least some species, passivity is not enough, and the attacks persist despite inactivity, presentation, or female odors.

Aggressive behaviors are also inhibited by fighting back. If the victim is successful in its counteraggression, the probability of its being attacked on future occasions is sharply diminished. Animals not only learn to consolidate attacking behaviors after victories, they learn nonattack sequences after defeats. There is ample evidence to indicate that one of the most effective ways to discourage attacks is to wage more vigorous counterattacks. In stable colonies, patterns of dominance and submission (based on victory or defeat) remain reasonably predictable over time. (However, as we observed earlier, dominance patterns are context and activity bound.)

There is a paradox in this pain-inhibition finding. It is understandable that pain—as experienced in a counterattack—*inhibits* aggression, but why does pain *elicit* aggression in the shock-elicitation studies, and why do some counterattacks stimulate *more* fighting? James Myer, at Johns Hopkins University, has suggested an explanation of the paradox. According to Myer, one key is the timing of the shock. In those instances where the shock is effective in inhibiting fighting, it is delivered when the animal is in the act of attacking or making preparatory movements for attacking. The behavior is thus disrupted because the shock stimulus elicits behavior (such as withdrawal and cringing) that interferes with attacking. In attack-elicitation demonstrations, however, the shock is delivered when the animals are neither attacking nor preparing to attack. Under these conditions, shock evokes biting and attacks (see Figure 10-5).

These findings concerning the importance of the timing of pain in the behavior sequence are consistent with everyday observations of fighting. Clearly, attack behavior can be effectively inhibited by strong retributive action (counterattack, pain,

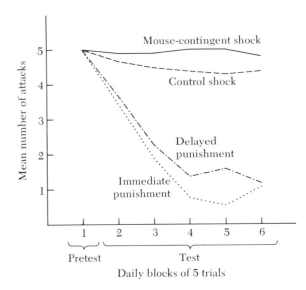

Figure 10-5. The effect of shock on the elicitation of attacks is a direct function of its timing. If the shock was made contingent on the presentation of another animal (*mouse-contingent*), or was unrelated to its presentation (*control*), the number of attacks that a rat performed against the newcomer was high. But if the shock occurred after an attack was in progress (*immediate* or *delayed punishment*), the frequency of attacks was sharply diminished. (From Myer. Copyright © 1968 by the American Psychological Association. Reprinted by permission.)

shock, punishment) by the victim. Like the initial attack, such action effectively disrupts the behavior of the attacker. Indeed, fighting seems to be adequately described as an "attack-elicitation-attack" feedback loop. The reciprocal attacks diminish, presumably, when the stimulus provided by one member of the pair is really painful or disabling.

In ontogeny, the capacity to control the pain-producing behavior of another individual through reciprocal behavior is of basic importance. When two animals are about evenly matched (as are littermates or same-age peers), the retributive potential of one is sufficient to counter the attacks (playful or otherwise) of the other. And a mother's reactions are sufficient to control and redirect infant approaches toward her that are too demanding or too vigorous. The net effect of reactive punishment is to decrease the probability of more vigorous attacks. Such a "balance of power" permits the occurrence of alternative responses, such as mutual grooming or following. Should one member of the dyad lack retributive potential, and should vigorous actions not be otherwise inhibited, one animal or the other may be destroyed. Maturation-paced changes in strength lead to gradual and sometimes deadly increases in the potential for hurting others.

The occurrence of attacks and reciprocal responses in ontogeny may also contribute to the development of "ritualized" forms of aggressive behavior. Actual physical attacks may not be necessary to inhibit the ongoing behaviors; events reliably associated with attacks may serve just as well. Accordingly, threats, menacing gestures, and preparatory physiological changes (bodily coloration, piloerection) can gain the capacity to signal attacks. Once the signal occurs, it elicits alternative, competing behavior.

How to Produce Peaceful Juveniles

Up to this point in the chapter, we have focused on how aggressive behaviors are established, maintained, and inhibited. What about the development of peaceful behaviors, particularly by preventing the establishment of attacks and fighting in the first place? It may come as a surprise to learn that "peaceful" interchanges are dominant in virtually all societies; most animals are peaceful most of the time. Even in those species that have a reputation for savageness, such as the hamadryas baboon, aggressive interchanges occur infrequently, if not rarely. Relative to other interchanges (such as play, grooming, social investigation, and passive "togetherness"), aggressive interchanges constitute but a small proportion of the total behaviors observed (less than 1–3 percent, depending on the species

studied). Such frequency is in keeping with the fact that aggressive acts require high levels of energy expenditure and that there are alternative, less expensive ways to alter the ongoing behavior of other individuals. [5]

Societal supports for peaceful behavior (roles, hierarchies) are found in all species, although the form that they take and the way in which they work differ markedly across species and subsocieties. Societal constraints, as enforced by a unit leader or dominant animal, become consolidated into the network of relationships in the society. Individual animals can also provide support for nonaggressive behavior (see Chapter 9). Some organisms are unlikely to behave in a hurtful fashion simply because they are physically ill-prepared (in terms of morphology and/or physiology), because of internal constraints, or because they are capable of provoking alternative actions (for example, as a result of female pheromones).

In addition to such supports for "peaceful" or nonaggressive interchanges, experiences in ontogeny can also decrease the likelihood that hurtful acts will occur. Instances where inherent species antagonisms are reversed provide some of the most dramatic illustrations of this developmental phenomenon. After being reared together, rats live peacefully with mice, as do cats with rats, dogs with cats, and sheep with dogs. The offbeat character of such relationships should not belie their significance—namely, demonstrating that the behaviors of the individuals can be markedly changed from what might be expected on the basis of their species membership.

---

[5] Such infrequency raises the question of whether the "problem of aggression" might be an anthropomorphic projection to animals of a human problem that has little relevance for animal societies. But it would be hazardous to equate frequency with importance. (An analogous case would be sexual behaviors, which are also observed infrequently.) Attacks help to realign relationships within group and societies, and, when they occur, they are most salient. The saliency may not merely be responsible for overestimating the prevalence of the behavior but may ensure that the acts will not be readily forgotten, either by participants or by observers.

However, early togetherness is no guarantee that either intraspecific or cross-specific pairings will be peaceful. Appearances can be deceptive, and photographs of peaceful cohabitation often create a false impression of its inevitability. The myths of Disneyland notwithstanding, rearing animals together that differ markedly in temperament and background can sometimes be disastrous (Cairns and Johnson, 1965; Johnson, 1972; Kuo, 1967). Various co-rearing studies indicate that dogs will, by change or design, destroy their smaller, less capable companions. Kuo (1967) discovered that he could ensure the survival of the alien animal (a rabbit) by punishing the dogs whenever they became too rough with their roommate. What happened if they were not punished? In the escalation of the "playful" wrestling and gnawing, the rabbit always came out the loser. Maturational changes require a continuing realignment of the relationship. The acts that were highly tolerable in a very young pup (gnawing, chewing, wrestling) can become increasingly harmful as the individual matures. But even the anticipation of harmful consequences does not necessarily inhibit the development of preferences. Independent preference tests indicate that young animals tend to approach their cohabitants, even though their previous interactions were destructive (Cairns and Johnson, 1965).

Returning to the prevention of aggression, why does cohabitation work, and why imperfectly? It would appear that co-rearing allows the development of response sequences that would not occur under ordinary rearing conditions. First, after having been reared with an alien species, animals do not become highly aroused by the presence of that species. (Arousal is a precursor of, or correlate of, attacks.) Rather, they are aroused by the *absence* of the alien species.

Second, co-rearing promotes the establishment of interaction sequences that are not harmful to either individual. Some of the interchanges are active (eating together, mutual grooming, play), and others are passive (sleeping side by side or merely being in each other's presence). The behaviors of each individual become organized around the distinctive cues provided by the other. Just as attack sequences can become consolidated, so can nonattack sequences.

Is *early* co-rearing necessary to achieve peaceful coexistence? For at least one species—the grey wolf—it is not. Ginsberg (1976) and his co-workers discovered that wolves can be tamed at maturity. These investigators observed animals at the Brookfield Zoo in Chicago and found that nonthreatening approach procedures could be used to gradually adapt the mature animals to human handlers (who wore protective clothing). The animals engaged in playful activity with the handlers, although some required a lengthy period of adaptation. One key to the success of such adaptation seems to be that aggressive behaviors toward humans never became established, and thus the development of nonassertive, nonhurtful interchanges was facilitated. Ginsberg (1976) also reports that the successful taming of a young wolf does not guarantee that it will remain docile as an adult. Again, maturational changes in structure and response capability demand a realignment of the relationship at each state of development.[6] Similar "inhibiting" effects in adulthood have been demonstrated in rats (Paul, 1972).

In summary, co-rearing is one basic way to limit the development of aggressive sequences. But interchanges are dynamic; they are affected by the changing characteristics of each participant as well as by the social structure in which the interactions occur. In intraspecific rearing, the "other"—usually littermates or the mother—is able to modify or suppress the more dangerous byproducts of play. In cross-specific rearing, help from the experimenter is often required to keep the relationship from degenerating into a brutal one. However it is achieved, a balance of power promotes the establishment of al-

[6] Recall the issue raised in Chapter 5 as to whether there are critical periods in the organization of interchanges. The wolf data suggest that the organization may occur at maturity if the first exposure to humans occurs at that time.

ternative, nonaggressive patterns. Throughout ontogeny, the societal structure transcends variations in individual experience; thus social control is not dependent solely on events internal or external to the individual.

"Therapy" and Change

The problems of "therapy" and change are critical ones for a developmental analysis because not all hurtful interactions can be prevented. What can be done, then, to reverse aggressive patterns after they have been permitted to become established and consolidated?

It should be observed that highly organized aggressive sequences typically are not easily modified. One problem is that hurtful behaviors, once established, tend to pre-empt other forms of social response. In cases of actual fighting, the problem is compounded because the relationship is terminated by the abrupt removal, submission, escape, or death of the other individual. Hence the behavior is not only consolidated, it is preserved. The consequences that it provokes tend to prevent the development of alternative patterns.

Despite these problems, aggressive sequences can be reliably disrupted, controlled, and/or inhibited. In light of the multiple ways that violent interchanges can be established, it is reasonable to assume that there should be multiple ways to modify them. Some of the procedures are biobehavioral, involving techniques that range from surgery (brain ablation, amputation, castration) to transient biochemical manipulation (tranquilization, hormonal injections). Although such methods can be highly effective, they all share the unfortunate feature of rendering the young animal physically handicapped, either permanently or temporarily. Happily, these effects are sometimes accompanied by powerful learning effects that take up when the medication wears off. For instance, a light drug administered to

a maternal ewe can temporarily promote her acceptance of an unfamiliar lamb, even though the infant would ordinarily be rejected. After the drug effects dissipate, the ewe typically continues to accept the infant lamb.

Other reversal procedures are basically behavioral. One of the most effective procedures is also the simplest: requiring the individual to continue to interact with other animals toward which it had earlier directed attacks. This procedure has been half-seriously called group therapy. As might be expected, there is usually an immediate outbreak of vigorous activity (including fighting) when the transplantation occurs, followed by a rapid decrement in the frequency and intensity of activity (including attacks). After an extended period of co-rearing, the previously aggressive animal (if it survives) tends to adopt the characteristics of the group with which it is placed (see Figure 2-3).

Why do attacks tend to diminish under conditions of "group therapy"? Direct observations of the phenomenon suggest that two different processes may be effective: (1) social habituation and the development of competing responses and (2) inhibition by counterattacks and punishment.

1. *Social habituation.* A diminution in aggressive activity occurs as the aggressive animal adapts to the cues and behavioral characteristics of the other animals, even if it dominates the group into which it is placed. The adaptation serves to (1) reduce the states of arousal provoked by the unfamiliar social stimuli, and (2) provide for a change in the kinds of interactions that occur. Hence the attack sequence is broken up and alternative, less vigorous behaviors take its place. Over time, the benign responses (sniffing, grooming, climbing, copulation) gradually become consolidated and replace the aggressive responses.

2. *Counterattacks and punishment.* A diminution in aggressive activity also occurs when one or more members of the group wage vicious counterattacks and the aggressive animal is defeated. Thereafter it not only ceases to initiate attacks but often

inhibits virtually all interchanges. The side effects of such "therapy" can be costly. Reproductive and grooming behaviors and exploratory activities are all diminished. In some animal groups (rodents, dogs, and monkeys) the "patient" is sometimes killed.

Both of these processes may be successful in reducing the likelihood of aggressive interchanges, but they have markedly different side effects. Both habituation and punishment can coexist in real life, and there is reason to believe that they are complementary in natural circumstances. For instance, in normal development, not only must new, nonpunitive interchanges become established, but the continuance of once benign but now hurtful behaviors must be discouraged. Where multiple patterns of interchange exist in a dyadic system, punishment of hurtful action sequences does not necessarily disrupt nonhurtful ones. Even brutal parents can be "loved," as can "difficult" and "aggressive" offspring.

Why Violence Occurs: A Common Interactional Process?

This chapter began with the curious and mildly sadistic question of how aggressive interchanges can be established and promoted. We found that they can be established in the absence of specific training and that they can be elicited by a wide range of social and nonsocial experiences. It seems useful now to return to that question and to comment on the relevance of the laboratory research on isolation to the normal development of aggressive behaviors. An obvious problem is that no mammalian young are reared in nature apart from others of their own kind, so the total isolate is only a laboratory creation. Hence the isolation-aggression phenomenon bears little if any relevance to the normal development of aggressive behavior.

Perhaps. But there is reason to believe that it would be more appropriate to view the isolation-aggression phenomenon as an exaggeration of processes that occur normally. Accordingly, the similarity of the interchanges by which "isolated" and "socially reared" animals become involved in fighting requires close scrutiny. The sequential analyses that have been performed point to the antecedent contribution of heightened psychobiological states (irritability and reactivity), regardless of whether isolation, territoriality, or physiological manipulations produce those states. Whether these psychobiological states are translated into aggressive acts depends, in part, on the behavior of the other animal or animals involved in the interchanges and the context of interaction. Although the manipulations by which the aggressive interactions are brought about may differ, the mechanisms that control them may be similar.

Summary

Behaviors that are painful to another organism do not have to be learned. The incidence of high-magnitude responses, such as biting, clawing, butting, and slapping, is determined by the structural and maturational status of the individual, as well as by its species. The capacity to produce pain is an inevitable byproduct of growth and development. But even infantile behaviors, when they persist beyond their time, can be painful for the mother (and others). Neither "reinforcement" nor "imitation" seems necessary for the initial establishment of hurtful interchanges.

But painful acts, once they occur in a relationship, are learnable. They can be either consolidated and maintained or inhibited and diminished. The outcome—consolidation or inhibition—is determined by the counteractions evoked by the behavior and the setting in which the interactions occur.

Aggression works. Even mildly hurtful acts can disrupt the behavior of the other individual and punish his ongoing activity. The fact that virtually all individuals, at some time in their development, become amply endowed with the capability to hurt others appears to guarantee the emergence of aggressive acts.

An overview of the literature on comparative development provided a preliminary outline of some major features of aggressive interactions.

■ Experiences during ontogeny provide the basis for the performance of the individual's primary interactional behaviors, including some that are "immature" forms of adult aggressive behaviors. Early aggressive interactions, surprisingly, are not necessary for the development of effective aggressive behaviors. Indeed, aggressive experiences with others during development structure and delimit the conditions under which hurtful behaviors occur. In addition to whatever specific effects occur, there are nonspecific effects of social experience. The young animal becomes adapted to the stimulation provided by others—in effect, habituated to their characteristics and to the characteristics of their species.

■ Multiple biophysical events contribute to the occurrence of aggressive interchanges. Biochemical, neural, genetic, pharmacological, and hormonal correlates have been identified. Moreover, the relation between structure and function is bidirectional. Chronic states of the individual (reactivity, arousal) are drastically modified by social interactions in development, and once the states are established, they affect subsequent interchanges.

■ However established, aggressive interchanges can be conditioned. One of the primary functions of experience with others in development is the control of hurtful behavior. Events that are immediately associated with pain rapidly acquire response-eliciting and response-inhibiting functions. One of the primary services of these signals is to redirect the behavior of others without attacking them.

■ Aggressive interchanges can be prevented, by biophysical modifications, social structure, or by experiences in development. Co-rearing does not automatically lead to mutual acceptance, but it can result in adaptation and the promotion of nonhurtful interchanges. In both intraspecific and interspecific rearing, relationships are dynamic and paced in part by the biophysical maturation rate of each participant. Not only must the individuals become adapted to each other, but high-magnitude responses (that can harm or maim) must be eliminated or redirected if the relationship is to be maintained.

■ Aggressive interchanges can be changed or relatively permanently modified, even after they have become firmly established in adulthood. The characteristics of the animals participating in the interchanges, and the reactions that they permit and evoke, significantly determine both the form of "therapy" and the speed at which it can proceed. The effective processes of change—habituation and punishment—have markedly different side effects, but in natural circumstances they are probably complementary.

The social networks into which the young are born contribute to the establishment, channeling, consolidation, and inhibition of aggressive behaviors. The effects can be direct (such as community attacks upon intruders or animals of lower status and the regulation and inhibition of attacks by high-ranking leaders), or they can be indirect (such as the establishment of territories and social hierarchies). Concurrent with the development of capabilities for hurtful actions, the young of most species are introduced into a social network that supports, inhibits, and channels those activities. To the extent that the network remains stable, there should be reasonable stability in the component interchanges.

The notion that mammalian species have a "drive" toward aggression—always a popular common-sense proposal—requires comment. The basic idea that there exists a force that impels each individual to attack others of its kind has considerable intuitive appeal. But, as the findings described in this chapter indicate, the problems of aggression are not that simple. Nor will they yield to pat solutions. In a broader sense, the problems of aggression are the problems of living. The study of the pathways of psychobiological and interactional influence in nonhumans has paved the way for a more adequate explanation of the development of aggressive interchanges among humans, the problem that will concern us in the next two chapters.

11

PSYCHOBIOLOGICAL FOUNDATIONS OF AGGRESSIVE BEHAVIOR IN HUMANS

William James's views on the adaptiveness of aggression were presented in Chapter 9. The quote included in that chapter stopped short, however; James was just getting warmed up to the topic. After observing that killing off a few obnoxious neighbors may have been a good thing in the course of human evolution, he concludes:

> Hence the gory cradle, the *bellum omnium contra omnes*, in which our race was reared; hence the fickleness of human ties, the ease with which the foe of yesterday becomes the ally of today, the friend of to-day the enemy of to-morrow; hence the fact that we, the lineal representatives of the successful enactors of one scene of slaughter after another, must, whatever more pacific virtues we may also possess, still carry about with us, ready at any moment to burst into flame, the smouldering and sinister traits of character by means of which they lived through so many massacres, harming others, but themselves unharmed (James, 1890, p. 410).

The flames of violence are getting easier to ignite, if recent F.B.I. *Crime Report* (1975) statistics are to be accepted as accurate (Figure 11-1). In the mid-1970's, arrests of teen-age boys and girls for committing violent crimes (criminal homicide, robbery, aggravated assault, rape) continued to increase. Approximately one-half of all arrests for violent crimes in the United States in 1974—46 percent—were arrests of persons 21 years of age and younger.

But the problems of human coerciveness and aggression are even broader than those implied by the dismal F.B.I. statistics. Acts of punishment and physical injury are commonplace in everyday life, although they make up only a small proportion of the total number of interchanges in which the child is involved. Children are both dispensers of and targets for a wide range of physical and symbolic injuries that are a normal part of their relationships with other children and adults. Our focus in this chapter and the next will be on the developmental process by which aggressive behaviors are established and the ways in which they are maintained and changed in the interchanges of childhood.

In the preceding chapters we found that aggressive acts are not always, and not even usually, maladaptive. The studies of nonhuman young indicated that one of the principal services of such acts is to control and direct the ongoing activities of other individuals. We might reasonably ask whether ag-

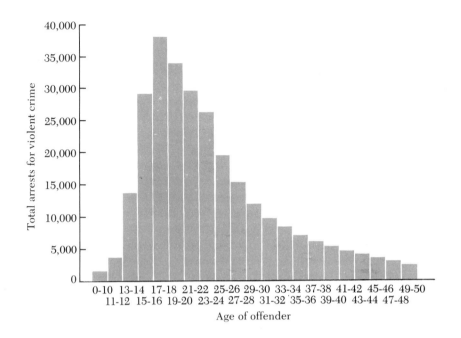

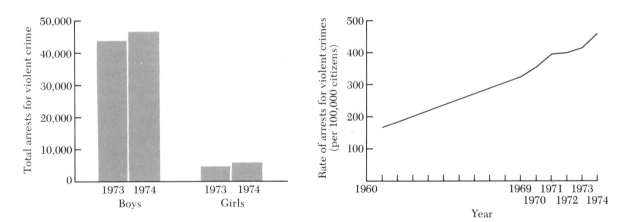

Figure 11-1. *Top:* total arrests for violent crimes as a function of the age of the offenders in the United States for one year. *Lower left:* comparisons between boys and girls (17 years old or younger) in terms of total number of arrests for violent crimes in two consecutive years. *Lower right:* there has been an almost linear increase in arrests in the United States for violent crimes in the recent past. (These data abstracted from *Crime in the United States*, 1975.)

gressive behaviors in children perform similar services. Furthermore, it was clear from these studies that the aggressive patterns of animals become consolidated and are maintained over time, independent of the conditions that originally led to their establishment. Does a similar generalization hold for children, despite their greater capability for symbolic communication and control?

To facilitate comparisons across species, the organization of this chapter and the next will parallel that of the preceding two chapters on the development of aggression in nonhumans. Accordingly, we will begin by tracing the development of the behavior and then examine how genetic, sexual, neurological, and chemical (drugs) events contribute to aggression. Chapter 12 is concerned with the synthesis of experience in social systems.

Ontogeny of Aggressive Behaviors in Children

Precursors in Infancy

Infants are intrinsically lovable, most of the time. Whatever punishment is normally given the infant in the first year of life is typically mild in intensity and is concerned with redirecting a specific behavior rather than penalizing the infant for it. In extreme circumstances, infants and young children are the victims of brutal aggression, leading to serious injury or death. Reliable data on the incidence of child abuse are hard to obtain because it is a private and relatively hidden crime. [1] But in California in the first 6 months of systematic recording (in 1967) there were 1,657 cases of child abuse that were se-

rious enough to warrant legal action (see Bakan, 1971; Gil, 1970; Helfer and Kempe, 1968; Parke and Collmer, 1975).

Attempts to trace the ontogeny of aggressive acts where infants and toddlers are the initiators have been handicapped by a failure of investigators to agree on what should be measured. The observer of preschool interchanges gets the impression that most acts that produce crying and fleeting unhappiness among children are not intended to hurt so much as they are intended to obtain a toy or gain a place. Since the definition of aggression requires that a subjective judgment be made by observers, whether the terms "assertive" or "aggressive" is applied to a given behavior depends on whose point of view is taken—that of the child doing the taking or that of the child being taken from. The following description of the activities of two 18-month-old infants illustrates the definitional problem:

> Clarissa walks up to Billy and grabs the block out of his hand. Billy tries, unsuccessfully, to grab it back, then begins to cry. Mr. _____, who didn't see the initial grab by Clarissa but did see Billy's apparent misbehavior, leads Billy to a chair on the other side of the room.

Should this act be labeled "assertive," "aggressive," or merely "possessive"? If the production of unhappiness or discomfort is the criterion, then the action sequence would be labeled aggressive. But if the intention to produce harm or injury is the criterion, it probably would not. Researchers who work with young children have tended to solve the definitional problem by focusing on the occurrence of particular disruptive behaviors, such as taking toys from, kicking, pushing, hitting, or yelling at, another child.

Half of the interchanges among children 12–18 months old observed in nursery school involve some act that might qualify as disruptive (mostly "taking toys") (Holmberg, 1977; Maudry and Nekula, 1939). The same children, however, exhibit few such behaviors in their interchanges with adults ("assertive" behaviors constitute only 5 percent of the total) (see

[1] Only estimates are available. A. Schuchter (1976) observes that "it is currently impossible to know the actual magnitude and nature of the problem of child abuse because of: (1) lack of uniform definitions, (2) combined abuse/neglect statistics, (3) lack of uniform reporting laws which specify who is to report and to whom, (4) differing statutory ages of the children to be reported, and (5) the role of individual discretion in reporting and validating child abuse."

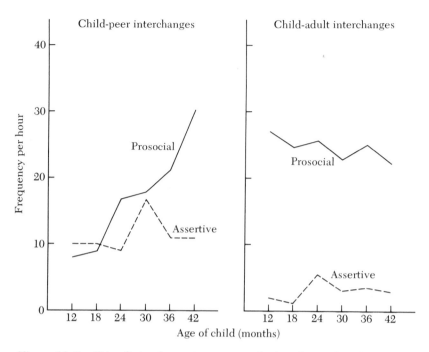

Figure 11-2. Naturalistic observations in preschools indicate that the rates of assertive and nonassertive ("prosocial") interchanges among children are about equal at 12 months of age, but are markedly different by 42 months (*left*). Interchanges among the same children with adults, however, show few assertive acts at any age (*right*). (From Holmberg, 1977, with permission.)

Figure 11-2). By the time the children are a year older (2½ years), the proportion of disruptive interchanges with peers has decreased to 20 percent, and disruptive interchanges with adults have remained very low (Holmberg, 1977; also Bronson, 1975).[2]

Analyses of disruptive interchanges among 1- to 2-year-old children suggest that most of them were not intended to hurt or to cause unhappiness so much as to gain possession of an object or a place or to continue an ongoing activity. Indeed, if the actions had been directed toward inanimate objects (for example, grabbing a toy from the floor or knocking a pillow off a chair to make room on it),

the behavior would not be labeled aggressive or assertive (Mueller and Lucas, 1975).

The matter of sex differences in assertive-aggressive action in infancy and early childhood requires some comment. That there are physiological differences between the sexes at birth cannot be disputed. Males, from birth to maturity, have a higher proportion of muscle tissues than girls (Ounsted and Taylor, 1972). However, as we will see later (Chapter 15), these differences are minimal before puberty; the mean difference is only 1–3 percent. There is some disagreement concerning the difference between the assertive-aggressive behaviors of infant boys and infant girls. Some investigators have reported substantial differences (Goldberg and Lewis, 1969), whereas other investigators have

---

[2] Note that the decrease is proportional to the total number of social acts. However, the absolute frequency (or rate per unit time) remains relatively constant from the first to the fourth year.

found minimal and negligible differences (Jacklin, Maccoby, and Dick, 1973; Maccoby and Jacklin, 1973; Van Lieshout, 1975). The failure of Holmberg (1977) to find differences in the behavior of boys and girls 2 years old and younger in day care centers is consistent with what appear to be basically overlapping distributions in male-female behavior at this age. The similarities between boys and girls in morphology and in physically assertive actions in the first two years are more impressive than the differences.

Aggression in Preschool-Age Children

During the preschool period (2-5 years of age), the proportion of physically aggressive encounters to nonaggressive ones tends to decrease as a function of age. Support for this empirical generalization is found in a large group of studies on the behavior of nursery school children conducted in the 1930's (Bott, 1934; Dawe, 1934; Jersild and Markey, 1935; Parten, 1932). The findings of the experiments of the 1970's are basically in agreement with those of the earlier studies (Rubin, Maioni, and Hornung, 1976; Smith and Green, 1975). Boys were found to be likely to become involved in aggressive encounters than girls—they were more often the initiators of as well as the targets of attacks (Smith and Green, 1975). Again, however, because there was overlap between the sexes, some researchers (Jersild and Markey, 1935) failed to find differences between the sexes with regard to aggression in children 2-5 years old.

A recent contribution by Willard Hartup (1974) at the University of Minnesota is useful because it distinguishes between the forms of aggressive behavior on the basis of age. Following the lead of Feshbach (1964) and Buss (1966), Hartup distinguishes between instrumental and hostile aggression. *Instrumental aggression* is object directed. For example, the child may injure or hurt another child in order to get his toy back, or to retain it. *Hostile*

aggression is person-directed; it is intended to produce harm or injury, not to obtain materials.

Analyses of 758 units of aggressive behavior by Hartup (1974) indicate that younger children (4-6 years of age) were more aggressive per unit of time than older ones (6-7 years of age). Moreover, the younger children showed proportionately more instrumental aggression than did the older children. Conversely, the older children were more likely to be hostile when aggression did occur. The two age groups also differed in their response to particular instigations. If a younger child was ridiculed or criticized by another, he tended to respond by hitting the other child about half of the time. Criticism of older children tended to produce reciprocal criticism 78 percent of the time, whereas hitting occurred only 20 percent of the time. Finally, the typical sex differences were observed: boys were more likely to behave aggressively (both hostile and instrumental) than girls at all age levels.

In general, as children grow older, there are fewer instances of aggression, and those that do occur are of a verbal rather than a physical nature. This outcome is consistent with age-paced changes in the child's cognitive status: children develop alternative ways of achieving what they previously achieved by pushing, shoving, and grabbing.

Situational factors also affect the amount and intensity of aggressive behavior. In three early studies that attempted to determine whether aggressive behavior is a function of social class, private (presumably middle-class) nursery schools were compared with public (lower-class) day care centers. Three different patterns were reported. Jersild and Markey (1935) found that the children in the private school were less likely to become involved in aggressive interactions than were the children in the public school. The investigators attributed this difference to the difference in the amount of supervision given in the two schools and in the extent to which quarrelsome interactions were tolerated. A second study (Muste and Sharpe, 1947) found that there were *more* instances of aggressive behavior in a private, university-affiliated school than in a public preschool in a lower-class neighborhood. These investigators explain that the probable reason for these results is that there is greater freedom of self-expression and a higher degree of active social participation among the children in the private school. A third study (Appel, 1942) found *no* consistent differences between private and public nursery schools. Why the apparent inconsistencies? What the overall results suggest is that the differences in the children's behavior reflect differences in the procedures of the teachers and in the way they structured their classrooms at least as much as they reflect differences in the socioeconomic background of the children. Macrae and Herbert-Jackson (1976) describe the effects of infant day care as "program specific." Furthermore, within a given preschool, the several activities (playing with blocks, arts, dramatic play) are differentially associated with vigorous, aggressive acts (Green, 1933; Shure, 1963).[3]

Finally, a comment on the cross-cultural generality of the findings on aggression is in order. A delegation of American psychologists recently visited some preschool nurseries in Mainland China and observed that the incidence of pushing, shoving, and other disruptive acts was minimal (Kessen, 1975). This was in sharp contrast to the activities observed in the typical nursery school in the United States and in England. Whether the differences across societies reflect the operation of contextual differences in the preschools per se, or whether they reflect differences in basic societal structure, cannot be determined by naturalistic observation.

Aggression in Middle Childhood

The frequency of physical attacks continues to be negatively correlated with age in middle childhood. In the Fels Research Institute longitudinal study,

Kagan and Moss (1962) found that there were not enough instances of unprovoked physical attacks in their sample of children 10 years old and older to permit a reliable plot of the behavior. Patterson and Cobb (1971) found only 2 or 3 instances of physical aggression per 1,000 interactions in a specially selected group of highly aggressive boys 6–12 years old. The behavior is not a frequent one, relative to the frequency of other interchanges. Physical attacks give way to verbal threats and denunciations, continuing a trend observed in the preschool period (Walters, Pearce, and Dahms, 1957). Sexual differentiation persists; that is, more boys than girls participate in activities that involve vigorous and hurtful physical contact. Cross-cultural comparisons confirm that such sex differences are not limited to Western societies. In all six societies studied by Whiting and her colleagues, boys were judged to be more aggressive than girls (Whiting, 1963; Whiting and Edwards, 1973).

In middle childhood, organized athletic activities that involve some degree of pain and injury (such as football, wrestling, and soccer) play a prominent role in the play behaviors of boys. In the absence of organized or sanctioned games, new "sports" are frequently devised by boys in this age group. Bandura (1973b) speculates that the "games" of childhood are seemingly used by some cultures as training schools for war. For example, in the Dugum Dani, a warrior society of the New Guinea highlands, young boys play war games that involve skewing seeds or impaling a hole with sharpened sticks. Older boys organized in teams battle one another with grass spears. The tactics are reasonably similar to those employed in war, except that the spears are too pliable to produce injury. The preoccupation with the materials and actions of war is not, of course, limited to boys in primitive tribes. Tin soldiers, chessmen, and, more recently, "bionic" men and G. I. Joes have been considered "acceptable" dolls for boys.

Our information on the frequency and intensity of real fighting (as opposed to playful fighting and sports) is distressingly incomplete. The reasons for

---

[3] Nonexperimental studies of preschool behavior cannot tell us whether quiet children are drawn to quiet activities, or whether the activities produce quiet children. Experimental studies of the type conducted by D. S. Patterson (1976—see Chapter 12) help distinguish between the two explanations.

incompleteness are not hard to find. The institutions in which children meet in organized groups (camps, schools, clubs) invariably prohibit violent behavior, and those who disobey the regulations are generally penalized. Consequently, the fighting that does occur is episodic, and, for the most part, is carried out where there is no direct observation.

The salience of aggression belies its frequency. "Attacks" are vivid events, even though they are infrequent. When one is a victim, the memories can be lifelong.

Aggression in Adolescence

As shown in Figure 11-1, physical assault is more frequent in teen-age males than in any other sex-age group. In their study of aggressive-antisocial adolescent boys in Oakland and Berkeley, California, Bandura and Walters (1959) found that their special group of delinquents considered toughness in street fighting to be a primary criterion by which they judged other boys and by which other boys judged them. An excerpt from one of the interviews illustrates this point:

Interviewer: Are there things about yourself that you're proud of, and wouldn't want to change?
Juvenile: Motorcycle riding.
Interviewer: Anything else?
Juvenile: Say, something like you're proud of? You probably wouldn't understand, but "stomping" I'm proud of because, I don't know, all the guys I hang around do that. Do you know what "stomping" is?
Interviewer: No, I don't.
Juvenile: Fighting with two feet without using your hands, see. I'm not trying to be conceited or anything, but I know I can use my feet better than all the guys I hang around with, so I wouldn't want to change that. Like my dad, he said, "If you know how to fight with your feet, then it's in your hands. You've got it made," or something like that. "You never need to be afraid of nobody."

There are marked differences in the frequency and intensity of aggressive acts, depending on where one lives in the United States (*Crime in the U.S.*, 1975). For instance, the incidence of arrest for violent crimes is twice as great in the eastern seaboard states (602 arrests per 100,000 population) as it is in the plains states (286 arrests per 100,000). The differences are not limited to regions: arrests for violence are approximately 8 times as frequent in cities as in rural areas (corrected for population differences). The powerful relationship between living circumstances and the probability of violence underscores the importance of the broader social supports for violent behavior that transcend individuals and the particular dyadic interactions in which they become involved.

Cross-cultural studies indicate that non-Western societies also differ in their attitude toward aggression in the young. The head-hunting Iatmul of New Guinea encourage brutal initiation rites for adolescent males. As Bandura and Walters (1963) have observed, the recipients of this treatment have excellent aggressive models to follow when it comes time for them to serve as the "initiators." Such approbation is not limited to initiation ceremonies. Following a successful head-hunting expedition, the decapitator is accorded a position of prestige and prominence.

In contrast, physical aggression is strongly frowned upon in another New Guinea culture, the Wogeo. If a fight does begin among children, they are usually led in an "opposite direction, presented with an axe, and told to take out their anger on a tree." As a result, "most of the big timber close to the village is . . . scarred" (Hogbin, 1945).

In arrests for violent crimes, large differences are found between males and females (see Figure

11–1). This outcome is consistent with other naturalistic studies (but not with some experimental ones; see below).

In summary, the normal development of aggressive behavior in humans parallels, superficially, the normal development of fighting in nonhuman animals. Specifically,

1.   In humans, as in nonhumans, the incidence of physical attacks tends to decrease with age and with the capacity to inflict injury.

2.   The relationship between the morphological and sexual status of the individual and the propensity to become involved in fighting interactions is seen in the behavior of both children and nonhumans. Males, beyond infancy and early preschool, are more likely to become involved in physically aggressive encounters than are females of the same age.

3.   In both humans and nonhumans, the occurrence of physical aggression is significantly dependent upon the social network in which the child is observed and the setting in which the interaction occurs. Contextual and interpersonal control is found from 12 months onward. A similar dependency has repeatedly been found, of course, in the analysis of fighting in nonhuman species.

The contrasts between humans and nonhumans are equally important. Human beings, unlike animals, can injure others with little or no physical involvement. Beginning in the preschool period, physical injury gradually gives way to verbal threats and attacks; the child finds that words can serve much the same function as physical aggression in interchanges, and often more effectively. To the extent that they disrupt the activity of another and produce withdrawal or behavioral redirection, words serve the same basic purposes for humans that attacks serve for animals. This is not to say that nonhuman species do not have signals that substitute for, ameliorate, or redirect physical attacks (Eibl-Eibesfeldt, 1970; Lorenz, 1966). In children, however, this capacity for symbolic expression of hostil-

ity is greatly expanded. Equally important are the kinds of acts that trigger retaliation and/or attack. Challenges to self-esteem, to plans and actions, and to status and social position can constitute, for humans, grounds for attack or defense (Feshbach, 1964).

Psychobiological Factors in the Development of Aggressive Behavior

Compared with the attention given to biophysical controls in animals, few studies of children have concentrated on their involvement in human aggressive interactions. This is unfortunate, not because there is any serious question about whether such controls operate in children, but because we still have a great deal to learn about *how* they operate to produce aggressive interchanges.

Most people who deal with children on a day-to-day basis would consider hardly newsworthy the finding that there is a correlation between children's biophysical states and their behavior. Even the most docile 5-year-old girl can become irritable and irritating if permitted to stay up considerably past her bedtime. Nor would parents (or children) be surprised to learn that a relationship exists between other temporary bodily states (fever, pain, "time since last meal") and the child's touchiness. And the more irritable children are, the more likely they are to become involved in quarrels and fights (Goodenough, 1931).

The operation of biophysical controls is not merely cyclical or episodic and short-term. Ontogenetic changes in morphology, biochemistry, and sensory capabilities clearly influence the amount and intensity of aggressive expression in a wide range of nonhuman species (Chapter 9). It seems possible that the same range of variables affects aggressive interactions in children. Moreover, because of age-paced changes in the capacity for symbolic and indirect forms of aggression in humans, ontogeny may play an even more important role in the control of aggressive behavior in humans than in other mammals.

Morphological Factors

Given the range of changes in physical structure that occur from birth to maturity, there can be little doubt that morphology accounts for some of the age-related variance in the frequency and intensity of attacks. The exact contribution of this variable is difficult to estimate, however, mainly because morphological changes are correlated with changes in cognitive development, which, in turn, are related to the differential social standards that are imposed upon the child.

One way to estimate the contribution of morphological factors is to analyze individual differences in physique while holding constant such variables as age and cognitive, social, economic, and situational differences. We know from comparative animal studies that there is a direct, modest correlation between such morphological characteristics as weight and musculature, on the one hand, and dominance in a relationship on the other. Not surprisingly, a similar but even more slender positive correlation holds for humans.

Two studies of dominance-aggressiveness in adolescent males confirm that morphology makes a difference. Boys in the Berkeley Growth Study who were the earliest to mature were more assertive, more active, and more frequently selected as leaders than were their slow-to-mature peers. (However, the ratings of "physique at maturity" were not correlated with "rate of maturation." So those who developed early were not necessarily mesomorphic—that is, having an athletic, muscular physique). But the personality dispositions observed at adolescence did persist, to a modest degree. When the males were retested at 30–40 years of age, the early-maturing males tended to score higher than late-maturing males on a self-report test of assertiveness and to be more likely to hold supervisory positions (Mussen and Jones, 1957).

Another thread of relevant evidence was reported by Sheldon and Eleanor Glueck (1950), who compared delinquent adolescents with a matched nondelinquent control group and found that the delinquents showed a stronger tendency toward mesomorphy than did the nondelinquents. Again, however, there was considerable overlap between the groups. Nor should morphology be expected to play a role of overwhelming importance in some of the more serious instances of human violence. We can be aggressive toward others—physically injure them—with minimal personal physical involvement. By using weapons and other devices capable of producing injury, men and women are freed from the limitations imposed by their physical structures. Hence experimental studies that employ electric shock as a means of punishing others show only modest and inconsistent differences between the men and women in aggressive behavior (Frodi, Macaulay, and Thome, 1977).

The Inheritance of Differences in Aggressive Dispositions

In Chapter 10, we found that individual differences in various measures of aggressive behavior were influenced by selective breeding. Analysis of the processes of development indicated that the pathways of genetic influence are multiple and that "aggression" is not inherited so much as are differential levels of activity and responsivity and rates of maturation.

Do we have any evidence to indicate that differences in aggressive behavior—or differences in characteristics that may be related to aggressive interchanges—are inherited in humans as well? Evidence of the heritability of temperament (affective disposition) has been found in studies where twins with identical chromosomal patterns (monozygotic twins) were compared with twins who had different genotypes (dizygotic twins). One of the most impressive studies using this technique was conducted in San Francisco by D. G. Freedman and B. Keller

(1963). These investigators tested 20 pairs of infants on a monthly basis during the first year of life to determine whether the identical twins were more similar to each other than were the fraternal twins. While the study was being conducted, neither the parents nor the investigators knew whether any given pair was monozygotic or dizygotic.

Appearance is not a reliable criterion of genetic identity. The physicians who delivered the infants were correct in only 10 of 19 cases, a level of accuracy that could be matched by flipping a coin. Whether infants were monozygotic or dizygotic was determined by 13 blood-group factors. This judg-

ment was made at the completion of the study, so that there was little opportunity for bias in the behavioral tests, even of the unconscious sort. Happily for the investigators, 11 of the 20 pairs proved to be fraternal and 9, identical. The 40 children were given two behavioral tests on a monthly basis throughout the first year: the "Infant Behavior Profile" (which covered such items as social orientation, tension, fearfulness, and general emotional tone) and the Mental and Motor Scales. Both tests were developed by Nancy Bayley at the National Institute of Mental Health.

The identical twins were found to be more similar to each other than the fraternal twins, at least on the items that were assessed in this study. Significant differences between the two types of twins were found in tests of motor activity: the monozygotic twins were clearly more similar to each other than were the dizygotic twins. The same outcome was obtained in the Bayley Infant Profile—within-pair differences were distinctly greater in the fraternal twins (see Figure 11–3).[4]

To what extent are early differences in activity/reactivity predictive of later differences in personality? R. Q. Bell and his collaborators at the National Institute of Mental Health (NIMH) conducted a longitudinal analysis of the relationship between certain patterns of infant behavior and subsequent activity in the preschool. Bell et al. (1971) found that the infant's response to tactile stimulation in the first week of life was moderately predictive of his reactivity to frustration 3½ years later. This finding

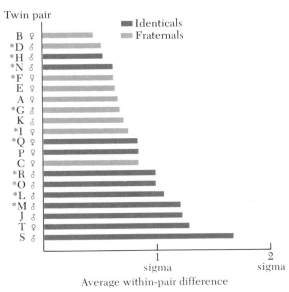

Figure 11–3. The differences between identical twin infants were less than those between nonidentical twins, according to the assessment on the Bayley mental and motor scales averaged to form a single distribution. Identical twins = dark gray; fraternal twins = light gray; two different experimenters, Dr. Freedman and Mrs. Keller, conducted the tests. (From Freedman and Keller. Copyright © 1963, by the American Association for the Advancement of Science. With permission.)

[4] Nichols and Broman (1974) have cautioned, however, that it may be "inappropriate to generalize infant twin studies to singleton populations" (p. 442). The problem is that (1) twins are more likely suffer neurological damage that nontwins (retardation is approximately 6 to 1 times more frequent, proportionally, in twins that in nontwins), and (2) there is a higher incidence of severe retardation among identical twins than among fraternal ones (Nichols and Broman, 1974). In other words, if one member of a twin pair is severely impaired, then the chances that the other member is also impaired are much higher for monozygotic twins than for dizygotic twins. The greater similarity at the very bottom of the scale, representing a small proportion of the twin sample, accounts for the difference in correlation between the monozygotic and dizygotic groups (Nichols and Broman, 1974).

of a positive relationship, though intriguing, must be balanced against the failure to predict later behavior on several other measures. A recent attempt at NIMH to replicate the finding yielded mixed, mostly negative, results (Yang and Halverson, 1976). A similar record of more misses than hits has been achieved by other longitudinal studies of personality from infancy through childhood (Kagan, 1971; Kagan and Moss, 1962; Thomas, Chess, and Birch, 1968)—see Chapter 22.

Another question concerns whether differences in aggressive interchanges that occur in later childhood and early adulthood reflect the operation of genetic factors. Here the evidence is less than compelling. A major problem is that the methods of human behavioral genetics have been unable to disentangle the obvious confounding of environmental and genetic influences. Genealogical analyses indicate that the disposition toward violence or criminality tends to run in families. But these methods fail to indicate what the effective process may be. As Fuller and Thompson (1960) comment in their review of the methods of human genetic analysis, the pedigree method "is fallible when dealing with well-defined character. With the complex subject of personality and temperament, it is even more so" (p. 231).

What do such kinship studies show? In general, that the closer the genetic relationship of two persons, the more similar are their test scores. This empirical generalization holds for those characteristics that are relevant to personality (for example, extraversion—Scarr, 1969; personality test performance—Gottesman, 1963) and mental illness (Rosenthal, 1970), as well as cognitive abilities (Jensen, 1969) and physical characteristics (Bayley, 1954).[5]

These data defy simple summary. About the most that might be said at this juncture is that the more closely related persons are in terms of genetic background, the more closely do their aggressive behaviors and correlated dispositions correspond. But the relationships are modest ones, and the explanation for them is unclear (that is, whether they are due to the operation of differences in psychobiological functioning, to the operation of the social system to which the individuals are exposed, or to some combination of the two).

The distinctive characteristics of the infant undergo multiple transformations prior to later childhood and adolescence. Once a reactive characteristic is expressed in a social interchange, its functional properties at any age are as dependent on the reactions of others as on the nature of the act itself. Hence it is not sufficient merely to demonstrate that some structural and reactive characteristics are heritable, because the relationship between early infant response dispositions and the development of assertive-aggressive patterns is not inevitable. As the Bell et al. (1971) study suggests, it is in the context of everyday interchanges that the inherent biases of the child are shaped, consolidated, and modified. A key to understanding genetic control is the systematic tracing of how constitutional characteristics mediate and influence the complex interchanges in which the child becomes involved.

Sex Chromosomes and Aggression

Closely related to heritability of temperament are differences in assertive-aggressive behavior that are sex linked. Feshbach (1970) compiled a tabular summary of studies that permit a comparison of males and females with respect to various forms of aggressive behavior (see Table 11–1). Despite the multiple definitions of aggression that were used in the studies, the results were remarkably consistent. In virtually all studies, boys were found to be more

[5] Nor is the direct evidence on the heritability of personality differences unambiguous. In Gottesman's (1963) careful work, monozygotic twins showed a greater similarity in performance on 25 percent (6/24) of the personality scales in which they were compared with dizygotic twins. However, on 17 percent of the scales (4/24), the fraternal pairs showed a greater similarity than did the identical pairs.

Table 11-1. Summary of 57 studies of sex differences in aggression.

Type of measurement	Number of studies where the aggression scores were higher for:		
	Girls	Boys	No difference
Direct observation	0	9	5
Ratings (by parents, teachers, peers)	0	9	1
Ratings (by self)	2	6	0
Experimental	0	9	1
Projective test (Thematic Apperception Test, etc.)	1	4	1
Fantasy test (doll play)	1	7	1
	—	—	—
Totals	4	44	9

NOTE: None of the four studies where girls were found to be more aggressive than boys indicated that the girls showed more physical aggression: The differences appeared on self-ratings of "prosocial" and "covert" aggression, and on two fantasy/projective test measures of verbal aggression.
SOURCE: Feshbach, 1970, with permission.

physically aggressive than girls. These results are consistent with the outcomes of studies of nonhuman mammals.[6] (Girls equal or surpass boys only when the measures are fantasy, projection, or self-ratings.)

A question that is relevant to the concerns of this chapter is whether chromosomal differences are responsible for the differences among boys who differ in assertiveness. In the past 20 years, procedures have been discovered that enable the relatively rapid and precise analysis of chromosomes in a single cell. The normal male sex chromosome is XY; the normal female, XX. Of particular interest has been the finding that some males who have all the normal male physical characteristics have one or more extra male chromosomes (that is, XYY instead of XY—rather than the normal complement of 46 chromosomes, these individuals have 47).

One provocative hypothesis is that males who have the extra Y chromosome are more likely to behave in an aggressive, antisocial manner. These males are more likely to be incarcerated than are males who have the normal set of chromosomes. The hypothesis has stimulated considerable controversy (Jarvik, Klodin, and Matsuyama, 1973). How, then, do XYY males differ from XY males?

First, there is general agreement that XYY males differ, on the average, from normal males in several ways. Males with this distinctive chromosomal pattern tend to be somewhat taller and more slender than XY males. They tend to be somewhat less bright, scoring typically at "borderline" scores on test of intelligence. They also tend to have a higher incidence of acne and associated skin disorders. But the popular stereotype of the XYY male as a tall, stupid man with acne and a murderous disposition is simply inaccurate.[7] The relationship between the physical characteristics, intelligence test perform-

---

[6] But the human-animal parallel is certainly not a perfect one. One discrepancy is that young (preadolescent) boys and girls show a difference in physical assertiveness that is as great as, if not greater than, that found in adult men and women (see Frodi et al., 1977). In most (but not all) nonhuman species, the species-typical differences in aggressiveness between prepubertal males and females are modest, whereas the differences between adult males and females are typically highly reliable.

[7] Contrary to popular belief, convicted mass-murderer Richard Speck (who seems to fit the XYY behavioral stereotype otherwise) is an XY male. Chromosomal analyses indicated a normal karyotype despite the abnormal behavior (Borgaonkar and Shah, 1974).

ance, and presence of an *XYY* chromosomal pattern is not strong enough, according to available reports, to permit reliable individual predictions (Borgaonkar and Shah, 1974; Money, 1970).

Second, there is also agreement that *XYY* males are more likely than *XY* males to be found in residential institutions, including prisons. This discovery was in large measure responsible for the generalization that *XYY* males were in prison because they are more aggressive and violent (see Jarvik et al., 1973). Persons are incarcerated for a good many reasons, only some of which have to do with violence or aggressiveness. When a careful comparison was made between type of crime (sex violations, nonpersonal crimes such as theft and bribery, crimes of violence) and chromosomal type, no relationship was found between aggressiveness and the presence of *XYY* (Borgaonkar and Shah, 1974). Moreover, when social class factors are taken into account, the proportion of *XYY* males in prisons is about the same as the proportion of *XY* males. In an authoritative and comprehensive review in the *Progress in Medical Genetics*, Borgaonkar and Shah (1974) therefore conclude that "the frequency of antisocial behavior of the *XYY* male is probably not very different from non-*XYY* persons of similar background and social class" (p. 188).

The most extensive single empirical evaluation of the *XYY* aggression hypothesis was recently made by an international body of scientists representing the fields of psychology, genetics, criminology, pediatrics, and gynecology.[8] They conducted an exhaustive analysis of the entire population of men born in Copenhagen, Denmark, in the 4 years between January 1, 1944, and December 31, 1947, inclusive. The aim was to identify the men born in this period who had an *XYY* and *XXY* chromosomal complement and to determine whether either of these

chromosomal patterns was associated with aggressive behavior in early adulthood. Since *XYY* men are typically taller than average, the researchers limited their analysis to tall men born in that period (184 cm and taller, or slightly over 6 feet). The men who qualified on the height criterion were studied for chromosomal pattern. This determination required individual contact, interviews, and the subject's cooperation in giving a buccal smear (from the mucuous membranes lining the cheek) and a blood sample from the ear lobe. Twelve *XYY* males, 16 *XXY* males, and 4,096 *XY* males were identified. There was a modest attrition in the sample due to death, uncooperativeness, or immigration (see Figure 11–4).

Were *XYY* males more likely to be criminal and/or aggressive than men who did not have this chromosomal pattern?[9] The data indicate that *XYY* males were more likely to have criminal records, but that they were not more likely to be violent or aggressive (see Tables 11–2 and 11–3). But why was the incidence of criminal arrests higher? Witkin et al. propose that the correlation between criminality and aggression is due primarily to the lower intelligence level of *XYY* and *XXY* males, since on all measures of intellectual functioning and the *XYY* and *XXY* males scored significantly below *XY* males. Whether this hypothesis is the full explanation cannot be determined from the results of the Copenhagen study. Witkin et al. (1976) conclude:

> The data from the documentary records we have examined speak on society's legitimate concern about aggression among XYY and XXY men. No evidence has been found that men with either of these sex chromosome complements are especially aggressive. Because such men do not appear to contribute particularly to society's problem with

---

[8] This multinational, multidisciplinary investigation is reported in Witkin, Mednick, Schulsinger, Bakkestrom, Christiansen, Goodenough, Hirschhorn, Lundsteen, Owen, Philip, Rubin, and Stocking (1976).

[9] The *XXY* chromosomal pattern was included because it was also a chromosomal aberration that occurs in phenotypic males. It has not, however, been proposed to be associated with heightened aggressiveness. The comparison of *XXY* and *XYY* provides a useful assessment of the effects of general chromosomal dysfunction on social behavior, as opposed to specific *XYY* effects.

aggressive crimes, their identification would not serve to ameliorate this problem (p. 554). [10]

Neurological and Biochemical Factors

The view that aggressive behavior comes about because of brain damage has received some support in both the clinical and the experimental literature. Studies of delinquents as well as adult criminals indicate that abnormal electroencephalographic (EEG) patterns, which are one sign of brain damage, are recorded more frequently in these groups than in comparable noncriminal populations (Gross, 1972; Mark and Ervin, 1970; McCord and McCord, 1956). At the clinical level, neurologists have reported a positive association between brain disease and violence, particularly of a sudden, impulsive sort (Gross, 1972). The notion that is most often proposed is the sensitization via neurological deficit. In this regard, Gross (1972) indicates that "the key concept is: organic brain disease→dyscontrol under minimal stimulation→ potential for violence" (p. 90). In other words, the brain-damaged person's threshold for aggressive behavior is lowered. Sudden, impulsive, and irrational violence has been associated, on an individual, case-study basis with a wide range of brain disorders (Mark and Ervin, 1970).

[10] This conclusion touches on ethics in XYY research with infants: should one report to parents that their infant has an abnormal chromosomal pattern? Giving such information to parents may not only induce anxieties, it may cause them to behave in ways that they would not have had the information not been given. Possibly changes in parental attitudes and the network of social influence could have a stronger impact than the extra chromosome. Biochemist Michael Mage (1975) offered a wry comment on the problem in *Science* magazine:

The controversy over the ethics of identification and study of individuals of XYY karyotype is an example of our fascination for the exotic problems to the neglect of common but more serious genetic conditions, such as the XY karyotype that afflicts roughly half of the human race, including the writer. Overwhelming statistical evidence indicates that the XY karyotype is associated with major social problems such as violent crime and war. If we are to provide medical and psychiatric assistance to XYY individuals, let us not neglect the XY's, who in aggregate present a much greater problem for the community (p. 299).

Although case histories are useful, we must be alert as well to those instances where brain damage does not lead to violent outbursts. In this regard, Bandura (1973a) notes that it is easy to overestimate the importance of brain damage if one singles out for analysis only those cases in which violence occurs. What about instances where there is brain injury but the person does not behave aggressively? Studies of normal populations, for instance, indicate that from 10 percent to 50 percent of the children examined show some signs of abnormality in their EEG patterns (Mark and Ervin, 1970). Further, studies of children who have demonstrable brain damage indicate that aggression and violence are not necessary outcomes of the defect. F. Graham and her colleagues at the University of Wisconsin (1962) studied children who had suffered injuries at birth that had resulted in varying degrees of brain damage. It was of particular interest that assertive-aggressive behavior was not an inevitable outcome of such injuries.

Nonetheless, that a relationship exists between some forms of brain disorder and violence cannot be denied. P. Gloor (1967), of the Montreal Neurological Institute, estimates that outbursts of rage occur in about 50 percent of the patients suffering from some types of psychomotor epilepsy and are sometimes triggered by the most trivial events. In some cases, the surgical cure of the epileptic condition results in a disappearance of this tendency toward unprovoked anger. Gloor theorizes that the rage is not an inevitable outcome of the brain stimulation. Rather, these responses are dependent upon the stimuli present in the environmental setting in which the stimulation occurs. He points out that the aggression associated with a seizure often occurs when the person is in a state of post-attack confusion. It typically occurs when the patient is "restrained by well-meaning people in an attempt to protect him." Changing the conditions for the arousal—through surgical or chemical intervention—should also diminish the likelihood that the individual will become involved in interactions that evoke the rage.

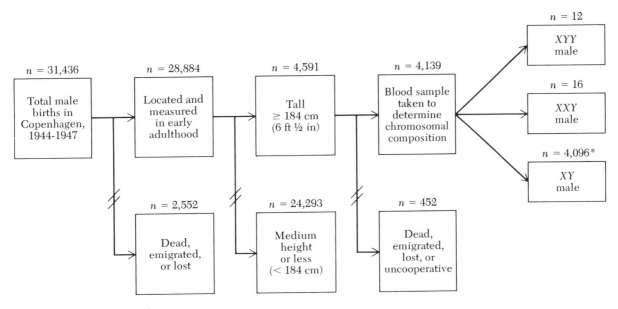

$*n=13$ chromosomal anomalies other than *XYY* or *XXY*
$n=2$ unaccounted for in study

Figure 11-4.   The steps taken to identify XYY, XXY, and XY males from all infants born in Copenhagen, Denmark, from January 1, 1944, to December 31, 1947. (From Witkin et al. Copyright © 1976, by the American Association for the Advancement of Science. With permission.)

Table 11-2.   Crime rates and mean values for background variables of *XY*'s *XYY*'s, and *XXY*'s in the Copenhagen study.

Group	Criminality		Army selection test			Educational index			Parental SES			Height (cm)		
	Rate (percent)	n	Mean	S.D.	n	Mean	S.D.	n	Mean	S.D.	n	Mean	S.D.	n
XY	9.3	4096	43.7	11.4	3759	1.55	1.18	4084	3.7	1.7	4058	187.1	3.0	4096
XYY	41.7*	12	29.7†	8.2	12	0.58*	0.86	12	3.2	1.5	12	190.8†	4.6	12
XXY	18.8	16	28.4†	14.1	16	0.81‡	0.88	16	4.2	1.8	16	189.8†	3.6	16

$*P < .01.$
$†P < .001.$
$‡P < .05.$
NOTE: Criminality refers to convictions for violations of the Danish penal code; the army selection test is a measure of intellectual functioning (higher scores mean better performance); the educational index refers to the highest grade achieved in school; and the parental SES refers to the father's occupation.
SOURCE: Witkin et al., 1976.

218

Table 11-3. Case reports of XYY and XXY men who were repeated offenders.

Nature of offenses of XYY's convicted on one or more criminal charges.

Case No. 2

This man is a chronic criminal who, since early adolescence, has spent 9 of 15 years in youth prisons and regular prisons. By far his most frequent criminal offense, especially in his youth, has been theft or attempted theft of a motor vehicle. Other charges included burglary, embezzlement, and procuring for prostitution. On a single occasion he committed a mild form of violence against an unoffending person; for this together with one case of burglary he received a sentence of around three-quarters of a year. This aggressive act was an isolated incident in a long period of chronic criminality. Except for this act, and the charge of procuring, all his nearly 50 offenses were against property, predominantly larceny and burglary. His single most severe penalty was somewhat less than a year in prison. Most of his crimes were committed in the company of other persons (BPP, 27).*

Case No. 3

This man committed two thefts, one in late adolescence, the second in his early 20's. The penalties for both were mild—a small fine for the first, and less than 3 months in prison for the second. His last offense was 7 years ago (BPP, 37).

Case No. 5

This man committed two petty offenses as a young adult, within a short time of each other (one the theft of a motor-assisted cycle, the other a petty civil offense), for which the penalties were detentions of approximately 2 weeks and less than 2 weeks, respectively. His last offense was committed 10 years ago (BPP, 28).

Case No. 7

This man committed his only criminal offenses in his 20's, within a short period of time: falsely reporting a traffic accident to the police and causing a small fire. On both occasions he was intoxicated. The penalty was probation. His last offense was committed 5 years ago (BPP, 25).

Case No. 12

This man was under welfare care as a child and has spent only three to four of the last 20 years outside of institutions for the retarded. He is an episodic criminal. When very young he committed arson. Later his crimes included theft of motor vehicles, burglary, larceny, and embezzlement. His more than 90 registered offenses were all against property, mostly theft and burglary. For crimes committed while he was out of an institution, the penalty imposed was placement in an institution for the mentally retarded. For crimes committed while he was in such an institution—once theft of a bicycle, another time theft of a quantity of beverage—he was continued in the institution (BPP, 18).†

Nature of offenses of XXY's convicted on one or more criminal charges.

Case No. 17

This man's only criminal offense, committed when he was well into his 20's, was that he attacked his wife in an exceptionally brutal way, without any provocation from her. This happened twice, within a very short interval, while he was under the influence of liquor. For this he was imprisoned for somewhat more than a year (BPP, 26).

Case No. 25

For criminal career of this man consisted of two offenses: the first, in late adolescence, a theft of edibles from a food store, for which he was placed on probation, the second the theft of a motor vehicle, for which he was given less than 3 weeks of simple detention. Both crimes were committed in company with others. The last occurred 7 years ago (BPP, 11).

Table 11-3. *(Continued)*

Nature of offenses of XYY's convicted on one or more criminal charges.

Case No. 27

This man has a short period of juvenile delinquency. His offenses included attempted theft and theft of a motor vehicle and a bicycle, burglary, and theft from a vending machine. On his first offense, in early adolescence, the charge was withdrawn and he was put under the care of child welfare authorities. His two other penalties consisted of withdrawal of charge on payment of a fine. Several of his offenses were committed in company with another person. The last occurred 10 years ago (BPP, 16).

*BPP is the army selection test score. Note that normal XY mean score is BPP 43.7

†Since this man was mentally retarded and spent many years in an institution for the retarded, he was not given a BPP at the draft board. The BPP of 18 was estimated by a stepwise linear regression, using a double cross-validity design, from the correlation between BPP scores and scores for the Wechsler Adult Intelligence Scale for the men in the individual case study.

SOURCE: Witkin et al., 1976.

Drugs and the Control of Aggressive Behavior

Brain surgery is not the only way to control assertiveness due to minimal brain damage. In adults, the same goal can be accomplished by the use of tranquilizing medications. This family of drugs began to be widely applied in this country in the mid-1950s and has since produced a revolution in the care and treatment of psychotic and severely neurotic patients, whether the disturbance has an organic basis or not. The happy feature of tranquilizers is that they can reduce anxiety even while the patient continues to experience delusions and hallucinations. Moreover, the patient is less likely to incur the wrath of others who must deal with him: the effects are socially bidirectional.

Tranquilizers are less effective when given to the minimally brain-damaged (hyperkinetic) child, for they frequently affect his attention and/or motivation in the classroom. Bradley (1937) discovered that this side effect was not produced when the hyperactive child was administered stimulant drugs instead of sedatives. Clinical observation further suggested not only that the child was calmed by the stimulant but also that he was able to focus his attention on the task at hand, such as completing his assignment. The outcome was interesting for an-

other reason. Amphetamines, the class of drugs used, typically have the opposite effect on adults, who use them as "pep" pills or appetite suppressants. Why they have a calming effect on children is still not known.

Amphetamines and their derivatives were originally prescribed for children suspected of having brain damage. More recently, they have been prescribed for virtually any child who shows extreme behavior patterns, regardless of presumed central nervous system involvement. The Food and Drug Administration has estimated (HEW Report, 1971) that some 150,000 to 200,000 children were treated with stimulant drugs in 1970.

How really effective are stimulants in diminishing assertive-aggressive activity? Authoritative opinion is divided on this question, although the bulk of the evidence indicates that the drugs do indeed reduce hyperactivity for some children. The hyperactivity reduction is greater in children who have been given stimulants than in children given a placebo (Aman and Sprague, 1974; Conners and Eisenberg, 1963). The extent to which scholastic performance is improved, however, remains controversial (see Grinspoon and Singer, 1973, for a comprehensive review). In addition, there is evidence of side effects, including a general growth suppression in some children. Presumably this result could come about because of the appetite-suppressing effect of the medication. There is also a concern that the drug may be addictive over the long run. Given these unfavorable side effects, it seems not surprising that many researchers and clinicians are concerned about long-term usage of the medication (Ross and Ross, 1976).

Anger

One other matter concerning psychobiology and the development of aggressive interchanges requires our attention, namely, the connection between anger and aggression. Acts of mild, intermediate, and extreme violence are usually assumed to go hand in hand with anger or fear. However, a question can be raised about whether the linkage between the emotion and the behavior is inevitable. Observations of 1½-year-old children indicate that they can be hurtful to others without getting "mad." Conversely, studies of the emotional states of adults indicate that frustration or anger gives rise to multiple reactions, only some of which should be labeled aggressive (Miller, 1941; Whiting, 1944). Anger can give rise to withdrawal, constructive actions, or pacification, according to the conditions under which it occurs and who is involved.

The essential problem is to determine how anger and certain interactional patterns become integrated in development and how the integration can be altered or redirected. The matter has multiple theoretical and practical implications. It is central to the problem of catharsis and how the mass media may influence aggression in children (Chapter 12), as well as how one might proceed with in the therapy of "angry" youngsters.

How does anger develop in the first place? The classic study on the development of emotional states was conducted some 45 years ago by Katherine Bridges (1933). Having set for herself the seemingly simple task of identifying the roots of emotions in young children, she observed institution-reared in-

fants who ranged in age from 1 month to 2 years. She found that the behavioral expressions of "anger" did not appear until the third or fourth month. Earlier in their development she had observed only variations in the intensity of "undifferentiated excitement" and distress.

Influential as this early study has been in shaping ideas about emotional development, it seems likely that the label given to a particular emotional display was strongly influenced by the circumstances that surrounded it. If the observers do not know what preceded the child's expressions, they cannot be sure whether it represents anger, fear, or excitement (Sherman, 1927). Second, and more important, as Knight Dunlap (1928) observed, emotions are not entities in themselves, and arousal states must be interpreted in the light of the settings and interactions in which they occur. More recently, Schachter and Singer (1962) extended this argument and showed that a given state of arousal will be given quite different labels (fear, anxiety, or anger) by the person who experiences it, according to his expectations and surroundings.

These observations seem to indicate that the development of anger is not a unitary process. Rather, it involves changes in the organization of the hormonal events associated with arousal *and* the capacity of the child to identify label his internal states. In view of the involvement of cognitive processes in identification and labeling, studies of the development of psychophysiological controls have thus begun to focus simultaneously on neurophysiological substrates and on the child's perceptual discrimination capabilities.

There remains the problem of the connection between arousal states and hurtful, assertive behavior. Three major positions have been taken on this issue, dating back to William James's (1890) classic analysis.

One view is that anger is the primary state and that aggression thus follows anger (anger→ aggression). If this is true, then control of aggression might proceed by controlling the occurrence of anger or hostility. Hence the child may be helped to redefine situations or acts that trigger emotional arousal so that they no longer elicit anger (Novaco, 1975). Alternatively, drugs may be used to decrease the child's readiness to be emotionally aroused.

A second view, originally offered by James and physiologist N. Langely, is that aggression precedes anger (aggression→anger). If this interpretation is accurate, then therapy should focus on the child's behavior, not his emotions. Hence efforts to produce changes in his behaviors might begin by operating directly on aggressive interchanges and include substitution of more peaceful or less provocative responses for ones that produce insult and injury, or removal of the provocations. This seems to be the strategy in behavioral therapy where new ways of responding are reinforced (Brown and Elliot, 1965).

A third view is that the actions and emotions should not be separated because, typically, the behavior and the emotional state augment each other. Accordingly, anger could be a stimulus for retributive actions, or it could emerge in the course of the escalation of the interchange. The bidirectional view is useful because it assumes that arousal states can wax and wane in the course of interchanges and that they serve in a dynamic fashion to support or to alter the children's acts and their outcomes.

Summary

Although we not been very successful in fighting back the "smouldering and sinister" flames of aggressive behavior, the information that has been gained over the past half century has helped to clarify the developmental bases for hurtful interchanges. In particular:

■ From the first to the fourth year of life there is a sharp reduction in the proportion of acts that might be broadly classified as assertive-aggressive. In one investigation (Holmberg, 1977), about one-half of the acts initiated by children 12–18 months of age with respect to other children involved behaviors that could potentially produce unhappiness or pain for the other child, but this proportion was significantly reduced by the fourth year.

■ Conclusions about the presence or absence of sex differences in assertive behaviors in very young children (0–2 years) remain controversial. By the third to fourth year and on through adolescence, researchers agree that boys are more likely to behave in a physically assertive-aggressive fashion than girls, even though an overlap between the sexes remains.

■ Events that reduce the threshold for emotional arousal (such as brain damage, or temporary states of hunger, sleepiness, and fever) tend to increase the probability of the occurrence of assertive-aggressive interchanges in children. Conversely, events that increase the threshold for arousal, such as certain drugs, decrease the likelihood of assertive-aggressive behavior.

Nonetheless, the correlation between arousal conditions and the occurrence of aggressive interchanges is only a modest one in children, in contrast to nonhumans. Some children, on becoming hungry or tired, do not become involved in assertive interchanges; they go to sleep. Similarly, not all or even most instances of brain damage lead to states of violence or rage. Nor are chromosomal disorders, such as the XYY pattern in males, related in any direct or simple way to aggressive behavior. And one cannot predict much better than chance whether patterns of reactivity observed in infancy will lead to aggressive interchanges in early and late childhood. Why not?

The answer is the same for children as for nonhuman young: psychobiological effects are translated into actions and counteractions that are shaped by the social network to which the individual is introduced. We now turn to an analysis of how aggressive interchanges develop and how they change throughout the lives of children.

12

AGGRESSIVE INTERCHANGES
IN CHILDREN:
THE SYNTHESIS OF EXPERIENCE

Picture yourself in a seafood restaurant, preparing to enjoy a dinner with friends: a father, mother, and their two children. Suddenly, the father slaps his 11-year-old son in the face, accidentally knocking his steamed clams to the floor in the process. The event is acutely embarrassing—to the family, to the waiters, and to almost everyone else in the restaurant—so you pretend to ignore it by peering under the table for the clams. As the mini-drama ends, the boy and his father are down on the floor retrieving their orders, which are still steaming.

To the observer the aggressive act—the slap—was the event that commanded attention. But what precipitated it? The observer probably is not aware that the victim himself had, moments before, been the aggressor. He had taunted his younger 6-year-old sister, who was in a pout because their mother had denied her request to order fried chicken instead of seafood. Following the taunt, the father had turned to the brother and reprimanded him by remarking, "That wasn't the smartest thing to say." Knowing that he was in the safety of a public place, the son unwisely retorted, "Yeah, so what?" Then came the slap and the embarrassing aftermath, and

the family eventually settled down to dipping clams and cracking lobsters.

What, then, was the real cause of the paternal aggression? Tracing backward in the interchanges, it could have been the mother's rigidity, the sister's pout, the brother/victim's taunting, the father's sarcasm, or the boy's wise talk. But all of these events were interrelated; each act in succession produced outcomes that triggered subsequent, more intense interchanges. Ultimately, the father and the boy found themselves entrapped in an escalation that they could not, or would not, stop. In a cogent analysis of such familial exchanges, G. R. Patterson (1976) has recently suggested that chronically aggressive children are both the "victims and architects" of their worlds. More generally, family exchanges are similar to other social interactions—including those between policeman and offender (Toch, 1969), between mother and offspring (Hinde, 1970), between animal and animal (Cairns and Scholz, 1973), and between child and child (Hall, 1973)—in short, almost all of life's relationships.

In this chapter we will examine the results of recent analyses of aggression in children. The questions that we will raise (How are aggressive children, or nonaggressive children, produced? How are the effects of experience consolidated or extinguished? How can aggressive behaviors be prevented and changed?) are roughly the same as those that we raised in our analysis of the development of aggressive behavior in nonhumans. Studies of children have also been concerned with such influences as the family and the media. Contemporary approaches to interactional analysis permit us to have a new perspective on these old questions.

We will consider first the principles that have been derived from the study of the behavior occurring in three age-developmental stages: early childhood, middle childhood, and adolescence. The aim will be to determine the extent to which common, or different, principles control aggressive interchanges at these different stages of human development.

Interactional Controls in Early Childhood

Recall that a key to understanding the establishment of aggression in nonhumans was the finding that aggressive behavior develops in the absence of any explicit training or specific attack-related experience. Detailed accounts of how the isolation experience affects the interaction patterns of animals indicated that it exaggerates processes that occur in normal development. Although the isolation experiment was helpful because it showed how aggressive animals can be produced, its basic importance was that it helped us to understand the development of "normal" or typical aggressive interchanges.

Studies of human development obviously cannot employ the isolation methodology. However, researchers have recently used the basic technique of interchange analysis to clarify how aggressive behavior develops in natural and in experimental settings.

Reciprocal Patterns in Aggressive Interchanges

According to interactional concepts, one of the determinants of whether a child behaves in an assertive manner is the social system in which his acts occur. The powerful effect of the behavior of the "other" was seen in positive social interchanges (Chapter 8). Will parallel effects occur in assertive or aggressive interchanges? William M. Hall attempted to answer this question in a doctoral dissertation at Indiana University (Hall, 1973). On the basis of the assumption of reciprocal influence—that the acts of children tend to elicit similar acts from others—Hall reasoned that, in a dyad, the assertive behaviors of one child are a major determinant of the other child's aggressiveness. Specifically, Hall argued that an escalation process occurs in pairs of children much like the one that occurs in pairs of nonhumans. in which assertive acts stimulate even more vigorous counter-responses.

Hall tested this hypothesis in an ingenious way. Before giving pairs of 6- to 7-year-old boys explicit instructions, he "programmed" one member of each pair to behave assertively by having him watch a motion picture. In the film the two "actors" escalated their interchanges to the point where they hit and threw their Bo-Bo dolls at each other (and at the cameraman). In the experiment proper, after one boy in each pair had seen the film and the other boy had seen no film, the two boys were placed in a large room with two big Bo-Bo dolls and told that they could do whatever they liked. The main question was whether the active member of the pair would entrap his partner into an escalating sequence in which both would become more assertive and aggressive, or whether the passive member of the pair could conceivably encourage his partner to "cool it" so that neither boy would behave aggressively.[1]

Hall found that the more active, aggressive partner was more effective in escalating the exchange

---

[1] Hall had other conditions (that will not be discussed here) that were designed to assess different aspects of the hypothesis.

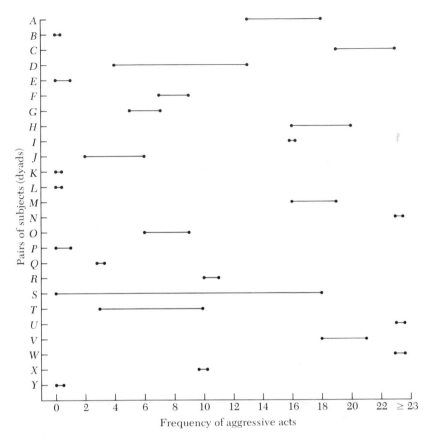

Figure 12-1. The correlation between nonpersonal aggressive acts observed among boys who were tested together was very high. Fifty boys tested in pairs (25 dyads, with one pair designated as *A*, another as *B*, and so on) were told that they could do whatever they wished in a room that contained, among other things, two large Bo-Bo dolls. Each dot in the above figure represents the number of occasions that a child threw, punched, or hit the dolls. The scores of the two members of each pair are shown on the same row and connected by lines (hence the shorter the line, the greater the similarity in the two children's behaviors). The correlation was high and positive ($r = +.82$) (from Hall, 1973).

than was the passive partner in de-escalating it. Hall's finding was consistent with earlier findings that the activity level of relatively inactive boys who are tested with highly active boys in free-play situations shows a dramatic increase (Hollenberg and Sperry, 1951; Kaspar and Lowenstein, 1971).

The reciprocal controls of aggressive activity were even stronger than Hall had originally expected. Regardless of the measure used, and regardless of the test conditions, there was a high correlation between the behaviors of the two members of the pair (see Figure 12-1 and Table 12-1). If one

Table 12-1. The information in Figure 12-1 can also be analyzed in terms of conditional probabilities. If one member of the pair (alpha) performs no aggressive act, then the probability that his partner (beta) will perform one or no aggressive act is $P = .86$. If alpha performs 23 or more aggressive acts, the probability that beta will perform one or less is $P = .00$.

		$\beta \leq 1$	$\beta \geq 23$
808°			
816°	$\alpha = 0$	.86	.00
820°	$\alpha \geq 23$	.00	.75

member continually banged his Bo-Bo doll into the other child's doll, his partner reciprocated with like behavior. The rule that guided the second child's behavior was, in effect, "If you want to act that way, so can I." Similarly, if one child was content simply to slam the doll against the wall and to tweak its nose, that was the dominant activity of the partner.

Cognitive Rules and Aggressive Interchanges

One of the most important results of Hall's experiment was the discovery that certain rules control interactions. Hall recorded the entire interchange on video tape so that he could later view it on closed circuit television and identify which acts encouraged or inhibited hitting. He discovered that the boys did not respond in an automatic, "tit-for-tat" fashion, as do animals, even though, on the whole, the behaviors of both members of a pair were quite similar. Thus, although there was a high correlation between the hitting scores within a pair (that is, if child *A* was aggressive, so was child *B*, and if child *A* was passive, so was child *B*), a par-

ticular act was not necessarily predictive of the partner's *immediate* response. Knowledge of the content of the immediately preceding action of the other child did not increase the accuracy of the prediction of what would be the next act of the subject.

How might there be reciprocity of action, without there also being a close interdependence of the acts of the two boys? The answer to this question may be the key to one of the nuclear issues of interactional analysis: how acts are synchronized. Hall's detailed examination of the second-by-second dependencies indicated that each boy's activities were primarily organized *within* each child (*intra*individual organization) and were secondarily organized around the framework provided by the actions of the other child (*inter*individual organization). At the interpersonal level, each pair of children tended to engage in the same "game"—that is, each child adopted the same activity as the other child, and followed the same rules. Different games were played in different pairs. Moreover, each participant fashioned his performance according to his own idiosyncratic style, which in turn was determined by organismic, experiential, and cognitive factors.

Hence the "synchrony" was simultaneously of two types: interpersonal and intrapersonal. The interpersonal coordination arose because the two children shared a common activity, as well as the roles and rules related to that activity. Hence the basic response pattern seemed to be organized at precise levels by intraorganismic factors, while the type of joint activity and its main features were coordinated by interpersonal events.

The recognition that children re-evaluate and revise the rules governing interchanges during the course of the interchange helps to explain otherwise puzzling data on the influence of toys and situations on social behavior. D. S. Patterson (1976) attempted to determine whether toys make children aggressive, or whether aggressive children are drawn to particular toys. In Patterson's experiment, same-sex trios of 5-year-olds were placed alternately in two different play areas. One play area was an "art materials" center; the other was a "blocks" center. Importantly, the trios were kept intact and the same three children were observed in both areas. If the nature of the materials controlled the social interchanges, then art materials should have led to quieter, more peaceful play than blocks. If, however, group composition was the controlling factor, then there should have been no difference between the two situations; boys would have behaved assertively and girls would have behaved quietly. Patterson observed different amounts of assertive play in the two situations. But the differences for the boys were opposite in direction from what is typically observed in nursery schools. The male trios showed considerably more assertive-aggressive play in the art center than in the block center. In the former, they had a virtual free-for-all: they tossed play dough against the walls and against each other; they smeared paint on themselves and on the floor; they made airplanes out of the drawing paper. They apparently learned early in the session that they could use the materials in any way that they wanted, so they did. The "rules" that the boys adopted for art were not the kind usually observed in nursery schools, but they played with the blocks in a reasonably normal fashion. The girls, on the other hand, behaved in both

laboratory settings in ways that were quite like those usually observed in nursery schools. The results of this experiment indicate not only that there are situational controls (laboratory versus classroom; blocks versus art materials), but that the expectations and acts associated with particular situations can be rapidly modified.[2]

Information by the Experimenter: Modeling

Doubtless one of the most reliable ways to produce aggressive or assertive acts experimentally in young children is through imitating or modeling another person's behavior (Bandura, 1971, 1973a; Bandura and Walters, 1963). Modeling studies would appear at first to be difficult to interpret within an interchange framework because only one child is usually involved, and the "aggressive" act is typically directed toward a large inflated "Bo-Bo doll" balloon (Cottrell, 1969). Nonetheless, the modeling phenomenon underscores the sheer power of observational learning which, when it occurs in interchanges, can be of great import in the control of social behavior.

The classic modeling studies with children of preschool and kindergarten age typically had two stages. First the child was permitted to view a depiction (filmed, televised, or live) in which a person or cartoon character directed unusual aggressive acts against a Bo-Bo doll or another person. After viewing the model's performance, the child was taken to a place similar to that just observed and permitted to play with the materials, which included a Bo-Bo doll. Ordinarily, the child duplicated many of the unusual acts that he observed, including the style in which they were performed. Among the general findings of experiments that used this procedure,[3] are the following:

---

[2] One trio of boys showed a great lack of insight by transferring their new, disruptive "game" with art materials back to the school setting. The art teacher immediately made clear whose rules applied: the boys sat in the corridor the rest of the morning.

[3] See Bandura, 1971 and 1973a, for careful reviews of this work. The procedure is discussed further in Chapter 19.

1. Boys and girls differ in their readiness to duplicate some of the more vigorous acts—boys are more assertive.

2. An act will be imitated less frequently if it is explicitly prohibited, either in the film or by the experimenter.

3. An act will be imitated more frequently if it is explicitly condoned, either in the film or by the experimenter.

4. Children will perform assaultive acts against "humanlike" clowns under some experimental conditions, indicating the relevance of modeling processes to interchanges.

5. Once imitation has been elicited, it is retained and the acts duplicated on tests given 6 months after the initial exposure.

Why does the modeling experiment work so well? According to a recent theoretical analysis by Bandura (1971), modeling is effective because it communicates information about how the child should behave. The presentation of a short film showing a salient activity appears to be an effective way of getting the message across. If the child is then left with a Bo-Bo doll and not given any further instructions, he usually tries to play the same kind of game. The modeling experiment may reflect processes that are basically parallel to the experiments of D. S. Patterson (1976) and W. M. Hall (1973) cited earlier. In these experiments, the child's partners were the agents of communication, and they entrapped the willing subject into interchanges in which assertive-aggressive actions were both tolerated and expected. The modeling experiment may perform the same service by using demonstrations and short films. What might happen when the interactional messages and the modeling messages (on television, movies) conflict? Which is more likely to control the child's behavior? We will return to this matter later in this chapter, in the discussion of the mass media and its potential influence.

Some comments are in order on two other major contributors to preschool aggression: situational influences and sex-typed activities.

Situational Influences

It has repeatedly been demonstrated that some preschool play areas and activities are more likely to be associated with aggressive play than others (Shure, 1963). Moreover, there are marked differences among preschools; the incidence of assertive-aggressive acts may be 2–3 times greater in one school than in another (Patterson, Littman, and Bricker, 1967). That situational influences have an effect is well documented, but how such an effect is achieved remains obscure. One possibility is that the situation "causes" or *supports* interchanges. A second possibility is that the setting (and materials in it) *elicits* vigorous interchanges, such that children may be self-selected by the material. For instance, rowdy boys may be drawn to football and passive ones may be drawn to art. Still a third possibility is that there is a two-way relationship between initial preferences and settings, such that once the selection is made, the children's interchanges will be shaped by the activities and persons present. Whatever the interpretation, in the normal classroom some materials (blocks, trucks) are more likely to be associated with vigorous activities than are painting and "playing house." These situational differences, in turn, appear to arise, at least in part, because of the shared interpretation among children as to the appropriate use of the materials (Patterson, 1976).

Strayer and Strayer (1976) have found that a stable hierarchy exists in the assertive-aggressive interchanges that occur during the free play of preschool-age children. Within an activity (such as free play), the interactional behavior of young children appears to be reasonably predictable; hence much of the "situational" support may be interpersonal.

Sex Differences

Although sex differences in aggressiveness in play are not present to a great extent in the very young (less than 2 years old), they appear consistently in children 4–5 years old. The questions of why and how these differences arise and how they are linked to other sex-typed play will be considered in Chapter 15.

Overall, the picture that emerges from the information in this section and Chapter 11 of how aggressive interchanges are produced in young children is reasonably clear. First, studies of infants indicate that assertive behaviors are likely to occur in their very early interchanges. Thereafter, these behaviors rapidly decrease in relative frequency, possibly because (1) the behavior is inhibited by others, and/or (2) children develop alternative ways to deal with others. Second, assertive behavior can apparently become a major part of the interchanges of young children in any given setting and relationship. This effect can be produced directly by the acts of other children, who exercise an immediate influence and thus entrap the child into increasingly more vigorous patterns. Or it can be accomplished by experimenters via filmed instructions or other prompting, which biases the relationship. In short, aggressive interchanges are likely to occur among young children even in the absence of special prompting, instructions, or imitation, unless feedback effects in the relationship or in the situation prohibit or redirect the pattern. Children learn quite early which behaviors are appropriate for one setting and relationship and not for others. But these rules, like the component behaviors themselves, are subject to continuing re-evaluation, and modification in early childhood.

Aggressive Interactions in Middle Childhood

Familial Controls

Some of the most promising attempts to plot the course of reciprocal controls have involved the study of highly aggressive young boys and their mis-

behavior in the home. An informative series of dyadic analyses was reported by G. R. Patterson at the Oregon Research Institute (Patterson and Cobb, 1971). The aim of the work was to investigate the social stimuli that elicit aggressive acts in boys 6–13 years of age who had been identified as pathologically assertive. The investigators report that the boys represented some of the most difficult cases that might be encountered in a child guidance clinic. Both the boys and their families (including both parents) were observed.

The observations were detailed and complete. The interactions among the members of each family were observed by two observers over a 2-week period for one hour each day, 5 days a week. To participate in the study, the family members had to cooperate by remaining either in the kitchen or in an adjoining room with the television turned off. No visitors were allowed, and no telephone calls were permitted. (The phone was taken off the hook.) The homes, in effect, were transformed into observational laboratories.[4]

Eliciting Events.   One objective of the study was to record exactly what happened immediately before and after each assertive-aggressive act. Each observer focused on one family member continuously for 5 minutes and recorded the actions of both the "target" member of the family and those with whom he interacted. After 5 minutes had passed, another member of the family was focused on, and so on.

What does one learn by focusing on the minutiae of interchanges in the homes of the families of aggressive children? First, even children with serious aggressive difficulties seldom commit blatantly aggressive acts in the home. Of the 117,033 interactions analyzed by Patterson and Cobb, only 273

---

[4] The reader might wonder why parents would agree to this kind of invasion of their private lives. Doubtless there were several reasons, including their feeling that they were contributing to understanding human behavior. But it seems likely that a common expectation was that they themselves would learn about better and more effective ways of handling their own children.

could be classified as negative physical behaviors. This category ("hits") included not only the aggressive child's beating his brothers and sisters and striking his parents, but their striking him (that is, spanking him). The negative physical behaviors occurred only 2 or 3 times in each thousand interactions (00.23 percent). Other observations of everyday interchanges in the preschool (Goodenough, 1931; Hartup, 1974) and in the school indicate that such infrequency is not uncommon. Aggressive behaviors are highly salient and memorable, but not particularly frequent.

Second, Patterson and Cobb (1971) found that in these families, negative behaviors begat negative behaviors. The analysis of interactional chains indicated that instances of *Hit* tended to be followed by *Hit*, regardless of which family member (mother, brother, or sister) initiated it. The exception was the father: his *Hits* did not elicit similar behavior from the boy.

How do these results compare with those of other studies of the interpersonal controls of the assertive-aggressive behaviors in boys? In a methodologically similar experiment, Raush (1965) carried out a sequential analysis of the relationships that occurred among hyperaggressive 9- to 12-year-old boys. Like Patterson and Cobb, he found that an unfriendly act was followed by an equally unfriendly one in 80 percent of the interchanges among aggressive boys and in 77 percent of the interchanges among "normal" boys. In both samples, hostility elicits reciprocal hostility, unless one individual is clearly more "powerful" than the other. The difference was that unfriendly acts occurred more frequently among the aggressive boys.

What other, less obvious behaviors elicit aggressive behavior in the family? The answer to this question is not simple; Patterson and Cobb's analysis suggests that it depends on who performs the act. In their study, the laughter of a younger brother or sister elicited more hitting by the target child, whereas the same behavior by an older sibling or by the parents caused no change in the child's rate of aggressive behavior. Similar person-specific reversals were observed for such categories as "crying," "ignoring," and "yelling": who performed an interpersonal act was as important as the nature of the act in controlling aggressive behavior.

Inhibiting Events. Although it is important to learn what provokes hitting, it is equally important to learn what inhibits it. In the experiment by Patterson and Cobb, virtually anything the father did to the target boy—even simply paying attention to him—diminished the probability that he would be aggressive. Maternal presence was somewhat less effective than father presence in decreasing the probability of aggressive acts. Other children, including siblings, varied in their effectiveness according to their age, sex, and, presumably, strength.

Terminating Events. The preceding discussion refers to antecedents for aggressive behaviors. What events terminate hitting once it has begun? In this sample, if the other person paid attention to, complied with, or showed no response whatever to the boy, the hitting tended to stop. So it appears that reciprocating kindness and compliance for hitting diminished the negative behavior. This interpretation is an important one and demands further investigation.

The Child as Architect. What is the role of the victim in an aggressive interchange? According to Patterson and Cobb, a large number of the punitive-aggressive sequences were triggered by the victim himself, even though at the end of the sequence he was often the loser. The investigators speculate that the child not only brought punishment on himself, but inadvertently trained his mother in the process:

> In the case of mothers, it is hypothesized that there are many grown women with no past history of Hitting, who are shaped by interactions with infants and children to initiate physical assaults. Presumably the shaping process is analogous to that provided by children, for children.

The mother learns that Hits terminate aversive child behavior. She may then be trained to display behavior of increasingly high aptitude as a function of the contingencies supplied by children. We also suspect that many of the child homicides reported are in fact the outcome of such training programs. A young woman, unskilled in mothering, is trained by her own children to carry out assaults that result in bodily injury to her trainers (p. 214).

Experimental Manipulations of the Family

Informative as direct observations in the home may be, they sometimes suffer from a lack of clarity of interpretation. Simply because the action of one person reliably occurs before that of another does not mean that there is a causal relationship between the two; they may both reflect the operation of a third variable that controls both occurrences. Similarly, the existence of a positive correlation between situations and behaviors is not sufficient to demonstrate that the circumstances "caused" the behaviors. The type of experimental procedures used is critical for teasing apart cause-effect relationships. In dyadic interactions, such procedures involve attempts to control (by holding effects constant or by randomization) all features of the interchange except those events that are considered essential for the effect. Characteristics of the interactive partner have been varied, as have features of the situation in which the interchanges take place.

The expectations and actions of both parents and children have been manipulated to determine whether and how the children's behaviors would be affected. In one recent study (Lobitz and Johnson, 1975), the families of aggressive boys and normal, "control" boys were observed in the home (as in the Patterson-Cobb work), but with a special twist. Before the observations, the parents were asked to make their children appear to be "good" (that is, to present the best picture they could). Before other

Table 12-2. Mean percentage of children's and parent's behaviors across experimental conditions.

Behavior and sample	Condition		
	"Good"	"Normal"	"Bad"
Child deviant acts			
Nonaggressive sample	4.3	6.3	11.0
Aggressive sample	7.0	7.8	16.0
Parent negative acts			
Nonaggressive sample	2.6	6.4	12.6
Aggressive sample	5.1	5.9	13.0
Parent positive acts			
Nonaggressive sample	88.3	81.8	63.3
Aggressive sample	84.1	82.1	71.6

NOTE: The entry in upper left means that 4.3% of the child's acts in the nonaggressive families could be classified as deviant ("deviant acts" to total acts) when the parents were instructed to make their child look "good."

SOURCE: Adapted from Lobitz and Johnson (1975).

observations were made, the same parents were asked to make their children appear "bad" (that is, to misbehave). To round out the picture and to provide baseline information, on other occasions the parents were instructed simply to interact with their children as they always did. The observers did not know about the special instructions—a sneaky deception that ensured that any effects obtained could not be explained away by observer bias. The results indicated that if the parents acted in a negative (critical, unkindly) fashion, they could make their children misbehave (see Table 12-2). But parents of clinic-referred aggressive boys were a little better at making their boys appear to be "bad" than were the parents of normal boys. In both cases, the children's behaviors were most disruptive. Explicit instructions to "fake good" were less successful. The parents of the clinic-referred aggressive boys were unable to induce any significant improvement relative to baseline behavior, and the parents of the normal boys did not fare significantly better, despite a high rate of positive statements.

More recently, Patterson and his co-workers (Patterson, 1979) in Eugene, Oregon, have explored a number of techniques by which to manipulate the control properties of particular interpersonal stimuli in order to provoke "coercive" acts in the child. One experimental strategy involves three phases:

1. Baseline 1. Identify in field observations which interpersonal events control coercive/noxious behaviors in particular children.

2. Manipulation. Change the stimuli that have been identified in phase 1 in order to determine whether there will be a concomitant increase (or decrease) in the child's coercive/noxious acts.

3. Baseline 2. Observe the child subsequently (when the presumed "controlling" events have returned to the normal or baseline level) to determine whether there is a parallel diminution in the child's coercive acts.

Patterson (1979) reports one such manipulation study where, for most children (9 out of 10), the controlling stimulus for whining during phase 1 was the act coded as "mother tease." When in phase 2 these nine mothers were directed to "tease," the incidence of the child's "whining" increased dramatically. In phase 3 (the second baseline), both the incidence of mother's teasing and child's whining returned to the original (baseline) levels.

Extrafamilial Control Systems

Social systems external to the family have been presumed to play a role of increasing importance in middle childhood in supporting and controlling assertive-aggressive behaviors. Although it seems intuitively obvious that other children and adults directly affect the child, the answer to the question of precisely how these social systems influence aggressive interchanges is not.

In one of the pioneering investigations of this question, M. and C. Sherif (1970) studied the social organization of fifth-grade boys who attended a summer camp for 6 weeks. In this field experiment, the Sherifs attempted to manipulate the feelings and attitudes of groups of children toward other groups from cooperation to hostility. All boys were assigned to one of two groups, which competed against each other for prizes and awards. Only one group could be the winner. The manipulation was strikingly "successful," in a negative way. Toward the end of the 6-week period, mild competition was transformed into an intense, bitter rivalry. It was not uncommon for fights to break out between members of the two groups.

After the rivalry was produced, the next step in the experimental procedure was to diminish it. This was done by requiring the two groups to cooperate. In one effective manipulation, the investigators rigged the camp so that the only means of transport for bringing in food—an old truck—broke down. To fix it, the two groups had to work together. The forced cooperation rapidly and effectively diminished the hostility and bitterness (see French et al., 1977).

The Sherif study underscores the fact that prevailing social attitudes and actions play a major role in determining the behavior of the individual members of a group. The result is not limited to experimental demonstrations. The success of most childhood organizations, from Girl Scouts to street gangs, is significantly enhanced by the spirit that develops among the members of the group.

Precisely how does the group qua group support and control the assertive behaviors of its members? First, it establishes the norms for the individual's behaviors and illustrates (by actions of members) those norms in the context. Second, it defines which targets are acceptable (scapegoats) and which forms of the behavior are acceptable in the microculture of which the individual is a part. The group as a group can act in more direct ways as well. In a very real way, the ongoing behaviors of a group become contagious—not through some mystical process of psychological infection, but as a result of the individual's participation in the activities of his fellows. In the course of such mutual exchanges, the behaviors and attitudes of a junior-high-school boy can be transformed into the activities that are acceptable to his friends but counter to the values of others in society, including his parents and teachers.

Information from the Experimenter: Reinforcement and Instruction

Two interesting laboratory studies of the reinforcement of aggressive behavior were conducted by the late R. H. Walters and his associates at the University of Toronto and at Waterloo University (Cowan and Walters, 1963; Walters and Brown, 1963). Walters devised a clownlike figure that could be used to reinforce hitting. When punched, slammed, or beaten, the device automatically recorded the frequency and intensities of the assaults. When the criterion was met for number and power of blows, the clown regurgitated a marble; the marble was the reinforcement event. To make sure that there was no misunderstanding about was expected, the clown had emblazoned across its stomach the words, "Hit Me."

The device was most effective in eliciting blows. Walters and his co-workers demonstrated some of the usual reinforcement contingency effects found in animals—notably, that a partial reinforcement schedule (where the child was rewarded for 1 of 6 blows) yielded greater resistance to extinction than continuous reinforcement. Further, it was found that children could be trained to hit the apparatus with greater or less intensity by different reinforcement procedures. But Cowan and Walters (1963) pointed out that the hitting was not merely an outcome of reinforcement; the 9- to 10-year-old boys vigorously hit the apparatus even when their actions were not initially reinforced. Further, many of the boys continued to hit the clown *even in extinction* (that is, absence of reinforcement). The boys kept

hitting the clown until their knuckles bled, and they stopped only because the experimenter told them to do so. Apparently the "Hit Me" sign was effective, as was the interest value of the game.

The results of this experiment and similar ones show that there are carry-over effects from one phase of an experiment to another. For instance, when the boys were given experience hitting the clown and were then tested together in another game, they were reliably more aggressive in the interpersonal game than boys who had no experience hitting the inanimate object (Walters and Brown, 1963). Moreover, when boys were differentially reinforced for high-magnitude hitting (that is, hard blows were reinforced), they were more likely to behave aggressively toward other children in the next game (Walters and Brown, 1963).

That the boys did not notice, or did not care, that reinforcement was stopped suggests that whatever effect reinforcement may have had, it was not essential once the child understood that hitting was acceptable and was expected. The reinforcement experiment is basically similar to the modeling experiment; both involve instructions from the experimenter (albeit indirect) as to what the child is supposed to do.

In overview, the findings reviewed in this section (on middle childhood) nicely parallel those in the preceding one (on children aged 3–7). Specifically, both experimental and field studies of both age groups of children indicate that there is a continuing differentiation of aggressive acts, according to the situation in which the interchange occurs, the other individual or individuals, and the nature of his or their actions. The likelihood of aggressive acts is increased when (1) the behavior is permitted by others in the setting or expected by them; (2) the behavior is provoked or elicited by the acts of others, especially those of a negative sort; and (3) the child is maintained in a setting or relationship in which aggressive behavior had occurred previously.

Interactional Experiences in Adolescence

Those who have analyzed the social controls of aggressive behavior in adolescence have identified several influences, including subcultural (Wolfgang and Ferracuti, 1967), family rearing (Bandura and Walters, 1959; McCord, McCord, and Zola, 1959), and constitutional (Glueck and Glueck, 1950). Here we shall focus on the social interactive processes by which these effects may be mediated and translated into behavior.

Escalation of Violent Interchanges

In his discussion of the process by which violent acts occur, criminologist Hans Toch (1969) cites the following account of the aggression that took place in the black ghettoes in the mid-1960's:

> The black kids and the white cops—their pride, their fear, their isolation, their need to prove themselves, above all their demand for respect— are strangely alike: victims both, prisoners of an escalating conflict that they didn't make and can't control (Toch, 1969, p. vii; quoted from *The London Observer*).

The few systematic accounts of aggressive esclation in adolescents are restricted to the behavior of seriously antisocial aggressive offenders. Among a group of "violent men," Toch identified a recurrent pattern whereby the acts of the police and the victim/ violator appear to mesh in such a way as to drive each other to increasingly more intense and dangerous responses. In one such instance, which occurred in Oakland, California, a teen-ager thought he was well within his legal rights when he did not immediately respond to a demand of a police officer. The 16-year-old initiated a semiplayful cat-and-mouse game with the policeman. The "game" became increasingly intense, until it was no game at all. The chase turned into one where each began to believe

the other to be exceedingly dangerous and to fear for his own life. When the officer finally threatened to shoot the boy, their perceptions almost became self-fulfilling.[5]

Obviously prior experiences and interchanges make a difference: not all teen-agers will dare to escalate an interchange with the police. The essential question is whether the escalation process is a general one, even though the content is limited by the particular background and prior experiences of the teen-ager.

Familial Support and Demands

Bandura and Walters (1959) asked why some boys, who appear not to be socially disadvantaged, show antisocial patterns of behavior. Accordingly, they studied adolescent boys who had histories of aggressive behavior. All the boys were of average intelligence and came from stable middle-class families. To determine the extent of familial influence, both parents and boys were interviewed simultaneously. These boys were matched with respect to age, IQ, residential area, and social class to a group of boys who had no record of aggressive behavior.

Although multiple differences in family attitudes and practices were identified in the comparisons of aggressive boys and nonaggressive boys, one of the most striking was the extent to which the parents of aggressive boys actively encouraged fighting (see

---

[5] Here are the two versions of what happened. The policeman:

> . . . so I run back to my vehicle, get on the radio and I told them that there was a possible 50-50 loose, which is from the Welfare and Institute's code, referring to a person that is mentally unbalanced. He had yelled something that in my opinion was a possible threat to my life, and I think that we should get somebody up there and flush him out before he hurts somebody (Toch, 1969, p. 106).

The boy; after the officer threatened to shoot him:

> . . . I was feeling pretty good right then cause I figured, "This cop, he's dumb. I haven't done anything wrong, I should give him trouble; he was giving me trouble, I should give him trouble." But, then, after he grabbed me, I says, "Oh no. This can't be, it's all over now. We're through playing games, I have to talk to him, now. He means business" (Toch, 1969, p. 108).

Table 12–3). Bandura and Walters illustrate the point in the following interview excerpt:

Interviewer: Have you ever encouraged Earl to use his fists to defend himself?
Father: Yes, if necessary. I told him many times that if someone wanted to fight with him and started the old idea of the chip on the shoulder, "Don't hit the chip, hit his jaw, and get it over with."

When the same question was put to the boy's mother, the answer was no less affirmative:

Interviewer: Have you ever encouraged Earl to use his fists to defend himself?
Mother: Oh yes, oh yes. He knows how to fight.

Apparently Earl's mother's perception was correct. When Earl was asked about school, the following exchange took place:

Interviewer: What if he [the teacher] gives you too much homework? Tells you to do something you think is unreasonable?
Boy: I hit one once and got suspended for it. I got suspended many times.
Interviewer: You mentioned you hit a teacher. What happened?
Boy: I said, "Hit, one, two, three." The teacher said, "Cut it out." He took me in the corner and bounced me around a bit, and I threw a stomp on him and hit him. That was about the eighth grade.

What was striking about these interviews was not merely that the family showed such frankness (or bravado), but that the parents apparently still approved aggressive behavior, even though their child

Table 12-3. Parents' encouragement of aggression: differences between parents of aggressive and control boys.

Parent	Aggressive group		Control group		
	Mean	S.D.	Mean	S.D.	p
Fathers	6.64	1.85	5.06	1.81	<.01
Mothers	5.37	1.95	4.12	1.25	<.01

SOURCE: Adapted from Bandura and Walters, Adolescent Aggression—A Study of the Influence of Child-Training Practices and Family Interrelationships. Copyright © 1959. The Ronald Press Company, New York.

had gotten into serious difficulty with the law. Bandura and Walters summarize their findings as follows:

It seemed that, in the aggressive boys' families, one or [the] other of the parents almost invariably encouraged aggression. Indeed, when the ratings of mothers and fathers were combined to provide an estimate of the total amount of encouragement to aggress that the boys received from their parents, a highly significant difference between the two groups of parents emerged (p. 115).

Information from the Experimenter: Obedience and the "Eichmann Effect"

A significant series of experiments concerning the extent to which normal college students will follow instructions to hurt other persons was conducted by Stanley Milgram (Milgram, 1974). The phenomenon is an awesome demonstration of the power of experimental demands. The students were told that they were to aid in an analysis of the effects of punishment on learning. Their job would be to teach another person a list of words and to punish him if he failed. The punishing apparatus that was to be used was a box clearly labeled as having a capacity to deliver shocks ranging from 15 volts to 450 volts. The 30 switches that were to be depressed were given such labels as *Slight Shock, Strong Shock, Extreme Intensity Shock,* and *Danger: Severe Shock.* Beyond this last designation were two switches simply marked *XXX* (see Figure 12-2).

In these experiments, the "learner" was in fact a skilled actor whose job was to feign extreme pain even though, of course, he had not been shocked at

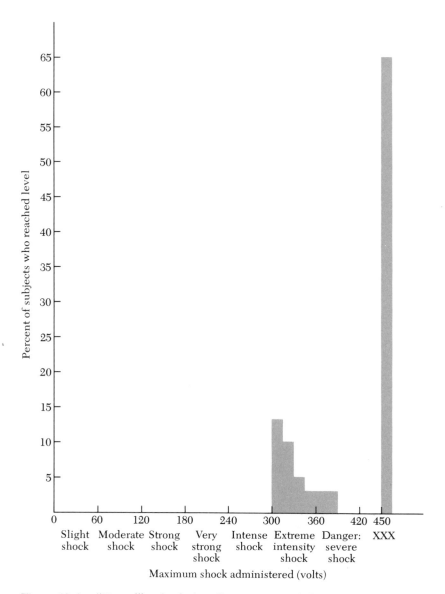

Figure 12-2. "Normal" individuals will agree to painfully shock and possibly injure another person, simply because they are instructed to do so by an authority. Virtually all the college students in this experiment administer shocks that they believed to be of extreme intensity (considerably beyond the level that they themselves would have tolerated), and the majority of them administered shocks that they believed to approximate 450 volts (labeled "Danger: Severe Shock") (data from Milgram, 1974).

all. The learner would typically emit painful groans at the administration of the 135-volt shock and at 150 volts would cry out, "Experimenter, get me out of here! I won't be in the experiment anymore! I refuse to go on." The situation got progressively worse. As Milgram describes it,

> At 315 volts, after a violent scream, the victim reaffirmed vehemently that he was no longer a participant. He provided no answers, but shrieked in agony whenever a shock was administered. After 330 volts he was not heard from, nor did his answers reappear. . . (p. 23).

Did the students simply refuse to go on? Some did, but they were in the minority. Most of them administered 330 volts and continued giving shocks until the terminal level, 450 volts, was reached. Recordings made during the experiment confirmed that the students actually believed that the learner was undergoing unbearable torture: the students hesitated, agonized, and expressed shame and guilt. Nonetheless, 50 percent to 85 percent of them followed instructions, even when they were told that the shock could be dangerous to the learner.

Milgram writes:

> The key to the behavior of subjects [the students] lies not in pent-up anger or aggression but in the nature of their relationship to authority. They have given themselves as instruments for the execution of his wishes; once so defined, they are unable to break free (p. 168).

The Control and Inhibition of Aggressive Interchanges

A major problem for families, and for other social groups, is to design a system that will promote spontaneous, vigorous, and free interchanges in children without their degenerating into hate and injury, on the one hand, or into passivity, submission, and withdrawal, on the other. Either pattern may have undesirable implications for future behavior. Indeed, clinically inhibited, overcontrolled persons have been thought to be vulnerable to conditions that provoke acts of uncontrolled violence (Megargee, 1966).

Origins of Peaceful Interchanges

One clue to the answer may lie in the comparison of the families of "normal," nonaggressive adolescent boys and aggressive ones. As we have already observed, Bandura and Walters (1959) found multiple differences between the practices followed in the families, including amount of punishment given for aggressive acting out, disagreements within the home, and the boys' resistance to parental restrictions. But these differences are not easy to interpret because they may have been determined by the boys' deviant behaviors, rather than vice versa. Obviously difficult boys are likely to provide more opportunities for punishment, to cause more familial disagreement, and to respond negatively to restrictions of any sort, including parental restrictions. One difference that cannot be explained away concerns the extent to which the parents of *nonaggressive* boys gave their sons explicit instructions as to how to avoid physical violence. Bandura and Walters (1959) found that the parents of the nonaggressive boys suggested alternative ways to deal with problems involving teachers or other boys such as talking with the teachers with whom they were having difficulty or working harder in class. As a last resort, the parent would intervene if he or she thought the boy was being treated unjustly. These families not only arranged conditions in the home to avoid the establishment of assertive-coercive ways of dealing with others, they continued to support non-assertive solutions to interpersonal conflicts throughout childhood and adolescence.

Another clue to how "assertive" interchanges can be avoided in young children may be found in cross-culture studies. The Chinese, for example, have apparently solved the problem of how to promote peaceful interchanges in the preschool. A delegation of American developmental psychologists to mainland China (Kessen, 1975) recently found that 3- to 5-year-old Chinese children interact with each other and with outsiders in a uniformly cheerful, outgoing manner. There is no grabbing or bickering and virtually no rowdiness. One impression communicated by the observers was that neither the teacher nor the parents permit the initial establishment of assertive behavior. The possibility that some of the early differences in assertiveness may reflect, in part, inherited differences in temperament cannot be dismissed (Freedman, 1974; Kagan, 1976). On the other hand, the extreme variations that have been observed across preschools in the United States (Chapt. 11) suggest that school organization in itself may be quite sufficient to explain the differences.

At a recent symposium on the control of aggression, a wide range of methods were discussed, from physiological and genetic manipulations, which seem not applicable to the human condition, to changes in conditions of peer interchanges and social support, which do (Knutson, 1973). Regarding the latter proposal, Bandura (1973b) states:

> Just as aggression is not rooted in the individual, neither does its control reside solely there. Humaneness requires, in addition to benevolent codes of self-reinforcement, social reinforcement systems that uphold compassionate behavior and discourage cruelty (p. 241).

The conclusion is an important one. But the problem of how to "discourage cruelty" is a difficult one, because the very acts that are intended to discourage cruel behavior can actually facilitate it. At this point we will examine the issues surrounding the use of punishment as a control technique.

The Special Problem of Punishment

In Chapter 10, we discussed the "paradox" of punishment, such that one and the same event, pain—

served to inhibit and to elicit aggressive behavior in animals. There is a similar paradox in the study of punishment in children. Child-rearing studies and direct observations of families indicate that frequent punishment is associated with a *heightened* likelihood of aggressive acting out in children (for example, Sears, Maccoby, and Levin, 1957).[6] Laboratory studies of punishment, on the other hand, indicate that it works to *diminish* the likelihood of aggressive actions (Parke and Deur, 1972). Punishment seems to inhibit aggressive behavior in the laboratory but to instigate aggressive behavior in the home. Why does seemingly the same stimulus—punishment—have opposite effects in the two different contexts?

Punishment in the Home.   One simple explanation for the positive correlation in the home and child assertive-aggressiveness is that the child may "earn" more punishment by his obnoxious, assertive behavior. His acts may demand a reciprocal response on the part of parents. There are other possibilities that are equally plausible. The parents, by virtue of their punitive acts, may provide excellent role models for aggressive behavior. In this regard, Owens and Straus (1975) found that persons who reported that they were treated in a punitive fashion as children tended, as adults, to condone the use of physical aggression as a means of dealing with others. Hence the generational transfer from parent to child of assertive-aggressive styles. Still another possible explanation for the positive correlation between punishment and the occurrence of aggressive behaviors focuses on the elicitation properties of aggressive acts. The punishment may provoke in the child states of arousal and anger, which are then expressed toward other children (including younger siblings). The "frustration-aggression" has been the focus of much

---

[6] Reviews of child-rearing research on aggression have recently appeared, including Feshbach, 1970; Yarrow et al., 1968; Martin, 1975; Becker, 1964. The work begins with the pioneering studies of R. R. Sears and his collaborators (Sears et al., 1953, 1957, 1965). The positive correlation between parental punishment and childhood aggressive behavior has not always been found (Yarrow et al., 1968).

attention (see Dollard, Doob, Miller, Mowrer, and Sears, 1939; Feshbach, 1964, 1970; Miller, 1941).

The recent theoretical analysis offered by G. R. Patterson (1979) also implies that a positive relationship should be obtained between punishment of children and the frequency of occurrence of assertive-aggressive acts. According to Patterson, the child's aggressive acts in the family are maintained by a negative reinforcement process. That is, the child learns that he can terminate punishment by counter-attacks. The problem is that other persons in the family system are also likely to learn the same thing, namely, to terminate his (the child's) assertiveness with counter-punishment. Thus evolves the "coercive" family system where each member's assertiveness is maintained by a negative reinforcement process and where punishment becomes both the primary means of control and a means of perpetuating further assertive-aggressive acts.

Which explanation is the "correct" one? The present data do not permit us to choose among the above possibilities with confidence. Indeed, a close examination of the "different" explanations suggest that they share more similarities than differences. The accounts are alike in one basic respect: namely, they all emphasize the capabilities for hurtful acts of one person to elicit hurtful acts from other persons in the family system. They all assume, further, the operation of a reciprocal process (except, perhaps, the modeling explanation). The differences between explanations arise in part because of different emphases on who in the family initiates the process. Earlier explanations focused on the actions of the parents (frustration-aggression, modeling) and the more recent ones focusing on the child (negative reinforcement, elicitation). In addition, Patterson's (1979) analysis explicitly recognizes that the immediate outcomes of punishment may be different from the long-term outcomes.

Punishment in the Laboratory. In contrast with child-rearing studies, laboratory experiments permit a precise assessment of the immediate effects of punitive events, but at a cost of removing the punishment events from the systems in which they ordinarily occur. Nonetheless, the studies have been informative in demonstrating that the effects of punishment depend on certain parameters, including:

1. *Intensity and timing.* Cheyne and Walters (1970) have reviewed an extensive series of studies on the relationship between (a) punishment effectiveness and (b) the timing of the punitive act and its intensity. While the complexity of the results precludes a simple generalization, it is clear that in children (as in animals, see Chapter 10) both variables control punishment effectiveness. Intense and immediate punishment can be a highly effective inhibitor of ongoing behavior.

2. *Role of elicitor or victim.* Shantz and his co-workers (Shantz and Pentz, 1972; Shantz and Voydanoff, 1973) have demonstrated that the targets of punishment make a difference in the child's likelihood of retaliation. In the study conducted by Shantz and Voydanoff, children aged 6–13 were read stories about various provocative incidents, which were described as perpetrated by other children or adults. In each story, information was also included about the nature of the child's retaliatory acts. The children were then asked to select the paddle with which each boy (the retaliator) should be spanked, on the assumption that the largest paddle would be selected when retaliation was seen as least acceptable. (The choices ranged from 12″ ping-pong-paddle-size shafts to shafts larger than baseball bats). In general, the boys' choices indicated that they considered it more acceptable to retaliate against other children than against parents, a belief that parents themselves try to indoctrinate (Sears et al., 1957).

3. *Child sensitivity.* Gordon Allport (1937) has remarked, on the matter of individual differences in personality, that the "heat that melts the butter can harden the egg." So it is with punishment. Recent studies suggest that anticipated punishment may have the opposite effect, depending on the timidity of the recipient. Peterson (1971) classified third-grade boys as "low aggressive" or "high aggressive" on the basis of their typical behavior. These children showed in the laboratory opposite levels of punishment towards peers, if retaliation seemed likely. Low aggressive boys *lowered* the levels of punishment given to peers, and high aggressive boys *increased* them.

To sum up, punishment can increase, decrease, or have no observable effect on the acts that preceded the punishment. Which outcome will be obtained depends on the social context in which both the aggressive act and the punishment occurs, as well as the parameters of the act (its intensity, timing, form), the individuals involved (their sensitivity, prior background), and the relationship that the persons bear to each other. Equally important, it makes a difference *when* and *where* the effects are observed. The immediate inhibiting effects observed in the laboratory can be replaced, at a subsequent time, by facilitating effects by virtue of the attitudes and network of relationships that the initial punitive acts supports. The unfortunate paradox is that the most effective control in the short run may be the most ineffective in the long run.

Some Applications

The revised view of development of aggressive behaviors from a psychobiological and interactive perspective sheds some new light on old problems, two of which can be commented on here: aggressive behavior continuity and the effects of the mass media.

The Continuity of Aggressive Behaviors

Only a small proportion of the population (approximately 6 percent) accounts for most of the antisocial aggression. The recidivism rate for arrests for delinquency, including crimes of an aggressive sort,

ranges from 55 percent to 80 percent, depending on the nature of the crime and prior offenses (*Crime in the United States*, 1975). A compelling issue concerns the development of more effective means for intervention and change.

To the extent that the aggressive behaviors of children are supported (either intentionally or unintentionally) by the social system of which they are a part, it seems reasonable to expect that significant changes in behavior will be produced by altering the system itself. In the case of smaller social units (such as families), this alteration can be readily produced if some members are amenable to change. Indeed, familial modification can be highly effective in altering a "problem" child's actions (see Patterson's review, 1979). But other social systems that support aggressive behavior are typically less susceptible to change. Such "larger systems" may involve the peer subgroup or the neighborhood ecology. To the extent that the child's assertive-aggressive behaviors are supported by these groups, they may be exceedingly difficult to modify *so long as the child is an active participant in those systems.* Perhaps this is why delinquency recidivism rates are so high. Techniques that are most successful in producing changes in behavior in one setting (such as the "training school" or "rehabilitation center") may have little enduring effect on the child's behavior when he is returned to the system whence he came. [7]

The explicit recognition of the situational relatively of the effects produced in "retraining" or "reformation" would seem at first blush to yield a dismal picture for their effectiveness. But not neces-

---

[7] Perhaps a more powerful example would be the Patricia Hearst/Tania/Patricia Hearst transformation. In each instance, the young woman seems to have been under intense and unrelenting social demands to act in a fashion that was consistent with the dominant views of the group of which she was then a part. Individuals, like societies, are susceptible to coercive persuasion. In this regard, Milgram (1974) recently observed:

The social psychology of this century reveals a major lesson: often, it is not so much the kind of person a man is as the kind of situation in which he finds himself that determines how he will act (p. 205).

sarily. The alternative would be to use the information as to why they are ineffective and to modify the follow-up operations accordingly. In particular, the preceding analyses of this chapter imply that enduring effects would depend on (a) modifying the original social system that gave rise to the behavior (b) introducing the child to another system that would support the new interchanges that have been established, (c) modifying the child's role in that system when he or she is re-introduced to it, or (d) modifying the child's response to other persons. [8]

The problem of generalization across settings and social systems brings us again to the nuclear issue of social development: change and continuity in interchanges. While it seems reasonable to expect that the same interchange learning considerations apply to aggressive behaviors as to nonaggressive ones (see Chapter 8), a potential (and major) difference between the two classes of actions is worthy of note. Assertive-aggressive behaviors have, regardless of the context in which they occur, high demand properties in eliciting behaviors from others. They are hard to ignore. Typically they have a high probability of eliciting counter-responses, although not necessarily of the same form. Once hostility occurs in a relationship, it tends to be self-fulfilling in producing reciprocal emotions. These considerations lead to the expectation that assertive or coercive actions should have a higher likelihood of generalizing across relationships and settings than noncoercive ones. The expectation has some support in the findings of S. Sherman (1975) and Yarrow and Waxler (1979), but the evidence is far too meager to be considered other than preliminary.

Perhaps an example would help clarify the matter. Recall the incident of the 16-year-old boy described earlier, where a cat-and-mouse game escalated into near fatal encounter with police. Prior to this incident, the boy had been "expelled from sev-

eral schools, in every case for fights involving serious damage to the other child" (Toch, 1969). The fights had reportedly begun because the boy had persistently harassed his potential opponents, apparently playing with them, as with the police officer, a cat-and-mouse game. The demand properties of the first "moves" in the game were such that their occurrence would yield preditable results, almost regardless of setting. The other person would be entrapped, and so would the boy.

The Effects of Television

It may seem curious to pick out television as a primary socializing influence for children as opposed, say, to school, church, or their peers (to name a few of the alternatives). Rightly or wrongly, TV has become the focus of a national concern on how the behavior and attitudes of children are shaped by forces outside of the immediate control of the family. The statistics on the matter of television viewing are surely compelling in that children spend as much time watching the electronic tube as they spend in school (approximately 3–4 hours each day, seven days a week). The matter is especially relevant to the development of aggressive behavior because (1) violence remains a favorite theme of television programs (including news programs), and (2) it has been repeatedly demonstrated in laboratory investigations that young children show a strong tendency to imitate aggressive behaviors (Bandura, 1973a).

Is television, then, a major cause for the increase in violence that was shown in Figure 11-1? The data are not conclusive. Field studies fail to yield a uniform set of findings. On the one hand, the thorough analysis of Feshbach and Singer (1971) indicates that "aggressive" programming on television yields no more aggressive behavior among boys in residential schools than does nonaggressive programming. Feshbach and Singer's work constitutes the most extensive experimental evaluation of the television induction effects in groups of teen-age boys. On the other hand, a positive correlation has been reported

---

[8] The last possibility—changing the child—brings us into matters of individual therapy which, while obviously relevant, would lengthen an already lengthy chapter if they were covered here. The interested reader should consult Novaco (1975) for further discussion of the problem.

between ratings of aggression at early maturity in men and watching violent TV programs in childhood (Eron, Huesmann, Lefkowitz, and Walder, 1972). The Eron et al. (1972) study permits at least two interpretations: (1) that the experience of having watched violence on television in childhood affected the individual's behavior when he reached adulthood; or (2) both the viewing habits of the individual in childhood and his behaviors at maturity reflect the influence of the family system of which he was a participant. Experimental studies of short-term influence support the possibility that there are indeed direct behavioral effects of watching television. For example, Steuer, Applefield, and Smith (1971) found that preschool children who were permitted to watch programs with an aggressive content tended to misbehave more in the classroom than children for whom aggressive content was deleted (see also Friedrich and Stein, 1973).

In the light of the controversies that remain in the interpretation of the data, it seems premature to attempt to draw strong conclusions about the multiple effects of television on aggressive behavior. In evaluating further research on the matter, the following points should be considered:

1.   Aggressive interactions are determined by a multiplicity of factors, with a major influence being the network of relationships that the child has established in the home and with peers. Values or attitudes depicted in the media may be supported, or canceled out, by influences that are operative in the child's immediate interchanges.

2.   Children's ability to draw inferences about the motives and intentions of other persons (including those shown on television) varies as a function of their developmental status (Collins, 1977). It is unclear, for instance, whether young children usually connect aggressive acts with the consequences that are produced by the acts.

3.   Television programs are a source of considerable information about when and where certain acts are to be performed (in the context of stories). They also provide information about the values held by the characters depicted and the social setting of which they are a part. There are wide differences among children (because of differences in developmental status, intelligence, and prior experience) in how, and how much of, this information is processed and retained.

4.   An influence that has a "trivial" effect on individual children can produce a significant effect on the society. In some areas of human experience, a modest change in societal standards and expectations can influence innumerable children via a change in the social systems in which they live. For an effect to produce profound implications, it is not necessary to find evidence for it in all or even most children.

What can be said then about the effects of television on the development of aggressive behavior? At this juncture it appears to be impossible to disentangle the media influence from that of the societal system of which it is a part. Children doubtless learn a great deal from the many hours that they spend in front of the television set, from the trivial (the precise schedule for their favorite programs, the names and roles of the main characters) to the significant (how persons behave in settings unfamiliar to them, what kinds of rules govern the behavior of other persons, new words and expressions, including some truths and half-truths about the world). Moreover, given a special setting (such as an experimental laboratory) where the information provided by television is highly salient for the child, the effect of television looms large relative to other contextual influences. But in the contexts of everyday life, it remains to be shown conclusively that the information provided by television does more than augment and support existing behaviors (if its serves even that function). We simply do not have the answers for some of the most important questions. One question in this last category concerns the effects that television observation has on the child's attitudes about the occurrence of aggressive—and prosocial—behaviors (see Stein and Friedrich, 1975).

Summary

An overview of this chapter and the preceding one suggest the following generalizations:

■ In their initial establishment, aggressive acts do not have to be "acquired." They occur inevitably, given the reciprocal nature of interchanges and the capabilities of normal children. Although hurtful acts come about without specific training, feedback from them provides for their integration into sequences in which the child controls the actions of others, and vice-versa.

■ The ground rules for childhood aggression—which assertive-aggressive acts are acceptable and which are not, in which relationships they are justified and in which relationships they are prohibited, when is it permissible to get hostile and angry and when one becomes only annoyed—are learned in the social systems of which the child is a part.

■ As the child moves from the family to nursery school to grade school and high schools, the interchanges in which he becomes involved provide for continued shaping, revision, and consolidation of attitudes and behaviors. Because contextual standards may vary, assertive-aggressive behaviors may become context-dependent. In the course of development, the child's interactive patterns become consolidated across the network of his or her relationships and hence become increasingly resistant to change.

■ Each child—as a unique and distinguishable individual—has an integrity and stability above and beyond momentary shifts in settings, biological states, and relationships. Behavioral adaptations achieved by the child in one setting and in one relationship—including one's attitudes and self-perceptions—become generalized to other settings and relationships. At least part of the stability seems maintained by the continuity of reactions of others to him and by his evoking from them common patterns. A hostile or insulting youngster is especially likely to create relationships in new settings that take on some of the negative properties found in prior ones. To the extent that children's orientation toward others becomes dominant, it appears that their actions can take on a self-fulfilling character and they become participant "architects" of the social systems in which they live.

13

SEXUAL DEVELOPMENT: BIOLOGICAL FOUNDATIONS

From an evolutionary perspective, sexual behavior is *the* basic social interchange; it is the essential behavioral component in the complex process of genetic recombination. In this chapter we will examine the development of the behavioral and biological substrate for this interchange.

Why Sex?

A good many animals and plants get along reasonably well without sexual reproduction. They adopt instead asexual forms of reproduction (such as parthenogenesis, where an egg develops into an embryo without having been fertilized). Asexual reproduction has one fatal disadvantage, however. Because of a reduction in diversity and adaptability, sooner or later asexual genetic informity leads to a "blind alley" in evolution.

In sexual reproduction, an individual receives a set of chromosomes from each of two parents and passes some proportion of these chromosomes on to his own offspring. Thus in each generation there is a recombination of genetic material, resulting in virtually unique patterns of genes for individuals and great biological diversity for populations. Those patterns that are best fitted for the circumstances of that generation and that era are typically favored in a natural selection process. When did sexual reproduction begin? Apparently the process is a primitive one. It is now known that bacteria and viruses, which were once thought to be asexual, bring together into one individual genetic materials that were derived from two others. Hence it is plausible to believe that sexual processes may have extended backward to the earliest forms of life.

Mammals, like most land animals, achieve genetic exchange via internal fertilization. They must develop, in each generation, some individuals whose structures, behaviors, and capabilities for social and physiological coordination will permit sexual synchronization with another member of the same species. Fundamental questions can be raised about the process by which individuals recognize others as being potential sexual partners and how each of them develops the capabilities to perform effectively. These issues bring us immediately to the problem of sexual determination in development.

Determinants of Male and Female

Until recently, sexual determination has been accepted at a popular level as being a clear-cut matter: a male is a male and a female is a female, with the classification having been irreversibly established at fertilization. Recent developmental and embryological analyses have shown the necessity for a reconsideration of this assumption—in particular, the necessity to distinguish between (1) chromosomal sex, (2) physiological/anatomical sex, as determined by internal and external sex organs, and (3) sexual behavior. Significant advances have come from the analysis of the processes by which anatomical and endrocrinological systems develop and how these systems in turn bias the individual's behavior.

Although a consideration of the genetic development of sexual structures may seem to take us far afield, the excursion will illustrate two quite significant points: that a bidirectionality exists between structure and function, and that there are "critical periods" in the sexual development of an organism.

Chromosomal Mechanisms

Chromosomal mechanisms operate to bias development in a masculine or feminine direction, causing certain embryos to develop into males and others to develop into females. The mechanism that is responsible in most cases is a pair of sex chromosomes that is present in all cells of the body. In one sex, the two chromosomes are alike in size, shape, and possibly function; in the other sex, one of the chromosomes differs from the other in function and typically in configuration and size. The mature reproductive cells (the gametes) of XX individuals always carry an X chromosome; those of XY individuals are of two kinds, bearing either an X or a chromosome Y chromosome. Thus, in the next generation, both XX and XY zygotes may be produced at fertilization. In mammals, including human beings, XX individuals are females and XY individuals are

males. (In birds, it is a different story in that females are heterogametic or XY, and males are homogametic or XX. For this reason, it has been said, loosely, that the "natural" state of mammals is female and that of birds is male.)

Developmental Mechanisms in Mammals

For at least a short time early in ontogeny, males and females are virtually bisexual; the distinctive male and female sexual organs arise out of a common structure. The bisexuality of the embryo's sex glands (*gonads*) is anatomical and, possibly, functional. The rudiments of the testes (male sex glands) occupy the inner portions of the embryonic gonads (the medulla), and the rudiments of the ovaries (female sex glands) are found in the outer portion of the gonads (the cortex). In males, there is both a progressive dominance of testicular growth and a suppression of ovarian development. The bisexual potential is not limited to the structure of the gonads. Both rudimentary Wolffian (male) and Müllerian (female) ducts for the gonads are found in embryonic males. Fetal growth in males is characterized by development of the Wolffian tract and the progressive disintegration of the Müllerian tract. The opposite pattern occurs in females: progressive development of Müllerian ducts and regression of Wolffian ducts.

Once differentiation takes place in the gonadal systems of mammals, it is permanent and irreversible. Such nonplasticity is not a firm rule for vertebrates. Certain birds and amphibians maintain the potentiality for the development of the reproductive system of the opposite sex throughout maturity. For instance, one of the two ovaries possessed by hawks and king doves remains in an bisexual state while the other ovary performs normal female functions (Gorbman and Bern, 1962). If the ovary becomes diseased, the "spare" gland can take on the male functions—that is, the "female" is thereby transformed into a male.

Recent studies indicate that in certain normal male mammals, some potential for bisexuality extends into maturity. On the basis of their studies of male hamsters, L. M. Kow, C. W. Malsbury, and D. W. Pfaff (1976) of Rockefeller University have proposed that "two different neural networks, one mediating male-typical and the other female-typical mating behavior," coexist in the nervous system of the normal male mammal (p. 39). The basis for their proposal is that (1) it is possible to stimulate female receptive postures (lordosis) in normal males; (2) lordosis in normal males is independent of copulation and mating in the same males; and (3) lordosis in normal males is functionally similar to that in normal females.

Bisexuality in normal males is not restricted to hamsters. Similar effects were reported for young primates by G. V. Hamilton (1914), who described how juvenile male macaque monkeys mounted and took turns being mounted in their sex play.

Hormonal Influences in Development: Females Can Be Masculinized

What is the trigger that determines whether an embryo will develop male or female characteristics? Embryological studies suggest that at least two triggers operate in early development. The first is genetic; in the presence of a Y chromosome, the gonad is differentiated into a fetal testis. The second trigger is hormonal; the fetal testis itself secretes a substance (or substances) that (1) facilitates masculine development and (2) inhibits feminine development. In the absence of appropriate concentrations of these testicular hormone(s), as in the case of the normal female fetus, the organism will develop as a female. It is via this second mechanism, hormonal control, that the fetus contributes to its own sexual development.

A series of experiments by W. C. Young and his colleagues demonstrated that this second mechanism can be triggered experimentally, hence, "turning on" male behavioral characteristics and "turning off" female characteristics, or vice-versa. The effects of hormonal secretions of the fetal gonads can be overridden and canceled out by externally administered hormones. Since steroid hormones—which include sexual hormones—pass through the maternal circulatory system to that of the infant, the fetus can be used as an experimental subject.

The first "guinea pigs" used in these experiments were, appropriately, unborn guinea pigs. If administered in sufficient quantity, the male hormone testosterone propionate effects profound changes in the development of the female fetus (Young, 1961). In female guinea pigs, a marked shift toward masculine structure and behavior at adulthood is obtained, along with a life-long suppression of feminine responsiveness and estrous cycling (Phoenix, Goy, Gerall, and Young, 1959). Testosterone propionate has, however, only a modest effect upon the behavior of males, shifting them in the direction of slightly stronger masculine responsiveness at adulthood. Examination of the morphological changes produced in the genital tracts of males and females indicates that these changes are consistent with the behavioral changes: the development of the male genital systems is only slightly accelerated; the development of the masculine characteristics of females is significantly enhanced. Prenatal hormonal treatment with male sex hormones, however, fails to disrupt or suppress the development of internal ducts in females. Because of the ambiguous nature of their internal and external sexual equipment, modified females are sometimes referred to as *pseudohermaphrodites* (masculinized females).

Essentially parallel outcomes have been obtained in embryological studies of other mammals. Both prenatal and early postnatal injections of androgens have a masculinizing effect on female rats. Gerall and Ward (1966) masculinized unborn female rats by injecting their mothers with a minute quantity (1–5 mg) of testosterone in the final trimester (days 14–22) of pregnancy. The modified offspring were masculinized to the extent that they had neither a vagina nor mammilary buds. On reaching maturity, the experimental "females" (as well as normal females) were given a series of testosterone injections to determine whether they would show masculine behavior. Whereas normal females simply developed an enlarged clitoris, the masculinized females developed an "evertible penile structure approximately equal in length and diameter to that of the normal male" (p. 372). During mating tests, the "females" used the extended clitoris much as the male uses its penis. In their observations, Gerall and Ward (1966) found that masculinized females exhibited a male "ejaculatory response" during mating tests with other females in estrus. They not only possessed the sexual structures of males; they behaved like males (see Figure 13-1).

The experimental demonstration of fetal masculinization is not limited to rats and guinea pigs. Goy and his co-workers (1968) at the Oregon Regional Primate Center masculinized female rhesus monkey fetuses by injecting the pregnant mothers with androgens (male sex hormones). Their findings indicate that many of the dimorphic behavioral characteristics of male and female monkeys are extensively influenced by the prenatal presence or absence of androgens. The nonsexual behavior of the masculinized female (for example, rough and tumble play and facial threats) falls between that of normal males and unmodified females. Observations of the infantile sexual behavior indicate that the tendency to mount and show pelvic thrusting is considerably more frequent among the masculinized than among normal females. The external genitalia are intersexual; that is, the modified females have an erectile organ that, though it is shorter than the normal phallus, is usable in a "normal" masculine fashion.

It has been well established that the timing of the injections is critical in determining the extent of masculinization that occurs and whether it will occur at all. The injections must be given during a formative period early in development. The interval of susceptibility varies with the species. In the case of guinea pigs, the injections must be given prenatally; in rats, postnatal treatment is effective if it occurs in the first 5 days after birth.

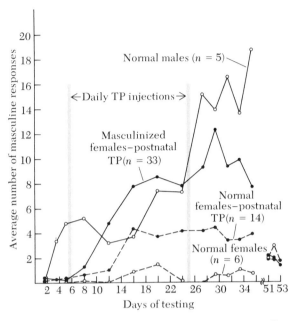

Figure 13-1. If female rats are masculinized prenatally, they adopt many of the sexual behaviors of normal males when tested at adulthood with the male hormone testosterone propionate (*TP*). The "masculine responses" included mounting another female and pelvic thrusting (*solid line, closed circles*). These behaviors are typically observed in males (*solid line, open circles*), but are not found in normal females (*dotted line, open circles*) and only moderately in females given only exogenous male hormones at maturity (*dotted line, closed circle*). Testing began when the subjects were 68–88 days old and continued for 53 days. *TP* injections were given daily from test day 6 to day 24; by 4 weeks after the last injections the female groups behaved similarly regardless of prenatal treatment. (From Gerall and Ward. Copyright © 1966, by the American Psychological Association. Reprinted by permission.)

Up to this point the discussion has been limited to mammals, a restriction that seems appropriate in light of the aims of this volume, on the one hand, and the basic similarity of the endocrinological mechanisms of the species within the class *Mammalia*, on the other (Barrington, 1975; Gorbman and

Bern, 1962). It is no accident that the hormonal effects obtained in rats and quinea pigs are similar to those obtained in monkeys. Comparative endocrinologists find close parallels across mammals in endocrine structure and function.

But I cannot resist the temptation to break the rule by noting that the problem of sexual differentiation has been achieved in various complex and ingenious ways during evolution. Lest we prematurely accept the proposition that mammals in general and humans in particular are more influenced by social factors than other animals, we should note the way that some fish have of determining their sex. One species, the "cleaner fish" of the Great Reef of Australia, is typically found in a harem-type social structure, with a single male dominating 3-6 mature females and their offspring. If the dominant male dies, he is replaced. The replacement is not surprising, but the way in which it is accomplished is. One of the females simply undergoes a sexual transformation and she/he takes over. Within 14-18 days, this new male is equivalent in all respects (behavior, appearance, and structure) to the old one. The recruit is not the youngest female in the group (presumably the most plastic and least set behaviorally and physiologically), but rather the oldest and most dominant female. Within 1½ to 2 hours after the death of the male, she/he begins special male aggressive display; within 2-4 days, male courting and

spawning; and within 14-18 days, actual sperm release and successful reproduction with the remaining females (see Figure 13-2).

Inversions (sexual reversal) are not uncommon in certain groups of fish (for example, the goldfish and swordtail fish, aquarium favorites, also change their sex) and birds, but the events that trigger the reversal are thought to be due to growth (maturation) or organic disease. In the case of the cleaner fish, the trigger is clearly a change in the animal's social role (Robertson, 1972).

Feminizing Males: Reversing the Switch

Can genetic males be feminized? Since the effective masculinizing agent for females is the presence of androgens at some critical phase of gonadal or neural development, it seems reasonable to expect that the absence of androgens at that period will demasculinize males. The validity of this proposition has been tested by using two procedures. First, male rats have been castrated at birth, or at systematic intervals following. The work of Grady, Phoenix, and Young (1965) demonstrated that if the operation is performed within 1-5 days after birth, then the males demonstrate a strong propensity toward feminine sexual behavior in adulthood—that is, they are receptive to other males when treated with

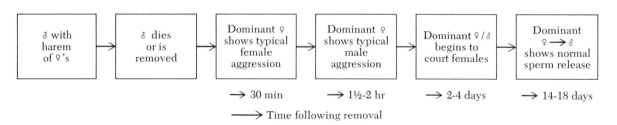

Figure 13-2. Sexual transformations occur in a coral reef fish when changes take place in the social organization of the colony. The female-male shift begins within 30 minutes following removal of the dominant male, and is complete within 14-18 days, when the female-now-male can produce sperm (from Robertson, 1972).

ovarian hormones in adulthood, and they are relatively nonresponsive to testosterone replacement therapy. Second, pregnant female dogs have been injected with an anti-androgen compound (Neumann and Steinbeck, 1972). The androgen-antagonistic biochemical destroys the effectiveness of male hormones for the fetal male pups: nipples develop, and the mammary glands react to ovarian hormone treatment in adulthood in a manner similar to that observed in female dogs. These effects were not obtained from pups whose prenatal development was normal and who were simply castrated after birth.

One of the more puzzling results of early hormonal manipulation is that large dosages of estrogen administered in the critical phase of sexual development *reduce* the capacity of the female rats to display female behavior at maturity. They do not become super-females; in fact, just the opposite occurs. On the other hand, removal of the ovaries at birth does not inhibit the expression of feminine sexual behavior in adulthood if the females are given appropriate hormone replacement therapy at maturity. In short, it appears that in the absence of male hormones, mammalian young maintain the capacity for some mature female behavior, whether their genetic sex is male or female. Self-produced ovarian hormones do not appear to be necessary for the development of the feminine genital tract or a propensity toward feminine sexual behavior. In the course of normal development, the male fetus produces androgen hormones that have a masculinizing influence upon the development of a variety of structures, including testicular development. But when this source of androgens is diminished—either by the administration of anti-androgen compounds or by early postnatal castration—the fetus develops female characteristics (Figure 13-3).[1] It should be emphasized that regardless of the procedures followed, feminized males are not complete females in terms of internal-external sexual equipment and

functions, or in terms of spontaneously producing all features of feminine behavior. They are in between: in structure, function, and behavior.

To summarize, in mammals the development of sexual organs (1) occurs within a limited period during the embryonic or early postnatal stages (depending on the maturation rate of the species), (2) is relatively irreversible when the developmental process is completed; (3) is under the direct control of hormonal as well as chromosomal mechanisms. But it must be underscored that the mammalian mechanisms represent only one of a range of possible solutions. When it is to the advantage of the species (such as the cleaner fish), the process (1) occurs at maturity, (2) is relatively reversible, and (3) is under the control of the social system of which the animal is a member.

Are Male Brains Different from Female Brains?

This question has had a special fascination for both the neurosciences and the social sciences, but, I suspect, for quite different reasons. Neuroscientists have attempted to identify the precise pathways and controls that operate in the nervous system to produce the distinctive features of male and female sexuality. Their attention has focused on the basic control centers in the brain, and their relation to the master gland of the endocrine system, the pituitary, and the male and female gonads (testes in the male, ovaries in the female). Questions concerning the internal control are several steps removed from the exceedingly complex issues of human male-female differences in cognition, intelligence, and personality. This is not to imply that the study of how the brain directs basic sexual functions is not important. Great advances have been made during the past 40 years toward understanding the biochemical and anatomical controls of sexuality. The development

---

[1] The opposite occurs in birds because the male is homogametic *(XX)* and the female is heterogametic *(XY)* (Adkins, 1975; Gorbman and Bern, 1962).

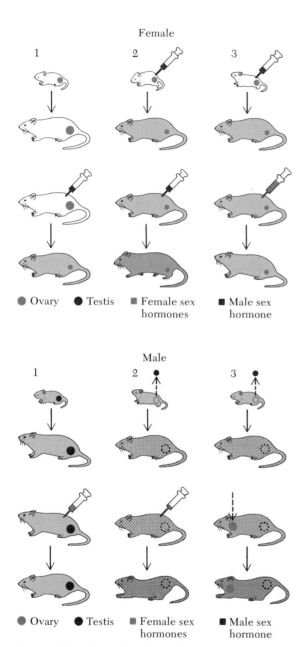

Female

● Ovary ● Testis ■ Female sex ■ Male sex
hormones hormone

Male

● Ovary ● Testis ■ Female sex ■ Male sex
hormones hormone

Figure 13-3. *Top:* Masculinized female rats were produced by injections of testosterone at birth. Column 1 shows a normal female that was injected with male hormones when mature; the animal exhibits some male behavior. Column 2 shows a female injected with male hormone in infancy; then reinjected at maturity, she exhibits

of the contraceptive pill is one of the most socially important consequences of this research.

The brain is appropriately seen as one component, albeit a rather important one, of a complex reciprocating system of sexual regulation. The three main structural components of the system are the pituitary gland (or hypophysis, as it is also called), the gonads, and the brain (principally the hypothalamus and preoptic areas). Linking these structures are hormones (blood-borne chemical messengers) and direct neural connections. The hormones produced by the pituitary and the gonads have a profound effect on the sexual functions and behaviors. They in turn control and are controlled by hypothalamic hormones or "releasing factors." Figure 13-4 summarizes some of these basic relationships.

Let us first consider the functions of the pituitary gland in establishing and maintaining male characteristics. Its role in maintaining the precision of the regulatory mechanism is basic: its secretions ensure a balance between the hormones of the several glands in the endocrine system. In males, at least two of the hormones released by the pituitary have as their target the gonads (testes): the luteinizing hormone (LH), and the follicle-stimulating hormone (FSH). Although separate functions have been defined for these gonadotropic hormones, they are often synergistic—that is, the presence of both is re-

full male sexual behavior. Column 3 shows that in spite of an injection of female hormone at maturity, the masculinized female fails to exhibit female sexual behavior. *Bottom:* Feminized male rats were produced by injections of estrogen and progesterone, or by ovary implants only, when the males have been castrated at birth and thereby deprived of testosterone during the critical first days of life. Column 1 shows that a normal male is not affected by the injection of female hormones at maturity. Column 2 shows that a castrated male that was similarly injected assumes the female's permissive sexual posture. Column 3 shows that the same behavior can be produced by implanting an ovary at maturity. (From S. Levine, "Sex differences in the brain." Copyright © 1966 by Scientific American, Inc. All rights reserved.)

quired for a given function. Singly and in combination with other hormones, they account for sperm production and for the release of male hormones (androgens) by the testes.

Androgens serve multiple functions, including maintaining the male sexual apparatus in working order, stimulating sexual dimorphism, contributing to the production of sperm, promoting growth, and regulating metabolism. A reciprocal feedback relationship obtains between testicular secretions of an-

drogens, on the one hand, and pituitary gonadotropin secretions, on the other. When critical levels of androgen concentrations in the blood are reached, gonadotropin release is suppressed, resulting in a reduction in the secretion of androgen. Natural disturbances of the regulatory mechanism are rare, but when they occur, the clinical disorders are often severe. They range from precocial development of sexual characteristics to perpetual immaturity.

The interaction between the brain, pituitary

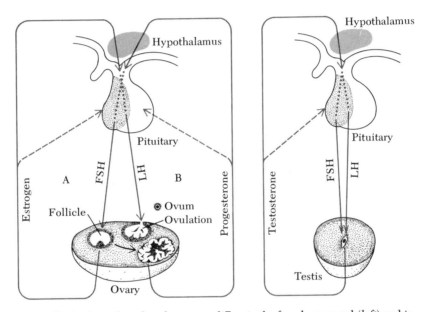

Figure 13-4. Interplay of sex hormones differs in the female mammal (*left*) and in the male (*right*). In the cyclic female system the pituitary gland initially releases a follicle-stimulating hormone (FSH) that cooperates with other hormones to make the ovary produce estrogen. The estrogen then acts on the hypothalamus of the brain to inhibit the further release of FSH by the pituitary and to stimulate the release of a luteinizing hormone (LH). This hormone both triggers ovulation and makes the ovary produce a second hormone, progesterone. On reaching the hypothalamus the latter hormone inhibits further pituitary release of LH, thereby completing the cycle. In the noncyclic male system the pituitary gland continually releases FSH and LH, which act together to stimulate the testes to produce and release testosterone; the latter hormone acts on the hypothalamus to stimulate further release of FSH and LH by the pituitary. Broken arrows represent the possibility that some of the feedback effects of the gonadal hormones take place in the pituitary directly (Davidson, 1977). (Adapted from S. Levine, "Sex differences in the brain." Copyright © 1966 by Scientific American, Inc. All rights reserved.)

gland, and sex glands in the maintenance and control of female sexual functions is somewhat more complicated because most mammalian females undergo cyclic periods of reproductive readiness. The gonadotropins, FSH and LH, act synergistically on the gonads (ovaries) to stimulate egg production and to control the release of estrogens (female sex hormones). Estrogens, in turn, act in a self-regulatory fashion to control the release of the gonadotropins FSH and LH by the pituitary.

Support for differences between male and female brains has been slow in coming. The evidence has implicated the anterior hypothalamic-preoptic region of the brain (Conrad and Pfaff, 1975; see the review by R. Lisk, 1967). Recent anatomical studies of the preoptic region of the brain have identified some of the features by which this area can be differentiated in males and females. Most of the differences that have been reported are relatively modest. Raisman and Field (1971) found that male and female brains differ basically in the type of neural connections that are formed, rather than in the intrinsic properties of the neurons themselves. This finding, if supported by the continuing work in the area, would be consistent with the basic sexual bipotentiality that has been identified in behavioral-physiological work (Kow et al., 1976). This area of research is still in a period of rapid expansion and facts are still accumulating.

For example, shortly after the preceding summary was written, F. Nottebohm and A. Arnold of Rockefeller University reported finding a "striking sexual dimorphism" in the brains of two species of songbirds: canaries and zebra finches (1976). The discovery is significant because it appears to be the first to suggest that gross sexual dimorphism exists in the vertebrate brain. The differences are located in the regions of the brain that control song production. The investigators observe that males have a complex song repertoire that is learned in development, but females do not produce songs. Female canaries will sing when administered male hormones, but their song is considerably less varied than that of males. Nottebohm and Arnold discov-

ered the gross difference between male and female brain structures—reflecting both larger cell size and a higher density of cells in the males—by tracing the neural pathways that are associated with song production. The differences were specific to song areas, and no reliable sex difference were found in brains of either species in those structures not related to song control, or in total brain weight. Hence the brain differences may possibly be viewed as being due less to sex differences than to song differences: singing birds (that happen to be male) versus non-singing birds (that happen to be female).

The Dual Role of Hormones: Organization and Activation

Up to this point in this discussion of hormones and sexual development, the focus has been on the sexual structural differences that are produced by gonadal secretions. The story of sexual development would be greatly simplified if these neural, structural, and biochemical variations were perfectly correlated with sexual behavior. But they are not. Hormones do affect the organization and activation of sexual behavior, but the type of influence they exert and the extent to which it is exerted varies with the animal's species, age, and sex.

According to W. C. Young (1961), gonadal hormones can play two distinct roles, depending upon the time in ontogeny at which they are introduced. In early development, they serve an organizational role, in that they "fix" the central nervous system template that guides future development and sets limits for future performance. In maturity, these hormones contribute directly to sexual behavior. In Young's words, at maturity "hormones might simply activate an individual to respond in accordance with the character of a substrate already established" (p. 1199). Other investigators had previously suggested that hormones perform one function or the other, but Young was the first to propose that they perform both.

Organization

There can be no doubt that the basic premise of the organizational-activational hypothesis is correct—that hormones do in fact serve a dual role according to the age-developmental level of the organism at the time of administration. The work of Young and his colleagues established that fetal or infant animals that had been castrated, then administered hormones, showed a differential response to hormonal injections at maturity. There is a major question, however, about the nature of the "substrate" that is organized by the hormones early in life. Is the substrate only in the central nervous system (the brain), or does it include the endocrine system and/or some of the "peripheral" sexual apparatus (including the internal and external genitalia)? Although the central nervous system has been seen as being the prime site for the substrate, recent evidence suggests that there may be more than a single substrate. A brief review of the possibilities follows.

Central Nervous System Substrate.   According to one proposal, a "template" is formed in the brain early in development that guides subsequent development and determines the limits of future performance. Once the template is established, it determines which hormones the organism will be responsive to, or will not be responsive to. The central neural template is presently a *hypothetical construct*, that is, a hypothesis has been formulated about the existence, in the brain, of an area that will eventually be fully described by histological and biochemical evidence. There are, indeed, several lines of evidence (some of which have already been discussed) that indicate that the preoptic/hypothalamic area is a likely site of such a template.

In addition to the brain, four other "semi-independent" mechanisms have been proposed to provide a "substrate" for later sexual performance.

The substrates for differences in sexual responsiveness may not be only in the brain.

Gonadal Substrate.   There is a pervasive influence of testosterone upon the genitals throughout the course of their development. Gonadal hormones present in infancy apparently sensitize the external genital structures for growth at later stages. Beach and Holz-Tucker (1949) found that whether male rats were castrated at birth or at 21 days of age did not affect their external genitalia at maturity: both groups were sexually immature. Replacement therapy (testosterone injections) at maturity, however, brought out significant differences between the two groups: the genital growth of the 21-day castrates greatly exceeded that of those castrated at birth. Apparently the androgens produced by the animals early in development primed the external genital structures for subsequent growth. This research also showed that androgens are required to maintain penis size at maturity. Castration leads to a reduction in the *balbus glandis* of dogs and to a weakening of the perineal muscles (which control phallic movement) in rats.

Reflexive Neural Substrate.   A third substrate is the neural network that controls reflexive sexual responding. Studies of paraplegic rats and dogs indicate that ejaculation and erection can be readily evoked by mechanical stimulation, even though all neural connections ascending to and descending from the brain have been severed. The recent work of Hart (1968, 1974) indicates that androgens directly influence this reflexive response. Implantation of testosterone in the spinal canal of castrated paraplegic rats produced an immediate increase in erection and ejaculation. Hart's work also indicates that brain centers or "templates" are not necessary for the evocation of primary masculine sexual responses. Indeed, basic sexual reflexes occur more readily in the animals whose spinal cords have been severed, suggesting that the brain might have an inhibitory effect on this reflex.

Sensory Substrate. A fourth substrate that gonadal hormones may help to organize in development is that which is involved in the establishment of particular sensory thresholds. As we will see in the next chapter, males and females are particularly responsive to olfactory and visual cues that communicate that members of the opposite sex of their species are receptive or sexually active. Precisely how do these stimuli develop the capacity to control the arousal level and sexual activity of members of the opposite sex? There is a possibility that the effects may be mediated at the site of the sensory receptor. Hence females may detect certain sex-related odors more readily than males (Carr, 1974).

Sexual Dimorphism. Androgens have a generalized effect upon the growth and metabolism of the animal (that is, not merely on the sex apparatus) in that castrated males are generally smaller and less strong than noncastrated siblings (Bevan, Daves, and Levy, 1960). Similarly, masculinized females tend to be heavier and more aggressive than normal females (Edwards, 1969). Such morphological changes produced by the hormones could have immediate effects on the nature of the interactions in which the animal becomes involved. In particular, gross differences in morphology could determine which one of two animals will assume the dominant role and which one will assume the submissive or receptive role. This "secondary" influence of hormonal administration may thus lead to the adoption of disparate behavior patterns in ontogeny, which would heighten the probability that corresponding patterns would occur in maturity.

In short, gonadal hormones in early development exert multiple effects in the course of development of an individual, and hence have multiple "targets." Although the basic premise of the organization hypothesis is agreed upon by investigators (that hormones administered early in development lead to the establishment of a substrate for subsequent responding), there is some disagreement over whether the organizing function of hormones is restricted to

a unitary neural substrate or whether it includes other "peripheral" substrates as well.

Activation

The second function of sexual hormones is to activate behavior—to fuel and ignite the biological machinery that has been established. Although there is support for this hypothesis, the relationship between hormones and behavior is rarely simple or direct.

Hormones and Masculine Behavior. If there were a one-to-one correspondence between level of male hormones and male sexual behavior, then castration (removal of the primary source of androgens) should sharply diminish or eliminate male sexual behavior. It often does not in the various mammalian species that have been studied (such as rats, dogs, cats, and primates). Castration inevitably eliminates masculine behavior only in rodents (Figures 13-5 and 13-6). The other species show a varied capacity for the maintenance of male sexual behavior, including copulation, in the absence of testicular secretions for periods ranging up to several years. Further, individuals differ in the extent to which they are influenced by castration (Luttge, 1971). The lack of a perfect correlation between male hormonal level and male sexual behavior is further illustrated by the failure of some sexually capable males to approach or show interest in sexually receptive females.

One determinant of the effects of castration is whether it occurs before or after sexual experience. If male dogs or cats are castrated prior to having mated, it is unlikely that they will develop species-typical sexual patterns. But if they are castrated following sexual experience, the behaviors will often persist (Beach, 1970; Rosenblatt, 1965—see Figure 13-7). This finding turns out to be a critical one because it indicates that there is a "consolidation" in sexual interchanges as well as in aggressive ones (Chapter 10).

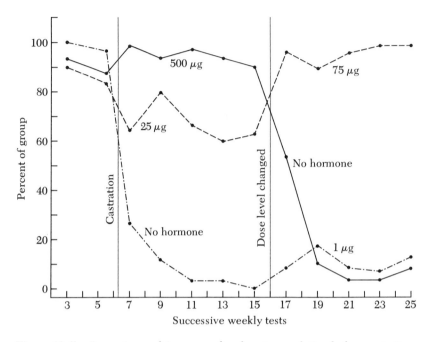

Figure 13-5. Percentages of 3 groups of male rats copulating before castration and after castration when members of different groups were receiving different daily dosages of testosterone propionate. (From Beach, copyright © 1969 by the American Psychological Association. Reprinted by permission.)

On the other hand, the correlation between male hormones and male sexual behavior is surely not inconsequential. In the course of normal development, striking changes in morphology and behavior occur in males at sexual maturity. These changes can, for the most part, be traced to gonadal secretion. Furthermore, injections of male hormones have *facilitated* (in Gottlieb's terminology, Chapter 5) "mature" male behaviors in "infantile" mammals and birds, including 3-day-old chicks (Andrew, 1975a, 1975b). In addition, when male hormones are administered to ovariectomized female rats, the temporarily masculinized females show many of the primary behavioral characteristics of adult males when permitted to interact with receptive females (Gerall and Ward, 1966).

Hormones and Feminine Behavior. In most "lower mammals," female sexual responsiveness is highly dependent upon the presence of ovarian hormones. In the absence of estrogen, female receptivity is sharply diminished (Beach, 1964). The sudden increase in feminine responsiveness at sexual maturation can be traced to the secretion of ovarian hormones. Furthermore, behavioral receptivity (and solicitiveness) can be produced in the adult female by administering appropriate dosages of ovarian hormones. In some circumstances, estrogen introduction paradoxically leads to masculine behavior, including, in rodents, mounting, thrusting, and intromission.

Estrogens appear to be less necessary to support receptivity in primate females, including humans,

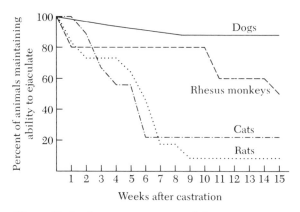

Figure 13-6. Species comparison of the percentage of animals maintaining the ability to ejaculate after castration. (From Hart, copyright © 1974 by the American Psychological Association. Reprinted by permission.)

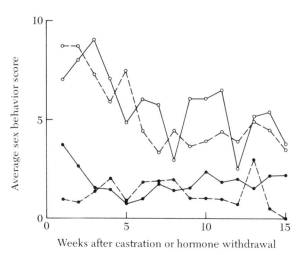

Figure 13-7. Mean sex-behavior scores for male cats before and after castration or cessation of androgen treatment. Some of the males had sexual experience (*open circles*) and some were sexually inexperienced (*closed circles*). The unbroken lines refer to postpuberal castrates and the broken lines refer to prepuberal castrates given androgen for 3 months (from Rosenblatt, 1965).

than in nonprimate females (Luttge, 1971). Female primates are receptive even when not in estrus (heat), or when ovariectomized. Nonetheless, in nonhuman female primates, estrogen (1) heightens receptivity, (2) heightens physical attractiveness, and (3) heightens promiscuousness. Both field studies and laboratory observations indicate that periods of heightened receptivity in the female correspond to her periods of physiological estrus. The physical changes that are correlated with onset of estrus (enlargement of and changes in coloration of the genital regions in primates, secretion of sexual odors) have effective signal properties for males (Luttge, 1971; Michael, Keverne, and Bonsall, 1971). In effect, females become more attractive to males. Johnson and Phoenix (1976) have shown that estrogen-treated female monkeys are more likely than untreated ones to actively seek out sexual partners and then to elicit advances from them.

Summary

In this chapter we have studied some of the interrelations between hormones, structure, and behavior

in sexual development. Recent study of these relationships indicates the following.

■ The connection between genes and sexual behavior is by no means direct, immediate, or inviolable. The processes that support male and female differentiation from the embryonic bisexual state are themselves formed in development, under the bidirectional control of chromosomal mechanisms and self-produced hormones.

■ Sexual development can be interrupted or redirected by changes in hormonal balance. The key biochemicals in this process—the gonadotropins and gonadal hormones—are critical not only for the initial organization of the reproductive system but for its activation and maintenance as well. Estrous cycles and states of sensitivity and responsiveness in the female, as well as sexual capacity and reactivity in the male, reflect variations in hormonal levels at maturity.

■ Attempts to identify the "substrate" that is organized by hormones early in development have focused primarily on the central nervous system, notably the anterior hypothalamic-preoptic region of the brain. In addition, certain other structural components of the reproductive system appear to become organized in development, including the gonads, reflexive pathways, and sensory sensitivities. Gonadal hormones also stimulate the growth of non-sexual tissues, and contribute to sex-related differences in body size (sexual dimorphism).

■ Male and female brains differ in structure and in functions, although these differences are modest and, insofar as evidence is now available, are specific to the areas that control sexual dimorphism in behavior and/or physiological function.

■ Endrocrinological research indicates that hormones are controlled by an intricate system that includes the pituitary gland, the brain, gonads, and other endocrine bodies. Perhaps most important for us is the fact that social events are part of the regulatory system. Social acts or states thus permit individuals to synchronize their sexual states and behaviors under multiple and diverse conditions.

■ This achievement of "social control" of hormones is not limited to mammals. We illustrated the way sexual status can be determined in fish at maturity by changes in social circumstances. Equally powerful functions of these events have been identified in birds (Lehrman, 1961), invertebrates (Wilson, 1975), and mammals.

In the next chapter we will examine how these social and sexual processes are interwoven in development and how the system may go awry.

14

INTERACTIONAL EXPERIENCE AND SEXUAL DEVELOPMENT: A COMPARATIVE PERSPECTIVE

In Chapter 13 we analyzed the biophysical and hormonal contributions to sexual development; in this chapter we will examine the role of social experiences. The twofold aim will be to trace how sexual-social interactions are affected by events that occur in development and to learn how these interactions can be modified and redirected at maturity.

Mammals have achieved spectacular diversity in mating patterns during evolution. It is nonetheless possible to classify mammalian mating-rearing strategies into five general types: one involving brief copulatory association, two kinds of harem systems (short-term and long-term polygyny), a colony structure that promotes dominance hierarchies, and a "family" system of monogamy (Crook, 1977). Remarkably, all five of the types appear among species of nonhuman primates. Furthermore, the monogamous family unit, though relatively rare in mammals, can be found in several of its orders, including coyotes (Carnivora), koalas (marsupials), and gibbons (primates). British ethologist John Crook has found that the particular mating-rearing pattern a species adopts in evolution seems to reflect its ecological circumstances and the maturational rate of its young, among other things. Monogamy, for instance, has evolved independently among coyotes and koalas (convergent evolution), possibly because both species have young who have a long period of dependency on the mother, and have a need for involvement by the male in food collection and infant care.

The general lesson to be learned from these evolutionary studies is that we will look in vain for *the* mating-rearing system in monkeys or apes that can be applied in a simple and direct way to human beings (Crook, 1977; Eisenberg, 1977). None exists. Comparative studies are required, nonetheless, to identify the general principles of mammalian sociosexual development. The "distinctively human" patterns of sexual behavior are themselves part of this broad outline of development.

Infantile and Juvenile Sexuality

The major components of adult sexual behavior are present, in at least incipient forms, in the behavioral repertoires of immature mammals. One of the first systematic studies of the "unlearned birth equipment" of babies was conducted by behaviorist John Watson (1926), who reported that newborn infants evidenced sexual excitability (erection of the penis) and sexual soothing (calming when they were stroked in erogenous areas). Infantile sexual behaviors can also be observed in other mammals, from guinea pigs to monkeys. Some of the outcomes are bisexual. The newborn male or female guinea pig, for instance, will assume a sexual receptivity posture (lordosis) not unlike that of the adult female when stroked in the genital regions. Bisexual behavior is also exhibited by young monkeys. G. V. Hamilton's (1914) observations of the bisexual activities of macaque monkeys were mentioned in the Chapter 13: young monkeys take turns at assuming the "active" (mounting and thrusting) and "passive" (being mounted) positions.

Studies conducted at the Wisconsin laboratory of H. F. Harlow (1965) indicate that some sexual differentiation of behavior is observable in rhesus monkeys by the third month of life. Males characteristically engage in rough-and-tumble play; females are more passive. Young rhesus males pursue, mount, and perform thrusting movements without having had relevant experience or specific training (Figure 14-1). The finding of reliable early differences between males and females does not mean, however, that they duplicate the actions of the adult. To the contrary, the sexual actions of the young are typically incomplete, fragmentary, and inept. Although these observations were made under laboratory conditions, they are generally consistent with observations of primates under free-ranging circumstances (see Kummer, 1968; Stephenson, 1975). One finds in other species (such as puppies) as well the early but incomplete differentiation of sexual roles and intersexual behavior (Scott and Fuller, 1965).

What is the long-term significance of these infantile sexual interchanges? The answer to this question can only be speculative in the absence of firm information. The speculations range from the possibility that the experience provides necessary preliminary

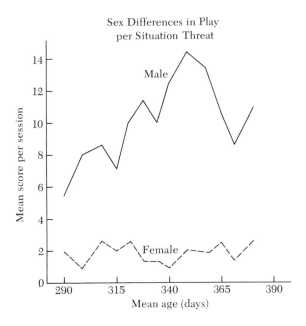

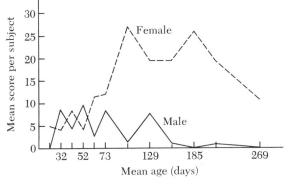

Figure 14-1. Sex differences in behavior are observed in laboratory-reared rhesus monkeys as early as the third month of life. *Top:* sex differences in threat responses associated with play fighting. *Bottom:* sex differences in the occurence of rigid postures, a species-typical indication of female receptivity (from Harlow, 1965).

experience in sexual coordination to the possibility that it helps the individual to determine appropriate mating choices to the possibility that it has no special function for later sexual behavior and simply represents activity appropriate to the individual's sex and age. Whatever might be the function of these early sexual activities—and it is not obvious that the same function is served for all species—their ubiquitous occurrence requires that the terms "sexually naive" and "sexually inexperienced" be used with caution. Although the individual may not have mated, most organisms have "sexual experience" of one sort or another at every stage of behavioral development, from infancy onward.

Isolation and Sexual Development

The isolation experiment has been one of the main tools used to measure the effects of social experience on sexual behavior. Like its parallel in neurological research—the ablation procedure—isolation has effects that are often more general than the investigator wishes to produce. As we have already seen, complete isolation of an individual from birth or weaning until adulthood results in a heightened irritability, a decreased tendency to remain with others of the same species, and an increased propensity to attack or withdraw from stimulation. Whatever effects the isolation procedure might have on sexual behavior are necessarily superimposed upon these other effects. Sexual dysfunctions resulting from isolation can be a consequence of such general behavioral disruption, a failure to develop appropriate sexual response patterns, a failure to select appropriate partners, or some combination of these.

The Sexual Interchange: Does It Take Two to Tango?

A puzzling discrepancy appeared in the scientific literature a few years ago that is relevant to the issue of sexual interchanges. G. Meier (1965) reported that rearing male rhesus monkeys in isolation does not inhibit species-appropriate mating behavior in adulthood. E. A. Missakian, working in the same laboratory 2–3 years later, examined the sexual behavior of the monkeys whom Meier had studied. Missakian (1969) found, however, virtually no instances of species-appropriate mating behavior. Two males that had been observed to mate in the earlier study and to father offspring were found to be sexually inept in the later study (see Table 14-1).

Table 14-1. Comparison of sexual performance of sexually deprived rhesus male monkeys studied by two investigators.

	Investigator			
Subject number	Meier, 1965		Missakian, 1969	
	Positive sperm test?*	Offspring?	Positive sperm test?*	Offspring?
43	Yes (1)	Yes (1)	Not tested	Not tested
49†	Yes (5)	Yes (1)	No (0)	No (0)
53†	Yes (21)	Yes (1)	No (0)	No (0)
62	Yes (2)	No	Not tested	Not tested

*Presence of sperm in the vaginal tract of the female with which the male was paired, indicating successful copulation.
†Monkeys tested in both series.

It is a rare event when two investigators independently study the same animals, and rarer still when they obtain opposite results. Clearly the animals behaved differently in the two studies. The question is why. One obvious possibility is that the animals' response capabilities changed during the 2- to 3-year interval between the two tests. What kind of changes could have occurred? Possibly the males had been rebuffed in their sexual behavior during the interval between the studies. Or perhaps they simply aged past their peak sexual effectiveness. (The latter possibility is unlikely, however, since the males were presumably reaching their sexual prime during the second test.)

A third possibility is that the conditions of testing—particularly those affecting partner selection—were different in the two studies. Whereas Meier selected only experienced females as partners, Missakian selected the female partners at random from a group that included both naive and experienced partners (personal communication, E. A. Missakian, 1969). The reactions of a female to the ineptness of an isolation-reared male might vary as a function of her prior experiences and her tolerance. Primate females are known to differ markedly in receptivity, and they develop strong preferences for and aversions to particular male partners (Stephenson, 1975). (This particular puzzle must remain unsolved, however, because we have no way of recovering information about what occurred in the years that intervened between the two studies. The Missakian observations suggest, however, that whether recovery from isolation is "complete" depends at least in part on the test circumstances.)

Does the receptivity of the partner affect the success of mating encounters in primates? The answer is yes (Rogers and Davenport, 1969). When isolated chimpanzee males were first paired with younger, isolation-reared females, virtually no sexual interactions were observed. But when the same males were placed with older, sophisticated females, they copulated on several occasions, and one of the females became pregnant (Rogers and Davenport, 1969).

The investigators report that "copulations were the result of the skill and persistence of the females who frequently effected intromission by trapping the male in a corner and backing into the erect penis" (p. 202). The effects of isolation can be ameliorated, with the partner's help.

One lesson to be learned is that sexual behavior is basically a dyadic interaction. When analyzing the effects of isolation—or any other manipulation—one must give explicit attention to the interaction between the states and behaviors produced by the procedure and the reactions provoked in the partner.

Isolation Sexual Development

The Effects of Isolation on Males.   The recognition that the development of sexual behavior is a fusion of social-contextual-organic influences helps to explain other effects of isolation on males. If a male rat is removed from his mother and littermates shortly after birth and is kept away from other members of his kind past sexual maturity, he does not respond "normally" when first presented to an estrous adult female. Instead of immediately performing species-typical patterns of pelvic mounting, isolated rats leap, climb over, and tunnel under the female. In their detailed study of isolated male rats, Gerall, Ward, and Gerall (1967) observed that intromission was not achieved "primarily because posterior mounting and, particularly, clasping of the flanks of the female were not performed" (p. 56). Although the males were apparently excited by the presence of the female, competing behaviors prevented complete copulation. Components of the mating act were present, but they were not sufficiently integrated so that intromission could be achieved. Similar results have been reported by investigators studying isolated male cats (Rosenblatt, 1965), monkeys (Mason, 1960; Harlow, 1965), and guinea pigs (Gerall, 1965).

But not all findings are consistent with these reports. Beach (1942) found that isolation did not disrupt the sexual performance of male rats relative to other forms of rearing (in exclusively male groups or in mixed-sex groups). The rats reared in isolation in fact mated faster and more often than did those maintained in the other conditions. These findings were later replicated and extended by Beach (1958).

How might this discrepancy be explained? Beach (1942) observed that the dimensions of the testing compartment played a role in determining whether aberrant mounting occurred. In smaller compartments, the female was more likely to assume the lordosis posture when she was backed against the corner or wall—that is, facing the male. Under these conditions, the inexperienced males were likely to mount the female's head or side. In larger compartments, the female assumed the receptive posture when the male pursued her from behind, and the orientation of the two was better suited for successful intromission. Seemingly trivial variations in the testing circumstances can have nontrivial effects. Some cases of pathological behavior may be partly the result of the testing circumstances.

Sexual "Therapy" for Males.

The effects of early rearing on sexual interchanges are not necessarily enduring. For instance, Gerall, Ward, and Gerall (1967) found that cohabitation with a receptive female for 3 weeks or less was sufficient to produce normal mating behavior in previously isolated male rats. Mere opportunity to cohabitate seems sufficient to establish successful mating behavior, regardless of prior isolation—see Figure 14-2 (Drori and Folman, 1967).

But not all mammalian males are easily rehabilitated. The first studies of partially or totally isolated monkeys, conducted in the Wisconsin laboratories by H. F. Harlow and his colleagues, indicated that rehabilitation can be difficult and unsuccessful. The initial attempts of Harlow (1965) failed, even though Harlow used a variety of ingenious procedures, including "group therapy" (placing the iso-

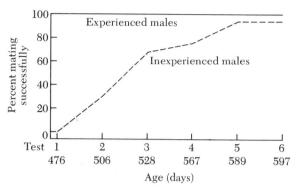

Figure 14-2. Male rats who were not mated until 16 months of age are initially ineffective in mating tests, compared with male rats who were reared with receptive females since weaning. From the age of 485 day onward, all males were maintained with receptive females between tests. Matings were observed in 15 of the 16 previously segregated males after approximately 3 months of cohabitation with females (data from Drori and Folman, 1967).

late with a large group of feral-reared adult male and female animals on a "monkey island" in a public zoo). Why the failure? In Chapter 5, the colony's behavior, and its possible rejection of the "outsider," was implicated. Further, the isolates may have been especially vulnerable to social rebuffs and stress. More recent attempts at "therapy" have been successful (Mason and Kenney, 1974; Novak and Harlow, 1975; Suomi and Harlow, 1972). Significantly, in all of them, there was (1) no colony rejection and (2) only mild partner stress and rebuff (see also Beach, 1970).

The Effects of Isolation on Females.

Rearing in isolation has generally been regarded as less devastating for the sexual behavior of females than for that of males (Beach, 1964). Female rats reared in complete isolation from birth until maturity demonstrate a capacity to mate, give birth, and adequately raise their offspring (Thoman and Arnold, 1968). This outcome may mean that the females were less affected by isolation than the males, or it may mean that aberrant tendencies existed but were rapidly reversed. Evidence that there is in fact some initial sexual dysfunction has been reported in isolated females of species as diverse as guinea pigs and rhesus monkeys (Harlow, 1965). The mating disturbances include a tendency to avoid males, and, if this were impossible, a failure to adopt a receptive position that would support mounting.

In some respects, females appear to be more influenced by social experience than males. For instance, studies of the odors of potential partners have shown that previous social experience has a greater effect on female rats than on male rats (Carr, Wylie, and Loeb, 1970). This finding, which is consistent with that obtained in the study of female mice (Bruce, 1966; Mainardi, Marsan, and Pasquali, 1965), suggests that female rodents are clearly responsive to the stimuli emitted by male rodents. The female mating pattern in the same species seems to be less vulnerable to disruption.

These considerations bring us to the more general problem of the ways in which experience contributes to sexual performance and sexual development.

The Integration of Psychobiological Contributions

In development, there is a continuing fusion between behavioral function and psychobiological structure. The bidirectionality of the relationship can be seen in the maintenance of sexual functions, the activity of hormones, and the selection of partners.

Maintenance: An Illustration of Bidirectionality in Structure and Function

In one of the few studies of the psychobiological consequences of long-term segregated rearing,

Drori and Folman (1964, 1967) found that significant anatomical differences exist between male rats continuously raised with other male rats and male rats raised with female rats. These investigators also noted differences in the size and weight of the accessory reproductive organs, including the penis, gonads, and the related musculature. The reproductive systems of the unmated males were atrophied relative to those of males that had been permitted continuous mating opportunities. These unmated males also performed poorly in a mating test conducted when they were 16 months (476 days) of age (Drori and Folman, 1964, 1967; Folman and Drori, 1966). Other studies suggest that males reared with other males eventually come to prefer same-sex partners (Beach, 1942; Jenkins, 1928).[1] These effects—both physiological and social—are reversible, however. Drori and Folman (1967) report that 3 weeks of cohabitation with females leads to recovery of species-typical male functions and physical characteristics (Figure 14-2).

Social Stimuli and Hormones

In view of the importance of gonadal hormones as controllers of sexual organization and activation, we might ask what controls the gonadal hormones. The internal interrelations are shown in Figure 13-4. The range of external events (environmental changes) that contribute to hormonal regulation include seasonal conditions, such as light duration and temperature, which determine onset of estrus (heat) in females and sexual vigor in males (Timiras, 1972).

Social stimuli have a direct influence from female hormonal secretions in both a disruptive and a facilitative sense. As an example of disruption, odors emitted by strange males can terminate pregnancy in recently impregnated female mice. The "pregnancy block" has been traced to a disruption of the

---

[1] These phenomena are consistent with the proposal that heterosexual stimuli play a "maintaining" role (see Chapter 5) for the sexual apparatus and behavior of the species.

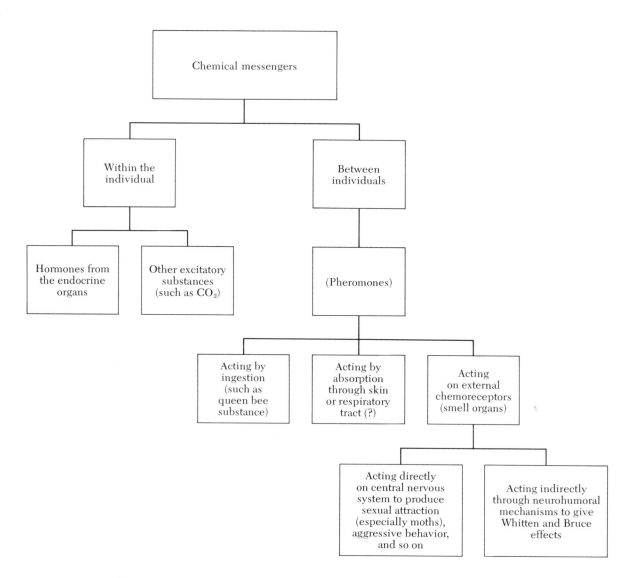

Figure 14-3. The term *pheromone* refers to a class of chemical substances by which some individuals influence the physiological states of others in the population. The effects of these substances on the regulation of social behavior have been observed in vertebrates and invertebrates. Special attention has been given to the effects of odoriferous substances produced by one sex on the physiology of the opposite sex (adapted from Etkin, 1964).

pattern of endogenous hormonal secretions required to maintain pregnancy (Adler and Zoloth, 1970; Parkes and Bruce, 1961). On the other hand, social stimuli can facilitate estrous, in that the odors produced by males are sufficient to provoke estrous cycles in females (Whitten, 1956). Figure 14-3 is an overview of the relations between the internal controls of hormones and external social controls exercised by pheromones (substances produced by organisms that directly influence the physiological processes of other organisms). The stimuli need not be chemical; they can be visual, mechanical, or somatosensory. For instance, a female pigeon can be induced to lay an egg merely by seeing a male courting her through a glass plate. Since the production of an egg by the ovary occurs only in response to the secretion of pituitary hormones, the sight of the male appears to be sufficient to trigger the necessary hormonal secretion (Lehrman, 1964). The phenomenon is more readily demonstrated in sexually experienced females than in naive ones (Lehrman, 1970; Michel, 1976). Apparently, hormones "learn"—that is, they can be conditioned.

More generally, the conditioning of hormonal release permits individuals to coordinate precisely their behaviors and sexual arousal states. In addition to whatever inherent biases operate, the range of stimuli that can gain the capacity to trigger arousal can be markedly expanded, and the organism might be seen as biologically "prepared" to learn some stimulus properties more readily than others. The conditioning experiences can sharpen whatever biases are already present and can potentially induce new preferences (Figure 14-4).

Psychobiological Bases for Preferences and Selection

Primates and other nonhuman mammalian males can mount, thrust, and ejaculate without having had

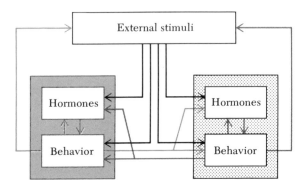

Figure 14-4. Interactions that appear to govern the reproductive-behavior cycle of doves. Hormones regulate behavior and are themselves affected by behavioral and other stimuli. And the behavior of each bird affects the hormones and behavior of its mate. The figure is general enough to describe other behavioral-hormonal-behavioral interactions, including those involved in nursing, fighting and reproduction in mammals (from D. Lehrman, 1964).

any special training or experience. The finding that components of sexual responses occur "spontaneously" given the presence of particular biochemical states should hardly be surprising in light of the information covered in the preceding chapter. Nor should the finding that patterns of sexual responding are relatively uniform within species. The psychobiological substrates for such sexual reactions are laid in the course of neural and morphological development.

But mating is a dyadic matter. The right responses must be elicited at the right time and with the right partner in order for successful reproduction to occur in mammals. It seems reasonable to expect that so basic a function should not depend entirely on an individual's experiences. There is, in fact, ample evidence that a variety of sensory biases support the individual's identification and preference for appropriate or receptive members of the opposite sex. Research on the matter of sensory biases has centered for the most part on olfactory, auditory, tactile, and visual stimulation.

Odor and Its Attraction Properties. Michael and his colleagues (1969, 1971) succeeded in isolating a vaginal secretion of receptive female monkeys and found that it is a strong attractant for males (1971). Similar results have been obtained in studies of rodents and dogs (Beach, 1975; Carr, 1974).

Does experience contribute to the establishment of a preference for certain odors? W. J. Carr and his co-workers at Temple University conducted systematic studies of the effect of olfactory stimuli on the sexual preferences of rats. (Carr, 1974, summarizes the results.) The findings are intriguing but are by no means simple. Inherent biases for odors are present in male and female rodents, but the pattern is not the same for the two sexes, nor is it the same at different age-developmental levels. Immature male rats treated with testosterone prefer odors from receptive females over those from nonreceptive females, regardless of whether they are reared in isolation or with their mother and littermates (Carr, Wylie, and Loeb, 1970). However, when immature females are presented with virtually the same conditions, the rearing circumstances (not the presence or absence of gonadal hormones) determines whether a preference will be demonstrated for intact or for castrated adult males. From their results, Carr et al. (1970) conclude that in immature rats, previous social experience "has a greater effect upon the females' response to sex odors than upon the males' response to sex odors"[2] (p. 57). Quite different results were reported by the same investigators when they studied adult rats in parallel test circumstances. Prior experience was found to have increased the rats' responsiveness to sex odors (Carr, 1970). Whatever may be the inherent response of rats to the odors of sexually active conspecifics, it is fused with a wide range of situational and experiential effects in the course of development. There is no reason to expect that the relations are less complex in other species, including primates.

---

[2] Note the earlier discussion in this chapter on the effects of social experience on females.

Auditory Signals. There are advantages to the mediation of mate identification by auditory signals: they leave no trace, permit great variation and individual identification, cover a limited geographic region, and are uninfluenced by lighting conditions and physical barriers (such as forests).

That primates identify their territories by their songs has now been firmly established (Marshall and Marshall, 1976). The gibbon, a small, slender, long-armed ape found in the East Indies and southern Asia, has been said to be man's fourth closest relative among extant genera. Gibbons sing a lot, and exceedingly well. Their songs are not impromptu, primitive productions, although certain elements are species-typical and constant throughout particular geographic regions. J. and E. Marshall recently toured Southeast Asia to record on tape the songs of the species of gibbons native to that region (Marshall and Marshall, 1976). They found that the songs were beautiful spectacles of nature—"the finest music uttered by a wild land mammal." Following is their description of a typical early morning performance:

> Each pair of gibbons daily advertises its territory by loud singing accompanied by gymnastics—a show of force. The female's great call dominates the half-hour morning bout. It is a brilliant theme lasting 20 seconds or more, repeated every 2 to 5 minutes. It swells in volume after soft opening notes, achieves a climax in pitch, intensity, or rapidity (at which time the gymnastics occur), then subsides. The male's shorter phrases, varying according to the species, either appear at appointed times during the great call, follow it as a coda, are interspersed between great calls (the female's opening notes command his silence during her aria), or are broadcast from his sleeping tree during a predawn chorus (p. 235).

The male's contribution extends over the 45 minutes or so until dawn; his embellishing phrases make it an elaborate though brief song. Tarzan notwithstanding, the male never sings the "great call"; that is the prerogative of the female. The Marshalls concluded that "the faithfulness of each species to its prescribed musical score, together with pronounced sexual divocalism, make the voices of gibbons seem a powerful guide to the isolation of species by appropriate pairing and restriction to territories." Once the characteristics of the song of the mate are learned, it can become an exceedingly powerful basis for individual identification.

Curiously, the *absence* of experience may enhance the effectiveness of auditory signals for some species. An important discovery was recently made concerning the mechanism by which the North American cowbird identifies potential mates (King and West, 1977). Mate identification is not as simple for cowbirds as for other vertebrates because they are a parasitic species whose young are reared by different birds. The cowbird female simply abandons the egg in the nest of one of over 100 different possible hosts. Hence the cowbird's earliest interactions are with birds of a different species than its own. If cowbirds become sexually imprinted to the host species—that is, select the host species for mating partners—the species wouldn't survive. Nonetheless, in the wild, they thrive.

How then do the cowbirds identify other cowbirds, particularly those that are ready to mate? King and West (1977) found that a male reared in isolation sings an abnormal song—a deficient production compared with the songs of male cowbirds that have been reared in the wild. However, this deficient song turns out to be a potent stimulus for eliciting sexual response in females of the species. On hearing this "inferior" song, all females of the species immediately assume a copulatory posture: wings lowered, neck arched, and feathers around the cloacal region separated. The special attractiveness of the abnormal song was found across the board—in females that had considerable sexual experience with normal males, in females reared in the wild, and in females reared in isolation. It works better than the normal male song (Figure 14-5). The results indicate that both male and female cowbirds have evolved a mechanism for identifying partners and eliciting species—appropriate sexual behavior that does not depend on preadult experience. Whether the effect is unique to cowbirds has not been determined. The abnormal songs of isolated males of other species have rarely been examined to ascertain whether they arouse females. If the songs sound imperfect to human ears, it has been assumed, perhaps wrongly, that they sound just as bad to female birds. In point of fact, the "abnormal" may be the most beautiful of all.[3]

Tactile Stimulation.   In contrast to the foregoing, the results that have been obtained with regard to tactile stimulation have not been surprising. Manipulating and licking the genitalia and surrounding exogenous regions evoke species-typical and sex-typical postures, produce sexual arousal, and stimulate sexual hormone release (Hart, 1974). The work of Kow, Malsbury, and Pfaff (1976) indicates that female golden hamsters will assume a receptive posture (lordosis) if stimulated at the rear of the body and if the level of female hormones in the system is sufficient. Stimulation of the face and head, however, disrupts lordosis. These findings are essentially consistent with those obtained in the study of other mammalian species. The erogenous areas of males directly reflect the hormones that were present in early development and at maturity. In rodents and dogs, castration diminishes the range of sensitive areas (Beach, 1965; Hart, 1974).

Surprisingly, sexual behavior can also *inhibit* pregnancy in rats, if copulation occurs soon after a prior mating. Sperm transport into the female uterus is disrupted if genital stimulation occurs within 5 minutes after mating; hence fertilization doesn't occur (Adler and Zolof, 1970).

---

[3] Note the similarity of this finding to that of the effects of isolation on the development of fighting. Isolated animals of many species have been found to be more effective in fighting than nonisolated animals (see Chapter 10).

Visual Stimulation.   Visual displays are used by primates to communicate threat and dominance, as well as states of sexual receptivity (Goodall, 1965; Stephenson, 1975). What is the role of experience in the development and interpretation of visual displays? There is evidence that they can be condi-tioned. For instance, experimental studies of ring-doves indicate that the evocative properties of visual stimuli are significantly enhanced if the doves have had mating experience (Michel, 1976; Lott, Scholz, and Lehrman, 1967).

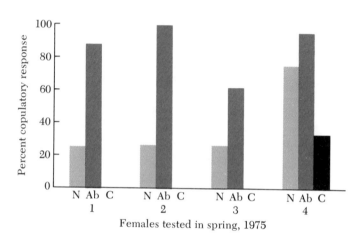

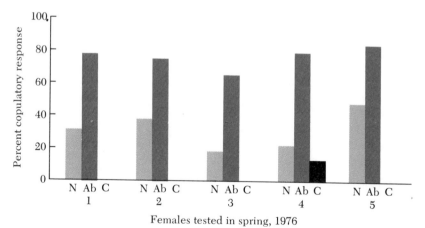

Figure 14-5.   The responsiveness of 4 female cowbirds tested in 1975 and 5 female cowbirds tested in 1976 to normal (N), abnormal (Ab), and control (C) calls (data from King and West, 1977).

The Effects of Experience: Coordination of Sexual Behavior Patterns and Mate Selection

We have seen that the organism has inherent biases that facilitate both coordination of sexual behavior and mate selection. To what extent are these biases sharpened and refined in development, or reversed by social experiences?

Play, Coordination, and Masturbation

Some primary findings concerning the effect of early play on later sexual interchanges in primates follow.

1.   The composition of the group that the young rhesus monkey associates with during the preadult period influences his readiness to perform heterosexual behavior patterns at maturity (Chamove, Rosenblum, and Harlow, 1973). Homosexual pairs apparently produce the least adequate sexual adjustment, and heterosexual pairs or familial groups produce the most adequate sexual adjustment (Chamove et al., 1973). Isolation, a special case of no interactional experience, significantly impairs performance, at least temporarily.

2.   Some races of squirrel monkeys, because of "normal" ecological conditions, engage in hardly any preadult sexual play. Nonetheless, members of this species are entirely adequate in adult reproduction and parental care (Baldwin and Baldwin, 1974).

3.   Even when disturbances in sexual behavior are produced by deprived rearing circumstances, these effects can be significantly modified by appropriate experiences at maturity (Novak and Harlow, 1975; Seay, Alexander, and Harlow, 1964).

These findings, particularly (2) and (3), are consistent with the conclusion that preadult heterosexual interchanges are not required for successful reproduction. The bulk of the evidence, including the Chamove et al. (1973) and Missakian (1969) work,

indicates that preadult social interactions have a facilitative impact for many primate species.

Related to the question of how sexual reflex components are coordinated within the individual is the question of how the sexual behaviors and arousal states are synchronized between two individuals. The available information on dyadic response chaining seems to indicate that the sexual responses of the individual reflect, in part, an adaptation to the responses of the potential mates that are available (Rogers and Davenport, 1969). And the more experience the individual has in responding to a particular partner, the more likely it is that the responses that evolve will be adapted to the responses of that partner. In brief, sexual interchanges tend to recur, and become consolidated, in a fashion parallel to nonsexual interchanges.

What if no sexual partners are available? Under such conditions, it is not unusual for the young animal to organize its sexual patterns with respect to itself. Among laboratory- or zoo-maintained primates, self-stimulation of the genitals is neither unusual nor uncommon. It occurs less frequently among primates in the wild. Why do animals masturbate—or why do they not masturbate more? The information that is currently available, fragmentary as it is, indicates that masturbation is shaped and supported by events in ontogeny. For animals reared in isolation, self-stimulation is functional and adaptive. Kuo (1967) found that male monkeys can be trained to masturbate orally if banana paste is applied to their penises. The treatment began when the animals were 1 month old, and oral masturbation was established within 2–3 months. Thereafter, the monkeys continued to masturbate without the paste. At the age of 1, the male monkeys were exposed to females. According to Kuo, the males attacked the females (5 subjects) or ignored them (2 subjects), all the while continuing to masturbate. More generally, behavior patterns, including sexual ones, which have become tightly organized with respect to self-produced stimuli seem highly resistant to change. Stereotyped rocking and self-clasping, also become firmly consolidated in isolated animals.

Choice of Sexual Partners:
Individual and Social Structure Factors

In some mammals, a minority, specific preferences for sexual partners are formed. Observations of closed societies of chimpanzees (Nowlis, 1941), free-ranging troops of Japanese macaque monkeys (Stephenson, 1975), colonies of dogs (Beach, Rogers, and Le Boeuf, 1968), one-male units of baboons (Kummer, 1968, 1971), and monogamous pairings in various species such as wolves indicate that enduring preferences can form for particular partners. Such observations raise the question of how animals choose, and why the preferences are maintained.

Social Structure and Mating Preferences. The social system seems to be a primary determinant of the nature and form of interchanges that occur. This observation is apparently as relevant to sexual interchanges as to aggressive, affiliative, and prosocial ones. In Chapter 9 it was noted that the dominance hierarchy is related to the mating that occurs in many mammalian societies. The alpha (top-ranked) male typically has priority in mating, as in other interchanges. Hence "preference" for a partner can hardly be divorced from the relative ranking of the individuals—both male and female—in the society. Social hierarchies control, among other things, sexual access.

Recent studies of the social structure of mating activity in Japanese macaque monkeys have extended our understanding of the role of social organization in the formation of mating preferences (Stephenson, 1975) In three separate sites on the island of Honshu, the social hierarchy of the troops could be described in terms of higher and lower classes of animals rather than merely higher and lower ranks of animals. Animals gained and maintained their class status by virtue of coalitions with other members of the class, and not merely by their own individual powers. G. R. Stephenson discovered that "higher-class" males prefer to mate with "higher-class" females and lower-class males prefer to mate with lower-class females. But the social class has its advantages, even among monkeys. The males that were members of the upper class intruded on and disrupted the consort activities of lower-ranking males. Upper-class males also tended to mate when it counted; that is, when the female had not yet conceived. (Only about 10 percent of the females had conceived when high-ranking males mated with them.) Conversely, low-ranking males consorted less frequently with upper-class females, and about half of their mating activity involved females already pregnant.

But the choice is not simply a male prerogative. Female Japanese macaques are active participants in the mate-selection process. Even high-ranking males can be rejected (or passively resisted), as the following observation of Kaminari, the first-ranking male in the leader class, illustrates.

> On the occasions when Kaminari was observed to push on a female's lower back as if to induce her to rock forward into a sexual present posture, the female did not raise her rump, but continued sitting. On several of these occasions, Kaminari continued to push on the female's back with enough force to literally bowl her over. When this happened, the female, rather than running away, simply righted herself and resumed sitting (Stephenson, 1975, p. 92).

Punishment and Mate Selection. The role of punishment in mate selection requires a brief comment. Recall that it has been observed that in natural settings, a considerable amount of discrimination training occurs throughout ontogeny. Indiscriminate mounting by young males is inhibited when the behavior elicits harsh, punishing attacks. One of the most prominent effects produced by the attacks is the inhibition of sexual behavior. The young hamadryas baboon, for instance, has ample opportunity to determine which conspecifics can be mounted and which can be only groomed. The punishment need not be administered only by the "violated" object. In one-male units, the dominant male punishes the member of his group that strays, thereby limiting the amount of promiscuity that occurs.

The function that punishment serves in the control of sexuality in dogs has been studied experimentally by Kuo (1967). Whenever a male puppy performed any sexual advances toward a grown female dog, the experimenter commanded "no-no." These words had previously been associated with an electric shock, and thus acquired strong negative reinforcement properties. Two to three weeks of this treatment was sufficient to inhibit the males' sexual advances toward the females. At maturity, the male dogs were asexual—they tolerated and were friendly to receptive females, but did not perform any sexual advances toward them. Kuo reports that these animals "would act as if they were bodyguards of the females in heat."

Critical Periods in the Organization of Sexual Interchanges

In our earlier consideration of biochemical controls, we found that the effect of hormones on the sexual behavior of mammals is determined by the stage in the individual's development at which they are introduced. Is the impact of social experiences also greater at one stage of development than at another? We have just seen that early experiences do indeed contribute in multiple ways to sexual behavior; they may result in inhibition, formation of social affiliations, integration of behavior, establishment of sensory preferences, and/or synchronization of acts between organisms.

At later stages of development, the impact of experience depends on the level of organization of the response, not merely on the age of the organism (see Chapter 5). "Critical" experiences can occur at infancy, puberty, or early maturity, depending on which aspect of sexual responding is under consideration. After sexual responses have been performed with respect to particular stimuli, and have become organized around them, they tend to recur regardless of the age of first exposure. Once the behavior pattern has become consolidated, inhibition or retraining is more difficult than if the pattern had not been permitted to become organized in the first place. Because of psychobiological changes in development, new channels of sexual expression are opened and old ones are inhibited. The linkages between age and sexual patterns are not inviolable; sexual interchanges can be organized or reorganized, in juveniles or in adults.

Summary

■ Some major elements of adult sexual behavior are present, in incipient forms, in the repertoires of immature mammals. Infant animals display a potential for bisexual behavior, along with an early but incomplete differentiation of sexual roles.

■ Sexual behavior at each developmental stage is appropriately viewed as being organized simultaneously at the individual and at the dyadic levels. Some of the apparent contradictions in the results of experimental investigations of the effects of isolation on the modifiability of early experiences can be resolved by attention to the actions of the partner and the dynamics of the interchange as well as to the subject.

■ Sexual interchanges require the integration of behavior and psychobiological states, for each individual, and the synchrony of action, for two individuals. Experience has been shown to play a role in the maintenance of sexual structures, and these structures, in turn, help to determine the nature and form of the sexual activity that occurs. More broadly, there is a continuing relationship between hormones and behavior, the choice of mating partners, and the stimuli that elicit sexual arousal.

■ Although species-typical sexual patterns do not have to be learned, they are learnable, and can be drastically modified through social experience or lack of it. In some species, learning appears to play a major role in the synchronization of the arousal states of individuals, in the sharpening of species-typical or alien preferences, in the identification of eligible and appropriate partners, and in the inhibition of sexual interchanges.

■ Depending on the social ecology and organization of the species, the role of experience in determining partner selection can be negligible (as in cowbirds) or powerful (as in primate societies).

■ In the organization of sexual interchanges, critical experiences can occur at infancy, puberty, or early maturity, depending on the nature and form of the activity involved.

■ Despite their commonalities with other inter-change patterns, sexual processes have some distinctive features of their own. More so than other social patterns, including aggression, sexual interchanges require precise coordination of the behaviors and arousal states of both members of the relationship. Analyses of the development of the synchronization indicate that in the normal course of events, innate biases are meshed with idiosyncratic experiences to produce particular actions, preferences, and choices. In primates, sexual experiences can augment, modify, or even cancel out the effects of biases.

15

GENDER-ROLE DEVELOPMENT IN CHILDREN

The Little Tailor is a child's fable about a gentleman who killed seven in one blow. The moral of the story is that you should be careful about whom you pretend to be because eventually you may become the person you impersonate. The fable is mentioned here because something happened when a group of children were inspired to dramatize the story. Under the direction of an insightful mother, some boys and girls 7–9 years of age were brought together to produce the play. They wrote the script, designed and sewed the costumes, assigned the roles, and memorized the parts. Predictably, the children from the beginning wanted to play sex-typed roles: the youngest girls wanted to be the princess and hand-maidens, and the boys wanted to be only the tailor and the giant. The reason for the one deviation from the traditional sex stereotype was that there were more girls than boys; thus one of the two giants had to be one of the 9-year-old girls. Traditional sex stereotypes seemed to be thriving in the 1970's, perpetuated by the children themselves (Figure 15-1).

But one incident cannot be so easily explained by sex-role prescriptions. Just before the play was to be performed at the downtown Senior Citizens Center, the girls in the group took advantage of the opportu-nity to "make themselves up" with quantities of lipstick and rouge. The two boys in the production, both semitough 9-year-olds who were more used to athletic uniforms than theatrical ones, were clearly uneasy. But it was not the "sissiness" of the play or the girls' use of cosmetics that bothered them. Rather, they were concerned lest they not be able to put on makeup too. When assured that it was all right to do so, these boys also put on lipstick and rouge. Only then did the play go on. Cultural and sexual stereotypes notwithstanding, the less "mascu-line" appearance was the one preferred by the boys in this circumstance.

Persons who deal with children in varied settings will doubtless not be surprised by such incidents, which reflect the power and the specificity of sex-role behaviors. Nonetheless, the stereotypes of a "real boy" and a "little lady" survive, still supported by television programs and commercials and many children's textbooks (Frueh and McGhee, 1975; Sternglanz and Serbin, 1974).

In the preceding chapters on sexual development not much was said about sex-role development and societal stereotyping. The reason is simply that the development of sexual behavior in animals has been

Figure 15-1. The cast of *The Little Tailor*.

viewed almost exclusively in terms of reproduction and species propagation. Hence the focus in animal investigations has been upon the ontogeny of behaviors directly associated with mating and fertilization. In research on sexual differences in children, the main issues have been the determinants of gender role and how it is reflected in the child's social and cognitive dispositions. Researchers have been reluctant to consider the implications of their research on

gender role for adult sexual behavior, including normal reproduction. Hence one body of theory and research on sexual behavior in humans is concerned with sex differences and gender-role establishment in children, and a second is concerned with the development of attitudes that affect adult sexual behavior and choice of partners. We will deal with each of the two major themes separately (sex-role development in this chapter, sexual development in the next), and integrate the information at the end of Chapter 16.

Masculinity and Femininity: Social Stereotypes or Scientific Constructs?

Sears(1965) has pointed out that the terms "masculinity" and "femininity" have certain shortcomings as scientific constructs.

The lack of exact definition of what behavior does or does not belong to a particular gender role has led to a peculiar consequence. In the eternal attempt to simplify classificatory problems, Western Civilization has almost always defined the two gender roles as opposites. Indeed, there are a number of behavior qualities that do seem to be polar opposites; e.g., activity-passivity, aggression-nonaggression, independence-dependence. These are abstractions, however, and even the simplest empirical investigation of what components constitute the behavior qualities of real people is sufficient to show that such abstractions do not have high internal coherency. *Masculinity and femininity are very complex personality qualities,*

without precise boundaries and with only the faintest centrality, and their definition requires careful attention to the operations of measurement (p. 135, my italics).

Sears' insightful comments underscore one of the basic problems that arise when terms and concepts are borrowed from common, everyday speech. They are not always effective vehicles for understanding the behaviors to which they refer. We have already encountered this problem in the discussion of aggression and dependency. What is gained from resonance with common experience and ease of communication tends to be canceled out because the mechanisms that control the behaviors to which they refer are obscured.

Sears's (1965) empirical analysis of masculinity and feminity in 5-year-old boys and girls illustrates a major shortcoming of the constructs. Preschool children were observed under various circumstances in the classroom and during play, and were also given tests designed to measure their status on a dimension of masculinity/femininity. The tests that were employed were selected because they were widely used for this purpose. The tests are briefly described in Table 15-1.

Table 15-1. Correlations among measures of gender role in preschool boys (*n* = 21) and girls (*n* = 19).

Measure \ Girls \ Boys	1	2	3	4	5	6
"It" test		−.06	+.13	−.03	+.09	+.10
Area usage	+.39		+.55	+.37	+.32	+.70
Pictures test	+.53	+.30		+.69	+.71	+.93
Toy preferences	−.03	−.03	+.20		+.36	+.76
Observer's ratings	+.01	−.01	+.29	+.09		+.74
Combined scores	+.42	+.48	+.78	+.47	+.57	

A brief description of the measures:
1. "It" test: Composed of three subtests, two of which involve the projective assessment of toy preference.
2. Area usage: Whether the child prefers "male" or "female" play areas in the preschool.
3. Pictures test: Choice by child of activity he or she prefers after viewing a picture of the activity.
4. Toy preferences: Types of toys that the child actually selects when given a choice of sex-typed toys.
5. Observer's ratings: Ratings by observers who knew the children well as to whether they were "highly sex typed" or evidenced "very little sex typing."
6. Combined scores: A composite score made up of the child's standing on all tests except the "It" Test.
SOURCE: Sears, 1965.

Since the tests were all supposed to measure the child's status on the masculinity/femininity dimension, it seems reasonable to expect that they should be rather highly correlated with each other; that is, a child classified as "highly feminine" on one test should be classified as "highly feminine" on the others. Such between-test correspondence was not obtained. Indeed, Table 15–1 shows that the several measures were negligibly related to each other. (Hence the child who would be classified as "slightly masculine" on one measure might well be labeled "moderately feminine" on another, and "masculine" on still a third.)[1]

Which test, then, is the "best" measure of masculinity/femininity? The answer to this question would seem to be of great importance for the furtherance of research. Parental characteristics that may predict the child's status on one measure obviously cannot predict status on other, independent measures. It has been difficult, however, to select the best measure because, on an a priori basis, they all seem reasonable and applicable. Indeed, it has been proposed that because the tests assess different aspects of the same quality (in the same way that a sculpture can be viewed from different perspectives), a combination of scores is required to obtain an adequate measure of masculinity/femininity.

But there is a possibility that the fault lies not with the measures of masculinity but with the construct itself. Perhaps the diversity of human behavior is such that there is no single bipolar dimension of masculinity and femininity on which each person can be placed. For example, a 10-year-old girl may, at different times of the week, participate in both "feminine" activities (play the violin, bake a cream pie) and "masculine" ones (build a fort, play baseball, swim a competitive 200-meter freestyle). A classification of the child on a feminine-masculine

dimension would differ according to the activities observed, and any "average" rating would likely be misleading. Hence Sears's conclusion that "masculinity and femininity are complex personality qualities . . . with only the faintest centrality." The implication is that these "complex qualities" do not cover a single dimension—with men and boys clustering at one end and women and girls at the other—but represent multiple dimensions and activities. If this analysis is correct, then no "single" test or combination score will do the job; what is required is a revision of the basic classification scheme itself (Hartup and Yonas, 1971).

What is unclear is precisely what direction such a revision should take. One possibility would be to rank each person separately on two dimensions—masculine and feminine. This solution has the advantage of recognizing that the qualities associated with men and women are not necessarily opposed, and that one person can embody some properties of each. S. Bem (1975) has suggested that the term *androgynous* be used to describe the sex roles of persons (man or woman, boy or girl) who have some of the desirable sex-role characteristics of both males and females. It is Bem's general hypothesis that "a nonandrogynous sex role can seriously restrict" the range of actions available to an individual. Hence children should be encouraged to be "both instrumental *and* expressive, both assertive *and* yielding, both masculine *and* feminine—depending upon the situational appropriateness of these various behaviors" (Bem, 1975, p. 634).

A second possibility, not inconsistent with the first, would be to follow Sears's suggestion and clarify the determinants of the "index behaviors" that have been viewed as measures of masculinity and femininity. Since these behaviors and attitudes are the stuff of which the stereotypes have been constructed, the clarification of their determinants should carry us a reasonable distance toward the goal of explaining how the "global" differences arise. An attempt should also be made to ascertain

---

[1] "It" has a masculine bias in that both boys and girls perceive "It" as being a boy; hence revisions have been proposed (Fling and Manosevitz, 1972).

what determines the child's own perceptions of himself/herself as a boy or girl, what these concepts ("boy," "girl") mean to the child, and how they affect the child's behavior. Such a strategy does not require that these measures be highly interrelated. Whether one activity influences the other, or whether they are controlled by common factors, can be resolved by empirical analysis.

These matters of research strategy and analysis might seem somewhat removed from the real task of determining the several contributors to sex-role differentiation. In fact, they are fundamental to identifying exactly *what* should be explained.

Sex-Typing in the Family System

It should not be surprising to learn that boys and girls typically prefer to play different kinds of games (Weisler and McCall, 1976); what may be surprising is that play-activity preferences appear to be the most reliable way to distinguish between boys and girls in terms of behavior (Fagot, 1974; Fein, Johnson, Kosson, Stork, and Wasserman, 1975; Fling and Manosevitz, 1972; Harper and Sanders, 1975; Sears, 1965; Sutton-Smith, Rosenberg and Morgan, 1963). Looking at Table 15-1, we find that all of the tests involved play either directly or indirectly. The Sears (1965) study is representative of other attempts to ascertain how gender roles are established. Typically a primary measure has been a description of the child's play activities and preferences (see Sutton-Smith and Rosenberg, 1970; and Maccoby and Jacklin, 1974, for reviews). This emphasis seems not to have been misplaced, because "play" constitutes a primary occupation of young children and, as such, is the activity in which the principal preferences and idiosyncracies should appear. Our first task, then, will be to examine how sex-typed activities are affected by societal, biological, and cognitive factors in the course of development.

Familial Support for Sex-Typing

Parents might be expected to be the first to make toys and games available to the child. In American families, the parents normally see to it that boys are given male playthings and clothes that girls are not, and vice-versa. Even today the father who buys Barbie dolls for his 2-year-old son might be considered unusual. Interviews conducted in toy stores in late 1975 indicated that (1) mothers buy more toys for children than fathers; (2) from infancy, the purchases are sex-typed; and (3) fathers and mothers are equally likely to make sex-typed purchases (M. J. West, unpublished study, 1976). In their study of 96 girls under 6 years of age, Rheingold and Cook (1975) found, as expected, that the toys, cars, and trucks in the boys' rooms far outnumbered those in the girls' rooms, from age 2 onward, and that girls' rooms had more dolls, doll houses, and other play "household" materials (Table 15-2).

The preferences of very young children for toys and furnishings are consistent with those of their parents. The toy choices and activities of boys and girls at about their second year (20 months) overlap

Table 15-2. Sex differences in furnishings and toys in rooms of children age 1-6.

Class of items	Mean number in 48 rooms of each sex		p value
	Male	Female	
Animal	6.8	5.0	$<.05$
Books	28.1	23.9	N.S.
Dolls	3.6	7.0	$<.001$
Ed-art materials	1.1	0.6	$<.05$
Floral furnishings	3.0	4.5	$<.001$
Furniture	6.2	6.3	N.S.
Musical objects	1.4	1.2	N.S.
"Ruffles"	0.9	2.0	$<.01$
Spatial-temporal	1.7	0.8	$<.001$
Sports equipment	1.0	0.4	$<.05$
Stuffed animals	4.1	4.4	N.S.
Toy animals	4.8	2.3	$<.01$

SOURCE: Adapted from Rheingold and Cook, 1975.

a good deal, but there are nonetheless reliable sex-typed differences in their play behaviors (Fein et al., 1975).

Parents and siblings contribute to the establishment and maintenance of sex-typed play activities in young children in at least three ways.

Acquisition of Toys, Games, and Furnishings. The initial decision for purchase or acquisition is ordinarily the prerogative of parents or older siblings (see, for instance, Rheingold and Cook, 1975), but the young child soon begins to exert some pressure on the selection process, as advertisers have come to understand.

Familial Interaction in Games. Familial influences are mediated not only by the toys that are made available, but by the ways in which other members of the family become involved with the child. The participation can take the form of tuition, as when the father teaches his son how to catch and throw a football or the mother shows her daughter how to sew or bake. Or the participation can be more immediate, as when siblings play together and, in the process, develop skill and competence. Do parents treat children differently in their play interactions? Yes. Parents attempt to elicit more "gross motor behavior" from boys than from girls (Maccoby and Jacklin, 1974). Fathers become involved in rough-and-tumble play with boys more than with girls, from school age onward (Tasch, 1952). Yarrow (1972) found that the differences occur as early as the fifth month of infancy. Parents tend to be more apprehensive about the physical well-being of their infant daughters than about that of their sons (Pedersen and Robson, 1969; Minton, Kagan, and Levine, 1971). Boys are also left on their own more, even at 18–24 months (Fagot, 1974). Later, fathers typically become involved in different games with boys than with girls, including baseball, basketball, and football. As we will see shortly in this chapter, such differences seem not based on the child's physical capabilities at these ages.

Social Standards. The parents and others in the child's immediate environment (which usually includes television) can also communicate, directly and indirectly, what the child is expected to like, and which activities are the best or most appropriate to play. The purchase and presentation of toys, as well as participation in an activity, are two channels by which norms can be communicated. And there are even more direct ways; for example, simply telling the child what is acceptable and what is not, and enforcing rules as to what and how the child should play. Playmates and adults outside the home can also influence the child's activities, depending upon how closely they are permitted to monitor his behavior. Wolf (1973) has recently shown that children imitate the play of other children, particularly if they are of the same sex.

Normative standards and children's preferences are not easily altered, especially those of boys. In follow-up work, Wolf (1973) attempted to vary the preferences of children aged 5–9 for sex-typed toys (a doll and a fire engine). Children of both sexes observed another child play with a sex-inappropriate toy. In half of the instances, the "model" (the child observed) was another child of the same sex, and in the remainder, the model was a child of the opposite sex. In general, the manipulation worked better for the girls than for the boys, in that girls more readily played with the "inappropriate" fire engine than did the boys with the doll. Modeling may not be sufficient to change a child's preference. Indeed, the cross-sex experience sometimes produced even stronger male preferences in boys. This outcome is consistent with the generalization that boys are less likely to accept, choose, or prefer sex-inappropriate toys or activities than are girls (see Maccoby and Jacklin, 1974, for a review of the evidence). Recall also that in *The Little Tailor*, the girls were willing to be the giant, but the boys showed little interest in being the princess or a handmaiden.

How does the more rigid parental standard for boys with regard to sex stereotyping for games and toys arise? One possibility is that parents, particularly fathers, have a double standard for their sons and daughters. Girls may be given a wider range of choices than boys and the father may become more upset if his son shows sex-inappropriate preferences. The interviews that have been conducted are consistent with this interpretation (Lansky, 1967; Fling and Manosevitz, 1972; Goodenough, 1957). Fling and Manosevitz (1972) found that both parents strongly discourage sex-inappropriate tendencies in their sons.

Maccoby and Jacklin (1974) have commented on these results:

> We may ask why it is that parents are more upset when a boy wants to wear lipstick or put on high heels than they are when a girl wants to paint a false moustache on her face or wear cowboy boots. Although the dynamics underlying this parental reaction are not clear, it would appear that feminine behavior in a boy is likely to be interpreted as a sign of possible homosexual tendencies, and, as such, it is a danger signal to parents and triggers powerful anxieties in them—perhaps especially in fathers (p. 339).

Maccoby and Jacklin speculate that the more rigid standard for boys may reflect a "realistic parental appraisal of the fact that homosexuality is considerably more common among males than females." Since boys are seen as being more at risk than girls, parents are assumed to be more likely to want to control boys' behavior. Cross-cultural investigations should be useful in determining the validity of this hypothesis and alternative ones.[2]

What happens if the child is surrounded from infancy only with games and toys appropriate for the opposite sex? No systematic experiments have been conducted, but clinical reports indicate that the child forms a preference for whatever is available. West (1967) cites a case in which a mother who dearly wanted a daughter, but who gave birth to identical twin boys, consoled herself by placing a "baby daughter" bracelet on the wrist of one of the boys. From infancy, this boy (whom the mother said was pretty enough to be a girl) was treated in a consistently different manner than his brother. When the latter took up football and swimming, the "pretty" boy was encouraged to remain with his mother. She retrospectively described him as a "sensitive, home-loving" type, who enjoyed playing with dolls, younger children, and girls.[3]

Siblings can influence the kinds of toys that are available and activities that the child prefers. In two-child families, girls who have a brother within 2–3 years of their own age tend to have more play interests of a masculine sort than do girls who have sisters in the same age range (Sutton-Smith and Rosenberg, 1970). Boys who have older brothers are typically more active and outgoing than are boys who do not (Longstreth, Longstreth, Ramirez, and Fernandez, 1975). As might be expected, the reverse is also true. Boys who have sisters close to their own age tend to have more feminine interests than do boys who have only brothers. If the siblings play together at all, such findings should not be considered unusual. In the normal course of events, such children become acquainted with, and skilled at, some of the activities ordinarily preferred by the opposite sex. Although other factors influence mutual sibling participation in play activities in large families, such as the size of the age gap between children and the sex of the oldest child, the results are consistent with these expectations (Sutton-Smith and Rosenberg, 1970).

---

[2] An additional possibility is that socialization demands are, in general, more stringent for boys than for girls of the same age. Pubertal rites, for instance, are typically more severe for passage from boyhood to manhood than from girlhood to womanhood. Hence the temptation to deviate from gender-role requirements may be greater for boys than for girls simply because the requirements are less rigorous, and strong parental and societal pressure may be necessary to keep the boys in line.

[3] At maturity, his brother had an entirely satisfactory heterosexual married life; however, the twin remained single and then settled into a pseudomarital relationship with a man of his own age (West, 1967). The problem of the continuity of influence is considered in more detail in the next chapter. It should be noted here that not all children who have opposite sex playthings develop unconventional sexual preferences; nor are all instances of sexual unconventionality associated with early play reversals.

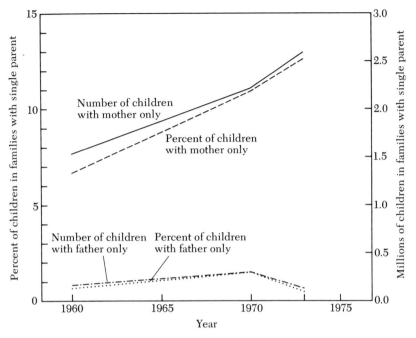

Figure 15-2. The total number (and percentage) of children 6 years old and younger who live in a home with only one parent (from Special Population Report, U.S. Census).

Effects of Family Disruption

One way to determine the effect of parental actions and attitudes on sex-role typing is to analyze what happens when either parent is absent. Not surprisingly, mothers are left to raise children in a fatherless family far more frequently than fathers are left with a motherless family. Moreover, the number of mothers who are sole "heads of households" is increasing dramatically (see Figure 15-2).

Father Absence. As in the case of other "natural" experiments, few firm conclusions can be offered about the effects of father absence on sex-role typing. The difficulty is that "father absence" can reflect a wide range of causes (death, divorce, war, job), durations and time of onset, and reasons for the

mother's not finding a new mate. Each of these factors may potentially affect the family interactions, sometimes in conflicting ways.

There is some support for the idea that the father's presence discourages femininity in boys and encourages femininity in girls (Biller, 1971). However, if the attitudinal support and behavior control typically provided by the father are provided by others in the family structure (older siblings, the mother, other adults), then the effect of father absence on sex-role typing seems negligible. Preoccupation with what the child is deprived of has unfortunately shifted attention away from the influences that he or she is exposed to during development. Analysis of the role that parents play in shaping sex-role behaviors might better focus on the influences that are present when the father is missing, such as the mother's attitudes and interactions among the siblings. Such an emphasis would be consistent with the view that the individuals with whom the child interacts, not the ones he or she is separated from, are the primary societal determinants of the child's sex-typed choices, attitudes, and behavior.

Divorce and Its Effects. Mavis Hetherington and her colleagues at the University of Virginia (Hetherington, Cox, and Cox, 1975) recently reported a longitudinal study of the effects that divorce has on the family and the actions of each of its members—father, mother, and children. Immediately following a divorce, parental expectations for mature behavior by the children declined, and the children were often given more freedom. In general, bedtimes were more erratic, and the children were more likely to get meals at irregular times and to arrive at school late or not at all. Fathers, on the average, took less responsibility for disciplining the children, and mothers took more. After 2 months of separation, the divorced mothers, as a group, used negative sanctions, (for example, telling them to "stop it") with their children about twice as often as did mothers of intact families. The divorced fathers behaved like "every day is Christmas": They used negative sanctions with their children almost half as frequently as fathers of intact families. Two years after the divorce, the systems had become restabilized; the mothers relied less on negative sanctions (perhaps because they were less necessary) and the fathers were less anxious to please. [4]

Hetherington et al. (1975) summarize their results as follows:

> When a father leaves the home following divorce, the family system is in a state of disequilibrium. Disorganization and disrupted family functioning seem to peak at one year and be restablizing by two years following the divorce. Stresses in family functioning following divorce are reflected not only in parent-child relations but in changes in life style, emotional distress, and changes in attitudes toward the self of the divorced couple. These changes in the parents may be mediating factors in changes in the child's behavior.

Communal Rearing. In the Israeli kibbutz, the *metapelet* is a specially trained woman who takes care of a small group of children during the entire day. In the late afternoon, after the day's work is done, the children return to their parents' apartments for a snack and spend some time with their parents. But at supper time, the children return to the children's house to eat with their peers, and they have no contact with the parents again until bedtime, in the children's house. How are these parents viewed by their children? On the average, very positively (Devereux, Shouval, Bronfenbrenner, Rodgers, Kav-Venaki, Kiely, and Karson, 1974). When the children were queried at age 11 or 12, they described *metapelet* as the agent of punishment, disapproval, and discipline; they saw their parents as warm, supportive, and encouraging. Compared with the attitudes that non-kibbutz-reared Israeli children expressed toward their parents, the kibbutz-reared children perceived their parents as equally supportive but considerably less critical. This perception is probably based in reality. When someone other than the parent is responsible for the discipline and long-term training of a child, whether because of divorce or because of social structure, it is apparently easier for the parent who is away to be more relaxed and approving. Sex-typing is apparently not disrupted by kibbutz rearing; traditional play preferences seem as strong in kibbutz-reared children as they are in non-kibbutz-reared children (Beit-Hallahmi and Rabin, 1977). [5]

---

[4] It should not be overlooked that the divorced families may have been equally "disorganized" *before* the separation.

[5] These investigators observed that the social organization of the kibbutz has undergone significant changes in the recent past, in the form of a return to more traditional patterns of child rearing in the home (in many communes, children are now permitted to sleep with the family) and traditional sex-role assignments for men and women. Since many persons who are now kibbutz adults were themselves reared in the kibbutz, it would follow that the earlier child-rearing practices did not eliminate sex-role differences.

Biophysical and Maturational Contributions to Sex-Typed Activities

In view of the sexual dimorphism of most mammalian species including humans, the different activity and play patterns of boys and girls appear to be determined by physiological factors. There is, as we shall see, reason to question this mild and plausible conclusion. Since these issues are about as controversial as they are complex, we will first review some elementary facts on sexual dimorphism in children. We will then examine differences in physical capabilities as reflected in competitive athletic activities. The aim is to determine when sexual dimorphism occurs, and to evaluate its effects on behavior.

Sexual Dimorphism

In an incisive discussion of sex differences, J. M. Tanner (1962) has distinguished between preadolescent and postadolescent sexual dimorphism in humans (see also Tanner, 1970). The physiological processes by which sex-differentiated maturity levels and growth rates are established in the preadolescent period are quite distinct from the hormonal processes that occur in adolescence and postadolescence.

Preadolescence. Consider first the preadolescent differences in size and growth. At birth and before, skeletal ossification (the most common indicator of physiological maturity) proceeds more rapidly in girls than boys. Girls maintain an edge in this index of maturity right up to adolescence. Boys are slightly larger at birth. (The difference is only 1–3 percent in length and about 4 percent in weight.) Boys tend to grow faster than girls in the first year of life, but from years 1–9 the rates of development of both sexes are virtually identical. Thus size differences between boys and girls in this age range are minor.

Skeletal and soft tissue growth follows the same pattern. Reliable though small differences in pelvic structure are visible in boys and girls at birth. Detailed analysis of limb growth also indicates that the male arm is longer than the female, due to a sex difference in development of the forearm. The difference is already established by age 2, and possibly earlier. Nonetheless, the absolute sex differences are modest in all skeletal dimensions prior to puberty.

Adolescence. Major sex differences in skeletal size and shape occur at puberty. Boys enter the adolescent growth spurt later than girls, and in the immediately pre-adolescent years the legs grow relatively fastest of all skeletal dimensions. Since the legs have an extra 2 years to grow before the adolescent spurt, boys have relatively longer legs than girls.

Sex differences in amount and distribution of muscular and fatty tissues also arise mostly at adolescence. Some of the most precise measurements of sexual dimorphism at different ages have been based on the amount of bone, muscle, and fat in the calf. From early childhood, boys tends to have slightly more bone and muscle in the calf than girls (Table 15-3). But the difference is small, and there is considerable overlap between boys and girls at age 7½. Attempts to classify boys and girls at that age solely on the basis of their calf X rays yield decisions that are slightly more accurate than would be obtained by flipping a coin. In contrast, the comparisons at age 17 permit classification of men and women with 95 percent accuracy.

Since the adolescent growth spurt of girls begins earlier than that of boys, girls are temporarily larger in practically all respects for about 2½ years. When boys are 10½ to 13 years of age, their growth spurt beings—just when that of girls beings to taper off. At the end of adolescence, the boys weigh approximately 10 percent more and are also 10 percent larger than girls (as indicated by length of limbs, chest breadth, and so on). The sex differences that occur at puberty are due chiefly to the differential action of the growth and sexual hormones.

Table 15-3. Bone and fat measurements (in millimeters) at greatest transverse diameter of calf, taken from X-rays.

| | Mean values at ages | | | |
	7½	10½	13½	Adult (19–70)
Boys				
Bone	25.86	29.77	35.03	39.38
Fat	11.41	12.51	13.27	10.78
Girls				
Bone	25.26	28.06	30.72	32.52
Fat	12.96	14.48	15.72	19.89

| | Increments (cross-sectional means) from ages | | |
	7½–10½	10½–13½	13½–Adult
Bone			
Boys	3.91	5.26	4.35
Girls	2.80	1.66	1.80
Fat			
Boys	1.10	0.76	−2.51
Girls	1.52	1.24	4.17

SOURCE: Tanner, 1962.

Athletic Differences and Similarities

The sizable athletic differences (in preference as well as performance) between preadolescent boys and girls seem to belie their biological similarities. The observed differences seem to be considerably greater than might be expected merely in terms of structure. Indeed, if morphology were the sole factor that determined activity—play or competitive—one might expect little if any sex differences prior to adolescence. But virtually all assessments of unrestricted play activity have revealed differences from the third year onward, and sometimes earlier (Maccoby and Jacklin, 1974). To distinguish between sex differences that are due to differences in morphology (such as large-muscle action, sensorimotor coordination) and those that are due to differences in social support (such as parental encouragement, so-

cial norms), we will now examine sex differences in athletics, particularly competitive swimming.

From the mid-1950's to the present, competitive swimming as an activity for boys and girls has increased in popularity: at least one million children of both sexes between the ages of 5 and 17 participate annually. Competitive swimming is of interest to us here because boys and girls train together, without bias, following virtually the same rigorous schedule according to their age, ability, and motivation. Maximal levels of performance are approached by extended year-round training; children commonly swim 3,000 yards and 1½ hours daily when they are 9–10 years old, and 10,000 yards and 3 hours each day when they are 13–14 years old. Since the criterion is speed, direct cross-sex comparisons can be made at different age levels even though boys rarely compete directly against girls.

Complete records of swimming times are kept by the Amateur Athletic Union. These times reflect the performances of the group of most advanced children, and presumably the most highly trained and motivated children, in each age-sex classification. There are negligible differences between males and females at 10 years of age, and sizable differences (approximately 10 percent to 12 percent) in favor of males in the older age groups.

The major conclusion to be drawn is that the development of sex differences in this activity directly parallels the development of sexual dimorphism. It is of interest to note that the speed differentials between boys and girls appear to be reasonably proportional to the differences in muscle-bone measurements, which are approximately 3–4 percent in preadolescence and 10–12 percent at adolescence. (But the speed differences are relative to the distances compared and the stroke covered. For example, in the 1976 Olympic Games, an East German woman established a world record in the 400-meter freestyle that the existing men's record for that distance exceeded by only 7 percent.) That a strong relationship exists between developmental changes in morphology and developmental changes in performance should not be surprising, and it is consistent with the general proposal that preadolescent girls are markedly similar to preadolescent boys in terms of their potential for large-muscle action of the sort required for swimming. Comparisons of younger children (5-9 years) confirm that the sex differences in performance are modest at the younger age levels.

These data are cited to illustrate that there is a major discrepancy between the findings on morphology and the findings of sex-typing that were discussed in the first part of this chapter. At the very time when there are slight differences in morphology between boys and girls (ages 3-10), major gender-role differences in play preferences and activity emerge. Although it has seemed plausible to explain sex-typed behavior differences in terms of sexual dimorphism, sex-typed behaviors appear at developmental levels when there is virtually no dimorphism. Nor are there large sex differences in a strenuous behavior that requires endurance and large-muscle coordination *if* training, motivation, and expectations are equal for preadolescent boys and girls.

How might this paradox be resolved? We might speculate that *the sex differences observed in gender-role behavior in preadolescents and younger children do not reflect the differences in morphology or in hormonal states that are present at that stage of development.* The sex differences are consistent, however, with the sexual dimorphism that is observed at adolescence and beyond. Hence the early sex differences in gender-role behavior might be seen as preparatory for and consistent with later sexual dimorphism, as opposed to being directly determined by it.

The Development of Sexual Concepts

What determines self-assignment of sexual identity? By the age of 2½, children have some rudimentary ideas about how boys and girls should behave and whether they themselves should be classified as a boy or a girl (Thompson, 1975). Even earlier, there are sex-typed differences in play and preferences (Fagot, 1974; Fein et al., 1975; Ross and Goldman, 1977a). This self-classification, once decided upon, may play a major role in determining the kinds of activities in which children permit themselves to become involved. The clarity of the concepts, their variety, and their subtlety for the child change over the course of ontogeny. Notions of what is "boyish" or "male" and "girlish" or "female" become more complex at each stage of childhood (Williams, Bennett, and Best, 1975).

Life-span studies indicate that adults (who are presumably most advanced in cognitive development and hence might be expected to be relative in their judgments) maintain traditional stereotypes about what is appropriate male and female behavior (Urberg and Labouvie-Vief, 1976). But recall the boys in *The Little Tailor* and the extent to which sex-role prescriptions are situation-specific in children. Adults are similar in that situations apparently play an important role in determining whether the responses of men and women are sex-typed. For instance, the responses of men and women to infants are sex-typed (women find babies more attractive than do men) if they are tested as part of a group. These differences are sharply diminished, or disappear, when individuals of each sex are tested alone—men report more attraction to babies when tested in private than when tested in groups (Berman, 1976).

The assignment of oneself to one category—boy or girl—occurs in conjunction with the establishment of the categories themselves. Exactly when in terms of chronological age the concept of masculinity-femininity develops, and when the self-assignment is made to one or the other category, of course vary among individuals. Spencer Thompson's recent work (1975) indicates that in most children a rudimentary concept of masculinity-femininity develops by the end of the third year of life (Table 15-4).

Table 15-4. Age at which sample of American children correctly use gender labels and identify sex-specific objects.

Test	Percent of questions answered correctly at each age		
	24 months	30 months	36 months
Correctly answer questions having to do with gender label (Are you a boy/girl? Are you going to be a daddy/mommy?).	44	70	76
Correctly identify sex-typed objects (things for girls and mothers and things for fathers or boys).	61	78	86
Appropriately label pictures as either boy or girl, man or woman, father or mother, brother or sister.	76	83	90
Accurately classify a picture of himself or herself as a male or a female.	55	75	95

SOURCE: Thompson, 1975.

Once the child's gender-role identification is established, "he is then in a position to identify what behavior is appropriate for his sex by observing what kinds of things males, as distinct from females, do and match of his own behavior to the conceptions that he has constructed" (Maccoby and Jacklin, 1974, p. 365). But at this age, children are typically not sure whether they will be the same sex when they grow up (Slaby and Frey, 1975). The concept is not a static one; it undergoes changes in both breadth and scope throughout childhood and adolescence.

There appears to be a continual attempt on the part of the child to match the behavior with the concept, leading to changes in both the behavior and the concept. This type of "self-socialization"—the attempt to accommodate the concept, the self-identity, and the behavior—is a basic phenomenon in sex-typing.

How do children resolve discrepancies that arise in development between their concept of masculine and feminine, their behaviors, and their concept of their own sexual identity? The developmental mechanisms by which these are synchronized—or discriminated—are still a matter of speculation. The following points are relevant.

1. The cultural stereotypes of what is appropriate male and female behavior are not static. They change for the society from one generation to the next, and they change for individuals over the course of their own development (Williams et al., 1975).

2. Children are active agents in the process of making their behaviors consistent with their self-concept. For instance, Jennings (1975) found that children prefer to hear and read about persons of the same sex, and that children choose roles (as in *The Little Tailor*) that correspond to their gender-role identity.

3. The social network of which the child is a part normally is a catalyst for the integration of the self-concept, the behavior, and the social norms. The burden of integration is not merely the child's to bear; on the contrary, the expectations of others and the interchanges that they provoke are ordinarily in accord with both the child's self-concept and society's norms. Safeguards operate at various levels of social organization to ensure that the consistency is maintained.

A final theoretical question is "Which comes first, sex-typed behavior or self-classification?" Does a child see himself or herself as a boy or girl before he or she behaves as one? Observations of the family suggest that the social network of which the child becomes a part is of prime importance, contributing to both the child's behavior and the child's sex-gender concept. Social influences can be mediated through multiple channels, including early parental concepts about the child. Regardless of which influence has early priority, the child's self-concept and behavior develop on a reciprocal basis throughout childhood. Once the self-classification is established, it continues to be affected by powerful social and cognitive constraints.

Sex Differences in Social Dispositions

The intensity of the political debate on the issue of the equality of the sexes virtually ensures that any firm statements on the matter will be challenged. A case in point is the controversy aroused by the work of two Stanford University psychologists, Eleanor Emmons Maccoby and Carol Nagy Jacklin. These investigators recently completed a thorough analysis of more than 1,600 articles pertaining to sex differences, published for the most part during the eight-year interval between 1966 and 1973. About three-fourths of the studies were of subjects 12 years of age and younger. Maccoby and Jacklin (1974) concluded that there are a number of unfounded beliefs about sex differences in social behavior, including the assumptions that: (1) girls are more "social" than boys, (2) girls are more suggestible than boys, (3) girls have lower self-esteem than boys, and (4) girls are affected more by heredity and boys are affected more by the environment. The one firm difference in the social behavior of males and females Maccoby and Jacklin found was that boys are more aggressive than girls. [6]

Maccoby and Jacklin's (1974) conclusions have been questioned on the grounds that (1) there are few differences between adult males and adult females in terms of aggression (Frodi, Macaulay, and

Thome, 1977); and (2) these investigators failed to identify sex differences in such characteristics as empathy, activity, dominance when in fact they exist (see Hoffman, 1977a, and Block, 1976, for a discussion of the issues). On the basis of our review of the studies of human aggressive interchanges (Chapter 11), at least one point is clear. Boys from age 2–3 through adolescence, as a group, are more likely than girls to become involved in physically aggressive interchanges. Beyond adolescence and through adulthood, moreover, men are more likely than women to be arrested for acts of personal injury and violence. When other measures are used, such as verbal or indirect aggression, the differences are attenuated or reversed (Feshbach and Sones, 1971). Moreover, in laboratory assessments of aggressive behavior (which involve, for instance, administering electrical shock to another subject), the differences between men and women are slight and inconsistent (Frodi et al., 1977).

Whether sex differences appear in assessments of other social dispositions (such as empathy, suggestibility) seems to depend on such factors as the measures used, the testing context, the size of the experimental sample, and the age, social class, and background of the children observed. The results defy a simple summary statement, other than the observation that boys and girls are "more human than otherwise"—that is, there is apparently great overlap between boys and girls on measures of these "social orientations," hence differences are difficult to detect when gross measures are used in small samples of heterogeneous groups. But as Block (1976) argues, without more definitive evidence than is now available, it is hazardous to conclude that some differences do not exist. The key to the sex-difference issue would seem to lie in the solution of the problem of how these social dispositions develop in any child, whether male or female.

Summary

Because of the quality of the data and the controversial nature of the issues surrounding gender-role

---

[6] We focus here only on the differences in social orientation discussed by Maccoby and Jacklin (1974). Their summary of the evidence suggests that there are differences in certain cognitive indicators, such as verbal skills, that could doubtless have implications for social behavior.

development, caution is required in the interpretation of the experimental results. However, some generalizations can be offered.

■ Little support has been found for the common-sense view that masculinity-femininity is a unitary, bipolar dimension. The evidence indicates that, although activities can be reliably classified, the contextual specificity of children's choices and preferences suggests that the characteristics subsumed by sexual stereotypes are multidimensional.

■ Studies of sex-typing in early childhood have relied greatly on measures of the child's play activities, play preferences, and playmates. Such an emphasis is not inappropriate, in that the child's play reveals much about his or her interests, style, disposition, and social orientation.

■ By 3–4 years of age, boys and girls usually differ in the kinds of play activities they choose, how they play, and with whom. By ages 5–6, these differences are large and consistent, even though there is minimal sexual dimorphism.

■ The social network to which the child is exposed from infancy onward appears to support activities, attitudes, and behaviors that are consistent with the gender classification to which the child was assigned at birth or shortly afterward. The interactions in which children engage act as a catalyst to integrate information about appropriate sexual behaviors, concepts, and expectations.

■ Children are not passive agents in this phase of social development. Their understanding of the concepts of "boy" and "girl" seem, at each stage of development, to sharpen and extend behavioral and attitudinal differences. Such self-socialization is relatively rudimentary at ages 3–4, befitting the concept-identification abilities of preschool children. The process continues at more subtle levels throughout childhood and adulthood.

■ Sex-typing in the play and interests of young children appears to be the result of societal anticipations of future biological differences rather than of actual biological differences. When preadolescent children are given equal opportunities and encouragement in competitive sports, even those requiring large-muscle coordination and endurance, sex differences are trivial prior to puberty. Girls are equally as competitive, achievement-oriented, and skilled as boys. However, sexual dimorphism at adolescence leads to differences in athletic performance that are roughly proportional to the differences in strength and morphology.

■ Whether there are differences in broad social dispositions—such as dependency, empathy, and social sensitivity—has remained controversial. Although the data with regard to differences between boys and girls in physically aggressive behavior are consistent, the results are less clear with regard to other measures of aggressive activity (indirect, verbal) and other measures of nonaggressive social dispositions. Apparently there is considerable overlap between boys and girls on these measures, and the finding of differences is highly dependent on what tests are used and the context of testing.

We observed early in this chapter that the study of sexual development in children reflects the efforts of researchers working in virtually two worlds: one concerned with normal gender-role development, and the other concerned with conventional and unconventional sexual practices in adulthood. There were precious few direct linkages between the subject matter covered in the preceding two chapters (Chapters 13 and 14) and the present one on gender-role development. From a biological-behavioral perspective, perhaps it would be more reasonable to look for evolutionary continuities in characteristics that are more directly related to reproduction and propagation. It is to this issue, and to the relationship between gender-role typing in childhood and sexual behaviors in adulthood, that we now turn.

16

DEVELOPMENT OF SEXUAL
BEHAVIOR IN HUMANS

Frederick C., age 7, . . . a clinging, fearful boy who was somewhat clumsy and compulsively clean, was not permitted to roam the neighborhood because of his mother's constant fear that he might be injured by the "rough" neighborhood boys. His mother also protected him against any anger from his large, imposing father who slept days and worked nights. Since she saw her son as helpless to achieve things by himself, she continued to bathe him herself, and even required that he change clothes with her in the woman's locker room at the public swimming pool. Roughness, noise, and physical risk were not allowed (Bates, Skilbeck, Smith, and Bentler, 1974, pp. 7-10).

Frederick comes to our attention primarily because he was one of 29 boys referred to the Gender Identity Project of the Department of Psychology of the University of California at Los Angeles. The complaint was that he acted more like a girl than a boy, which may not seem too surprising in light of his mother's behavior. Two questions arise about Fred and the general developmental issues of which his background is representative. One is the issue of developmental determinants: what caused the be-

havior? The other concerns prognosis: what are the implications of early gender-role characteristics for adult sexual behavior and adjustment?

In the preceding chapter, we considered the problems of gender typing. In this companion chapter, we will take up the issues of how sexual development proceeds, and how it is related to the gender role of the child.

Sexual Differentiation

To begin, we should recall some of the facts that were covered in Chapter 13. Mammals from mice to men have in common some basic genetic and hormonal processes related to the development of sex differences.

Genetic Mechanisms

In human beings, the number of chromosomes is 46 in both sexes: 22 pairs of autosomes (nonsex chromosomes) and a single pair of X chromosomes in females and 22 pairs of autosomes and an X and a Y chromosome in males. In approximately 3–4 births out of a thousand, infants are born with more or less than 46 chromosomes and the abnormality occurs in the sex chromosomes. We have already discussed one anomaly at length—the XYY pattern. Two other sex chromosome variations occur with sufficient frequency in humans to have been studied extensively. They are:

1. XXY *Klinefelter's syndrome.* Persons who have an extra X chromosome are phenotypic males (that is, they have a basically masculine sexual apparatus, masculine appearance, and masculine names). They differ from normal XY males in that they are sterile and typically remain sexually immature. They may be seen as having either an extra Y or an extra X chromosome, but the male chromosome always dominates the female one. Even when 48 or 49 chromosomes are present, with the extra ones being X chromosomes (*XXXY* or *XXXXY*), the individuals develop as males, but constitute a population "at risk with respect to psychopathology of almost any type," according to Money and Ehrhardt (1972). There is a high rate of severe retardation among persons with Klinefelter's syndrome. The frequency of Klinefelter's syndrome is approximately one in 400 newborn males.

2. XO *Turner's syndrome.* Persons with only one sex chromosome, XO, develop as phenotypic females. The internal sex organs are those of a female but they are incomplete, and the individuals remain sexually infantile due to ovarian deficiency and are sterile. They are also physically short of stature (usually 4½ to 5 feet tall) and often have anomalies of the cardiovascular system. Fortunately, Turner's syndrome rarely occurs (one birth in 3,000), and some of its symptoms can be reversed by estrogen therapy. The sterility cannot be reversed.

Apparently one X chromosome cannot do the work of two, for if it could, XO females would develop normal sexual functions. Similarly, the Y chromosome and the processes that it triggers apparently cannot cancel out entirely the effects of an pair of X chromosomes. Hence normal sexual development in both males and females depends on an equilibrium between the two sex chromosomes and the remaining chromosomes (the autosomes).

Hormonal Mechanisms: Organization in Prenatal Development

Even in persons who have the normal quota of sex chromosomes, sexual development is dependent on hormonal events that occur early in prenatal development. The human embryo is like other mammalian embryos in that it is bisexual early in development; differentiation (of the gonad, then the internal reproductive structure, and finally the external genitals) does not begin until about the sixth week after conception. Self-produced androgens have multiple effects during this period, such as inhibition of female anatomical development, stimulation of the development of internal and external male genitalia, and differentiation of central nervous system pathways.

It is of interest to examine some ways that the process of differentiation can be disrupted. One type of anomaly is the masculinization of the fetuses that have female (*XX*) genotypes. Male-type genital development can occur in genetic (*XX*) female fetuses that have been exposed to androgens from internal and external sources during the critical weeks (6–12) of gestation. The maternal (or fetal) adrenal cortex may malfunction and produce a surplus of androgens during this critical phase of anatomical differentiation, or progestin may be administered during the first third of pregnancy (to prevent miscarriages). Any of these events can masculinize the developing female fetus. [1]

----

[1] See the discussion by Money and Erhardt (1972), Neumann and Steinbeck (1972), and Hutt (1972).

Money and Ehrhardt (1972) studied the play preferences and play of girls who had been masculinized in utero by hormones. In their interests and activities, these girls tended to be more tomboyish than their sisters and girls selected as normal matched controls. The mothers of these children were also interviewed and according to the maternal reports, the masculinized daughters were less interested in feminine activities such as doll play than were their normal daughters. According to Money and Ehrhardt, the "most likely hypothesis to explain the various features of tomboyism in fetally masculinized genetic females is that their tomboyism is a sequel to a masculinizing effect on the fetal brain" (p. 103). There is the additional possibility that the familial role for the masculinized daughter may have promoted tomboyish pursuits, particularly if the parents had been aware of the partial masculinization at birth. What should be emphasized, however, is that all of the girls, both masculinized and normal, were quite stable in their identities as females. The gender that the children considered themselves to be was that which was assigned at birth or shortly afterward. The masculinized girls were tomboyish, but they were tomboyish girls.

The opposite effect—the anatomical feminization of XY males—can be produced if the influence of male hormones is blocked during the critical period of sexual differentiation. In the "androgen insensitivity" syndrome, the genetic male (XY) is unable to utilize (is insensitive to) self-produced androgens (Money and Ehrhardt, 1972). Because of a genetic deficiency, the target cells are insensitive to the androgens that are produced. Being unable to respond to the male sex hormones, the fetus differentiates morphologically as a female except for the internal sexual structures. Except for their XY chromosomal pattern and discordant internal sexual apparatus and sterility, these genetic males are indistinguishable from normal females in appearance, attitudes, and behavior at maturity. Often it is only after marriage that the infertility, and consequently the anomaly, are discovered.

Hormonal Mechanisms: Activity at Puberty

Puberty, or sexual maturity, is marked by the onset of menarche in girls and the production and release of mature sperm in boys. It generally occurs between ages 10-18 in girls and ages 12-20 in boys (Timiras, 1972). The gradual appearance of secondary sex characteristics (changes in voice, hair growth and distribution, body configuration) is controlled by hormonal processes (Chapter 13). Various environmental conditions have been shown to influence growth processes in general and sexual hormone release in particular. For instance, puberty occurs earlier in rodents that have proper nutrition, are exposed to constant light, and are born in spring or summer. Conversely, puberty occurs later in animals that suffer from malnutrition, are exposed to constant darkness, and are born in autumn or winter.

Environmental conditions also influence the onset of puberty in humans. Although such conditions can influence the time of onset of puberty, they play only a permissive or supporting influence. No specific environmental stimulation other than that normally encountered by adolescent males and females, is required for puberty to begin at the usual ages (10-18 and 12-20). The age of onset of menarche has been gradually lowered over the past 100 years. This trend is consistent with the gradual increments in height that have occurred over the same period. Moreover, the trend is not restricted to a single part of the world or to a single culture. Presumably, it reflects a general improvement in nutrition and health care.

Human beings, no less than other mammalian young, find it unnecessary to "learn" the basic components of reproduction and sexual arousal. Although sexual expression is limited by physiological and maturational factors, there is considerable plasticity in both the nature of that expression and the choice of partners. It is with respect to these matters—choice of activity and partner and attitudes—that experiential factors appear to be of considerable importance.

Varieties of Sexual Expression

Men and women have proved to be almost as inventive in their sexual behaviors as they have in other areas of human experience. Comparisons across cultures (and over time in Western societies) indicate that the rules by which sexual behaviors are regulated are variable to an extraordinary degree, as are the modal or accepted practices. Some of the more obvious deviations from the Western societal standard of a monogamous relationship with a partner of the opposite sex are found in the societies of the South Pacific. Among the Marind Anim, a head-hunting people of New Guinea, boys and girls are strictly segregated in early adolescence in households other than those of their parents. From the onset of puberty until marriage, the boy's primary sexual expressions are homosexual and masturbatory and are seen, in this society, as part of a normal developmental phase. The adult males enjoy both heterosexual expression in marriage and homosexual experiences with other men and boys (Money and Ehrhardt, 1972).

In contrast with males, females of the Marind Anim apparently do not become involved in homosexual relationships. Sexual experience is reserved for marriage, which is a single-mate relationship. Some extramarital activity occurs, but these encounters are also regulated. For instance, the young bride must have sexual intercourse with the male members of her husband's clan as a part of the wedding ceremony.

Obviously, it is not necessary to travel to exotic societies to identify a wide range of sexual activities. In recent years, subgroups have been formed in the United States by persons who share a preference for sexual expressions that differ markedly from societal norms of what is "conventional." Similarly, individuals who have been isolated from members of the opposite sex for extended periods, as in prison, may develop forms of sexual expression and interchange that vary markedly from heterosexual forms (Money and Ehrhardt; Ward and Kassebaum, 1965).

The lesson that cross-cultural and cross-societal comparisons teaches us is that humans are capable of a variety of forms of sexual expression, and that one practice does not necessarily preclude others, either at the same time or later in development. The practice (or practices) adopted depends significantly on subcultural expectations and individual living circumstances. In at least some societies, such as the Polynesian East Bay society, "normal" sexual development progresses from homosexual to bisexual and heterosexual expression (Davenport, 1965). There is considerable modifiability of sexual behavior over development. Moreover, this modifiability may be dictated by the mores of the society. In the Marind Anim and East Bay peoples, homosexual, then bisexual and heterosexual behavior occur *in accord with* societal expectations. In the United States, homosexuality and bisexuality occur *despite* social mores.

Developmental Determinants of Heterosexual Partner Selection

There are substantial differences among societies on probably the most important dimension of mate selection—the extent to which there is freedom of choice. The possibilities range from laissez-faire societies, where the individual is legally free to select a partner without economic, religious, or racial constraints, to societies where the selection is made independently of the individual, either before birth or early in childhood. But "permissive" societies are not as free as they are purported to be, and most "restrictive" societies provide loopholes that permit individual choice. Implicit or explicit guides are typically established concerning the sex, age, race, kinship, and socioeconomic status of appropriate partners.

In societies where relative freedom of choice is openly endorsed (as in the United States), such variables as physical attractiveness, health, wealth, and status have been shown to play a role in the selection process (Ford and Beach, 1951; Rosenblatt,

1974). With regard to personality and social behavior characteristics, it has been repeatedly demonstrated that like begets like: persons are attracted to potential mates who have similar values, interests, and attitudes (Byrne, 1971; Murstein, 1971).

Why does similarity affect mate selection? It seems reasonable to expect that persons who share common values, interests, and backgrounds more readily find common grounds for a relationship than those who do not. Hence several investigators have emphasized the importance of propinquity in the selection of mates (see Byrne, 1971; Huston, 1974).

But propinquity and mutuality of interests do not explain why one selects as a mate from only a small number of the persons whom one knows best, and avoids sexual relationships with those who are known best of all: the members of one's immediate family. The incest taboo is widespread, having been found in all human cultures that have been studied (Lindzey, 1967). In addition, close semifamilial relationships between boys and girls often, but not always, diminish the probability of sexual ties at maturity. Children raised in the same peer group within a kibbutz, for instance, very rarely marry each other. In his analysis of 2,769 marriages of second-generation kibbutz-reared adults, Shepher (1971) found that there were no intra-peer-group marriages. Co-rearing appears to diminish the attractiveness of the other child as a sexual partner (Shepher, 1971).

An instance where the co-rearing does not keep the children from marrying each other may be instructive. Wolf (1968, 1970) has described a practice sometimes followed in Taiwan, where a young girl lives with the lower-class family of her husband-to-be as though she were his sister. The girls are forced Cinderella-like into early drudgery. Attitudes and feelings engendered in both the boys and the girls may not be compatible with the later requirements for mutual respect. These marriages prove to be less stable and more susceptible to breakup and adultery, and less productive of children than are conventional marriages between members of the same socioeconomic class. Part of the reason for the troubled marriages may be the economic differen-

tial of the children rather than the rearing circumstance per se. Early togetherness is no guarantee for marital bliss any more than species cohabitation assures peaceful coexistence.

Why the "incest" taboo? As Lindzey (1967) has argued, societies may prohibit the mating of close kin for genetic reasons. Diversity in the genetic background of partners may serve the dual function of (1) limiting the number of recessive, debilitating characteristics that appear in the population; and (2) producing *heterosis* (an increase in vigor and reproductive capacity). There are nongenetic considerations as well. The social reorganization necessitated by intrafamilial mating could disrupt or destroy the existing network of relationships within the family or, in the kibbutz, the "extended family" of peers. Economic factors—such as sharing resources or gaining prestige by virtue of marital ties—have also been proposed as a reason for incest prohibitions. No definitive answer can yet be offered with regard to the question of why the incest taboo exists among humans. Indeed, early togetherness may inhibit later sexual arousal, for "who wants to marry her brother?" as one of Wolf's (1968) Chinese informants put it (see Chapter 21 for further comments).

Development of Sexual Arousal

Do humans have species-typical biases that influence the identification of appropriate and receptive partners? The evidence on this matter is inconclusive and has been the subject of considerable speculation. Apart from somatosensory (tactile) stimuli, which clearly have an inherent, unconditioned capability for producing sexual arousal (Watson, 1926; Masters and Johnson, 1966), we have scant basis for concluding that a given stimulus has an inherent capacity to elicit arousal. Virtually any environmental event can be shown to produce sexual arousal for some persons under some circumstances (Kinsey et al., 1953). And there are exceedingly wide variations among persons in the events that they find arousing.

A major problem in identifying "inherent" or species-typical biases is that sexual arousal states in human beings are readily conditioned, in both males and females. The problem is to determine whether some stimulus dimensions are more readily conditioned than others—a matter on which our present information is woefully incomplete.

Three issues concerning the development of sexual arousal require comment here: (1) the vulnerability of children to the conditioning of arousal, (2) male-female differences in the conditioning of arousal, and (3) the independence of sexual arousal of sex hormones.

Are Children More Vulnerable?   The question of whether children are more easily conditioned to sexual stimuli than adults is critical for the law as well as for psychology. The assumption of greater childhood vulnerability is not a new one, and it is the basis of many of the statutes that have been enacted with regard to pornography (Cairns, Paul, and Wishner, 1962). Despite the obvious importance of the susceptibility question, few answers can be offered at this time. The problem is simply that little reliable information is available on the course of sexual conditioning processes in children and adolescents. The assumption of the greater vulnerability of children is plausible, and it accounts in part for the age-graded censorship standards of movies (rated G to X). It is also consistent with the proposal that behaviors and emotional arousal tend to become organized around, and consolidated with respect to, particular social events. But if one excludes anecdotal case-study reports, firm evidence on the conditioning of early sexual arousal is lacking.

Male-Female Differences.   One issue that has been investigated is the relative susceptibility of males and females to arousal by abstract stimuli. Kinsey and his collaborators (1953) argued that women are sexually aroused by pornography less readily than men, but are aroused by more "polite" and acceptable materials, such as love stories. This conclusion seems entirely consistent with self-reports, as well as with the results of studies of which sex patronizes "adult" bookstores and movies, and which sex buys movie magazines and watches soap operas. But apparently Kinsey's conclusion was premature. Studies conducted recently in Germany and the United States clearly indicate that if the technique is sufficiently sensitive, and if the males and females are reasonably experienced sexually, hard-core pornography appears to be sexually stimulating to both men and women, and to about the same degree (Gebhard, 1973; Schmidt, Sigusch, and Schafer, 1973). Moreover, pornographic stimulation is more likely to lead to action by women than by men, and more college-age women than men reported increased frequency of intercourse following the experimental exposure to pornography. The results of recent studies give a hint as to why Kinsey et al. (1953) obtained the findings they did: although many women are aroused by pornography, more women than men are distressed and disgusted by it (Heiman, 1975; Schmidt, Sigusch, and Schafer, 1973).

Sex Hormones and Sexual Arousal.   It should be observed that sexual arousal and performance are not dependent on the presence of sex hormones in either men or women (Chapter 13). Once established, patterns of sexual expression can be maintained even in the absence of such hormones (Luttge, 1971). Studies of whether homosexuals differ from heterosexuals in terms of hormonal secretion yield conflicting results (Dörner, Rhode, Stahl, Krell, and Masius, 1975), indicating that whatever hormonal differences are present, they are subtle and difficult to detect.

Developmental Contributions to Sexual Unconventionality

To understand normal, species-typical sexual development, it is instructive to examine instances of variations from it. What are the developmental determinants of the various forms of adult sexual expression, and is there a relation between gender identification in children and sexual unconventionality in adulthood?

Unconventionality in sexual behavior is not uncommon in American society; Kinsey and his associates (1948) reported that 37 percent of the American men studied had had some homosexual contact leading to orgasm by the time they were 45 years old. The corresponding figure for occasional homosexuality in American women was smaller (13 percent). Although the Kinsey data were collected 30 years ago, they are consistent with more recent surveys. Today, obligatory or exclusive male homosexuals (as contrasted with men who have had some sexual experience but who are primarily heterosexual in orientation) constitute roughly 2–6 percent of the population.[2]

To what extent do developmental events contribute to the individual's basic sexual orientation—heterosexual, bisexual, or homosexual? Speculations about the developmental determinants of these forms of adult sexual expression have centered around parental contributions (Acosta, 1975).

Familial Influences on Homosexual Development

According to a major psychoanalytic interpretation of the origin of homosexuality in men, the choice is determined by a particular family constellation. Specifically, the mother is seen as a domineering figure and is close-binding and seductive with her son and husband. The father is seen as weak, passive, and detached and/or hostile toward his son (Bieber, Dain, Dince, Drillich, Grand, Gundlach, Kremer, Rifkin, Wilbur, and Bieber, 1962; Gundlach, 1969). The individual later rejects heterosexual partners and channels his sexual expression toward males.

How accurate is this depiction? The work of R. B. Evans (1969) at the Loma Linda (California) School of Medicine is representative of the kind of study that has attempted to evaluate the hypothesis. This investigator gained the cooperation of 43 homosexual and 142 heterosexual American-born, Caucasian men between the ages of 22 and 47 who lived in the Los Angeles area. The homosexual sample had been recruited through the auspices of One, Inc.; the heterosexual control group had been participating in a study of cardiovascular disease. None of the men in either group had sought psychotherapy. All men were given a 27-item questionnaire designed to obtain information about their childhood experiences. The differences between the two groups in their response to the questionnaire were clear-cut. The homosexual group reported "negative" feelings toward the family. The homosexuals viewed their mothers as frigid and puritanical and likely to interfere with heterosexual activity; they recalled hating and not respecting their fathers. These results are consistent with those of a previous study of psychoanalytic patients who were being treated for homosexual behavior (Bieber et al., 1962; see also Thompson, Schwartz, McCandless, and Edwards, 1973). Evans commented that it was noteworthy that the results of the two studies were so similar, despite major differences in the level of observation. In the earlier investigation, the homosexuals were not interviewed; their psychoanalyst filled out the questionnaire.

Do these findings indicate that poor relationships caused the homosexual orientation? Possibly. But the child's orientation may have produced the familial difficulties as much as vice-versa. It may be the case that the homosexuals, as children, contributed significantly to their parents' responses, making it difficult for their parents to establish close relationships with their sons. In this regard, Evans (1969) writes that the proposal that the

> . . . father of a homosexual son becomes detached and/or hostile because he does not understand or

---

[2] These estimates are as subject to error today as when they were originally reported by Kinsey et al. (1948).

is disappointed in the son is just as tenable as that the son becomes homosexual because of the father's rejection. Similarly, that a mother may be more intimate with and bind her homosexual son more closely because of the kind of person he is, is just as reasonable as the idea that he becomes homosexual because she is too binding or intimate (p. 134).

In support of the child-causality view, Evans (1969) observes that the specific items of his questionnaire having to do with childhood play experiences and fear revealed the differences between homosexual and heterosexual men more clearly than did items that assessed general relationships with the mother and father. In the first type of question, each man was asked whether as a boy he had played baseball and other competitive games, played mostly with girls, avoided fights, was clumsy, was afraid of getting hurt, and was a "lone wolf." Fewer homosexual than heterosexual men described themselves as having conformed to part of the male stereotype as children. But when the family items are considered there was considerable overlap between the two groups. Many adult homosexuals reported having had entirely normal and pleasant relationships with their parents and, conversely, many heterosexual men reported having had extremely unpleasant family relationships. Evans proposes that a poor father-son relationship may be a consequence of the failure of the son to adopt masculine behaviors and attitudes, as much as it is an antecedent of the failure. [3] This does not mean, obviously, that all

boys whose behavior does not fit the male stereotype are predestined to adopt unconventional sexual behavior at maturity. Nor do the data reveal what proportion of the boys who exhibit unconventional behavior is likely to adopt a homosexual orientation at adulthood.

Three comments are in order concerning these studies. First, the information was derived from the recollections of adult males. Memories can fail, or they can be colored by the quality of current relationships. If the man happens to be at odds with his family at the time of the interview, possibly because they disapprove of his current behavior, he may view the past in an especially dim light. To clarify etiology, retrospective studies must be combined with prospective ones that follow individuals from birth to adulthood.

Second, until the recent past, there has been only meager information on the etiology of lesbianism. Recent studies indicate that female homosexuals reported disturbed family relationships more frequently than do female heterosexuals (Loney, 1972; Thompson et al., 1973). As with men, situational factors play a major role in determining the occurrence of the behavior (Ward and Kassebaum, 1965).

Third, a shortcoming of retrospective studies of early social experience is that the influence of persons other than the parents is usually omitted from the analysis. It seems likely that the peer-group and familial relationships of the individual at each stage of development help to determine the social-sexual behaviors that he or she prefers. But retrospective analyses have not been very helpful in identifying the positive impact of peers in the adoption of unconventional sexual patterns.

Effeminate Boys and Their Families

To correct for some of the shortcomings of retrospective studies, there has been a renewed effort to study children who are "at risk" for later unconventional sexual behavior. The Gender Identity Project at UCLA has provided useful information concern-

---

[3] Evans (1969) implies that the homosexual group was predisposed toward this sexual orientation because of inherent or constitutional differences from the nonhomosexual group. Studies of the blood relatives of homosexuals indicate that there is a correlation between the adoption of homosexuality and the closeness of the relationship to the homosexual subject. Wilson (1975) discusses the evidence and addresses the obvious problem: how can homosexual biases be retained in the gene pool if homosexuals do not reproduce themselves? Wilson (1975) tentatively offers an explanation in terms of kinship selection (that homosexuals, by their altruistic actions, enhance the survival of their close kin, who can reproduce). The alternate, environmentalist's hypothesis would be that the family group that promotes unconventional sexual behavior in one of its members is likely to promote the same behavior in others.

ing a group of 29 boys who were referred to the project by teacher, physician, or social worker for diagnosis and/or treatment. Frederick C., the 7-year-old whom we met at the beginning of this chapter, was included in the project. Attempts to identify a family constellation associated with male effeminacy were not successful. Nevertheless, there seemed to be a greater incidence of family disturbance in this group than in a random sample of boys who came from families that can be most appropriately described as normal (in terms of interests, attitudes, and behaviors). The researchers conclude that:

> At this point, despite fairly intensive clinical study of gender-problem boys and their families, firm conclusions cannot be drawn about the family patterns associated with boyhood gender abnormalities (Bates et al., 1974, p. 15).

Other studies have also failed to find any consistent family patterns in the etiology of gender-role anomalies (Acosta, 1975; Green and Money, 1960; Green, 1974). The failure to find a single general constellation is consistent with the contention of Green (1974) that all feminine boys are not the same, and should not be grouped together. Green notes that there are multiple routes into these orientations. One of the routes may be the progressive removal from peer activities, including those involving athletics. Bates and Bentler (1973) report a highly reliable difference between effeminate and noneffeminate boys in athletic interest. The investigators speculate that effeminate boys may simply retain the less-masculine play patterns of early childhood, and thus may fail to develop more age- and sex-appropriate ones. (Although this developmental view is intriguing, it does not take into account the possibility that the play patterns of the preschool boys may also differ markedly.)

Continuity of Gender-Role Deviance

Is an effeminate boy likely to show unconventional sexual behavior in adulthood? Longitudinal studies (which identify clinic-referred effeminate boys in childhood and trace them into early adulthood) indicate that effeminate behavior sometimes does continue (Bates et al., 1974) and that it is statistically associated with various forms of adult sexual unconventionality (Green, 1974; Green and Money, 1964; Zuger and Taylor, 1969). Nonetheless, a significant number of effeminate boys establish normal sexual relationships in adulthood. Similarly, longitudinal studies of clinic referrals overlook those individuals who are reasonably adjusted in both childhood and adulthood, and who choose homosexual expression at maturity.

Attempts to treat gender-problem boys and their families have met with varying degrees of success. Bates et al. (1974) used a multilevel approach. The techniques were diverse. Interviews were conducted with both parents, and the fathers and their sons were taken on group outings to bowling alleys and miniature golf courses. The boys were taught how to play new sports and how to get along with other children. The investigators found that "most of the families treated showed noticeable gains." A year and a half after treatment, the boys seemed happier, less effeminate, and more able to get along with other children. The investigators point out that effeminacy, for most of these clinic-referred boys, was part of a general inability to get along with their peers. The feminine behavior was also typically encouraged, either directly or indirectly, by one or more members of the family system; hence the reason for including both the parents and the children in the treatment.

Summary

The information on the developmental controls of human sexual expression is incomplete, and speculations on this critical issue abound. The studies that are available permit us to take the first tentative steps toward a coherent view of one part of the process—that having to do with mate selection. On the basis of available information, it appears that sexual orientation (whom the individual prefers as a sexual partner) and sexual preferences (what activities are preferred) are established in the course of development. The orientation and preferences come about in a sequential, probabilistic series of events that take place over time; there is not a magic moment when a single experience consolidates the individual's sexual activity and preferences for life. The several critical developmental phases include:

■ The prenatal period, when the sexual structures are formed under the bidirectional influence of genes and hormones.

■ Birth and infancy, when societal-parental judgments are made concerning the gender classification of the child on the basis of sexual phenotype and expectations about the child's future behavior.

■ The preschool ages (3–5 years), when the child establishes and consolidates a gender self-concept and gender-appropriate behavior. Both the child's self-concept and behavior are supported by the acts and expectations of others with whom the child interacts (within and outside the family system).

■ Middle childhood (roughly 6–11 years), when social influences continue and children establish a network of peer relations that influence their ideas and behaviors on a variety of matters, including sexual ones.

■ Adolescence, when the primary psychobiological capabilities for mature sexual expression emerge, along with the appearance of secondary sexual characteristics. Influences in the social network continue to operate in the selection of the sexual activities, if any, that will be performed, when, and with whom.

■ Early adulthood, when sexual patterns reflect a fusion of a person's preferences, capabilities, and opportunities, along with interactional and societal demands.

Events in each of these phases seem to help to determine, but do not irrevocably fix, the nature of the biases and preferences that the individual will adopt in succeeding phases. There is a continuing interplay among influences (early and present) and a realignment with the individual's current attitudes and preferences.

With regard to the issue of the development of homosexual preferences, the data support Bell's (1973) conclusion that homosexuality involves a large number of widely divergent experiences, developmental, sexual, social, and psychological, and that even after a person has been labeled "homosexual" on the basis of his or her preferred sexual object there is little that can be predicted about that person on the basis of that label (Bell, 1973, p. 24).

The interpersonal and social dynamics that are conducive to the plasticity and nonplasticity of sexual orientation at maturity have yet to be firmly established. In those cultures where age-related changes in form of sexual expression and choice of partner are the norm, the "conventional" expression includes homosexual, bisexual, and heterosexual patterns. Possibly because plasticity of partner and activity are expected, they typically occur. In the United States, sexual orientations tend to become consolidated in early maturity and to remain stable unless there is a marked change in living circumstances (such as imprisonment) or interactional relationships (Acosta, 1975). Although such results point to the importance of the network of other persons whose attitudes and behaviors support the choices, there is strong evidence that the individual's own preferences become firmly stabilized by early maturity. These preferences, in turn, can determine which network the individual enters and remains in.

17

MORE ON RECIPROCITY
IN INTERCHANGES:
ALTRUISM, COOPERATIVENESS,
AND MORALITY RECONSIDERED

Tsz-Kung put to him the question, "Is there one word upon which the whole life may proceed?" The Master replied, "Is not reciprocity such a word?—What you do not yourself desire, do not put before others."

—*The Confucian Analects, XV.23*
(Translated by W. Jennings, 1895)

Social development has been described in this volume in terms of the establishment, maintenance, and transformation of interchange patterns during ontogeny. In this chapter we will "step into" the organization of relationships to ask why and how synchrony and reciprocity emerge or fail to emerge. This question requires that we make explicit a proposition that has been implicit in the preceding chapters concerning the dependence of interchanges on the psychobiological and cultural systems in which they are embedded. Then we will review attempts that have been made to sharpen our understanding of reciprocal processes by tracing their development and ubiquity. A special concern will be the role of reciprocity in the occurrence of altruistic and cooperative interchanges.

The passage from *The Confucian Analects* reflects both the simplicity and the subtlety of the issues. The Master's answer to the question of Tsz-Kung was beautifully succinct, but it was another question. In a larger sense, the contents of this chapter address that second question, namely, the properties and limits of reciprocity.

Reciprocity: Its Breadth, Limits, and Development

"Everyone knows" that children influence each other. Beyond that truism lie complex and subtle issues as to how they affect one another, and why. What does synchrony observed in mother-infant interchanges have to do with synchrony observed in later childhood? Are the same processes involved, and does the earlier interchange relate to the later one? More specifically, how does reciprocity that occurs in one relationship generalize to other ones? We have considered these questions in earlier chapters and have offered some tentative answers for them with respect to specific research issues. At this point it will be useful to place the phenomena of reciprocity into a broader context and then review some ideas that have emerged regarding the development of interchange processes in children.

Some Distinctions Among Terms

First I will review some distinctions among the terms that have been used to describe how interchanges are organized. One advantage in clarifying the similarities and differences in concepts is that it draws attention to processes that may have been overlooked in other discussions. In any case, it is now appropriate to highlight certain distinctions between synchrony, reciprocity, complementarity, and imitation.

Synchrony refers to a property of interactions which obtains when one person's acts are coordinated with and supportive of the ongoing activity of another individual. Synchrony is the most general term of the four, referring to the occurrence of mutually supported, coordinated action. Are all interactions by definition synchronous? No, because not all coordinated actions (interactions) involve mutual support for ongoing activities. We have discussed, for instance, interactions that involve acts that disrupt the ongoing behaviors of another person. Such

dissynchronous acts as punishment may involve the disruption of behavior. Or the acts of one person in the interaction may neither support nor disrupt the activities of the other person. A mother's ignoring the temper tantrum of her 2-year-old child could be viewed as an interaction in which her activity was *asynchronous* with that of the child. (In this instance, synchrony may involve the unhappy requirement that the mother perform acts that would support and maintain the tantrum behavior.)

Reciprocity is the most difficult of these four organizational concepts to define because it has carried so much surplus meaning in the past. Two properties of the term—relational activity and similarity—figure importantly in its interactional definition. The relational aspect is captured in the German expression for reciprocal, *sich hin- und herbewegen* (meaning literally, "movement there and here"). This connotation of the term is possibly the reason why many writers have used "reciprocal" as a synonym for "interaction." The second property of reciprocity—similarity—seems to be implied by the passage cited at the beginning of this chapter, namely, that one's acts may eventually breed counteracts of a similar sort. For us, then, reciprocity can be said to occur *when the acts of two or more persons support each other in a relationship and their actions become similar to each other.* Accordingly, reciprocity can be seen as one type of interchange synchrony, namely, a synchrony that is associated with a high level of similarity in the actions or expressions of the participants.

Two other terms, complementary and imitation, require comment because of their overlap with reciprocity. *Complementary* (or complementarity) also refers to supportive "movement back and forth" and hence identifies another way that interchanges can be synchronized. But complementary acts, unlike reciprocal ones, differ from each other in some key quality in order for the sequence to be completed. Examples would be, say, a complementary question-answer sequence or a nursing-suckling one, where the roles of the two persons are different but each contributes to the ongoing activity of the other person.[1]

The final term, *imitation,* has as its key property the occurrence of a unique similarity (identity) between the acts of one person and those of another (Bandura and Walters, 1963). But unlike the terms that we have just discussed (synchrony, reciprocity, complementary), imitation does not require a "back and forth" activity, where each member of the relationship affects the other. Indeed, the basic studies of imitation have been noninteractional, in that the aim has been to demonstrate how the acts of one person (the model) can influence the responses of another person (the subject). A major challenge for contemporary theory has been to determine how this special case of interpersonal influence fits into the dynamic conditions that operate in the interchanges of everyday life (Chapter 19).

The work of the past ten years has yielded a reasonable outline of when reciprocal patterns occur and when they do not. We will turn now to an overview of the main findings of that research.

The Ubiquity of Reciprocity

In earlier discussions of reciprocal processes, we focused on their occurrence in social patterns. Parallel phenomena have been identified as well in primary features of language, cognitive, emotional, and motor expressions.

Reciprocity in Language.   Recent findings in developmental psycholinguistics indicate that persons often adjust their communications to fit the capabilities and characteristics of those with whom they speak. Some of the adjustments are obvious. Mothers talking to their young children adopt a simplier and distinctive language style compared to their normal patterns. The utterances are shorter, the words easier, and there are attempts to expand and structure the child's speech (Moerk, 1976; Nelson, 1973; Seitz and Stewart, 1975; Snow, 1972). Similarly, older children teaching younger ones attempt to talk at the younger child's level (Shatz and Gelman, 1973). Other adjustments are more subtle—such as the patterns of pauses and turn-talking observed in children's interchanges (Welkowitz, Cariffe, and Feldstein, 1976). The burden of adjustment is typically borne by the more "competent" member of the relationship, namely, the one who is more able to adjust his communication patterns. In any case, one can typically deduce significant features of the second child's behavior merely by tracking the course of the verbal activity of one of the participants.

What functions does the synchrony serve for the child? Seitz and Stewart (1975) observe that:

> When mothers perceive a child as "trying to talk," they respond with modifications, especially expansions, designed to help him say what he is trying to say. Thus, imitations allow the child with limited language to engage his mother in conversation. The fortuitous byproducts of this reciprocity include maternal language that is tied to the young speaker's interests and language level. This enables the child to exert an active influence on his language environment so that it changes with his increasing competence (p. 768).

Hence the reciprocity seems to be both diagnostic and facilitative in language development.

Reciprocity in Cognitive Functioning.   If a child's language development can be facilitated by interchanges, can children's cognitive abilities be accelerated by interacting with older or more advanced children? Although the sense of the discussion up to this point suggests that the answer should be affirmative, it isn't so obvious that it has been accepted

---

[1] It should be noted that the distinction between reciprocal and complementary pivots on the judgment of "similar" and "different." Where the line is drawn between the two categories depends on the level of abstraction or dimension employed. Consider the expressions of two children in a question-and-answer sequence. In terms of the content of what is said, their acts are clearly different, hence complementary. But if their activities are considered on other dimensions (such as topic, loudness of utterance, whether talking or nonverbal), their acts may be seen as similar, hence reciprocal.

in everyday activities, including the design of schools and the planning of families. Who will benefit, say, from an arrangement where children of differing abilities or different ages are placed in the same classroom? Will the younger children be accelerated by the interchanges, or will the older ones be retarded? Or will both ages come out ahead because the more advanced children will be required to take an "older" role with respect to the younger children? The meager evidence available on the matter suggests that under some circumstances, both children may benefit: the younger from having been given help and structured guidance, and the older ones by virtue of having performed an "adult" role (see, for instance, Cicirelli, 1975). It seems likely, however, that the direction, magnitude, and uniformity of the relationship depends greatly on the context in which the interchanges occur.

A rather intriguing hypothesis that was offered recently by Zajonc and Marcus (1975) concerns the reciprocity of siblings in intellectual functioning. It has been known that the oldest and/or only child in a family tends to achieve slightly higher grades and SAT scores, on the average, than other children (see Jones, 1954). Zajonc and Marcus proposed that this superiority comes about because of the reciprocal impact of interchanges. Whereas the oldest child (or the only child) interacts primarily with the parents, younger siblings interact with both the parents and the older siblings. Hence, oldest and/or only children should be at an advantage relative to the middle-born and youngest ones. The same argument may be offered to explain why identical twins tend to score lower on the verbal sections of tests of scholastic potential than do nonidentical twins and siblings (Jones, 1954). Because identical twins often develop reciprocal and private communication signals with their twin, the opportunity and need to develop more advanced communication patterns may be diminished. Too much synchrony, or too little variety, may retard cognitive development.

Reciprocity in Emotional Expression and Empathy.
Observations of young children in preschool settings indicate that there is indeed considerable reciprocity in emotional expression. L. Sherman (1975) found, for instance, that "gleeful" episodes in the classroom were contagious, in that children would rapidly spread through the group. Does the same phenomenon also occur in the two-person interactions of children; does laughter beget laughter, and anger, anger? Preliminary observations of children indicate that the mutual engagement of emotional states commonly occurs with dyadic pairs in everyday life, in that the positive expressions of one child in an interchange are associated with similar feelings expressed by the other child, and negative expressions in one with negative expressions in the other (personal communication, Louisa Rogoff, 1977). It may be that the majority of the child's intense emotional states—either positive or negative—occur *primarily* in interactional contexts and are associated with the acts or anticipated acts of the other person.

The problem of reciprocal emotional expression brings us to the special issue of empathy, and the vicarious participation of the child in the feelings of other persons. The matter is relevant to the phenomena of reciprocity in that it refers to the capability of one person to experience similar emotions of another, although there may be no actual interchange between the two. As Hoffman (1977b) points out, this capability seems to require certain basic cognitive capabilities for the recognition of feelings in others and, possibly, the ability to take the role of the other person. Although there is no question about *whether* the capacity for empathy develops, it is unclear as to *when* (at what age) the child is capable of empathy. Borke (1973) finds that even young children (3 years of age) are capable of "empathetic awareness" (ratings of affect shown in slides), while a later onset has been proposed by other investigators (Chandler and Greenspan, 1972). [2]

---

[2] Hoffman (1977a) also notes that some of the discrepancies among studies of empathy appear to reflect the different measurement techniques that are employed. See "Age of Onset" section later in this chapter.

Reciprocity in Motor Actions. In most games, it is essential that children's motor responses are coordinated: playing catch or playing pat-a-cake are similar in that they both require a synchrony in motor actions. But there are less obvious ways than in games that the motor acts of one individual directly affect those of another. Coaction refers to the finding that the joint participation of two or more persons in an activity yields a heightened level of performance relative to the levels reached by the same persons acting alone. Children swim and run faster when in groups or in competition than when alone, and their performance on simple, repetitive activities (from winding fishing reels to solving elementary arithmetic problems) is facilitated when working together relative to when working alone. Why does such interactive participation make a difference? Zajonc's (1965) explanation emphasized that joint participation may heighten the "generalized drive" level of the participants and hence energize the activities of each member so that the acts are performed with greater intensity and involvement. Although the proposal has shortcomings as an explanation for all features of interpersonal influence, it has special merit in pointing to the relationship between emotional states of the interacting persons and the intensity of the motor acts that they perform.

Reciprocity in Social Patterns. We have commented on the different kinds of reciprocity in social behavior in preceding chapters. A tabular summary of some of the more relevant research is given in Table 17-1. Three general points are suggested by the table. First, the magnitude of correlation between the acts of two or more children is typically high, underscoring the power as well as the ubiquity of the phenomenon. Second, the findings are primarily from studies of young children in laboratories and in the preschool—conditions that can provide some restrictions that enhance behavioral similarity. However, sufficient work has been conducted in nonlaboratory contexts to confirm that the effects are not limited by age-sex conditions. Third, reci-

procity is not inevitable. In the case of certain patterns of response, such as physical aggression, the other child's tendency to react with a similar action may not be heightened; indeed, it may be diminished (Hall, 1973; S. Sherman, 1975). Such findings remind us that interchanges are not always synchronous, nor are all synchronous interchanges reciprocal. Indeed, the boundary conditions for reciprocity should be as helpful in understanding its general properties as are illustrations of its ubiquity.

Some Limits on Reciprocity and Synchrony

Think of a child in a crowded playground with several different activities going on around him. With whom will he synchronize, or will he become involved in any synchronized interactions? A moment's reflection on what our imaginary child would do—or what we ourselves actually do—suggests that what is usually done in such settings is to ignore others or to inhibit a response to their actions. If such selection did not occur, each child might be obligated to rush frantically from one reciprocal activity to another. Hence the first line of control on whether or not to reciprocate is attentional and intentional.

But even when the child is involved in an interchange, there are some general conditions in which he fails to reciprocate or even fails to act in a synchronous fashion. Four conditions that have been identified in research are summarized below:

1. Most acts of adult caretakers toward infants are not reciprocated simply because the infants do not have the relevant behaviors in their repertoires. Instead, as Seitz and Stewart (1975) indicate, the mother enters the child's system at the level at which the child is capable of responding. The more general condition is that there are occasions where children cannot reciprocate because of limitations due to developmental status.

2. Social or cultural expectations may require that similar acts should *not* occur. Marked differ-

Table 17-1. Synchronous controls of social interchanges: some illustrations.

Source	Subjects	Actions Measured	Design	Statistical Analysis	Relationship Observed	Comments
Bott, 1934	Preschool children	"Initiations"	Naturalistic preschool	High positive correlation ($r \geq .80$). (Children who initiate to others tend also to be recipients of initiations.)	Mutual similarity	An early demonstration of high reciprocity, but confounded with activity level of child.
Anderson, 1939	Kindergarten children	"Dominance"	Naturalistic preschool	High positive correlation ($r \geq .70$). (Dominant acts toward others are associated with dominant acts toward self.)	Mutual similarity	Observations made across settings and persons.
Raush, 1965	Hyperaggressive and normal adolescent boys	"Friendly"	Naturalistic	Information analysis, transitional probabilities. ("Friendly" acts beget "friendly" acts; "unfriendly" acts beget "unfriendly" ones.)	Mutual similarity	Effect of setting analyzed separately.
Kohn, 1966	Preschool children	"Initiations"	Naturalistic preschool	High positive correlation ($r = .77$). (Analysis same as Bott, above.)	Mutual similarity	Observations made across settings and persons.
Kohn, 1966	Preschool children	"Positive initiations"	Naturalistic preschool	High positive correlation ($r = .68$).	Mutual similarity	Observations made across settings and persons.
Sherman, 1975	Preschool boys and girls	Play patterns	Laboratory "naturalistic"	High positive correlation ($r \geq .80$), conditional probabilities. (Verbal and nonverbal communication begets like communication.)	Mutual similarity, nonreciprocity for direct physical assertiveness.	Setting held constant, triads.

Table 17-1. (*Continued*)

Source	Subjects	Actions Measured	Design	Statistical Analysis	Relationship Observed	Comments
Hall, 1973	First-grade boys	"Aggression"	Experimental laboratory	High positive correlation, ($r \geq .80$) conditional probabilities. (Nonpersonal aggressive acts beget nonpersonal aggressive acts.)	Mutual similarity for nonpersonal assertiveness, nonreciprocity for direct physical "hits."	Experimental manipulation of one child's activity to determine effects on the other.
Quilty, 1975	First-grade children and an adult	Cooperation	Experimental laboratory	Conditional probabilities.	Child adopts similar or different activity, depending on directions.	Experimental manipulation of the strategy expected of the child.
Patterson, 1976	Preschool boys and girls	Assertive	Laboratory "naturalistic"	High positive correlation ($r \geq .90$), conditional probabilities (Nonpersonal aggressive acts beget nonpersonal aggressive acts.)	Mutual similarity	Setting held constant.

ences in the roles of two persons (produced by cultural, familial, sex, or age factors) can limit the extent to which similar acts are expected to beget similar acts. There are obvious differences between the roles of the teacher and the student, between the parent and the child, between the therapist and the patient, and so on. There role differences, in turn, dictate certain rules of the interchange, including when it is appropriate (or inappropriate) to reciprocate, obey, imitate, or act independently (Quilty, 1975).

3. The acts in the interchange may elicit behaviors that are complementary rather than reciprocal. For instance, questions call for answers, not further questions. Vigorous hits may demand self-defense, appeals for help, and/or requests to cease (Hall, 1973). Complications arise because some features of the behaviors of two persons may be similar (such as their emotional expression or content of the conversation), although other features may be different (complementary to each other). In addition there are acts that permit either reciprocal or complementary expression. Kindness can elicit reciprocal kindness, or complementary selfishness, according to the background and characteristics of each participant.

4. The child may choose *not* to respond in a synchronous fashion and may instead select a dissyn-

chronous act (inhibiting the ongoing behavior of the other individual) or an asynchronous one (not supportive of the ongoing behavior of the other individual but not inhibiting the behavior). The ability to not respond reciprocally, even though one has the capabilities for it, may be of considerable .importance in socialization.

Asynchrony can be a key in the control of escalating and emotion-producing interchanges. If the parent remains calm, despite increases in the emotional intensity and negative actions of the child, the likelihood of escalation and agression is diminished (Patterson, 1979). More generally, the ability to inhibit reciprocation appears to be of great importance in parents dealing with children, young or old. Otherwise, fretful and irritable infants would inevitably produce fretful and possibly abusive parents, and provocative acts by adolescents would inevitably elicit counter-provocation by authorities (such as the encounters described in Chapter 12). Nor is the matter simply one of child-rearing. John Gottman (personal communication, July 1977) has preliminary findings indicating that the ability for husband/ wife pairs to remain asynchronous in emotional expression may contribute to stability and harmony in marriages. When one spouse becomes angry or upset, the other spouse responds in a like manner in distressed marriages and in a moderating, nonreciprocal fashion in nondistressed marriages.

Why Synchrony and Reciprocity?

Evolutionary Considerations. At an evoluntionary level of analysis, the answer to the question of why reciprocal and synchronous responding occurs early in life may appear self-evident. Mammalian young would be at grave risk for survival if they were not synchronized shortly after birth. The "machinery" of the mammalian organism—the biological equipment of both mother and infant—was designed in evolution to promote the enmeshing of their behaviors and needs. The hormonal states and morpho-

logical structures of the mother, as well as the sensory, motor, and nervous systems of the infant, are seemingly "made" for each other. A different answer could be offered to explain the ubiquity of social synchrony even in the absence of obvious biological supports for the interchange. Social integration of the sort required for living in family groups and larger units presupposes a capability for synchronizing social actions, and this capability may have evolved in the phyletic history of human beings.

The concept of *reciprocal altruism* has been proposed to explain the seeming genetic illogic of altruistic acts (which may require the giving of one's own life) toward persons who are unrelated to the altruist. Altruism toward relatives makes good genetic sense, as Hamilton (1964) pointed out, because the closer the relationship, the more likely it is that the beneficiary will share a significant proportion of his genes with the altruist. Hence one's success in transmitting one's genes to the next generation can be enhanced by helping close relatives. This argument has been extended by R. L. Trivers (1971, 1974) and E. O. Wilson (1975) to account for acts of altruism even when the beneficiary is unrelated to the individual who makes the sacrifice. According to conditions outlined by Trivers (1971), altruistic acts call forth in the recipient further acts of altruism. These reciprocal altruistic acts in turn can benefit the reproductive potential of the altruist or persons who are closely related to him.

Functional Considerations. A second, more familiar level of analysis is that concerned with the immediate controls and functions of the activity. Again, we can ask: Why reciprocity and synchrony? In infancy, the synchronous interchanges between mothers and their offspring are clearly supported by the biological states of both (Chapters 3 and 6). But beyond infancy (2 years and older), it is unclear in terms of proximal mechanisms as to why interactional reciprocity should be ubiquitous when there are few biological supports for it.

A partial answer to the proximal question is suggested by an examination of what modifications are necessary in order for the child's behaviors to become synchronized with those of another person. To the extent that the ongoing activity of the other individual follows a pattern or "theme," it will place constraints on what activities of the child can be synchronous, and vice-versa. Hence the interpolated acts of each person must be modified to "fit" the essential theme (pattern) of the other person's ongoing behavior. But when this is done, the acts of the two persons will become more similar on some dimensions. And the more tightly integrated or synchronized are the behaviors of the child with another person, the more likely it is that they should share essential features of each other's behavior (including emotional states, language, and attitudes and expectations). Thus interpersonal reciprocity is a byproduct of interpersonal synchrony.

The answer is only partial because it begs the question of why children would choose to organize their behavior around that of other persons in the first place. What is so attractive about interacting with other persons as opposed to not interacting with them? On this matter, only speculations have been offered. Possibly the most reasonable (and the most widely adopted) proposal is the *interpersonal bias* hypothesis: that other persons provide salient and contingent events that recruit the child's attention, curiosity, and activity (see Cairns, 1966a; Gewirtz, 1972; Mason, 1979; Rheingold, 1966). Human beings have the distinctive capabilities of being able to process information about another's activities, of responding, instantly, in ways that are immediately relevant to the other's acts, and of provoking counter-responses that support one's own activities. Accordingly, these properties may combine to make the actions of other persons the preferred basis for behavior organization. The range of synchrony that is observed in the child's behavior should then be jointly determined by (1) the child's ability to process information about other persons and to respond contingently and flexibly to their actions, and (2)

these capabilities in the others with whom the child interacts.

This last corollary of the interpersonal bias hypothesis provides a perspective from which to trace the course of the development of synchronized interchange in children, the overview of which we shall now discuss.

The Developmental Course

I hope that it is not too tedious to note again that interchange synchrony is not a property of the individual but of the relationship between individuals. Otherwise puzzling findings on the development of synchrony become entirely reasonable when there is a shift in perspective from the infant to the relationships in which infants are involved. Consider, for instance, the surprising finding of Margaret Holmberg (1977) that children from 1 to $3\frac{1}{2}$ years of age show few changes in the $2\frac{1}{2}$ years in the number of complex interchanges involving adults. (See Figure 17-1.) Holmberg's observations were made in the day-to-day interactions of nursery schools, and the children interacted with a variety of adults in a wide range of circumstances. But a child at 42 months of age is obviously more socially competent than an infant. Why then no change? Holmberg's results indicate that even though the child is undergoing continuous modification, the adult's responses are also being modified in order to maintain the synchrony of the relationship. Holmberg writes:

> At the younger ages it is again the adult who sets the pace and makes the necessary adjustments to maintain the interchange. The teacher picks up on the response of the child (names what the child points to, offers another puzzle as the child completes the first one), thus indicating a sensitiveness to child capabilities and response level. Even when the child initiates (runs to greet the teacher) the teacher responds with a request to engage in an activity (work a puzzle) which is fairly certain to maintain the interchange (pp. 100–101).

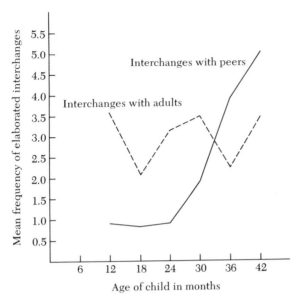

Figure 17-1. Frequency of elaborated interchanges (as determined by length and variability of interchange) among children who range in age from 12 to 42 months of age. The number of such interchanges increased sharply over development when the other person was a peer but did not change reliably when the other person was an adult (from M. C. Holmberg, 1977, with permission).

Hence the burden of complex social interchange rests not merely with the child but with the other participant's capability to identify ongoing behaviors and adjust to them. In child-child interactions, younger children (12–18 months old) cannot, or do not, make the appropriate adjustments. By 30 months of age, however, same-age peers are more adept at the art of enmeshing their acts. One then observes a sharp increase in the number of complex synchronous interchanges that occur naturally among peers (see Figure 17-1).

Parallel instances of ontogenetic pacing and equilibrium occur in the social interchanges of nonhuman mothers and their offspring (Chapter 3) and in the language of infants and adults. Longitudinal investigations of younger children (6 to 12 months) indicate that similar readjustments occur in the

mother-infant social interchanges. With the increasing capabilities of infants to respond flexibly to maternal initiations, their "games" grow more complex, and there is a greater reliance on verbal instructions to control and direct the infant's behaviors (Gustafson, 1977).

Rudolph Schaffer (1977) has provided a useful catalogue of the ways in which mothers shape the dialogue they have with their infants, from that of a passive "adapter" to the cues provided by the child to an active "facilitator" and "controller" of the direction of the relationship. Schaffer emphasizes that one of the more widely adopted (yet rarely acknowledged) techniques for facilitation had to do with the way that parents design the environment in which the children live and thereby elicit new techniques of relating.

Peer-Peer Interchanges

A significant series of studies by Mueller and his colleagues at Boston University provides a preliminary outline as to what kinds of interpersonal competence occur during the first 5 years of life (see Mueller, Bleier, Krakow, Hegedus, and Cournoyer, 1977; Mueller and Brenner, 1977; Mueller and Lucas, 1975). Mueller and Lucas (1975) describe three primary stages in the development of peer interchanges: (I) simple, object-centered contacts, (II) peer-oriented, and (III) complex-sustained interchanges. In stage I, children as young as one year old can be simultaneously drawn to the same toy, and interchanges may occur as a byproduct of mutual play with that toy. Object-centered actions, such as playing with a toy train where each child squats down and "toots" the whistle on it, can provide the opportunity for the onset of mutual play. Although in this initial stage interchanges are "lacking in an orientation toward influencing the behavior of peers themselves" (p. 236), contacts centered around objects permit the children to reach mutual social accommodations.

In stage II, occurring in the second year of life, mutual dependencies arise in the absence of objects.

Mueller and Lucas (1975) suggest that these interactions may be called "intercoordinated secondary circular reactions."

Consider, for example, this interchange between Bernie (13 months) and Larry (15 months):

> Larry sits on the floor and Bernie turns and looks toward him. Bernie waves his hand and says "da," still looking at Larry. He repeats the vocalization three more times before Larry laughs. Bernie vocalizes again and Larry laughs again. Then the same sequence of one child saying "da" and the other laughing is repeated twelve more times before Bernie turns away from Larry and walks off. Bernie and Larry become distracted at times during the interchange. Yet when this happens the partner reattracts attention either by repeating his socially directed action or by modifying it, as when Bernie both waves and says "da," reengaging Larry (p. 241).

A qualitative difference between interchanges at this stage of development and subsequent ones is that children begin to maintain and mutually control the directionality of the patterns.

In stage III, the key advance is that the children take complementary roles with respect to each other. One child is the giver, the other is the receiver; one throws a ball, the other receives or retrieves it. Mueller and Lucas propose that at this stage children are able to switch their roles. This complex pattern of interchange has been observed in children 18-24 months of age. As Mueller and Lucas point out, "role taking may or may not be uniquely human; but in either case it is the product of a developmental process" (p. 255).

The observations of Mueller and his colleagues have been collaborated and extended by other investigators (see Eckerman, 1979; Ross and Goldman, 1977a).

Age of Onset and the Relativity of Context

In contrast with the field studies that we have just discussed, well-controlled laboratory investigations of cooperative and reciprocal behaviors have usually concluded that children were not capable of these patterns until 6 or 8 years of age (Bryan and London, 1970; Cook and Stingle, 1974; Fishbein, 1976; Kagan, 1974; Kagan and Madsen, 1971). Why the difference in age of onset? The key factor appears to be the context of observation and the nature of the task employed. Laboratory investigations rigidly constrain the child's actions by controlling the kinds of ways that the child can behave cooperatively or competitively (such as having the children play a modified form of checkers). Observations of children in everyday life, however, assess "spontaneous" acts of cooperation and reciprocation; there are multiple ways that the child can be seen as having reciprocated, cooperated, or competed. Markedly different results in terms of age of onset of these patterns are obtained, depending upon the context of observation. Flavell (1977) observed that the differences were so great that

> children of *grade* three or four often communicate egocentrically in the tasks of the first tradition [laboratory]; children of *age* three or four often communicate nonegocentrically in the contrived situations of the second [field] (p. 174, italics in the original).

In the typical laboratory assessment study, the children must learn the rules of the experimenter's game before they can act reciprocally or competitively; in the usual observation study, the experimenter must learn the rules of the children's games.

A recent laboratory study that was also observational helps to clarify the age-of-onset problem. Dennis MacCombie (1978) placed pairs of children (selected at random from the same classroom) into a laboratory room and gave them a free choice of several activities: a dart game, paper to draw on, musical instruments to play, an indoor basketball hoop and a mini-ball to play with, and so on. The youngest pairs of children were 5 years old, and the oldest were 9 years old. Given the wide array of interests and capabilities of children in these age groups, one might expect that a good many of them might select their "favorite" game, regardless of what the partner did. Quite the opposite. In all age-

and sex-groups studied, most pairs of children very rapidly joined the partner's activity (Figure 17-2a). Seventy percent became involved in the same activity within *10 seconds after entering the room*. And if one child switched activities, the other typically followed suit within 10 seconds (Figure 17-2b). In accord with what one might expect from observational studies of children in nonlaboratory settings, the 5-year-old pairs synchronized their activities as much as the older children, and there were no differences between boys and girls. In a companion study, MacCombie (1978) used the same procedure to demonstrate parallel effects among children as young as 2 years of age (see also Eckerman, 1979).

We might conclude that laboratory constraints do not always inhibit synchrony. Indeed, for some laboratory arrangements, such as MacCombie's (1978), the amount of reciprocity may be exaggerated relative to what might be observed in a similar relationship outside the laboratory. The facilitation would come about if the children were placed in an unfamiliar setting and left free to do "anything you want," or instructions to that effect. Under these conditions, the behavior of each child might be expected to take on heightened directional properties for the other child because there are few other reliable guides available. The general lesson is that synchrony and reciprocity are relative not only to the acts and competencies of the other person but also to the physical and social constraints of the context in which the observations are made. A corollary is that statements about "age of onset" of interactional phenomena—including reciprocity and cooperation—are necessarily misleading in that they focus on only one attribute of a single child.

Nonreciprocity and the Escape from Synchrony

Before leaving the issues of reciprocity and development, we should note that reciprocal responding can sometimes produce unhappy and disastrous consequences. Toch's (1969) accounts of how men escalate to murderous violence is a case in point. If ill-tempered acts of children inevitably· elicited negative and abusive reactions in parents, and this in turn triggered further hateful reactions in children, survival would be hardly possible (or worth the effort). What protects us from a continuous round-robin of aggression? Children indeed have a strong tendency to reciprocate negative acts as well as positive ones. Although it is constructive to focus on the beneficial consequences of the reciprocity principle, it would be ill-advised not to attend as well to its undesirable outcomes.

Perhaps the problem of social development is not to achieve synchrony—that is assured in early infancy—but to escape from its constraints. Failure to match one's responses to another's, and the ability to select alternative pathways that do not escalate in intensity, become significant accomplishments for the person as he or she approaches maturity. To achieve consistency, the child must be able at some points to escape the boundaries of reciprocity (Chapter 22).

Some Implications for Moral Behavior Development

The progress that has been made in the understanding of reciprocal processes has provided a new perspective on the problem of how moral behaviors and attitudes develop. "Honesty," "altruism," and "selfishness" refer to "prosocial" actions and intentions that are clearly basic to the human condition. Unfortunately the terms also carry with them considerable surplus meaning, including value judgments about the actions and emotions to which they refer. This seems to be another instance in which the terms that we have available to identify important actions may not be the best vehicles for understanding how they develop. In this section we will examine the development of prosocial activities and interchanges (later, in Chapter 20, we will take up the issue of the development of moral judgments).

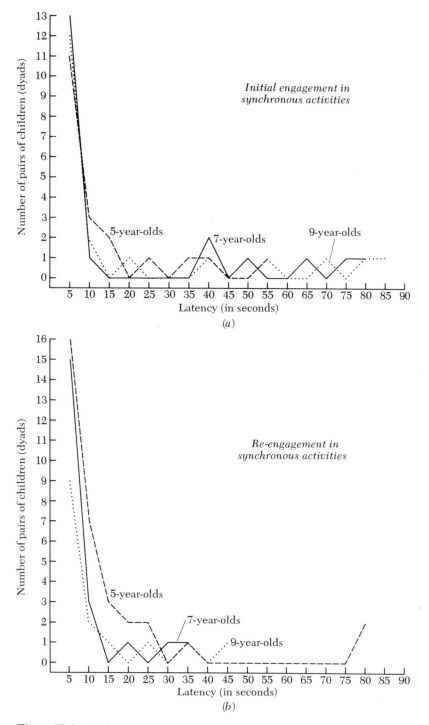

Figure 17-2. (*a*) Latency to joint participation in an activity among children who have been placed in pairs in an experimental room. (*b*) Latency to join in new activity if one member of the pair switches within the first minute in the experimental setting (from D. J. MacCombie, 1978, with permission).

The Specificity of Moral Conduct

The foundational studies on the behavioral development of honesty, altruism, and kindness were completed some 50 years ago in the United States by
Hugh Hartshorne and Mark May (1928). The studies, funded by the Institute for Religious and Social
Education, had as one of their primary aims the
assessment of the effectiveness of the institutions of
society (such as churches, Sunday schools, service
organizations) in supporting these values and the determination of how they might do their work better.
The first problem for Hartshorne and May was to
develop a technique for measuring such characteristics in children. Previous investigations had relied
primarily upon questionnaires, a procedure that
Hartshorne and May rejected partly on the grounds
that the child's answers may have revealed only
how capable he was of determining what was expected of him, and how aware he was of their purpose. A better criterion, they proposed, was the
child's actual conduct. Following this reasoning,
they attempted to devise tests that seemed, at least
on the surface, to measure several aspects of morality and integrity. Hence "honesty" was measured by
the child's truthfulness and resistance to cheating in
various settings, and charity and altruism were assessed by the child's generosity under different circumstances. The general method is illustrated by
one of the tests of "honesty," which I summarize
here:

> The child was brought into the gym and told
> about a school competition for physical fitness,
> where the "fittest" boys and girls would receive
> medals and other prizes. Then the youngster was
> given the tasks, one of which involved "chinning"
> himself. On the first trial, in front of the examiner,
> the child chinned himself as many times as he
> could. Finishing that, the now-fatigued youngster
> was instructed, "Now, while I attend to the next
> boy, you can go ahead and see how many times
> you can chin. You may have two trials. Remem-
> ber what you did on each trial. The best record
> counts." However, the immediate fatigue effect
> in this activity is so great that improvement after

> the first trial would be improbable. To the extent
> that a significant increase is later reported by the
> child, the probability that he "fudged" the truth
> is very high.

Other tests measured cheating more directly (as by
counting the number of times the child changed his
scores on an intelligence test).

Over 10,000 children were tested, and some retested, to determine their honesty, generosity, and
service to others. The child's scores on each test
were correlated with the others, and with the
child's ethnic, sociocultural, familial, and religious
background. However, this exhaustive attempt to
identify the roots of honest and altruistic behavior
floundered at the outset. The investigators found
that the characteristics were surprisingly specific to
the situations and relationships in which they were
measured. Although the children tended to get similar scores if they were given the same test twice,
different tests of the same trait were not correlated
very highly with each other. For example, the fact
that a child consistently cheated on athletic tests
permitted only a modest prediction of his tendency
to cheat on arithmetic and intelligence tests. The
children who cheated on the vocabulary tests were
not necessarily the ones who cheated on the arithmetic tests, and vice-versa.

On the basis of these data, Hartshorne and May
concluded:

> Even after the principle of honesty is understood
> [by the child], the deceptive aspect of certain acts
> may not be noticed until one's attention is drawn
> to them. One may be meticulously honorable in
> his relations with his neighbours but steal a ride
> on the streetcar without thinking himself a thief.
> Acts are not accurately labeled because they
> were not completely analyzed. Consequently, an
> otherwise honest man may be shocked and in-
> sulted when his sharp business practices are
> called stealing or his purchase of votes, political
> corruption.

Our conclusion, then, is that an individual's
honesty or dishonesty consists of a series of acts
and attitudes to which these descriptive terms apply. The consistency with which he is honest or

dishonest is a function of the situations in which he is placed in so far as (1) these situations have common elements, (2) he has learned to be honest or dishonest in them, and (3) he has become aware of their honest or dishonest implications or consequences (p. 380).

According to Hartshorne and May (1928), the most powerful determinants of moral conduct were to be found in the immediate situation (which included the actual constraints in the setting, the prevalent attitudes about the behaviors, and the child's interpretation or awareness of the implications of his actions in the setting). Various experimental findings seemed consistent with that generalization. Hartshorne and May found, for instance, that cheating on a given test could be controlled by varying such factors as likelihood of detection, ease with which the dishonest act could be performed, and whether or not other children cheated. Reciprocal controls were implicated by the finding that dishonesty was five to ten times more frequent in some classrooms than in others. But not all of the controls were external and situational; certain internal factors (including task competence and intelligence) were associated with honesty across situations. Hence the more competent the child was in performing a given activity, the less likely he was to be dishonest.

The sheer variability of the scores—that is, the fact that one and the same child may be judged honest on the vocabulary test, dishonest on the "chinning" test, and a "fudger" on party games—works against finding consistent relationships with some stable quality of the individual or his background. For this reason, it should not be surprising that negligible correlations were obtained between the child's test scores and such factors as Sunday school attendance, service club membership, and other social obligations.

Specificity Reconsidered

Hartshorne and May's *Studies in the Nature of Character* (1928) remains controversial even after half a century, despite repeated replication (Dudycha, 1936; Lehmann and Whitty, 1934). A major problem, as Bem and Allen (1974) have observed, is that the findings defy intuition. Most persons *feel* that there is a strong continuity in their actions and motives, especially those that reflect basic values. Hence the results have been especially puzzling, although sophisticated re-evaluations of the work seem to yield conclusions that were not greatly different from the original ones. One of the problems in the original work is that the investigators may have used statistical procedures that underestimated the generality of the characteristics. A careful statistical reanalysis of the original data was completed by Roger Burton (1963). Using more powerful techniques of statistical analysis than were available in 1928, Burton factor-analyzed the original correlational matrices. He found that commonalities across measures were higher in the recalculated analysis than in the original one, indicating that children who were honest in one situation were more likely than chance to be honest in another situation. However, the commonalities across settings were still only modest.

Burton concluded that stable individual differences accounted for a statistically reliable, but proportionally small, source of variance. This "small" effect is, as we shall see, of some importance in providing a basis for making judgments as to whether a person is kind or unkind, honest or dishonest, and altruistic or selfish.

Studies that have adopted measures similar to those of Hartshorne and May have, for the most part, yielded conclusions similar to theirs [Bem and Allen (1974) discuss the evidence, as does Mischel (1973)]. But the measures employed make a difference. If one does not use measures of the child's actual *conduct* in situations but employs instead *ratings* made by observers, there is greater stability in differences between individuals. That is, if one asks human judges to make an overall rating of the child's "helpfulness" or "concern for others," one obtains better cross-situational predictions (as to whether child A will be judged as more helpful than child B) than if one attempts to predict only on the basis of the child's actual conduct in the two situations.

Why should ratings yield greater consistency than measures of actual behavior? At least part of the answer seems to lie in the capabilities of humans to duplicate the feat of Burton's (1963) statistical analysis, but to do it with even greater accuracy because they have more information available. That is, judges apparently take into account the powerful contextual and reciprocal processes that control the child's behavior in the situation, and they adjust for these constraints in making ratings. Direct observations of behavior make no such adjustments. Thus "conduct" may provide a good measure of what the child actually does but a poor measure of what may be enduring, idiosyncratic dispositions (see Chapter 22).

Developing a Concern for Others

Now that some uncertainty has been removed on whether general dispositions contribute to the child's interchanges, we can return to the question that was posed 50 years ago and is still relevant today: How can one encourage children to have a concern for the welfare of others? Marion Yarrow and her colleagues at the National Institute of Mental Health provide one answer to this question in their attempt to instill in preschool children 3½ to 5½ years of age a helpful, sympathetic orientation toward others. These investigators (Yarrow, Scott, and Waxler, 1973) point out that altruism is not a specific form of behavior; rather, it includes a "diversity of responses—helping, sharing, defending, rescuing, sympathizing, and undoubtedly more" (p. 241). They contrasted a variety of techniques, each of which on the surface might be expected to increase the child's concern for others. They ranged from simple make-believe incidents performed in a diarama (miniature play theater, similar to a dollhouse) where the "teacher" expressed feelings and acts of helpfulness, to contrived incidents where the

child was given direct training in helping to relieve distress in others. Yarrow et al. (1973) found that the training was effective in heightening the children's tendency to give help or show concern, but that most of the effects were specific to the materials on which the training had been given. That is, if the child was trained to be helpful on the diarama, he was likely to be helpful if tested on the diarama but not if he were tested elsewhere, such as in real-life distress situations. In the light of the specificity findings of Hartshorne and May, such limited effects of training should not be surprising.

But not all of the outcomes were specific ones. If the children had been given a combination of all training procedures, plus an additional two weeks of interaction with a teacher who herself expressed a sympathetic and helpful attitude, they exhibited a generalized tendency to show sympathetic concern for other persons. That is, kindly interactions in themselves were not sufficient, nor was special didactic training alone effective: the combination was required. Yarrow et al. thus conclude that "only a very generalized form of altruism in the adult led to generalized altruism in the child" (p. 255).

At first it appears that there is a wide gulf between the early specificity conclusion of Hartshorne and May (1928) and those of Yarrow et al. (1973). But is it really wide? Recall that the earlier investigators proposed that honest behavior could generalize if (1) the child had learned the relevant standards and the actions that correspond to those standards, and (2) if the child was aware of their application in a given situation and relationship. Yarrow and her colleagues seem to have found support for those conclusions. If the training was specific, so were the outcomes in the child's later behaviors. But if the children were given ample experience in interchanges where considerable concern had been shown for their own welfare, and if the children were given direct tuition and guidance as to when and where "altruistic" concern should be demonstrated, then the effects generalized. Apparently an integration of behavior with the child's understanding as to when the behavior is appropriate is necessary for generalized effects to be demonstrated.

Is that all? Recent attempts to come to grips with the problem of the development of a concern for others have implicated the roles of the emotional reaction of the child and the extent to which the child identifies with the emotional state of the other ("empathy"). Accordingly, Martin Hoffman (1975) has proposed that altruistic actions arise from a strong empathy for the plight of other persons. Without a sympathetic emotional response in the child, the likelihood of altruistic action would presumably be diminished. As Hoffman (1975) points out, there is some evidence that children one and two years of age can respond sympathetically to other persons. According to Hoffman, if children perform acts that relieve distress in persons with whom they sympathize, both child and recipient benefit. The original state of arousal in the "other" may be reduced, and the sympathetic arousal in the child may be diminished. As children develop competencies in responding to the needs of others, they can be guided by a strong motive to exercise these skills in helping them (see also Aronfreed, 1968).

Hoffman's proposal reminds us again of the hazards of divorcing the child's actions from the cognitive and emotional states that support the actions. He also points up the need to clarify how emotional states develop, and how these states are linked to the occurrence of behaviors. However, the story is still incomplete. Milgram (1974) and others find that feelings of empathy do not lead one always to help others, and that helping others is not always associated with sympathetic distress.

The Flow of Control: What Determines Directionality?

Now we will turn to a question on the flow of interactional control that has been implicit in much of the content of this chapter: Who—or what—determines the nature of an interchange when persons of different response dispositions are brought together? In other words, who "calls the shots" (i.e., determines the course of the relationship)—the child who turns his other cheek or the child who smites it? In dealing with the matter and the issues that it raises, one should first review the more general controls on the nature of interchanges.

The Regulation of Social Patterns

Interpersonal events provide only one class of events (albeit an important class) that contributes to the ongoing organization of social behavior. The nature of an interaction may also be determined by internal constraints that operate on one or both members of the relationship, or by noninteractional external physical and cultural constraints. Both kinds of control can influence directionality, depending on which features of the relationship one chooses to focus upon. To illustrate, an infant's behavior is typically less likely to change because of social stimulation than is the mother's, *within* a given interchange. Because the neonate has fewer alternative action patterns available, the mother adjusts more to the baby (to his movement patterns, vocalizations, facial expressions) than vice-versa. But as Schaffer (1977) points out, mothers routinely produce highly significant changes in the infant's internal condition by effecting changes in his state (as by feeding, placing in a bath or crib, changing diapers). Who then controls whom? In this relationship, the answer depends on which aspects of the interchange one analyzes: the momentary behaviorial adjustments within the interchange or the changes in state. In the first instance, it is often the infant who controls by virtue of his own internal constraints and those that he places on the adult; in the second, it is usually the mother who controls by virtue of how she "designs" the world to which the infant adapts.

Nor are extrainteractional control biases necessarily biological or physical. In relationships where there are clear discrepancies between the social roles of the participants—teacher-pupil, therapist-patient, father-son, older-younger—societal biases can support the dominance of one individual's acts relative to another. Though the internal course of such interchanges may be bidirectional—as in the mother-infant relationship—its major themes and course can be determined unequally by virtue of societal expectations and institutional constraints that operate on all members of the interchange. On a broader scale of social organization, the nature of the social system and the range of interchanges favored by it reflect political, economic, and ecological constraints.

A descriptive summary of the potential sources of regulation of interactional behaviors is provided in Table 17-2 and Figure 17-3. The diagram shows that the interactional sequences that one observes are in fact regulated by internal, organismic events of the various participants as well as by contextual and social systems rules (in addition to the actions and expectations that the interchange generates in each participant).

To simplify matters, in Figure 17-3 I have plotted an interchange that consists of only two children to illustrate how it is embedded in social context (including the supervisory-controlling role of other persons, the physical setting, and the rules of the social system) as well as in an organismic context (the developmental status of each child and their momentary status and enduring dispositions). The children, say, could be in a classroom, the "other" could be a teacher, and the social system could be

Table 17-2. Contributors to interchange regulation and organization: some illustrative influences.

Internal Constraints	→	Interactional Constraints	→	Contextual Constraints	→	Social System Constraints
Developmental status (ability to form expectations and to perform actions)		Interpersonal acts (momentary actions of each child, and interpretation given to them by the other)		Physical setting (manipulanda available to support interchanges)		Prescriptions and proscriptions (societal rules for acceptable interchanges shared by all members of the relationship)
Personal dispositions (individual differences in reactivity, intelligence, personality, and style)		Interactional theme (whether activity is relatively noninteractive, such as reading or daydreaming, or interactive, such as conversations and play)		Contextual discriminanda (background cues that support and direct the occurrence of particular interchanges)		Ecological considerations (including economic and political factors) that apply to entire system
Momentary status (short-term fluctuations in state or activity readiness for each person; biological rhythm of each interactor)		Interactional relationship (whether between older and younger child, peers, parent-infant, and so on)		Social agents (presence of other persons, including teachers, parents, peers who are not directly involved in the interchange but who serve as catalysts for synchrony)		Roles and role behaviors (societal guides for who performs what behaviors in any given interchange, according to sex, age, position, and so on)

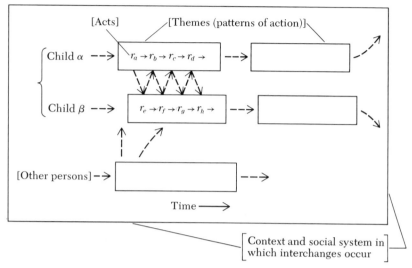

Figure 17-3. The embeddedness of interchanges. The regulatory properties of another person's acts are relative to the immediate context (social/nonsocial) and the broader societal system, as well as to the nature of an ongoing theme of activity itself and to each person's internal constraints (see also Table 17-2).

the rules and conventions that are shared among all of the participants. Or it could be in the home, where the children are siblings and the "other" is a parent. (Table 17-2 illustrates some of the major sources of regulations.)

Recognition of the multiple sources of interchange control helps to make explicit that interchange analysis requires attention to macrosocial as well as internal events. The lesson is that narrow focus on the details of interchanges can be, for most purposes, incomplete and misleading.

The Competition Between Social Patterns

If an interchange can be shown to be regulated wholly by noninteractional factors, whether organismic, contextual, or societal, directionality of interactional control is not an issue. Typically, however, such constraints permit ample flexibility within the relationship so that the "theme" of the interchange can be determined by one or the other participant.

And there is considerable room for competition when, say, two peers are brought together into a new relationship, or when previously established social roles (between parent and child) undergo modification in the course of normal development.

The empirical data on the "flow of control" issue are limited, but they suggest some overall pattern. Studies of children in middle and early childhood indicate that:

1. The more active child influences the less active one rather than vice-versa (Kaspar and Lowenstein, 1971).
2. The child who performs salient, vigorous acts tends to be more influential than the child who does not (Hall, 1973; D. Patterson, 1976).
3. "Gleeful" acts promote further "glee" and disruption on the part of preschool children (L. Sherman, 1975; S. Sherman, 1975).
4. Coercive and punitive acts tend, in general, to dominate over quiet and nonassertive ones (Parke, 1977b; Patterson, 1979).

5.   Children actively recruit each other's participation. Attempts may be made, for example, to make the ongoing activity more attractive so the other child won't change to a new one, or by inviting, entreating, or coercing the other child to join them in a new activity (MacCombie, 1978).

The theoretical proposition that seems relevant to the direction-of-effects problem can be derived from the interpersonal bias hypothesis (that social events are more salient, intrusive, and more readily enmeshed than nonsocial ones). A corollary of the bias hypothesis is that social events themselves should differ in terms of their effectivensss in ordering and organizing social behavior. Specifically, if two children are engaged in different activities immediately prior to entering an interchange, and their activities differ in terms of salience, intrusiveness, or coerciveness, then the activity that they adopt together should be the one that ranks highest on these dimensions.

How well do the actual findings fare with respect to what one might expect on theoretical grounds? Reasonably well, if one takes into account (1) the meager data that are available on the problem, and (2) the elementary nature of the relevant theory. Exactly how elementary the proposition is can be appreciated if one assumes that the corollary is universally applicable. What would then keep all relationships from giving way to the most vigorous and coercive theme? Such considerations point up the necessity for viewing interactions in terms of the other regulatory forces that operate, including constraints in the social and ecological context.

A Developmental Perspective on Synchrony

Research of the past decade has provided a fresh perspective on the issues of interpersonal organization and directionality. Seven key points of this perspective are:

1.   Behavior is organized throughout development from the prenatal period onward. Organization is not something that the child must develop or achieve in his behavior; it is inherent in living.

2.   At each stage of ontogeny, behavior organization has multiple sources. In postnatal development, it reflects the integrated operation of internal, intraorganismic sources with extraorganismic ones (including constraints provided by interactional events, the context, and the social system). Hence behavior organization does not necessarily depend on the presence of social stimuli, even though they become of increasing importance in development in directing the child's activities.

3.   A strong bias toward social synchrony was presumably adaptive in the evolution of human beings (and for other species with similar adaptive demands). Among other things, the bias facilitates survival in infancy, reproduction at maturity, and communication at all stages.

4.   From birth onward, social acts tend to play a key role in behavior organization because they are (a) more readily enmeshed with ongoing activities of the child, and (b) are more compelling (salient, intrusive) than are nonsocial events.

5.   A corollary of the preceding point is relevant to the problem of the directionality of children's activities when other, noninterpersonal sources of internal and external control are roughly equivalent. Accordingly, more readily enmeshed, salient, and/or coercive patterns should usually dominate over patterns that rank lower on these dimensions.

6.   Once two persons are synchronized in the performance of an activity, reciprocity (i.e., enhanced similarity) is a typical though not inevitable outcome. It is typical because synchronization usually elicits further mutual similarities on emotional, communicative, and/or motor dimensions in order for each person to become more adequately fitted to (enmeshed in) the ongoing behaviors of the other. However, reciprocity is not inevitable; synchronization may permit (or even require) complementary acts by the other person.

7.   As important as synchrony is in evolution and ontogeny, a major achievement occurs when children develop interpersonal competencies that permit them to sometimes escape from synchrony. This accomplishment is a prerequisite for interpersonal autonomy and independence; it permits the child to maintain interpersonal orientations that transcend immediate contextual and social constraints.

The preceding points outline, in a reasonably coherent fashion, the ideas that recent developmental researchers can agree upon. There remain gaps in the proposals, especially concerning the direction-of-influence issue, and the empirical evaluation of the ideas has only just begun.

Summary

Recent empirical studies on the regulation of interactions of children permit us to extend the implications of the perspective for everyday life and development. Some of the relevant findings that we covered in this chapter are as follows:

■   High levels of interactional organization, including evidence for synchrony and reciprocity, can be observed in the early maternal infant relationship, as well as other relationships in which adults are involved.

■   The developmental course of reciprocal acts depends, moreover, upon the capabilities and activities of the other person. Different developmental curves can be found, for instance, in interchanges with adults than in those with peers over the first three years of life.

■   From the third year, the acts of peers are exceedingly important in predicting the direction, nature, and outcome of an individual's activities, particularly in settings where there are no compelling external guidlines. Reciprocities are ubiquitous across response systems, appearing in linguisitic, motor, cognitive, emotional, and social patterns.

■   Differences among investigations when the capability for "reciprocal" or "cooperative" first appears in relations with peers seems to reflect basic differences in the kinds of devices employed. In "natural" everyday interchanges, evidence of peer reciprocity has been found in the second year. But in some complex laboratory (and nonlaboratory) games, the onset of cooperation and competition is considerably later.

■   "Situational specificity" has been often observed in studies of "prosocial" acts (such as helping others, kindness, honesty), presumably because of the powerful impact of external constraints (including immediate contextual and societal norms, and interpersonal actions) upon the child's actual conduct.

■   Nonetheless, significant consistencies in interpersonal conduct can be identified, and these consistencies can be enhanced by providing children with multiple interpersonal experiences and explicit tuition as to when and where the attitudes and behaviors are relevant. Generalization and continuity are not automatic, they are supported through experience.

An overview of the issues of reciprocity obviously does not provide a succinct answer to the Master's question. Perhaps the problem is that scientific analyses, no matter how refined they may become, will never reveal the only pathway to the "whole life."

IV

THEORIES AND PROCESSES OF SOCIAL DEVELOPMENT

Now that we have examined the major social adaptations that occur in the course of development, we can take a second look at the proposals that have been offered to explain the origin and plasticity of interchanges.

Four of the chapters in Part IV focus on the central orientations to social development. We will consider, in turn, the processes emphasized by psychobiological (Chapter 18), social learning (Chapter 19), cognitive-developmental (Chapter 20) and ethological (Chapter 21) theories. The concepts that have evolved reflect, in part, the intimate relationship between the aims of an orientation and the methods that it adopts. By way of introduction, you may find it useful to consult Figure 2-6 (at the end of Chapter 2). The figure provides a first approximation to the task of this section, but it is only an approximation. Closer examination of the processes assumed by each orientation is required if we are to go beyond superficial statements about their similarities and differences.

Accordingly, each of the four chapters begins with a summary of the major concepts and concerns of the orientation. To a limited extent, I have noted the "new directions" being explored (which is a risky and speculative business because of the rapid transformations now taking place). At the end of Chapters 18, 19, 20, and 21 appears a section entitled "Contributions to the Developmental Synthesis." These are not to be regarded as summary statements because they are too selective; they may be more properly viewed as a judgment on what the orientation has contributed to the emerging synthesis on social development. Taken as a whole, the propositions provide the framework for the modern orientation.

In Chapter 22, we will examine the problem of social behavior continuity and changes in children, a matter that lies at the heart of the study of social development. I regret that it was not possible to include a parallel chapter on continuity in the social development of nonhuman mammals; for the present, Chapter 5 must stand as an incomplete substitute. A central theme of this book has been that success in understanding the phenomena and processes of social continuity and change demands an integrated view of interchange patterns over time, contexts, and relationships. It seems altogether fitting, then, that we should conclude with an evaluation of this nuclear issue.

18

PSYCHOBIOLOGICAL FOUNDATIONS
OF SOCIAL DEVELOPMENT

Behavioral ontogenesis is the backbone of comparative psychology. Shortcomings in its study inevitably handicap other lines of investigation from behavioral evolution and psychogenetics to the study of individual and group behavior.

—*Schneirla (1966), p. 283*

The animal of Schneirla's studies is . . . a productively different kind of animal from the ethologist's wind-up toy, awaiting its releaser, or from the operant-behaviorist's feathered and furry computers, so susceptible to programming and read-out.

—*Piel (1970), p. 6*

In this chapter we will examine the theoretical underpinnings and implications of psychobiology for social development and evaluate some of its strengths and shortcomings. The contributions of developmental psychobiology to the developmental synthesis are summarized in the final section. I begin with the psychobiological orientation because it is generally regarded as being the principal developmental approach to social behavior. Despite its limitations—which include, unfortunately, a short shrift of child social development—it provides the foundation for the contemporary developmental perspective on social interchanges.

Holistic Theory and the Organization of Behavior

"Developmental psychobiology" is a bulky title. "Holistic theory" might be a preferred alternative label for the orientation if it were not that the term "holistic" usually introduces as much confusion as clarification. That is a pity, because the idea that it stands for is not inherently complicated; it is just unfamiliar. Holistic refers to the need to consider the organism and its behavior as a whole—not as a functioning "gene machine" that is made up of confederations of genetic elements, nor as a discrete social entity that serves an assigned role function for the society. According to the "holistic" orientation (developmental psychobiology), behavior is appropriately viewed as an integral feature of a biological-social system. Hence the key to understanding development lies in understanding how biological, interactional, and social components become fused during the course of ontogeny.

To appreciate the significance of this proposal (which as we shall find is not universally accepted), it is useful to illustrate its emergence in biology. Experimental advances in the 1920s in embryology raised questions about the validity of the two then-dominant theories of embryogenesis (actually, there were more than two, but that is another, more lengthy story). On the one hand, mechanistic models held that the end-product of development was predetermined by a genetic program, and that ontogenesis proceeded in a unidirectional, invariant fashion with information being transmitted from gene to structure to function. On the other hand, vitalism assumed that development was directed and coordinated by transcendent, goal-directed forces that were self-correcting even if the timing of the mechanism was somehow retarded, or accelerated. In a discovery that challenged both positions, Hans Spemann (1938) found that the essential "character" of living cells was highly dependent on the context in which they matured. For instance tissues that normally would become part of the skin at maturation would, if transplanted to the brain during a critical phase of embryonic development, become adequately functioning components of the nervous system in the adult animal. Hence the context of embryological development played a crucial role in determining the very structure and functions of individual cells—the end products of development were not predetermined entirely by either genetic activity or by "transcendent" forces. In this regard, von Bertalanffy (1933) wrote:

Neither of these views [mechanistic or vitalistic] is justified by the facts. We believe now that the solution of this antithesis in biology is to be sought in an organismic or system theory of the organism which, on the one hand, in opposition to machine theory, sees the essence of the organism in harmony and coordination of the processes among one another, but, on the other hand, does not interpret this coordination as Vitalism does, by means of a mystical entelechy, but through the forces immanent in the living system itself (pp. 177–178).

Accordingly, von Bertalanffy (1933) proposed that the "developmental germ is to be conceived as a unitary system" and that "the organism is not a secondary unit in which single cells play the most important role, but the primary unity and wholeness of the individual prevails in all stages of its life" (p. 179).

Although organismic theory has since become broad enough to encompass a wide range of views and problems (see von Bertalanffy, 1968), its original concern was with the question of "What directs development?" The answer, simply stated, is the organism. Development is directed by the constraints that are inherent in the relationship among elements of the living system as they act upon themselves and upon each other. These "elements" can be either cells, clusters of cells, or entire subsystems, such as those formed by hormonal processes. The kernel idea is that the development and functioning of components of the organism depend on the reciprocating system of which they form parts. The mutual regulation among components permits, among other things, the possible feedback to the original source and self-regulation.

Organismic theory was highly compatible with the Darwinian perspective of evolution as a dynamic, adaptive process. According to the organismic account, development is equally dynamic. The direction in which any component develops is not dependent solely upon its own chemical and physical properties, nor upon its own genetic program or "set-goal," but upon these properties in terms of their relationship to the organism of which they are a part. Speeman's surprising demonstrations of the plasticity of cell-structure and functions during embryogenesis provided incontrovertible proof of the value of the perspective for embryology.

The influence of the view has not been limited to embryology. The concepts of feedback, coordination, and mutual regulation rapidly became (or already were) indispensable for several areas of modern biology, from developmental neurobiology and endocrinology to physical ecology and population biology. Advances, say, in the study of hormonal function demanded an appreciation of the mutual controls that operated in the organism. At quite a different level, systems analyses of the interdependence of species and their environments provided the foundation for contemporary ecology (von Bertalanffy, 1968).

Behavior Development and Organismic Theory

The impact of the organismic perspective upon psychology was neither immediate nor pervasive. The dominant behavior theories of the time—covering the half century from about 1915 through 1965—did not consider development to be a major problem. Psychological views of learning, motivation, and cognition proceeded, for the most part, independently of movements in the biological sciences. Although there were hot disputes among proponents for the different theories of learning, they were family quarrels. As a group, most learning theories shared common assumptions about the deterministic and mechanistic nature of development (Chapter 19).

A few dissenters nonetheless pursued the implications of the view that behavior is an essential component of the organismic system, and that its development can be understood only in terms of other biological and social features of the system (Baldwin, 1902). It followed that the "system" in which the organism developed was not merely under the skin. The organization must be broadened to include feedback with other organisms and the social network. Accordingly, organismic theory becomes a special case of a more general organizational perspective on how development—including social development—proceeds.

Just as Speeman's experimental work had underscored the need for the organismic perspective in embryological development, the work of T. C. Schneirla and Z.-Y. Kuo helped to lead the way for an organizational orientation to the problems of behavioral development. The problem that Schneirla tackled was to unravel the complex social structure of army ants, one of the "truly social" species (Wilson, 1975). These insects are highly coordinated in virtually all phases of their adaptation: in their raids, where "scouts" return with up-to-date information and "lieutenants" keep the troops in line; in forming "bivouacs" for coordinated living arrangements; in feeding the young during the periods when their needs are greatest and in serving their queen with feasts at precisely the correct time in her reproductive cycle; in their migrations, which occur at optimal intervals in terms of food supply. How do the insects maintain this complex social organization? The puzzle becomes more perplexing when it is recognized that the workers are so stereotyped in the behavior that they will march themselves to death in a circular mill if they are placed on a flat surface. Nonetheless, the social organization of ants has remained stable for literally millions of years (Haskins, 1970).

Schneirla's field studies in Panama and laboratory investigations at the American Museum of Natural History provided a new insight on the origin and controls of this "intelligent" behavior. He tested the assumption that the colony organization does not arise from any one source; rather, the complex social system was seen as the outcome of the interdependence of events that occurred in the brood, workers, queen, and the ecological constraints. Schneirla identified a pattern of relationships that in their totality provided elegant support for a developmental approach. Schneirla (1971) discovered, for instance, that a primary trigger for large raids was the heightened activity of the developing larvae. The larvae emerged from the quiescent phase, their activity aroused the workers to raids, and the raids eventually led to migration. When the ontogenetic-paced activity of the brood diminished, the raids ceased and the nomadic phase ended. Similarly, the queen's reproductive periods were shown to be related to the worker and brood activity. Surplus food and worker attention is directed toward the queen when the needs of the brood diminish, thereby triggering events associated with her ovulation cycle. With respect to reproduction, Schneirla (1957) concluded: "The cyclic pattern thus is self-rearoused in a feedback fashion, the product of a reciprocal relationship between queen and colony functions, not of a timing méchanism endogenous to the queen."

Z.-Y. Kuo focused on the problem of the origin of behavior: when and how does it first arise? He was concerned with the issue of how "instinctive" behaviors in birds develop, including the highly coordinated movement, pecking, and vocalization patterns that are observed shortly after hatching. He assumed that these coordinated movements were appropriately understood in the light of organismic changes in central nervous system, morphological, *and* behavioral functions. In other words, he tested the far-fetched proposal that the behavior of the embryo provided feedback to help direct subsequent development of the chick.

The story of how Kuo explored the implications of his proposal is a fascinating one that is best told by Kuo himself (a short version is found in Kuo, 1967). He first had to overcome a number of obstacles, including the problem of how to keep embryos alive while also viewing their development inside the egg (he produced a "window" by removing the shell but keeping the internal membranes intact). Kuo then was able to plot, from the onset of gestation to hatching, all movement patterns in the egg, including the first stages of walking, pecking, and wing activity. On the basis of these observations, he concluded that the activity of the organism itself was influential in determining the direction of development, including leg coordination and pecking. Some of Kuo's speculations have not been upheld

because he did not give sufficient weight to the effects of spontaneous central nervous system innervation in producing cycles of activity and inactivity (see Oppenheim, 1973). But his conclusion that behavioral feedback controls some features of embryonic development has been strikingly confirmed. For example, failure to permit leg movement in the embryo has been found to be associated with ossification of the joints and difficulty in post-hatching locomotion (Drachman and Coulombre, 1962). Self-produced vocal calls by the embryo facilitate the development of immediate post-hatching species-preferences (Gottlieb, 1976b).

As compelling as were Schneirla's and Kuo's demonstrations of the utility of the developmental approach, they had little immediate impact upon psychological theorizing. There were doubtless several reasons for the lack of direct and early influence, not the least of which was the aversion of many psychologists to the "biological" underpinnings of the orientation. Full recognition of the orientation had to wait until behavioral theories came to grips with another biological orientation to behavior, that of ethology.

The Guiding Principles

Before dealing with the themes, issues, and shortcomings of the psychobiological approach, we should review its major principles. To call developmental psychobiology a theory, however, would be misleading. "Orientation" would be a more appropriate term, since the major contributors to the approach have not presented a cohesive theoretical model so much as a set of principles to guide the analysis of developmental phenomena.

Two of the guidelines are metatheoretical in that they deal with biases as to how explanatory concepts should be evaluated and as to how research should proceed. Schneirla and his colleagues have consistently stood for the need for parsimony in explanation. One of the problems that they find with "instinctual" explanations, for instance, is that they require special drives and dispositions to explain behaviors that might be efficiently (and parsimoniously) explained in terms of general quantitative principles of development. The second metatheoretical bias concerns the preference for induction in scientific explanation. One should begin with an analysis of a behavior's development, controls, and consequences before offering explanations about its origins and determinants. This view can be contrasted with the then-dominant psychological tradition of formal hypothesis testing, where much of the research seemed designed to *demonstrate* principles as opposed to *discovering* them.

Beyond these attitudes toward theory and research, the psychobiological orientation can be described by the following six principles:

1.   Behavior, whether social or nonsocial, is appropriately viewed in terms of an organized system, and its explanation requires a "holistic" analysis. Accordingly, T. C. Schneirla (1966) has written:

> The developmental contributions of the two complexes, maturation and experience, must be viewed as *fused* (i.e., as inseparably coalesced) at all stages in the ontogenesis of any organism. This holistic theory conceptualizes all processes of progressive organization in consecutive early stages of development as fused, coalescing maturational and experiental functions (pp. 288–289; author's emphasis).

2.   The system of which behavior is a part is not merely "organismic" but for some functions, particularly social behaviors, it must be expanded to include the acts of other organisms and the reciprocal relationships that are formed with them. Bidirectional and feedback effects can potentially occur across several levels. The basic structure-function bidirectionality in embryogenesis is seen as a special case of a more general organizational principle. Its operation can be seen as well in the synchronized activities between the individual and other organisms, and in the relationships between organisms and their environment. Behavior development is probabilistic, not fixed by genes or by early experience.

3.   There is a continuity in development, such that the organization at one stage provides the basis for organization at the next succeeding stage. This does not mean, however, that all processes persist throughout life, nor does it mean that behaviors must remain stable across stages. To the contrary, development is essentially a dynamic process that promotes reorganization and adaptation across time. J. Rosenblatt and D. Lehrman (1963) illustrate this principle when they write:

> Our approach to the analysis of the problems of maternal behavior is a developmental one. The processes underlying the organization of the behavior of an animal at any developmental age, or at any stage of a cyclically-varying pattern, appear to us to be best illuminated by analyzing the ways in which that age (or stage) influences or gives rise to succeeding ones. The relationships among those processes and influences which persist through several stages, those continuous through the life of the animal, and those specific to different stages are often complex. Their analysis involves the simultaneous consideration of events at different biological and psychological levels. These may include physiological events which are themselves organized at different levels (for example, central nervous regulation, local sensitivities and reactions, regulation of endocrine secretion, specific effects of hormones, and so on), and psychological processes of varying complexity, ranging from reaction to simple forms of stimulation to behavior patterns characterizing interindividual (that is, social) situations (p. 9).

4.   The last sentence in the above quotation points to the fourth guiding principle: the need for multiple levels of analysis. This need is a direct corollary of the assumption that there are interlocked systems associated with the control of behavior, from neurobiological events to socio-cultural ones. The investigator must be prepared to operate simul-

taneously on different levels of analysis in order to achieve an adequate account of behavioral phenomena. The spirit of the principle was captured by Kuo (1967) when he wrote:

> Thus, from the standpoint of the epigenetic behaviorist, the relationship between the behaving organism and its environment is an extremely complex and variable dynamic process. It goes deeper and beyond the molar level. As we shall see in the following chapters, *behavior* is far more than the visible muscular movements. Besides such movements the morphological aspect, the physiological (biophysical and biochemical) changes, the developmental history of the animal, and the ever-changing environmental context are interwoven events which are essential and integral parts of behavior. In our study of behavior all such events must be investigated in a coordinated way. In other words, *the study of behavior is a synthetic science* (p. 25).

5. The fifth guideline deals with the problem of generalizing one's observations. Behavioral investigators frequently compare two species with respect to some characteristic (such as aggression in monkeys and man), or they compare early behavior with later behavior in the same individuals. In such comparisons, behavior should be viewed in terms of the organization of which it is a part, and one must be as sensitive to differences as to similarities. What appears to be the "same" activity at two different stages or in two different species may be similar in only superficial properties. Seemingly the same activity (such as fighting) may have different determinants, produce different consequences, and serve different functions within the social organization. In other words, comparisons should be *polythetic* [made on the basis of the organization of which the activity is a part, not a single characteristic (Jensen, 1967)]. To illustrate, Schneirla (1966) proposed that it is inappropriate to generalize about social behavior between species that have a *biosocial* basis for social organization (with strong dependence on biological controls, such as army ants) and species that have a *psychosocial* basis for organization (with strong dependence on psychological processes, in-

cluding social interactions and learning, such as mammals).

6. The sixth and final principle is that the organism is continuously active and adaptive throughout the course of development. The embryo and neonate assimilate features of the environment to themselves, and accommodate to others. Moreover, the adaptational processes continue throughout development from birth to maturity.

Although this last principle is of great importance to the psychobiological position, it requires explication in (a) the meaning of adaptation, (b) the direction that adaptation takes in development, and (c) the limits of adaptation. The problem of meaning follows from the fact that developmental adaptation—the fitting of characteristics of organisms to their surrounds—is a relative judgment. It is relative to what system is involved and the circumstances in which adaptation is assessed. An isolate-reared animal's hormonal system, say, may be well adapted for living in a nonsocial environment but poorly adapted for social interchanges. More generally, it is meaningless to refer to an "adapted" organism, without specifying what components are adapted to what circumstances (see also "evolutionary adaptation," Chapter 21).

The second problem—that of the direction of adaptation—was answered in part by organismic theories (von Bertalanffy, 1933; 1968). The direction is toward greater "harmony" and coordination among the components of the organism. Hence an unusual component—such as a nonresponsive environment that might be provided by isolation—may require adjustments on the part of the individual's behavior to bring it into harmony with respect to present living circumstances. Similarly, the "abused" infant monkey must bring its actions into harmony with those of the punitive parent in order to adapt. The assumption of continuing adaptation also suggests that new levels of performance can be achieved, if the environment requires it and the internal constraints of the organism permit it.

This brings us to the third problem—the limits of developmental adaptation. How far can the system be moved from what is "normal" for the species? Such a question has not been a critical problem for most psychobiological investigators because the question has simply not seemed to be relevant for their primary experimental work, which was to trace the course of normal development. The unstated assumption seems to have been that normal was in fact optimal, so there would be scant reason to attempt to improve upon it. Kuo, a significant figure in this orientation, emphasized the potential malleability of behavior in development. He argued that not all activities (or organisms) are equally open to external influence, nor are all activities equally susceptible to influence at different developmental stages (Kuo, 1967). Nonetheless, Kuo has been commonly (and unfairly) accused of arguing that an organism's behavior is infinitely malleable during the course of development (see, for instance, Eibl-Eibesfeldt, 1975).

Major Themes: Innateness, Normal Development, and Neophenotypes

Nowadays, investigators of animal social development subscribe to most, if not all, of the tenets of the organismic approach. An attempt to review all of the major themes and accomplishments of the approach would therefore be beyond the scope of this volume. Nonetheless, there are three areas of concern that help to illustrate what the developmental psychobiological orientation stands for, and what it stands against. These areas are the role of the concept of innateness, the nature of "normal" development, and the establishment of neophenotypes.

Innate, Developed, or Both

I mentioned earlier that the emergence of modern conceptions of ethology helped to bring developmental psychobiology to the forefront. The dispute revolved around the question of how one might explain the biological basis of behavior: from an evolutionary perspective in terms of innate, inherited dispositions and pre-programmed individual differences, or from a developmental perspective, in terms of the processes that control behavior during the lifetime of the individual.

Schneirla, Kuo, and their colleagues stood firmly against what they considered to be simplistic instinctive explanations of such behaviors as aggression, social attachment, and maternal care. They argued that the concept of instinct provided answers at just the point that more questions were called for.

Daniel Lehrman's early contribution on this matter opened the debate. He wrote:

> The "instinct" is obviously not present in the zygote. Just as obviously it is present in the behavior of the animal after the appropriate age. The problem for the investigator who wishes to make a closer analysis of behavior is: how did this behavior come about? The use of "explanatory" categories such as "innate" and "genetically fixed" obscures the necessity of investigating developmental *processes* in order to gain insight into the actual mechanisms of behavior and their interrelations. The problem of development is the problem of the development of new *structures* and activity *patterns* from the resolution of the interaction of existing ones, within the organism and its internal environment, and between the organism and its outer environment. At any stage of development, the new features emerge from the interactions within the *current* stage and between the *current* stage and the environment. The interaction out of which the organism develops is *not* one, as is so often said, between heredity and environment. It is between *organism* and environment! And the organism is different at each different stage of its development (Lehrman, 1953, p. 345).

On the other side of the fence (and the Atlantic), ethologists pointed to the primacy of evolution in determining behavior. Just as morphological features of the organism can become adapted through successive generations, so can social activities, particularly if they were related to the survival and procreation. Hence a major concern of ethology, in the early stages, was to identify innate and instinctive behavioral dispositions, and to distinguish between *behavioral homologies* and *behavioral analogies*. (Behavioral homologies refer to similarities between species that are due to a common ancestry; behavioral analogies are similarities between species that arise because of similar adaptational requirements rather than similar ancestry.) Studies in behavioral evolution and behavioral genetics have demonstrated overwhelming support for the basic proposition that virtually *any* behavioral disposition in animals can be shown to be influenced by evolutionary adaptations.

How then was the dispute resolved? Or can it be? In a most sensitive and thoughtful review of the problem written some seventeen years after the paper quoted above, Lehrman (1970) observed that much of the debate between ethologists and psychobiologists hinged on "differences in their conception of what is an important problem and what is a trivial one or rather what is an interesting problem and what is an uninteresting one" (p. 19). The major difference was that the developmental psychobiologists were concerned with the functional and immediate determinants of behavior, and ethologists were concerned with its evolutionary determinants. The two levels are sometimes called *proximal* and *ultimate* levels of explanation.

The difference between the aims and goals of developmental psychobiologists and those of ethologists reflected a more general schism in biology between functional and evolutionary biologists. As E. O. Wilson (1975) put it, the two groups usually behave as if they dwell in different lands. The aim of the functional biologist is to find out how the organism functions, and his tools in the search are anatomical, biochemical, neural embryological, and behavioral analyses. His goal is to identify proximal causes of the phenomena. Evolutionary biologists, on the other hand, try to find out why and how the machinery evolved in phylogeny. Its goal is to elucidate how species respond to environmental stresses by genetic evolution through natural selection. For evolutionary biology, the aim is to clarify "ultimate causation." Since the relationship between the time scales of the two levels of analysis is remote—a single organism's lifetime or milliseconds versus a species' "lifetime" or eons—Wilson understandably despairs of their being linked in the foreseeable future.

Happily, contemporary psychobiologists and ethologists are more optimistic about the possible linkages (see Chapter 21). Indeed, the resolution to the "nature-nurture" issue lies in the recognition that developmental and evolutionary explanations must support each other and that information from one level of analysis can be of great value in guiding and correcting work on the other level (Hinde, 1970).

Normal Development

Recent progress in understanding the origins of "instinctive" behavior patterns has been one of the causes for optimism. Following rigorous inductive procedures, psychobiological investigators have been able to unravel the developmental controls of a wide range of behavior patterns, from reproduction in the ring-dove to maternal behavior in rats and social preferences of kittens. The aim of the analyses was to take up where the evolutionary concepts of innate or fixed action patterns left off, namely, to provide an account of the immediate controls of the activity in the organism's life history.

Investigators whose work with children fit within the framework of developmental psychobiology have chosen, for the most part, to study nonverbal infants. Studies of the normal, adaptive features of development by Rheingold, Hay, and West (1976), for example, have been of great importance in clarifying the ontogeny of exploratory and sharing behaviors. The orientation is less often represented in studies of older children, however. An important exception is the longitudinal work of Thomas, Chess, and Birch (1968), where an explicit attempt was made to clarify the nature of the transactions that occur from infancy through childhood (see Chapter 22).

Neophenotypes

One of the more provocative implications of the organismic-organizational orientation is that individuals become in development more perfectly fitted to their immediate surrounds. As I mentioned earlier, there has been relatively little interest among psychobiological investigators in pursuing the possibilities of this implication beyond its application to the "fine tuning" of species-typical behaviors.

Nonetheless, Z.-Y. Kuo has boldly argued that one of the main aims of the developmental approach should be the establishment of new ways of adapting, or *neophenotypes*. His proposal is that appropriate arrangements of contextual conditions of rearing and living can produce drastic modifications in "typical" behaviors. Once established, they can profoundly influence members of the next generation by virtue of the values, attitudes, and/or behaviors of the parents. Kuo in fact demonstrated the possible "cultural" transmission of food preferences and some social behaviors. But the broader implications of the psychobiological orientation for enhancing social adaptation have been rarely explored, even though this issue touches as directly upon the peculiar problems of human beings as does any other concern of the approach. Why this avenue of research has not been more vigorously explored remains a mystery.

Incompleteness of the Developmental Psychobiological Orientation

Shortcomings in the psychobiological formulation are primarily ones of omission, or incompleteness. One of the reasons for a big gap in the orientation has been that the problems of social development in children beyond infancy have seldom been explored by investigators operating within this theoretical framework. Hence the view is least complete in those areas that child developmentalists find most important. Perhaps it is for this reason that its powerful implications for child social development have often been overlooked.

Two other unsolved problems for the orientation deserve attention: the clarification of how experiences influence later social adaptation, and how ontogeny and phylogeny are related.

Experience and Learning

Psychobiologists have been reluctant to tackle the esoteric concepts of learning. Consequently, there is a failure to specify how learning processes interact with psychobiological ones. Kuo (1967) has taken the most extreme position on this issue by arguing that concepts of learning have outlived their usefulness. In a similar vein, Gottlieb (1976b) concludes that "traditional forms of learning (habituation, conditioning, and the like) have not proven very useful in explaining the species-typical development of behavior . . ." (p. 232).

As Schneirla (1966) saw it, the problem has been that "experience" has been too narrowly defined in the past so that it included only "learning" effects. He observed that experience could have effects on biological structures and their organization, via changes in hormonal states, physical structures, and sensory responsiveness. Nonetheless, learning cannot be removed from the picture, for it is one of the routes by which experience has major effects in "psychosocial" animals.

Psychobiological studies of sexual and maternal activities have pointed to the large carry-over effects of prior experience. Once an activity has become organized by the experience of the young animal's having performed it, the activity often becomes easier to elicit and harder to eliminate. Rosenblatt (1975) has thus proposed that a distinction must be made between the conditions that are required to establish an activity, such as sexual behavior or maternal caretaking, and those that are required for eliciting the activity once it has been established. Hormonal states that are associated with parturition clearly accelerate the initial establishment of maternal care patterns in several species. But once the activities occur, they are maintained with minimal hormonal contributions. Similarly, castration has different effects on sexual performance in male cats and dogs, depending on their prior sexual experience (Rosenblatt, 1965). Animals that had mated prior to castration typically continue to perform adequately (for varying periods of time) even after gonad removal. But animals with no mating experience prior to castration tend never to establish the activity. Whether these "experience" induced effects are due to learning or other biological-structural consequences of the experience has not yet been determined.

Developmental psychobiologists are clearly tempted to become more precise about the nature of experience and learning processes in development (Bateson, 1976; Gottlieb, 1976a). Hence Gottlieb (1976a) introduced the distinction between the kinds of influences that experience may have upon behavior—facilitation, maintenance, and induction. These terms describe the three major possible roles of experience: to facilitate the appearance of some function in ontogeny, to maintain a function in such a way as to keep it on course in ontogeny, and to induce or be necessary for the introduction of a function in ontogeny. Although these terms don't tell how or why experience has these effects, they provide a new window through which one can observe learning and nonlearning processes.

Parallels in Ontogeny and Phylogeny

Developmental psychobiologists have been accused, with some justification, of having ignored the problems of phylogeny (Lorenz, 1965). The justification is not complete, however. Schneirla (1966) made the "theoretical considerations of probable evolu-

tionary relationships" a fundamental guide for directing studies of ontogenesis. Similarly, Lehrman (1970) points out that he and others in the developmental psychobiological tradition have been sensitive to the operation of evolutionary factors in all features of their work. While these counterarguments have merit, there has been a clear failure among psychobiologists to come to grips with a problem central to behavioral evolution: What is the relationship between ontogeny and phylogeny?

The answer, for at least some who view the issue from an evolutionary perspective, is that the course of development as well as its major outcomes are determined by evolutionary forces. Accordingly, much of social development is "pre-programmed" according to a "genetic blueprint." Bowlby's (1973) and Ainsworth's (1972) view of social attachment is consistent with such a view, and this is related to their belief that a disruption of the natural, preadapted course is likely to produce negative consequences. Dawkins (1976) argues that the details of the developmental process are "irrelevant to evolutionary considerations" (p. 66).

The "phylogeny determining ontogeny" view can be contrasted with de Beer's (1958) concept that the relationship should be the other way around; that is, variations in ontogenesis can provide the essential mechanisms for evolutionary change. How can ontogeny influence phylogeny? According to one evolutionary hypothesis, major changes in the phyletic series may be produced by modest *heterochronies*, or alterations in the rate of maturation of particular organismic features (de Beer, 1958; Gould, 1977). Changes in timing can be multiplied in development so as to produce massive changes in structure and function. For instance, it has been proposed that a key event in the phylogeny of human beings has been the delay in the closing of the sutures of the skull of man, relative to the timing of skull closure in man's primate ancestors. This *neoteny* (retention of an infantile characteristic of the ancestral species into the adulthood of the descendant) presumably permitted the human brain to continue to develop through adolescence and into early adulthood, thereby providing the preconditions for a complex neural network and distinctively human capabilities. Another illustration of the neotenization of behavior might include the evolution of species and sex differences in bighorn sheep (the descendant species retain some infantile characteristics of the ancestral species, and females retain many of the immature characteristics of males; see Geist, 1971). The general view that ontogeny can affect phylogeny through variations in maturational timing can be diagrammed as

$$\triangle \text{ Ontogeny} \longrightarrow \triangle \text{ Phylogeny}$$

The problem remains for developmental psychobiologists to specify precisely what relations may exist between developmental timing (heterochrony) and changes in behavioral evolution. One provocation proposal has been that the plasticity of human behavior reflects a more general "syndrome of immaturity" that has been produced by the neotenization of man's ancestors (Mason, 1979). With the onset of maturity delayed, human beings can have more time to learn complex patterns of social organization and develop more varied cognitive skills. "Immaturity" benefits the organism by extending the periods that it is plastic and susceptible to environmental influences. While the proposal is an attractive one, it raises the question of whether "immaturity" in itself is sufficient. There are, for instance, ample cases of extended immaturity in nonhuman species without any apparent gain in their social complexity or cognitive competence.

Another proposal is suggested by the effects of heterochrony on component characters (subsystems) of the organism and considering how these effects may contribute to producing a truly novel organism. Neoteny (extended immaturity) is only one outcome that changes in developmental timing can produce; the appearance of component characters can also be *accelerated* (can develop sooner in the descendant species than in the ancestral one). The neotenization of key components and the acceleration of others can produce novel behavioral outcomes. For instance, human beings are not merely

immature longer than the ancestral species; they can perform some "adult" discriminations of primates at a very early age (2–3 years). Hence human language could result from the happy combination of a morphological neoteny (which promotes high flexibility of activity and movement) combined with a cognitive acceleration (which promotes symbolic learning and discrimination).

Both proposals are speculative, and which one is correct remains to be determined. However, the more general point on evolution is not speculative (Gould, 1977; King and Wilson, 1975). Modest differences in the timing of the onset of components can produce marked changes (in structure and behavior) in the successive phases of the individual's life and in successive generations of the species. The unsolved problem for developmental psychobiology is to specify how this phenomenon relates to behavioral evolution.

Contributions to the Developmental Synthesis

Developmental psychobiology has required a drastic shift in traditional perspectives on social development because of its insistence that social behavior should be viewed as one component of an organismic-organizational system. The shift brought about a re-evaluation of the usefulness of static, unidirectional concepts of learning on the one hand and preadapted, fixed concepts of behavioral evolution and early experience on the other. The clash in ideas has yielded a fresh approach to the problem of how social behaviors become initially established.

Our summary of the major points of psychobiology may have been easier if they had been given in axiomatic form by the theorists themselves. They were not. The investigators whom I have called developmental psychobiologists have been more concerned with demonstrating the power of their ideas in the inductive analysis of phenomena than with theory building. They first of all share a commitment to rigorous induction in scientific work and to parsimony in the evaluation of theoretical constructs. To guide investigations, the orientation has adopted the following six principles on the nature of development:

■ Behavior is appropriately viewed in terms of an organized system, and its explanation requires a "holistic" analysis.

■ In the developmental analysis of social interactions and social organization, intraorganismic factors often play a primary role in eliciting and maintaining changes while, conversely, social interchanges and other experiences feedback to modify biological states and behavior potentials.

■ There is a continuity in development, such that the organization at one stage provides the basis for organization at the next succeeding stage.

■ Because of the holistic nature of development, multiple levels of analysis are required; the study of behavior is a synthetic science.

■ Comparisons across species, or across time, require a polythetic analysis (attention to the dissimilarities as well as the similarities of the functions that a given pattern plays in the social organization of which it is a part).

■ The organism is continuously adaptive and active throughout the course of development, not merely in its early stages; hence development continues to be bidirectional and probabilistic throughout the lifespan.

These principles capture much of what is current in contemporary views of the developing organism, whether the references are from human infancy or from animal behavior. In addition, a major theme of the developmental psychobiological orientation has been the explanation in precise, developmental terms of the determinants of various kinds of normal behavior, particularly those patterns that are so universal for the species that they are called innate.

The principles provide a foundation for a theory and not a theory itself; the approach is more appropriately viewed as an orientation. In failing to deal explicitly with the issues of learning and with the problems of cognitive development in children, it falls short of a general model of social development. Developmental psychobiology also leaves open the problem of behavioral evolution and its possible parallels with development. As we shall find in the next three chapters, these issues have been the main concern of other perspectives on social development.

19

SOCIAL LEARNING THEORIES

Social learning theories have undergone radical changes in the past ten years. A major overhaul of core learning concepts was required to bring them into line with contemporary shifts in the conception of what is the essential nature of the child—from a view of the child as being an object molded by familial and cultural forces, to the view of the child as an interactive, information-processing organism capable of both influencing the environment and being influenced by it. The nature of the revisions and their implications for the developmental synthesis are the subject of this chapter.

Social learning theories have historically been the most significant force in shaping ideas about social development in children. The concepts are still crucial even though it is now generally accepted that they cannot stand alone. The plan of this chapter is to clarify first the several different orientations to social learning and to trace briefly their evolution over the past half century. To highlight the nature of the conceptual changes that have occurred, I will focus on the effects of the reformulation on two key social learning concepts—imitation and social reinforcement. After some comments on what appear to

be the most promising trends in the area, I will summarize their contributions to the emerging developmental synthesis.

Evolution of Social Learning Theories

Despite impressions to the contrary, there is no single "social learning theory"; there are several. The business of building behavior theories has been the primary occupation of a good many psychologists during the past 50 years. The problem would be less difficult if there were unanimity on the question of how organisms learn. There is not. Competing theories of animal conditioning and learning emphasize quite distinct and sometimes contradictory processes (see Hilgard and Bower, 1974). These emphases, in turn, give rise to different views on how social behaviors are established in ontogeny. The evolution of social learning theories can be divided into three different stages or "generations" (see Figure 19-1).

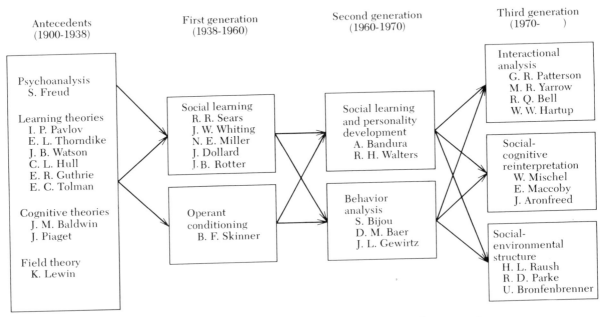

| Antecedents (1900-1938) | First generation (1938-1960) | Second generation (1960-1970) | Third generation (1970-) |

Figure 19-1. The evolution of social learning theories: some significant contributors.

First-generation social theories were basically of two types: one drawn from a synthesis of psychoanalytic concepts of personality and Hullian-Pavlovian learning ideas, and the other based on operant reinforcement principles. The synthesis came about primarily as a result of the work of a group of young theorists working at Yale University—including J. Dollard, N. Miller, R. R. Sears, O. H. Mowrer, and J. Whiting—in the late 1930's. Working within the then-dominant Hullian framework of learning, they succeeded in translating some of the more cogent psychoanalytic proposals into the language of learning theory. In the process of translation, the hypotheses were stated with sufficient precision to permit their experimental evaluation (Dollard, Doob, Miller, Mowrer, and Sears, 1939). This seminal work provided the theoretical basis for social learning accounts of child-rearing (Sears, Whiting, Nowlis, and Sears, 1953; Sears, Maccoby, and Levin, 1957; Sears, Rau, and Alpert, 1965), cross-cultural analyses (Whiting and Child, 1953), and per-

sonality development (Dollard and Miller, 1950; Miller and Dollard, 1941).

The other first-generation social learning model was that of B. F. Skinner (1953, 1971), who extended operant reinforcement principles to the problems of human behavior. Skinner developed a coherent view of man, the central assumption being that behavior can be predicted, shaped, and controlled by varying environmental reinforcement contingencies. His views, like the earlier one of J. B. Watson (1928), were boldly stated and pregnant with implications for living. In North America, Skinner's proposals have had some influence on virtually all institutions concerned with children, from families and schools to prisons and hospitals. The concept of reinforcement resonated with common sense ideas about rewards, and the methods were simple and, for some problems, remarkably effective.

Of the second-generation social learning theories, doubtless the most influential has been that formulated by Albert Bandura and Richard H. Walters and included in their pivotal monograph, *Social Learning and Personality Development* (1963). This theory has since been expanded and revised by Bandura (1965, 1969, 1971, 1973a and b), and has also been effectively applied to a wide range of therapeutic and educational problems. Although these theorists owed a debt to both first generation social learning models, they differed from them on two main issues. First, Bandura and Walters (1963) argued that social learning concepts should be closely tied to the basic phenomena and ideas of learning theory and should rely less on the mere redefinition of psychoanalytic concepts. In particular, they were wary of the motivational concepts borrowed from the psychoanalytic tradition. Second, Bandura and Walters observed that social learning explanations for behavior establishment in terms of social drive and social reinforcement were tenuous at best. They proposed that the problem of establishment could be solved by imitation or psychological modeling. The latter proposal became a cornerstone for the social learning position, a matter that we will explore in depth in the next section.

Another second-generation branch of social learning theory followed directly from the basic operant conditioning position (Bijou and Baer, 1961, 1965; Gewirtz, 1961). The position taken by these writers is appropriately viewed as second generation because it introduces concepts that had not been anticipated in the original formulations. One of the more important advances for us was the introduction of the concept of reciprocal reinforcement and control in an interchange. To put it simply, the child can reinforce the mother as well as the mother her child. This extension of the interactional model provided the impetus for much of the current work on interchanges.

The third-generation models are not as readily defined. Perhaps it is too early to expect a clear delineation of positions, or, equally likely, the trend is toward less encompassing but more precise explanations of specific phenomena. The major theoretical trends are shown in Figure 19-1, and "third-

generation" developments will be discussed later in this chapter.[1]

So much for the family tree of social learning theories. The fact that Figure 19-1 represents a kind of genealogy underscores that the models share a common intellectual ancestry. The points of similarity are as important as are the differences. First, all social learning accounts begin with the assumption that social behaviors are established, maintained, and changed primarily through learning processes. Although psychobiological processes may be acknowledged or mentioned, it is rare that social learning treatments have paid more than lip-service to developmental (maturational) controls. Second, the learning processes that have been implicated— including secondary drives, modeling, and social reinforcement—have been assumed to apply to all ages studied; there is a "general learning process" assumption (Sameroff, 1975). Third, the formulations have been evaluated almost exclusively in terms of phenomena that can be observed in children and, typically, in children who can communicate verbally. The proposals have rarely been applied to other species.

Now we can take a closer look at how social learning models have dealt with the issues of social behavior establishment, maintenance, and change.

Establishment of Social Behaviors: Learned Motives, Response Shaping, and Modeling

Establishment by Learned Drives

According to the Yale theorists and, later, Sears et al. (1953), social behavior patterns such as dependency and aggression were established as a consequence of learned motives. What, in turn, leads to

---

[1] Significant omissions from this brief overview include two pivotal volumes: N. Miller and J. Dollard's *Social Learning and Imitation* (1941); and J. B. Rotter's *Social Learning and Clinical Psychology* (1954). These books helped pave the way for the introduction of imitation and cognitive concepts into social learning theories.

the establishment of the motives? Surprisingly, this question was never satisfactorily resolved, either in the basic learning formulations of Clark Hull (1943, 1951) or in the work of social learning theorists. One of the more thoughtful attempts to come to grips with the problem appears in Sears et al. (1953). But their proposal on how the motives of dependency and aggression are learned (or unlearned) has not been pursued, and there is no need to dwell on it here (see Brown, 1961, and Bolles, 1967), for further discussions of the problem).

Despite a lack of clarity about their origins, learned drives proved to be highly flexible explanatory devices for first-generation social learning theories. They were employed to describe why children differed in aggressiveness, dependency, achievement striving, socialness, anxiety, and a host of other social behaviors. The usage was extended by taking into account that certain drives were incompatible and that anxiety could conflict with and inhibit other motives. Hence dependency-anxiety was employed to explain antisocial aggressive behavior (Bandura and Walters, 1959) and therapy failures (Cairns, 1961). But critical analysis of this usage, and other problems associated with social motivation, led to a gradual, then sharp, decline in the popularity of the concepts. What went wrong? We have earlier (in Chapters 8 and 12) commented on some of the problems, including the multidimensionality of the concepts and their failure to yield consistent relationships. Because of logical gaps in the theory, and its lack of power in predicting empirical phenomena, the concept of learned motivation has been laid aside in most modern social learning models. (But not all. For an important exception, see Feshbach's [1964] sophisticated use of the concept in the discussion of aggressive control.)

Establishment by Response Shaping

The other first-generation theory—that of B. F. Skinner—proposed a radically different solution to social pattern establishment. Skinner assumed that behaviors are established and molded by the environmental contingencies that are present when the response is organized: "operant conditioning shapes behavior as a sculptor shapes a lump of clay" (Skinner, 1953). By selective control of the reinforcement events that occur, the behavior can be gradually "sculpted" by successive approximations to a criterion state. The idea of a gradual shaping of behavior grew out of convincing demonstrations of the power of selective reinforcement to produce novel or species-atypical behaviors in pigeons, rats, piglets, and chickens. Skinner applied the concept to explain the development of "normal" behaviors in children as well, as indicated by the following:

> Through the reinforcement of slightly exceptional instances of his behavior, a child learns to raise himself, to stand, to walk, to grasp objects, and to move them about. Later on, through the same process, he learns to talk, to sing, to dance, to play games—in short, to exhibit the enormous repertoire characteristic of the normal adult (Skinner, 1953, p. 93).

The role of social reinforcement in the operant conditioning process should be underscored. Just as "primary reinforcement" events—such as food pellets and water—are used to control the acts of nonhumans, "social reinforcement," in the form of attention, affection, and approval, were seen as the basic reinforcers of the social acts of children.

Despite the practical success of the reinforcement-shaping proposal, its adequacy as a general explanation for behavioral development has suffered attacks both from within and from without the operant movement. From within, K. Breland and M. Breland (1961) have observed that the most dramatic instances of behavioral shaping in animals rely for their success upon the response propensities of the species. Over time, the environmental contingencies tend to be superseded by the species-typical actions of the individuals. For instance, obedient piglets who receive reinforcement for depositing wooden tokens into a piggy bank (what else?) eventually begin to play with and "root" the tokens (dig them into the earth with their snouts).rather than deposit them *despite continued reinforcement*. The eventual dominance of species-typical behaviors was interpreted by the Brelands to reflect an "instinctual drift" in behavior—that is, an evolutionary adaptation gradually superseding a developmental adaptation. According to this concept, reinforcement contingencies may temporarily deflect basic behaviors from their natural course, but the phyletic adaptation would eventually win out.

From "without," studies of motor development show that walking, grasping, smiling, and crawling, may develop in the absence of specific reinforcement contingencies or training—quite contrary to B. F. Skinner's original speculation. Although "reinforcement" experiences can *facilitate* the appearance of certain motor patterns (Zelazo, Zelazo, and Kolb, 1972; McGraw, 1939), they are not necessary for the *induction* of the behavior (see Gottlieb, 1976a). More generally, the original statement of the operant conditioning model did not give much credit to organismic contributions to the achievement of basic behavioral competencies, whether social or nonsocial.

The third major criticism of selective reinforcement explanation for establishment was offered by Bandura (1962), who observed that selective reinforcement was, for human beings, an enormously inefficient, costly, and time-consuming process. He argued that there were much more rapid and effective ways to establish novel behaviors, with imitation being a principal one. Bandura's arguments had the advantage of appealing to commonsense, and they underscored the problems of directly generalizing concepts of animal learning to human behavior.

Establishment by Imitation

The concept of selective reinforcement was not rejected in the next major development in social learning theory; it was assigned a more limited role in maintaining behavior. For induction, the concept of imitation was revived by Miller and Dollard (1941) after having been in limbo for the better part

of the century (Baldwin, 1902). Nonetheless, Albert Bandura (1962) deserves major credit for establishing the concept as part of modern social learning theory and for stimulating the most systematic and ingenious analyses of its characteristics and limits in children.

In the original statement (Bandura, 1962; Bandura and Walters, 1963), modeling was described as the process by which the child acquires new behavior—behavior that has an "extremely low or zero probability of occurrence." There was the additional experimental requirement that the child's action must match some highly distinctive features of the model's behavior. For instance, merely opening a door after another person has opened it does not qualify as modeling. Such an act could be an instance of response elicitation (elicitation of an action *already* in the repertoire) or disinhibition (permitting an act to occur that had been previously punished). But opening a door by pushing the knob with one's nose, just like the model had done, is modeling by any name.

Bandura and Walters (1963) also revised the relationship between establishment and maintenance. Their view was that reinforcement is *not* necessary for initial learning by observation. However, reinforcement was seen by Bandura and Walters to play a major role in the continuation of behavior. Thus a two-process model was proposed: establishment comes about through imitation, and maintenance comes about through reinforcement.

Left open in *Social Learning and Personality Development* was how the mere observation of a novel behavior that is processed through the visual sensory apparatus can be translated into a new motor coordination that matches the activity that was observed. Such a translation seems commonplace in our experience, but perceptual learning theories have just begun to come to grips with this issue of such cross-modality learning (see Gibson, 1969). Bandura and Walters suggested that the visual image might produce a perceptual blueprint which, in turn, translated visual input into motor output.

Later critics charged that the explanation was hardly adequate:

> The research on observational learning and imitation is very important, but Bandura and Walters do not integrate it into the main body of S–R [stimulus-response or behavior] theory. Just how does imitation occur? What events intervene between the stimulus (model) and the response (imitation)? Is there a tendency for any stimulus to be imitated? If not, what differentiates a model from a stimulus? The exploration of these problems is necessary for the development of a good social-learning theory. At the moment, the justification for the concept of imitation is merely that it occurs, not that it is related to the other concepts in the theory (Baldwin, 1967, p. 480).

As Baldwin's questions imply, mere imitation seems not sufficient to explain a great many instances of "new act" acquisition or establishment—such as the establishment of a new motor skill. Consider how one learns the forehand stroke in tennis. The coordinated act that looks smooth and natural when performed by Chris Evert or Bjorn Borg on television seems unnatural when one first attempts it on his own. The unnatural becomes natural only after many hours of practice to strengthen the triceps and forearm and wrist muscles, increase the sensitivity to changes in stroke and ball-speed variation, and perfect balance and timing. Similar requirements hold for other skilled motor performances in childhood, from holding a spoon to pronouncing "banana" and riding a bicycle. To attribute the establishment of these "new" skills simply to modeling takes for granted (hence overlooks) the coordination of the several motor, attentional, and sensory processes that are involved.

Modeling as Information Processing: The Cognitive Solution

Partly in response to such criticism, more detailed accounts were offered on the nature of modeling processes. In a restatement of modeling theory, Bandura (1971) lists four intermediate sub-processes: (a) whether or not the child pays attention to the model's activity, (b) whether the child recalls the activity, (c) how motivated the child is to perform the activity, and (d) whether the child has the necessary skills to perform what he observes. Perhaps more important, he proposes that the information communication function of the model's behavior is the effective factor in imitation. Bandura (1971) writes:

> Most contemporary interpretations of learning assign a more prominent role to cognitive functioning in the acquisition and regulation of human behavior than did previous explanatory systems. Social learning theory . . . assumes that *modeling influences operate principally through their informative function*, and that observers acquire mainly symbolic representations of modeled events, rather than specific stimulus-response associations (p. 16, italics in original).

This position represents a significant departure from the earlier proposal that the modeling process is guided by merely a perceptual blueprint and anticipated reinforcement (or its omission). In the cognitive reformulation, the model is a communicator who informs the observer which acts should be performed and when and how they should be performed. Whether the "message" is successful in producing effects in the observer depends on whether the child (a) attends to the model, (b) remembers what he did, (c) wants to imitate, and (d) has the necessary skills available to imitate the model's behavior.

The cognitive reinterpretation helps to explain otherwise puzzling findings, including:

1. Verbal instructions can be substituted for visual demonstrations, and for some purposes, they are more effective than visual demonstrations. (Information is the key, not the modality.)

2. Most acts of skill are not imitated, and if an attempt is made, the behavior is often a poor copy

of the original. (See d above; child lacks component behaviors.)

3. Infants do not imitate with the flexibility or skill that is observed in preschool children or older children (Meltzoff and Moore, 1977). (Infants have shorter attention spans, poorer memories, and fewer skills.)

4. Animals are extremely limited in their ability to imitate novel physical acts through visual observation (Mason and Hollis, 1962; Crawford and Spence, 1939). On the other hand, primates with relatively advanced symbolic capabilities, such as the great apes (Mason, 1976), show some talent for learning through observation, and some, but not all, song-bird species learn their distinctive songs by hearing other birds.

But there remain some puzzling questions. Does the occurrence of imitation in newborn babies mean that they are more advanced cognitively than has been supposed to be the case (Meltzoff and Moore, 1977)? Why can the zebra finch and parrot imitate songs and verbal statements when, say, dogs seem unable to imitate much of anything? Close examination of the several phenomena that have been called imitation suggest that even though they are alike in one characteristic (similarity between model and observer), they appear to differ in other properties. For instance, recent reports of imitation in human newborns indicate that the activities imitated, such as sticking out the tongue or opening the mouth, are surely not novel acts for the babies. There is scant basis for concluding that the infant is learning a new response that shares some features peculiar to that of the model. Further, imitation in song-birds differs from imitation in children in that for birds, reproduction is rarely instantaneous (the delay between exposure and imitation ranges from hours to months; Todt, 1976), it does not require cross-modality transfer, and the song or patterns are relatively inflexible once learned. Such findings underscore that similarity in outcome does not require similarity in process. The differences among the several demonstrations of imitation strongly suggest

that more than one process is involved and that a single explanation will not cover them all.

Social Learning and Social Behavior Establishment: An Evaluation

The revised view that imitation in children involves information transmission helps to answer some of the questions that Baldwin (1967) raised, and some that he did not. The revision nonetheless leaves open and unanswered the most compelling issues surrounding the original question of how social behavior patterns are established in the life of each individual. The recognition of the subprocesses of modeling (as information processing) moves the problem back one step and leads one to ask of the theory: How do *components* of social action arise in development? No clear answer to this question is offered within the model, although several possibilities exist, ranging from a reconsideration of the earlier proposals of selective reinforcement and social motives to the adoption of the proposals of developmental psychobiology or evolutionary theories. What, then, does the modeling proposal achieve? It provides a compelling account of how the social patterns of children are rapidly and effectively reorganized and redirected, thus promoting efficient adaptation to new circumstances and new relationships. It does not, however, serve as a powerful or generally applicable account of social behavior establishment, if establishment refers to the origin of basic patterns of aggressive, sexual, or affiliative responding.

Maintenance and Change: Social Reinforcement

Beyond establishment, the other central issues for developmental theories are maintenance and change. Reinforcement—particularly social reinforcement—has been assumed to be of major importance for both functions. Social reinforcement has been defined, for practical purposes, to include expressions of approval, attention, and approbation. The concept was initially offered to bridge the gap between general theories of animal learning and the complexities of children's social behavior. The assumption was that these interpersonal events could serve the same reinforcing functions for children that nonsocial, biologically relevant events (such as pellets and water) do for hungry rats and thirsty pigeons. The advantage to developing an analogue of this sort is that it permits learning theory formulations to be extended to problems and outcomes that are relevant for human beings. In any case, that was the hope. Social reinforcement has played a role of major importance for social learning theories, from the early formulations of Dollard and Miller (1950) to the contemporary statements of Mischel (1973) and Patterson (1979).

In view of the centrality of the concept, it should not be surprising, perhaps, that a great number of investigations have been concerned with its nature and origins. But if the number of such studies is not surprising, the outcomes have been. The research provides us with another example in which the empirical analysis of a foundational concept has forced its major re-evaluation and revision. As in the case of modeling, the shift has been away from a unidirectional, mechanistic view of the concept to one that emphasizes its informational and interchange properties.

The shift in conception reflects the sensitivity of social learning investigators to the results of their research. Scores of innovative studies were completed in attempts to define and clarify the properties of social reinforcement (see reviews by Stevenson, 1965, and Parton and Ross, 1965). Much of the early work was devoted to the question of whether differences in the effectiveness of social reinforcement could be traced to differences in a "social drive" or a "need for approval." (Apparently not, because contrary to the drive analogue, social reinforcer "satiation" can lead to a paradoxical increase in effectiveness. See Eisenberger, Kaplan, and Singer, 1974; Gewirtz, 1967; Warren and Cairns, 1972.) More recent laboratory and field studies have attempted to clarify why social reinforcement works, and why it does not. Some of the more relevant findings are:

1. Laboratory investigations indicate that social reinforcement in the form of attention and approval is not as effective as it is purported to be. Expressions of social approval, including praise such as saying "great" or "fine," have a surprisingly modest effect on what and how rapidly the child learns (see overview in Paris and Cairns, 1972). In some instances, positive reinforcement has been shown to *retard* learning, possibly because the child's attention is distracted (Spence, 1971). The effectiveness of social events seems to depend less on their "intrinsic" reward properties than upon conditions specific to the laboratory circumstance (such as the instructions given to the child, the nature of the task, and the child's expectations). Furthermore, virtually all manipulations that draw attention to the informational properties and meanings of the words serve to heighten the effectiveness of praise expressions. Merely telling a 9-year-old child, for instance, that "whenever I say 'good' or 'right,' that means your're performing correctly" can transform a previously ineffective outcome into one that is highly effective (Cairns, 1967; Redd et al., 1975).

2. Field studies of children's behavior in school settings raise questions about whether social reinforcement events play an important regulatory role everyday life. Classroom observations indicate that teachers are reasonably effective in organizing and regulating children's activities. But social reinforcement rarely occurs following the acts of individual children in the course of a day. How is control exercised if not by social reinforcement? Observations strongly suggest that the key factor is how teachers organize or structure activities—defining when and how and where children should be studying and playing. Children, in turn, support one another in maintaining the expected activity.

Microanalyses of the actual functions of approval in interchanges indicate, further, that the occurrence of social reinforcement does *not* typically produce continuation of the activity (see Patterson and Cobb, 1971). Rather than repeat the activity that elicited approval, children typically consider approval to be a signal to go on to the next activity. Accordingly, Patterson and Cobb (1971) distinguish between the immediate effects of reinforcement and their long-term effects in interchanges (see also Chapter 8).

3.   Social reinforcement works best when children are aware of the contingency between the reward and what they are supposed to learn. If the person is unaware of the relationship, there is typically scant evidence of learning (Spielberger and DeNike, 1966). Such outcomes have been interpreted, reasonably enough, to be in conflict with the original assumption that social reinforcement was automatic and occurred independently of the child's awareness. Furthermore, noncontingent usage can diminish the effectiveness of rewards (Babad and Weisz, 1977).

4.   Contrary to a first-generation social learning position (Skinner, 1953), punishment works. As in the case of positive social reinforcement, the information associated with the occurrence of punishment, whether as criticism or as physical pain, influences its effectiveness (Cheyne and Walters, 1970; Parke, 1977). The clearer the message that punishment communicates, the more effective it is in behavior control. Support for this generalization has been obtained in studies of children in the home, classroom, and laboratory (Parke, 1977; Paris and Cairns, 1972). Moreover, explicit statements of punishment (such as the word "wrong") are typically less ambiguous and more effective in short-term control than are seemingly comparable expressions of praise (such as "right").

The whole of the findings—not a single feature considered alone—has discredited the simple analogue that social reinforcement is to learning in children what reinforcement is to conditioning in animals. Furthermore, the results have forced a reformulation of the concept of social reinforcement (which, as it was originally proposed, was nei-

ther social nor reinforcing). The contemporary view is that social reinforcement events help to regulate learning to the extent that they communicate information to the child about what is to be learned. The communicative properties of social events are not inherent nor are they entirely fixed and unchangeable; rather, they are defined and redefined in the context of everyday experience. Hence the regulatory capabilities of approval and attention vary across settings, social relationships, and the communication networks in which they occur.

New Directions in Social Learning Theory

In commenting on the revisions in social learning formulations, I am running the risk of overlooking some of the more significant advances because they have just gotten underway. But the changes that we can identify unambiguously are important enough. The "new directions" that I will discuss here concern the attempts to reformulate the theory in terms of emphasizing the role of interactions, cognitive processes, and the eliciting and organizing properties of the environment in social behavior regulation.

Interactional Analysis

A proposition that has now been accepted by virtually all contemporary statements of social learning is that social phenomena require interactional analyses (Sears, 1951). The sentiment is expressed in various ways, one of the more articulate being Mischel's (1973) recent statement:

The proposed cognitive social learning approach to person variables emphasizes most strongly the need to study the individual's behavior in specific interaction with particular conditions. Indeed, the conceptualization of behavior, whether psychologist defined (as in research) or subject defined (as in clinical, individually oriented assessment), must be embedded in relation to the specific conditions in which the behavior occurs. Rather than talk about "behavior," it may be more useful to conceptualize behavior-contingency units that link specific patterns of behavior to the conditions in which they may be expected (p. 278).

Rather the same ideas were expressed by Patterson (1979) in his overview of the need for the interactional treatment of aggressive behavior. Focusing on aggressive behavior patterns in young boys, Patterson saw the aggressive child as both victim and architect of a coercive family system. Coercive or assertive behaviors occur in children when parental threats and warnings are used to inhibit their actions. These threats, in turn, merely encourage the very acts they were designed to prevent. Hence, the child helps to design his own family environment.

An interaction methodology has the additional advantage of permitting the investigator to identify controlling events more precisely than do methods that focus solely on individuals taken alone. Patterson and Cobb (1971) have argued in this regard that there is no serious alternative to the detailed analysis of interchanges:

A proper study of man's behavior requires that we observe man in his natural habitat and focus upon the minutiae which describe the changes in his behaviors as he confronts and is confronted by the other people in this world. It is those variables which produce changes in his immediate, continuing behavior which are of interest (p. 125).

Social-Cognitive Reinterpretations

Another direction that social learning approaches have taken is reflected in explicit attempts to synthesize social learning processes with cognitive ones. The effects of this theoretical shift are seen most sharply in the reintepretation of social reinforcement and modeling processes, but similar shifts of emphasis are to be found in the analysis of conscience development (Aronfreed, 1968), how the delay of reinforcement affects behavior (Mischel, 1973), and the development of sex-roles (Maccoby and Jacklin, 1974). Moreover, interactional analyses of children have underscored the need to attend to their mutual expectations as well as mutual actions.

The reasons for, and content of, the cognitive reformulation have already been covered in this chapter and elsewhere (Chapters 8, 12, and 15). Two comments are called for on the broad implications of the reformulation. First, it should be noted that social learning theories have retained a primary commitment to the principle of parsimony, which, simply stated, is not to employ a complex cognitive process when a simple, noncognitive one will do the job. Hence the basic concepts of conditioning and learning continue to play a central role in social learning theories, whatever their generation.

Second, some confusion has been generated within social learning models because old terms (social reinforcement, modeling, delay of gratification) have been retained but they have been given quite new interpretations and emphases. The change in interpretation itself is not so bad because it was obviously called for, but the retention of the old terms for new processes can be quite misleading. A continuity with earlier learning theories is often implied and cannot be justified.

Structures and Organization

A third "new direction" of social learning theories is their recognition of the role that social and environmental systems play in social behavior regulation. The emphasis on the organizing properties of the social system and the environment does not replace earlier emphases on their reinforcing properties; it supplements attention to outcomes by drawing attention to the eliciting and supportive properties of antecedent conditions.

Of the major shifts in social learning emphasis, this one is most difficult to identify as being different from what behavior theorists knew all along. In one of the early contributions to general learning theory, E. C. Tolman (1932) proposed that environmental events could serve two different functions in the organization and support of behavior. They can support an activity by virtue of being directly involved in its performance ("manipulanda"), or they can elicit an activity by signaling when it should be performed ("discriminanda"). Other theorists, including B. F. Skinner (1938), clearly recognized the directing and eliciting role of environmental events. The work of Kurt Lewin (1935)—although Lewin can scarcely be considered a learning theorist— seems to be an antecedent for current emphases. For Lewin, the immediate situation (or better, how the child perceived the situation) was of *primary* importance in understanding the direction and nature of behavior.

Nowadays virtually all social learning theories explicitly recognize the contextual regulation of social behavior. Raush's comments on the matter and the problems that it raises for "static" trait concepts, such as dependency, seem to be representative of the social learning position. He writes:

> Children are, for example, no more taught not to be dependent than they are taught not to urinate. What they are taught are right and wrong times and places. For some parents and for some cultures, as compared to others, there are more wrong places, and in that sense one might speak of quantitatively greater or lesser amounts of expression or inhibition. But this is a rather different matter than presumed quantities of traits (Raush, 1965, p. 498).

The contextual relativity to which Raush refers has been amply demonstrated (see Chapters 8 and 17). But recognition of situational controls merely states the problem. What seems required of social learning theory are positive steps towards its solution. Three of the steps that could be taken are: (1) formulating a taxonomy of situations or contexts to which children are typically exposed in development, (2) specifying the general rules by which environments produce and maintain particular social patterns, and (3) defining the mediators that pro-

mote generalization of the child's social behaviors across settings and thereby promote stability.

For children, one can hardly divorce the regulatory properties of the environment from those of social systems. John Paul Scott (1977), one of the prime movers in the area of behavior genetics, recently argued that the interdependence of social systems and the environments in which they occur is inevitable. Scott writes that

> . . . almost all behavior that is exhibited by members of highly social species such as man is expressed within social relationships. What little solitary behavior remains is expressed within social contexts derived from these relationships. This means that, as far as behavior is concerned, *the concept of the independent individual is a myth* (pp. 327–328, italics in original).

Scott concludes in a corollary of this view that the concept of an independent environment is equally mythical insofar as social behavior genetics is concerned.

Social learning writers have arrived at a similar conclusion (see Bandura, 1973a; Mischel, 1973; Patterson, 1979). But recognition of the control properties of social systems does not explain how they exercise their effects. Precisely the same questions may be asked about the nature of social systems as we asked about the nature of environments (how they may be effectively classified, rules by which they operate on individuals, and processes by which the child's behavior is generalized from one system, such as the family, to another, such as the school, and back again). Social learning investigations of these issues have just begun (see Bronfenbrenner, 1977; Parke, 1978).

Unresolved Issues and Unfinished Business

Whether one chooses to call the gaps in the explanation "failures" or "unfinished business" depends upon one's view of the vitality of social learning theories. The evolution of the perspective indicates that its principal architects have been responsive to the results of the research that the position has generated as well as to advances in related areas of science. Hence the approach has maintained its hegemony in the discipline despite the fact that it is not a developmental theory (i.e., one for which maturational changes are a central focus).

Three of problems that remain to be resolved include: (1) how to achieve an integration with developmental perspectives of social development, (2) formulation of concepts to account for learning in interchanges, and (3) some conceptual housecleaning.

1. A shortcoming common to all generations of social learning is that they only pay lip-service to the concept of the child as a developing, changing organism. A correlated oversight is to ignore the maturation-paced changes that are woven into virtually all features of the child's social adaptation. A reasonable case can be made for the proposition that most of the serious problems confronting the orientation follow directly from its nonorganismic, nondevelopmental stance. The problems include the failure to come up with a convincing explanation of the origin of social behaviors, the apparent lack of applicability of the concepts to nonhuman species, and the failure to take into account age-related changes in cognitive capabilities of the child. Compare these "shortcomings" with the "strengths" of organismic theories that we covered in Chapter 18. The major problems for social learning theories are the areas of strength for organismic ones, and vice-versa.

2. The second unfinished task for social learning views concerns the job of building an adequate theory of how interchanges are learned and organized, changed and generalized. We have discussed the problems of formulating a dynamic account of interchange learning, transformation, and generalization in earlier chapters (see Chapters 6, 8, 12, and 17). Some plausible solutions were offered in the context of particular problems of attachment, social organization, aggression, and reciprocity. These issues lie at the heart of the development synthesis and are ones that social learning theories are uniquely prepared to explore.

3. The harshest criticism that can be leveled at social learning theories is that they offer a convincing explanation—for everything. A large stockpile of learning concepts has accumulated in three generations of theory building (including some nebulous and tautological ones), and few have been discarded. If one set of concepts fails to explain a given finding, another set can be called into action. Although such flexibility is admirable, the theory becomes virtually impossible to falsify. And if a theory cannot be shown to be wrong, one must have questions about whether its explanations are accurate or merely plausible. Some further conceptual housecleaning is in order. It could profitably proceed along the lines that have emerged in the mini-theories of conscience (Aronfreed, 1968), aggression (Patterson, 1979), and peer relations (Hartup, 1970).

Contributions to the Developmental Synthesis

Social learning theories have evolved in three generations, and they continue to evolve still. What might be said about the accomplishments of social learning models to date? In brief, they remain our primary source for hypotheses on how the behaviors of children are reciprocated, regulated, and consolidated. Despite their shortcomings, they provide a foundation for understanding how the social behaviors of children become adapted to each other and to the social systems of which they become a part. They provide the key to understanding the interactional "fine tuning" from which personal distinctiveness and developmental adaptation proceed. Specific interchange learning mechanisms were discussed in Chapters 8, 12, 15, and 17. These concepts have been of nuclear importance for the developmental synthesis.

In reviewing the general proposals of recent social learning formulations, it is useful to recall that they have been derived from, and apply most directly to, verbally competent children (3 years of age and older). Of these general proposals, the following seem likely to continue to be influential for understanding social interchanges in children:

■ The social behaviors of children are appropriately viewed in terms of the relationships, settings, and social systems in which they occur. The child's social actions vary as a function of situational and interpersonal demands and, hence, can become relatively distinctive to both circumstances and relationships.

■ The child's ability to discriminate among relationships and settings, and to form expectations about them, changes as a function of age and experience. Hence what a child learns from an interchange is relative to his cognitive abilities, prior experiences, and the settings in which the interchanges occur.

■ Generalization across settings and relationships is a joint function of the common features that the child perceives in them and the range of social patterns that the child has available in his repertoire. The greater the identity (or, perceived identity) of the situation-relationship, the greater the likelihood of generalizing interchange patterns across situations-relationships.

■ The child's expectations help to determine (1) whether he will initially enter a new setting or relationship, and (2) his initial actions and reactions in new settings and relationships. However, once the child is in a new context, the reciprocal controls that operate in that setting will contribute significantly to the type, direction, and intensity of behavior observed.

■ Changes in the form and type of the child's interchanges can be brought about by modifying the social system in which he is placed or from which he is permitted to choose. The effective processes of change may involve information communicated symbolically (by instructions, modeling, social rewards, or punishment) or they may involve constraints that occur in the interchange or the physical environment.

■ Interchange patterns recur, become consolidated, and are generalized. Social behavior is thus both conservative and adaptive, in that there is a continuous interplay between the demands of the contemporary setting and the carryover effects of previous experience.

These proposals are concerned with the maintenance and change (regulation) of the social behaviors of children, and it is in these areas that social learning statements have proved to be most powerful. Synthesized with companion principles (Chapters 18, 20, and 21) from organismic and evolutionary models, they provide framework for dealing with the problem of how children become adapted to the multiple relationships of childhood.

20

COGNITIVE DEVELOPMENT AND SOCIAL BEHAVIOR

The reorganization of social learning concepts from an informational perspective provides a stepping-stone to discussion of the social development implications of the cognitive theories of Jean Piaget (1932, 1952), Heinz Werner (1948), and Lawrence Kohlberg (1969). In this chapter we will consider (1) some assumptions that are common to cognitive approaches, (2) social development research themes that they have generated, (3) certain problems that remain to be solved, and (4) new directions relevant to social behavior. In the concluding section I will summarize the contributions of the orientation to the developmental synthesis. The concepts of cognitive development are, as Flavell (1977) observes, prone to "distortion, oversimplification, and misunderstanding" when they are presented briefly. The reader can consult Flavell (1977), Phillips (1975), Shantz (1975), and the original sources themselves for additional information.

Basic Concepts

The Organismic Perspective on Cognitive Development

Langer (1969) described the cognitive-developmental view of man as an "organic lamp" theory. This label accurately captures the idea that this view of cognitive development is fundamentally an organismic theory—one whose basic concepts are analogous to those of developmental biology.

Attempting to review the multiple theoretical and empirical contributions of Jean Piaget, much less those of other contributors to the organismic view of cognitive development, would take us too far away from our main task. Perhaps it isn't necessary. Although Piaget's theory is complex, and has theoretical implications that extend beyond development to epistemology, the basic assumptions most relevant for social development can be stated succinctly (if incompletely):

1. Cognitive development (i.e., the development of intelligence or the ability to organize one's cognitions abstractly) follows principles that are analogous to those of general biological development.

2. Intelligence requires distancing oneself from the "here and now," the events in the immediate present. Hence cognitive development can be described in terms of successive stages of "de-centering" one's cognitions (mental events) from immediate sensations and perceptions in order to achieve abstract representations of those experiences.

3.   The cognitive structures of the child ("schemata") undergo progressive and invariant sequential organization during development. Cognitive development thus involves an integration of earlier cognitive structures into a hierarchy of increasing complexity (simple, undifferentiated structures must precede complicated, differentiated ones).

Piaget's theory uses organismic principles, but it is not a biological theory of cognitive development. The theory thus has not been concerned with the neural substrate of intelligence, nor with evolutionary causation. It is analogous to biological development because the cognitive structures of the child ("schemata") are assumed to undergo reorganization during ontogeny in ways that parallel organismic development. Cognitive reorganization is stimulated by both internal and external changes; it permits the child to achieve an equilibrium between modifications in his existing schemata and variations in his perceptions of himself and the external world. The schemata not only promote the processing of information from the environment (assimilation), they are progressively reorganized as a result of the stimulation (accommodation).

According to Piaget, cognitive reorganization follows predictable and invariant sequences, where the child graduates in stages from a dependence on immediate sensation in infancy to conceptual independence and abstraction in adolescence. Earlier schemata are integrated into subsequent ones, and it is these integrations that permit the child's mental representations to become independent of the constraints of "here-and-now" stimulation.

Some of the most compelling evidence in support of Piaget's theory involves counterintuitive demonstrations that young children are in fact "bound" by their perceptions. Before 7 months of age infants seem to equate their not being able to see an object with its ceasing to exist, and 4-year-old children can be easily fooled about how many objects are present (in laboratory tests) because they center their attention on the salient properties of length or height instead of number. In both instances, slightly older children make more "intelligent" judgments. Babies

11–18 months of age begin to treat objects as being "permanent" even though they can't be seen, and older children (7–8 years) "de-center" their perceptions and begin to use information about number and mass.

What accounts for the invariant sequences in cognitive development? Piaget's theory emphasizes the joint, bidirectional operation of internal change and the stimulating environment in bringing about differentiation and integration. It is not simply a "maturational" theory, because the actual ages at which the stages occur are less fundamental for the account than the fact that the reorganization is lawful and invariant. The sensorimotor stage must precede the preoperational stage, and these in turn must occur prior to the concrete operational stage and that of formal operations. There is thus a hierarchical integration of stages. Heinz Werner's (1948) "orthogenetic principle"—the idea that global, undifferentiated stages precede differentiated, integrate ones—places a similar emphasis on the developing organism in a dynamic environment.

Not all cognitive development theories agree with Piaget's emphasis on the active role of the environment in organizing changes. According to Langer (1969), the role is a passive one: "The environment, then, in organic lamp theory is merely the occasion for or scene of, and not the cause of agent of, development. It provides the nourishment or context for the child's emotional and cognitive digestion, which is necessary for autogenesis" (p. 157). (The term autogeneis means for Langer that cognitive development is established and directed by endogenous factors). The difference in emphasis upon the active (Piaget) vs. passive (Langer) role of stimulation in bringing about developmental change is parallel to the difference between unidirectional vs. bidirectional emphases in psychobiological development (Chapter 19).

Implications for Social Development

How, then, does cognitive-developmental theory account for the establishment of social behaviors in the child? This question brings us to the assumption of *cognitive primacy:* that the child's cognitions—of himself and of others—are the primary determinants of his social behavior. Kohlberg's (1969) description of the interrelationship of sex-role identity, imitation, and social attachment-dependency is perhaps the clearest statement of this assumption. Consider, for example, sex-role identification. Kohlberg argues that the child's basic sex-role behavior is largely the *result of* self-categorization as a male or female made early in development (p. 431). This categorization comes about because of age-related changes "in complex modes of cognitive organization" and not because of particular social labeling or reinforcement experiences. Once the identity is established, the child seeks out models that exemplify the sex with which he has identified because of their perceived similarity to himself. Behavior acquisition is thus subsequent to and dependent upon establishment of the sex concept. In the course of imitation, the child's desire to be more like and approved by the model leads to increased dependency upon and attachment to that model.

The presumed sequence of events—from cognition of one's self as male or female to imitation to social attachment—is diagrammed in Figure 20-1

(right). Kohlberg points out that this sequence is opposite(!) to what has been assumed to be the course of sex-typing development by "neopsychoanalytic" social learning theories. In such models, the child first establishes a social bond, then he is motivated to produce in his own behavior characteristics of the same-sex parent, and from this selective-reproduction of parental behaviors, sex-identity arises (see Figure 20-1, left). Kohlberg's diagrams admittedly oversimplify both cognitive and social learning theories; nonetheless, they capture a meaningful difference in the emphases of the two orientations.

More generally, Kohlberg's (1969) propositions on the relationship between cognitive development and social behavior can be outlined as follows:

1. There is a cognitive primacy in social behavior. Social cognitions and the stage of an individual's cognitive development determine both the establishment and the maintenance of basic social behaviors, from sex typing and modeling to aggression and attachment.

2. Cognitive development, and hence social development, proceeds in qualitative stages, and a "more advanced stage is not simply an addition to a

Neopsychoanalytic	Cognitive-Developmental
1. Child's dependency based on care-taking and affection.	1. Child's imitation of competent and interesting behavior of adult.
↓	↓
2. Imitation as a substitute for parental nurturance.	2. Desire for normative conformity, i.e., a sense of shared standards for behavior, desires to imitate.
↓	↓
3. Internal normative conformity in order to maintain self-approval based on 2.	3. Dependency, i.e., persistent sense of need for guidance and approval by the model.

Figure 20-1. L. Kohlberg's comparison of "neo-psychoanalytic" and "cognitive-developmental" views of the relationship between imitation and social dependency. Kohlberg attributes the left-side position to Sigmund Freud, and the right-side position to James Mark Baldwin (1902) (from Kohlberg, 1969, with permission).

less advanced stage, but represents a reorganization of less advanced levels" (Rest, Turiel, and Kohlberg, 1969).

3. There is a sequential invariance in cognitive-social development, in that the attainment of an advanced stage is dependent on the attainment of each of the preceding stages.

4. The sequential invariance is due to the major role played by endogenous maturational factors that govern the pace of accommodation and assimilation, as well as the patterns of behavioral reorganization, throughout ontogeny.

In addition, Lawrence Kohlberg has effectively revived the concept of the self as an organizing, active agent in socialization. Following the ideas of J. M. Baldwin (1902), Kohlberg has consistently emphasized that developmental changes in cognition and social behavior are inseparably fused in the child's self concept.

To what extent are these assumptions shared by cognitive-developmental approaches in general? A fine-grained comparison of the similarities and differences among cognitive theories is beyond the scope of this chapter. It may be sufficient to note that the two most controversial assumptions of the four are the first (on cognitive primacy) and the last (on autogenesis). Disagreements arise because the organismic foundation of both Piaget's and Werner's approaches presupposes significant bidirectionality in development, an assumption that is inconsistent with unidirectionality in either genetic or cognitive influence.

Illustrations of Research Themes: Moral Development and Social Cognition

Jean Piaget deserves major credit for formulating modern cognitive-developmental theory, and for devising research methods for evaluating its adequacy. In contrast to social learning and psychobiological approaches, cognitive-developmental techniques rely heavily upon questionnaires or in-depth interviews for primary data. Piaget argued that the reasons a child offers for his actions are more important than the actions themselves, because the same behavior might come about for quite different reasons, and different behaviors might reflect the same reason or intent. The method offers several advantages, not the least of which are flexibility and the potential to probe beyond simple observation. Nonverbal tests are employed, of course, with nonverbal or preverbal children (3 years and younger). The methods have been applied to virtually all problems of social development, with two of the most active areas being moral development and social cognition.

Moral Development and Moral Judgment

Moral reasoning has been extensively investigated by Lawrence Kohlberg (1969) and his collaborators. The research follows directly from Piaget's (1932) classic study, with some standardization of procedures and an extension of the concepts and methods. Kohlberg and his coworkers developed a scale of moral judgment and used it to determine (a) whether the moral reasoning of children progressed in qualitative stages, and (b) whether there was a sequential invariance in the appearance of the stages (that is, whether the sequence would occur regardless of the experiences and cultural background of the children).

How does one go about measuring "moral judgment"? Kohlberg's solution (following Piaget, 1932) was to assess the quality or abstractness of a child's answers to stories that posed hypothetical ethical conflicts. Once measured, moral "maturity" (that is, level of moral judgments) can be correlated with other variables, such as the child's age, culture, and other measures of cognitive development. The construction and format of the *Scale* are similar to those of standard story-completion techniques used in personality assessment. Each of the 9 different stories that make up the *Scale* involves some kind of moral dilemma. The critical aspect of the child's response to the dilemma is not its "correctness" or "incorrectness" but the level of abstraction at which it is rationalized. To illustrate, one of Kohlberg's moral dilemma stories concerned the fictional account of Heinz, whose wife was dying, and for whom drugs were prohibitively expensive. Out of desperation, Heinz broke into the pharmacy and stole the drugs. The examiner asks, "Should the husband have done that? Why?" The answer that the child gives to explain Heinz's actions are categorized into one of 6 stages of moral maturity, 3 of which are illustrated below:

Stage 1. *Premoral: Punishment and obedience orientation.* An absolutistic, nonmotivational view which limits the individual's perspective to consequences as opposed to intentions. One might be in favor of stealing by offering the reason that "If his wife dies, he will get into trouble," or in favor of not stealing, offering the reason that "If you steal the drug, then you'll get caught and get sent to jail."

Stage 4. *Morality of conventional code conformity: Authority maintaining.* Adoption of societal standards, and reflection of the expected values of others toward the action or the application of a stereotyped rule of society ("law and order"). Such reasons would be: "No matter how noble that cause, there is a violation of a basic biblical commandment if the property if another person were taken."

Stage 6. *Morality of self-accepted moral principles: Individual principles of conscience.* Internalization of principles that are used to guide one's acts and thinking, even though these may contradict "accepted" or popular norms. For example: "Heinz would fail to live to the dictates of his own conscience if he did not exhaust every alternative in trying to save his wife's life," or, "Heinz would forever condemn himself for placing his own needs before the needs

of the society of which he was a participating member."

Two questions are whether the child's stage of moral judgment bears a direct relationship to his cognitive level of development (measured roughly by age), and whether his judgments are consistent across questions, as would be expected if there were sequential invariance.

What does the *Moral Judgment Scale* reveal? The overall merits of quasi-clinical interviews as a means of assessing cognitive-developmental theory have been controversial since Piaget first introduced the procedure. Nor has Kohlberg's extension of the method escaped criticism (see, for instance, Kurtines and Greif, 1974). Nonetheless, there is found a clear trend, across cultures, for children's judgments to become increasingly more abstract up to about 16 years (Kohlberg, 1969). No firm conclusions, however, may be drawn with respect to the assumption of an invariant sequence of changes. One puzzling finding, for instance, is that a child may seem to operate at two (or more) different levels, according to which story is analyzed.

Some of the problems may lie in the methods, not the theory. Kurtines and Greif (1974) point out that the *Moral Judgment Scale* hardly meets the standards that such a widely cited research tool might be expected to meet. They note that the *Scale* employs intuitive scoring standards, leaves many of the details of administration to the discretion of the examiner, and has uncertain reliability (the child's scores may fluctuate greatly over short periods). Kurtines and Greif (1974) conclude that "the research done within this framework is beset with a multitude of problems which detract from the model's usefulness" (p. 468).

It is with respect to the cognitive primacy assumption, however, that our information on moral development is least adequate. The developmental changes in moral *judgments* of children are impressive, but it is unclear whether there is a corresponding change in their moral *conduct*, or whether cognitive changes indeed precede behavioral ones.

Social Cognition

The issues of social cognition—how the actions of others are interpreted, how children perceive the roles of other persons, how social stereotypes are formed, how the cognitive stage of the child influences his social behaviors—have provided a central research theme for theories of cognitive development. The areas of research stimulated by the approach have been diverse, covering topics from role perception and communication to the origins of attachment (see Shantz, 1975, for an excellent review). Some of the more intensely researched areas include:

1. *Role perception and communication.* John Flavell and his collaborators (Flavell, Botkin, Fry, Wright, and Jarvis, 1968) explored the proposal that children 4-6 years old are unable to "de-center" themselves from their self-perceptions in order to take the perspective of another person. Using innovative experimental methods, these investigators attempted to determine when in development children were able to place themselves in the role of another person, and to communicate from that perspective. Role taking (having the child explain what another person would see or understand) is clearly age-dependent, according to Flavell, et al. (1968), with younger children (4–5 years old) performing quite poorly. Further studies of the phenomenon indicate that role taking is highly dependent on the nature of the tasks and the familiarity of the child with them (see Shantz, 1975). A similar relativity of age of onset to the kind of task employed has been observed in studies of empathy (Hoffman, 1975) and role reciprocity and communication (Mueller and Lucas, 1975; see Chapter 17).

2. *Sex-role stereotyping.* Kohlberg's (1966) view of sex-role development requires that the child's concept of gender roles should be age-related, with male-female differentiation to be relatively independent of social experiences, and abstract properties appearing relatively late in development. Presumably these outcomes should transcend the norms of particular societies. There is indeed considerable similarity across societies in what gender role stereotypes children form, and when they are formed (Best, Williams, Cloud, Davis, Robertson, Edwards, Giles, and Fowles, 1977). In three different countries where comparable procedures were employed (Ireland, England, and the United States), 5-year-old children tend to come up with different adjectives to describe males ("strong," "cruel," "coarse") than females ("softhearted," "sentimental"). Older children showed an even sharper distinction between male and female stereotypes. The 8–12-year-olds (both boys and girls) used more adjectives to distinguish males from females, and there is some suggestion that the adjectives referred to more abstract properties of personality ("appreciative," "meek," "independent"). The work yields indirect, but intriguing, support for the contentions of cognitive-developmental theories (but does not exclude social learning explanations).

3. *Interpretation of social actions.* According to cognitive-developmental theory, the child's perception of a social act should change as a function of cognitive stage. This proposal has multiple implications for research, including studies of the effects of television. Accordingly, Collins, Brendt, and Hess (1974) observed that the question of how television affects children's behaviors and attitudes should begin with an analysis of what they perceive and what interpretations are given to the action. Children 5-7 years old, for example, typically have only a fragmentary understanding of television programs that involve violence. Collins et al. found that younger children focused on the salient and vigorous actions and sometimes upon the consequences that were provoked, but they rarely perceived (or recalled) the motivational sequence that gave rise to the behavior. The lesson is the "effects" of television for young children may be quite different from the effects that are produced in older persons, even when the same program is viewed and even when the same "message" is communicated.

4. *Object constancy and attachment.* The infant's attainment of object permanence (when in-

fants begin to view objects as having an existence independent of their perception of them) has been seen as a prerequisite for the establishment of a social attachment (Ainsworth, 1972; Schaffer, 1977). The logic underlying this proposal seems straightforward enough: children must perceptually differentiate themselves from their mothers and establish an idea of her as a permanent, independent being before they can relate to her as another person. Although the proposition is plausible, investigators have found considerable difficulty in finding persuasive support for it (review by Flavell, 1977). The problems are (a) there is no strong correlation between stages of object permanence and measures of social attachment; (b) some indices of attachment, such as infants' preference for their mothers, occurs at 4 months of age, considerably before the onset of the concept of objects; and (c) a wide range of nonhuman species of questionable cognitive competence nonetheless develop strong and lasting social bonds with respect to their mothers. Flavell's (1977) recent comments sum up the problem:

> It is virtually impossible on logical grounds to imagine how these two developments, object concept and social attachment, could proceed in mutual isolation, neither having any effect on the other. At the same time, it has so far been surprisingly difficult to demonstrate empirically any object-concept basis for the formation of social attachments; in fact, we are not even quite sure precisely what sort of link between the two developments we ought to expect on theoretical grounds. The issue rests where most issues in cognitive development tend to rest—stubbornly encamped in midair (p. 60).

Some Unsolved Problems

Cognitive-developmental theory has played a major role in reshaping the direction of contemporary child psychology. But as Flavell's (1977) remarks

suggest, stubborn problems remain. Three of the major ones will be discussed in the following paragraphs: (1) the unclarity about how transitions in cognitive stages are achieved, (2) the failure to explain the relationship between social cognition and social behavior, and (3) the inattention to the linkages between cognitive development and broader issues of biological development and evolution.

1. The first problem stems from the essential unclarity in the cognitive position as to how transitions in mental development are achieved, and how new cognitive stages are generated and reorganized from earlier ones. In a brief but candid appraisal of the position, Langer (1969) notes the concepts of accommodation and assimilation imply that new stages are "more differentiated and integrated" versions of earlier ones. But these concepts are descriptions rather than explanations because they fail to provide a precise account of the necessary and sufficient conditions for the transitions to occur. The problem is particularly important when cognitive transitions are used to explain social behavior changes, such as the onset of sexual behaviors, attachment behavior dimunition, and variations in the expression of hostility. Presumably each of these changes is paced by more fundamental changes in cognitive schemata. But what causes the cognitive schemata to change? What accounts for the failure of some persons to move beyond the intermediate stages of cognitive development? Although the assumption of autogenesis seems to answer some of these questions by implying that these transitions are preprogrammed or maturationally determined, autogenesis does not explain the powerful role that social systems play in the direction and control of social development.

2. There remains an uncertainty within the theory and within empirical studies as to the nature of the relationship between social cognitions and social behavior. What is the link between what a child says and what he does? Do persons who have attained a high level of moral reasoning on the *Moral Judgment Scale* behave in a highly moral fashion?

Apparently not, according to Mischel and Mischel (1976). The low correlations between "reasoning" scores and conduct are consistent with converging lines of information on the matter, including findings that (a) ethical conduct is usually specific to the setting in which it is observed (Chapter 17); (b) delinquent aggressive boys differ only modestly from nondelinquent boys in measures of conscience (Bandura and Walters, 1959); (c) intelligence is correlated with criminal behavior in complex ways, but one of the stable relationships is between educational level attained and type of crime (embezzlement is a crime for brighter offenders).

But the failure to find a direct correspondance between moral reasoning and moral conduct is only part of the problem. Similar questions can be raised about other measures of social cognition and their relevance to the child's behavior. One problem is to identify precisely the pathways by which experiences in social interchanges and in the social system give rise to expectations about social behavior and the rules that govern it in specific relationships. The other problem is to clarify the several ways that the child's perceptions of himself, others, and the relationships that they bear to each other, influence his behavior.

There now seems to be ample grounds on which to reject the cognitive primacy hypothesis in its simple form (that social behavior is merely a reflection of social cognition). Piaget's theory of accommodation and assimilation would have it that there should exist bidirectional relationship: that social experiences should give rise to social cognition, and vice-versa. The theory leaves open, perhaps wisely, how the interrelationships proceed. It seems wise because the problems may not be resolved at the general level but at the specific ones, due to the changing capabilities of the child and the social systems of which he is a part.

3. I observed at the beginning of this chapter that cognitive-developmental theory was not a biological theory of cognition because, among other things, it was not concerned with such matters as brain-neurological development or with evolution.

However, some speculations on the issue have been offered. By making the establishment of self-concept a prerequisite for the development of social attachment in infants, Kohlberg's model seems to imply that a similar cognitive achievement is necessary for social bonding in nonhuman species. Accordingly, Kohlberg (1969) writes that "the more social species are also (a) the more cognitive species, (b) the more imitative species, and (c) the more playful (primary competence motivated) species" (p. 462).

This proposal is not generously supported by studies of behavior evolution and behavior development. In an exhaustive survey of animal societies, E. O. Wilson (1975) concludes that the prototypic truly social groups—in terms of distribution of work, establishment of roles, and complexity and efficiency of organization—are the insect societies of ants and wasps. How do ants do it? As we observed earlier (Chapter 18), their organization is achieved interdependence of development-paced changes in the brood, hormonal and breeding cycles of the queen, and foraging and care-taking activities of the workers in the colony. Detailed analyses of maternal-infant interactions in nonhuman mammals suggests, as well, that biophysical states in both mother and infant support early behavioral synchrony, the development of preferences, and bonding. Concepts of cognitive development cannot be denied in ants, but they don't seem to add much to the explanation either.

How might cognitive-developmental approaches be integrated more closely than they have been to evolutionary and developmental psychobiological views? The tentative steps toward the answer to this question have been taken by investigators coming at the problem from the direction of evolutionary biology. Hans Kummer (1971), for instance, speculates that increases in the complexity of the social interchanges of man's ancestors may have been responsible for an evolutionary increase in cognitive capacity. Kummer's argument thus reverses the directionality of the proposal that higher levels of cognitive organization gave rise to more complex social organization. Similarly, Julian Jaynes (1976) has proposed that the human consciousness reflects, in part, an evolutionary adaptation to changes in social organization of humans that occurred in the relatively recent past (3000 to 4500 years ago).

At an ontogenetic (proximal) level of analysis, the task remains to determine how morphological-hormonal changes are coordinated with cognitive changes to support the phenomena of early social development. Work on the cognitive-behavioral integration in both infancy and later childhood is required if these issues are to be rescued from hanging in mid-air.

New Directions

Of particular relevance for issues of social development are three major "new directions" in cognitive-developmental theory. These are its integration with the more general approaches of cognitive psychology, the new life that it has provided for symbolic interactional approaches to social behavior, and basic advances that have been made in the conceptualization of intentionality and motivation.

Cognitive Development and Cognitive Psychology

In its first forty years, cognitive-developmental theory proceeded almost independently of the main stream of the experimental work in psychology concerned with perception, cognition, and memory. The two areas of study—cognitive-developmental theory and cognitive psychology—have two quite different roots. The concepts of cognitive-developmental theory grew out of a biological analogy to mental growth in children, and the concepts and approaches of cognitive psychology were derived from longstanding traditions in psychology and philosophy on the nature of perception and memory.

Until the recent past, there has been scant overlap between the areas at the empirical or theoretical level. Despite differences in methods, orienting attitudes, and concepts, the two areas deal with common problems. It seems likely that work in cognitive psychology may help to answer some of the more compelling questions raised by cognitive-developmental theory, and vice-versa. Of immediate relevance to cognitive-developmental concerns are recent contributions on the development of memory, attention, and language.

The cross-fertilization of ideas is likely to invigorate both areas. Consider the key problem of the relationship between early cognitive and early social development. As A. Baldwin has observed:

> In the very young child the cognitive representation is relatively narrow and focused on some momentarily salient aspect of the immediately perceptible environment; it is strongly dependent upon the momentary state of the child, such as his drive state, his emotional state, his specific orientation, and upon the ongoing action of the moment (p. 327).

In effect, the "cognitive representation" of children 1–3 years old, including concepts of sex role and personality, are diffuse and not clearly defined. As the child matures and gains experience, the concepts become more precise, integrated, and "neutralized" with regard to momentary emotional state. This process, Baldwin (1969) argues, follows the general ground rules of developmental learning and generalization. To better understand the processes of concept identification and concept establishment, Baldwin argues, one must turn to the contributions of experimental studies of learning, memory, and language acquisition.

Baldwin's proposal has considerable merit. Rather than view studies of memory and language as being foreign territory, the findings on the development of memory and other cognitive processes would be integrated with changes in social behavior. Studies of the development of perceptual, discrimination, and language-memory abilities have begun to yield some promising leads. For instance, work on memory organization confirms that children 3–4 years of age do indeed have concepts around which they can organize both their perceptions and their memory (Ornstein, 1978). But they do not necessarily use the concepts effectively unless they are given hints and directions. Unlike older children and adults, who readily organize concepts in a memory task, preschool and kindergarten children choose inefficient and ineffective strategies. Because the young child's concepts of classes of events are relatively diffuse and easily modified, it seems reasonable to expect that his concepts of social relationships and of himself will also be reasonably open and vulnerable to modification.

Symbolic Interactionism and Cognitive Development

While experimental studies of memory and discrimination have begun to provide insights into the nature of concept identification and control processes, they have not provided many guidelines, as yet, on how concepts of interpersonal relations arise. Such matters have been a principal concern of symbolic interactional theories. In this regard, sociologist Leonard Cottrell (1969) has written insightfully on the emergence of the "self-other" system. Cottrell begins with the assertion that "the self should be conceived of not as a 'thing' but as a process" (p. 549). Interchanges with others lead to the emergence of a "self-other system" in which the child learns to expect certain acts from others as well as particular responses to his own acts. The child thus develops attitudes toward oneself as well as toward others. As Mead (1934) and Sullivan (1953) have emphasized, the "self" and "other" concepts are relative to the relationships and settings to which the individual has been exposed— hence Cottrell's emphasis on the "self" as a process rather than as an entity.

A reasonable goal for the immediate future will be to extend studies of concept identification into the naturalistic context to facilitate the study of in-

terpersonal adaptation and the self-concept. Such a step is long overdue; if taken, it will breathe fresh life into traditional experimental approaches to cognitive development and provide needed information about the concept identification processes of children in their most crucial adaptations. This step was originally proposed by James Mark Baldwin, who began with the assumption that mental development and social development are inseparably fused because "we are members one of another" (Baldwin, 1902).

Intentions, Expectations, and Actions

A third new direction of cognitive theory has been to clarify the relations between intentions, expectations, and actions. One objection that careful writers have to the use of such terms as "intention" and "expectation" in a systematic account of behavior is that they may provide only the illusion of an explanation. That is, the explanation of "why" a child acts in a particular way may be that he "intended to do it" or that he "wanted to," without specifying why he intended to or wanted to. If the reason were clearly specified, "intention" and "expectation" would be superfluous. Skinner (1971) has emphasized the danger of attributing actions to the "autonomous man" within, whose desires and intentions are beyond empirical analysis, and beyond science.

While the hazards are great, those of ignoring the cognitive controls of social behaviors are even greater. "Intentions" or "expectations" may be ascertained by a variety of means. Simply asking children what they think may be one of the most convenient but, in fact, one of the least reliable, ways to establish intentions.

In a recent treatment of the problem of intentionality, Francis Irwin (1971) has described rules for judging whether or not a given act was intentional. The advantage of Irwin's rules is that they do not require that the individual be able to speak; they can thus be applied to nonverbal species and human infants as well as to older children and adults. Although Irwin's solution is a complex one, couched in the language of symbolic logic, his ideas can be briefly described. He distinguishes among the *situation* in which behavior occurs, the *act* of the individual, and the *outcome* produced by the act. Irwin assumes that outcomes can be independently scaled on an "affective scale" in terms of being most preferred or least preferred. He assumes that expectancies arise (based on past experience) as to which acts of an individual will produce which outcomes. It is the relationship among (1) the individual's choice of acts, (2) his preference for a particular outcome, and (3) his expectancy that a particular act will produce a particular outcome that permits a judgment of whether a particular act was intentional. Such a judgment requires the precise identification of the act-outcome expectancy, on the one hand, and of the individual's preference for that outcome or its alternative, on the other.

In everyday life, information on act-outcome expectancies and preferences is not easy to come by. But, as Irwin demonstrates, under laboratory conditions we can ascertain precisely both expectancies and preferences. Preferences are determined by the individual's relative rankings of outcomes, and expectancies, by his differential choice of acts that reliably differ in the outcomes they produce. Specifically, Irwin defines intentionality as follows:

> By definition, act *a* is intentional if and only if its occurrence depends upon a preference for some differential outcome, *o*, over another differential outcome, o', upon the expectancy that *o* will result from *a* rather than some alternative act, a', and upon an expectancy that o' will result from a' rather than *a*.

Irwin's model makes it possible to determine a person's expectancies, preferences, and intentions by analyzing the situation, the person's behavior, and the outcome. As the above quote indicates, the criteria for definition are severe and cannot be easily or superficially applied in human affairs. The development of innovative procedures to anchor empirically the concepts of "intention" and "preference" in the typical everyday interchanges of children has just begun.

Contributions to the Developmental Synthesis

A synthesis of cognitive-developmental concepts with those of social learning and psychobiology is now in the making. Developmental studies of the social interchanges of children have forced attention to the "imprecise" concepts of expectancy, intention, and rules. These are concepts that behavioral psychologists have shied away from—not because they considered them unimportant, but because they considered them treacherous. Now that the Piagetian approach has helped break down some of the inhibitions about using cognitive concepts, they have come to the forefront. In cognitive-developmental theory, social behavior development cannot be divorced from the child's development of cognitions relevant to that behavior. Although the cognitive-developmental position has specific weaknesses (in failing to clarify how transitions between cognitive stages occur, and to explain the relation between cognitions and 'behavior'), it has forced attention to the correspondence between how children perceive and think, and how they behave. The cognitive-developmental approach has also facilitated the introduction of work of symbolic interactionists, on the one hand, and cognitive psychology, on the other, into the mainstream of developmental theory.

The contributions of the orientation to the developmental synthesis include the following:

■ The child's capabilities for making discriminations and forming concepts (about himself, about others around him, and about situations in which he is placed) change as a function of age and experience. Initially, the child's concepts are imprecise, transitory, and relatively inconsistent. In later childhood, concepts (including those concerned with social interaction) become more abstract and transcendant.

■ The self-concept and expectancies regarding the behaviors of others develop during interactions (both direct and vicarious) as well as through direct evaluations and training. These concepts, like those of a nonsocial kind, are relative to the settings and relationships that the child has experienced and are thus susceptible to change.

■ The child's expectations initially determine which social acts he will perform, and when he has a choice, which situations he will become involved in. Once he is involved in a relationship or situation, however, the interchanges that occur will shape his behaviors, attitudes, and expectations.

■ Neither unidirectional view of cognitive-social development—whether "cognitive" primacy or "social" primacy—seems justified by an organismic perspective, or by the facts. Direct analyses of the social adaptations of young children suggest that social rules and expectancies become interwoven with actions quite early in life. It has long been recognized that qualitative shifts occur in cognitive development following predictable (and possibly invariant) sequences. Contemporary studies of social ontogeny suggest that there are parallel stages in social behavior, although they have been less formally defined. A major job for research in the 1980's will be to trace bidirectional regulation of these two processes (interactive and cognitive) in the first five years of childhood.

21

ETHOLOGY AND EVOLUTION

Embryos undergo development; ancestors have undergone evolution, but in their day they also were the products of development.

—de Beer (1958), p. 1

If readers graded behavioral theories in terms of inherent interest, ethology would be a hands-down winner. Some of the most compelling science nonfiction of the past 25 years has been written by ethologists on the lifestyles and behavior patterns of diverse species: from the bighorn sheep in British Columbia to the hamadryas baboons in North Africa; from the chimpanzees of the Gombi Reserve in Uganda to the prairie dogs of North Dakota; from the feral sheep of the Soay Islands in the Northern Atlantic to the elephants, mountain gorillas, and lions of South Africa. The description of the behavior of species in their natural environments (ethograms) is a necessary step if ethology is to achieve its goal of determining how behavior patterns have evolved.

Ethology is the subdiscipline of biology concerned with the biological bases of behavior, including its evolution, causation, function, and development. The critical extension of evolutionary theory to behavior was largely ignored by biology until the issues were forcefully presented to European scientists by Konrad Lorenz (1935) and, later, to English-speaking biologists and psychologists by Niko Tin-

bergen (1951). Modern ethology now encompasses and provides direction for virtually all European (and many non-European) investigations of animal behavior, from neurobiological and physiological studies to developmental and ecological ones.

In this chapter I will focus on the *concepts* of ethology instead of its empirical contributions. The latter assignment—reviewing the ethological findings relevant to social development—was a major task of the rest of this volume. Here I will outline some ideas that underlie ethological investigations of social behavior and trace their revisions to see they have been fused with other concepts of human behavior. Because of the concerns of this book, I have selected for special attention the proposals of human ethology. For a broader picture of the multiple contributions of ethology and ethologists, the reader may want to consult one of the several volumes now available on the topic (Brown, 1975; Hinde, 1970; Eibl-Eisbesfeldt, 1975; Tinbergen, 1972a). In the final section of the chapter, the distinctive contributions of ethology to the developmental synthesis will be summarized.

Basic Themes: Evolution and Observations in the Natural Setting

Although a family tree of ethological theory would show as many branches as that of social learning theory, ethologists share at least two basic orientations—theoretical and methodological. The principal theoretical commitment is to the proposition that phylogenetic adaptations are significant determinants of social behavior patterns and motivations in animals, both human and nonhuman. The methodology follows directly from this theoretical orientation, in that the procedures are designed to identify the adaptive actions of the species in the conditions in which it is normally found. Although ethologists are thus committed to observations of unrestrained behavior, they also devise experiments to precisely control particular components in order to clarify the structure and intrinsic properties of action patterns and correlated motives.

The following comments by M. R. A. Chance, a British ethologist, on the scope and limits of ethology appeared in the *Human Ethology Newsletter* (May, 1975):

> The behavioural sciences came into existence as a result of historical accident and not logical requirements, otherwise ethology would have been the first, not the last, discipline to emerge, because observation and description are what is needed before analysis. Ethology is the observation of unrestrained behaviour or, where this is not possible, behaviour isolated as far as possible in a known way from its natural setting. . . . This leads to the description of the behaviour by whatever framework of units or measures is theoretically justifiable.
>
> Description of the behaviour requires the use of correct language. Then only does descriptive accuracy become possible, the object of which, in the first instance, should be the delineation of behaviour structure, since only then are we apprised of what exists and what may then be analysable. A knowledge of structure *must* precede analysis in causal or functional terms (Kummer,

1971). Hence, logically it is biologically based, i.e., it is concerned initially with species in their natural environment. Like any other part of biology, the theory of evolution is the theoretical background. This is a heuristic aid but not a universal explanation.

Chance's statement emphasizes (1) ethology's concern with the structure of "normal" behavior in a natural setting, and (2) ethology's commitment to evolutionary mechanisms. The comment that the evolutionary perspective is "not a universal explanation" should not be skipped over, because not all ethologists would agree with it. Indeed, they disagree as to whether the explanation of behavior in evolutionary terms is sufficient, or whether a proximal analysis of development is also required. I. Eibl-Eibesfeldt (1975), for one, has assigned an exclusive explanatory role to evolutionary mechanisms. Similarly, E. O. Wilson (1975) has proposed that evolutionary influences are the *primary* causes of behavior. Other ethologists, including N. Tinbergen (1972a) and R. Hinde (1970), consider both proximal and evolutionary analyses to be necessary. For Tinbergen, the issues of causation can be divided into three separate questions that differ primarily in the time scale involved, each of which is concerned with "what makes this happen?" First, there are short-term cycles in behavior (such as the tendency to eat, mate, defend territory), and one might ask what controls the onset and termination of such behaviors by examining the physiological and behavioral "machinery" that underlie them. Second, the individual's whole life can be considered as the cycle, and changes in behavior over the entire course of development can be studied to identify causes. Third, evolutionary changes in behavior occur as generations follow each other, and the time unit may be an eon. Tinbergen (1972a) points out that even though there is some overlap, causation studies refer to "three different problems" (p. 138) that require quite different research strategies. As Tinbergen describes the present state of affairs, a major trend of modern ethology has been to become deeply involved in the first two questions (in addition to maintaining its distinctive focus on evolutionary causation of behavior).

Concepts of Classical Ethology

Like the first three orientations that we discussed, ethology is a "living" theory, and any brief description of its concepts is apt to be misleading because the concepts themselves are undergoing critical evaluation, extension, and revision. As a starting point, I will describe certain of the key concepts introduced by Lorenz and Tinbergen in their efforts to describe behavioral "structures" and to explain how they evolved. The problem, as Tinbergen (1972a) put it, was to determine how behavior patterns could be treated as organs—as components of the individual's equipment for survival. The initial concepts were concerned with homologies (similarities due to common ancestry) in action, in motivation, and in developmental process.

Behavioral Units of Evolution. *Fixed action patterns* (FAP) have been called "innate skills" (Eibl-Eibesfeldt, 1975). Essentially, they can be defined as innate behaviors that serve major survival functions for the species—such as retrieval of eggs by the graylag goose, crying by the human infant, nest building by lovebirds, and nut opening by red squirrels.

What is the evidence that these acts are innate, and hence qualify as fixed action patterns? The appropriate criteria for innateness have long been the subject of debate; however, an act is generally agreed by ethologists to be innate if it is (1) stereotyped in form across individuals within a species, (2) established in the absence of relevant prior experience, (3) universal for the species, and (4) relatively uninfluenced by subsequent experience and learning. For example, as we saw in Chapter 6, infants smile at 6–8 weeks of age in a particular and predictable fashion when there is mild environmental change (and crying, to intense changes). The smiling occurs even in blind and deaf children,

emerging at approximately the same age as in normal children. Even though the frequency of the behavior can change with experience and with a change in conditions, the form of the expression remains relatively invariant across cultures (Freedman, 1974).

Key or *sign stimuli* are the cues by which fixed action patterns are released. These key stimuli are the result of phylogenetic adaptations of the organism, whereby particular events acquire the capability to trigger *innate releasing mechanisms* (IRM). The analogy of a key opening a lock has been used by Lorenz (1966) to describe the releasing process. Precisely what is released by the IRM? According to Eibl-Eibesfeldt's description of classical ethology, a neurosensory IRM allows central impulses to proceed to motor effectors (to activate the FAP) only when certain key stimuli occur.

In this system, not only are the motor patterns determined by phylogenetic adaptation, but so are the key stimuli that have the capacity to elicit the motor patterns. A major preoccupation of early ethological research was to catalogue, by means of detailed behavioral inventories or ethograms, the range of fixed action patterns and innate releasing mechanisms that occur in the species.

Are these concepts still employed by ethologists? Yes and no, depending on which ethologists and which concepts. Certainly a major concern of ethology remains to establish principles by which behavior has evolved, and a critical step has been to trace the occurrence of "fixed", or better, "modal" action patterns in related species (Barlow, 1968). On the other hand, contemporary ethological approaches have moved beyond the stage of cataloguing such patterns to undertaking analyses of their function, causation, and development (Immelmann, 1975). In addition, contemporary investigators, including Klopfer (1976), have argued persuasively for the need to employ more critical standards in attempts to distinguish among species similarities due to a common ancestry or to a common function.

Motivational Adaptations in Evolution. Ethological studies have been equally concerned with motivation, and how it is that propensities for action can be determined by phylogenetic adaptations. The theoretical underpinning for the concept of heritable drives—each with an action-specific energy source that required periodic discharge—were described by Lorenz in his early work (1973, first published in 1939). The ideas were later extended in the semipopular volume *On Aggression*, in which Lorenz defines the relationship between fixed action patterns and innate drives in the "great parliament" of instincts:

> The everyday, common, "cheap," fixed motor patterns which I have called the "little servants of species preservation" are often at the disposal of more than one of the "big drives." Particularly the behavior patterns of locomotion, such as running, flying, swimming, etc., also those of pecking, gnawing, and digging, can be used in the service of feeding, reproduction, flight, and aggression, which we will here call the "big drives." Because the little servants play a subsidiary part of "common final pathways" to various superior systems, in particular to the above-mentioned "big four," I have called them tool activities (p. 85).

The "big four" drives—hunger, aggression, reproduction, and flight—are proposed by Lorenz to be the basic motivations of all organisms and arise because of phylogenetic adaptations. The observed behaviors emerge as a result of continuing conflicts and compromises between these sources of energy. Accordingly, the task of ethological motivational analysis is to determine which major drives are in conflict in the performance of a given adaptive behavior.[1]

Do human beings have instinctive drives and innate behavioral propensities? According to some recent ethological statements, such as Eibl-Eibesfeldt (1975), the answer is strongly affirmative. The social behavior of humans is even more under the control of innate forces than that of nonhumans:

> This ethological knowledge, based on animal studies, can contribute to a better understanding of human behavior, and K. Lorenz recognizes this as "essentially the most important task" of the branch of science he founded. This is so because *in species that are mentally more advanced behavior to conspecifics is determined to a greater extent by innate components and less by learning than is their behavior toward the environment.* "That this is unhappily so even in man," Lorenz (1950, p. 431) writes, "is expressed drastically by the discrepancy between the enormous success in controlling the external environment and the crushing inability to solve intraspecific problems" (Eibl-Eibesfeldt, 1975, p. viii, my italics).

This conclusion is much the same as that reached by William James in 1890. In his classic *Principles of Psychology*, James argued that it was likely that inborn behaviors were more numerous and pervasive in human beings than in animals. The revival of this belief has been associated with the rapid recent growth of human ethology as a branch of ethology.

The concept of heritable drives, along with the proposals of action-specific energy and drive conflict, are now highly controversial. While many ethologists follow Hinde's (1970) lead in rejecting the idea of global social drives (such as aggression) and the correlated concept of specific energy, other classical ethologists are willing to entertain if not entirely endorse the motivational arguments (see Eibl-Eibesfeldt, 1975). The problems that unitary, global social drives present for ethology are not unlike the ones that they present for social learning theory (Chapter 19).

Homologous Processes: The Critical Period Hypothesis. Lorenz (1935) early proposed that not only were behavioral units (FAPs) subject to evolutionary survival pressures, but so were the processes by which the behavior patterns are acquired. The idea was, and still is, an important one for evolutionary accounts of behavior. It implies, among other things, that the predisposition to learn can evolve differ-

---

[1] A distinction has been drawn between innate behavior patterns and instinctual drives. Instinctual drives (such as aggression, gregariousness) are assumed to have their own inborn energy source that strives for expression toward a particular goal or activity. Innate behavior patterns, on the other hand, are not seen as endowed with action-specific energy and must be elicited by particular stimuli under particular conditions. Hinde's (1970) discussion further clarifies this distinction.

ently in different species, according to their survival demands. The specific proposal that Lorenz offered was that there was a *critical period* early in the life of some precocial birds when they were most susceptible to learning the characteristics and stimulus properties of their species. The period was critical because the effects produced by experiences in the post-hatching hours were proposed to be irreversible.

Lorenz's proposal was widely applied and, perhaps inevitably, widely misinterpreted. Because of its loose application (by ethologists and nonethologists) to species and to issues quite remote from those involved in the original conception, the concept became muddled and the term ambiguous. Presently there is a general preference in ethology to employ the term "sensitive period" to refer to the hypothesis that *the effects that experiences produce upon adult social behavior depend on the age-developmental stage at which they occur* (Bateson, 1978).

Are there in fact sensitive periods in social development? In birds, it depends on which species one observes. In the zebra finch, there is now strong evidence to support both of the two key criteria of Lorenz, early susceptibility and adult irreversibility (Immelmann, 1972). The persistence of the preferences established in the males of this species in the first 30 days post-hatching extend literally for years. For other species of birds, however, sensitive periods for social preferences occur later in life or not at all (King and West, 1977). A study of the social ecology and social organization of the species often suggests a straightforward reason as to why such differences exist. In the case of the zebra finch, the very rapid acquisition of filial preferences in the month following hatching meshes with the observation that in this species, there is virtually no interaction between the parents and their young after the first 30 days. If the young are to learn the distinctive characteristics of their parents and their species, it must be fast or not at all. For other birds, such as the parasitic cowbird that is foster-reared in nature, the establishment of an irreversible sexual preference in early post-hatching experience would be a disaster for the species. Hence an early sensitive period would be counteradaptive.

Is there a homology between the sensitive periods of birds and those that might be found in mammals? Because behavioral processes (unlike anatomical structures) leave no fossil records, we have no direct evidence on the matter. The indirect evidence, however, argues against any causal ancestral relationship. There are several problems, and one of the most compelling is simply that birds differ significantly among themselves in this process. Whether a given parallel is obtained depends on which birds are chosen for comparison: species that show strong evidence for a sensitive period for filial bonding, species that show a gradual development of bonds, or species for which the problem of species and sexual identification is solved by other mechanisms.

Now that the question of whether sensitive periods actually exist has been resolved (they do, but not necessarily in the same form or in an equivalent fashion for even closely related species), a cautious re-examination is being made of the functions that they serve and the mechanisms by which they operate. Bateson (1978), for instance, has proposed that preferences established in the sensitive period serve principally to inhibit inbreeding. At adulthood, birds may be able to recognize which mates to *avoid* (brothers or sisters) rather than approach. More generally, the question can be raised as to why an individual's choices should be constrained by very early experiences as opposed to later ones. The answer to this question—as well as to questions concerning the mechanisms by which sensitive periods operate—remains unanswered.

Ethology and Human Social Development

Despite uncertainties about the nature of behavioral homologies, the evolution of human behavior has become an increasingly explicit theme in the writings of ethologists. The contributions on this issue sort themselves into three categories: "ethologism," child ethology, and the ethological-psychoanalytic synthesis. It would be unfair to mix up these approaches to social development, because despite some overlap, they differ markedly in terms of aims, scientific merit, and logical development. For this reason, I shall consider them separately.

Ethologism

The scientific acceptance of revolutionary views of social behavior has often been associated with (and preceded by) aggressive and provocative presentations to the public. Since the public has supported the research, either directly or indirectly, and will be eventually influenced by its conclusions, either directly or indirectly, public disclosure is surely not a bad thing. But sometimes the techniques are. To ensure that the ideas are not ignored, they are often presented in such an extravagant form that they become caricatures of the scientific theory advocated. Usually the major theorists act as their own spokesmen (as did Sigmund Freud for psychoanalysis and John B. Watson for behaviorism), but sometimes the task is taken up by a protégé (as did G. J. Romanes for Darwinian theory). Ethology has had it both ways. Konrad Lorenz, a prime mover in modern ethology, has presented the popular case for ethology in several publications in German and English (most notably, *On Aggression*, 1966), and ethological investigators (such as Desmond Morris, in *The Naked Ape*, 1967) have written cleverly about the evolution of the human sexual condition and other matters.

How can one know whether a given work is supposed to be a scientific contribution or one aimed at informing and broadcasting the perspective? There is no simple formula (except, maybe, interest value and readability). Problems arise when intriguing but modestly researched claims proceed without due regard for scientific restraints, and when no clear distinctions are made between fanciful speculations, theoretical hypotheses, and empirical findings. The problems become compounded in dealing with hazy issues of development because it is unclear to the reader where informed reporting leaves off and unsubstantiated beliefs begin. Niko Tinbergen's insightful comments on the matter are worthy of attention:

> Recently, the application of Ethology to the study of man has been given worldwide publicity by Konrad Lorenz's *On Aggression* and Desmond Morris' *The Naked Ape*. As I have pointed out elsewhere, these books, while in many respects of great importance, have had two undesirable effects. On the one hand, they have led to an uncritical acceptance of their bold but not sufficiently substantiated extrapolations to Man—an attitude which Callan has recently called "ethologism." On the other hand, professional students of human behaviour have, in rejecting some of Lorenz's and Morris' claims, thrown away the baby with the bathwater, and so the Ethology of Man finds itself at the moment in a false position: over-acclaimed by many, shrugged off by others (Tinbergen, 1972b, p. vii).

Ethological Studies of Child Behavior

The application of ethological methods and ideas to the study of child social behavior has burgeoned in the 1970's, with Great Britain being the center of activity and its influence radiating to North America and the European continent (see Hutt and Hutt, 1970; Blurton Jones 1972; McGrew, 1972; and Schaffer, 1977). The work has proceeded on several fronts, ranging from the plotting of the social structures of preschool classrooms to parent-child interactions and the cross-cultural study of emotional development and expression. By employing direct observation methods to the study of children and the social systems of which they are a part, child ethologists have scored two significant accomplishments. First, they combined with a parallel movement emanating from behavioral approaches in North America to breathe fresh life into the analysis of child social development. Second, they provided some of the substance needed to evaluate ethological assumptions regarding the evolution of human behavior.

So far, however, few new conceptual formulations have arisen in child ethology, with the exception of the psychoanalytic synthesis, which we will consider in the next section. Research has been concerned for the most part with applying traditional ethological concepts and methods to children. Its two-fold aim has been to plot the structure and course of child development in the surroundings in which it typically occurs, and to identify possible evolutionary origins of sexual, cultural, and racial differences. Perhaps because of the second aim, initial ethological studies of children tended to treat them as if they were nonverbal primates, with great attention given to nonverbal communication and bodily movements. The limitations of this methodological restriction have become increasingly clear, and a trend in present studies has been to give greater attention to what a child says and what is said to the child (Strayer and Strayer, 1976) and what others expect of them.

What conceptual ideas might we reasonably expect to grow out of research in child ethology? To the extent that ethologists continue to take into account the interactions of children and the role of verbal communications in regulating them, major changes in ethological formulations may be required to incorporate the findings. Indeed, it seems inevitable that human ethology will move toward a more comprehensive understanding of cognitive development. This move, in turn, should promote a reconsideration of the mechanisms by which human cognitions have evolved (see Jaynes, 1976; Kummer, 1971).

The Ethological-Psychoanalytic Synthesis

The first serious attempt—and still by far the most influential—to extrapolate the implications of ethology to human behavior was pioneered by psychoanalyst John Bowlby (1958). Bowlby's life's work has been development of a comprehensive explanation of the origins of psychopathology and his major hypothesis has been that a primary cause is a disrupted mother-infant relationship. Bowlby's systematic tracing of the reasons why disruption of the bond may be critical brought him to a reconsideration of the issue from an evolutionary perspective. This reconsideration, in turn, permitted Bowlby (1969, 1973) and his colleagues (Ainsworth, 1972; Schaffer and Emerson, 1964) to attempt to achieve an integration of psychoanalytic theory and ethological concepts.

Psychoanalysis and ethology would seem to make an odd couple. At first blush, the combination would seem to be based on convenience rather than true compatibility. Psychoanalysis was founded as a branch of medicine concerned with the diagnosis and treatment of human behavioral and mental aberrations; ethology was founded as a branch of zoology concerned with the evolution of species-specific natural behavior patterns. Obscured by these different aims and methods is the fact that the orientations share the same biological heritage and a similar commitment to the study of the immanent forces that motivate behavior.

Both Freudian and Lorenzian theory (the classical statements of psychoanalysis and ethology, respectively) approach behavior from a biological perspective, and both assume that motives are instinctive and operate within a closed system of energy distribution. Even though Lorenz considered the aggressive drive to be primary in his "parliament of instincts," and Freud assumed libidinal drives to be basic, both systems share the assumption that primary motivations are instinctive and have action-specific energy that demands expression or sublimation. Equally important, they shared a belief in the primacy and significance of early experiences in the control of social patterns. The psychoanalytic concept of fixation (in psychosexual stages) roughly parallels the ethological concept of sensitive periods in terms of its emphasis on the highly durable effects of early social experience.

In light of these basic commonalities, it was perhaps inevitable that the two orientations should be merged, and that the resulting synthesis should have a significant impact on the study of social behavior, both normal and pathological. The merger provided new strength for both orientations: evolutionary theory gave new authority to psychoanalytic hypotheses, and psychoanalytic demonstrations of relevance to human behavior underscored that ethology was not limited to nonhuman animal behavior. Bowlby deserves credit for having outlined how the synthesis might proceed, and for serving as a catalyst in instigating novel lines of research to evaluate its validity.

Ethological-psychoanalytic theory can be divided into two separable though related parts: (1) an account of how social attachment behaviors initially arise, and (2) an account of how deprivation of maternal care of discontinuities in a child's relationship with his mother figure lead to psychopathological states. First, how does the mother-infant social attachment arise? Briefly, actions in the innate repertoire of the infant are synchronized with those of the mother, thus establishing the foundation for the bond. Because of phylogenetic adaptations, the infants has "genetic blueprint" to form an exclusive attachment with his principal caretaker, normally his mother. Hence, the mother's actions are key stimuli that elicit fixed action patterns in the infant, and vice versa. In Lorenz's terminology, the actions are "little servants." So the smile of the infant can elicit reciprocal smiling and caretaking by the mother; involuntary separation can provoke protest vocalization in the infant, which elicits attention by the mother. Such "synchrony" of action leads to the development of the firm mutual expectancies on the part of both the child and his caretaker, and to the strengthening of the affectional bond between them. Once the attachment bond is established, it promotes activation of an internal control system that serves to regulate the multiple behavioral manifestations of attachment, including the maintenance of an optimal distance from the mother and the fear of strangers. These "attachment behaviors" are modifiable; the "attachment structure" endures.

Second, how does anxiety (including related forms of psychopathology such as extreme distress, excessive anger, depression) develop? Bowlby answered this question early in his career, in an influential report commissioned by the World Health Organization: "What is believed to be essential for mental health is that the infant and young child should experience a warm, intimate and continuing relationship with his mother (or permanent mother-substitute) in which both find satisfaction and enjoyment" (Bowlby, 1952). The solution to the essential issue of psychopathology—the origin of anxiety—is to be found in disturbances to the early mother-infant relationship. Accordingly, anxiety and related states of disturbance are elicited by separation or fear of separation from the object of attachment. If the separation is permitted to extend, or if repeated separations occur, the child will become increasingly vulnerable to anxiety. As Bowlby (1973) indicates, the principal thesis can be stated precisely: "whether a child or adult is in a state of security, anxiety, or distress is determined in large part by the accessibility and responsiveness of his principal attachment figure" (p. 23). Separation-produced anxiety augments states of anger and aggression, which in turn provoke additional interpersonal stress. Such a vicious pattern of events presumably provides inevitable difficulty for the child in personal relationships and sets the stage for personality disorganization in adulthood.

Bowlby remains within the general framework of psychoanalysis, but introduces concepts of modern ethology to deal with the establishment and regulation of the attachment bond. The explanation of psychopathy remains essentially psychoanalytic except the root conflicts concern attachment rather than sex. Bowlby also shares the classical emphasis on the importance of the early experiences of infants and children. However, on the important question of when adjustment processes cease (that is, whether social plasticity is limited to infancy and early childhood or whether it persists into maturity), the theory is equivocal. On the one hand, some statements in *Attachment and Loss* (1973) suggest early fixedness:

> There is reason to believe that after a very prolonged or repeated separation during the first three years of life detachment can persist indefinitely (p. 12). . . . Their (Robertson and Robertson, 1971) experience has served to reinforce them in the view, which we have long shared, that separation is dangerous and whenever possible should be avoided (p. 22).

But in the same volume, later malleability is also suggested:

> The view adopted here . . . holds that the period during which attachment behaviour is most readily activated, namely from about six months to about five years, is also the most sensitive in regard to the development of expectations of the availability of attachment figures; but that nevertheless sensitivity in this regard persists during the decade after the fifth birthday, albeit in steadily diminishing degree as the years of childhood pass (p. 203).

Taken together, these passages reflect a relaxation of earlier held beliefs concerning the primacy and irreversibility of the early maternal-infant affectional relationship. Nonetheless, the theme that was expressed in the 1952 work remains dominant: a significant variation from the "normal" relational pattern in early life can be expected to produce subsequent pathological behavior.

Bowlby's attachment theory has had a catalytic impact on research. Some of the more influential work was conducted by Bowlby's colleagues at Tavistock Institute (Rudolf Schaffer, Mary Ainsworth, Christopher Heinicke, and James and Jane Robertson), and that work has stimulated research throughout the world on social development in humans, including much of the research cited in Chapters 6 and 7.

But on substantive grounds, the research of the past 25 years has failed to provide convincing support for a major premise of the theory: that mental health depends on the nature of the social bond that the child formed with his mother in infancy and early childhood. The premise leads to a pair of correlated hypotheses: one is that a warm, loving relationship between the mother and her infant will result in normal emotional development; the other is that the absence of warm, loving relationship, or interruptions of it, either brief or lengthy, will predispose the child to anxiety, anger, and hostility in later relationships. Neither assumption has won either conclusive or unequivocal support.

Both hypotheses require longitudinal information so that the later histories of children who have markedly different relationships with their mothers in infancy can be evaluated. "Crucial" studies on the matter are difficult to come by for both methodological and theoretical reasons (see Chapter 7, and compare Clarke and Clarke, 1976, with Klaus and Kennell, 1976). The problem of disentangling early effects in humans from later ones is formidable. If, for instance, the mother-infant relationship was in some way disturbed because of the mother's inattention, it may seem likely to expect that the later mother-child relationship would be strained for the same reason. But if the child has difficulties outside the home, which relationship should be blamed: the early, the late, or both? In one respect, the hypotheses seem grounded on a firm empirical base. The incidence of delinquency and psychopathology is higher among persons whose family relations were disturbed than among those whose families were not (see Bowlby, 1973). But there appears to be little specificity in the linkages between the disorder and the timing and nature of the familial disruption. Moreover, the factors that might account for these correlational findings have been confounded, so that maternal separation typically is associated with other plausible explanations for behavior disturbance. It remains for investigators in this tradition to either provide compelling tests of the hypotheses or to suggest revisions of them.

Nonetheless, the theory has achieved enormous success in stimulating innovative studies of children at home and in laboratory settings, and has inspired a new focus on cross-cultural infancy research and cross-specific work. It has, in effect, helped to re-shape contemporary views of the social behavior of infants and young children. The reformulation em-phasizes the biological foundations of interactive and attachment phenomena, the need to view the organism as part of a social system, and the rel-evance of evolutionary models and perspectives to understanding human behavior.

Sociobiology and the Evolution of Behavior

Not all of the credit for recent developments in clarifying the evolution of behavior should be given to ethology. In North America, there has been a convergence of biological disciplines concerned di-rectly or indirectly with behavior (principally ecol-ogy and population biology). This has led to the for-mation of a new major subarea of biology, *sociobiology*, which has been defined by E. O. Wil-son (1975) as the "study of the biological bases of all social behavior." The degree of overlap between this definition and that of ethology suggests, appro-priately, that these two fields share a good deal in common in methods and goals. But there are certain differences that are relevant to the study of social development. In this brief review of sociobiology, I will touch only a few of the conceptual issues: the reader can consult one of the following sources for further information: *The Evolution of Behavior* (Brown, 1975); *Sociobiology, The New Synthesis* (Wilson, 1975); or *The Selfish Gene* (Dawkins, 1976).

De-Coupling Development and Evolution

Biological studies can be organized typically into one or the other branch of the science—evolution-ary biology or molecular biology. This distinction is of particular importance for a major spokesman for sociobiology, E. O. Wilson, because of his classifica-tion of ecology and population biology into one branch, and developmental studies (including virtu-ally all of the work of psychology, experimental em-bryology, and behavioral endocrinology) into the other. Furthermore, Wilson does not foresee that the concepts and ideas of evolutionary biology will, in the foreseeable future, have any direct relevance for molecular biology, or vice-versa. Hence he pro-poses that developmental studies and theories should be "decoupled" from sociobiology.

This bold conclusion is a logical outcome of Wil-son's view that the evolution of behavior is appro-priately pursued by the study of social structures of species and populations, not of individuals and their interactions—thus the term sociobiology (sociology-biology) instead of psychobiology. This focus on so-cial structure instead of developmental process is not a mere artifice. To the contrary, Wilson ob-serves that the leap between gene and social behav-ior is fraught with more pitfalls, intellectual and em-pirical, than between gene and social structure. Since the societal structure of a species is reasonably stable across generations while the social behaviors of an individual are surely not, the former has seemed more susceptible to the concepts and mathematics of population biology. I should add that Wilson's view on decoupling development and evolution is widely shared (see Dawkins, 1976; Lor-enz, 1965) but not universally shared (Gould, 1977).

Evolutionary Adaptation

What aspects of societal organization are analyzed by sociobiolgists? Virtually all of its basic features, including reproductive patterns (whether monoga-mous or polygamous, etc), nature of the social struc-ture (whether in social hierarchies or autonomous subunits, territorial or nonterritorial), and whether or not specific roles exist in the society (to help, to forage, to give birth). These differences in social structure, in turn, may be related to the ecological demands to which the species is normally exposed.

Evolutionary adaptations, which are, by definition, genetic and occur in populations over generations, can be contrasted with *functional adaptations,* which are nongenetic and occur within a single individual over a lifetime or shorter periods of time. This distinction is an important one because in developmental studies (which occupy most of this book) we have dealt with functional adaptations in ontogeny, such as fitting into a new social relationship or learning new coordination patterns.

Consider how environments can provide the conditions for the evolution of particular reproductive patterns (whether to breed prolifically or selectively, whether to have more than one mate, whether to breed offspring that mature rapidly or slowly, and so on). Presumably some environments may favor rapid reproduction by the society (by breeding more and producing more eggs or babies), a reproductive "strategy" that is called "r-selection." Other environments may favor breeding with great efficiency and parental care in meeting the needs of the offspring, a reproductive strategy that is called "K-selection." Which sort of environment might be expected to support which reproductive strategy? According to one evolutionary model, highly variable environments that change during the course of the year from abundant, lush conditions to barren, sparsely vegetated ones (as in certain regions of the arctic or in the African savanna) should support r-selection. For such species, the best policy would be: "Be fruitful and multiply, fast." On the other hand, overcrowding could become a problem in lush, abundant environments that show little change during the course of the year (as might be found in, say, a tropical forest). When density is a primary factor limiting population growth, the species might be expected to favor a K-selection reproduction strategy. Hence the species should produce fewer offspring, but the young should have relative long periods of immaturity and should benefit from excellence in parental care.

How well do these predicted correlations between reproductive patterns and environmental conditions hold up? Despite the breadth of the hypothesis and the number of factors that might influence reproductive patterns, one finds overall a rough matching of pattern with environment in various species, including some primate societies and birds (see Brown, 1975; Crook, 1970; Wilson, 1975). The match, however, falls considerably below perfect, and detailed analyses of primate societies yield considerably less than stable relationships.

Space limitation prohibits giving a detailed analysis of the other major applications of sociobiological/evolutionary models to the occurrence of aid-giving in rearing, to altruism, to parent-child conflict, and to other nonparental stable patterns of interchange that have been presumed to have evolved. There is presently considerable controversy about the precise evolutionary mechanisms involved, because of the open-ended nature of the current theories of behavior evolution. One of the more interesting proposals has been considering these interchange and reproductive patterns to represent *evolutionarily stable strategies,* or ESS. An ESS is defined as "a strategy which, if most members of a population adopt it, cannot be bettered by an alternative strategy" (Dawkins, 1976, p. 74). What makes the proposal an evolutionary one is the assumption that the "strategy" is a "preprogrammed behavioural policy." It is, in other words, a genetic propensity to take particular roles in an interaction. The provocative feature of this proposal is that it recognizes the interactional nature of social behavior and social organization *within* the context of evolutionary adaptations (see Maynard Smith, 1974; and Dawkins, 1976). Further consideration of the technical details would take us too far afield.

Recoupling Evolution and Development

Can developmental and evolutionary orientations be integrated, or must they be decoupled, as some sociobiological theorists have proposed? The advantages to a separation are not trivial. The fields are immense, and it might be a waste of resources to attempt to become involved in the methods, ideas, and terminology of other disciplines, especially if there were meager hope of one's being related to the other. It would also save a great deal of misunderstanding and debate about *the* origin of behavior—whether innate or developed—because there would be the explicit acceptance that the answer depended on which level the analysis was employed.

But there are also disadvantages to a cleavage of fields and concepts. One of the more unfortunate practices in evolutionary discussions of behavior has been to use terms that have been borrowed from descriptions of human personality and emotions, such as altruism, selfishness, cooperation, and spitefulness, and to redefine them to refer to concepts of population genetics. Subtle problems arise when these redefined concepts are then reintroduced to the interpersonal processes from whence they came, with the new, altered meanings. One may possibly speak of an "altruistic gene" or an "aggressive gene" at the level of population biology and species social structure. But it is a hazardous business to imply that the multiple and complex psychological processes to which these terms refer in the interactions of individuals can be likewise explained. Furthermore, introduction of a concept of "reciprocal altruism" without an appreciation of the multiple other reciprocities and how they arise can be misleading.

On a more general level, some psychobiological theorists have argued that the course of evolutionary change in species' behaviors may be identified by a detailed analysis of their ontogenies (see Chapter 18). Accordingly, a functional/evolutionary divorce would be a theoretical disaster for both areas. Instead of explaining social behavior in terms of evolutionary forces, social development would be accepted as a major force in social evolution.

Before we leave this topic, it is of interest to note the closing comments in S. Gould's recent review on the relations between ontogeny and phylogeny. Gould (1977) writes:

> I predict that this debate [on the role of heterochrony in producing evolutionary changes] will define the major issue in evolutionary biology for the 1980s. I also believe that an understanding of regulation must lie at the center of any rapprochement between molecular and evolutionary biology; for a synthesis of the two biologies will surely take place, if it occurs at all, on the common field of development (p. 408).

A similar conclusion may be offered for the special problems of social evolution and social development.

Contributions to the Developmental Synthesis

Just as there is no single social learning theory, there is no single statement that accurately sums up the ethological position. But two major themes are shared by virtually all investigators who call themselves ethologists. One is the concern with behavioral evolution, and the belief that comparative observations may shed light on the social behaviors of related species. The other theme is that behavior is best analyzed under "natural" conditions. The theoretical and methodological themes fit together, in that the observation of species in their natural habitats, without artificial constraints, should permit the identification of innate, heritable characteristics. Both themes stand in sharp contrast to the traditional theories and methodologies of child development, which were concerned neither with evolution nor with natural observation.

The ethological-psychoanalytic synthesis adds still another theme: that of developmental psychopathology. The phenomena of infancy and early childhood, the infant's "protest" on being separated from his mother and his "fear" of strangers, are considered to be prototypic of adult human depression, anxiety, anger, and sorrow.

The ethological-psychoanalytic view that innate developmental pacemakers determine the nature and course of the child's interchanges has had, and doubtless will continue to have, great impact on studies of social development in human infants. However, attempts to account for individual differences in susceptibility to psychopathology (because of early disruptions of the attachment relationships) are based on slender empirical evidence (see Chapters 6 and 7).

More important for the developmental synthesis, the critical issues of behavior evolution have been discovered anew because of the emphases and findings of ethology. The phenomena of evolutionary adaptations can no longer be ignored in developmental analyses, even if they do not readily fit existing ideas. A key advance follows from the recognition that social phenomena can be analyzed at two levels—ontogenetic and phyletic—and that different concepts may be legitimately employed at the two levels. Hence social patterns may be seen as developing in an individual's lifetime (over years) or they may be viewed as evolving over a species "lifetime" (over thousands or millions of years). Moreover, ontogenetic analyses are biased toward the identification of individual differences by virtue of their focus on how the individual uniquely adapts during the course of development. Evolutionary analyses, on the other hand, are biased toward finding group similarities because of their attention to how the species had adapted to its environment in phylogeny.

In conclusion, the following propositions must be added to the developmental synthesis:

■ Studies of the social behavior of a species in its natural habitat are needed to establish the nature and course of typical development; hence they are prerequisites for both evolutionary and developmental analyses. Although the identification of the "natural habitat" for human beings is virtually impossible because of the range of environments in which man may be found, ethological methods are nonetheless required for the study of child social development. A precise account of the normative course of social development is as fundamental for the establishment of ontogenetic principles as it is for the establishment of evolutionary ones.

■ The existence of universal and species-typical social patterns that appear to be adaptive in the ontogeny of the species (including human beings) strongly implicates the role of biological pacemakers in social development. Biological influences operate through multiple routes, however. The effects may be produced directly (via bidirectional changes related to modifications of hormonal, morphological, or cognitive status) or indirectly (such as by societal expectations regarding anticipated differences at maturity, see Chapter 15).

■ Therefore the proper study of the determinants of social interchanges requires attention to be given to both evolutionary and developmental processes. Even though the processes may be usefully explored at two different levels of analysis, they must ultimately yield concepts and findings that are mutually supportive and complementary.

22

CONTINUITY AND CHANGE
IN SOCIAL DEVELOPMENT

However closely psychical changes may conform to law, it is safe to say that individual histories and biographies will never be written in advance no matter how "evolved" psychology may become.

—*James (1890), Vol. II, pp. 576–577*

The matters of continuity and change have been addressed, directly and indirectly, throughout this book and it seems fitting that it should close with a re-examination of when human social behavior can be predicted and when it cannot. It has been observed, half seriously, that human behavior is about as predictable as the weather. In other words long-range forecasting, whether of rain or behavior, is a risky business. Exactly how risky and probabilistic is illustrated by the following biographical profiles:

Zane Calvin[1] was reared in the eastern United States and enjoyed the educational and social advantages that are associated with a family whose income is in the upper 1 percent. His father was a prosperous attorney, and for a period was president of a principal railroad serving New York

City. In high school and college, Zane developed an opportunistic though thoroughly pleasant way of dealing with others. Following graduation from college, he entered a Ph.D. program in psychology, where he rapidly gained a reputation for being a well-informed, witty lecturer, and a well-organized, promising researcher.

Xeno Bennett grew up on the other side of the country, literally and figuratively. He lived in a medium-sized community, the son of a nurse and small business owner. Xeno was well coordinated physically, and in high school was an outstanding athlete, well liked by his companions, both male and female. He was a lackluster student, and though he entered junior college after high school, he did poorly and dropped out. He was then employed in a succession of short-term jobs, such as the grading of old automobile carcasses for retreading.

---

[1] The proper names used in all descriptions are fictitious; otherwise, the descriptions are accurate to my best knowledge.

Yolanda Addison was the daughter of a successful neurosurgeon. In secondary school, her fellow students regarded her as being pleasant and bright, though somewhat on the serious side. Upon entering the university, she declared a major in sociology and psychology, and became especially interested in working with young children in nursery school and kindergarten. But she was not merely a serious student who enjoyed working with children; she became involved in various campus activities, including the "protest" movements that rippled periodically across the campus.

Although the information provided on each person is sketchy, it may seem sufficient to enable us to make some general predictions about their eventual adjustments to life. The odds may suggest that Zane would have become a popular college instructor and perhaps departmental chairman or dean; that Xeno would have become a marginal working class type, who relived past glories by watching televised football with his high school buddies; and that Yolanda would teach preschool for a year or two before entering graduate school or becoming a housewife who was vitally concerned with local and national political issues. These predictions are disappointingly off target. There were some clues in the biographies—but precious few—that would permit us to predict the status of the persons at mid-life: one had become a successful banker; one had become a spiritual leader of the counterculture; and one had become the subject of an international manhunt after committing acts of terrorism.

Zane Calvin completed his graduate training and accepted a teaching position at a major university in the eastern United States. One of his several research projects concerned the investigation of the hallucinogenic properties of LSD, mescaline, and other psychomimetic drugs at a time (the early 1960's) when their use was legal and little was known about long-term effects. Partly because of the research, Calvin and a colleague were forced to leave their teaching positions. They continued drug investigations in various locations, but the work ran into difficulties, including legal ones.

Calvin eventually dropped out of the project, and, seeking new directions for life, studied Hindu practices and beliefs with a guru in whom he had great confidence. Calvin adopted a new name, Pukka Sadhu, and, after returning to the United States, became a well-known lecturer, author, and spiritual figure.

Xeno Bennett's troubles in junior college were followed by a family tragedy: his mother died and his father became increasingly incapacitated. A maternal aunt and uncle invited Xeno to live in their home on the condition that he attend the local university. The first year at the university was tenuous for Xeno, but with considerable tutorial help from his relatives he achieved above-average grades. Gradually developing reasonable achievement standards and study habits, he did quite well through the junior year. At that time, concerns about financial matters and restraints placed upon him led to his withdrawal from school and entry into the management training program of a large banking firm. By the age of thirty, he had been promoted to a key management position in the firm.

While Yolanda Addison was still an undergraduate, she became a dedicated participant in political protests that became increasingly extreme. The splinter group with which she became affiliated became alienated from the broader community and turned to radical forms of expression. To date, the organization has claimed responsibility for multiple acts of terrorism, including several murders and the kidnapping and execution of a major industralist. At age 27, Yolanda is thought to be one of the leaders of the group. She is presently being sought by the police of several Western European countries.

Although it may be possible to make better-than-chance matchings across the two sets of selections, it seems unlikely that the early information would have provided the basis for predicting the actual careers and social adaptations of the persons. The critical information relevant to predictions was not intentionally omitted from the first selections; rather, it simply was not available at the time that they were 19–21 years of age. In each case, major choices, and environmental changes occurred afterwards. The reversals of prediction were most startling in the case of Addison and Bennett, where their social actions at maturity seem to be in sharp contrast with those to which they had been exposed in development. Nonetheless, once they were established in their new roles, the actions that they followed fit the circumstances and relationships to which they were then exposed, whether as a member of a terrorist group or of the banking community.

It is tempting to try to pinpoint the "critical" determining events in each person's life. In the case of Pukka Sadhu, it might be argued that entrapment with psychedelic drugs (via legitmate research) was a major turning point. For Bennett, the uprooting from the network of relationships in his home and the demand to adapt to a new and virtually foreign set of standards might have been the key. In the case of Addison, it could be argued that she was a terrorist by default, that her primary concerns were political idealism and that she had been forced by events into terrorism. But it is easy to offer plausible post hoc explanations as to why persons behave as they do. The temptation is to selectively emphasize consonant events and to ignore or explain away dissonant ones.

How might the predictions have been made more accurate, *or could they have been?* The inherently probablistic nature of development may preclude precise predictions, as the passage from James's *Principles of Psychology* (1890) suggests. On the average, however, one would have been accurate in predicting that Calvin's peers would become respected teachers and researchers (they have, in fact), and that the best estimates for future accomplishments of persons with Bennett's and Addison's backgrounds should have been their accomplishments in the past. To sharpen forecasting, it doubtless would have been useful to have known the social-cultural environment to which Addison, Calvin, and Bennett would eventually be introduced. If it were known that Bennett, say, would have been translocated to a more challenging intellectual context and given help in adapting to it, the prediction might have been totally different than if it were known that he would remain in his home town.

But how could it have been predicted that a college professor would become a sadhu? On closer analysis, it might be argued that Calvin's transformation was the least radical of the three, in that Pukka Sadhu performed many of the same functions (lecturing to persons of college age, writing books, giving personal counsel) that Calvin would have performed in an academic setting. Perhaps, beneath the surface, the motivation and essential psychological needs of each person remained unchanged, although their expression was not anticipated.

The aim of this chapter is to summarize the implications of the developmental synthesis for these issues of continuity and change. Following a brief overview of the main proposals that have been offered to explain continuity, I will outline the contemporary developmental perspective on the issue. One virtue of the developmental synthesis is that it promotes more precise statements than heretofore available by indicating when and why major shifts in social adaptation are likely to occur, and when and why some interpersonal characteristics are likely to remain relatively unchanged.

Why Continuity?

A debate has been in progress throughout most of the present century on whether continuity in social development is due to internal influences (motives, traits, or physiological structures) or external (environmental) influences.

The first point of view is represented by Gordon Allport (1937) and his concept of the functional autonomy of motives. According to this concept, social acts that begin as means to an end can become ends in themselves, and, once established, "acquire a stranglehold." Consistent with his emphasis on the ultimate and irreducible uniqueness of personality,

Allport (1937) proposed a general law by which he attempted to explain how both consistency and uniqueness come about. He argues that the motives of an adult grow out of antecedent motives, but become functionally independent of them. A person becomes what at first he pretended to be:

> . . . the smiling professional hostess who grows fond of her once irksome role and is unhappy when deprived of it; the man who for so long has counterfeited the appearance of self-confidence and optimism that he is always driven to assume it; the prisoner who comes to love his shackles. Such *personae*, as Jung observes, are often transformed into the real self. The mask becomes the animus (Allport, 1937, pp. 206–207).

The principle of functional autonomy was seen by Allport to be the "declaration of independence" for the psychology of personality, presumably because behavior was no longer regulated by adaptational demands.

The idea that general motives can be acquired, and then can become essentially permanent aspects of personality, is similar to the ideas contained in other models (see Table 22-1). Social learning theory proposes that motives are acquired by being paired with the induction and reduction of primary drive states, and classical psychoanalytic theory holds that motives arise because of an interaction between psychobiological forces and early experiences. Most dynamic personality theories, including that of Bowlby (1969) and Ainsworth (1972), assume that the internal structures underlying social behaviors are strongly influenced by early familial experiences. For Allport, motives can become functionally autonomous both early in life and in later maturity. Because the theory specifies that actions which were once functional will later be performed for their own sake instead of for the consequences that they produce, a very large (but finite) number of motives become possible.

But the proposal that continuity comes about because of the operation of internal structures of personality needs and motivation is but one end of a continuum of theoretical possibilities. At the other

end of the continuum, it has been proposed that personal consistency is most appropriately viewed in terms of environmental constancy. Hartshorne and May (1928) provided a clear statement of the key role of contextual factors when they wrote:

> Not only does character not consist of a sum of virtues, but the virtues themselves are not psychological entities with any real existence. They are not acts. They are classifications of acts. To attribute to a man who acts honestly a faculty or trait of honesty is like explaining the act of remembering by referring it to some faculty of memory, which our popular systems of mnemonics are supposed to develop as one would train a muscle. Of course some people remember better than others, but to refer this difference to some mysterious and specialized power of memory is to stuff our ignorance with words. Similarly, to say that an honest act is caused by a man's honesty is like saying that it is cold because the temperature has fallen. Some men, it may be, can learn to be honest more easily than others because of real mental differences the nature of which we are not as yet aware; but whatever honesty a man possesses resides not in a secret reservoir of honest virtue nor in the ideal of honesty which he may hold before himself as worthy of his best effort, but in the quality of acts he performs (pp. 378–379).

The position has been given a modern statement by Mischel (1973; see also Chapters 17 and 19). He has cogently argued that one should not speak of "behavior" but of "behavior-contingency units" because it is meaningless to attempt to describe behaviors independent of the contexts and relationships in which they may be expected.

By way of summary, Table 22-1 outlines the range of proposals that have been offered and, roughly, their placement with respect to several key dimensions that extend beyond the external-internal control controversy. I provide the outline with some hesitation because of the hazards of lifting a construct from the context of the theory in which it was established, and thereby distorting its meaning. It can be used nonetheless to demonstrate that the problem of "why continuity" has been tackled from a wide range of theoretical perspectives and that the assumptions that have been entertained (on whether a characteristic is innate, age-dependent, biologically based, and mode of development) are not interdependent. The summary also points out that (a) a significant proportion of the proposals have been nondevelopmental, and (b) few attempts have been made to account for *both* change and continuity over the lifespan of the person. This table is brief and incomplete, and the reader may wish to consult Bloom (1964) and Wohlwill (1973) for further discussion, including the "overlap hypothesis" that Anderson (1939) proposed to account for continuities in motor and cognitive development. We now turn to the outcome of the attempts of contemporary developmentalists to explain both social continuity and change.

Continuity and Change from a Developmental Perspective

An emerging developmental perspective to continuity and change has been adopted in one form or another by most contemporary investigators. The ideas should not seem novel to the reader; indeed, they have appeared in various sections in this book. The problem for developmental models is to explain continuity, not change, since ontogeny necessarily involves modification. Developmental orientations have investigated maturational, interactional, and societal-generational sources of change. None of these domains can be expected to remain constant throughout the life of the individual, and changes in one domain can trigger changes in another. Consider, for instance, the pervasive effects of age-related changes. Modifications in the child's sensorimotor and cognitive competencies elicit, typically, modifications in interchange patterns, and possibly vice-versa. Even if the social-cultural context remains relatively unchanged over a generation (which is unlikely these days), an individual child's

status in the society surely will not remain unchanged over ontogeny. Given the dynamic nature of social development, the challenge is to explain why continuities occur, not why changes are observed.

How, then, do individual consistencies arise in social development? Five factors that support continuity of social behavior over development have been identified:

1. *Social network*. In the light of the importance of reciprocal controls on the social actions of the child, reliable predictions to other settings and later developmental states require information about the social networks in which the child will participate and their relations to the present one. If all other factors are equal, similarities in the child's social actions from one point in time to a future time should be the greatest when the social systems are similar over the two times. Conversely, drastic changes in the social adaptation requirements should produce concomitant changes in the child's social behavior. Consistencies in social settings promote consistencies in social behaviors.

2. *Evocation*. The child is not a passive agent in the process. Individual children may evoke common responses across time by virtue of their stimulus properties (sex or gender role, size age, race) or by virtue of their social actions. Obviously, some stimulus properties are likely to remain constant over time and across settings; others are likely to change. Sex classification, say, is in most cases highly stable while physical characteristics, such as height and weight, are likely to change over the course of development. Similarly, the social patterns of children can evoke common responses. The loud assertive child can re-create for himself similar environments and reactions across several different contexts and time intervals.

3. *Choices*. The child may also behave in ways that help to promote continuity in social settings and relationships by virtue of his choices and preferences. Although attachment is considered the prototype of the child's attempt to preserve the familiar and avoid the unfamiliar, a comparable process can

Table 22-1. Continuity proposals compared on five developmental dimensions.

Examples of proposals	Induction[a]	Age-dependent[b]	Biological Structure[c]	Internal-external control[d]	Mode of development[e]	References
"Evolutionarily stable strategies" (ESS) of aggression, altruism, selfishness	Preprogrammed	Independent	Implied	Internal/External	Nondevelopmental	Dawkins, 1976; Maynard Smith, 1974; Trivers, 1974; Wilson, 1975
"Instinctual drives" for aggression, mating, with action-specific energy	Preprogrammed	Independent	Implied	Internal	Nondevelopmental	Eibl-Eibesfeldt, 1975; Lorenz, 1969; McDougall, 1908; Tinbergen, 1951
"Innate releasing mechanisms" that are triggered by particular sign-stimuli	Preprogrammed	Independent	Sometimes explicit	Internal	Nondevelopmental	Lorenz, 1966; Tinbergen, 1951
"Temperament differences" and heritable differences in reactivity	Innate-Constitutional	Dependent	Explicit	Internal/external	Transactional	Bell, 1968; Thomas, Chess, and Birch, 1968; Sameroff, 1975
Stable societal and macrosocial norms that operate across time and settings	Experiential	Dependent	Unspecified	External	Age-related societal norms and roles	Bronfenbrenner, 1977: Nesselroade and Baltes, 1974
"Functional autonomy" of motives in human personality	Experiential	Dependent	None	Internal	Motive learning	Allport, 1937
"Secondary motives" in the behavior regulation of children	Experiential	Dependent	Unspecified	Internal	Motive learning (early)	Sears, Whiting, Nowlis, and Sears, 1953

Phenomenon						Reference
"Control systems" in the establishment and regulation of attachment	Preprogrammed/Experiential	Dependent	Unspecified	Internal	System establishment (early)	Bowlby, 1969; Ainsworth, 1972
"Situational specificity" of moral conduct (altruism, honesty) in children	Experiential	Independent	None	External	Nondevelopmental	Hartshorne and May, 1928
"Behavior-contingency units" of social behavior in stable environments	Experiential	Independent	Unspecified	External/Internal	Nondevelopmental	Mischel, 1973; Bandura, 1969
"Sensitive period" for irreversible mating preferences in birds	Preprogrammed/Experiential	Dependent	Implied	Internal	Arrest	Lorenz, 1935; Immelmann, 1972
"Fixation" and "regression" in the development of psychopathology	Experiential/Preprogrammed	Dependent	Unspecified	Internal	Arrest	Freud, 1933
"Reinstatement" of early experience by stimulation at maturity	Experiential	Dependent	Unspecified	Internal	Arrest	Campbell and Jaynes, 1966

[a] Whether the continuities arise by virtue of preprogrammed factors and are relatively uninfluenced by individual experience, or whether they are dependent upon the unique experiences of the individuals.
[b] Whether the process by which the structures underlying continuity are age-dependent (must occur at a sensitive or critical phase of development), or whether the process is age-independent.
[c] Whether the continuities reflect the operation of an explicitly defined biological structure or function, or whether there is no attempt to link continuities to biological status.
[d] Whether the continuity is assumed to reflect internal or external factors.
[e] Whether continuity is assumed to reflect nondevelopmental factors, early development arrest, consolidation, or continuing transaction.

occur throughout development in the maintenance of friendships and the choice of activities. Once the choices are made, reciprocal processes permit the child to adapt to the demands of the new relationship and situation. Obviously, not all choices preserve continuity. Some, as in the case of religious conversion, marriage, or joining a political movement, can produce radical changes.

4. Biological constraints and maturation. At each developmental stage (and for some characteristics, across developmental stages), the child is predisposed to perform particular social acts by virtue of biological constraints. These constraints include those of a basic physiological nature (including endocrine gland and neural activity) that may support differences in activity levels, reactivity, and other "emotional" or temperament differences. They also include biological differences related to motor, cognitive, linguistic, and perceptual capabilities. Hence similarities in a child's interactions across two or more time intervals may arise simply because the child is not competent to make different responses, or because the perceptual-cognitive discriminations necessary for formulating new responses are not yet in the repertory.

5. Consolidation. Children (and older persons as well) tend to repeat a social act or pattern if the conditions for its prior elicitation recur, and social sequences become consolidated by virtue of their repeated occurrence. Once consolidated, social interchanges will be elicited by fewer cues than were originally required for establishment and hence will be more readily generalized to new settings and maintained in old ones. Such consolidation also provides a major experiential basis for the maintenance of individual differences, and thereby constitutes a major mechanism for social continuity.

The developmental perspective is necessarily a bidirectional (transactional) one. The child's interchanges and organismic status at any point in time are seen as contributing to, but not wholly determining, his status and interchanges at succeeding times. The weight that must be given to any one of the five factors in maintaining continuity is relative:

(a) to the magnitude in change of any one of them and (b) to the point in ontogeny and organization of behavior at which the changes occur. Hence the reason that "biographies cannot be written in advance" is that the course of development is essentially probabilistic. To the extent that the probabilities are given explicit definition for the present and for future times, predictions into succeeding time intervals can be sharpened.

In accord with an organismic analysis, the unique social adaptations of children are multiply determined. Supports for individual consistency may occur in the child, in other persons, in their interchanges, and in the social-cultural milieu. Nor are the factors independent of each other. If one had known, for instance, the social network into which Xeno Bennett was thrust at early maturity, one would have been tempted to offer predictions about the nature of his subsequent choices and what social patterns might consolidate quite different from the predictions that would have been made from his earlier background.

The fact that we can be surprised by failures to predict correctly (as possibly was the case for Calvin, Bennett, or Addison) suggests our intuitions about such matters may not be wholly random. Indeed, they are not. Common sense predictions usually reflect one's hunches about the kinds of situations in which the child will be placed, as well as educated guesses about what may be the child's emerging capabilities, choices, and preferences. One can become educated in such guesses to the extent that one has information about the special capabilities of the person, the likely environment in which the person will develop, and the typical trajectory of development and expectations of the society.

The developmental model points to ways that common sense judgments may be improved upon. In order to transform an informal subjective analysis into a more accurate predictive one, precise information is needed about the nature of the social systems that are most likely at each stage of development, and the likely conditions for decision-making, evocation, and social pattern consolidation. Such a requirement presupposes information about the normal (that is, typical) course of social development for children in general and for those who differ with regard to the above sources for continuity. Separate explanations are not required for continuity and change: Both outcomes can follow from the same developmental processes.

How might the adequacy of the developmental account be evaluated? Unfortunately, most of the studies available on social continuity and change in children either do not provide findings relevant to the above propositions, or they are relevant only in a negative sense (that of providing evidence for change). Accordingly, before summarizing the empirical findings, it is necessary to review the main problems encountered in the assessment of social and nonsocial continuities.

Semantic, Measurement, and Methodological Issues in Empirical Studies of Continuity

What might at first seem to be a straightforward though tedious task of testing and retesting children at different points in time in order to obtain information about the continuity of social behavior has proved to be anything but straightforward. Because of problems that have arisen in definition, measurement, and method, the empirical study of social continuity has become a complex, controversial business.

The Multiple Meanings of Continuity

One of the problems is semantic. The central term—*continuity*—has been used to refer to quite different phenomena by different investigators, producing, for both students and investigators, a kind of semantic minefield. Six of the meanings are listed in Table 22-2, along with certain properties of the

term as it has been used. Two of the usages refer to the persistence over time of some quality of the individual. *Intraindividual continuity* refers to the absolute stability of some characteristic. The child's early performance or classification with respect to some characteristic is the criterion for judging whether or not later performance or classification is the same or different. A scale may be employed that is not dependent on the "relative performance" of other same-age children. *Interindividual continuity* refers to the stability of the child's placement in a group when that placement is assessed over two or more time intervals. For this usage, continuity means that the difference among individuals is stable over time, not that the characteristic itself is necessarily stable. The failure to recognize these distinctions (between interindividual continuity and intraindividual continuity; between stability of a characteristic and stability of a difference with respect to a characteristic) has been responsible for considerable confusion in the theoretical and empirical literature.

Four other overlapping usages of the term have not helped to clarify matters. *Organizational continuity* refers to the appearance of continuity in various definitions of development in order to emphasize that the organism undergoes continuous change from conception to birth to maturity to death. Given these definitions (see Kuo, 1967, for example), it is meaningless to refer to a lack of continuity. More detailed analyses of the theoretical concepts of stages of development suggest, however, that qualitative, noncontinuous shifts occur in behavior organization (Sameroff, 1975). *Factor structure continuity* refers to whether or not there is a stability in the structural relationships that are obtained when one correlates a set of variables among themselves at two different ages (Emmerich, 1964). Here the concern is with the continuing relevance of a psychological dimension and with whether or not the dimension remains relevant at different ages, even though the observations from which a child's status on that dimension may change over time. The statistical technique called factor matching has been em-

Table 22-2. Concepts of continuity.

Concept	Criterion	Examples	Principal Measures
Intraindividual continuity (absolute stability)	Whether specific properties of individual or interchange remain stable	Sex-role classification, mental age scores	Mean differences, within-individual variability
Interindividual continuity (relative stability)	Whether the child's placement in a group (peer group, normative group) remains stable	Relative standing in terms of assertive behavior, IQ	Correlations, deviation from the mean
Organizational continuity	Whether ontogenetic linkages are continuous from conception to death	Abstraction about the nature of development	No measure
Factor structure continuity	Whether same structural relations are obtained in variables assessed at two different ages	Comparison of factor analyses at two different ages	Factor matching; analysis of contributing variables
Process continuity	Whether a given psychological or biological process is continuous throughout development	Sensitive periods in development; learning of preferences or attitudes	Various
Societal continuity	Whether the societal structure (including norms, standards for behavior, roles) remain unchanged	Changes in norms for intelligence tests and personality scales	Various

ployed in attempts to identify whether dimensions remain constant or whether they shift (see Wohlwill, 1973, pp. 368–375, for an analysis of this usage). *Process continuity* refers to whether or not a given underlying process, either biological or psychological, is continuously active across the full span of development, or whether the process is noncontinuous or phasic (showing cyclic activity and inactivity). Finally, *societal* or *generational continuity* refers to the persistence of certain characteristics in a society over time. Here the focus is upon changes or stabilities in societal values, roles, traditions, or experiences from one time period to another. These societal stabilities or changes may serve to support or modify individual differences or individual characteristics.

Problems arise when these meanings of continuity appear interchangeably, as sometimes has been the case. Continuity at one level (as in, say, the continuous activity of learning processes or continuity of development change) may imply discontinuity in behavioral characteristics and in differences among individuals, and vice-versa. A solution to the semantic confusion may involve, as a first step, the use of the full label (for example, intraindividual continuity, or process continuity) when there might be any doubt.

It may have occurred to the reader that since virtually all behaviorial characteristics of the individual undergo drastic change over time from birth to maturity, the concept of "intraindividual continuity" is nearly meaningless. If, say, a very bright 5-

year-old's performance on a standard measuring scale of intelligence actually remained stable over a 10-year period, in that roughly the same items were passed and were failed over the two occasions, this "brilliant" preschool child would be a "severely retarded" teenager. Why? Obviously, he would have been expected to gain new competencies in addition to the childlike ones. And even though the term "fearfulness" may be used to describe the behavior of a child at 2, 4, 8, and 16 years of age, the actual behaviors from which fearfulness is assumed change markedly. The normal "fearful" acts of the 2-year-old might be viewed as severely neurotic or psychotic symptoms if they were observed in a teenage boy or girl.

Two comments are called for on this observation that change is an essential property of development. First, the pervasiveness of age-related changes in behavior has led to the development of measurement techniques and measurement transformations that eliminate or control for differences related to maturation in order to highlight individuality. A main virtue of such procedures is that they permit the investigator to separate differences between individuals from differences between ages. (The IQ score gained great popularity, in part, because it was presumed to be constant over time, even though the child's actual capabilities changed greatly.) Second, a plausible argument can be made that a major task of developmental research is to devise measurement systems that permit one to assess the social behavior changes more precisely, not eliminate them. This conflict in goals brings us to the problem of measurement and the efforts that have been made to cope with the dilemma of how to measure both individuality and change in a dynamic organismic system.

Some Issues of Measurement: Scores, Ratings, and Transformations

How investigators choose to measure social behaviors can determine whether or not developmental

changes will be preserved or eliminated.[2] Measurement decisions also play a major role in determining whether evidence for stability in individual differences is likely to be obtained. The steps that are taken at each stage of the measurement process—classifying discrete observations into categories, combining entries in the various categories to form a scale, transforming the information derived from different ages, situations, and sexes to form a common basis for comparison—can magnify or eliminate developmental variations.

Consider the problem of classification. To bring order into a changing, dynamic world where no two acts are identical, the first step of measurement is classification or determining which acts are similar and representative of the same characteristic and which acts are not. Classification of social behavior is difficult enough when the organism itself is not undergoing changes. One must form explicit criteria as to what acts belong together as being representative of, say, aggression, when a major consideration of similarity is not only the form of the behavior but the intention of the actor. The problems of forming judgments are magnified when children of different ages are compared on what is presumably the same characteristic. The most economical schemes—in the sense of considering a wide range of seemingly different acts of children at different ages to be functionally equivalent—may also be the ones most likely to obscure or eliminate developmental changes in actual form and expression. Although a single dimension might facilitate cross-age comparisons, one runs the danger of blurring distinctions between quite different behavioral expressions and dispositions. Broad categories, such as "aggression," can obscure developmental differences in the actual behaviors and, as a byproduct, risk the presumption of a single dimension when in fact two or more may be involved. On the other hand, too narrow a defini-

[2] I will aim for only an intuitive grasp of the issues because a detailed coverage would catapult us into a discussion of measurement theory that is beyond the scope of this book. Interested readers may wish to consult one of the recent volumes that deal with these matters, including Sackett, 1978, and Wohlwill, 1973.

tion can result in multiple discrete categories that serve to obscure systematic trends and continuities that are in fact present in the data. The point is that theoretical decisions made at the first stage of data collection serve to predetermine the nature of conclusions that can be reached.

To illustrate, consider how one might study the development of individual differences in "cooperation" in the preschool. Two basically different procedures have been employed, sometimes by the same investigator. One technique involves the precise assessment of actual behaviors of children and those with whom he interacts (such as buttoning the coat of a younger child; continuing to build with blocks when told to put them away, etc.). Once recorded, the separate behaviors can be placed into multiple categories and then combined in various different ways in order to describe the anatomy of "cooperation" as it is expressed in individual children. Whether there is a single dimension or several depends on the form of the data and explicit decisions on the part of the investigator. Continuities can be explored by comparing discrete activities and interactions across time, or by using dimensional scores. The effects of differences in settings and relationships on cooperation can be controlled experimentally, by comparing particular settings and interchanging partners, or statistically, by performing appropriate mathematical transformations. In any case, each step in the analysis requires additional decisions on the part of the investigator beyond those made in the initial collection of the data.

The second technique is simpler and more economical. Most of the above steps, and in some instances all of them, are combined into a single step. For instance, if the investigator can accept the assumption that most persons understand what is meant by "cooperation," he might devise a rating scale that ranges from "one" to "five," where a score of "one" is defined as uncooperative, "three" as somewhat cooperative, and "five" as highly cooperative. The range of scales that one can employ depends on the ability of raters to make reliable discriminations and on the interests and aims of the

investigator. The teacher or some other person who knows the child well might be asked to make the judgments, and these could be collected at different time intervals to determine persistence or change. [3] (Variations in the form of how such judgments are obtained include the use of personality checklists, forced-choice descriptions, and a wide range of similar devices.)

As we observed in Chapter 17, the two different methods can yield quite different conclusions. Why? Although there is still some debate on the actual reasons, the main differences lie in the aims of the techniques and the kinds of transformations that are required at the very first step of data recording. One procedure requires a precise record of what actually occurs, with a minimum of interpretation by the observer as to the role of age, sex, context, and eliciting circumstances in determining the behavior. It is just the opposite in the case of ratings. Judges are required to make these interpretations (on the basis of their subjective norms) in order to arrive at a judgment. To permit a focus on the child's idiosyncratic characteristics, the effects of other "ephemeral" contributions to that characteristic are discounted (eliminated) at the first stage of recording. The key to the success of ratings (which have been a primary technique for the study of personality traits and other enduring characteristics) is the adequacy of the observer in (1) identifying the standard for evaluation, (2) recognizing and taking into account interactional and contextual factors that influence the behavior, and (3) determining how much of the characteristic is enduring and personal and how much is situational, relational, and nonenduring. Because of the number of transformations that are required, Mischel (1973) observes that "the

---

[3] The above description is, of course, a much simplified version of the steps that are actually taken by a researcher in the construction of the assessment device. Indeed, the design of behavior rating scales is an exceedingly complex task, requiring attention to the definition of the criterion, scaling of the alternatives, and standardization and validation of the procedural measure. The requirements for the observer, however, are similar in that the success of the procedure depends on the skill of the person who ultimately makes judgments about particular children.

study of global traits may ultimately reveal more about the cognitive activity of the trait theorist than about the causes of behavior (p. 264)." But despite their obvious drawbacks for the study of social development (the obvious one being that the effects of developmental change are eliminated), rating scale procedures possess some distinct advantages in detecting consistencies in social behavior that more precise assessments obscure. Evidence to support that expectation will be covered later in the chapter.

Issues of Method

Longitudinal methods are required to study the persistence of both individual characteristics and individual differences. The methods are not only expensive and tedious, but raise a number of practical problems when applied to human beings (see Kessen, 1960). Briefly, the problems include attrition of the sample because of lack of interest, moving, or death; contamination after repeated testing, so the child remembers what to expect from one test to another or the rater recalls his previous ratings; "halo" effects, where the relationship between experimenter and subject becomes a factor in the nature of the scoring or the child's actual behaviors, and so on.

But apart from these commonly recognized problems, there is a deficiency in how the problem of continuity has usually been conceived. Ordinarily, the task has been construed as to try to predict, on the basis of an individual's initial status on some characteristic, what his later status on that characteristic should be. But if a developmental model of continuity is correct, the child's early status should be only one component in the equation. For social interchanges, other components must include the nature of the social network in which development can be presumed to occur, the distinctive psychobiological constraints that will be operative, as well as the nature of the transitions that might be expected. Hence methods that assess only the child's

early status on the characteristic, and leave out information about the nature of the social systems in which developmental transformations are likely to occur, will necessarily be handicapped.

Empirical Outcomes in Studies of Behavioral Continuity

Behavioral continuities from birth to maturity have been plotted for only a small range of human behaviors. Moreover, the techniques that have been employed have been largely restricted to studies of the persistence of individual differences over time. Wohlwill (1973) remarks that this definition of continuity accounts for "99.9% of the work on the problem," an estimate that is quantitatively inaccurate but poetically defensible. Hence we cannot expect the work to reveal much about the actual properties of the behaviors that undergo change or how they are transformed in ways that may preserve or eliminate individual differences. Further, the studies have been typically limited to the assessment of a single characteristic of children at two (or more) points in time. Few efforts have been made to explore continuity of other properties of the developing system of which the individual behaviors are a part (including interactional, contextual, societal, and biological components) that presumably are melded with the characteristic in development. Thus a narrow basis has typically been employed in formulating predictions.

Despite these limitations, the results of longitudinal studies of the persistence of individual differences are informative and worthy of careful study. I am including the summary findings from studies of cognitive and motor pattern continuity—with, of course, studies of social behavior continuity—for a couple of reasons. First, the developmental perspective implies that certain nonsocial aspects of the child's behavior should be less susceptible to situational and interactional variation than are social behaviors. Second, and more important, social behavior within a developmental orientation cannot be divorced from ontogenetic changes in biological, motor, and cognitive processes. They are fused in the course of development.

Empirical Continuity in Cognitive Development

Studies of the persistence of individual differences in intelligence test performance constitute the most extensive body of information available on the continuity of a psychological characteristic. Despite differences among investigators in their research strategies, types of tests used, and opinions on what "intelligence tests" actually measure, their results have yielded a consensus on two major points:

1. The shorter the interval between two tests, the more likely it is that the children's relative positions in the distributions of scores will be similar.
2. The older the children are at the time of the initial test, the less likely it is that their positions relative to each other will change over a given interval of time between two tests.

As several writers have pointed out (see Bloom, 1964; Jones, 1954), the magnitude of the product moment coefficient (which provides an index of individual difference continuity) is affected by several factors. These include the "spread of talent" in the group studied with respect to intelligence test scores (it's easier to shift one's standing in a homogeneous group than in a heterogeneous one), the reliability of the test procedures (tests have different reliabilities, according to the parts that are used), and various other test-related and nontest events. Nonetheless, it is possible to predict the relative standing of individuals at early maturity, with reasonable accuracy, from early adolescence. Infancy and childhood test scores, however, provide a less adequate basis for prediction (see Figure 22-1).

Even when there are reasonably stable differences among individuals (as reflected in correlation coefficients demonstrating a reliable relationship be-

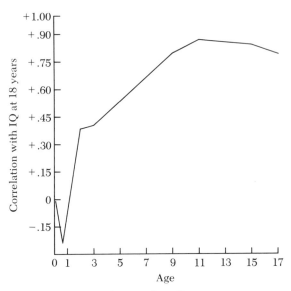

Figure 22-1. Correlations of intelligence test scores at each age with intelligence scores at age 18. Data from 27 cases that were repeatedly tested from 3 months of age through early adulthood (from Bayley, 1949, Table 6).

tween the first and later tests), sizable changes in the scores of individual children are not uncommon. In this regard, McCall, Applebaum, and Hogarty (1973) report that 50% of the children studied from age 3 to age 17 show a shift of 28 IQ points or more from the early to the later test. A smaller but nonetheless significant proportion of the total sample, $1/7$ of the children, showed shifts of 40 IQ points or more. Such increases could mean a change from "borderline defective" to "bright normal" or "superior," or vice-versa. Hence the most carefully standardized behavioral measure available to psychologists indicates that radical changes in test ranking can occur in the normal course of development.

Can one accurately predict, on the basis of a test given to an infant, what his intelligence test performance would be at maturity? The answer is no, except in extreme cases of organic defect or brain disease. Indeed, examination of a child at 8 months does not permit one to predict reliably the language the child will speak, much less how well he will speak it and use its concepts. But if a broader base is used for prediction, such as the parent's social class or occupation, quite reliable predictions can be made at birth. For instance, the correlation of children's IQ's at age 17 with parental educational level (average number of years of school both parents have completed) ranges from $r = .50$ to $r = .60$ (Jones, 1954; McCall, 1977). In such cases, one can achieve quite respectable predictive correlations, even though the infant's early performance on tests of intelligence is ignored. Leaving aside the issue of "why" for the moment, the lesson is that children's standings on intelligence tests at 17 years can be reliably predicted at birth, *or before*, if the index of prediction captures a significant feature of the genetic-interactional-societal system in which development occurs.

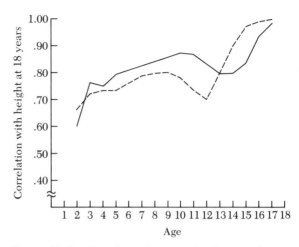

Figure 22-2. Correlation between height at each age and height at maturity (age 18) for females (*dashed line*) and males (*solid line*) (from Bloom, 1964, based on data reported by Tuddenham and Snyder, 1954, with permission).

Empirical Continuities in Sensorimotor and Physical Development

The patterns of individual difference continuity obtained in studies of physical growth and sensorimotor development are generally consistent with the two empirical principles cited in the study of intelligence test performance. The correspondence is not perfect, however. Early predictions are not always worse than later ones, nor are increases in the interval between tests always associated with decreases in the accuracy of prediction. One problem is adolescence. Individual differences in onset of the growth spurt and in rate of growth can play havoc with otherwise consistent trends in prediction. Figure 22-2 illustrates the problem. For both boys and girls, preadolescent height differences provide better predictions of height differences at age 18 than do corresponding differences in adolescence. This finding conflicts with both generalizations, in that predictions about relative standing at early maturity are more accurate over a long time span than a short one, and status at an earlier age can be a better

predictor than status at adolescence. Otherwise, note that at virtually all ages the correlations between early and late height status are impressively high.

It is a different story when one attempts to plot the reliability of predictions of individual difference in dimensions of early neurobehavioral development. In one of the more detailed studies of the continuity of the infant's neurological condition, Alex Kalverboer (1975) examined a sample of 150 children born in and around Groningen, The Netherlands, in the mid-1960's. Complete neonatal neurological examinations were given to the children, and it was known that none of them suffered severe neurological disorders at birth. There were, however, significant differences that could be detected in the neurological examination with respect to the neurological syndromes of hyperexcitability ("high amplitude tremor," "hyperkinesis"), apathy ("depression of nervous functions," "difficult to arouse"), and hemisyndrome (when three or more asymmetries in reaction were found).

Do these differences at and shortly after birth predict subsequent behavior patterns? Kalverboer reports that there is no immediate correlation between any of these features of birth activity and reactivity and later behaviors, whether they are assessed in the school and preschool, in the laboratory, or even in subsequent neurological assessments. The Netherlands data do not stand alone on this point: As we have observed earlier (Chaper 11), predictions of later activity/reactivity from scores derived in early postnatal or infancy tests are negligible (Sameroff and Chandler, 1975). Kalverboer (1975) offers the interesting suggestion that children with demonstrable neurological disorders may be able to achieve the same end results in behavior as children without disorders; they just go about it in a different way. Hence developmental studies should be concerned as much with the ways "that children and adults structure and organise their behaviour" as with the end results (p. 98).

A parallel argument has been offered by Thomas, Chess, and Birch (1968) in their studies of why "temperamental" differences observed in infancy are maintained or are eliminated in the course of development. "Temperamental" corresponds, roughly, to what Kalverboer labels as hyperexcitable patterns. Detailed analyses of the interactions between the children and their parents indicate that the adjustments made by the parents to the children, and the attitudes that arose, were significant determinants of whether or not temperamental children continued to be difficult. Focus only on the child's attributes or the parental caretaking attitudes in isolation was not sufficient; attention had to be given to the reciprocal transactions that occurred during the course of development to determine whether or not subsequent problems in adjustment would arise (Thomas et al., 1968). To this conclusion Kalverboer (1975) adds that the transactions between neurological-temperamental conditions and social behavior must be studied in specific settings and relationships if one is to achieve precise predictions.

Relevant also are questions regarding the persistence of styles of moving, talking, and coordination. How continuous are individual differences in sensorimotor coordination and skill? The relevant findings that have been reported in animal behavior studies—from the retention of song patterns and dialects in birds to the persistence of stereotyped rocking patterns in isolated monkeys—suggest that long-term continuity is not unusual.

Short-term continuities in sensorimotor coordination—in both absolute levels and in individual differences—are impressive. The optimal performances of children in various athletic activities, from running 50 yards to swimming 100 meters, seldom vary more than 6 percent in any month's interval. How long do special skills persist, such as typing, riding a bicycle, or playing a violin? Unfortunately, few systematic studies have been made on the memory and recovery of such skills over years. Intuitively, it seems that our ability to recall—but not necessarily to perform—such complex coordinations is remarkable. So is the ability to pronounce words of a language that has not been used for years, even if the meanings of the words have been forgotten. One hypothesis consistent with the developmental perspective is that these skills are retained in their original forms because their organization, once established, is relatively uninfluenced by variations in societal, interactional, and contextual factors. In other words, there are few pressures to change that are external to the organism. Muscle atrophy and disuse can, of course, make for disappointing results if a sensorimotor skill is not practiced.

Empirical Continuities in Social Development

The rather orderly picture of individual difference continuities in cognitive and motor-expressive patterns is less neatly duplicated by the results of studies of social behavior continuity. Why the greater variability in studies of social development? Part of the problem lies in the measurement techniques that have been employed, and part of it is in the dynamic nature of the social patterns themselves. In line with our earlier comments on the difference between behavioral analyses and rating scale procedures, the results of studies using these two general measuring techniques will be covered separately.

Behavior Assessments. Because of the essential changeability of the form and functions of interchange patterns over the course of development, investigators of human behavior have infrequently tried to employ the same standard tests and measures at different age levels. As we noted in Chapter 6, attempts to predict whether an "insecure" infant at 9 to 12 months as measured in standard assessments of maternal attachment will be an insecure child in the preschool at three years have yielded few significant findings. For that matter, one cannot predict with confidence individual differences in specific attachment behaviors over a 12-month interval. If the time interval between tests is short and the test is standard, however, predictions based on individual differences in specific behaviors are relatively stable.

These findings provide a pattern that is consistent with other studies of infants and young children, even though they were not concerned expressly with attachment. When attempts have been made to obtain precise measurements by observing the same children in the same context on two days in a row, high levels of day-to-day prediction are possible. These predictions include choice of companions, activity performed, and manner of interacting among 5-year-old boys and girls. (S. Sherman, 1975). A decay in the magnitude of the prediction coefficients is obtained if the amount of time between observations is extended to three weeks, *even if the context and companions remain the same* (S. Sherman, 1975).

Studying mother-infant pairs in their homes, Green (1977) discovered some details of interchanges that were reliable and persistent in the first year of life. Mother-infant dyads in which relatively large numbers of social initiations occurred at 6 months (infant's age) were observed to have relatively more social initiations at 8 months. Similarly, the relative standings of the pairs persisted from the 8th- to the 12th-month observations. But the correlation over the full half year (from 6 to 12 months) was not statistically reliable. Was the consistency in the interchange maintained primarily by mothers or by infants? In a reanalysis of his data, Green (1977) determined that the consistencies were supported principally by the actions of the mothers rather than by the actions of the infants. It was her talking, initiations, and so on that remained stable.

In part, the empirical generalizations that were offered to describe the results of cognitive studies seem to hold as well for studies of social interchange continuity. The earlier the assessment in the child's life, the less reliable the predictions over a given interval; and the longer the interval between observations, the less reliable the predictions. But there are major differences. First, in social interaction analyses, the typical time interval between observations is usually brief because the behaviors themselves are modified and can no longer be observed. Second, the predictive correlations involving social acts are typically smaller and decay more rapidly than those involving nonsocial behaviors. Third, the observations that have been reported typically hold constant the context, the members of the interchange, or both. Variations in either of these dimensions tend to further diminish the magnitude of the correlation.

Ratings of Social Patterns and Dispositions. Rating scale procedures have provided some of the most powerful and compelling support for the persistence of individual differences in social behavior patterns. It may seem paradoxical that subjective, global procedures should demonstrate continuity when precise, objectives ones do not. The paradox gives way when it is recognized that the main purpose of rating techniques is to identify stable differences. They are less useful in identifying how these differences may arise, what accounts for them, and how they may be maximized or eliminated.

To illustrate, consider recent demonstrations of the stability of the classification of infants and their mothers into types of "attachment" (Waters, 1978). Fifty infants and their mothers were observed on two occasions (at 12 months and 18 months) in a laboratory setting under standard conditions where the mothers left and then reentered the experimental room. Several kinds of individual measures were available, including discrete activities of looking toward the mother, crying, and other such activities that have sometimes been considered to be indicative of attachment. Waters (1978) included a second level of analysis, where children were rated with respect to such characteristics as "proximity seeking" (trying to reach mother or another adult), "contact resisting" (negative behavior by infant when adult comes into contact with him) and three other scales that were presumed to assess attachment. Finally, a third level of analysis, more global than the first two, was employed. The infant's relationship to his mother was classified into one of three global categories, called A, B, and C. Unfortunately, the precise basis for classification was not described in Waters' (1978) report, other than to indicate that Group B was "the modal classification for middle class one-year-olds; in past research approximately 65% of a sample typically placed in this group"; and that Groups A and C are "often termed 'anxiously attached' " (see Ainsworth, 1973).

As might be expected from our previous discussions of the properties of rating scales, the stability of the ratings exceeded that of individual measures (although the stability of individual differences in crying was not separately reported). The most impressive finding, however, concerned the ability of judges to classify the infant-mother pairs into the same categories, despite a 6-month interval between tests—48 of the 50 infant-mother pairs were reassigned to the same A-B-C categories on the two tests. How did the judges do it? Since they had the entire session to use in forming the classification decision, and because information from the mother as well as the infant was contained in the session, one can only speculate about what features of the rela-

tionship in addition to infant crying and maternal avoidance were used. It may include activities of the mother (who, Green, 1977, has found, is a catalyst for consistency), temperamental differences in infants (whether they were quiet or highly excitable), physical characteristics of mother and infant, or a host of other properties of the behavior of the two that capture some feature of their relationship. Further exploration of this phenomenon is called for, including the identification of the critical defining characteristics.

Use of rating scales to assess the stability of individual differences in older children and young adults has achieved varying degrees of success. E. S. Schaefer (Schaefer, 1975) finds high levels of persistence of individual differences in ratings on several dimensions of social behavior over the six years of elementary school (first grade to sixth grade). This work, involving over 500 children in several different elementary schools and their teachers (who served as raters), consistently yields correlations on such characteristics as "extraversion" and "hostility" that range between $r = .50$ and $r = .60$. Block (1971) reports that some dimensions on which low-level positive correlations are obtained over a period from adolescence to adulthood (accounting for approximately 6 to 9 percent of the variance). Studies of the persistence of individual differences from "birth to maturity" indicate, however, that attempts to generalize across settings and relationships as well as across time typically yield predictive correlations that are very modest and inconsistent across investigations (see Kagan, 1971; Kagan and Moss, 1962; Sears, 1961; Yarrow, Campbell, and Burton, 1968).

A Comparison Across Social and Nonsocial Consistencies

In overview, the persistence of individual differences—whether over the short term or the life span—is considerably lower in the case of social behavior characteristics than in the case of cognitive and motor ones. Why? On the face of it, one would expect that the same developmental considerations that apply to social behaviors would apply to nonsocial ones as well. It seems likely that some of the reasons for the differences are methodological, while others pertain to the essential differences between the properties of actions that occur in interchanges and those which are nonsocial. Among the more frequently cited possibilities are the following:

1. The goal of most tests of cognitive and motor development is to measure the child's *optimal* performance, while the goal of social interchange and personality assessments is to measure *representative* performance. This difference in aim is important because it permits the researcher to design standardized and well-defined conditions for the assessment of intelligence, coordination, perception, and the like. But, to obtain truly representative samples of social behavior, it is necessary to use unobtrusive yet sensitive measures that apply in a variety of circumstances. One negative byproduct of this state of affairs is that measures of social behavior and personality have typically been less reliable and more vulnerable to error in both the early and later tests. It is simply easier to measure height and strength than aggression and friendliness, and doubtless with greater accuracy.

2. The evidence further suggests that there is a higher level of specificity—situational, relational, and time—in the interactional patterns of children than in the noninteractional ones. William James offered the observation that a man "has as many different social selves as there are distinct groups of persons about whose opinion he cares" (1890, p. 204, Vol. 1). This view is consistent with what has now become an impressive body of information regarding the contextual and social specificity of interchanges. It is also consonant with speculations about why rating measures tend to yield more "consistent" results with regard to interindividual differences than do more precise behavioral assessment techniques: ratings tend, in general, to explicitly eliminate situational sources of variance.

It seems also to be the case that cognitive and sensorimotor patterns are less influenced by variations in context and conditions of assessment. Once organized, the primary "supports" for such activities as mental calculations, gross motor movements, strength, and the like can be seen as mostly internal and part of a within-organism feedback system. But it should be noted that even these activities are influenced by changes in social context, and sometimes markedly. Indeed, the performance of activities in familiar surroundings typically conveys some advantage to the performer, whether the performer is a musician, a student, an athlete, or a prairie dog in its home territory.

3. In relation to the previous point, it seems plausible to suppose that social interactions are more likely affected and reorganized by the transactions that occur during the course of development than are nonsocial patterns. Unfortunately, there is not much direct evidence on this point because there have been few systematic studies of transactional change. The indirect evidence—on the rapid decay of individual difference correlations, on the reversal and modification of early experiences, and on the rechanneling of temperamental differences—seems consistent with the proposal. Nor can interactions be interpreted independent of changes in the cultural-social context of which they are a part. The recent finding of Nesselroade and Baltes (1974) that significant changes occur in the "normal" patterns of personality test profiles of adolescents in a period as short as two years underscores the importance of viewing social behavior changes in their cultural-social context. Absolute changes (intraindividual) may be required to maintain relative continuity (interindividual) because the reference group in society is undergoing change.

Again, it would be a mistake to view cognitive behaviors as developing independently of changes in the cultural milieu. Shifts in the "average" performance of American draftees in the First and Second World Wars were great enough that the "average" performance in 1917 would fall in the "borderline defective" range in 1941 (Jones, 1954). More recently, changes in average Scholastic Aptitude Test (SAT) performance in the opposite direction have been observed.

A Critique and Some Guides

Those who aspire to study continuities in social development are immediately confronted with a paradox. The problem is that change is an essential property of development, and virtually all features of children undergo modifications in ontogeny. Nonetheless, continuity would seem to be essential for individual uniqueness, organization, and the maintenance of behavioral integration. The paradox is this: How can continuity and persistence be achieved in an organismic system that necessarily undergoes maturational, interactional, and cultural-social change?

I observed earlier that solution to the problem has been retarded by subtle and not-so-subtle issues, some of which are the result of attempts to ignore or gloss over the basic paradox. Although the developmental perspective represents a significant advance over its predecessors in this regard, the proposal has been criticized for other shortcomings, apparent and real. We shall close this chapter with a few comments on the nature of the criticisms, and indicate what new directions the proposal suggests.

One argument that has been advanced within psychology is that it is inappropriate to discuss the developmental and biological substrates of social behavior because so little is known about how they operate. Rather, attention should be given to the establishment of behavioral principles where our information is secure and less speculative. The argument can be answered by questioning both of its premises—do we really lack information about the biological controls of social behavior, and are neo-behavioristic accounts of social behavior adequate? Recent texts, synthesizing information from the

fields of zoology, sociology, and psychology, indicate that the first premise is surely wrong. In any case, lack of background in biological disciplines is no excuse for ignoring them. Nor is it a justification for leaving them out of a systematic account of social development when maturational/morphological factors are clearly implicated.

A second criticism is that the developmental solution, by virtue of its emphasis on the inevitability of change, is inconsistent with one's intuitions about continuity and personal stability. This criticism represents an unfortunate (though common) misunderstanding of the developmental view. It is, in fact, as much concerned with the issues of persistence as change. Hence the answer to such criticism is that the developmental explanation is appropriately described by Gottlieb's (1976a) phrase "probablistic epigenesis." Each individual is indeed unique, in that the organization of his social (and nonsocial) patterns is a personal mosaic of multiple demands. The developmental explanation is an attempt to outline the general principles by which the uniqueness arises; hence it describes the rules for both change and continuity.

A third criticism is that internal controls—such as genetic determinants—are given short shrift by developmental analyses. In light of the importance of evolutionary processes, should they not be given more consideration? The answer is that developmental analyses focus on the proximate mechanisms that control social behavior. They do not deny the importance of evolutionary processes or genetic contributions, but attempt to clarify how they operate and are operated upon. Indeed, a goal of developmental analyses has been to specify not only how evolution and genetic processes control social behavior, but how social development controls evolution and genetic processes. The two sets of mechanisms must ultimately prove to be mutually supportive.

One last objection cannot be answered so easily. It is an attack on the level of specificity of developmental theory, and it raises the critical question of whether the perspective yields clear-cut predictions. Can the proposal be tested in a way that might lead to its own rejection? No matter that other positions are themselves vague: The inadequacy of these predecessors cannot be considered an excuse for failing to offer critical predictions.

Certain features of the orientation are explicit enough to permit the investigation of specific proposals, and to provide criteria for their acceptance or rejection. In particular, the proposals discussed in Parts II and III of this book regarding the establishment and modification of affiliative, aggressive, and sexual patterns of interchange can be readily evaluated. So can proposals on the consolidation of interchanges and the presumed determinants of interchange synchrony.

Vagueness arises when one deals with the concepts of developmental transactions in the abstract. Accordingly, one might ask how the major sources of continuity—social system, evocation, psychobiological constraints, choices, and prior and ongoing consolidation experiences—are melded at any particular time in development. What sources will dominate, and when? What weight must be given to any given source in the bidirectional process? Although the theory specifies that the nature of the influence will differ according to the interactional pattern, or the time in the child's life at which the observations are made, it leaves open the details of which patterns and which times. More precise, possibly quantitative, statements of the developmental perspective are needed to facilitate its elaboration, expansion, and correction.

Some General Guidelines

One of the major contributions of the developmental perspective is that it provides guides for what kinds of questions should be asked and for what sorts of research strategies should be employed to solve the continuity-change paradox. In order to unravel the nature of ontogenetic transactions, it is necessary to adopt research techniques that reveal the details of the interchanges that occur during the course of normal development. This means, among other things, the study of the interchanges of individual children should be concerned with the year-to-year as well as the minute-by-minute bases for behavior organization and transaction. In addition, the measures employed must be sufficiently precise to yield information about the changes that occur and how these serve to preserve or modify more general bases of social organization.

The developmental perspective also provides guides for what kinds of questions are less meaningful and what procedures should be regarded with skepticism. Specifically, the traditional techniques used to identify the persistence of individual differences have not, to date, been effective in helping researchers solve the essential problems of social continuity. All too often the issues have been obscured at the first level of analysis by defining the variables in such a way as to eliminate the effects of developmental change. Even when "positive" correlations are obtained, they typically fail to yield information about the bases for the relationship. By focusing on individual *differences* in characteristics, instead of the development of the *actual* interchange characteristics, only meager information has been obtained on the course of development of the relevant social behaviors.

Finally, the developmental perspective requires a comprehensive view of the individual child, on the one hand, and the systems of which the child is a part, on the other. It also implies that the solution of the essential problems of social development requires a broader base of information and scientific competence than has previously been assumed to be necessary. In short, the study of social continuity cannot be divorced from cognitive and emotional changes that persons undergo over their lifespans, nor from the familial and social systems in which they live. The analysis of how these developmental processes are integrated promises to be a major task for the behavioral sciences over the next two decades.

REFERENCES

Acosta, F. X. Etiology and treatment of homosexuality: A review. *Archives of Sexual Behavior,* 1975, **4,** 9-29.

Ader, R. Effects of early experiences on emotional and physiological reactivity in the rat. *Journal of Comparative and Physiological Psychology,* 1968, **66,** 264-268.

Adkins, E. K. Hormonal basis of sexual differentiation in the Japanese quail. *Journal of Comparative and Physiological Psychology,* 1975, **89,** 61-71.

Adler, N. T., and Zoloth, S. R. Copulatory behavior can inhibit pregnancy in female rats. *Science,* 1970, **168,** 1480-1482.

Ahmad, S. S., and Harvey, J. S. Long-term effects of septal lesions and social experience on shock-elicited fighting in rats. *Journal of Comparative and Physiological Psychology,* 1968, **66,** 596-602.

Ainsworth, M. D. S. The development of infant-mother interaction among the Ganda. In B. M. Foss (ed.), *Determinants of infant behavior: II.* New York: Wiley, 1963.

Ainsworth, M. D. S. *Infancy in Uganda: Infant care and the growth of love.* Baltimore: The Johns Hopkins University Press, 1967.

Ainsworth, M. D. S. Object relations, dependency, and attachment: A theoretical review of the infant-mother relationship. *Child Development,* 1969, **40,** 969-1025.

Ainsworth, M. D. S. Attachment and dependency: A comparison. In J. L. Gewirtz (ed.), *Attachment and dependency.* New York: Wiley, 1972.

Ainsworth, M. D. S. The development of infant-mother attachment. In B. M. Caldwell and H. N. Ricciuti (eds.), *Review of child development research* (Vol. 3). Chicago: University of Chicago Press, 1973.

Ainsworth, M. D. S., and Bell, S. M. Infant crying and maternal responsiveness: A rejoinder to Gewirtz and Boyd. *Child Development,* 1977, **48,** 1208-1216.

Alberts, J. R. Huddling by rat pups: Group behavioral mechanisms of temperature regulation and energy conservation. *Journal of Comparative and Physiological Psychology,* 1978, **92,** 231-245.

Alberts, J. R., and Galef, B. G., Jr. Olfactory cues and movement: Stimuli mediating intraspecific aggression in the wild Norway rat. *Journal of Comparative and Physiological Psychology,* 1973, **85,** 233-242.

Aleksandrowicz, M. K., and Aleksandrowicz, D. R. "Obstetrical pain-relieving drugs as predictors of infant behavior variability": A reply to Federman and Yang's critique. *Child Development,* 1976, **47,** 297-298.

Alexander, G., and Williams, D. Maternal facilitation of a sucking drive in newborn lambs. *Science,* 1964, **146,** 665-666.

Alloway, T., Pliner, P., and Krames, L. (eds.), *Attachment behavior.* New York: Plenum Press, 1977.

Allport, G. W. *Personality: A psychological interpretation.* New York: Holt, Rinehart, and Winston, 1937.

Altmann, M. The role of juvenile elk and moose in the social dynamics of their species. *Zoologica,* 1960, **45,** 35-39.

Altmann, M. Naturalistic studies of maternal care in moose and elk. In H. L. Rheingold (ed.), *Maternal behavior in mammals.* New York: Wiley, 1963.

Aman, M. G., and Sprague, R. L. The state-dependent effects of methylphenidate and dextroamphetamine. *The Journal of Nervous and Mental Disease,* 1974, **158,** 268-279.

Anderson, H. H. Domination and integration in the social behavior of young children in an experimental play situation. *Genetic Psychological Monographs,* 1939, **21,** 287-385.

Anderson, J. E. The limitations of infant and preschool tests in the measurement of intelligence. *Journal of Psychology,* 1939, **8,** 351-379.

Anderson, W. H., Jr. Self-control as used in a delay of gratification paradigm with children. Unpublished doctoral dissertation, State University of New York at Stony Brook, Stony Brook, New York, 1974.

Andrew, R. J. Effects of testosterone on the behavior of the domestic chick I. Effects present in males but not in females. *Animal Behavior,* 1975(a), **23,** 139-155.

Andrew, R. J. Effects of testosterone on the behavior of the domestic chick II. Effects present in both sexes. *Animal Behavior,* 1975(b), **23,** 156-168.

Appel, M. H. Aggressive behavior of nursery school children and adult procedures in dealing with such behavior. *Journal of Experimental Education,* 1942, **11,** 185-199.

Ardrey, R. *The territorial imperative.* New York: Atheneum, 1966.

Arling, G. L., and Harlow, H. P. Effects of social deprivation on maternal behavior of rhesus monkeys. *Journal of Comparative and Physiological Psychology,* 1967, **64,** 371-377.

Aronfreed, J. *Conduct and conscience: The socialization of internalized control over behavior.* New York: Academic Press, 1968.

Aronson, L. R. Hormones in reproductive behavior: Some phylogenetic considerations. In A. Gorbman (ed.), *Comparative endocrinology.* New York: Wiley, 1959.

Ascione, F. R. The effects of continuous nurturance and nurturance withdrawal on children's behavior. *Child Development,* 1975, **46,** 790-795.

Atkinson, R. C., and Estes, W. K. Stimulus sampling theory. In R. D. Luce, R. R. Bush, and E. G. Galanter (eds.), *Handbook of mathematical psychology:* II. New York: Wiley, 1963.

Atz, J. W. The application of the idea of homology to behavior. In L. R. Aronson, E. Tobach, D. S. Lehrman, and J. S. Rosenblatt (eds.), *Development and evolution of behavior: Essays in memory of T. C. Schneirla.* San Francisco: Freeman, 1970.

Azrin, N. H., and Holz, W. C. Punishment. In W. K. Honig (ed.), *Operant behavior: Areas of research and application.* New York: Appleton-Century-Crofts, 1966, 380-447.

Babad, E. Y., and Weisz, P. Effectiveness of social reinforcement as a function of contingent and noncontingent satiation. *Journal of Experimental Child Psychology,* 1977, **24,** 406-414.

Bacon, W. E., and Stanley, W. C. Reversal learning in neonatal dogs. *Journal of Comparative and Physiological Psychology,* 1970, **70,** 344-350.

Baer, D. M. Wolf, M. M., and Risley, T. R. Some current dimensions of applied behavior analysis. *Journal of Applied Behavior Analysis,* 1968, **1,** 91-97.

Bakan, D. *Slaughter of the innocents: A study of the battered child syndrome.* Boston: Beacon Press, 1971.

Bakeman, R., and Brown, J. V. Behavioral dialogues: An approach to the assessment of mother-infant interaction. *Child Development,* 1977, **48,** 195-203.

Baldwin, A. L. *Theories of child development.* New York: Wiley, 1967.

Baldwin, A. L. A cognitive theory of socialization. In D. A. Goslin (ed.), *Handbook of socialization theory and research.* Chicago: Rand McNally, 1969.

Baldwin, A. L., and Baldwin, C. P. The study of mother-child interaction. *American Scientist,* 1973, **61,** 714-721.

Baldwin, J. D., and Baldwin, J. I. Exploration and social play in squirrel monkeys (*Saimuri*). *American Zoologist,* 1974, **14,** 303-315.

Baldwin, J. M. *Mental development in the child and the race.* New York: Macmillan, 1894.

Baldwin, J. M. *Social and ethical interpretations in mental development: A study in social psychology* (3d ed.). New York: Macmillan, 1902. (Originally published, 1897.)

Baldwin, J. M. (ed.). *Dictionary of philosophy and psychology* (3 vols.). New York: Macmillan, 1901-1905.

Bandura, A. Social learning through imitation. In M. R. Jones (ed.), *Nebraska Symposium on Motivation*

(Vol. 10). Lincoln: University of Nebraska Press, 1962.

Bandura, A. Behavioral modification through modeling procedures. In L. Krasner and L. P. Ullmann (eds.), *Research in behavior modification*. New York: Holt, Rinehart, and Winston, 1965, 310-340.

Bandura, A. *Principles of behavior modification*. New York: Holt, Rinehart, and Winston, 1969.

Bandura, A. (ed.). *Psychological modeling: Conflicting theories*. Chicago: Aldine-Atherton, 1971.

Bandura, A. *Aggression: A social learning analysis*. Englewood Cliffs, N.J.: Prentice-Hall, 1973(a).

Bandura, A. Social learning theory of aggression. In J. Knutson (ed.), *The control of aggression*. Chicago: Aldine, 1973(b).

Bandura, A. Behavior theory and the models of man. *American Psychologist*, 1974, **29**, 859-869.

Bandura, A. *Social learning theory*. Englewood Cliffs, N.J.: Prentice-Hall, 1977.

Bandura, A., and Walters, R. H. *Adolescent aggression*. New York: Ronald, 1959.

Bandura, A., and Walters, R. H. *Social learning and personality development*. New York: Holt, Rinehart, and Winston, 1963.

Barker, R. G. (ed.). *The stream of behavior*. New York: Appleton-Century-Crofts, 1963.

Barker, R. G. Explorations in ecological psychology. *American Psychologist*, 1965, **20**, 1-14.

Barlow, G. W. Ethological units of behavior. In D. Ingle (ed.), *Central nervous system and fish behavior*. Chicago: University of Chicago Press, 1968.

Barnett, S. A. *The rat: A study of behavior*. Chicago: Aldine, 1963.

Barnett, S. A. Letter to the editor. *Newsweek*, December 3, 1973.

Barrett, D. J., and Yarrow, M. R. Prosocial behavior, social inferential ability, and assertiveness in children. *Child Development*, 1977, **48**, 475-481.

Barrington, E. J. W. *An introduction to general and comparative endocrinology*. Oxford: Clarendon Press, 1975.

Bates, J. Effects of children's nonverbal behavior upon adults. *Child Development*, 1976, **47**, 1070-1088.

Bates, J., and Bentler, P. Play activities of normal and effeminate boys. *Developmental Psychology*, 1973, **9**, 20-27.

Bates, J., Skilbeck, W. M., Smith, K., and Bentler, P. Gender role abnormalities in boys: An analysis of clinical ratings. *Journal of Abnormal Child Psychology*, 1974, **2**, 1-16.

Bateson, P. P. G. Relation between conspicuousness of stimuli and their effectiveness in the imprinting situation. *Journal of Comparative and Physiological Psychology*, 1964, **58**, 407-411.

Bateson, P. P. G. The characteristics and context of imprinting. *Biological Reviews*, 1966, **41**, 177.

Bateson, P. P. G. Specificity and the origins of behavior. In J. Rosenblatt, R. A. Hinde, and C. Beer (eds.), *Advances in the study of behavior* (Vol. 6). New York: Academic Press, 1976.

Bateson, P. P. G. Early experience and sexual preferences. In J. B. Hutchison (ed.), *Biological determinants of sexual behaviour*. London: Wiley, 1978.

Bayley, N. Consistency and variability in the growth of intelligence from birth to eighteen years. *Journal of Genetic Psychology*, 1949, **75**, 165-196.

Bayley, N. Some increasing parent-child similarities during the growth of children. *Journal of Educational Psychology*, 1954, **45**, 1-21.

Bayley, N. *Bayley scales of infant development: Birth to two years*. New York: Psychological Corp., 1969.

Beach, F. A. Comparison of copulatory behavior of male rats raised in isolation, cohabitation, and segregation. *Journal of Genetic Psychology*, 1942, **60**, 121-136.

Beach, F. A. Normal sexual behavior in male rats isolated at fourteen days of age. *Journal of Comparative and Physiological Psychology*, 1958, **51**, 37-38.

Beach, F. A. Biological bases for reproductive behavior. In W. Etkin (ed.), *Social behavior and organization among vertebrates*. Chicago: University of Chicago Press, 1964.

Beach, F. (ed.). *Sex and behavior*. New York: Wiley, 1965.

Beach, F. A. Locks and beagles. *American Psychologist*, 1969, **24**, 971-989.

Beach, F. A. Coital behavior in dogs: VI. Long-term effects of castration upon mating in the male. *Journal of Comparative and Physiological Psychology, Monographs*, 1970, **70** (3, Pt. 2).

Beach, F. A. Behavioral endocrinology: An emerging discipline. *American Scientist*, 1975, **63**, 178-187.

Beach, F. A., and Holz-Tucker, A. M. Effects of different concentrations of androgen upon sexual behavior in castrated male rats. *Journal of Comparative and Physiological Psychology*, 1949, **42**, 433-453.

Beach, F. A., and Levinson, G. Effects of androgen on the glans penis and mating behavior of castrated male rats. *Journal of Experimental Zoology*, 1950, **114**, 159-168.

Beach, F., Rogers, C., and Le Boeuf, B. Coital behavior in dogs: Effects of estrogen on mounting by females. *Journal of Comparative and Physiological Psychology*, 1968, **66**, 296-307.

Becker, W. C. Consequences of different kinds of parental discipline. In M. L. Hoffman and L. W. Hoffman (eds.), *Review of child development research* (Vol. 1). New York: Russell Sage Foundation, 1964.

Becker, W. C., Thomas, D. R., and Carnine, D. *Reducing behavior problems: An operant conditioning guide for teachers.* Urbana, Ill.: Educational Resources Information Center Clearinghouse on Early Childhood Education, 1969.

Beckwith, L. Relationships between infants' social behavior and their mothers' behavior. *Child Development*, 1972, **43**, 397-411.

Behan, J. M. *Dogs of war.* New York: Scribners, 1946.

Beit-Hallahmi, B., and Rabin, A. I. The kibbutz as a social experiment and as a child-rearing laboratory. *American Psychologist*, 1977, **32**, 532-541.

Bekoff, M. The development of social interaction, play, and metacommunication in mammals: An ethological perspective. *Quarterly Review of Biology*, 1972, **47**, 412-434.

Belkin, E. P., and Routh, D. K. Effects of presence of mother versus stranger on behavior of three-year-old children in a novel situation. *Developmental Psychology*, 1975, **11**, 400.

Bell, A. Homosexualities: Their range and character. In J. K. Cole and R. Dienstbier (eds.), *Nebraska Symposium on Motivation* (Vol. 21). Lincoln: University of Nebraska Press, 1974.

Bell, R. Q. A reinterpretation of the direction of effects in studies of socialization. *Psychological Review*, 1968, **75**, 81-95.

Bell, R. Q. Stimulus control of parent or caretaker by offspring. *Developmental Psychology*, 1971, **4**, 63-72.

Bell, R. Q., Weller, G. M., and Waldrop, M. P. Newborn and preschooler: Organization of behavior and relations between periods. *Monographs of the Society for Research in Child Development*, 1971, **36**, (142, Whole Nos. 1-2).

Bell, S. M., and Ainsworth, M. D. S. Infant crying and maternal responsiveness. *Child Development*, 1972, **43**, 1171-1190.

Bem, D. J., and Allen, A. On predicting some of the people some of the time: The search for cross-situational consistencies in behavior. *Psychological Review*, 1974, **81**, 506-520.

Bem, S. L. Sex role adaptability: One consequence of psychological androgyny. *Journal of Personality and Social Psychology*, 1975, **31**, 634-643.

Berger, S. M. Conditioning through vicarious instigation. *Psychological Review*, 1962, **69**, 450-466.

Berghe, L. van den. Naissance d'un gorille de montagne à la station de zoologie expérimentale de Tshibata. *Folia Scientifica Africae Centralis*, 1959, **5**, 81-83.

Berk, L. E. Effects of variation in the nursery school setting on environmental constraints and children's modes of adaptation. *Child Development*, 1971, **42**, 839-869.

Berkowitz, L. Words and symbols as stimuli to aggressive responses. In J. F. Knutson (ed.), *The control of aggression.* Chicago: Aldine, 1973.

Berman, P. W. Social context as a determinant of sex differences in adult's attraction to infants. *Developmental Psychology*, 1976, **12**, 365-366.

Bernstein, I. Role of dominant male rhesus monkey in response to external challenges to the group. *Journal of Comparative and Physiological Psychology*, 1964, **57**, 404-406.

Bertalanffy, L. V. *Modern theories of development: An introduction to theoretical biology.* New York: Harper & Brothers, 1962. (First published in 1933.)

Bertalanffy, L. V. *General system theory: Foundations, development, applications.* New York: G. Braziller, 1968.

Best, D. Williams, J. E., Cloud, J. M., Davis, S. W., Robertson, L. S., Edwards, J. R., Giles, H., and Fowles, J. Development of sex-trait stereotypes among young children in the United States, England, and Ireland. *Child Development*, 1977, **48**, 1375-1384.

Bevan, D., Daves, W., and Levy, G. W. The relation of castration, androgen therapy and pre-test fighting experience to competitive aggression in male C57BL/10 mice. *Animal Behaviour*, 1960, **8**, 6-12.

Bibring, E. The development and problems of the theory of instincts. *International Journal of Psychoanalysis*, 1969, **50**, 293-308.

Bieber, I., Dain, H. J., Dince, P. R., Drellich, M. G., Grand, H. G., Gundlach, R. H., Kremer, M. W., Rifkin, A. H., Wilbur, C. B., and Bieber, T. B. *Homosexuality: A psychoanalytic study.* New York: Basic Books, 1962.

Bigelow, B. J. Children's friendship expectations: A cognitive-developmental study. *Child Development*, 1977, **48**, 246-253.

Bijou, S. W., and Baer, D. M. *Child development*, Vol. 1: *A systematic and empirical theory.* New York: Appleton-Century-Crofts, 1961.

Bijou, S. W., and Baer, D. M. *Child development.* Vol. 2: *Universal stage of infancy.* New York: Appleton-Century-Crofts, 1965.

Biller, H. B. *Father, child, and sex role: Paternal determinants of personality development.* Lexington, Mass.: Heath Lexington Books, 1971.

Bindra, D. A motivational view of learning, performance, and behavior modification. *Psychological Review,* 1974, **81,** 199–213.

Birch, H. G., and Clark, G. Hormonal modification of social behavior: IV. The mechanism of estrogen-induced dominance in chimpanzees. *Journal of Comparative and Physiological Psychology,* 1950, **43,** 181–193.

Blakemore, C. Developmental factors in the formation of feature extracting neurons. In F. O. Schmitt and F. G. Worden (eds.), *The neurosciences: Third study program.* Cambridge, Mass.: MIT Press, 1973.

Blanchard, R. J., and Blanchard, D. C. Effects of hippocampal lesions on the rat's reaction to a cat. *Journal of Comparative and Physiological Psychology,* 1972, **78,** 77–82.

Blanchard, R. J., and Blanchard, D. C. Aggressive behavior in the rat. *Behavioral Biology,* 1977, **21,** 197–224.

Blanchard, R. J., Blanchard, D. C., and Fial, R. A. Hippocampal lesions in rats and their effect on activity, avoidance, and aggression. *Journal of Comparative and Physiological Psychology,* 1970, **71,** 92–102.

Blanchard, R. J., Mast, M. and Blanchard, D. C. Stimulus control of defensive reactions in the albino rat. *Journal of Comparative and Physiological Psychology,* 1974, **88,** 81–88.

Blauvelt, H. Dynamics of the mother-newborn relationship in goats. In B. Schaffner (ed.), *Group processes: Transactions of the First Conference.* New York: Macy Foundation, 1955.

Block, J. *Lives through time.* Berkeley: Bancroft Books, 1971.

Block, J. H. Debatable conclusions about sex differences. *Contemporary Psychology,* 1976, **21,** 517–522.

Bloom, B. S. *Stability and change in human characteristics.* Chicago: University of Chicago, 1964.

Bloom, K., and Esposito, A. Social conditioning and its proper control procedures. *Journal of Experimental Child Psychology,* 1975, **19,** 209–222.

Blurton Jones, N. (ed.) *Ethological studies of child behavior.* Cambridge: Cambridge University Press, 1972.

Bock, D. R., and Kolakowski, D. Further evidence of sex-linked major-game influence on human spatial visualizing ability. *American Journal of Human Genetics,* 1973, **25,** 1–14.

Bolles, R. C. *Theory of motivation.* New York: Harper & Row, 1967.

Bolles, R. C. Reinforcement, expectancy, and learning. *Psychological Review,* 1972, **79,** 394–409.

Borgaonkar, D., and Shah, S. The XYY chromosome male—or syndrome? *Progress in Medical Genetics,* 1974, **10,** 135–222.

Borke, H. The development of empathy in Chinese and American children between three and six years of age: A cross cultural study. *Developmental Psychology,* 1973, **9,** 102–108.

Bott, H. McM. *Personality development in young children.* Toronto: University of Toronto Press, 1934.

Bowers, K. S. Situationism in psychology: An analysis and a critique. *Psychological Review,* 1973, **80,** 307–336.

Bowlby, J. Forty-four juvenile thieves: Their characters and home-life. *International Journal of Psychoanalysis,* 1944, **25,** 19–52 and 107–127.

Bowlby, J. *Maternal care and mental health* (2d ed.). Geneva: World Health Organization, 1952.

Bowlby, J. The nature of the child's tie to his mother. *International Journal of Psychoanalysis,* 1958, **39,** 350–373.

Bowlby, J. *Attachment and loss.* Vol. 1: *Attachment.* New York: Basic Books, 1969.

Bowlby, J. *Attachment and loss.* Vol. 2: *Separation.* New York: Basic Books, 1973.

Bowlby, J., Ainsworth, M. D. S., Boston, M., and Rosenbluth, D. The effects of mother-child separation: A follow-up study. *British Journal of Medical Psychology,* 1956, **29,** 211–247.

Brackbill, Y. Extinction of the smiling response in infants as a function of reinforcement schedule. *Child Development,* 1958, **29,** 114–124.

Brackbill, Y. Cumulative effects of continuous stimulation on arousal level in infants. *Child Development,* 1971, **42,** 17–26.

Brackbill, Y. Continuous stimulation and arousal level in infancy: Effects of stimulus intensity and stress. *Child Development,* 1975, **46,** 364–369.

Bradley, C. The behavior of children receiving Benzedrine. *American Journal of Psychiatry,* 1937, **94,** 577–585.

Bradley, C., and Bowen, M. Amphetamine (Benzedrine) therapy of children's behavior disorders. *American Journal of Orthopsychiatry,* 1941, **11,** 92–103.

Brandt, E. M., and Mitchell, G. Pairing preadolescents with infants (*Macaca mulatta*). *Developmental Psychology,* 1973, **8,** 222–228.

Brazelton, T. B., Tronick, E., Adamson, L., Als, H., and Wise, S. Early mother-infant reciprocity. In M. E. Hofer (ed.), *Ciba Foundation Symposium,* No. 33. Amsterdam: ASP, 1975.

Breland, H. M. Birth order, family size, and intelligence. *Science,* 1974, **184,** 114.

Breland, K., and Breland, M. The misbehavior of organisms. *American Psychologist*, 1961, **16**, 681-684.

Brendt, T. J. The effect of reciprocity norms on moral judgment and causal attribution. Paper read at the Biennial Meeting of the Society for Research in Child Development, New Orleans, March 1977.

Bridges, K. M. B. A study of social development in early infancy. *Child Development*, 1933, **4**, 36-49.

Bronfenbrenner, U. Toward an experimental ecology of human development. *American Psychologist*, 1977, **32**, 513-531.

Bronson, F., and Desjardins, C. Steroid hormones and aggressive behavior in mammals. In B. E. Eleftheriou and J. P. Scott (eds.), *The physiology of aggression and defeat*. New York: Plenum Press, 1971.

Bronson, F., and Eleftheriou, B. E. Adrenal response to fighting in mice: Separation of physical and psychological causes. *Science*, 1965, **147**, 627-628.

Bronson, G. W. Infant's reactions to an unfamiliar person. In L. J. Stone, H. T. Smith, and L. B. Murphy (eds.), *The competent infant: Research and commentary*. New York: Basic Books, 1973.

Bronson, W. C. Developments in behavior with age-mates during the second year of life. In M. Lewis and L. A. Rosenblum (eds.), *The origins of behavior: Friendship and peer relations*. New York: Wiley, 1975.

Brookhart, J., and Hock, E. The effects of experimental context and experiential background on infants' behavior toward their mothers and a stranger. *Child Development*, 1976, **47**, 333-340.

Brooks, J., and Lewis, M. Infants' responses to strangers: Midget, adult, and child. *Child Development*, 1976, **47**, 323-332.

Brown, J. L. *The evolution of behavior*. New York: Norton, 1975.

Brown, J. S. Problems presented by the concept of acquired drives. In M. R. Jones (ed.), *Current theory and research in motivation, A symposium*. Lincoln: University of Nebraska Press, 1953.

Brown, J. S. *The motivation of behavior*. New York: McGraw-Hill, 1961.

Brown, J. W., Bakeman, R., Snyder, P. A., Fredrickson, W. T., Morgan, S. T., and Hepler, R. Interactions of black inner-city mothers with their newborn infants. *Child Development*, 1975, **46**, 677-686.

Brown, P., and Elliot, R. Control of aggression in a nursery school class. *Journal of Experimental Child Psychology*, 1965, **2**, 103-107.

Brown, R. W. *Social psychology*. New York: Free Press, 1965.

Bruce, H. M. Smell as an exteroceptive factor. *Journal of Animal Science*, 1966, **25**, 83-89.

Bryan, J. H., and London, P. Altruistic behavior by children. *Psychological Bulletin*, 1970, **73**, 200-211.

Burton, R. V. Generality of honesty reconsidered. *Psychological Review*, 1963, **70**, 481-499.

Buss, A. H. Instrumentality of aggression, feedback, and frustration as determinants of physical aggression. *Journal of Personality and Social Psychology*, 1966, **3**, 153-162.

Byrne, D. *The attraction paradigm*. New York: Academic Press, 1971.

Caggiula, A. R. Shock-elicited copulation and aggression in male rats. *Journal of Comparative and Physiological Psychology*, 1972, **80**, 393-397.

Cairns, R. B. The influence of dependency inhibition on the effectiveness of social approval. *Journal of Personality*, 1961, **29**, 466-488.

Cairns, R. B. Antecedents of social reinforcer effectiveness. Paper presented at the Biennial Meeting of the Society for Research in Child Development, Berkeley, Calif., April 1963.

Cairns, R. B. Attachment behavior of mammals. *Psychological Review*, 1966(a), **73**, 409-426.

Cairns, R. B. Development, maintenance, and extinction of social attachment behavior in sheep. *Journal of Comparative and Physiological Psychology*, 1966(b), **62**, 298-306.

Cairns, R. B. The information properties of verbal and nonverbal events. *Journal of Personality and Social Psychology*, 1967, **5**, 353-357.

Cairns, R. B. Meaning and attention as determinants of social reinforcer effectiveness. *Child Development*, 1970, **41**, 1067-1082.

Cairns, R. B. Attachment and dependency: A psychobiological and social learning synthesis. In J. L. Gewirtz (ed.), *Attachment and dependency*. New York: Wiley, 1972.

Cairns, R. B. Fighting and punishment from a developmental perspective. In J. K. Cole and D. D. Jensen (eds.), *Nebraska Symposium on Motivation* (Vol. 20). Lincoln: University of Nebraska Press, 1973.

Cairns, R. B. The ontogeny and phylogeny of social interactions. In M. Hahn and E. C. Simmel (eds.), *Evolution of communicative behaviors*. New York: Academic Press, 1976.

Cairns, R. B. Beyond social attachment. The dynamics of interactional development. In T. Alloway, P. Pliner, and L. Krames (eds.), *Attachment behavior*. New York: Plenum Press, 1977.

Cairns, R. B. (ed.). *The analysis of social interactions: Methods, issues, and illustrations*. Hillsdale, N.J.: Erlbaum Associates, 1979.

Cairns, R. B., and Green, J. A. How to assess personality and social patterns: Observations or ratings? In

R. B. Cairns (ed.), *The analysis of social interactions: Methods, issues, and illustrations.* Hillsdale, N.J.: Erlbaum Associates, 1979.

Cairns, R. B., and Johnson, D. L. The development of interspecies social preferences. *Psychonomic Science*, 1965, **2**, 337–338.

Cairns, R. B., and Milakovich, J. T. Is aggression learned? Indiana University, 1971.

Cairns, R. B., and Nakelski, J. S. On fighting in mice: Ontogenetic and experiental determinants. *Journal of Comparative and Physiological Psychology*, 1971, **71**, 354–364.

Cairns, R. B., and Ornstein, P. A. Developmental psychology. In E. Hearst (ed.), *The first century of experimental psychology.* Hillsdale, N.J.: Erlbaum Associates, 1979.

Cairns, R. B., Paul, J. C. N., and Wishner, J. Sex censorship: The assumptions of anti-obscenity laws and the empirical evidence. *Minnesota Law Review*, 1962, **46**, 1009–1041.

Cairns, R. B., and Scholz, S. D. The plasticity of social preferences, Indiana University, 1970.

Cairns, R. B., and Scholz, S. D. On fighting in mice: Dyadic escalation and what is learned. *Journal of Comparative and Physiological Psychology*, 1973, **85**, 540–550.

Cairns, R. B., Sherman, S. J., Buck, N. L., Holmberg, M. C., and Patterson, D. S. Interchanges in the preschool: Stability, multiplicity, and contextual relativity. (In Preparation.)

Cairns, R. B., and Werboff, J. A. Behavior development in the dog: An interspecific analysis. *Science*, 1967, **158**, 1070–1072.

Calhoun, J. B. Disruption of behavioral states as a cause of aggression. In J. Cole and D. Jensen (eds.), *Nebraska Symposium on Motivation* (Vol. 20). Lincoln: University of Nebraska Press, 1973.

Campbell, B. A. Developmental studies of learning and motivation in infra-primate mammals. In H. W. Stevenson, E. H. Hess, and H. L. Rheingold (eds.), *Early behavior: Comparative and developmental approaches.* New York: Wiley, 1967, 43–71.

Campbell, B. A., and Jaynes, J. Reinstatement. *Psychological Review*, 1966, **73**, 478–480.

Campos, J. J., Emde, R. N., Gaensbauer, T., and Henderson, C. Cardiac and behavioral interrelationships in the reactions of infants to strangers. *Developmental Psychology*, 1975, **11**, 589–601.

Cantor, N. L., and Gelfand, D. M. Effects of responsiveness and sex of children on adults' behavior. *Child Development*, 1977, **48**, 232–238.

Carmichael, L. The onset and early development of be-

havior. In L. Carmichael (ed.), *Manual of child psychology* (2d ed). New York: Wiley, 1954.

Caron, A. J., Caron, R. F., Caldwell, R. C., and Weiss, S. J. Infant perception of structural properties of the face. *Developmental Psychology*, 1973, **9**, 385–399.

Carpenter, G. Visual regard of moving and stationary faces in early infancy. *Merrill-Palmer Quarterly*, 1974, **20**, 181–194.

Carr, W. J. Pheromonal sex attractants in the Norway rat. In L. Krames, P. Pliner, and T. Alloway (eds.), *Nonverbal communication.* New York: Plenum Press, 1974.

Carr, W. J., Wylie, N. R., and Loeb, L. S. Responses of adult and immature rats to sex odors. *Journal of Comparative and Physiological Psychology*, 1970, **72**, 51–59.

Casler, L. Maternal deprivation: A critical review of the literature. *Monographs of the Society for Research in Child Development*, 1961, **26** (2, Whole No. 80).

Cavior, N., and Dekecki, P. R. Physical attractiveness, perceived attitude similarity, and academic achievement as contributors to interpersonal attraction among adolescents. *Developmental Psychology*, 1973, **9**, 44–54.

Cavior, N., and Lombardi, D. A. Development aspects of judgment of physical attractiveness in children. *Developmental Psychology*, 1973, **8**, 67–71.

Chamove, A. S., Rosenblum, L. A., and Harlow, H. F. Monkeys *(Macaca mulatta)* raised only with peers. A pilot study. *Animal Behaviour*, 1973, **21**, 316–325.

Chandler, M. J., and Greenspan, S. Ersatz egocentrism: A reply to H. Borke. *Developmental Psychology*, 1972, **7**, 104–106.

Charles, D. C. Ability and accomplishment of persons earlier judged mentally deficient. *General Psychology Monograph*, 1953, **47**, 3–71.

Charlesworth, R., and Hartup, W. W. Positive social reinforcement in the nursery school peer group. *Child Development*, 1967, **38**, 993–1002.

Cheyne, J. A., and Walters, R. H. Punishment and prohibition: Some origins of self-control. In *New directions in psychology* (Vol. 4). New York: Holt, Rinehart, and Winston, 1970.

Church, R. M. The varied effects of punishment on behavior. *Psychological Review*, 1963, **70**, 369–402.

Cicirelli, V. G. Effects of mother and older sibling on the problem-solving behavior of the younger child. *Developmental Psychology*, 1975, **11**, 749–756.

Cicirelli, V. G. Mother-child and sibling-sibling interactions on a problem-solving task. *Child Development*, 1976, **47**, 588-596.

Clarke, A. M., and Clarke, A. D. B. The formative years. In A. M. Clarke & A. D. B. Clarke (eds.), *Early experience: Myth and evidence*. London: Open Books Publishing Ltd., 1976.

Clore, G. L., and Byrne, D. A reinforcement-affect model of attraction. In T. L. Huston (ed.), *Foundations of interpersonal attraction*. New York: Academic Press, 1974.

Coates, B. White adult behavior toward black and white children. *Child Development*, 1972, **43**, 143-154.

Coates, B., Anderson, E. P., and Hartup, W. W. Interrelations and stability in the attachment behavior of human infants. Paper presented at the meeting of the Society for Research in Child Development, Minneapolis, April 1971.

Coates, B., Anderson, E. P., and Hartup, W. W. Interrelations in the attachment behavior of human infants. *Developmental Psychology*, 1972(a), **6**, 218-230.

Coates, B., Anderson, E. P., and Hartup, W. W. The stability of attachment behaviors in the human infant. *Developmental Psychology*, 1972(b), **6**, 231-237.

Cochran, M. M. A comparison of group day and family child-rearing patterns in Sweden. *Child Development*, 1977, **48**, 702-707.

Cohen, L. J. The operational definition of human attachment. *Psychological Bulletin*, 1974, **81**, 207-217.

Cohen, L. J., and Campos, J. J. Father, mother, and stranger as elicitors of attachment behaviors in infancy. *Developmental Psychology*, 1974, **10**, 146-154.

Collias, N. E. The analysis of socialization in sheep and goats. *Ecology*, 1956, **37**, 228-239.

Collins, W. A. Effects of temporal separation between motivation, aggression, and consequences: A developmental study. *Developmental Psychology*, 1973, **8**, 215-221.

Collins, W. A. Temporal integration and inferences about televised social behavior. Paper read at the Biennial Meeting of the Society for Research in Child Development, New Orleans, March 1977.

Collins, W. A., Berndt, T. J., and Hess, V. L. Observational learning of motives and consequences for television aggression: A developmental study. *Child Development*, 1974, **45**, 799-802.

Condon, W. S., and Sander, L. W. Synchrony demonstrated between movements of the neonate and adult speech. *Child Development*, 1974, **45**, 456-462.

Conners, C. K., and Eisenberg, L. The effects of methylphenidate on symptomatology and learning in disturbed children. *American Journal of Psychiatry*, 1963, **120**, 458-463.

Conrad, L. C. A., and Pfaff, D. W. Axonal projections of medial preoptic and anterior hypothalamic neurons. *Science*, 1975, **190**, 1112-1114.

Conway, E., and Brackbill, Y. Delivery medication and infant outcome: An empirical study. In W. A. Bowes, Jr., Y. Brackbill, E. Conway, and A. Steinschneider (eds.), The effects of obstetrical medication on fetus and infant. *Monographs of the Society for Research in Child Development*, 1970, **35**, 24-34 (4, Serial No. 137).

Cook, H., and Stingle, S. Cooperative behavior in children. *Psychological Bulletin*, 1974, **81**, 918-933.

Corah, N. L. Differentiation in children and their parents. *Journal of Personality*, 1965, **33**, 300-308.

Cornelius, S. W., and Denney, N. W. Dependency in day-care and home-care children. *Developmental Psychology*, 1975, **11**, 575-582.

Corter, C. M., Rheingold, H. L., and Eckerman, C. O. Toys delay the infant's following of his mother. *Developmental Psychology*, 1972, **6**, 138-145.

Cottrell, L. S. The analysis of situational fields in social psychology. *American Sociological Review*, 1942, **7**, 370-382.

Cottrell, L. S., Jr. Interpersonal interaction and the development of the self. In D. A. Goslin (ed.), *Handbook of socialization theory and research*. Chicago: Rand McNally, 1969.

Cowan, P. A., and Walters, R. H. Studies of reinforcement of aggression: I. Effects of scheduling. *Child Development*, 1963, **34**, 543-551.

Crawford, M. P., and Spence, K. W. Observational learning of discrimination problems by chimpanzees. *Journal of Comparative Psychology*, 1939, **27**, 133-147.

Creutzfeldt, O. D., and Heggelund, P. Neural plasticity in visual cortex of adult cats after exposure to visual patterns. *Science*, 1975, **188**, 1025-1027.

Crime in the United States. Washington, D.C.: Government Printing Office, 1975.

Cronbach, L. J. *Essentials of psychological testing* (2d ed.). New York: Harper, 1970.

Crook, J. H. Social organization and the environment: Aspects of contemporary social ethology. *Animal Behaviour*, 1970, **18**, 197-209.

Crook, J. H. On the integration of gender strategies in mammalian social systems. In J. S. Rosenblatt and B. R. Komisaruk (eds.), *Reproductive behavior and evolution*. New York: Plenum Press, 1977.

Crook, J. H., Ellis, J., and Goss-Custard, J. Mammalian

social systems: Structure and function. *Animal Behaviour,* 1976, **24,** 261–274.

Crowcroft, P. *Mice all over.* Chester Springs, Pa.: Dufour Editions, 1966.

Daniels, J. D., and Pettigrew, J. D. Development of neuronal responses in the visual system of cats. In G. Gottlieb (ed.), *Neural and behavioral specificity.* New York: Academic Press, 1976.

Dank, B. M. Six homosexual siblings. *Archives of Sexual Behavior,* 1971, **1,** 193–204.

Darling, F. F. *A herd of red deer: A study in animal behavior.* New York: Oxford University Press, 1937.

Darwin, C. R. *The expression of the emotions in man and animals.* New York: Appleton, 1873.

Davenport, R. K., Menzel, E. W., and Rogers, C. M. Maternal care during infancy: Its effect on weight gain and mortality in the chimpanzee. *American Journal of Orthopsychiatry,* 1961, **31,** 803–809.

Davenport, W. Sexual patterns and their regulation in a society of the Southwest Pacific. In F. Beach (ed.), *Sex and behavior.* New York: Wiley, 1965.

Davidson, J. M. Reproductive behavior in a neuroendocrine perspective. In J. S. Rosenblatt and B. R. Komisaruk (eds.), *Reproductive behavior and evolution.* New York: Plenum Press, 1977.

Davitz, J. R. The effects of previous training on profrustration behavior. *Journal of Abnormal and Social Psychology,* 1952, **47,** 309–315.

Dawe, H. C. An analysis of two hundred quarrels of preschool children. *Child Development,* 1934, **5,** 139–157.

Dawkins, R. *The selfish gene.* Oxford: Oxford University Press, 1976.

de Beer, G. *Embryos and ancestors* (3d ed.) London: Oxford University Press, 1958.

DeFries, J. C., and McClearn, G. E. Social dominance and Darwinian fitness in the laboratory mouse. *American Naturalist,* 1970, **104,** 408–411.

Denenberg, V. H. The mother as a motivator. In W. Arnold (ed.), *Nebraska symposium on motivation* (Vol. 19). Lincoln: University of Nebraska Press, 1971, 69–93.

Deur, J. L., and Parke, R. D. Effects of inconsistent punishment on aggression in children. *Developmental Psychology,* 1970, **2,** 403–411.

De Valois, R. L., and Jacobs, G. H. Primate color vision. *Science,* 1968, **162,** 533–540.

Devereux, E. C., Shouval, R., Bronfenbrenner, U., Rodgers, R., Kav-Venaki, S., Kiely, E., and Karson, E. Socialization practices of parents, teachers, and peers in Israel: The kibbutz versus the city. *Child Development,* 1974, **45,** 269–281.

De Vore, I. *Primate behavior: Field studies of monkeys and apes.* New York: Holt, Rinehart, and Winston, 1965.

deVries, M. The cultural relativity of toilet training readiness: A perspective from East Africa. *Pediatrics,* (in press).

Dollard, J., Doob, L. W., Miller, N. E., Mowrer, O. H., and Sears, R. R. *Frustration and aggression.* New Haven: Yale University Press, 1939.

Dollard, J., and Miller, N. E. *Personality and psychotherapy: An analysis in terms of learning, thinking, and culture.* New York: McGraw-Hill, 1950.

Dörner, G., Rohde, W., Stahl, F., Krell, L., and Masius, W. A neuroendocrine predisposition for homosexuality in men. *Archives of Sexual Behavior,* 1975, **4,** 1–8.

Doyle, A. Infant development in day care. *Developmental Psychology,* 1975, **11,** 655–656.

Drachman, D. B., and Coulombre, A. J. Experimental clubfoot and arthrogryposis multiplex congenita. *Lancet,* 1962, **283,** 523–526.

Drori, D., and Folman, Y. Effects of cohabitation on the reproductive system, kidneys and body composition of male rats. *Journal of Reproduction and Fertility,* 1964, **8,** 351–359.

Drori, D., and Folman, Y. The sexual behavior of male rats unmated to sixteen months of age. *Animal Behavior,* 1967, **15,** 20–24.

Dudgeon, P. Intellect in brutes. *Nature,* 1879, **20,** 77.

Dudycha, G. J. An objective study of punctuality in relation to personality and achievement. *Archives of Psychology,* 1936, **29** (Serial no. 204), 54–57.

Dunlap, K. Emotion as a dynamic background. In M. L. Reymert (ed.), *Feelings and emotions: The Wittenberg Symposium.* Worcester, Mass.: Clark University Press, 1928.

Dweck, C. S. Sex differences in the meaning of negative evaluation in achievement situations: Determinants and consequences. In C. S. Dweck (Chairman), *Negative evaluation and feedback: Impact and implications for the agent and recipient.* Symposium presented at the meeting of the Society for Research in Child Development, Denver, April 1975.

Eaton, G. G. The social order of Japanese macaques. *Scientific American,* 1976, **235,** 96–106.

Eaton, J. W., and Weil, R. J. *Culture and mental disorders.* New York: Free Press, 1955.

Eckerman, C. O. The human infant in social interaction. In R. B. Cairns (ed.), *The analysis of social interactions: Methods, issues, and illustrations.* Hillsdale, N.J.: Erlbaum Associates, 1979.

Eckerman, C. O., and Whatley, J. L. Infant's reactions to

unfamiliar adults varying in novelty. *Developmental Psychology*, 1975, **11**, 562-566.

Eckerman, C. O., Whatley, J. L., and Kutz, S. L. Growth of social play with peers during the second year of life. *Developmental Psychology*, 1975, **11**, 42-49.

Edwards, D. A. The organization and activation of aggression in male and female mice. Unpublished doctoral dissertation, University of California, Irvine, 1968.

Edwards, D. A. Early androgen stimulation and aggressive behavior in male and female mice. *Physiology and Behavior*, 1969, **4**, 333-338.

Eibl-Eibesfeldt, I. The fighting behavior of animals. *Scientific American*, 1961, **205**(6), 112-122.

Eibl-Eibesfeldt, I. Ontogenetic and maturational studies of aggressive behavior. In C. D. Clemente and D. B. Lindsley (eds.), *Aggression and defense: Neural mechanisms and social patterns*. Vol. 5: *Brain function*. Berkeley: University of California Press, 1967.

Eibl-Eibesfeldt, I. *Ethology: The biology of behavior*. New York: Holt, Rinehart, and Winston, 1970.

Eibl-Eibesfeldt, I. *Ethology: The biology of behavior* (2d ed.). New York: Holt, Rinehart, and Winston, 1975.

Einsiedel, A. E. The development and modification of object preferences in domestic White Leghorn chicks *(Gallus gallus)*. Unpublished doctoral dissertation, Indiana University, 1973.

Einsiedel, A. E. The development and modification of object preferences in domestic White Leghorn chicks. *Developmental Psychobiology*, 1975, **8**, 533-540.

Eisenberg, J. F. The evolution of the reproductive unit in the class *Mammalia*. In J. S. Rosenblatt and B. J. Komisaruk (eds.), *Reproductive behavior and evolution*. New York: Plenum, 1977.

Eisenberger, R., Kaplan, R. M., and Singer, R. D. Decremental and nondecremental effects of noncontingent social approval. *Journal of Personality and Social Psychology*, 1974, **30**, 716-722.

Elkind, D., and Dabek, R. F. Personal injury and property damage in the moral judgments of children. *Child Development*, 1977, **48**, 518-522.

Elliot, D. G. *A review of the primates* (Vol. 2). New York: American Museum of Natural History, 1913.

Emde, R. N., and Koenig, K. L. Neonatal smiling and rapid eye movement states. *American Academy of Child Psychiatry*, 1969, **8**, 57-67.

Emmerich, W. Continuity and stability in early social development. *Child Development*, 1964, **35**, 311-332.

Eron, L. D., Huesmann, L. R., Lefkowitz, M. M., and Walder, L. O. Does television violence cause aggression? *American Psychologist*, 1972, **27**, 253-263.

Estes, W. K. Comments on Dr. Bolles's paper. In M. R. Jones (ed.), *Nebraska symposium on motivation* (Vol. 6). Lincoln: University of Nebraska Press, 1958, 33-34.

Estes, W. K. Stimulus-response theory of drive. In M. R. Jones (ed.), *Nebraska symposium on motivation* (Vol. 6). Lincoln: University of Nebraska Press, 1958.

Etaugh, C., Collins, G., and Gerson, A. Reinforcement of sex-typed behaviors of two-year-old children in a nursery school setting. *Developmental Psychology*, 1975, **11**, 255.

Etkin, W. Types of social organization in birds and mammals. In W. Etkin (ed.), *Social behavior and organization among vertebrates*. Chicago: University of Chicago Press, 1964.

Evans, R. B. Childhood parental relationships of homosexual men. *Journal of Consulting and Clinical Psychology*, 1969, **33**, 129-135.

Ewbank, R., Meese, G. B., and Cox, J. E. Individual recognition and the dominance hierarchy in the domestic pig: The role of sight. *Animal Behaviour*, 1974, **22**, 473-480.

Fagan, J. F. III. Infants' recognition of invariant features of faces. *Child Development*, 1976, **47**, 627-638.

Fagot, B. I. Sex differences in toddlers' behavior and parental reaction. *Developmental Psychology*, 1974, **10**, 554-558.

Falender, C. A., and Heber, R. Mother-child interaction and participation in a longitudinal intervention program. *Developmental Psychology*, 1975, **11**, 830-836.

Fantz, R. Pattern vision in newborn infants. *Science*, 1963, **140**, 296-297.

Fantz, R. Visual perception and experience in early infancy: A look at the hidden side of behavioral development. In H. Stevenson, E. Hess, and H. L. Rheingold (eds.), *Early behavior: Comparative and developmental approaches*. New York: Wiley, 1967.

Federman, E. J., and Yang, R. K. A critique of "Obstetrical pain-relieving drugs as predictors of infant behavior variability." *Child Development*, 1976, **47**, 297-298.

Fein, G. G. Children's sensitivity to social contexts at eighteen months of age. *Developmental Psychology*, 1975, **11**, 853-854.

Fein, G., Johnson, D., Kosson, N., Stork, L., and Wasserman, L. Sex stereotypes and preferences in the toy choices of twenty-month-old boys and girls. *Developmental Psychology*, 1975, **11**, 527-528.

Feitelson, D., Weintraub, S., and Michaeli, O. Social interactions in heterogeneous preschools in Israel. *Child Development*, 1972, **43**, 1249-1259.

Feshbach, N. D. Cross-cultural studies of teaching styles in four-year-olds and their mothers. In A. D. Pick (ed.), *Minnesota Symposia on Child Psychology* (Vol. 7). Minneapolis: University of Minnesota Press, 1973.

Feshbach, N. D., and Sones, G. Sex differences in adolescent reactions toward newcomers. *Developmental Psychology*, 1971, **4**, 381-386.

Feshbach, S. The function of aggression and the regulation of aggressive drive. *Psychological Review*, 1964, **71**, 257-272.

Feshbach, S. Aggression. In P. H. Mussen (ed.), *Carmichael's manual of child psychology*. (3d ed.), Vol. 2. New York: Wiley, 1970.

Feshbach, S., and Singer, R. D. *Television and aggression: An experimental field study*. San Francisco: Jossey-Bass, 1971.

Fishbein, H. D. *Evolution, development, and children's learning*. Pacific Palisades, Calif.: Goodyear Publishing Co., 1976.

Fitzgerald, H., and Brackbill, Y. Classical conditioning in infancy: Development and constraints. *Psychological Bulletin*, 1976, **83**, 353-376.

Flavell, J. H. *The developmental psychology of Jean Piaget*. Princeton: Van Nostrand, 1963.

Flavell, J. H. *Cognitive development*. Englewood Cliffs, N.J.: Prentice-Hall, 1977.

Flavell, J. H., Botkin, P. T., Fry, C. L., Wright, J. W., and Jarvis, P. E. *The development of role-taking and communication skills in children*. New York: Wiley, 1968.

Fleener, D. E. Attachment formation in humans (Doctoral dissertation, Indiana University, 1967). Ann Arbor, Mich.: University Microfilms No. 6872-12.

Fleener, D. E. Experimental production of infant-maternal attachment behaviors. *Proceedings, 81st Annual Convention, American Psychological Association*, 1973, **8**, 57-58.

Fleener, D. E., and Cairns, R. B. Attachment behavior in human infants: Discriminative vocalizations on maternal separation. *Developmental Psychology*, 1970, **2**, 215-223.

Fling, S., and Manosevitz, M. Sex typing in nursery school children's play interests. *Developmental Psychology*, 1972, **7**, 146-152.

Floody, O. R., and Pfaff, D. W. Aggressive behaviors in female hampsters: The hormonal basis for fluctuations in female aggressiveness correlated with estrous state. *Journal of Comparative and Physiological Psychology*, 1977, **91**, 443-464.

Flynn, J. P. Patterning mechanisms, patterned reflexes, and attack behavior in cats. In J. K. Cole and D. D. Jensen (eds.), *Nebraska symposium on Motivation* (Vol. 20). Lincoln: University of Nebraska Press, 1973.

Folman, Y., and Drori, D. Effects of social isolation and female odours on the reproductive system, kidneys and adrenals of unmated male rats. *Journal of Reproduction and Fertility*, 1966, **11**, 43-50.

Ford, C. S., and Beach, F. A. *Patterns of sexual behavior*. New York: Academic Press, 1951.

Fouts, G. T. The effects of being imitated and awareness of the behavior of introverted and extroverted youth. *Child Development*, 1975, **46**, 296-300.

Fouts, G. T., Waldner, D. N., and Watson, M. W. Effects of being imitated and counterimitated on the behavior of preschool children. *Child Development*, 1976, **47**, 172-177.

Freedman, D. G. An ethological approach to the genetical study of human behavior. In S. G. Vandenberg (ed.), *Methods and goals in human behavior genetics*. New York: Academic Press, 1965.

Freedman, D. G. *Human infancy: An evolutionary perspective*. New York: Halsted Press, 1974.

Freedman, D. G., and Keller, B. Inheritance of behavior in infants. *Science*, 1963, **140**, 196-198.

Freedman, D. G., King, J. A., and Elliot, O. Critical period in the social development of dogs. *Science*, 1961, **133**, 1016-1017.

French, D. C., Brownell, C. A., Graziano, W. G., and Hartup, W. W. Effects of cooperative, competitive, and individualistic sets on performance in children's groups. *Journal of Experimental Child Psychology*, 1977, **24**, 1-10.

Freud, A., and Dann, S. An experiment in group upbringing. *Psychoanalytic Study of the Child*, 1951, **8**, 127-168.

Freud, S. *New introductory lectures on psycho-analysis*. New York: Norton, 1933.

Freud, S. *Collected papers*. New York: Basic Books, 1959.

Freud, S. *Drei Abhandlungen zur Sexualtheorie*. (2d ed.) Vienna: Deuticke, 1910. (Translated as *Three essays on the theory of sexuality*, 1962).

Friedrich, L. K., and Stein, A. H. Aggressive and prosocial television programs and the natural behavior of preschool children. *Monographs of the Society for Research in Child Development*, 1973, **38** (Serial No. 151).

Friedrich, L. K., and Stein, A. H. Prosocial television and young children: The effects of verbal labeling and role playing on learning and behavior. *Child Development*, 1975, **46**, 27-38.

Frodi, A., Macaulay, J., and Thome, P. R. Are women always less aggressive than men? A review of the experimental literature. *Psychological Bulletin*, 1977, **84**, 634-660.

Frueh, T., and McGhee, P. E. Traditional sex role development and amount of time spent watching television. *Developmental Psychology*, 1975, **11**, 109.

Fullard, W., and Reiling, A. M. An investigation of Lorenz's "babyness." *Child Development*, 1976, **47**, 1191-1193.

Fuller, J. L. Cross-sectional and longitudinal studies of adjustive behavior in dogs. *Annals of the New York Academy of Sciences*, 1953, **56**, 214-224.

Fuller, J. L. Experiential deprivation and later behavior. *Science*, 1967, **158**, 1645-1652.

Fuller, J. L., and Clark, L. D. Genetic and treatment factors modifying the postisolation syndrome in dogs. *Journal of Comparative and Physiological Psychology*, 1966, **61**, 251-257.

Fuller, J. L., and Fox, M. W. The behaviour of dogs. In E. S. E. Hafez (ed.), *The behavior of domestic animals* (2d ed.). Baltimore: Williams and Wilkins, 1969.

Fuller, J. L., and Thompson, W. R. *Behavior genetics*. New York: Wiley, 1960.

Gagnon, J. H. Scripts and the coordination of sexual conduct. In J. K. Cole and R. R. Dienstbier (eds.), *Nebraska Symposium on Motivation* (Vol. 21). Lincoln: University of Nebraska Press, 1974.

Galef, B. G., Jr. Aggression and timidity: Responses to novelty in feral Norway rats. *Journal of Comparative and Physiological Psychology*, 1970, **70**, 370-381.

Galst, J. P., and White, M. A. The unhealthy persuader: The reinforcing value of television and children's purchase-influencing attempts at the supermarket. *Child Development*, 1976, **47**, 1089-1096.

Gardner, D. B., Hawkes, G. R., and Burchinal, L. G. Noncontinuous mothering in infancy and development in later childhood. *Child Development*, 1961, **32**, 225-234.

Garn, S. M. Body size and its implications. In L. W. Hoffman and M. L. Hoffman (eds.), *Review of child development research* (Vol. 2). New York: Russell Sage Foundation, 1966.

Garvey, C., and Bendebba, M. Effects of age, sex, and partner on children's dyadic speech. *Child Development*, 1974, **45**, 1159-1161.

Garvey, C., and Hogan, R. Social speech and social interaction: Egocentrism revisited. *Child Development*, 1973, **44**, 562-568.

Gavrin, J. B., and Sacks, L. S. Growth potential of preschool-aged children in instituted care: A positive approach to a negative condition. *American Journal of Orthopsychiatry*, 1963, **33**, 399-408.

Gebhard, P. H. Sex differences in sexual response. *Archives of Sexual Behavior*, 1973, **2**, 201-214.

Geist, V. *Mountain sheep: A study in behavior and evolution.* Chicago: University of Chicago Press, 1971.

Gelfand, D. M., Hartmann, D. P., Lamb, A. K., Smith, C. L., Mahan, M. A., and Paul, S. C. The effects of adult models and described alternatives on children's choice of behavior management techniques. *Child Development*, 1974, **45**, 585-593.

Gerall, A. A., and Ward, I. L. Effects of prenatal exogenous estrogen on the sexual behavior of the female albino rat. *Journal of Comparative and Physiological Psychology*, 1966, **62**, 370-375.

Gerall, H. D. Effects of social isolation and physical confinement on motor and sexual behavior of guinea pigs. *Journal of Personality and Social Psychology*, 1965, **2**, 460-464.

Gerall, H. D., Ward, I. L., and Gerall, A. A. Disruption of the male rat's sexual behaviour induced by social isolation. *Animal Behaviour*, 1967, **15**, 54-58.

Gershman, H. The evolution of gender identity. *Bulletin of the New York Academy of Medicine*, 1976, **43**, 1000-1018.

Gesell, A., and Amatruda, C. S. *Developmental diagnosis.* New York: Hoeber, 1947.

Gesell, A. L., and Thompson, H. *Infant behavior: Its genesis and growth.* New York: McGraw-Hill, 1934.

Gewirtz, J. L. A learning analysis of the effects of normal stimulation privation, and deprivation on the acquisition of social motivation and attachment. In B. M. Foss (ed.), *Determinants of infant behavior.* New York: Wiley, 1961.

Gewirtz, J. L. Deprivation and satiation of social stimuli as determinants of their reinforcing efficacy. In J. P. Hill (ed.), *Minnesota symposium on child psychology* (Vol. 1). Minneapolis: University of Minnesota Press, 1967.

Gewirtz, J. L. (ed.). *Attachment and dependency.* New York: Halsted Press, 1972.

Gewirtz, J. L., and Boyd, E. F. Does maternal responding imply reduced infant crying? A critique of the 1972 Bell and Ainsworth report. *Child Development*, 1977(a). **48**, 1200-1207.

Gewirtz, J. L., and Boyd, E. F. Experiments on mother-infant interaction underlying mutual attachment acquisition: The infant conditions the mother. In T. Alloway, P. Pliner, and L. Krames (eds.), *Attachment behavior.* New York: Plenum, 1977(b).

Gewirtz, J. L., and Gewirtz, H. B. Stimulus conditions, infant behaviors, and social learning in four Israeli child-rearing environments: A preliminary report illustrating differences in environment and behavior between the "only" and the "youngest" child.

In B. M. Foss (ed.), *Determinants of infant behaviour* (Vol. 3). London: Methuen, 1965.

Gewirtz, J. L., and Stingle, K. G. Learning of generalized imitation as a basis for identification. *Psychological Review*, 1968, **75**, 374–397.

Gibson, E. J. *Principles of perceptual learning and development*. New York: Appleton-Century-Crofts, 1969.

Gil, D. G. *Violence against children: Physical child abuse in the United States*. Cambridge: Harvard University Press, 1970.

Ginsberg, B. Evolution of communication patterns in animals. In E. C. Simmel and M. E. Hahn (eds.), *Communicative behavior and evolution*. New York: Academic Press, 1976.

Glickman, S. E., and Schiff, B. B. A biological theory of reinforcement. *Psychological Review*, 1967, **74**, 81–109.

Gloor, P. Discussion of Kaada's paper, "Brain mechanisms related to aggressive behavior." In C. D. Clemente and D. B. Lindsley (eds.), *Aggression and defense: Neural mechanisms and social patterns* (*Brain Function*, Vol. 5). Berkeley and Los Angeles: University of California Press, 1967.

Glueck, S., and Glueck, E. *Unraveling juvenile delinquency*. New York: Commonwealth Fund, 1950.

Goldberg, S., and Lewis, M. Play behavior in the year-old infant: Early sex differences. *Child Development*, 1969, **40**, 21–32.

Goldfarb, W. Psychological privation in infancy and subsequent adjustment. *American Journal of Orthopsychiatry*, 1945, **15**, 247–255.

Goodall, J. Chimpanzees of the Gombe stream reserve. In I. DeVore (ed.), *Primate behavior*. New York: Holt, Rinehart, and Winston, 1965, 425–473.

Goodenough, E. W. Interest in persons as an aspect of sex differences in the early years. *Genetic Psychology Monographs*, 1957, **55**, 287–323.

Goodenough, F. L. *Anger in young children*. Minneapolis: University of Minnesota Press, 1931.

Gorbman, A., and Bern, H. A. *A textbook of comparative endocrinology*. New York: Wiley, 1962.

Gottesman, I. I. Heritability of personality: A demonstration. *Psychological Monographs*, 1963, **77** (Whole No. 572).

Gottlieb, G. Species identification by avian neonates: Contributory effect of perinatal auditory stimulation. *Animal Behavior*, 1966, **14**, 282–290.

Gottlieb, G. Conceptions of prenatal behavior. In L. R. Aronson, E. Tobach, D. S. Lehrman, and J. S. Rosenblatt (eds.), *Development and evolution of behavior: Essays in memory of T. C. Schneirla*. San Francisco: Freeman, 1970.

Gottlieb, G. *Development of species identification in birds: An inquiry into the prenatal determinants of perception*. Chicago: University of Chicago Press, 1971.

Gottlieb, G. Development of species identification in ducklings: I. Nature of perceptual deficit caused by embryonic auditory deprivation. *Journal of Comparative and Physiological Psychology*, 1975(a), **89**, 387–399.

Gottlieb, G. Development of species identification in ducklings: II. Experiential prevention of perceptual deficit caused by embryonic deprivation. *Journal of Comparative and Physiological Psychology*, 1975(b), **89**, 675–684.

Gottlieb, G. Development of species identification in ducklings: III. Maturational rectification of perceptual deficit caused by auditory deprivation. *Journal of Comparative and Physiological Psychology*, 1975(c), **89**, 899–912.

Gottlieb, G. The roles of experience in the development of behavior and the nervous system. In G. Gottlieb (ed.), *Neural and behavioral specificity*. New York: Academic Press, 1976(a).

Gottlieb, G. Conceptions of prenatal development. *Psychological Review*, 1976(b), **83**, 215–234.

Gottman, J., Gonso, J., and Rasmussen, B. Social interaction, social competence, and friendship in children. *Child Development*, 1975, **46**, 709–718.

Gould, S. J. *Ontogeny and phylogeny*. Cambridge, Mass.: Harvard University Press, 1977.

Goy, R. W. Organizing effects of androgen on the behaviour of rhesus monkeys. In R. P. Michael (ed.), *Endocrinology and human behavior*. London: Oxford University Press, 1968.

Grady, K., Phoenix, C. and Young, W. Role of the developing rat testis in differentiation of the neural tissues mediating mating behavior. *Journal of Comparative and Physiological Psychology*, 1965, **59**, 176–182.

Graham, F. K., Ernhart, C. B., Thurston, D., and Craft, M. Development three years after perinatal anoxia and other potentially damaging newborn experiences. *Psychological Monographs*, 1962, **76**, No. 522.

Green, E. H. Group play and quarreling among preschool children. *Child Development*, 1933, **4**, 302–307.

Green, J. A. A developmental analysis of mother-infant interactions: Changes in infant behaviors and capabilities. Unpublished masters thesis, University of North Carolina at Chapel Hill, 1977.

Green, J. A., and Cairns, R. B. Postpartum aggression in female mice: Experiential and dyadic controls. Paper read at the Annual Meeting of the American

Psychological Association, Washington, D.C., September, 1976.

Green, R. *Sexual identity conflict in children and adults.* New York: Basic Books, 1974.

Green, R., and Money, J. Incongruous gender role: Nongenital manifestations in prepubertal boys. *Journal of Nervous and Mental Disease*, 1960, **131**, 160-162.

Green, R., and Money, J. Prepubertal, morphologically normal boys demonstrating signs of cross-gender identity: A five year followup. *American Journal of Orthopsychiatry*, 1964, **34**, 365-366.

Green, R., and Stoller, R. J. Two monozygotic (identical) twin pairs discordant for gender identity. *Archives of Sexual Behavior*, 1971, **1**, 321-327.

Greenberg, D. J., and O'Donnell, W. J. Infancy and the optimal level of stimulation. *Child Development*, 1972, **43**, 639-645.

Griffiths, R. *The abilities of babies: A study in mental measurement.* New York: McGraw-Hill, 1954.

Grinspoon, L., and Singer, S. B. Amphetamines in the treatment of hyperkinetic children. *Harvard Educational Review*, 1973, **43**, 515-555.

Grobstein, P., and Chow, K. L. Receptive field organization in the mammalian cortex: The role of individual experience in development. In G. Gottlieb (ed.), *Neural and behavioral specificity.* New York: Academic Press, 1976.

Gross, M. D. Violence associated with organic brain disease. In J. Fawcett (ed.), *Dynamics of violence* (2d ed.). Chicago: American Medical Association, 1972, 85-91.

Grossman, S. P. Aggression, avoidance, and reaction to novel environments in female rats with ventromedial hypothalamic lesions. *Journal of Comparative and Physiological Psychology*, 1972, **78**, 274-283.

Grubb, P., and Jewell, P. A. Social grouping and home range in feral soay sheep. *Symposium of the Zoological Society of London*, 1966, No. 18, 179-201.

Guhl, A. M. Social inertia and social stability in chickens. *Animal Behaviour*, 1968, **16**, 219-232.

Guhl, A. M., and Fischer, G. J. The behaviour of chickens. In E. S. E. Hafez (ed.), *The behaviour of domestic animals* (2d ed.). Baltimore: Williams and Wilkins, 1969.

Gundlach, R. H. Childhood parental relationships and the establishment of gender roles of homosexuals. *Journal of Consulting and Clinical Psychology*, 1969, **33**, 136-139.

Gustafson, G. E. Social interactions in 18-month-old children: Distinctions among familiar adults and peers. Paper read at the Fourth Annual Southeastern Conference on Human Development, Nashville, Tenn., 1976.

Gustafson, G. E. A longitudinal study of infants' interactions with their mothers: Some contributions of locomotor and social development. Unpublished master's thesis, University of North Carolina at Chapel Hill, 1977.

Hafez, E. S. E., Cairns, R. B., Hulet, C. V., and Scott, J. P. The behavior of sheep and goats. In E. S. E. Hafez (ed.), *The behavior of domestic animals* (2d ed.). Baltimore: Williams and Wilkins, 1969.

Hall, C. S. The genetics of behavior. In S. S. Stevens (ed.), *Handbook of experimental psychology.* New York: Wiley, 1951.

Hall, W. G. Weaning and growth of artificially reared rats. *Science*, 1975, **190**, 1313-1315.

Hall, W. M. Observational and interactive determinants of aggressive behavior in boys. Unpublished doctoral dissertation, Indiana University, 1973.

Hamilton, G. V. A study of sexual tendencies in monkeys and baboons. *Journal of Animal Behavior*, 1914, **4**, 293-318.

Hamilton, L. W. Intrabox and extrabox cues in avoidance responding: Effect of septal lesions. *Journal of Comparative and Physiological Psychology*, 1972, **78**, 268-273.

Hamilton, W. D. The genetical theory of social behavior, I, II. *Journal of Theoretical Biology*, 1964, **7**, 1-52.

Hann, N., Langer, J., and Kohlberg, L. Family patterns of moral reasoning. *Child Development*, 1976, **47**, 1204-1206.

Harlow, H. F. The nature of love. *The American Psychologist*, 1958, **13**, 673-685.

Harlow, H. F. The development of affectional patterns in infant monkeys. In B. M. Foss (ed.), *Determinants of infant behaviour.* London: Methuen, 1961.

Harlow, H. F. Sexual behavior in rhesus monkeys. In F. A. Beach (ed.), *Sex and behavior.* New York: Wiley, 1965.

Harlow, H. F., and Harlow, M. K. The affectional systems. In A. M. Schrier, H. F. Harlow, and F. Stollnitz (eds.), *Behavior of nonhuman primates: Modern research trends* (Vol. 2). New York: Academic Press, 1965.

Harlow, H. F., and Rosenblum, L. Maturational variables influencing sexual posturing in infant monkeys. *Archives of Sexual Behavior*, 1971, **1**, 175-180.

Harlow, H. F., and Zimmerman, R. R. Affectional responses in the infant monkey. *Science*, 1959, **130**, 421-432.

Harper, L. V., and Sanders, K. M. Preschool children's use of space: Sex differences in outdoor play. *Developmental Psychology*, 1975, **11**, 119.

Hart, B. L. Sexual reflexes and mating behavior in the male rat. *Journal of Comparative and Physiological Psychology*, 1968, **65**, 453–460.

Hart, B. L. Gonadal androgen and sociosexual behavior of male mammals: A comparative analysis. *Psychological Bulletin*, 1974, **81**, 383–400.

Hart, B. L., and Haugen, C. M. Activation of sexual reflexes in male rats by spinal implantation of testosterone. *Physiology and Behavior*, 1968, **3**, 735–738.

Hartlage, L. C. Sex-linked inheritance of spatial ability. *Perceptual and Motor Skills*, 1970, **31**, 610.

Hartshorne, H., and May, M. A. *Studies in the nature of character*. Vol. 1: *Studies in deceit*. New York: Macmillan, 1928.

Hartshorne, H., May, M. A., and Maller, J. B. *Studies in the nature of character*. Vol. 2: *Studies in service and self-control*. New York: Macmillan, 1929.

Hartup, W. W. Dependence and independence. In H. W. Stevenson (ed.), *Child psychology: The Sixty-Second Yearbook of the National Society for the Study of Education* (Part 1). Chicago: University of Chicago Press, 1963.

Hartup, W. W. Peer interaction and social organization. In P. H. Mussen (ed.), *Carmichael's manual of child psychology* (3d. ed.), Vol. 2. New York: Wiley, 1970.

Hartup, W. W. Aggression in childhood developmental perspectives. *American Psychologist*, 1974, **29**, 336–341.

Hartup, W. W., and Yonas, A. Developmental psychology. *Annual Review of Psychology*, 1971, **22**, 337–392.

Haskett, G. J. Modification of peer preferences of first-grade children. *Developmental Psychology*, 1971, **4**, 429–433.

Haskins, C. P. Researches in the biology and social behavior of primitive ants. In L. R. Aronson, E. Tobach, D. S. Lehrman, and J. S. Rosenblatt (eds.), *Development and evolution of behavior: Essays in memory of T. C. Schneirla*. San Francisco: Freeman, 1970.

Haskins, R. Effect of kitten vocalizations on maternal behavior. *Journal of Comparative and Physiological Psychology*, 1977, **91**, 830–838.

Hay, D. F. Following their companions as a form of exploration for human infants. Unpublished doctoral dissertation, University of North Carolina, Chapel Hill, 1975.

Hebb, D. O. Heredity and environment in mammalian behaviour. *British Journal of Animal Behaviour*, 1953, **1**, 43–47.

Hebb, D. O. Comment on altruism: The comparative evidence. *Psychological Bulletin*, 1971, **76**, 409–410.

Heiman, J. *Responses to erotica: An exploration of physiological and psychological correlates of human sexual responses*. Unpublished doctoral dissertation, State University of New York at Stonybrook, 1975.

Hein, A., and Diamond, R. M. Locomotory space as a prerequisite for acquiring visually guided reaching in kittens. *Journal of Comparative and Physiological Psychology*, 1972, **81**, 394–398.

Heinicke, C., and Westheimer, I. *Brief separations*. New York: International Universities Press, 1966.

Held, R., and Hein, A. Movement-produced stimulation in the development of visually guided behavior. *Journal of Comparative and Physiological Psychology*, 1963, **56**, 872–876.

Helfer, R. E., and Kempe, C. H. (eds.). *The battered child*. Chicago: University of Chicago Press, 1968.

Hellman, I. Sudden separation and its effect followed over twenty years: Hampstead Nursery follow-up studies. *Psychoanalytic Study of the Child*, 1962, **17**, 159–174.

Hersher, L., Moore, A. U., and Richmond, J. B. Effect of postpartum separation of mother and kid on maternal care in the domestic goat. *Science*, 1958, **128**, 1342–1343.

Hersher, L., Richmond, J. B., and Moore, A. U. Modifiability of the critical period for the development of maternal behavior in sheep and goats. *Behaviour*, 1963, **20**, 311–320.

Herzog, E., and Sudia, C. E. Children in fatherless families. In B. M. Caldwell and H. N. Ricciuti (eds.), *Review of child development research* (Vol. 3). Chicago: University of Chicago Press, 1973.

Hetherington, E. M., Cox, M., and Cox, R. Beyond father absence: Conceptualization of effects of divorce. Presented at the meeting of the Society for Research in Child Development, Denver, April, 1975.

Hicks, D. J. Imitation and retention of film-mediated aggressive peer and adult models. *Journal of Personality and Social Psychology*, 1965, **2**, 97–100.

Hilgard, E. R., and Bower, G. H. *Theories of Learning* (4th ed.). New York: Appleton-Century-Crofts, 1974.

Hinde, R. A. Influence of social companions and of temporary separation on mother-infant relations in rhesus monkeys. In B. M. Foss (ed.), *Determinants of infant behavior IV*. London: Methuen (New York: Wiley), 1969.

Hinde, R. A. *Animal behavior: A synthesis of ethology and comparative psychology* (2d ed.). New York: McGraw-Hill, 1970.

Hinde, R. A., and Spencer-Booth, Y. The behavior of social living rhesus monkeys in their first two and a half years. *Animal Behaviour*, 1967, **15**, 169–196.

Hinde, R. A., and Spencer-Booth, Y. Effects of brief separation from mother on rhesus monkeys. *Science,* 1971, **173,** 111–118.

Hinde, R. A., and Stevenson-Hinde, J. (eds.). *Constraints on learning: Limitations and predispositions.* New York: Academic Press, 1973.

Hinde, R. A., and White, L. E. Dynamics of a relationship: Rhesus mother-infant ventro-ventral contact. *Journal of Comparative and Physiological Psychology,* 1974, **86,** 8–23.

Hoffman, L. W. Effects of maternal employment on the child: A review of the research. *Developmental Psychology,* 1974, **10,** 204–228.

Hoffman, M. L. Developmental synthesis of affect and cognition and its implications for altruistic motivation. *Developmental Psychology,* 1975, **11,** 607–622.

Hoffman, M. L. Personality and social development. *Annual Review of Psychology,* 1977(a), **28,** 295–321.

Hoffman, M. L. Sex differences in empathy and related behaviors. *Psychological Bulletin,* 1977(b), **84,** 712–722.

Hogan, R. Theoretical egocentrism and the problem of compliance. *American Psychologist,* 1975, **30,** 533–540.

Hogbin, H. I. Marriage in Wogeo, New Guinea. *Oceania,* 1945, **15,** 324–352.

Hokanson, J. E. Psychophysiological evaluation of the catharsis hypothesis. In E. I. Megargee and J. E. Hokanson (eds.), *The dynamics of aggression: Individual, group, and international analyses.* New York: Harper and Row, 1970.

Hollenberg, E., and Sperry, M. Some antecedents of aggression and effects of frustration in doll play. *Personality,* 1951, **1,** 32–43.

Holmberg, M. C. Social interchanges in the second and third year. Symposium paper read at the Meeting of the Southeastern Conference on Human Development, Nashville, Tenn., 1976.

Holmberg, M. C. The development of social interchange patterns from 12 to 42 months: Cross-sectional and short-term longitudinal analyses. Unpublished doctoral dissertation, University of North Carolina at Chapel Hill, 1977.

Homans, G. C. *The human group.* New York: Harcourt, Brace, 1950.

Hore, B. D., Nicolle, F. V., and Calnan, J. S. Male transsexualism: Two cases in a single family. *Archives of Sexual Behavior,* 1973, **2,** 317–321.

Horney, K. *The neurotic personality of our time.* New York: Norton, 1937.

Hoving, K. Laboratory studies of aggression in children. Bowling Green University, 1975.

Hull, C. L. *Principles of behavior: An introduction to behavior theory.* New York: Appleton-Century-Crofts, 1943.

Hull, C. L. *Essentials of behavior.* New Haven: Yale University Press, 1951.

Hunt, J. McV. *Intelligence and experience.* New York: Ronald, 1961.

Hunt, J. McV. Foreword. In Yarrow, L. J., Rubenstein, J. L., and Pedersen, F. A. (with Jankowski, J. J., Durfee, J. J., and Fivel, M. W.) *Infant and environment: Early cognitive and motivational development.* Washington, D.C.: Hemisphere Publishing, 1975.

Huston, Ted L. (ed.). *Foundations of interpersonal attraction.* New York: Academic Press, 1974.

Hutt, C. *Males and females.* Baltimore: Penguin, 1972.

Hutt, S. J., and Hutt, C. *Direct observation and measurement of behavior.* Springfield, Ill.: Charles C. Thomas, 1970.

Hyde, J. S., and Ebert, P. D. Correlated response in selection for aggressiveness in female mice: I. Male aggressiveness. *Behavior Genetics,* 1976, **4,** 421–427.

Immelmann, K. Sexual and other long-term aspects of imprinting in birds and other species. In D. S. Lehrman, R. A. Hinde, and E. Shaw (eds.), *Advances in the study of behavior* (Vol. 4). New York: Academic Press, 1972.

Immelmann, K. Ecological significance of imprinting and early learning. *Annual Review of Ecology and Systematics,* 1975, **6,** 15–37.

Irwin, F. W. *Intentional behavior and motivation: A cognitive theory.* Philadelphia: Lippincott, 1971.

Jacklin, C. N., Maccoby, E. E., and Dick, A. E. Barrier behavior and toy preference: Sex differences (and their absence) in the one-year-old child. *Child Development,* 1973, **44,** 196–200.

Jacobs, B. S., and Moss, H. A. Birth order and sex of sibling as determinants of mother-infant interaction. *Child Development,* 1976, **47,** 315–322.

Jakibchuk, Z., and Smeriglio, V. L. The influence of symbolic modeling on the social behavior of preschool children with low levels of social responsiveness. *Child Development,* 1976, **47,** 838–841.

James, W. *The principles of psychology* (Vol. 1). New York: Macmillan, 1890.

James, W. T. Social organization among dogs of different temperament, terriers and beagles, reared together. *Journal of Comparative and Physiological Psychology,* 1951, **44,** 71–77.

Jarvik, L., Klodin, V., and Matsuyama, S. Human aggression and the extra Y chromosome: Fact or fantasy? *American Psychologist,* 1973, **28,** 674–682.

Jaynes, J. *The origin of consciousness in the breakdown of the bicameral mind.* Boston: Houghton Mifflin, 1976.

Jenkins, M. The effect of segregation on the sex behavior of the white rat as measured by the obstruction method. *Genetic Psychological Monographs*, 1928, **3**, 457–571.

Jennings, S. A. Effects of sex-typing in children's stories on preference and recall. *Child Development*, 1975, **46**, 220–223.

Jennings, W. *The Confucian analects: A translation.* New York: G. Routledge & Sons, 1895.

Jensen, A. R. How much can we boost IQ and scholastic achievement? *Harvard Educational Review*, 1969, **39**, 1–123.

Jensen, D. D. Polythetic operationism and the phylogeny of learning. In W. C. Corning and S. C. Ratner (eds.), *Chemistry of learning: Invertebrate research.* New York: Plenum Press, 1967.

Jensen, G. D., Bobbitt, R. A., and Gordon, B. N. The development of mutual independence in mother and infant pigtail monkeys, *Macaca nemestrina.* In S. A. Altmann (ed.), *Social communication among primates.* Chicago: University of Chicago Press, 1967.

Jensen, G. D., and Tolman, C. W. Mother-infant relationship in the monkey, *Macaca nemestrina:* The effect of brief separation and mother-infant specificity. *Journal of Comparative and Physiological Psychology*, 1962, **55**, 131–136.

Jersild, A. T., and Markey, F. V. Conflicts between preschool children. *Child Development Monographs*, 1935, No. 21.

Johnson, D., and Phoenix, C. Hormonal control of female sexual attractiveness, proceptivity and receptivity in rhesus monkeys. *Journal of Comparative and Physiological Psychology*, 1976, **90**, 473–483.

Johnson, R. *Aggression in man and animals.* Philadelphia: Saunders, 1972.

Jones, H. C. The environment and mental development. In L. Carmichael (ed.), *Manual of child psychology* (2d ed.). New York: Wiley, 1954.

Jones, M. C. The later careers of boys who were early- or late-maturing. *Child Development*, 1957, **28**, 113–128.

Jones, S. J., and Moss, H. A. Age, state, and maternal behavior associated with infant vocalizations. *Child Development*, 1971, **42**, 1039–1051.

Kaada, B. Brain mechanisms related to aggressive behavior. In D. C. Clemente and D. B. Lindsley (eds.), *Aggression and defense.* Berkeley: University of California Press, 1967.

Kagan, J. The determinants of attention in the infant. *American Scientist*, 1970, **3**, 298–305.

Kagan, J. *Change and continuity in infancy.* New York: Wiley, 1971.

Kagan, J. Emergent themes in human development. *American Scientist*, 1976, **64**, 186–196.

Kagan, J., and Moss, H. A. *Birth to maturity: A study in psychological development.* New York: Wiley, 1962.

Kagan, S. Field dependence and conformity of rural Mexican and urban Anglo-American children. *Child Development*, 1974, **45**, 765–771.

Kagan, S., and Madsen, M. C. Cooperation and competition of Mexican, Mexican-American, and Anglo-American children of two ages under four instructional sets. *Developmental Psychology*, 1971, **5**, 32–39.

Kalverboer, A. F. *A neurobehavioural study in pre-school children.* Philadelphia: Lippincott, 1975.

Kaspar, J. C., and Lowenstein, R. The effect of social interaction on activity levels in six- to eight-year-old boys. *Child Development*, 1971, **42**, 1294–1298.

Kaufmann, J. H. Field observations of the social behavior of the eastern grey kangaroo, *Macropus giganteus.* *Animal Behaviour*, 1975, **23**, 214–221.

Kawai, M. Newly acquired precultural behavior of the natural troops of Japanese monkeys on Koshima Islet. *Primates*, 1965, **6**, 1–30.

Kay, H. Channel capacity and skilled performance. In F. A. Geldard (ed.), *Defense Psychology.* New York: Macmillan, 1962.

Kay, H. The development of motor skills from birth to adolescence. In E. A. Bildeau (ed.), *Principles of skill acquisition.* New York: Academic Press, 1969.

Keller, M. F., and Carlson, P. M. The use of symbolic modeling to promote social skills in preschool children with low levels of social responsiveness. *Child Development*, 1974, **45**, 912–919.

Kessen, W. Research design in the study of developmental problems. In P. H. Mussen (ed.), *Handbook of research methods in child development.* New York: Wiley, 1960.

Kessen, W. (ed.), *Childhood in China.* New Haven: Yale University Press, 1975.

King, A. P., and West, M. J. Species identification in the North American cowbird: Appropriate responses to abnormal song. *Science*, 1977, **195**, 1002–1004.

King, J. A. Closed social groups among domestic dogs. *Proceedings, American Philosophical Society*, 1954, **98**, 327–336.

King, J. A. Social behavior, social organization, and population dynamics in a black-tailed prairie dog town in the black hills of South Dakota. *Contributions from the Laboratory of Vertebrate Biology*, No. 67. Ann Arbor, 1955.

King, J. A. Relationship between early social experience and adult aggressive behavior in inbred mice. *Journal of Genetic Psychology*, 1957, **90**, 151–166.

King, J. A. The social behavior of prairie dogs. *Scientific American*, 1959, **201** (No. 4), 128–140.

King, M., and Wilson, A. C. Evolution at two levels in humans and chimpanzees. *Science*, 1975, **188**, 107–116.

Kinsey, A. C., Pomeroy, W. B., and Martin, C. E. *Sexual behavior in the human male*. Philadelphia: Saunders, 1948.

Kinsey, A. C., Pomeroy, W. B., Martin, C. E., and Gebhard, P. H. *Sexual behavior in the human female*. Philadelphia: Saunders, 1953.

Kinsey, K. P. Social behavior in confined populations of the Allegheny woodrat, *Neotoma floridana magister*. *Animal Behaviour*, 1976, **24**, 181–187.

Klaus, M. H., and Kennell, J. H. *Maternal-infant bonding: The impact of early separation or loss on family development*. St. Louis: Mosby, 1976.

Kleck, R. E., Richardson, S. A., and Ronald, L. Physical appearance cues and interpersonal attraction in children. *Child Development*, 1974, **45**, 305–310.

Klinghammer, E. Factors influencing choice of mate in altricial birds. In H. W. Stevenson, E. H. Hess, and H. L. Rheingold (eds.), *Early behavior: Comparative and developmental approaches*. New York: Wiley, 1967.

Klopfer, P. H. Evolution, behavior, and language. In M. E. Hahn and E. C. Simmel (eds.), *Communicative behavior and evolution*. New York: Academic Press, 1976.

Klopfer, P. H., Adams, D. K., and Klopfer, M. S. Maternal imprinting in goats. *Proceedings of the National Academy of Science*, 1964, **52**, 911–914.

Klopfer, P. H., and Hailman, J. P. *An introduction to animal behavior: Ethology's first century*. Englewood Cliffs, N.J.: Prentice-Hall, 1967.

Klopfer, P. H., and Klopfer, M. S. Maternal "imprinting" in goats: Fostering of alien young. *Zeitschrift für Tierpsychologie*, 1968, **25**, 862–866.

Knutson, J. *The control of aggression*. Chicago: Aldine, 1973.

Kohlberg, L. A cognitive-developmental analysis of children's sex-role concepts and attitudes. In E. E. Maccoby (ed.), *The development of sex differences*. Stanford: Stanford University Press, 1966.

Kohlberg, L. Stage and sequence: The cognitive-developmental approach to socialization. In D. A. Goslin (ed.), *Handbook of socialization theory and research*. Chicago: Rand McNally, 1969.

Kohn, M. The child as a determinant of his peers' approach to him. *Journal of Genetic Psychology*, 1966, **109**, 91–100.

Kopfstein, D. The effects of accelerating and decelerating consequences on the social behavior of trainable retarded children. *Child Development*, 1972, **43**, 800–809.

Korner, A. F., and Thoman, E. B. The relative efficacy of contact and vestibular-proprioceptive stimulation in soothing neonates. *Child Development*, 1972, **43**, 443–453.

Kovach, J. K., Paden, P., and Wilson, G. Stimulus variables in the elicitation and short-range reversibility of early approach and following responses. *Journal of Comparative and Physiological Psychology*, 1968, **66**, 175–178.

Kow, L. M., Malsbury, C., and Pfaff, D. Lordosis in the male golden hamster elicited by manual stimulation: Characteristics and hormonal sensitivity. *Journal of Comparative and Physiological Psychology*, 1976, **90**, 26–40.

Kraemer, H. C., Korner, A. F., and Thoman, E. B. Methodological considerations in evaluating the influence of drugs used during labor and delivery on the behavior of the newborn. *Developmental Psychology*, 1972, **6**, 128–134.

Krebs, D. Infrahuman altruism. *Psychological Bulletin*, 1971, **76**, 411–414.

Kuhn, T. S. *The structure of scientific revolutions* (2d ed.). Chicago: University of Chicago Press, 1970.

Kummer, H. *Social organization of hamadryas baboons: A field study*. Chicago: University of Chicago Press, 1968.

Kummer, H. *Primate societies*. Chicago: Aldine-Atherton, 1971.

Kummer, H., and Kurt, F. Social units of a free-living population of Hamadryas baboons. *Folia Primat.*, 1963, **1**, 4–19.

Kuo, Z. Y. The genesis of the cat's responses to the rat. *Journal of Comparative Psychology*, 1930, **11**, 1–35.

Kuo, Z. Y. Ontogeny of embryonic behavior in aves: I. The chronology and general nature of the behavior in the chick embryo. *Journal of Experimental Zoology*, 1932, **61**, 395–430.

Kuo, Z. Y. Studies on the basic factors in animal fighting: III. Hormonal factors affecting fighting in quails. *Journal of Genetic Psychology*, 1960, **96**, 217–223.

Kuo, Z. Y. *The dynamics of behavior development: An epigenetic view.* New York: Random House, 1967.

Kurtines, W., and Greif, E. B. The development of moral thought: Review and evaluation of Kohlberg's approach. *Psychological Bulletin,* 1974, **81,** 453–470.

Kuttner, R. An hypothesis on the evolution of intelligence. *Psychological Reports,* 1960, **6,** 283–289.

Lagerspetz, K. M. J., and Hautojärvi, S. The effect of prior aggressive or sexual arousal on subsequent aggressive or sexual reactions in male mice. *Scandinavian Journal of Psychology,* 1967, **8,** 1–6.

Lagerspetz, K. M. J., and Lagerspetz, K. Y. H. Changes in the aggressiveness of mice resulting from selective breeding, learning and social isolation. *Scandinavian Journal of Psychology,* 1971, **12,** 241–248.

Lagerspetz, K. Y. H., Tirri, R., and Lagerspetz, K. M. J. Neurochemical and endocrinological studies of mice selectively bred for aggressiveness. *Scandinavian Journal of Psychology,* 1968, **9,** 157–160.

Lamb, M. E. Father-infant and mother-infant interaction in the first year of life. *Child Development,* 1977, **48,** 167–181.

Langer, J. *Theories of development.* New York: Holt, Rinehart, and Winston, 1969.

Lansky, L. M. The family structure also affects the model: Sex-role attitudes in parents of preschool children. *Merrill-Palmer Quarterly,* 1967, **13,** 139–150.

Latané, B., Cappell, H., and Joy, V. Social deprivation, housing density and gregariousness in rats. *Journal of Comparative and Physiological Psychology,* 1970, **70,** 221–227.

Lawick-Goodall, J. van. Behaviour of free-living chimpanzees of the Gombi Stream area. *Animal Behaviour Monographs,* 1968, **1** (Part 3), 161–311.

Leakey, L. S. B. Development of aggression as a factor in early human and pre-human evolution. In C. D. Clemente and D. B. Lindsley (eds.), *Aggression and defense: Neural mechanisms and social patterns (Brain function,* Vol. 5). Berkeley and Los Angeles: University of California Press, 1967.

Le Boeuf, B. J., and Peterson, R. S. Social status and mating activity in elephant seals. *Science,* 1969, **163,** 91–93.

Lebowitz, P. S. Feminine behavior in boys: Aspects of its outcome. *American Journal of Psychiatry,* 1972, **128,** 1283–1289.

Lee, C. T., and Griffo, W. Progesterone antagonism of androgen-dependent aggression-promoting pheromone in inbred mice *(Mus musculus). Journal of Comparative and Physiological Psychology,* 1974, **87,** 150–155.

Lee, C. T., and Naranjo, N. N. The effects of castration and androgen on social dominance of BALB/cJ male mice. *Physiological Psychology,* 1974, **2,** 93–98.

Lehmann, H. C., and Witty, P. A. Faculty psychology and personality traits. *American Journal of Psychology,* 1934, **46,** 486–500.

Lehrman, D. S. A critique of Konrad Lorenz's theory of instinctive behavior. *Quarterly Review of Biology,* 1953, **28,** 337–363.

Lehrman, D. S. Hormonal regulation of parental behavior in birds and infrahuman animals. In W. C. Young (ed.), *Sex and internal secretions* (3d ed.). Baltimore: Williams and Wilkins, 1961.

Lehrman, D. S. The reproductive behavior of ring doves. *Scientific American,* 1964, **211** (No. 5), 48–54.

Lehrman, D. S. Some semantic and conceptual issues in the nature-nurture problem. In L. R. Aronson, E. Tobach, D. S. Lehrman, and J. S. Rosenblatt (eds.), *Development and evolution of behavior: Essays in memory of T. C. Schneirla.* San Francisco: Freeman, 1970.

Lerner, R. M. "Richness" analyses of body build stereotype development. *Developmental Psychology,* 1972, **7,** 219.

Lerner, R. M., and Korn, S. J. The development of body-build stereotypes in males. *Child Development,* 1972, **43,** 908–920.

Lerner, R. M., and Schroeder, C. Physique identification, preference, and aversion in kindergarten children. *Developmental Psychology,* 1971, **5,** 538.

Levine, L., Diakow, C. A., and Barsel, G. E. Interstrain fighting in male mice. *Animal Behaviour,* 1965, **13,** 52–58.

Levine, S. Sex differences in the brain. *Scientific American,* 1966, **214** (No. 4), 84–90.

Lev-Ran, A. Gender role differentiation in hermaphrodites. *Archives of Sexual Behavior,* 1974(a), **3,** 391–424.

Lev-Ran, A. Sexuality and educational levels of women with late-treated andrenogenital syndrome. *Archives of Sexual Behavior,* 1974(b), **3,** 27–32.

Levy, D. Primary affect hunger. *American Journal of Psychiatry,* 1937, **94,** 643–652.

Lewin, K. *A dynamic theory of personality.* New York: McGraw-Hill, 1935.

Lewis, M., and Ban, P. Stability of attachment behavior: A transformational analysis. Paper presented at the meeting of the Society for Research in Child Development, Minneapolis, April 1971.

Liddell, H. S. Post-Pavlovian development in conditional reflexes. In M. A. B. Brazier (ed.), *The central nervous system and behavior.* New York: Josiah Macey, Jr., Foundation, 1959.

Lindzey, G. Some remarks concerning incest, the incest taboo, and psychoanalytic theory. *American Psychologist*, 1967, **22**, 1051-1059.

Lippman, W. A., Jr. (ed.). *Official rules for competitive swimming*. Indianapolis: Amateur Athletic Union of the United States, 1975.

Lisk, R. D. Sexual behavior: Hormonal control. In L. Martini and W. F. Ganong (eds.), *Neuroendocrinology* (Vol. 2). New York: Academic Press, 1967.

Littenberg, R., Tulkin, S. R., and Kagan, J. Cognitive components of separation anxiety. *Developmental Psychology*, 1971, **4**, 387-388.

Lobitz, W. C., and Johnson, S. M. Parental manipulation of the behavior of normal and deviant children. *Child Development*, 1975, **46**, 719-726.

Loney, J. Background factors, sexual experiences and attitudes towards treatment in two "normal" homosexual samples. *Journal of Consulting and Clinical Psychology*, 1972, **38**, 57-65.

Longstreth, L. E., Longstreth, G. V., Ramirez, C., and Fernandez, G. The ubiquity of big brother. *Child Development*, 1975, **46**, 769-772.

Lorenz, K. Z. Der Kumpan in der Umwelt des Vogels. *Journal of Ornithology*, 1935, **83**, 137-213; 289-413.

Lorenz, K. Z. The companion in the bird's world. *Auk*, 1937, **54**, 245-273.

Lorenz, K. Z. Ganzheit und Teil in der tierischen und menschlichen Gemeinschaft. *Studium Gen.*, 1950, **3**, 455-499. (Quoted from Eibl-Eibesfeldt, 1975).

Lorenz, K. Z. The comparative study of behavior. In K. Lorenz and P. Leyhausen (eds.), *Motivation of human and animal behavior: An ethological view*. New York: Van Nostrand, 1973. (First published in 1939, translated by B. A. Tonkin.)

Lorenz, K. Z. *Evolution and modification of behavior*. Chicago: University of Chicago Press, 1965.

Lorenz, K. Z. *On aggression*. New York: Harcourt, Brace, and World, 1966.

Lorenz, K. Z. Analogy as a source of knowledge. *Science*, 1974, **185**, 229-234.

Lott, D., Scholz, S., and Lehrman, D. S. Exterioceptive stimulation of the reproductive system of the female ring dove *(Streptopelia risoria)* by the mate and by the colony milieu. *Animal Behaviour*, 1967, **15**, 433-437.

Luttge, W. G. The role of gonadal hormones in the sexual behavior of the rhesus monkey and human: A literature survey. *Archives of Sexual Behavior*, 1971, **1**, 61-93.

Lynn, D. B. *The father: His role in child development*. Monterey, Calif.: Brooks Cole, 1974.

Maas, H. The young adult adjustment of twenty wartime residential nursery children. *Child Welfare*, 1963, **42**, 57-72.

Maccoby, E. E. Stability and change in attachment-to-mother during the third year of life. Paper presented at the meeting of the Society for Research in Child Development, Minneapolis, April 1971.

Maccoby, E. E., and Feldman, S. S. Mother-attachment and stranger-reactions in the third year of life. *Monographs of the Society for Research in Child Development*, 1972, **37** (1, Whole No. 146).

Maccoby, E. E., and Jacklin, C. N. Stress, activity, and proximity seeking: Sex differences in the one-year-old child. *Child Development*, 1973, **44**, 34-42.

Maccoby, E. E., and Jacklin, C. N. *The psychology of sex differences*. Stanford: Stanford University Press, 1974.

Maccoby, E. E., and Jacklin, C. N. Personal consistency in the context of mutual influence. Unpublished manuscript, 1976.

Maccoby, E. E., and Masters, J. C. Attachment and dependency. In P. H. Mussen (ed.), *Carmichael's manual of child psychology* (3d ed.), Vol. 2. New York: Wiley, 1970.

MacCombie, D. J. An analysis of the teaching styles of four-year-old boys and girls from two social classes. Unpublished honors thesis, Indiana University, 1973.

MacCombie, D. J. Infant vocalization in a mother-infant interaction setting. Unpublished manuscript. University of North Carolina, 1974.

MacCombie, D. J. The development of synchrony in children's interchanges. Unpublished doctoral dissertation, University of North Carolina at Chapel Hill, 1978.

MacCombie, D. J., and Cairns, R. B. Early experience and social plasticity: Reducing aggression in isolation-reared mice. Paper read at the Annual Meeting of the American Psychological Association, Chicago, September 1975.

MacDonnell, M. F., and Flynn, J. P. Control of sensory fields by stimulation of hypothalamus. *Science*, 1966, **152**, 1406-1408.

Mackintosh, J. H., and Grant, E. C. The effect of olfactory stimuli on the agonistic behaviour of laboratory mice. *Zeitschrift für Tierpsychologie*, 1966, **23**, 584-587.

Macrae, J., and Herbert-Jackson, E. Are behavioral effects of infant day care program specific? *Developmental Psychology*, 1976, **12**, 269-270.

Madow, L. *Anger*. New York: Charles Scribner's Sons, 1972.

Mage, M. Harvard XYY study. *Science*, 1975, **187**, 298-299.

Mainardi, D., Marsan, M., and Pasquali, A. Causation of sexual preferences of the house mouse. *Atti Della Societa Italiana di Scienze e del Museo Civico di Storia Naturale di Milano*, 1965, **104**, 325–338.

Mandler, G. The interruption of behavior. In D. Levine (ed.), *Nebraska Symposium on Motivation* (Vol. 12). Lincoln: University of Nebraska Press, 1964.

Marantz, S. A., and Mansfield, A. F. Maternal employment and the development of sex-role stereotyping in five- to eleven-year-old girls. *Child Development*, 1977, **48**, 668–673.

Mark, V. H., and Ervin, F. R. *Violence and the brain.* New York: Harper and Row, 1970.

Marler, P. Communication in monkeys and apes. In I. DeVore (ed.), *Primate behavior: Field studies of monkeys and apes.* New York: Holt, Rinehart, and Winston, 1965.

Marler, P. On animal aggression: The roles of strangeness and familiarity. *American Psychologist*, 1976, **31**, 239–246.

Marler, P., and Mundinger, P. Vocal learning in birds. In H. Moltz (ed.), *The ontogeny of vertebrate behavior.* New York: Academic Press, 1971.

Marshall, J. T., Jr., and Marshall, E. R. Gibbons and their territorial songs. *Science*, 1976, **193**, 235–237.

Martin, B. Parent-child relations. In F. D. Horowitz (ed.), *Review of child development research* (Vol. 4). Chicago: University of Chicago Press, 1975.

Mason, W. A. The effects of social restriction on the behavior of rhesus monkeys: I. Free social behavior. *Journal of Comparative and Physiological Psychology*, 1960, **53**, 582–589.

Mason, W. A. Determinants of social behavior in young chimpanzees. In A. M. Schrier, H. F. Harlow, and F. Stollnitz (eds.), *Behavior of nonhuman primates* (Vol. 2). New York: Academic Press, 1965.

Mason, W. A. Motivation aspects of social responsiveness in young chimpanzees. In H. W. Stevenson, E. H. Hess, and H. L. Rheingold (eds.), *Early behavior: Comparative and developmental approaches.* New York: Wiley, 1967.

Mason, W. A. Scope and potential of primate research. In J. H. Masserman (ed.), *Science and psychoanalysis.* Vol. 12: *Animal and human.* New York: Grune and Stratton, 1968.

Mason, W. A. Environmental models and mental modes: Representational processes in the great apes and man. *American Psychologist*, 1976, **31**, 284–294.

Mason, W. A. Social ontogeny. In P. Marler and J. G. Vandenbergh (eds.), *Social behavior and communication.* New York: Plenum Press (in press).

Mason, W. A., and Hollis, J. H. Communication between young rhesus monkeys. *Animal Behaviour*, 1962, **10**, 211–221.

Mason, W. A., and Kenney, M. D. Redirection of filial attachments in rhesus monkeys: Dogs as mother surrogates. *Science*, 1974, **183**, 1209–1211.

Masters, J. C., and Wellman, H. M. The study of human infant attachment: A procedural critique. *Psychological Bulletin*, 1974, **81**, 218–237.

Masters, W. H., and Johnson, V. E. *Human sexual response.* Boston: Little, Brown, 1966.

Maudry, M., and Nekula, M. Social relations between children of the same age during the first two years of life. *Journal of Genetic Psychology*, 1939, **54**, 193–215.

Maurer, D., and Salapatek, P. Developmental changes in the scanning of faces by young infants. *Child Development*, 1976, **47**, 523–527.

Maynard Smith, J. The theory of games and the evolution of animal conflict. *Journal of Theoretical Biology*, 1974, **47**, 202–221.

Mayr, E. *Animal species and evolution.* Cambridge, Mass.: Harvard University Press, 1963.

McCall, R. B. Childhood IQ's as predictors of adult educational and occupational status. *Science*, 1977, **197**, 482–483.

McCall, R. B., Appelbaum, M. I., and Hogarty, P. S. Developmental changes in mental performance. *Monographs of the Society for Research in Child Development*, 1973, **38** (Serial No. 150).

McClintock, C., and Nuttin, J. Development of competitive game behavior in children across two cultures. *Journal of Experimental Social Psychology*, 1969, **5**, 203–218.

McCord, W., and McCord, J. *Psychopathy and delinquency.* New York: Grune and Stratton, 1956.

McCord, W., McCord, J., and Zola, I. K. *Origins of crime: A new evaluation of the Cambridge-Somerville youth study.* New York: Columbia University Press, 1959.

McDougall, W. *An introduction to social psychology.* London: Methuen, 1908.

McGraw, M. B. Swimming behavior of the human infant. *Journal of Pediatrics*, 1939, **15**, 485–490.

McGrew, W. C. *An ethological study of children's behavior.* New York: Academic Press, 1972.

Mead, G. H. *Mind, self, and society.* Chicago: University of Chicago Press, 1934.

Mead, M. A. cultural anthropologist's approach to maternal deprivation. In *Deprivation of maternal care.* Public Health Paper No. 14. Geneva: World Health Organization, 1962.

Megargee, E. I. Undercontrolled and overcontrolled personality types in extreme antisocial aggression. *Psychological Monographs*, 1966, **80** (Whole No. 611).

Meier, G. W. Other data on the effects of social isolation during rearing upon adult reproductive behaviour in the rhesus monkey *(Macaca mulatta)*. *Animal Behaviour*, 1965, **13**, 228-231.

Meltzoff, A. N., and Moore, M. K. Imitation of facial and manual gestures by human neonates. *Science*, 1977, **198**, 75-78.

Michael, R. P. Effects of gonadal hormones on displaced and direct aggression in rhesus monkeys of opposite sex. In S. Garattini and E. B. Siggs (eds.), *Aggressive behavior*. Amsterdam: Excerpta Medica, 1969.

Michael, R. P., Keverne, E. B., and Bonsall, R. W. Pheromones: Isolation of a male sex attractant from a female primate. *Science*, 1971, **172**, 964-966.

Michel, G. Role of mate's previous experience in ring-dove hormone-induced incubation. *Journal of Comparative and Physiological Psychology*, 1976, **90**, 468-472.

Michenbaum, D. Unpublished manuscript. University of Waterloo, 1972.

Miczek, K. A., and Grossman, S. P. Effects of spatial lesions on inter- and intraspecies aggression in rats. *Journal of Comparative and Physiological Psychology*, 1972, **79**, 37-45.

Milakovich, J. T. Factors influencing aggressive behavior in mice. Unpublished M. A. thesis, Indiana University, 1970.

Milgram, S. *Obedience to authority: An experimental view*. New York: Harper and Row, 1974.

Miller, N. E. The frustration-aggression hypothesis. *Psychological Review*, 1941, **48**, 337-342.

Miller, N. E., and Dollard, J. *Social learning and imitation*. New Haven: Yale University Press, 1941.

Miller, R. S., and Morris, W. N. The effects of being imitated on children's responses in a marble-dropping task. *Child Development*, 1974, **45**, 1103-1107.

Minton, C., Kagan, J., and Levine, J. A. Maternal control and obedience in the two-year-old. *Child Development*, 1971, **42**, 1873-1894.

Mirsky, A. F. The influence of sex hormones on social behavior in monkeys. *Journal of Comparative and Physiological Psychology*, 1955, **48**, 327-335.

Mischel, W. *Personality and assessment*. New York: Wiley, 1968.

Mischel, W. Continuity and change in personality. *American Psychologist*, 1969, **24**, 1012-1018.

Mischel, W. Toward a cognitive social learning reconceptualization of personality. *Psychological Review*, 1973, **80**, 252-283.

Mischel, W., and Mischel, H. A cognitive social learning approach to morality and self-regulation. In T. Lickona (ed.), *Morality: Theory, research, and social issues*. New York: Holt, Rinehart, and Winston, 1976.

Missakian, E. Reproductive behavior of socially deprived

male rhesus monkeys *(Macaca mulatta)*. *Journal of Comparative and Physiological Psychology*, 1969, **69**, 403-407.

Moerk, E. L. Processes of language teaching and training in the interactions of mother-child dyads. *Child Development*, 1976, **47**, 1064-1078.

Moltz, H. Some effects of previous breeding experience on the maternal behavior of the laboratory rat. In L. R. Aronson, E. Tobach, D. S. Lehrman, and J. S. Rosenblatt (eds.), *Development and evolution of behavior: Essays in memory of T. C. Schneirla*. San Francisco: Freeman, 1970.

Moltz, H., Geller, D., and Levin, R. Maternal behavior in the totally mammectomized rat. *Journal of Comparative and Physiological Psychology*, 1967, **64**, 225-229.

Monahan, L. C. Mother-infant and stranger-infant interaction: An ethological analysis. Unpublished doctoral dissertation, Indiana University, 1975.

Money, J. Sexual dimorphism and homosexual gender identity. *Psychological Bulletin*, 1970, **74**, 425-440.

Money, J., and Ehrhardt, A. A. *Man and woman, boy and girl*. Baltimore: The Johns Hopkins University Press, 1972.

Money, J., and Wolff, G. Sex reassignment: Male to female to male. *Archives of Sexual Behavior*, 1973, **2**, 245-250.

Morgan, C. L. *Habit and instinct*. London: Edward Arnold Publishers, Ltd., 1896.

Morris, D. *The naked ape: A zoologist's study of the human animal*. New York: McGraw-Hill, 1967.

Moss, H. A. Coping behavior, the need for stimulation, and normal development. *Merrill-Palmer Quarterly*, 1965, **11**, 171-179.

Moss, H. A. Sex, age, and state as determinants of mother-infant interaction. *Merrill-Palmer Quarterly*, 1967, **13**, 19-37.

Moyles, E. W., and Wolins, M. Group care and intellectual development. *Developmental Psychology*, 1971, **4**, 370-380.

Mueller, E. The maintenance of verbal exchanges between young children. *Child Development*, 1972, **43**, 930-938.

Mueller, E. Bleier, M., Krakow, J., Hegedus, K., and Cournoyer, P. The development of peer verbal interaction among two-year-old boys. *Child Development*, 1977, **48**, 284-287.

Mueller, E., and Brenner, J. The origins of social skills and interactions among playgroup toddlers. *Child Development*, 1977, **48**, 854-861.

Mueller, E., and Lucas, T. A developmental analysis of peer interaction among toddlers. In M. Lewis and

L. A. Rosenblum (eds.), *Friendship and peer relations*. New York: Wiley, 1975.

Mugford, R. A., and Nowell, N. W. Pheromones and their effect on aggression in mice. *Nature*, 1970, **226**, 967–968.

Munroe, R. L. *Schools of psychoanalytic thought: An exposition, critique, and attempt at integration*. New York: Dryden Press, 1955.

Murstein, B. (ed.), *Theories of attraction and love*. New York: Springer, 1971.

Mussen, P. H., and Jones, M. C. Self-conceptions, motivations and interpersonal attitudes of late and early maturing boys. *Child Development*, 1957, **28**, 243–256.

Muste, M., and Sharpe, D. Some influential factors in the determination of aggressive behavior in pre-school children. *Child Development*, 1947, **18**, 11–28.

Myer, J. S. Associative and temporal determinants of facilitation and inhibition of attack by pain. *Journal of Comparative and Physiological Psychology*, 1968, **66**, 17–21.

Mykytowycz, R. Further observations on the territorial function and histology of the submandibular cutaneous (chin) glands in the rabbit, *Oryctolagus cuniculus* (L.). *Animal Behaviour*, 1965, **13**, 400–412.

Neilon, P. Shirley's babies after fifteen years. *Journal of Genetic Psychology*, 1948, **73**, 175–186.

Neisser, U. *Cognitive psychology*. New York: Appleton-Century-Crofts, 1967.

Nelson, K. Structure and strategy in learning to talk. *Monographs of the Society for Research in Child Development*, 1973 (Serial No. 149).

Nesselroade, J. R., and Baltes, P. B. Adolescent personality development and historical change: 1970–1972. *Monographs of the Society for Research in Child Development*, 1974, **39** (Serial No. 154).

Neumann, F., and Steinbeck, H. Influence of sexual hormones on the differentiation of neural centers. *Archives of Sexual Behavior*, 1972, **2**, 147–162.

Newcomb, T. M. *Consistency of certain extrovert-introvert behavior patterns in 51 problem boys*. New York: Columbia University, Teachers College, Bureau of Publications, 1929.

Nichols, P. L., and Broman, S. H. Familial resemblance in infant mental development. *Developmental Psychology*, 1974, **10**, 442–446.

Nottebohm, F., and Arnold, A. P. Sexual dimorphism in vocal control areas of the songbird brain. *Science*, 1976, **194**, 211–213.

Novaco, R. W. *Anger control: The development and evaluation of an experimental treatment*. Lexington Mass.: Lexington Books, 1975.

Novak, M. A., and Harlow, H. F. Social recovery of monkeys isolated for the first year of life: I. Rehabilitation and therapy. *Developmental Psychology*, 1975, **11**, 453–465.

Nowlis, V. Companionship preference and dominance in the social interaction of young chimpanzees. *Comparative Psychological Monographs*, 1941, **17** (1, Whole No. 85).

Oden, S., and Asher, S. R. Coaching children in social skills for friendship making. *Child Development*, 1977, **48**, 495–506.

O'Kelly, L. W., and Steckle, L. C. A note on long-enduring emotional responses in the rat. *Journal of Psychology*, 1939, **8**, 125–131.

Oppenheim, R. W. Prehatching and hatching behavior: Comparative and physiological consideration. In G. Gottlieb (ed.), *Behavioral embryology*. New York: Academic Press, 1973.

Ornstein, P. A., (ed.) *Memory development in children*. Hillsdale, N.J.: Erlbaum Associates, 1978.

Ornstein, P. A., Naus, M. J., and Liberty, C. Rehearsal and organizational processes in children's memory. *Child Development*, 1975, **46**, 818–830.

Osofsky, J. D., and Danzger, B. Relationships between neonatal characteristics and mother-infant interaction. *Developmental Psychology*, 1974, **10**, 124–130.

Ounsted, C., and Taylor, D. C. *Gender differences—their ontogeny and significance*. London: Churchill, 1972.

Owens, D. J., and Straus, M. A. The social structure of violence in childhood and approval of violence by adults. *Aggressive Behavior*, 1975, **1**, 193–211.

Paris, S. G. Integration and inference in children's comprehension and memory. In F. Restle, R. Shiffrin, J. Castellan, H. Lindman, and D. Pisoni (eds.), *Cognitive theory* (Vol. 1). Hillsdale, N.J.: Erlbaum Associates, 1975.

Paris, S. G., and Cairns, R. B. An experimental and ethological analysis of social reinforcement with retarded children. *Child Development*, 1972, **43**, 717–729.

Parke, R. D. Parent-infant interaction progress, paradigms and problems. In G. P. Sackett (ed.), *Observing behavior*. (Vol. 1): *Theory and applications in mental retardation*. Baltimore: University Park Press, 1978.

Parke, R. D. Punishment in children: Effects, side effects, and alternative strategies. In Hom, H. L., Jr., and Robinson, P. A., (eds.), *Psychological processes in early education.* New York: Academic Press, 1977.

Parke, R. D., and Collmer, D. A. Child abuse: An interdisciplinary analysis. In E. M. Hetherington (ed.), *Review of child development research* (Vol. 5). Chicago: University of Chicago Press, 1975.

Parke, R. D., and Deur, J. L. Schedule of punishment and inhibition of aggression in children. *Developmental Psychology*, 1972, **7**, 266-269.

Parkes, A. S., and Bruce, H. M. Olfactory stimuli in mammalian reproduction. *Science*, 1961, **134**, 1049-1054.

Parry, M. H. Infants' responses to novelty in familiar and unfamiliar settings. *Child Development*, 1972, **43**, 233-237.

Parten, M. B. Social participation among preschool children. *Journal of Abnormal and Social Psychology*, 1932, **27**, 243-269.

Parton, D. A., and Ross, A. O. Social reinforcement of children's motor behavior: A review. *Psychological Bulletin*, 1965, **64**, 65-73.

Passman, R. H., and Weisberg, P. Mothers and blankets as agents for promoting play and exploration by young children in a novel environment: The effects of social and nonsocial attachment objects. *Developmental Psychology*, 1975, **11**, 170-177.

Patterson, D. S. Social ecology and social behavior: The development of differential usage of play materials in preschool children. Paper read at the Fourth Annual Southeastern Conference on Human Development, Nashville, Tenn., 1976.

Patterson, G. R. A basis for identifying stimuli which control behaviors in natural settings. *Child Development*, 1974, **45**, 900-911.

Patterson, G. R. The aggressive child: Victim and architect of a coercive system. In L. A. Hamerlynck, L. C. Handy, and E. J. Mash (eds.), *Behavior modification and families:* I. *Theory and research.* New York: Brunner/Mazell, 1976.

Patterson, G. R. A performance theory for coercive family interaction. In R. B. Cairns (ed.), *The analysis of social interactions: Methods, issues, and illustrations.* Hillsdale, N.J.: Erlbaum Associates, 1979.

Patterson, G. R., and Cobb, J. A. A dyadic analysis of "aggressive" behaviors. In J. P. Hill (ed.), *Minnesota Symposium on Child Psychology* (Vol. 5). Minneapolis: University of Minnesota Press, 1971.

Patterson, G. R., Littman, R. A., and Bricker, W. Assert-ive behavior in children: A step toward a theory of aggression. *Monographs of the Society for Research in Child Development*, 1967, 32 (Whole No. 113).

Paul, L. Predatory attack by rats: Its relationship to feeding and type of prey. *Journal of Comparative and Physiological Psychology*, 1972, **78**, 69-76.

Paul, L., Miley, W. M., and Mazzagatti, N. Social facilitation and inhibition of hunger-induced killing by rats. *Journal of Comparative and Physiological Psychology*, 1973, **84**, 162-168.

Pavlik, L. G. Features of conditioned reflex activity in sheep. *Fiziol. Zh. SSSR* (Trans.), 1958, **44**, 45-49.

Pawlowski, A. A., and Scott, J. P. Hereditary differences in the development of dominance in litters of puppies. *Journal of Comparative and Physiological Psychology*, 1956, **49**, 353-358.

Payne, R., Anderson, D. C., and Murcurio, J. Preshock-produced alterations in pain-elicited fighting. *Journal of Comparative and Physiological Psychology*, 1970, **71**, 258-266.

Pedersen, F. A., and Bell, R. Q. Sex differences in preschool children without histories of complications of pregnancy and delivery. *Developmental Psychology*, 1970, **3**, 10-15.

Pedersen, F. A., and Robson, K. S. Father participation in infancy. *American Journal of Orthopsychiatry*, 1969, **39**, 466-472.

Pederson, D. R., and Ter Vrugt, D. The influence of amplitude and frequency of vestibular stimulation on the activity of two-month-old infants. *Child Development*, 1973, **44**, 122-128.

Perry, D. G., and Bussey, K. Self-reinforcement in high- and low-aggressive boys following acts of aggression. *Child Development*, 1977, **48**, 653-657.

Peterson, R. Aggression as a function of expected retaliation and aggression level of target and aggressor. *Developmental Psychology*, 1971, **5**, 161-166.

Phillips, J. L. *The origins of intellect: Piaget's theory* (2d ed.). San Francisco: Freeman, 1975.

Phoenix, C. H., Goy, R. W., Gerall, A. A., and Young, W. C. Organizing action of prenatally administered testosterone propionate on the tissues mediating mating behavior in the female guinea pig. *Endocrinology*, 1959, **65**, 369-382.

Piaget, J. *The moral judgment of the child.* London: Routledge and Kegan Paul, 1932.

Piaget, J. *The origins of intelligence in children* (M. Cook, Trans.). New York: International Universities Press, 1952. (Originally published, 1936).

Piel, G. The comparative psychology of T. C. Schneirla.

In L. R. Aronson, E. Tobach, D. S. Lehrman, and J. S. Rosenblatt (eds.), *Development and evolution of behavior: Essays in memory of T. C. Schneirla.* San Francisco: Freeman, 1970.

Pinneau, S. R. The infantile disorders of hospitalism and anaclitic depression. *Psychological Bulletin,* 1955, **52,** 429–452.

Poole, T. B., and Morgan, H. D. R. Aggressive behavior of male mice *(Mus musculus)* towards familiar and unfamiliar opponents. *Animal Behaviour,* 1975, **23,** 470–479.

Postman, L. The history and present status of the law of effect. *Psychological Bulletin,* 1947, **44,** 489–563.

Powell, D. A., and Creer, T. L. Interaction of developmental and environmental variables in shock-elicited aggression. *Journal of Comparative and Physiological Psychology,* 1969, **69,** 219–225.

Prechtl, H. F. R. Problems of behavioral studies in the newborn infant. *Advances in the Study of Behavior,* 1965, **1,** 75–98.

Premack, D. Toward empirical behavior laws: I. Positive reinforcement. *Psychological Review,* 1959, **66,** 219–233.

Preston, D. G., Baker, R. P., and Seay, B. Mother-infant separation in the patas monkey. *Developmental Psychology,* 1970, **3,** 298–306.

Pringle, M. L. K., and Bossio, V. A study of deprived children: Intellectual, emotional and social development of deprived children. *Vita Humania,* 1958, **1,** 66–92.

Quilty, R. F. Modeling as an interchange strategy. Unpublished doctoral dissertation, Indiana University, 1973.

Quilty, R. F. Imitation as a dyadic interchange pattern. *Scandinavian Journal of Psychology,* 1975, **16,** 223–239.

Rabin, A. I. *Growing up in the kibbutz.* New York: Springer, 1965.

Rabin, A. I. Kibbutz adolescents. In J. F. Rosenblith and W. Allinsmith (eds.), *The causes of behavior: Readings in child development and educational psychology* (2d ed.). Boston: Allyn and Bacon, 1966.

Rabinowitz, F. M., Moely, B. E., Finkel, N., and McClinton, S. The effects of toy novelty and social interaction on the exploratory behavior of preschool children. *Child Development,* 1975, **46,** 286–289.

Rachlin, H. *Behavior and learning.* San Francisco: Freeman, 1976.

Raisman, G., and Field, P. M. Sexual dimorphism in the preoptic area of the rat. *Science,* 1971, **173,** 731–733.

Raush, H. L. Interaction sequences. *Journal of Personality and Social Psychology,* 1965, **2,** 487–499.

Rebelsky, F., and Hanks, C. Fathers' verbal interaction with infants in the first three months of life. *Child Development,* 1971, **42,** 63–68.

Redd, W. H., Morris, E. K., and Martin, J. A. Effects of positive and negative adult-child interactions on children's social preference. *Journal of Experimental Child Psychology,* 1975, **19,** 153–164.

Redican, W. K., and Mitchell, G. A longitudinal study of paternal behavior in adult male rhesus monkeys: I. Observations on the first dyad. *Developmental Psychology,* 1973, **8,** 135–136.

Rekers, G. A., Amaro-Plotkin, H. D., and Low, B. P. Sex-typed mannerisms in normal boys and girls as a function of sex and age. *Child Development,* 1977, **48,** 275–278.

Rest, J., Turiel, E. and Kohlberg, L. Level of moral development as a determinant of preference and comprehension of moral judgments made by others. *Journal of Personality,* 1969, **37,** 225–252.

Reuter, J., and Yunik, G. Social interaction in nursery schools. *Developmental Psychology,* 1973, **9,** 319–325.

Rheingold, H. L. The modification of social responsiveness in institutional babies. *Monographs of the Society for Research in Child Development,* 1956, **21** (2, Whole No. 63).

Rheingold, H. L. Maternal behavior in the dog. In H. L. Rheingold (ed.), *Maternal behavior in mammals.* New York: Wiley, 1963.

Rheingold, H. L. The development of social behavior in the human infant. In H. W. Stevenson (ed.), *Concept of development. Monographs of the Society for Research in Child Development,* 1966, **31** (5, Serial No. 107).

Rheingold, H. L. Infancy. *International encyclopedia of the social sciences* (Vol. 7). New York: Crowell-Collier and Macmillan, 1968.

Rheingold, H. L. The social and socializing infant. In D. A. Goslin (ed.), *Handbook of socialization theory and research.* Chicago: Rand McNally, 1969.

Rheingold, H. L., and Bayley, N. The later effects of an experimental modification of mothering. *Child Development,* 1959, **30,** 363–372.

Rheingold, H. L., and Cook, K. V. The contents of boys' and girls' rooms as an index of parents' behavior. *Child Development,* 1975, **46,** 459–463.

Rheingold, H. L., and Eckerman, C. O. The infant separates himself from his mother. *Science*, 1970, **168**, 78–83.

Rheingold, H. L., and Eckerman, C. O. Fear of the stranger: A critical examination. In H. W. Reese (ed.), *Advances in child development and behavior* (Vol. 8). New York: Academic Press, 1973.

Rheingold, H. L., Hay, D. F., and West, M. J. Sharing in the second year of life. *Child Development*, 1976, **47**, 1148–1158.

Ribble, M. A. *The rights of infants.* New York: Columbia University Press, 1943.

Rieder, C. A., and Reynierse, J. H. Effects of maintenance condition on aggression and marking behavior of the Mongolian gerbil *(Meriones unguiculatus)*. *Journal of Comparative and Physiological Psychology*, 1971, **75**, 471–475.

Roberts, W. W., and Bergquist, E. H. Attack elicited by hypothalamic stimulation in cats raised in social isolation. *Journal of Comparative and Physiological Psychology*, 1968, **66**, 590–595.

Robertson, D. R. Social control of sex reversal in a coral-reef fish. *Science*, 1972, **177**, 1007–1009.

Robertson, J., and Robertson, J. Young children in brief separation: A fresh look. *Psychoanalytic Study of the Child*, 1971, **26**, 264–315.

Rogers, C. M., and Davenport, R. K. Effects of restricted rearing on sexual behavior of chimpanzees. *Developmental Psychology*, 1969, **1**, 200–204.

Romanes, G. J. *Mental evolution in animals.* New York: Appleton, 1884.

Rose, S. A., Blank, M., and Spalter, I. Situational specificity of behavior in young children. *Child Development*, 1975, **46**, 464–469.

Rosenblatt, J. S. Effects of experience on behavior in male cats. In F. A. Beach (ed.), *Sex and behavior.* New York: Wiley, 1965.

Rosenblatt, J. S. Learning in newborn kittens. *Scientific American*, 1972, **227** (No. 6), 18–25.

Rosenblatt, J. S. The significance of the resolution of maternal and aggressive responses to pups for the organization of maternal behavior in the rat. In L. Paul (Chairman), *Interactions between affectional bonds and aggressive responses.* Symposium presented at the meeting of the Eastern Psychological Association, New York, April 1975.

Rosenblatt, J. S., and Lehrman, D. S. Maternal behavior of the laboratory rat. In H. L. Rheingold (ed.), *Maternal behavior in mammals.* New York: Wiley, 1963.

Rosenblatt, P. C. Cross-cultural perspective on attraction. In T. C. Huston (ed.), *Foundations of interpersonal attraction.* New York: Academic Press, 1974.

Rosenblum, L. A., and Kaufman, I. C. Variations in infant development and response to maternal loss in monkeys. *American Journal of Orthopsychiatry*, 1968, **38**, 418–426.

Rosenblum, L. A., and Harlow, H. F. Approach-avoidance conflict in the mother-surrogate situation. *Psychological Reports*, 1963, **12**, 83–85.

Rosenthal, D. *Genetic theory and abnormal behavior.* New York: McGraw-Hill, 1970.

Rosenthal, M. K. Attachment and mother-infant interaction: Some research impasses and a suggested change in orientation. *Journal of Child Psychology and Psychiatry and Allied Disciplines*, 1973(a), **14**, 201–207.

Rosenthal, M. K. The study of infant-mother environment interaction: Some comments on trends and methodology. *Journal of Child Psychology and Psychiatry and Allied Disciplines*, 1973(b), **14**, 301–317.

Ross, D. M., and Ross, S. A. *Hyperactivity: Research, theory, and action.* New York: Wiley, 1976.

Ross, G., Kagan, J., Zelazo, P., and Kotelchuck, M. Separation protest in infants in home and laboratory. *Developmental Psychology*, 1975, **11**, 256–257.

Ross, H. S., and Goldman, B. D. Establishing new social relations in infancy. In T. Alloway, P. Pliner, and L. Krames (eds.), *Attachment behavior.* New York: Plenum, 1977(a).

Ross, H. S., and Goldman, B. D. Infants' sociability toward strangers. *Child Development*, 1977(b), **48**, 638–642.

Rosvold, H. E., Mirsky, A. F., and Pribram, K. H. Influence on amygdalectomy on social behavior in monkeys. *Journal of Comparative and Physiological Psychology*, 1954, **47**, 173–178.

Roth, L. L., and Rosenblatt, J. S. Changes in self-licking during pregnancy in the rat. *Journal of Comparative and Physiological Psychology*, 1967, **63**, 397–400.

Rothchild, L. The corpus luteum-pituitary relationship: The association between the cause of luteotrophin secretion and the cause of follicular quiescence during lactation: The basis for a tentative theory of the corpus luteum-pituitary relationship in the rat. *Endocrinology*, 1960, **67**, 9–41.

Rotter, J. B. *Social learning and clinical psychology.* New York: Prentice-Hall, 1954.

Routh, D. K., and Schroder, C. S. Standardized playroom measures as indices of hyperactivity. *Journal of Abnormal Child Psychology*, 1976, **4**, 199–207.

Rubin, K. H., Maioni, T. L., and Hornung, M. Free play behaviors in middle- and lower-class preschoolers: Parten and Piaget revisited. *Child Development*, 1976, **47**, 414–419.

Rumbaugh, D. M., Gill, T. V., Glaserfeld, E. von, Warner, H., and Pisani, P. Conversations with a chimpanzee in a computer-controlled environment. *Biological Psychiatry*, 1975, **10**, 627–641.

Rutter, M., *Maternal deprivation reassessed*. Harmonsworth: Penguin, 1972.

Sackett, G. P. Some persistent effects of different rearing conditions on preadult social behavior of monkeys. *Journal of Comparative and Physiological Psychology*, 1967, **64**, 363–365.

Sackett, G. P. (ed.). *Observing behavior, Vol. 1: Theory and applications in mental retardation*. Baltimore: University Park Press, 1978.

Saltz, R. Effects of part-time "mothering" on IQ and SQ of young institutionalized children. *Child Development*, 1973, **44**, 166–170.

Salzen, E. A., and Meyer, C. C. Imprinting: Reversal of a preference established during the critical period. *Nature*, 1967, **215**, 785–786.

Salzen, E. A., and Meyer, C. C. Reversibility of imprinting. *Journal of Comparative and Physiological Psychology*, 1968, **66**, 269–275.

Sameroff, A. J. Early influences on development: Fact or fancy? *Merrill-Palmer Quarterly*, 1975, **21**, 267–294.

Sameroff, A. J., and Chandler, M. Reproductive risk and the continuum of caretaking casualty. In F. D. Horowitz, M. Hetherington, S. Scarr-Salapater, and G. Siegel (eds.), *Review of child development research* (Vol. 4). Chicago: University of Chicago, 1975.

Santrock, J., Smith, P. C., and Bourbeau, P. E. Effects of social comparison on aggression and regression in groups of young children. *Child Development*, 1976, **47**, 831–837.

Scarr, S. Genetic factors in activity motivation. *Child Development*, 1966, **37**, 663–673.

Scarr, S. Social introversion-extraversion as a heritable response. *Child Development*, 1969, **40**, 823–832.

Schachter, S., and Singer, J. E. Cognitive, social, and physiological determinants of emotional state. *Psychological Review*, 1962, **69**, 379–399.

Schaefer, E. S. Major replicated dimensions of adjustment and achievement: Cross-cultural, cross-sectional, and longitudinal research. Paper read at the annual meeting of the American Educational Research Association, Washington, D.C., April 1975.

Schaffer, H. R. *Mothering*. Cambridge, Mass.: Harvard University Press, 1977.

Schaffer, H. R., and Emerson, P. F. The development of social attachments in infancy. *Monographs of the Society for Research in Child Development*, 1964, **29** (3, Whole No. 94).

Schlottmann, R. S., and Seay, B. Mother-infant separation in the Java monkey *(Macaca irus)*. *Journal of Comparative and Physiological Psychology*, 1972, **79**, 334–340.

Schmidt, G., Sigusch, V., and Schafer, S. Responses to reading erotic stories: Male-female differences. *Archives of Sexual Behavior*, 1973, **2**, 181–199.

Schneirla, T. C. Theoretical consideration of cyclic processes in Doryline ants. *Proceedings of the American Philosophical Society*, 1957, **101**, 106–133.

Schneirla, T. C. Behavioral development and comparative psychology. *Quarterly Review of Biology*, 1966, **41**, 283–302.

Schneirla, T. C. *Army ants: A study in social organization*. San Francisco: Freeman, 1971.

Schneirla, T. C., and Rosenblatt, J. S. Behavioral organization and genesis of the social bond in insects and mammals. *American Journal of Orthopsychiatry*, 1961, **31**, 223–253.

Schneirla, T. C., Rosenblatt, J. S., and Tobach, E. Maternal behavior in the cat. In H. L. Rheingold (ed.), *Maternal behavior in mammals*. New York: Wiley, 1963.

Schoggen, P. Environmental forces in the everyday lives of children. In R. G. Barker (ed.), *The stream of behavior*. New York: Appleton-Century-Crofts, 1963.

Scholz, S. D. The effects of brief separations upon maternal behavior and infant development. Unpublished doctoral dissertation, Indiana University, 1974.

Schuchter, A. *Prescriptive package: Child abuse intervention*. Washington, D.C.: U.S. Government Printing Office, 1976.

Schwartzbaum, J. S., Green, R. H., Beatty, W. W., and Thompson, J. B. Acquisition of avoidance behavior following septal lesions in the rat. *Journal of Comparative and Physiological Psychology*, 1967, **63**, 95–104.

Schwarz, J. C., Strickland, R. G., and Krolick, G. Infant day care: Behavioral effects at preschool age. *Developmental Psychology*, 1974, **10**, 502–506.

Schwarz, J. C., and Wynn, R. The effects of mother's presence and previsits on children's emotional reaction to starting nursery school. *Child Development*, 1971, **42**, 871–881.

Scott, J. P. Social behavior, organization and leadership in a small flock of domestic sheep. *Comparative Psychological Monographs*, 1945, 18 (Serial No. 96).

Scott, J. P. *Aggression*. Chicago: University of Chicago Press, 1958.

Scott, J. P. Critical periods in behavioral development. *Science*, 1962, **138**, 949-958.

Scott, J. P. Agonistic behavior of mice and rats: A review. *American Zoologist*, 1966, **6**, 683-701.

Scott, J. P. Comparative psychology and ethology. *Annual Review of Psychology*, 1967, **18**, 65-86.

Scott, J. P. Social genetics. *Behavior Genetics*, 1977, **7**, 327-346.

Scott, J. P., and Fuller, J. L. *Genetics and the social behavior of the dog*. Chicago: University of Chicago Press, 1965.

Sears, R. R. A theoretical framework for personality and social behavior. *American Psychologist*, 1951, **6**, 476-483.

Sears, R. R. Relation of early socialization experiences to aggression in middle childhood. *Journal of Abnormal and Social Psychology*, 1961, **63**, 466-492.

Sears, R. R. Dependency motivation. In M. R. Jones (ed.), *Nebraska Symposium on Motivation* (Vol. 11). Lincoln: University of Nebraska Press, 1963.

Sears, R. R. Development of gender role. In F. A. Beach (ed.), *Sex and behavior*. New York: Wiley, 1965.

Sears, R. R. Attachment, dependency, and frustration. In J. L. Gewirtz (ed.), *Attachment and dependency*. New York: Wiley, 1972.

Sears, R. R. Your ancients revisited: A history of child development. In E. M. Hetherington (ed.), *Review of child development research* (Vol. 5). Chicago: University of Chicago Press, 1975.

Sears, R. R., Maccoby, E. E., and Levin, H. *Patterns of child rearing*. New York: Harper, 1957.

Sears, R. R., Rau, L., and Alpert, R. *Identification and child rearing*. Stanford: Stanford University Press, 1965.

Sears, R. R., Whiting, J. W. M., Nowlis, V., and Sears, P. S. Some child-rearing antecedents of aggressive and dependency in young children. *Genetic Psychology Monographs*, 1953, **47**, 135-234.

Seay, B., Alexander, B. K., and Harlow, H. Maternal behavior of socially deprived rhesus monkeys. *Journal of Abnormal and Social Psychology*, 1964, **69**, 345-354.

Seay, B., Schlottmann, R. S., and Gandolfo, R. Early social interaction in two monkey species. *Journal of General Psychology*, 1972, **87**, 37-43.

Seitz, A., and Stewart, C. Imitation and expansions: Some developmental aspects of mother-child communi-cations. *Developmental Psychology*, 1975, **11**, 763-768.

Seligman, M. E., and Hager, V. L. (eds.). *Biological Boundaries of Learning*. Englewood Cliffs, N.J.: Prentice Hall, 1972.

Selinger, H. E., and Bermant, G. Hormonal control of aggressive behavior in the Japanese quail (*Coturnix coturnix japonica*). *Behaviour*, 1967, **28**, 255-268.

Senn, M. J. E. Insights on the child development movement in the United States. *Monographs of the Society for Research in Child Development*, 1975, **161** (Whole No. 161).

Shantz, C. U. The development of social cognition. In E. M. Hetherington (ed.), *Review of child development research* (Vol. 5). Chicago: University of Chicago Press, 1975.

Shantz, D. W., and Pentz, T. Situational effects on justifiableness of aggression at three age levels. *Child Development*, 1972, **43**, 274-281.

Shantz, D. W., and Voydanoff, D. A. Situational effects on retaliatory aggression. *Child Development*, 1973, **44**, 149-153.

Shatz, M., and Gelman, R. The development of communication skills: Modifications in the speech of young children as a function of listener. *Monographs of the Society for Research in Child Development*, 1973 (Serial No. 152).

Shaw, C. R., and McKay, H. *Juvenile delinquency and urban areas*. Chicago: University of Chicago Press, 1942.

Shelton, W. C., and Slaby, R. G. Infant social preferences based on distal interaction. Paper read at the Biennial Meeting of the Society for Research in Child Development, Denver, Colorado, April 1975.

Shepher, J. Mate selection among second-generation kibbutz adolescents and adults: Incest avoidance and negative imprinting. *Archives of Sexual Behavior*, 1971, **1**, 293-307.

Sherif, M., and Sherif, C. W. Motivation and intergroup aggression: A persistent problem in levels of analysis. In L. Aronson, E. Tobach, D. Lehrman, and J. Rosenblatt (eds.), *Development ane evolution of behavior*. San Francisco: Freeman, 1970.

Sherman, L. W. An ecological study of glee in small groups of preschool children. *Child Development*, 1975, **46**, 53-61.

Sherman, M. The differentiation of emotional responses in infants. I. Judgments of emotional responses from motion picture views and from actual observation. *Journal of Comparative Psychology*, 1927, **7**, 265-284.

Sherman, M. The differentiation of emotional responses in

infants: II. The ability of observers to judge the emotional characteristics of the crying of infants and the voice of an adult. *Journal of Comparative Psychology*, 1927, **7**, 335-351.

Sherman, S. J. Social interchanges in children: Formation, stability, and contextual constraints. Unpublished doctoral dissertation. University of North Carolina, Chapel Hill, 1975.

Shirley, M. M. *The first two years: A study of twenty-five babies: Vol. 2. Intellectual development.* Minneapolis: University of Minnesota Press, 1933.

Shure, M. B. Psychological ecology of a nursery school. *Child Development*, 1963, **34**, 979-992.

Siegel, A. E. The influence of violence in the mass media upon children's role expectation. *Child Development*, 1958, **29**, 35-56.

Siegel, A. E., and Haas, M. B. The working mother: A review of research. *Child Development*, 1963, **34**, 513-542.

Siegelman, M. Parental background of male homosexuals and heterosexuals. *Archives of Sexual Behavior*, 1974, **3**, 3-18.

Skarin, K., and Moely, B. E. Altruistic behavior: An analysis of age and sex differences. *Child Development*, 1976, **47**, 1159-1165.

Skeels, H. M. Adult status of children with contrasting early life experiences. *Monographs of the Society for Research in Child Development*, 1966, **31** (3, Whole No. 105).

Skinner, B. F. *The behavior of organisms: An experimental analysis.* New York: Appleton-Century-Crofts, 1938.

Skinner, B. F. *Science and human behavior.* New York: Macmillan, 1953.

Skinner, B. F. *Beyond freedom and dignity.* New York: Knopf, 1971.

Slaby, R. G., and Frey, K.S. Development of gender constancy and selective attention to same-sex models. *Child Development*, 1975, **46**, 849-856.

Smith, F. V., Van-Toller, C., and Boyes, T. The "critical period" in the attachment of lambs and ewes. *Animal Behavior*, 1966, **14**, 120-125.

Smith, P. K., and Green, M. Aggressive behavior in English nurseries and play groups: Sex differences and response of adults. *Child Development*, 1975, **46**, 211-214.

Snow, C. E. Mother's speech to children learning language. *Child Development*, 1972, **43**, 549-565.

Solomon, R. L. Punishment. *American Psychologist*, 1964, **12**, 239-253.

Solyom, L., and Miller, S. A differential conditioning procedure as the initial phase of the behavior therapy of homosexuality. *Behavior Research and Therapy*, 1965, **3**, 147-160.

Sostek, A. M., and Anders, T. F. Effects of varying laboratory conditions on behavioral-state organization in two- and eight-week-old infants. *Child Development*, 1975, **46**, 871-878.

Southwick, C. H., Siddiqi, M. F., Farooqui, M. Y., and Pal, B. C. Effects of artificial feeding on aggressive behavior of rhesus monkeys in India. *Animal Behavior*, 1976, **24**, 11-15.

Spalding, D. Instinct: With original observations on young animals. *Macmillans Magazine*, 1873, **27**, 282-293.

Spelke, E., Zelazo, P., Kagan, J., and Kotelchuck, M. Father interaction and separation protest. *Developmental Psychology*, 1973, **9**, 83-90.

Spemann, H. *Embryonic development and induction.* New Haven: Yale University Press, 1938.

Spence, J. T. Do material rewards enhance the performance of lower-class children? *Child Development*, 1971, **42**, 1461-1470.

Spielberger, C. D., and DeNike, L. D. Descriptive behaviorism versus cognitive theory in verbal operant conditioning. *Psychological Review*, 1966, **73**, 306-326.

Spitz, R. A. Hospitalism: An inquiry into the genesis of psychiatric conditions in early childhood. *Psychoanalytic Study of the Child*, 1945, **1**, 53-74.

Spitz, R. A. *The first year of life.* New York: International Universities Press, 1965.

Spitz, R. A., and Wolf, K. M. The smiling response: A contribution to the ontogenesis of social relations. *Genetic Psychology Monographs*, 1946(a), **34**, 57-125.

Spitz, R. A., and Wolf, K. Anaclitic depression. *Psychoanalytic Study of the Child*, 1946(b), **2**, 313-342.

Sroufe, L. A. and Waters, E. The ontogenesis of smiling and laughter: A perspective on the organization of development in infancy. *Psychological Review*, 1976, **83**, 173-189.

Sroufe, L. A., and Wunsch, J. P. The development of laughter in the first year of life. *Child Development*, 1972, **43**, 1326-1344.

Staffieri, J. R. Body build and behavioral expectancies in young females. *Developmental Psychology*, 1972, **6**, 125-127.

Stafford, R. E. Sex differences in spatial visualization as evidence of sex-linked inheritance. *Perceptual and Motor Skills*, 1961, **13**, 428.

Stayton, D. J., and Ainsworth, M. D. S. Development of separation behavior in the first year of life: Protest, following, and greeting. *Developmental Psychology*, 1973, **9**, 213-225.

Stein, A. H. The effects of sex-role standards for achievement and sex-role preference on three determinants of achievement motivation. *Developmental Psychology*, 1971, **4**, 219-231.

Stein, A. H., and Friedrich, L. K. Impact of television on children and youth. In E. M. Hetherington (ed.), *Review of child development research* (Vol. 5). Chicago: University of Chicago Press, 1975.

Stein. A., Pohly, S., and Mueller, E. The influence of masculine, feminine, and neutral tasks on children's achievement behavior, expectancies of success, and attainment values. *Child Development*, 1971, **42**, 195-207.

Stephenson, G. R. Social structure of mating activity in Japanese macaques. In S. Kondo, M. Kawai, A. Ehara, and S. Kawamura (eds.), *Symposia of the Fifth Congress of the International Primate Center*. Tokyo: Japan Science Press, 1975.

Sternglanz, S. H., and Serbin, L. A. Sex role stereotyping in children's television programs. *Developmental Psychology*, 1974, **10**, 710-715.

Steuer, F. B., Applefield, J. M., and Smith, R. Televised aggression and the interpersonal aggression of pre-school children. *Journal of Child Experimental Psychology*, 1971, **11**, 442-447.

Stevenson, H. W. Social reinforcement with children. In L. P. Lipsitt and C. C. Spiker (eds.), *Advances in child development and behavior*. Vol. 2. New York: Academic Press, 1965.

Stolz, L. M., et al. *Father relations of war-born children*. Stanford: Stanford University Press, 1954.

Strayer, F. F., Bovenkerk, A., and Koopman, R. F. Social affiliation and dominance in captive squirrel monkeys (*Saimuri sciurcus*). *Journal of Comparative and Physiological Psychology*, 1975, **89**, 308-318.

Strayer, F. F., and Strayer, J. An ethological analysis of social agonism and dominance relations among pre-school children. *Child Development*, 1976, **47**, 980-999.

Sullivan, H. S. Conceptions of modern psychiatry. *Psychiatry*, 1940, **3**, 1-117.

Sullivan, H. S. *The interpersonal theory of psychiatry*. New York: Norton, 1953.

Suomi, S. J., Collins, M. L., and Harlow, H. F. Effects of permanent separation from mother on infant monkeys. *Developmental Psychology*, 1973, **9**, 376-384.

Suomi, S. J., and Harlow, H. F. Social rehabilitation of isolate-reared monkeys. *Developmental Psychology*, 1972, **6**, 487-496.

Sutton-Smith, B., and Rosenberg, B. G. *The sibling*. New York: Holt, Rinehart, and Winston, 1970.

Sutton-Smith, B., Rosenberg, B. G., and Morgan, E. E. The development of sex differences in play choices in preadolescence. *Child Development*, 1963, **34**, 119-126.

Svare, B., and Gandelman, R. Postpartum aggression in mice: Experimental and environmental factors. *Hormones and Behavior*, 1973, **4**, 323-334.

Swift, J. Effects of early group experience: The nursery school and day nursery. In M. Hoffman and L. Hoffman (eds.), *Review of child development research* (Vol. 1). New York: Russell Sage Foundation, 1964.

Syme, L. A., Syme, G. J., Waite, T. G., and Pearson, A. J. Spatial distribution and social status in a small herd of dairy cows. *Animal Behavior*, 1975, **23**, 609-614.

Tanner, J. M. *Growth at adolescence*. Oxford: Blackwell Scientific Publications, 1962.

Tanner, J. M. Physical growth. In P. H. Mussen (ed.), *Carmichael's manual of child psychology* (3d. ed.), Vol. 2. New York: Wiley, 1970.

Tasch, R. J. The role of the father in the family. *Journal of Experimental Education*, 1952, **20**, 319-361.

Taylor, A. Deprived infants: Potential for affective adjustment. *American Journal of Orthopsychiatry*, 1968, **38**, 835-845.

Taylor, A. L. The development of children's social interaction behaviors in a game situation. Unpublished doctoral dissertation, University of Cincinnati, 1975.

Tees, R. C. Perceptual development in mammals. In G. Gottlieb (ed.), *Neural and behavioral specificity*. New York: Academic Press, 1976.

Tennes, K. H., and Lampl, E. E. Stranger and separation anxiety in infancy. *Journal of Nervous and Mental Diseases*, 1964, **139**, 247-254.

Thoman, E. B., and Arnold, W. J. Effects of incubator rearing with social deprivation on maternal behavior in rats. *Journal of Comparative and Physiological Psychology*, 1968, **65**, 441-446.

Thoman, E. B., Barnett, C. R., and Leiderman, P. H. Feeding behaviors of newborn infants as a function of parity of the mother. *Child Development*, 1971, **42**, 1471-1483.

Thoman, E. B., Leiderman, P. H., and Olson, J. P. Neonate-mother interaction during breast-feeding. *Developmental Psychology*, 1972, **6**, 110-118.

Thoman, E. B., Turner, A. M., Leiderman, P. H., and Barnett, C. R. Neonate-mother interaction: Effects of parity on feeding behavior. *Child Development*, 1970, **41**, 1103-1111.

Thomas, A., Chess, S. and Birch, H. G. *Temperament and behavior disorders in children*. New York: New York University Press, 1968.

Thomas, A., Chess, S., Birch, H. G., Hertzig, M. E., and Korn, S. *Behaviorial individuality in early childhood*. New York: New York University Press, 1963.

Thompson, N. I., Schwartz, D. M., McCandless, B. R., and Edwards, D. A. Parent-child relationships and sexual identity in male and female homosexuals and heterosexuals. *Journal of Consulting and Clinical Psychology*, 1973, **41**, 120-127.

Thompson, S. Gender labels and early sex role development. *Child Development*, 1975, **46**, 339-347.

Thurstone, L. L., and Peterson, R. C. Motion pictures and the social attitudes of children. In *Motion pictures and youth*. New York: Macmillan, 1933.

Timberlake, W., and Allison, J. Response deprivation: An empirical approach to instrumental performance. *Psychological Review*, 1974, **81**, 146-164.

Timiras, P. S. *Developmental physiology and aging*. New York: Macmillan, 1972.

Tinbergen, N. *The study of instinct*. Oxford: Clarendon Press, 1951.

Tinbergen, N. Some recent studies of the evolution of sexual behavior. In F. Beach (ed.), *Sex and behavior*, New York: Wiley, 1965.

Tinbergen, N. *The animal in its world: Explorations of an ethologist*. London: Allen & Unwin, 1972(a).

Tinbergen, N. Foreword. In N. Blurton Jones (ed.), *Ethological studies of child behaviour*. Cambridge: Cambridge University Press, 1972(b).

Tinbergen, N. Ethology and stress diseases. *Science*, 1974, **185**, 20-26.

Tinklepaugh, O. L., and Hartman, C. G. Behavioral aspects of parturition in the monkey, *M. rhesus*. *Journal of Comparative Psychology*, 1930, **11**, 63-98.

Tobach, E., Gianutsos, J., Topoff, H. R., and Gross, C. G. *The four horsemen: Racism, sexism, militarism, and social Darwinism*. New York: Behavioral Publications, 1974.

Toch, H. *Violent men: An inquiry into the psychology of violence*. Chicago: Aldine, 1969.

Todt, D. Social learning of vocal patterns and modes of their application in grey parrots *(Psittacus erithacus)*. *Zeitschrift für Tierpsychologie*, 1976, **39**, 178-188.

Tolman, E. C. *Purposive behavior in animals and men*. New York: Century, 1932.

Trivers, R. L. The evolution of reciprocal altruism. *Quarterly Review of Biology*, 1971, **46**, 35-37.

Trivers, R. L. Parent-offspring conflict. *American Zoologist*, 1974, **14**, 249-264.

Tronick, E. D., Als, H., and Brazelton, T. B. Mutuality in mother-infant interaction. *Journal of Communications*, 1977, **27**, 74-79.

Tuddenham, R. D., and Snyder, M. M. Physical growth of California boys and girls from birth to 18 years. *Child Development* **1**, No. 2. Berkeley: University of California Press, 1954.

Tulkin, S. R. An analysis of the concept of cultural deprivation. *Developmental Psychology*, 1972, **6**, 326-339.

Tulkin, S. R., and Kagan, J. Mother-child interactions in the first year of life. *Child Development*. 1972, **43**, 31-41.

Uhrich, J. The social hierarchy in albino mice. *Journal of Comparative Psychology*, 1938, **25**, 373-413.

Ulrich, R. E., and Azrin, N. H. Reflexive fighting in response to aversive stimulation. *Journal of the Experimental Analysis of Behavior*, 1962, **5**, 511-520.

Ulrich, R. E., Hutchinson, R. R., and Azrin, N. H. Pain-elicited aggression. *Psychological Record*, 1965, **15**, 111-126.

U. S. Bureau of the Census, *Current Population Reports*, Series p-23, No. 50, "Female Family Heads." Washington, D.C.: Government Printing Office, 1974.

U. S. Department of Health, Education, and Welfare. *Preprimary enrollment*, October 1974. Washington, D. C.: Government Printing Office, 1975.

Urberg, K. A., and Labouvie-Vief, G. Conceptualizations of sex roles: A life span developmental study. *Developmental Psychology*, 1976, **12**, 15-23.

Vale, J. R., Vale, C. A., and Harley, J. P. Interaction of genotype and population number with regard to aggressive behavior, social grooming, and adrenal and gonadal weight in male mice. *Communications in Behavioral Biology*, 1971, **6**, 209-221.

Valenstein, E. S. Steroid hormones and the neuropsychology of development. In R. L. Isaacson (ed.), *The neuropsychology of development: A symposium*. New York: Wiley, 1968.

Valenstein, E. S., Cox, V. C., and Kakolewski, J. W. Reexamination of the role of the hypothalmus in motivation. *Psychological Review*, 1970, **77**, 16-31.

Van Lieshout, C. F. M. Young children's reactions to barriers placed by their mothers. *Child Development*, 1975, **46**, 879-886.

Wahler, R. G. Infant social attachments: A reinforcement theory interpretation and investigation. *Child Development*, 1967, **38**, 1079-1088.

Waldrop, M. F., and Halverson, C. F. Jr. Intensive and extensive peer behavior: Longitudinal and cross-sectional analyses. *Child Development*, 1975, **46**, 19-26.

Walters, J., Pearce, D., and Dahms, L. Affectional and aggressive behavior of preschool children. *Child Development*, 1957, **28**, 15-26.

Walters, R. H. Some conditions facilitating the occurrence of imitative behavior. In E. C. Simmel, R. A. Hoppe, and G. A. Milton (eds.), *Social facilitation and imitative behavior*. Boston: Allyn and Bacon, 1968.

Walters, R. H., and Brown, M. Studies of reinforcement of aggression: III. Transfer of responses to an interpersonal situation. *Child Development*, 1963, **34**, 563-571.

Walters, R. H., and Parke, R. D. Social motivation, dependency and susceptibility to social influence. In L. Berkowitz (ed.), *Advances in experimental social psychology* (Vol. 1). New York: Academic Press, 1964.

Walters, R. H., and Parke, R. D. The role of the distance receptors in the development of social responsiveness. In L. P. Lipsitt and C. C. Spiker (eds.), *Advances in child development and behavior* (Vol. 2). New York: Academic Press, 1965.

Ward, D. A., and Kassebaum, G. G. *Women's prison: Sex and social structure*. Chicago: Aldine, 1965.

Warren, V. L., and Cairns, R. B. Social reinforcement satiation: An outcome of frequency or ambiguity? *Journal of Experimental Child Psychology*, 1972, **13**, 249-260.

Waters, E. The reliability and stability of individual differences in infant-mother attachment. *Child Development*, 1978 (in press).

Waters, E. and Sroufe, A. The stability of individual differences in attachment. Paper read at the Biennial meetings of the Society for Research in Child Development, New Orleans, March 1977.

Watson, J. B. What the nursery has to say about instincts. In C. Murchison (ed.), *Psychologies of 1925*. Worcester, Mass.: Clark University Press, 1926.

Watson, J. B. *Psychological care of infant and child*. New York: Norton, 1928.

Weisler, A., and McCall, R. B. Exploration and play: Résumé and redirection. *American Psychologist*, 1976, **31**, 492-508.

Welch, B. L. Discussion of "aggression, defense, and neurohumors." In C. D. Clemente and D. B. Lindsley (eds.), *Aggression and defense: Neural mechanisms and social patterns*. Vol. 5. *Brain function*. Los Angeles: University of California Press, 1967.

Welker, W. I. Factors affecting aggregation of neonatal puppies. *Journal of Comparative and Physiological Psychology*, 1959, **52**, 376-380.

Welkowitz, J., Cariffe, G., and Feldstein, S. Conversational congruence as a criterion of socialization in children. *Child Development*, 1976, **47**, 269-272.

Werner, H. *Comparative psychology of mental development*, (rev. ed.). Chicago: Follett, 1948.

West, D. J. *Homosexuality*. Chicago: Aldine, 1967.

White, B. L., and Held, R. Plasticity of sensorimotor development. In J. F. Rosenblith and W. Allinsmith (eds.), *The causes of behavior: II*. Boston: Allyn and Bacon, 1966.

Whiting, B. B. *Six cultures: Studies of child rearing*. New York: Wiley, 1963.

Whiting, B. B., and Edwards, C. P. A cross-cultural analysis of sex differences in the behavior of children three through eleven. *Journal of Social Psychology*, 1973, **91**, 171-188.

Whiting, B. B., and Whiting, J. W. *Children of six cultures: A psycho-cultural analysis*. Cambridge, Mass.: Harvard University Press, 1974.

Whiting, J. W. M. The frustration complex in Kwoma society. *Man*, 1944, **44**, 140-144.

Whiting, J. W. M., and Child, I. L. *Child training and personality*. New Haven: Yale University Press, 1953.

Whitten, W. K. Modification of the oestrous cycle of the mouse by external stimuli associated with the male. *Journal of Endocrinology*, 1956, **13**, 399-404.

Wiesner, B. P., and Sheard, N. M. *Maternal behaviour in the rat*. Edinburgh: Oliver and Boyd, 1933.

Wiley, R. H. Territoriality and nonrandom mating in the sage grouse, *Centrocercus urophasianus*. *Animal Behaviour Monographs*, 1973, **6** (Part 2), 87-169.

Willems, E. P. An ecological orientation in operation. *Merrill-Palmer Quarterly*, 1965, **11**, 317-343.

Willems, E. P., and Raush, H. L. (eds.), *Naturalistic viewpoints in psychological research*. New York: Holt, Rinehart, and Winston, 1969.

Williams, C. D. The elimination of tantrum behavior by extinction procedures. *Journal of Abnormal and Social Psychology*, 1959, **59**, 269.

Williams, J. E., Bennett, S. M., and Best, D. L. Awareness

and expression of sex stereotypes in young children. *Developmental Psychology*, 1975, **11**, 635-642.

Wilson, E. O. *Sociobiology: The new synthesis.* Cambridge, Mass.: Harvard University Press, 1975.

Witkin, H. A., Mednick, S. A., Schulsinger, F., Bakkestrom, E., Christiansen, K. O., Goodenough, D. R., Hirschhorn, K. O., Lundsteen, C., Owen, D. R., Philip, J., Rubin, D. B., and Stocking, M. Criminality in XYY and XXY men. *Science*, 1976, **193**, 547-555.

Wohlwill, J. F. *The study of behavioral development.* New York: Academic Press, 1973.

Wolf, A. P. Adopt a daughter-in-law, marry a sister: A Chinese solution to the problem of the incest taboo. *American Anthropologist*, 1968, **70**, 864-874.

Wolf, A. P. Childhood association and sexual attraction: A further test of the Westermarck hypothesis. *American Anthropologist*, 1970, **72**, 503-515.

Wolf, T. M. Effects of live modeled sex-inappropriate play behavior in a naturalistic setting. *Developmental Psychology*, 1973, **9**, 120-123.

Wolff, P. H. Observations on the early development of smiling. In B. M. Foss (ed.), *Determinants of infant behavior:* II. New York: Wiley, 1963.

Wolff, P. H. The natural history of crying and vocalization in early infancy. In B. M. Foss (ed.), *Determinants of infant behavior:* IV. London: Methuen, 1969.

Wolfgang, M. E., and Ferracuti, F. *The subculture of violence.* London: Tavistock, 1967.

Wolins, M. Young children in institutions. *Developmental Psychology*, 1970, **2**, 99-109.

World Health Organization. *Deprivation of maternal care.* Public Health Paper No. 14. Geneva: WHO, 1962.

Wright, H. F. *Recording and analyzing child behavior.* New York: Harper and Row, 1967.

Wynne-Edwards, V. C. *Animal dispersion in relation to social behaviour.* Edinburgh: Oliver and Boyd, 1962.

Yang, P. K., and Halverson, C. F., Jr. A study of the "inversion of intensity" between newborn and a preschool-age behavior. *Child Development*, 1976, **47**, 350-359.

Yang, R. K., Zweig, A. R., Douthitt, T. C., and Federman, E. J. Successive relationships between maternal attitudes during pregnancy, analgesic medication during labor and delivery, and newborn behavior. *Developmental Psychology*, 1976, **12**, 6-14.

Yarrow, L. J. Maternal deprivation: Toward an empirical and conceptual re-evaluation. *Psychological Bulletin*, 1961, **58**, 459-490.

Yarrow, L. J. Separation from parents during early childhood. In M. Hoffman and L. Hoffman (eds.), *Review of child development research.* New York: Russell Sage, 1964.

Yarrow, L. J. The development of focused relationships during infancy. In J. Hellmuth (ed.), *Exceptional infant: The normal infant* (Vol. 1). Seattle: Special Child Publications, 1967.

Yarrow, L. J. Attachment and dependency: A developmental perspective. In J. L. Gewirtz (ed.), *Attachment and dependency.* Washington, D.C.: V. H. Winston, 1972.

Yarrow, L. J., and Goodwin, M. S. Effects of change in mother figure during infancy on personality and development. Progress Report, 1963. Family and Child Services, Washington, D.C.

Yarrow, L. J., and Goodwin, M. S. The immediate impact of separation: Reactions of infants to a change in mother figures. In L. J. Stone, H. T. Smith, and L. B. Murphy (eds.), *The competent infant: Research and commentary.* New York: Basic Books, 1973.

Yarrow, L. J., Goodwin, M. S., Manheimer, H., and Milowe, I. D. Infancy experiences and cognitive and personality development at ten years. In L. J. Stone, H. T. Smith, and L. B. Murphy (eds.), *The competent infant: Research and commentary.* New York: Basic Books, 1973.

Yarrow, M. R. Campbell, J. D., and Burton, R. V. *Child rearing: An inquiry into research and methods.* San Francisco: Jossey-Bass, 1968.

Yarrow, M. R., Scott, P. M., and Waxler, C. Z. Learning concern for others. *Developmental Psychology*, 1973, **8**, 240-260.

Yarrow, M. R., and Waxler, C. Z. Observing interaction. In R. B. Cairns (ed.), *The analysis of social interactions: Methods, issues, and illustrations.* Hillsdale, N.J.: Erlbaum Associates, 1979.

Yarrow, M. R., Waxler, C. Z., and Scott, P. M. Child effects on adult behavior. *Developmental Psychology*, 1971, **5**, 300-311.

Yerkes, R. M. *Chimpanzees: A laboratory colony.* New Haven: Yale University Press, 1943.

Young, W. C. The hormones and mating behavior. In W. C. Young (ed.), *Sex and internal secretions* (3d ed.). Baltimore: Williams and Wilkins, 1961.

Zajonc, R. B. Social facilitation. *Science*, 1965, 269-274.

Zajonc, R. B. *Social psychology: An experimental approach.* Belmont, Calif.: Wadsworth, 1966.

Zajonc, R. B. (ed.), *Animal social psychology: A reader of experimental studies.* New York: Wiley, 1969.

Zajonc, R. B., and Marcus, G. B. Birth order and intellectual development. *Psychological Bulletin*, 1975, **82**, 74-88.

Zajonc, R. B., Reimer, D. J., and Hausser, D. Imprinting and the development of object preference in chicks by mere repeated exposure. *Journal of Comparative and Physiological Psychology*, 1973, **83**, 434-440.

Zelazo, P. R. Smiling to social stimuli: Eliciting and conditioning effects. *Developmental Psychology*, 1971, **4**, 32-42.

Zelazo, P. R., Zelazo, N. A., and Kolb, S. "Walking" in the newborn. *Science*, 1972, **176**, 314-315.

Zuckerman, S. *The social life of monkeys and apes.* London: Kegan Paul, 1932.

Zuger, B., and Taylor, P. Effeminate behavior present in boys from early childhood: II. Comparison with similar symptoms in non-effeminate boys. *Pediatrics*, 1969, **44**, 375-380.

Name Index

Subject Index